Bed & Breakfast U.S.A.

1 9 9 9

B&Bs can be your home away from home! Complete with hundreds of listings, all with reasonable rates, this indispensable directory gives you the keys to America's most popular alternative to impersonal hotels and shows you why B&Bs are the *only* way to travel. Offering friendly, home-style places to stay for business travelers, family vacationers, and anyone looking for a way to really see the country, this information-packed book will be every traveler's constant companion.

◆

"For those who have embraced the B&B way to travel, there is no going back to hotel high-rises and motel monotony."—*Time*

◆

PEGGY ACKERMAN is the director of the Tourist House Association of America, Inc., a national association of over 1,100 members. She lives in Greentown, Pennsylvania.

Bed & Breakfast
U.S.A.
1999

PEGGY ACKERMAN

Tourist House Association of America, Inc.

A PLUME BOOK

PLUME
Published by the Penguin Group
Penguin Putnam Inc., 375 Hudson Street, New York, New York 10014, U.S.A.
Penguin Books Ltd, 27 Wrights Lane, London W8 5TZ, England
Penguin Books Australia Ltd, Ringwood, Victoria, Australia
Penguin Books Canada Ltd, 10 Alcorn Avenue, Toronto, Ontario, Canada
M4V 3B2
Penguin Books (N.Z.) Ltd, 182–190 Wairau Road, Auckland 10, New Zealand

Penguin Books Ltd, Registered Offices:
Harmondsworth, Middlesex, England

Published by Plume, an imprint of Dutton NAL,
a member of Penguin Putnam Inc.

First Printing, January, 1999

10 9 8 7 6 5 4 3 2 1

 REGISTERED TRADEMARK—MARCA REGISTRADA

LC card number: 86-649303

Printed in the United States of America

Set in Palatino and Optima
Designed by Stanley S. Drate/Folio Graphics Co. Inc.

If you want to be listed in future editions of this guide, DO NOT WRITE TO
PLUME OR PENGUIN. See page 583 for a membership application, or write to:
    Tourist House Association of America, Inc.
    Greentown, PA 18426
Applications will be accepted until March 15, 1999.

The book you are holding is the result of one woman's hard work and big dreams. In 1974, Betty Revits Rundback began thinking about how to celebrate the American Bicentennial in 1976. She decided to take her family of seven on a cross-country tour, but didn't like the idea of staying in motels night after night. She wanted her children to really see the country, and to get to know its people along the way. Remembering back to her own childhood, when the house down the road offered comfortable lodging and a bountiful breakfast to travelers, she set out to create a similar experience. She never expected to spend months at the New York Public Library doing it! But that's exactly what she did, going through every telephone directory in America to find listings of family-style guesthouses, contacting all the owners individually, and finally assembling them into a pamphlet in time for the Bicentennial. With the information Betty had gathered, she founded the Tourist House Association of America, which she ran enthusiastically and successfully until her death on July 4, 1990. My wife, Peggy, now continues her work of bringing together guests and hosts from around the world. We dedicate this book to her, in loving memory of her warmth, compassion, and spirit.

—Peggy and Michael Ackerman

Contents

Reservation service organizations appear here in boldface type.

Reservation service organizations appear here in boldface type.

Reservation service organizations appear here in boldface type.

Reservation service organizations appear here in boldface type.

Reservation service organizations appear here in boldface type.

Reservation service organizations appear here in boldface type.

Reservation service organizations appear here in boldface type.

Reservation service organizations appear here in boldface type.

Reservation service organizations appear here in boldface type.

Reservation service organizations appear here in boldface type.

Reservation service organizations appear here in boldface type.

Reservation service organizations appear here in boldface type.

Reservation service organizations appear here in boldface type.

Reservation service organizations appear here in boldface type.

Reservation service organizations appear here in boldface type.

Reservation service organizations appear here in boldface type.

Reservation service organizations appear here in boldface type.

Reservation service organizations appear here in boldface type.

Reservation service organizations appear here in boldface type.

Reservation service organizations appear here in boldface type.

Reservation service organizations appear here in boldface type.

Reservation service organizations appear here in boldface type.

Reservation service organizations appear here in boldface type.

Reservation service organizations appear here in boldface type.

Reservation service organizations appear here in boldface type.

Reservation service organizations appear here in boldface type.

Reservation service organizations appear here in boldface type.

Reservation service organizations appear here in boldface type.

Reservation service organizations appear here in boldface type.

Reservation service organizations appear here in boldface type.

Preface

If you are familiar with earlier editions of *Bed & Breakfast U.S.A.*, you know that this book has always been a labor of love. It is very gratifying to see how it has grown from the first sixteen-page edition, titled *Guide to Tourist Homes and Guest Houses*, which was published in 1975 and contained forty individual listings. Twenty-four years later, the twenty-first revised edition lists 814 homes and 60 reservation agencies, giving travelers access to over 20,000 host homes. This spectacular success indicates how strongly the concept of the guesthouse has recaptured the fancy of both proprietors and travelers.

Although we do not list grand hotels, rental properties, or campground compounds, we do list an exciting amount of smaller bed and breakfasts and inns, and a small percentage of higher-priced inns. But make no mistake—we still dedicate most of this book to meeting the needs of our readers, which means listing only those B&Bs with reasonably priced accommodations. In the years of doing this book, we have found that you can pay a reasonable amount of money and enjoy the bed and breakfast experience just as much as a very chic inn, and in most cases enjoy more personal contact with your hosts. We have given a great deal of thought to what we feel a B&B should be and are focusing on our original definition: an owner-occupied residence with breakfast included at a fair rate, where a visitor is made to feel more like a welcome guest than a paying customer.

Because of personal experience and letters from our readers, *Bed & Breakfast U.S.A.* will not accept properties where the host does not reside on the premises, rental properties, B&Bs with more than fifteen guest rooms, rates exceeding $35 where six people or more share a bath, rates exceeding $45 where five people share a bath, or rates without breakfast included. Higher-priced B&Bs and inns will only be included according to space availability.

This is not a project for which listings have been compiled just for the sake of putting a book together; bigger isn't necessarily better. *Bed & Breakfast U.S.A.* is a product of a membership organization whose credo is "Comfort, cleanliness, cordiality, and fairness of cost." We solicit and rely on the comments of our readers. For this purpose, we include a tear-out form on page 593. We genuinely appreciate comments from guests—negative if necessary, positive when warranted—and we do follow up. We want to hear from you!

All of the B&Bs and inns described in this book are members of the Tourist House Association of America, Inc., Greentown, Pennsylvania 18426, phone: (888) 888-4068. THAA dues are $40 annually.

PEGGY ACKERMAN
Tourist House Association of America, Inc.

January 1999

Even after careful editing and proofreading, errors occasionally occur. We regret any inconvenience to our readers and members.

Acknowledgments

A special thanks to all the travel writers and reporters who have brought us to the attention of their audiences.

To my family, Mike Ackerman, Travis Kali, and Justin Ackerman, the three men in my life—thank you for all the encouragement and support you have shown; to Mary Kristyak Donnelly, a superb mother, grandmother, and best friend—I admire you so; to Bill Donnelly, dad and joke teller; to the grandmothers, Ann Revits and Helen Kristyak.

A final note of thanks to my editor, Leslie Jay, for her deeply appreciated assistance. Never too much, always a smile.

1

Introduction

Bed and breakfast is the popular lodging alternative to hotel high-rises and motel monotony. B&Bs are either private residences where the owners rent spare bedrooms to travelers, or small, family-operated inns offering a special kind of warm, personal hospitality. Whether large or small, B&Bs will make you feel more like a welcome guest than a paying customer.

The custom of opening one's home to travelers dates back to the earliest days of Colonial America. Hotels and inns were few and far between in those days, and wayfarers relied on the kindness of strangers to provide a bed for the night. Which is why, perhaps, there is hardly a Colonial-era home in the mid-Atlantic states that does not boast: "George Washington Slept Here!"

During the Depression, the tourist home provided an economic advantage to both the traveler and the host. Travelers always drove through the center of town; there were no superhighways to bypass local traffic. A house with a sign in the front yard reading "Tourists" or "Guests" indicated that a traveler could rent a room for the night and have a cup of coffee before leaving in the morning. The usual cost for this arrangement was $2. The money represented needed income for the proprietor as well as the opportunity to chat with an interesting visitor.

In the 1950s, the country guesthouse became a popular alternative to the costly hotels in resort areas. The host compensated for the lack of hotel amenities, such as private bathrooms, by providing comfortable bedrooms and bountiful breakfasts at a modest price. The visitors enjoyed the home-away-from-home atmosphere; the hosts were pleased to have paying houseguests.

The incredible growth in international travel that has occurred over the past 30 years has provided yet another stimulus. Millions of Americans now vacation annually in Europe, and travelers have become enchanted with the bed and breakfast concept so popular in England, Ireland, and other parts of the Continent. In fact, many well-traveled Americans are delighted to learn that we "finally" have B&Bs here. But, as you now know, they were always here—just a rose by another name.

Bed and breakfasts are for:

- **Parents of college kids:** Tuition is costly enough without the added expense of Parents' Weekends. Look for a B&B near campus.
- **Parents traveling with children:** A family living room, playroom, or backyard is preferable to the confines of a motel room.
- **"Parents" of pets:** Many proprietors will allow your well-behaved darling to come, too. This can cut down on the expense and trauma of kenneling Fido.
- **Business travelers:** Being "on the road" can be lonely and expensive. It's so nice, after a day's work, to return to a home-away-from-home.
- **Women traveling alone:** Friendship and conversation are the natural ingredients of a guesthouse.
- **Skiers:** Lift prices are lofty, so it helps to save some money on lodging. Many mountain homes include home-cooked meals in your room rate.
- **Students:** A visit with a family is a pleasant alternative to camping or the local "Y."
- **Visitors from abroad:** Cultural exchanges are often enhanced by a host who can speak your language.
- **Carless travelers:** If you plan to leave the auto at home, it's nice to know that many B&Bs are convenient to public transportation. Hosts will often arrange to meet your bus, plane, or train for a nominal fee.
- **Schoolteachers and retired persons:** Exploring out-of-the-way places is fun and will save you money.
- **History buffs:** Many B&Bs are located in areas important to our country's past. A number have the distinction of being listed on the National Register of Historic Places.
- **Sports fans:** Tickets to championship games are expensive. A stay at a B&B helps to defray the cost of attending out-of-town events.
- **Antique collectors:** Many hosts have lovely personal collections, and nearby towns are filled with undiscovered antique shops.
- **House hunters:** It's a practical way of trying out a neighborhood.
- **Relocating corporate executives:** It's more comfortable to stay in a real home while you look for a permanent residence. Hosts will often give more practical advice than professional realtors.
- **Relatives of hospitalized patients:** Many B&Bs are located near major hospitals. Hosts will offer tea and sympathy when visiting hours are over.
- **Convention and seminar attendees:** Staying at a nearby B&B is less expensive than checking into a hotel.

And everyone else who has had it up to here with plastic motel monotony!

What It Is Like to Be a Guest in a B&B

The B&B descriptions provided in this book will help you choose the places that have the greatest appeal to you. A firsthand insight into local culture awaits you; imagine the advantage of arriving in New York City or San Francisco and having an insider to help you sidestep the tourist traps and direct you to that special restaurant or discount store. Or explore the countryside, where fresh air and home-cooked meals beckon. Your choice is as wide as the U.S.A.

Each bed and breakfast listed offers personal contact, a real advantage in unfamiliar environments. You may not have a phone in your room or a TV on the dresser. You may even have to pad down the hall in robe and slippers to take a shower, but you'll discover that little things count.

- **In Williamsburg, Virginia, a visitor from Germany opted to stay at a B&B to help improve her conversational English. When the hostess saw that she was having difficulty understanding directions, she personally escorted her on a tour of Old Williamsburg.**
- **In Pennsylvania, the guests mistakenly arrived a week prior to their stated reservation date and the B&B was full. The hostess made a call to a neighbor who accommodated the couple. (By the way, the neighbor has now become a B&B host!)**
- **In New York City, a guest was an Emmy Award nominee and arrived with his tuxedo in need of pressing. The hostess pressed it; when he claimed his award over nationwide TV, he looked well groomed!**

Expect the unexpected, such as a pot of brewed coffee upon your arrival, or fresh flowers on a nightstand. At the very least, count on our required standard of cleanliness and comfort. Although we haven't personally visited all of the places listed, they have all been highly recommended by chambers of commerce or former guests. We have either spoken to or corresponded with all of the proprietors; they are a friendly group of people who enjoy having visitors. They will do all in their power to make your stay memorable.

Our goal is to enable the traveler to crisscross the country and stay only at B&Bs along the way. To achieve this, your help is vital. Please take a moment to write us of your experiences; we will follow up on every suggestion. Your comments will serve as the yardstick by which we can measure the quality of our accommodations. For your convenience, an evaluation form is included at the back of this book.

Cost of Accommodations

Bed and breakfast, in the purest sense, is a private home, often referred to as a "homestay," where the owners rent their spare bedrooms to travelers. These are the backbone of this book.

However, American ingenuity has enhanced this simple idea to include more spectacular homes, mansions, small inns, and intimate hotels. With few exceptions, the proprietor is the host and lives on the premises.

There is a distinction between B&B homestays and B&B inns. Inns are generally defined as a business and depend upon revenue from guests to pay expenses. They usually have six or more guest rooms, and may have a restaurant that is open to the public. The tariff at inns is usually higher than at a homestay because the owners must pay the mortgage, running expenses, and staff, whether or not guests come.

Whether plain or fancy, all B&Bs are based on the concept that people are tired of the plastic monotony of motels and are disappointed that even the so-called budget motels can be quite expensive. Travelers crave the personal touch, and they sincerely enjoy "visiting" rather than just "staying."

Prices vary accordingly. There are places listed in this book where lovely lodging may be had for as low as $40 a night, and others that feature an overnight stay with a gourmet breakfast in a canopied bed for $95. Whatever the price, if you see the sign ❂, it means that the B&B has guaranteed its rates through 1999 to holders of this book, so be sure to mention it when you call or write! (If there is a change in ownership, the guarantee may not apply. Please notify us in writing if any host fails to honor the guaranteed rate.)

Accommodations vary in price depending upon the locale and the season. Peak season usually refers to the availability of skiing in winter and water sports in summer; in the Sunbelt states, winter months are usually the peak season. Some B&Bs require a two-night weekend minimum during peak periods, and three nights on holiday weekends. Off-season rate schedules are usually reduced. Resorts and major cities are generally more expensive than out-of-the-way places. However, B&Bs are always less expensive than hotels and motels of equivalent caliber in the same area. A weekly rate is usually less expensive than a daily rate. Special reductions are sometimes given to families (occupying two rooms) or senior citizens. Whenever reduced rates are available, you will find this noted in the individual listings.

Meals

Breakfast: *Continental* refers to fruit or juice, rolls, and a hot beverage. Many hosts pride themselves on home-baked breads, home-made preserves, as well as imported teas and cakes, so their Continental breakfast may be quite deluxe. Several hosts have regular jobs outside the home, so you may have to adjust your schedule to theirs. A "full" breakfast includes fruit, cereal and/or eggs, breakfast meats, breads, and a hot beverage. The table is set family-style and is often the highlight of a B&B's hospitality. Either a Continental breakfast or full breakfast is included in the room rate unless otherwise specified.

Other Meals: If listed as "available," you can be assured that the host takes pride in his or her cooking skills. The prices for lunch or dinner are usually reasonable but are not included in the quoted room rate unless clearly specified as "included."

Making Reservations

- Reservations are a MUST or you may risk missing out on the accommodations of your choice. Reserve *early* and confirm with a deposit equal to one night's stay. If you call to inquire about reservations, please remember the difference in time zones. When dialing outside of your area, remember to dial the digit "1" before the area code.

- Many individual B&Bs now accept charge cards. This information is indicated in the listings by the symbols MC for MasterCard, AMEX for American Express, etc. A few have a surcharge for this service, so inquire as to the policy.

- Cash or traveler's checks are the accepted method of paying for your stay. Be sure to inquire whether or not tax is included in the rates quoted so that you will know exactly how much your lodging will cost.

- Rates are based on single or double occupancy of a room as quoted. Expect that an extra person(s) in the room will be charged a small additional fee. Inquire when making your reservation what the charge will be.

- If a listing indicates that children or pets are welcome, it is expected that they will be well behaved. All of our hosts take pride in their homes and it would be unfair to subject them to circumstances in which their possessions might be abused or the other houseguests disturbed by an unruly child or animal.

- Please note that many hosts have their own resident pets. If you are allergic or don't care to be around animals, inquire before making a reservation.
- In homes where smoking is permitted, do check to see if it is restricted in any of the rooms. Most hosts object to cigars.
- Where listings indicate that social drinking is permitted, it usually refers to your bringing your own beverages. Most hosts will provide ice; many will allow you to chill mixers in the refrigerator, and others offer complimentary wine and snacks. A few B&B inns have licenses to sell liquor. Any drinking should not be excessive.
- If Yes is indicated in the listings for airport/station pickup, it means that the host will meet your plane, bus, or train for a fee.
- Feel free to request brochures and local maps so that you can better plan for your visit.
- Do try to fit in with the host's house rules. You are on vacation; he or she isn't!
- A reservation form is included at the back of this book for your convenience; just tear it out and send it in to the B&B of your choice.

Cancellations

Cancellation policies vary from one B&B to another, so be sure to read the fine print on the reservation form. Many require a 15-day notice to refund the entire deposit, after which they will refund only if the room is rebooked. When a refund is due, most keep a processing fee and return the balance. A few keep the deposit and apply it to a future stay.

While these policies may seem harsh, please keep in mind that B&Bs are not hotels, which commonly overbook and where no-show guests can easily be replaced. Your host may have turned down a prospective guest, and may have bought special breakfast food in anticipation of your visit and should not be penalized. If you feel you've been unfairly treated in a cancellation situation, please do let us know.

B&B Reservation Services

There are many host families who prefer not to be individually listed in a book, and would rather have their houseguests referred by a coordinating agency. The organizations listed in this book are all members of the Tourist House Association. They all share our standards regarding the suitability of the host home as to cordiality, cleanliness, and comfort.

The majority do a marvelous job of matching host and guest according to age, interests, language, and any special requirements. To get the best match, it is practical to give them as much time as possible to find the host home best tailored to your needs.

Many have prepared descriptive pamphlets describing the homes on their rosters, the areas in which the homes are located, and information regarding special things to see and do. *Send a self-addressed, stamped, business-size envelope to receive a descriptive directory by return mail along with a reservation form for you to complete.* When returning the form, you will be asked to select the home or homes listed in the brochure that most appeal to you. (The homes are usually given a code number for reference.) The required deposit should accompany your reservation. Upon receipt, the coordinator will make the reservation and advise you of the name, address, telephone number, and travel instructions for your host.

A few agencies prepare a descriptive directory and *include* the host's name, address, and telephone number so that you can contact the host and make your arrangements directly. They charge anywhere from $2 to $11 for the directory.

Several agencies are *membership* organizations, charging guests an annual fee ranging from $5 to $25 per person. Their descriptive directories are free to members and many of them maintain toll-free telephone numbers for reservations.

Most reservation services have a specific geographic focus. The coordinators are experts in the areas they represent. They can often make arrangements for car rentals, theater tickets, and touring suggestions, and offer information in planning a trip best suited to your interests.

Most work on a commission basis with the host, and that fee is included in the room rates quoted in each listing. Some make a surcharge for a one-night stay; others require a two- or three-night minimum stay for holiday periods or special events. Some will accept a credit card for the reservation, but the balance due must be paid to the host in cash or traveler's checks.

All of their host homes offer a Continental breakfast, and some may include a full breakfast.

Many reservation services in the larger cities have, in addition to the traditional B&Bs, a selection of apartments, condominiums, and houses *without hosts in residence*. This may be appealing to those travelers anticipating an extended stay in a particular area.

Statewide services are listed first in the section for each state. City or regionally based organizations are listed first under the heading for that area. For a complete description of their services, look them up under the city and state where they're based.

NOTE: When calling, do so during normal business hours (for that time zone), unless otherwise stated. Collect calls are not accepted.

2

How to Start Your Own B&B

What It's Like to Be a Host

Hosts are people who like the idea of accommodating travelers and sharing their home and the special features of their area with them. They are people who have houses too large for their personal needs and like the idea of supplementing their income by having people visit. For many, it's a marvelous way of meeting rising utility and maintenance costs. For young families, it is a way of buying and keeping that otherwise-too-large house, as well as a way of furnishing it, since many of the furnishings may be tax deductible. Another advantage is that many state and local governments have recognized the service that some host families perform. In browsing through this book you will note that some homes are listed on the National Historic Register. Some state governments allow owners of landmark and historical houses a special tax advantage if they are used for any business purpose. Check with the Historical Preservation Society in your state for details.

If you have bedrooms to spare, if you sincerely like having overnight guests, if your home is clean and comfortable, this is an opportunity to consider. It is a unique business because *you* set the time of the visit and the length of stay. (Guesthouses are not boarding homes.) You invite the guests at *your* convenience, and the extras, such as meals, are entirely up to you. You can provide a cup of coffee, complete meals, or just a room and shared bath. Remember that your income may be erratic and should not be depended upon to pay for monthly bills. However, it can afford you some luxuries.

Although the majority of hosts are women, many couples are finding pleasure in this joint venture. The general profile of a typical host is a friendly, outgoing, flexible person who is proud of his or her home and hometown. The following information and suggestions represent a guideline to consider in deciding whether becoming a B&B host is really for you.

There are no set rules for the location, type, or style of a B&B. Apartments, condos, farmhouses, town houses, beach houses, vacation cottages, houseboats, mansions, as well as the traditional one-family dwelling are all appropriate. The important thing is for the host to be on the premises. The setting may be urban, rural, or suburban, near public transportation or in the hinterlands. Location is only important if you want to have guests every night. Areas where tourism is popular, such as resort areas or major cities, are often busier than out-of-the-way places. However, if a steady stream of visitors is not that important or even desirable, it doesn't matter where you are. People will contact you if your rates are reasonable and if there is something to see and do in your area, or if it is near a major transportation route.

Setting Rates

Consider carefully four key factors in setting your rates: location, private versus shared bath, type of breakfast, and your home itself.

Location: If you reside in a traditional resort or well-touristed area, near a major university or medical center, or in an urban hub or gateway city, your rates should be at least 40 percent lower than those of the area's major motels or hotels. If you live in an out-of-the-way location, your rates must be extremely reasonable. If your area has a "season"—snow sports in winter, water sports in summer—offer off-season rates when these attractions are not available. Reading through this book will help you to see what the going rate is in a situation similar to yours.

The Bath: You are entitled to charge more for a room with private bath. If the occupants of two rooms share one bath, the rate should be less. If more than five people must share one bathroom, you may have complaints, unless your rates are truly inexpensive.

The Breakfast: Figure the approximate cost of your ingredients, plus something for your time. Allow about $2 to $3 for a Continental breakfast, $4 to $5 for a full American breakfast, and then *include* it in the rate.

Your Home: Plan on charging a fair and reasonable rate for a typical B&B home, one that is warm and inviting, clean and comfortable. If your home is exceptionally luxurious, with king-size beds, Jacuzzi baths, tennis courts, or hot tubs, you will find guests who are willing to pay a premium. If your home is over 75 years old, well restored, with lots of antiques, you may also be able to charge a higher rate.

The Three Bs—Bed, Breakfast, and Bath

The Bedroom: The ideal situation for a prospective host is the possession of a house too large for current needs. The children may be away at college most of the year or may have left permanently, leaving behind their bedrooms and, in some cases, an extra bath. Refurbishing these rooms does not mean refurnishing; an extraordinary investment need not be contemplated for receiving guests. Take a long, hard look at the room. With a little imagination and a little monetary outlay, could it be changed into a bedroom *you'd* be pleased to spend the night in? Check it out *before* you go any further. Are the beds comfortable? Is the carpet clean? Are the walls attractive? Do the curtains or shades need attention? Are there sturdy hangers in the closet? Would emptying the closet and bureau be an impossible task? Is there a good light to read by? A writing table and comfortable chair? Peek under the bed to see if there are dust balls or old magazines tucked away. While relatives and friends would "understand" if things weren't perfect, a paying guest is entitled to cleanliness and comfort.

Equip the guest bureau or dresser with a good mirror, and provide a comfortable chair and good reading light. The clothes closet should be free of your family's clothing and storage items, and stocked with firm, plastic hangers, a few skirt hangers, and some hooks. Sachets hung on the rod will chase musty odors. Provide room-darkening shades or blinds on the windows. And if your house is located on a busy street, it is wise to have your guest bedrooms in the rear. Paying guests are entitled to a good night's rest! If your tap water is not tasty, it is thoughtful to supply bottled water.

If the idea of sprucing up the room has you overwhelmed, forget the idea and continue to be a guest rather than a host! If, however, a little "spit and polish," replacement of lumpy mattresses and sagging springs, and freshening the room in general present no problem, continue!

Mattresses should be firm, covered with a mattress pad, attractive linens, and bedspread. Although seconds are OK, good-quality linens are a wise investment, since cheap sheets tend to pill. Offer a selection of pillows of various firmnesses—a choice of down or fiberfill is the ultimate in consideration! Twin beds are often preferred, since many people do not wish to share a bed. Sofa beds are really not comfortable and should be avoided. Is there a bedside lamp and night table on each side of the bed? Bulbs should be at least 75 watts for comfortable reading. A luggage rack is convenient for guests and keeps the bedspread clean. Provide a varied assortment of books, current magazines in a rack, a local newspaper, and some information on what's doing in your town along with a map. If yours is a shared-bath accommodation, do provide a well-lit mirror and convenient electric outlet for makeup and shaving purposes. It will take the pressure off the bathroom! A fresh thermos of ice water and drinking glasses placed on an attractive dresser tray is always appreciated. Put it in the room while the guest is out to dinner, right next to the dish of hard candy or fruit. A fancy candlestick is a pretty accessory and a useful object in case of a power failure. Dresser drawers should be clean and lined with fresh paper. A sachet, flashlight, and a pad and pencil are thoughtful touches. For safety's sake, prohibit smoking in the bedroom. Besides, the odor of tobacco clings forever. Always spray the bedroom with air freshener a few minutes before the guest arrives. On warm or humid days, turn on the air conditioner as well.

From time to time sleep in each guest room yourself. It's the best test.

The Breakfast: Breakfast time can be the most pleasant part of a guest's stay. It is at the breakfast table with you and the other guests that suggestions are made as to what to see and do, and exchanges of experiences are enjoyed. From a guest's point of view, the only expected offering is what is known as a Continental breakfast, which usually consists of juice, roll, and coffee or tea.

Breakfast fare is entirely up to you. If you are a morning person who whips out of bed at the crack of dawn with special recipes for muffins dancing in your head, muffins to be drenched with your homemade preserves followed by eggs Benedict, an assortment of imported coffees or exotic teas—hop to it! You will play to a most appreciative audience. If, however, morning represents an awful intrusion on sleep, and the idea of talking to anyone before noon is difficult, the least you should do is to prepare the breakfast table the night before with the necessary mugs, plates, and silverware. Fill the electric coffeepot and leave instructions that the first one up should plug it in; you can even hook it up to a timer so that it will brew automatically!

Most of us fall somewhere in between these two extremes. Remember that any breakfast at "home" is preferable to getting dressed, getting into a car, and driving to some coffee shop. Whether you decide upon a Continental breakfast or a full American breakfast, consisting of juice or fruit, cereal or eggs, possibly bacon or sausage, toast, rolls, and coffee or tea, is up to you. It is most important that whatever the fare, it be included in your room rate. It is most awkward, especially after getting to know and like your guests, to present an additional charge for breakfast.

With so many of us watching calories, caffeine, and cholesterol, be prepared to offer unsweetened and/or whole grain breads, oat-bran cereals and muffins, and brewed decaf coffee or tea. It is also thoughtful to inquire about your guests' dietary restrictions and allergies. Whatever you serve, do have your table attractively set.

Some Suggestions

- Don't have a messy kitchen. If you have pets, make sure their food dishes are removed after they've eaten. If you have cats, make sure they don't walk along the countertops, and be certain that litter boxes are cleaned without fail. Sparkling clean surroundings are far more important than the decor.
- Let guests know when breakfast will be served. Check to see if they have any allergies, diet restrictions, or dislikes. Vary the menu if guests are staying more than one night.
- Do offer one nonsweet bread for breakfast.
- Consider leaving a breakfast order sheet in each room with a request that it be returned before guests retire. It might read:

We serve breakfast between 7 AM and 10 AM. Please check your preference and note the time at which you plan to eat.

☐ Coffee ☐ Tea ☐ Decaf ☐ Milk ☐ Toast ☐ Muffins
☐ Sweet Rolls ☐ Orange Juice ☐ Tomato Juice ☐ Fruit Cup

The Bath: This really is the third B in B&B. If you are blessed with an extra bathroom for the exclusive use of a guest, that's super. If guests will have to share the facilities with others, that really presents no problem. If it's being shared with your family, the family must always be "last in line." Be sure that they are aware of the guest's importance; the guest, paying or otherwise, always comes first. No retainers, used Band-Aids, or topless toothpaste tubes are to be carelessly left on the sink. The tub, shower, floor, and toilet bowl are to be squeaky clean. The mirrors and chrome should sparkle, and a supply of toilet tissue, fresh soap, and unfrayed towels goes a long way in reflecting a high standard of cleanliness. Make sure that the grout between tiles is free of mildew and that the shower curtain is unstained; add nonskid tape to the tub. Cracked ceilings should be repaired. Paint should be free of chips, and if your bath is wallpapered, make certain no loose edges mar its beauty.

Although it is your responsibility to check out the bath at least twice a day, most guests realize that in a share-the-bath situation they should leave the room ready for the next person's use. It is a thoughtful reminder for you to leave tub cleanser, a cleaning towel or sponge, and bathroom deodorant handy for this purpose. A wastepaper basket, paper towels, and paper cups should be part of your supplies. Needless to say, your hot water and septic systems should be able to accommodate the number of guests you'll have without being overtaxed. Call the plumber to fix any clogged drains or dripping faucets. Make sure that there are enough towel bars and hooks to accommodate the towels of all guests. Extra bathroom touches:

- Use liquid soap dispensers in lieu of bar soap on the sink.
- Provide a place for guests' personal toilet articles; shelves add convenience and eliminate clutter.
- Give different colored towels to each guest.
- Supply each guest room with its own bath soap in a covered soap dish.
- Provide guests with one-size-fits-all terry robes.

The B&B Business

Money Matters: Before embarking upon any business, it's a good idea to discuss it with an accountant and possibly an attorney. Since you'll be using your home for a business enterprise there are things with which they are familiar that are important for you to know. For instance, you may want to incorporate, so find out what the pros and cons are. Ask about depreciation. Deductible business expenses may include refurbishing, furnishings, supplies, printing costs, postage, etc. An accountant will be able to guide you with a simple system of record keeping. Accurate records will help you analyze income and expense, and show if you are breaking even or operating at a profit or a loss.

Taxes: Contact your state department of taxation requesting specific written information regarding tax collection and payment schedules. Get a sales tax number from your county clerk. If you rent rooms less than 15 days a year, you need not report the B&B income on your federal return. Income after the fourteenth day is taxable, and you can take deductions and depreciation allowances against it. If the revenues from running the B&B are insignificant, you can call it "hobby income" and avoid taxes. However, you can't qualify as a business and may lose other tax advantages.

Record Keeping: Open a B&B checking account and use it to pay expenses and to deposit all income, including sales tax associated with the B&B. Write checks whenever possible for purchases; get dated receipts when you can. Estimate the cost of serving breakfast and multiply it by the number of guests you feed annually; keep track of extra expenses for household supplies and utilities.

The Case for Credit Cards: Many guests prefer to stay now and pay later; business travelers like the easy record keeping for their expense sheets. Even if you don't wish to accept them on a regular basis, credit cards give you the opportunity to take a deposit over the phone when there isn't time to receive one by mail. The cost is negligible, generally 4 percent.

If you do accept a last-minute reservation without a credit card number to guarantee it, make certain the caller understands that if they don't show up, and you have held the room for them, you will have lost a night's rent. You may also remind the caller that if they aren't there by a mutually agreed-upon time, you may rent the room to someone else. Needless to say, it is equally important for you to remain at home to receive the guests or to be on hand for a phone call should they get lost en route to your home.

Insurance: It is important to call your insurance broker. Some homeowner policies have a clause covering "an occasional overnight paying guest." See if you will be protected under your existing coverage and, if not, what the additional premium would be.

Every home should be equipped with smoke detectors and fire extinguishers. All fire hazards should be eliminated; stairways and halls should be well lit and kept free of clutter. If you haven't already done so, immediately post prominently the emergency numbers for the fire department, police, and ambulance service.

Safety Reminders: Equip guest bedrooms and bathrooms with nightlights. Keep a flashlight (in working order!) in each bedroom, in case of power failure. Bathrooms should have nonslip surfaces in the tub and shower, and handholds should be installed in bathtubs. Keep a well-stocked first aid kit handy and know how to use it. Learn the Heimlich Maneuver and CPR (cardiopulmonary resuscitation). Periodically test smoke detectors and fire extinguishers to make certain they are in working order.

Regulations: If you have read this far and are still excited about the concept of running a B&B, there are several steps to take at this point. As of this writing, there don't seem to be any specific laws governing B&Bs. Since guests are generally received on an irregular basis, B&Bs do not come under the same laws governing hotels and motels. And since B&Bs aren't inns where emphasis is on food rather than on lodging, no comparison can really be made in that regard either. As the idea grows, laws and regulations will probably be passed. Refer to the back of *Bed & Breakfast U.S.A.* to write to your state's office of tourism for information. The address and phone number are listed for your convenience. You might even call or write to a few B&Bs in your state and ask the host about his or her experience in this regard. Most hosts will be happy to give you the benefit of their experience, but keep in mind that they are busy people and it would be wise to limit your intrusion upon their time.

If you live in a traditional, residential area and you are the first in your neighborhood to consider operating a B&B, it would be prudent to examine closely the character of houses nearby. Do physicians, attorneys, accountants, or psychologists maintain offices in their residences? Do dressmakers, photographers, cosmeticians, or architects receive clients in their homes? These professions are legally accepted in the most prestigious communities as "customary house occupations." Bed and breakfast has been tested in many communities where the question was actually brought to court. In towns from La Jolla, California, to Croton-on-Hudson, New York, bed and breakfast has been approved and accepted.

Zoning boards are not always aware of the wide acceptance of the B&B concept. Possibly the best evidence that you could present to them is a copy of *Bed & Breakfast U.S.A.*, which indicates that it is an accepted practice throughout the entire country. It illustrates the caliber of the neighborhoods, the beauty of the homes, and the fact that many professionals are also hosts. Reassure the zoning board that you will accept guests only by advance reservation. You will not display any exterior signs to attract attention to your home. You will keep your home and grounds properly maintained, attractive, and in no way detract from the integrity of your neighborhood. You will direct guests to proper parking facilities and do nothing to intrude upon the privacy of your neighbors.

After all, there is little difference between the visit of a family friend and a B&B guest, because that is the spirit and essence of a B&B. Just as a friend would make prior arrangements to be a houseguest, so will a B&B guest make a reservation in advance. Neither would just drop in for an overnight stay. We are happy to share letters from hosts attesting to the high caliber, honesty, and integrity of B&B guests that come as a result of reading about their accommodations in this book. There are many B&Bs extending hospitality throughout the United States, and the number is increasing geometrically every day.

You should also bring along a copy of *Bed & Breakfast U.S.A.* when you go to visit the local chamber of commerce. Most of them are enthusiastic, because additional visitors mean extra business for local restaurants, shops, theaters, and businesses. This is a good time to inquire what it would cost to join the chamber of commerce.

The Name: The naming of your B&B is most important and will take some time and consideration because this is the moment when dreams become reality. It will be used on your brochures, stationery, and bills. (If you decide to incorporate, the corporation needs a name!) It should somehow be descriptive of the atmosphere you wish to convey.

Brochure: Once you have given a name to your house, design a brochure. The best ones include a reservation form and can be mailed to your prospective guests. The brochure should contain the name of your B&B, address, phone number, best time to call, your name, a brief description of your home, its ambience, a brief history of the house if it is old, the number of guest rooms, whether or not baths are shared, the type of breakfast served, rates, required deposit, minimum stay requirement if any, dates when you'll be closed, and your cancellation policy. Although widely used, the phrase ''Rates subject to change without notice'' should be avoided. Rather, state the specific dates when the rates will be valid. A deposit of one night's stay is acceptable, and the promise of a full refund if cancellation is received at least two weeks prior to arrival is typical. If you have reduced rates for a specific length of stay, for families, for senior citizens, etc., mention it.

The Rate Sheet should be a separate insert so that if rates change, the entire brochure need not be discarded. Mention your smoking policy. If you do allow smoking inside the house, do you reserve any bedrooms for nonsmokers? Don't forget to mention the ages of your children, and describe any pets in residence. If you don't accept a guest's pet, be prepared to supply the name, address, and phone number of a reliable local kennel.

If you can converse in a foreign language, say so, because many visitors from abroad seek out B&Bs; it's a marvelous plus to be able to chat in their native tongue. Include your policy regarding children, pets, or smokers, and whether you offer the convenience of a guest refrigerator or barbecue. It is helpful to include directions from a major route and a simple map for finding your home. It's a good idea to include a line or two about yourself and your interests, and do mention what there is to see and do in the area as well as proximity to any major university. A line drawing of your house is a good investment since the picture can be used not only on the brochure but on your stationery, postcards, and greeting cards as well. If you can't have this taken care of locally, write the Tourist House Association. We have a service that can handle it for you.

Take your ideas to a reliable printer for his professional guidance. Don't forget to keep the receipt for the printing bill since this is a business expense.

Confirmation Letter: Upon receipt of a paid reservation, do send out a letter confirming it. You can design a form letter and have it offset-printed by a printer, since the cost of doing so is usually nominal. Include the dates of the stay; number of people expected; the rate, including tax; the cancellation policy; as well as explicit directions by car and, if applicable, by public transportation. A simple map reflecting the exact location of your home in relation to major streets and highways is most useful. It is a good idea to ask your guests to call you if they will be traveling and unavailable by phone for the week prior to their expected arrival. You might even want to include any of the house rules regarding smoking, pets, or whatever.

Successful Hosting

The Advantage of Hosting: The nicest part of being a B&B host is that you aren't required to take guests every day of the year. Should there be times when having guests would not be convenient, you can always say you're full and try to arrange an alternate date. But most important, keep whatever date you reserve. It is an excellent idea at the time reservations are accepted to ask for the name and telephone number of an emergency contact should you have to cancel unexpectedly. However, *never* have a guest come to a locked door. If an emergency arises and you cannot reach your prospective guests in time, do make arrangements for someone to greet them, and make alternate arrangements so that they can be accommodated.

House Rules: While you're in the thinking stage, give some thought to the rules you'd like your guests to adhere to. The last thing you want for you or your family is to feel uncomfortable in your own home. Make a list of House Rules concerning arrival and departure during the guests' stay, and specify when breakfast is served. If you don't want guests coming home too late, say so. Most hosts like to lock up at a certain hour at night, so arrange for an extra key for night owls. If that makes you uncomfortable, have a curfew on your House Rules list. If smoking disturbs you, confine the area where it's permitted.

Some guests bring a bottle of their favorite beverage and enjoy a drink before going out to dinner. Many hosts enjoy a cocktail hour too, and often provide cheese and crackers to share with guests. B&Bs cannot sell drinks to guests since this would require licensing. If you'd rather no drinks be consumed in your home, say so.

Many hosts don't mind accommodating a well-behaved pet. If you don't mind, or have pets of your own, discuss this with your guests before they pack Fido's suitcase. Your House Rules can even be included in your brochure. That way, both host and guest are aware of each other's likes and dislikes, and no hard feelings are made.

Entertaining: One of the most appealing features of being a guest at a B&B is the opportunity to visit in the evening with the hosts. After a day of sightseeing or business, it is most relaxing and pleasant to sit around the living room and chat. For many hosts, this is the most enjoyable part of having guests. However, if you are accommodating several people on a daily basis, entertaining can be tiring. Don't feel you'll be offending anyone by excusing yourself to attend to your own family or personal needs. The situation can be easily handled by having a room to which you can retreat, and offering your guests the living room, den, or other area for games, books, magazines, and perhaps the use of a television or bridge table. Most guests enjoy just talking to one another since this is the main idea of staying at a B&B.

The Telephone: This is a most important link between you and your prospective guests. As soon as possible, have your telephone number included under your B&B name in the white pages. It is a good idea to be listed in the appropriate section in your telephone directory yellow pages. If your home phone is used for a lot of personal calls, ask the local telephone company about call-waiting service, or think about installing a separate line for your B&B. If you are out a lot, give some thought to using a telephone answering device to explain your absence and time of return, and record the caller's message. There is nothing more frustrating to a prospective guest than to call and get a constant busy signal, or no answer at all. Request that the caller leave his or her name and address so that you can mail a reservation form. This will help eliminate the necessity of having to return long-distance calls. If the caller wants further information, he or she will call again at the time you said you'd be home.

B&B guests don't expect a phone in the guest room. However, there are times when they might want to use your phone for a long-distance call. In your House Rules list, suggest that any such calls be charged to their home telephone. Business travelers often have telephone charge cards for this purpose. In either case, you should keep a telephone record book and timer near your instrument. Ask the caller to enter the city called, telephone number, and length of call. Thus, you will have an accurate record should a charge be inadvertently added to your bill. Or, if you wish, you can add telephone charges to the guest bill. A telephone operator will quote the cost of the per-minute charge throughout the country for this purpose.

Maid Service: If you have several guest rooms and bathrooms, you may find yourself being a chambermaid as part of the business. Naturally, each guest gets fresh linens upon arrival. If a guest stays up to three days, it isn't expected that bed linen be changed every day. What is expected is that the room be freshened and the bath be cleaned and towels replaced every day. If you don't employ a full-time maid you may want to investigate the possibility of hiring a high school student on a part-time basis to give you a hand with the housekeeping. Many guests, noticing the absence of help, will voluntarily lend a hand, although they have the right to expect some degree of service, particularly if they are paying a premium rate.

Keys: A great many hosts are not constantly home during the day. Some do "hosting" on a part-time basis, while involved with regular jobs. There are times when even full-time hosts have to be away during the day. If guests are to have access to the house while you are not on the premises, make extra keys and attach them to an oversize key chain. It is also wise to take a key deposit of $50 simply to assure return of the key. Let me add that in the 16 years of my personal experience, as well as in the opinions of other hosts, B&B guests are the most honest people you can have. No one has ever had even a washcloth stolen, let alone the family treasures. In fact, it isn't unusual for the guest to leave a small gift after a particularly pleasant visit. On the other hand, guests are sometimes forgetful and leave belongings behind. For this reason it is important for you to have their names and addresses so that you can return their possessions. They will expect to reimburse you for the postage.

Registering Guests: You should keep a regular registration ledger for the guest to complete before checking in. The information should include the full name of each guest, home address, phone number, business address and telephone, and auto license number. It's a good idea to include the name and phone number of a friend or relative in case of an emergency. This information will serve you well for other contingencies, such as the guest leaving some important article behind, an unpaid long-distance phone call, or the rare instance of an unpaid bill. You may prefer to have this information on your guest bill, which should be designed as a two-part carbon form. You will then have a record and the guest has a ready receipt. (Receipts are very important to business travelers!)

Settling the Bill: The average stay in a B&B is two nights. A deposit equal to one night's lodging is the norm; when to collect the balance is up to you. Most guests pay upon leaving, but if they leave so early that the settling of the bill at that time is inconvenient, you can request the payment the previous night. You might want to consider the convenience of accepting a major credit card, but contact the sponsoring company first to see what percentage of your gross is expected for this service. If you find yourself entertaining more business visitors than vacationers, it might be something you should offer. Most travelers are aware that cash or traveler's checks are the accepted modes of payment. Accepting a personal check is rarely risky, but again, it's up to you. You might include your preference in your brochure.

Other Meals: B&B means that only breakfast is served. If you enjoy cooking and would like to offer other meals for a fee, make sure that you investigate the applicable health laws. If you have to install a commercial kitchen, the idea might be too expensive for current consideration. However, allowing guests to store fixings for a quick snack or to use your barbecue can be a very attractive feature for families traveling with children or for people watching their budget. If you can offer this convenience, be sure to mention it in your brochure. (And be sure to add a line to your House Rules that the guest is expected to clean up.) Some hosts keep an extra guest refrigerator on hand for this purpose.

It's an excellent idea to keep menus from your local restaurants on hand. Try to have a good sampling, ranging from moderately priced to expensive dining spots, and find out if reservations are required. Your guests will always rely heavily upon your advice and suggestions. After all, when it comes to your town, you're the authority! It's also a nice idea to keep informed of local happenings that might be of interest to your visitors. A special concert at the university or a local fair or church supper can add an extra dimension to their visit. If parents are visiting with young children they might want to have dinner out without them; try to have a list of available baby-sitters. A selection of guidebooks covering your area is also a nice feature.

The Guest Book: These are available in most stationery and department stores, and it is important that you buy one. It should contain designated space for the date, the name of the guest, home address, and a blank area for the guest's comments. They generally sign the guest book before checking out. The guest book is first of all a permanent record of who came and went. It will give you an idea of what times during the year you were busiest and which times were slow. Second, it is an easy way to keep a mailing list for your Christmas cards and future promotional mailings. You will also find that thumbing through it in years to come will recall some very pleasant people who were once strangers but now are friends.

Advertising: Periodically distribute your brochures to the local university, college, and hospital, since out-of-town visitors always need a place to stay. Let your local caterers know of your existence since wedding guests are often from out of town. If you have a major corporation in your area, drop off a brochure at the personnel office. Even visiting or relocating executives and salespeople enjoy B&Bs. Hotels and motels are sometimes overbooked; it wouldn't hurt to leave your brochure with the manager for times when there's no room for their last-minute guests. Local residents sometimes have to put up extra guests, so it's a good idea to take an ad out in your local school or church newspaper. The cost is usually minimal. Repeat this distribution process from time to time so that you can replenish the supply of brochures.

Check the back of this book for the address of your state tourist office. Write to them, requesting inclusion in any brochures listing B&Bs in the state.

The best advertising is being a member of the Tourist House Association since all member B&Bs are fully described in this book, which is available in bookstores, libraries, and B&Bs throughout the United States and Canada. In addition, it is natural for THAA, Inc., members to recommend one another when guests inquire about similar accommodations in other areas. The most important reason for keeping your B&B clean, comfortable, and cordial is that we are all judged by what a guest experiences in any individual Tourist House Association home. The best publicity will come from your satisfied guests, who will recommend your B&B to their friends.

Additional Suggestions

Extra Earnings: You might want to consider a few ideas for earning extra money in connection with being a host. If guests consistently praise your muffins and preserves, you might sell attractively wrapped extras as take-home gifts. If you enjoy touring, you can plan and conduct a special outing, off the beaten tourist track, for a modest fee. In major cities, you can do such things as acquiring tickets for theater, concert, or sports events. A supply of *Bed & Breakfast U.S.A.* for sale to guests is both a source of income and gives every THAA, Inc., member direct exposure to the B&B market. Think about offering the use of your washer and dryer. You may, if you wish, charge a modest fee to cover the service. Guests who have been traveling are thrilled to do their wash or have it done for them "at home" rather than wasting a couple of hours at the laundromat.

Several hosts tell me that a small gift shop is often a natural off-shoot of a B&B. Items for sale might include handmade quilts, pillows, potholders, and knitted items. One host has turned his hobby of woodworking into extra income. He makes lovely picture frames, napkin rings, and footstools that many guests buy as souvenirs to take home. If you plan to do this, check with the Small Business Administration to inquire about such things as a resale license and tax collection; a chamber of commerce can advise in this regard.

Transportation: While the majority of B&B guests arrive by car, there are many who rely on public transportation. Some hosts, for a modest fee, are willing to meet arriving guests at airports, train depots, or bus stations. Do be knowledgeable about local transportation schedules in your area, and be prepared to give explicit directions for your visitors' comings and goings. Have phone numbers handy for taxi service, as well as information on car rentals.

Thoughtful Touches: Guests often write to tell us of their experiences at B&Bs as a result of learning about them through this book. These are some of the special touches that made their visit special: fresh flowers in the guest room; even a single flower in a bud vase is pretty. One hostess puts a foil wrapped piece of candy on the pillow before the guest returns from dinner. A small decanter of wine and glasses, or a few pieces of fresh fruit in a pretty bowl on the dresser are lovely surprises. A small sewing kit in the bureau is handy. Offer guests the use of your iron and ironing board, rather than having them attempt to use the bed or dresser. Writing paper and envelopes in the desk invite the guest to send a quick note to the folks at home. If your house sketch is printed on it, it is marvelous free publicity. A pre-bed cup of tea for adults and cookies and milk for children are always appreciated.

By the way, keep a supply of guest-comment cards in the desk, both to attract compliments as well as to bring to your attention the flaws in your B&B that should be corrected.

Join the Tourist House Association of America, Inc.: If you are convinced that you want to be a host, and have thoroughly discussed the pros and cons with your family and advisers, complete and return the membership application found at the back of this book. Our dues are $40 annually. The description of your B&B will be part of the next edition of *Bed & Breakfast U.S.A.* Paid-up members receive a complimentary copy of *Bed & Breakfast U.S.A.* You will also receive the THAA, Inc.'s newsletter; regional seminars and conferences are held occasionally and you might enjoy attending. And, as an association, we will have clout should the time come when B&B becomes a recognized industry.

Affiliating with a B&B Reservation Agency: There are 60 agencies listed in *Bed & Breakfast U.S.A.* If you do not care to advertise your house directly to the public, consider joining one in your area. Membership and reservation fees, as well as the degree of professionalism, vary widely from agency to agency, so do check carefully.

Prediction of Success: Success should not be equated with money alone. If you thoroughly enjoy people, are well organized, enjoy sharing your tidy home without exhausting yourself, then the idea of receiving compensation for the use of an otherwise dormant bedroom will be a big plus. Your visitors will seek relaxing, wholesome surroundings, and unpretentious hosts who open their hearts as well as their homes. Being a B&B host or guest is an exciting, enriching experience.

3

B&B Recipes

The recipes that follow are B&B host originals. They've been cho-sen because of the raves they've received from satisfied B&B guests. The most important ingredient is the heartful of love that goes into each one.

We always have a good response to our request for favorite break-fast recipes. Although we could not publish them all this time, we will use most of them in future editions.

Tea Scones

3 c. all-purpose flour
$^1/_2$ c. sugar
4 tsp. baking powder
$^1/_2$ tsp. salt
$^1/_2$ c. butter or margarine
1 tbsp. orange or lemon zest

$^1/_2$ c. raisins or currants
2 eggs
Approximately $^1/_4$ c. milk
Butter, strawberry jam, and Devon
   cream, for serving

Preheat the oven to 450°F. In a large bowl, combine the flour, sugar, baking powder, and salt. Cut in the butter or margarine to make a crumblike texture. Stir in the orange zest and raisins. Beat the eggs in a 1-cup measure, then add enough milk to reach 1 cup. Lightly stir the egg mixture into the dry mixture to form a soft dough. Roll out the dough to a $^1/_2$-inch thickness. Cut into 2-inch rounds with a cutter. Place on a lightly greased cookie sheet and bake for 15 minutes. Serve with butter, strawberry jam, and Devon cream. Makes 12–16 scones.

Dorrington B&B, White Rocks, B.C., Canada

Duck's Nest Eggs

$^3/_4$ c. crumbled corn bread
1 c. chopped ham
$1^1/_2$ c. grated sharp cheese
$1^1/_2$ c. milk
6 large eggs, lightly beaten

1 tsp. hot sauce
1 tsp. Pickapeppa sauce
$^1/_4$ tsp. salt
$^1/_4$ tsp. pepper

Preheat the oven to 375°F. Coat 6 individual baking dishes, 6 inches long, 3 inches wide, one inch deep, with nonstick cooking spray. Place a layer of cornbread in each dish, followed by a layer of chopped ham and a layer of cheese. Combine the remaining ingredients, then pour over the top of each dish. Bake for 20 to 25 minutes, until brown and puffy. Serves 6.

Bay Breeze Guest House, Fairhope, Alabama

Nancy's Cranberry Coffee Cake

1 c. sugar
1 tbsp. butter
1 large egg
1 c. milk
2 c. all-purpose flour
3 tsp. baking powder

1/2 tsp. salt
1/2 to 3/4 of 16-oz. can whole cranberry
   sauce
1/2 cup chopped walnuts
1 tsp. cinnamon, and sugar, for
   topping

Preheat the oven to 350°F. In a large bowl, cream together the sugar, butter, and egg. Add the milk and dry ingredients. Pour the batter into 2 greased 8-inch cake pans. Spoon 1/2 cup of cranberry sauce over the top, then gently swirl it into the batter. Top with the leftover sauce and sprinkle generously with the nut topping. Bake for 20 to 25 minutes. Serve hot or cold. Serves 8–12.

Nancy's Auberge, Martha's Vineyard, Massachusetts

Pecan Pie Bars

3 c. all-purpose flour
1/2 c. sugar
1 c. margarine
1/2 tsp. salt
4 large eggs, lightly beaten

1 1/2 c. corn syrup
1 1/2 c. sugar
3 tbsp. margarine, melted
1 1/2 tsp. vanilla
2 1/2 c. chopped pecans

Preheat the oven to 350°F. Grease a 15 × 10 × 1-inch baking pan. In a large bowl with a mixer set at medium speed, beat the flour, sugar, margarine, and salt until the mixture resembles coarse crumbs; press firmly and evenly into the prepared pan. Bake for 15 to 20 minutes. While the crust is baking, prepare the filling. In a large bowl, stir the eggs, corn syrup, sugar, melted margarine, and vanilla until blended. Stir in the pecans. Spread evenly over the hot crust. Bake for 20 to 25 minutes or until set. Cool on a wire rack. Makes 48 bars.

Dear's Rest B&B, Ozark, Missouri

Pumpkin Chocolate Chip Muffins

1²/₃ c. all-purpose flour
1 c. granulated sugar
1 tbsp. pumpkin pie spice
¹/₄ tsp. baking powder
1 tsp. baking soda

¹/₄ tsp. salt
1 c. chocolate chips
2 large eggs
1 c. plain pumpkin puree
¹/₂ c. butter or margarine, melted

Preheat the oven to 350°F. In a medium bowl, combine the first 7 ingredients. In a separate bowl, beat the eggs, then add the pumpkin and butter or margarine and whisk until well blended. Pour over the dry ingredients and mix until moistened. Spoon into muffin cups and bake for 20 to 25 minutes. Makes 12 muffins.

Snow Goose Inn, Grove City, Pennsylvania

Almond Ham Croissants

4 croissants
6 tbsp. softened cream cheese
4 slices ham
9-oz. jar orange marmalade
¹/₃ c. orange juice
5 large eggs
1 c. half-and-half

1 tsp. almond extract (do not leave this out or substitute)
¹/₄ cup toasted almonds
Strawberries or raspberries and mandarin orange sections, for garnish

Cut the croissants in half lengthwise and spread the softened cream cheese over the bottom halves. Place a slice of ham on each one, then transfer to a 12 × 9-inch ovenproof dish. Combine the marmalade and orange juice and spread over the ham, reserving enough to be used as a glaze for the tops of the croissants. Place the tops on the croissants. In a medium bowl, beat the eggs, half-and-half, and almond extract until well blended, then pour over the croissants. Refrigerate overnight. Remove the croissants from the refrigerator 30 minutes before baking and preheat the oven to 350°F. Bake the croissants for 15 minutes, then spoon the remaining marmalade mixture on top and sprinkle with the toasted almonds. Continue baking for an additional 5 to 10 minutes, until the egg mixture is set. Serve hot, garnished with strawberries or raspberries and mandarin orange slices. Serves 4.

Austin's Wildflower Inn, Austin, Texas

Grand Marnier Soufflé Pancakes

6 large eggs, separated
2 c. small-curd cottage cheese
1/4 c. canola oil
5 tbsp. freshly squeezed orange juice
  (must be fresh)
1 tbsp. grated orange zest
1 tbsp. Grand Marnier

1 1/2 tbsp. sugar
4 tsp. baking powder
1/2 tsp. salt
1/4 c. finely chopped pecans
Pure maple syrup or fresh strawberry
  sauce, for serving

Place the egg yolks and all of the remaining ingredients except for the egg whites and pecans in a food processor and blend until smooth. Transfer the batter to a large bowl and set aside to rest for at least 30 minutes. In another large bowl, beat the egg whites until stiff. Fold in the pecans and egg whites. Spoon about 1/4 cup batter per pancake onto a hot buttered griddle and cook until browned on both sides, watching carefully to avoid burning. If desired, finished pancakes can be held in a warm oven for a few minutes. The texture will become a bit firmer upon standing. Serve with pure maple syrup or fresh strawberry sauce. Serves 6.

Sampson Eagon Inn, Staunton, Virginia

Sweet Tomato Chutney

1 whole bulb garlic, peeled and
  chopped
2 1-inch pieces fresh ginger, peeled and
  chopped
1 1/2 c. red wine vinegar
2 lbs. fresh tomatoes, skinned, or 1 lb.
  12 oz. canned whole tomatoes

1 1/2 c. sugar
1 1/2 tsp. salt
1/4–1/2 tsp. cayenne pepper, to taste
2 tbsp. golden raisins
2 tbsp. blanched slivered almonds
Cream cheese and crackers, for serving

Put the garlic, ginger, and 1/2 cup of the vinegar in a food processor and process until smooth. In a large, heavy-bottomed pot, combine the tomatoes (with their liquid if using canned tomatoes), the remaining 1 cup vinegar, the sugar, salt, and cayenne pepper. Bring to a boil. Add the puree from the food processor and simmer, uncovered, for 2 to 3 hours, until the chutney thickens and a film clings to a spoon when dipped into it. Stir occasionally at first and more frequently as it thickens; you may need to lower the heat as the liquid diminishes. Add the raisins and almonds. Simmer, stirring, for another 5 minutes. Turn off the heat and let cool. The chutney should be as thick as honey. Bottle in clean containers and refrigerate. Makes about 2 cups. Serve with cream cheese and crackers.

A B&B at Llewellyn, Lexington, Virginia

Rhubarb Muffins

1/2 c. buttermilk	1 tsp. baking soda
1 medium egg	1 tsp. baking powder
1/2 c. vegetable oil	1/4 tsp. salt
2 tsp. vanilla	1 1/2 c. diced rhubarb
2 1/2 c. all-purpose flour	1/2 c. chopped pecans
1 1/4 c. brown sugar	

Topping

1 1/4 tsp. melted margarine	1 heaping tbsp. all-purpose flour
1/3 c. white sugar	1 tsp. cinnamon

Preheat oven to 400°F. Beat together the buttermilk, egg, oil, vanilla, flour, brown sugar, baking soda, baking powder, and salt. Add the rhubarb and nuts. Spoon into greased muffin cups about 2/3 of the way to the top. Combine the melted margarine, sugar, flour, and cinnamon, and sprinkle over the muffins. Bake for 18 to 20 minutes. Makes 24 muffins.

Rummel's Tree Haven B&B, Sebewaing, Michigan

Blueberry Banana Muffins

1 egg	1/3 c. sugar
1/2 c. buttermilk	2 tsp. baking powder
1/2 c. vegetable oil	1 tsp. baking soda
1 ripe banana	1 tsp. salt
2 c. all-purpose flour	1 1/2 c. frozen blueberries

Preheat the oven to 400°F. In a blender, combine the egg, buttermilk, vegetable oil, and banana until smooth. Sift the dry ingredients into a medium bowl. Add the frozen blueberries and the banana mixture and stir until the flour is moistened (batter will be lumpy). Fill 12 greased muffin cups about 3/4 of the way to the top. Bake for about

20 minutes, until golden brown. Immediately remove the muffins from the pan. Makes 12 muffins.

The Blue Door B&B, Del Mar, California

Cornmeal Soufflé

3 tbsp. butter
2 tbsp. chopped green onion
1¼ c. milk
¾ c. Monterey Jack cheese

¼ c. yellow cornmeal
½ tsp. oregano
4 large eggs, separated

Preheat the oven to 350°F. In a medium saucepan, melt the butter. Add the green onion and sauté until softened. Add the milk, cheese, cornmeal, and oregano, and stir until the cheese is melted. Remove from the heat and stir in the egg yolks to blend. In a medium bowl, beat the egg whites to soft peaks, then fold them into the cornmeal mixture. Pour into 2 pint-size soufflé dishes. Set the soufflé dishes in a pan and add enough water to reach 1½ inches up the sides. Bake for 45 minutes or until the top is dry. Serves 4.

The Heirloom Circa 1863 B&B Inn, Ione, California

Creamed Beef on Toast

1 lb. ground round beef
1 tsp. oregano
1 tsp. dried basil
Salt and pepper, to taste
4 tbsp. chopped onion

1 stick margarine or butter
¼ cup all-purpose flour
2 c. hot milk
1 tbsp. Worcestershire sauce
Toast or biscuits, for serving

In a heavy 10- to 12-inch skillet over medium heat, cook the beef with the oregano, basil, salt, and pepper until browned. Remove the meat from the skillet. In the same skillet, sauté the onion in the margarine for about 5 minutes. Add the flour and stir with a wooden spoon for about 1 minute. Heat the milk until just hot but not boiling, then pour into the skillet all at once, stirring constantly with a whisk until thickened. Remove the skillet from the heat and add the Worcestershire sauce and meat mixture. Serve over toast or biscuits. Creamed beef can be kept warm on a low setting in the oven for 2 hours. Serves 4.

Papaya Paradise B&B, Kailua, Oahu, Hawaii

Sour Cream Pancakes with Blueberry Sauce

4 large eggs	2 tbsp. sugar
1 pint sour cream	1 tsp. baking soda
6 heaping tbsp. all-purpose flour	$^1/_2$ tsp. salt

Blueberry Sauce

2 c. fresh or frozen blueberries	$^1/_4$ tsp. pumpkin pie spice
$^1/_2$ c. light corn syrup	Salt to taste
1 tbsp. water	1 tbsp. lemon juice
2 tbsp. cornstarch	

To make the pancakes, in a medium bowl, beat the eggs. Add the remaining ingredients and beat well. Spoon about $^1/_4$ cup batter per pancake on a lightly greased griddle and cook at 325°F until browned on both sides. If desired, hold the pancakes in a warm oven while preparing the sauce.

To make the sauce, in a medium saucepan, combine the blueberries and light corn syrup. Add the water, cornstarch, pumpkin pie spice, and salt. Bring to a boil over medium heat, stirring constantly. Boil 1 minute. Remove from the heat and stir in the lemon juice. Spoon the warm sauce over the pancakes. Serves 4.

Juniper Hill Farm, Dubuque, Iowa

Beef and Bean Round-Up

$1^1/_2$ lb. ground beef	16-oz. can baked beans
$^1/_4$ c. chopped onion	10-oz. can refrigerated flaky biscuit
1 c. barbecue sauce	dough
1 tbsp. brown sugar	$^1/_2$ c. shredded Cheddar cheese

Preheat the oven to 375°F. In a large skillet over medium heat, brown the ground beef and onion, then drain. Stir in the barbecue sauce, brown sugar, and beans, and heat until bubbly. Pour into a $2^1/_2$-quart casserole. Separate the dough into 10 biscuits, then cut each biscuit in half crosswise. Place the biscuits over the hot meat mixture, cut side down and in spoke fashion around the edge of the casserole. Sprinkle the cheese over the biscuits. Bake for 22 to 25 minutes or until the biscuits are golden brown. Serves 6.

Oak Square Plantation, Port Gibson, Mississippi

Sampler's Steamy Apple Pudding

1 1/2 c. sifted all-purpose flour
1 tsp. baking soda
1/4 tsp. salt
1/2 tsp. cinnamon
1/2 tsp. nutmeg
1/4 tsp. cloves
1/4 c. softened butter

1 c. sugar
2 large eggs, beaten
4 medium apples, pared and shredded
1/2 c. raisins
Boiling water
Light cream, for serving

Grease a 1 1/2-quart heatproof bowl. Into a small bowl, sift flour, baking soda, salt, and spices; set aside. In a large bowl, beat the butter, sugar, and eggs until smooth and light. Stir in the apples and raisins. Stir the flour mixture into the fruit mixture and mix well. Turn into the prepared bowl. Cover the surface of the pudding with a double thickness of wax paper. Cover the top of the bowl completely with aluminum foil and tie the edge securely with twine. Place the bowl on a trivet in a Dutch oven. Pour the boiling water around the bowl to come halfway up the side. Cover the Dutch oven and bring the water to a boil. Reduce the heat and simmer for 2 hours. Remove the bowl to a wire rack and let stand for 5 minutes. With a spatula, gently loosen the edge of the pudding from the side of the bowl. Invert onto a serving dish. Serve warm with cream. Serves 6–8.

Williamsburg Sampler Bed & Breakfast, Williamsburg, Virginia

4

Wheelchair Accessible Listings

Although this chapter is small, within a few years *Bed & Breakfast U.S.A.* hopes to have listings from all fifty states and Canada. The requirements are fairly simple. To be listed in this section, all B&Bs must have easy-access entrances and exits. Doorways must be wide enough to admit a wheelchair—36 inches should be wide enough. Toilets and tubs must have reach bars. If the bathroom has a shower, reach bars and a built-in seat are preferable. Wheelchairs should be able to fit under the breakfast table; 26 inches is high enough. It's also a good idea to check to see what kind of activities are available. Many parks, restaurants, shopping areas, museums, beaches, etc. have wheelchair accessibility. If you or someone you know has a B&B that is wheelchair accessible, please turn to page 583 for further details.

Kern River Inn Bed & Breakfast ✪
P.O. BOX 1725, 119 KERN RIVER DRIVE, KERNVILLE, CALIFORNIA 93238

Tel: **(760) 376-6750; (800) 986-4382**	Open: **All year**
Best Time to Call: **8 AM–8 PM**	Reduced Rates: **Available**
Hosts: **Jack and Carita Prestwich**	Breakfast: **Full**
Location: **50 mi. NE of Bakersfield**	Credit Cards: **AMEX, MC, VISA**
No. of Rooms: **1**	Pets: **No**
No. of Private Baths: **1**	Children: **Welcome**
Double/pb: **$89–$99**	Smoking: **No**
Single/pb: **$79–$89**	Social Drinking: **Permitted**

Stay in a charming riverfront B&B in a quaint Western town within Sequoia National Forest. Jack and Carita specialize in romantic, relaxing getaways. Their accessible room has a queen bed and a Piute-style, wood-burning fireplace. (Your hosts provide the wood.) Native American pictures and macramé wall hangings accent the room's Southwestern color scheme of beige, mauve, and sage green. The bathroom has grab bars; the full-size, mirror-doored closet has shelving that can be reached from a wheelchair.

Redwood Reflections ✪
4600 SMITH GRADE, SANTA CRUZ, CALIFORNIA 95060

Tel: **(408) 423-7221**	Reduced Rates: **10% Seniors, Disabled**
Best Time to Call: **Evenings**	Breakfast: **Full**
Hosts: **Ed and Dory Strong**	Credit Cards: **MC, VISA**
Location: **70 mi. S of San Francisco**	Pets: **No**
No. of Rooms: **1**	Children: **Welcome**
No. of Private Baths: **1**	Smoking: **No**
Suite: **$100**	Social Drinking: **Permitted**
Open: **All year**	

Nestled on 10 private acres of giant redwoods, Redwood Reflections offers one wheelchair-accessible room with a private bath and patio. A romantic Roman tub for two has a transfer seat and adjustable shower head. Grab bars for toilet and tub, 36-inch doors, and a roll-in vanity provide accessibility and safety. Guests are invited to concoct favorite goodies and listen to old-time piano music in an ice cream parlor featuring 1920s collectibles and a 100-year-old potbelly stove. A full breakfast is served and dietary restrictions can be observed. Santa Cruz is a wheelchair-friendly town and offers an amusement park, wharf with fine restaurants, and a 2-mile coastline sidewalk. The Monterey Bay Aquarium and two state parks are great accessible day excursions.

On Golden Pond Bed & Breakfast
7831 ELDRIDGE, ARVADA, COLORADO 80005

Tel: **(303) 424-2296**	Credit Cards: **AMEX, DISC, MC, VISA**
Host: **Kathy Kula**	Pets: **No**
Location: **15 mi. W of Denver**	Children: **No**
Suite: **$100**	Smoking: **No**
Open: **All year**	Social Drinking: **Permitted**
Reduced Rates: **10% weekly, seniors**	Foreign Languages: **German**
Breakfast: **Full**	

A secluded retreat tucked into the Rocky Mountain foothills, this custom-built, two-story brick home has dramatic views of mountains, prairies, and downtown Denver. Birds and other wildlife are drawn to the ten-acre grounds, which have a fishing pond and hiking trails. After a full breakfast, stroll along the garden path, bicycle by the creek, swim laps in the pool, or ride horses into the foothills. Then join Kathy for a late afternoon kaffeeklatsch. Conclude the day with a soak in the hot tub. The suite has a Jacuzzi tub and fireplace.

Bed & Breakfast Honolulu Statewide ✪

3242 KAOHINANI DRIVE, HONOLULU, HAWAII 96817
bnbshi@alohabnb.com; www.aloha-bnb.com

Tel: **(800) 288-4666; (808) 595-7533;**
  fax: **(808) 595-2030**
Best Time to Call: **8 AM–5 PM**
  Mon.–Fri., 8 AM–Noon Sat.
Coordinator: **Mary Lee**
States/Regions Covered: **Hawaii**
  Statewide

Rates (Single/Double):
  Modest: **$45–$55/$45–$60**
  Average: **$55–$70/$55–$75**
  Luxury: **$75 up/$75 up**
Credit Cards: **DISC, MC, VISA**

This home-based family service, started in 1982, pays careful attention to visitors who want to be more than tourists. That's made it Hawaii's largest statewide agency, listing more than 700 rooms, 10 wheelchair-friendly, on all islands. Many agencies have membership fees and directories; this one doesn't! When you call the 800 number, use the E-mail address, or fax Bed & Breakfast Honolulu, Mary Lee can match your needs, desires, and pocketbook to her computerized listings. This service's size lets her offer very favorable rates on rental cars and inter-island air.

Trinity Hills Farm B&B—Stained Glass Studio ✪

10455 OLD LOVELACEVILLE ROAD, PADUCAH, KENTUCKY 42001

Tel: **(800) 488-3998**
Best Time to Call: **10 AM–10 PM**
Hosts: **Mike and Ann Driver, Jim and
  Nancy Driver**
Location: **12 mi. W of Paducah**
Suites: **$80–$105**
Open: **All year**
Reduced Rates: **Available**

Breakfast: **Full**
Credit Cards: **DISC, MC, VISA**
Pets: **Sometimes**
Children: **Welcome**
Smoking: **No**
Social Drinking: **Permitted**
Airport Pickup: **Yes**

Share the serenity of the Drivers' 17-acre retreat. This three-story home offers amenities for romantic getaways and family retreats, and features one room for guests with disabilities. Your hosts have installed a chair-lift on both staircases to provide access to your suite. There is also an outdoor ramp. The room was specifically designed to meet your needs. Breakfast may include strawberry pecan waffles, blueberry pancakes, strata, and quiche.

Amanda's B&B Reservation Service ✪

1428 PARK AVENUE, BALTIMORE, MARYLAND 21217

Tel: **(410) 225-0001; fax: (410) 728-
  8957**
Best Time to Call: **8:30 AM–5:30 PM**
  Mon.–Fri.
Coordinator: **Betsy Grater**

States/Regions Covered: **Annapolis,
  Baltimore, Delaware, District of
  Columbia, Maryland, New Jersey,
  Pennsylvania, Virginia, West Virginia**

Rates (Double):
 Modest: **$85**
 Luxury: **$100–$150**

Credit Cards: **AMEX, DISC, MC, VISA**
Descriptive Directory of B&Bs: **$5**

The roster of this reservation service includes eight sites designed for visitors with disabilities—five in downtown Baltimore, two in Annapolis, and one in Chesapeake City.

The Allen House
18 ALLEN PLACE, SCITUATE, MASSACHUSETTS 02066

Tel: **(617) 545-8221**
Best Time to Call: **Mornings; evenings**
Hosts: **Christine and Iain Gilmour**
Location: **32 mi. SE of Boston**
No. of Rooms: **1**
No. of Private Baths: **1**
Double/pb: **$99–$169**

Open: **All year**
Breakfast: **Full**
Pets: **No**
Children: **Welcome, over 12**
Smoking: **No**
Social Drinking: **Permitted**
Airport/Station Pickup: **Yes**

With views of the village center, this white gabled Victorian overlooks the yacht harbor. When the Gilmours came to the United States in 1976, they brought along the lovely furniture of their native Great Britain. English antiques fill the house. They also imported British rituals: tea is a frequent celebration. For breakfast, Christine, a professional caterer, offers standards such as waffles and pancakes, as well as gourmet treats. The Allen House is distinguished by good music and good food. Iain, an accomplished musician, cheerfully shares the large library of classical music.

The Wildwood Inn ✪
121 CHURCH STREET, WARE, MASSACHUSETTS 01082

Tel: **(413) 967-7798; (800) 860-8098**
Best Time to Call: **After 10 AM**
Hosts: **Fraidell Fenster and Richard Watson**
Location: **8 mi. N of Mass. Pike (I-90), Exit 8**
No. of Rooms: **1**
No. of Private Baths: **1**
Double/pb: **$60–$90**

Open: **All year**
Reduced Rates: **Weekly**
Breakfast: **Full**
Credit Cards: **AMEX, DC, MC, VISA**
Pets: **No**
Children: **Welcome, over 6**
Smoking: **No**
Social Drinking: **Permitted**

This Queen Anne Victorian is furnished with American Primitive antiques, heirloom quilts, and early cradles. The first-floor bedroom is easily accessible from a roofed ramp leading directly to the accommodation. The beds can be arranged as twins or a king-size to meet most personal living styles. Both the room and the shower of the bath have grab bars for easy access. The shower is also equipped with a seat. For the hearing-impaired there is a strobe smoke detector. All the doors are equipped with lever-style handles. The room and bath are themed in birds and waterfowl, with air conditioning in summer. All the first-floor common areas are easily reached from this room, including the romantic fireplaced parlor, and spacious dining room overlooking a lovely garden, bird feeders, and birdbaths. Start off your day with a hearty New England breakfast before you venture out to Old Sturbridge Village, Old Deerfield, the Basketball Hall of Fame, or the 100-acre park behind the Inn with its paved roads and rustic pathways. Abundant information about recreational activities is kept at the Inn to meet the varying needs of our guests. Your comfort and relaxation are your hosts' most important goals.

Market Sleigh Bed & Breakfast ✪
BOX 99, 57 SOUTH MAIN STREET, LOGANVILLE, PENNSYLVANIA 17342-0099

Tel: **(717) 428-1440**	Reduced Rates: **After 3rd day**
Best Time to Call: **3–6 PM**	Breakfast: **Full**
Hosts: **Judy and Jerry Dietz**	Credit Cards: **MC, VISA**
Location: **7 mi. S of York**	Pets: **No**
No. of Rooms: **2**	Children: **Welcome (no crib)**
No. of Private Baths: **1**	Smoking: **No**
Suite: **$65–$85; $20 each additional person**	Social Drinking: **Permitted**
Open: **All year**	Minimum Stay: **2 nights convention weekends**

This bed and breakfast takes its name from the 19th-century sleigh sitting by the entrance as if stranded after the snow melted. A peaceful night's sleep and a hearty farmer's breakfast await you. Walk the paths of the 22-acre farm through the meadows, enjoy the stream and the quiet of the woodland, or just relax near the water garden and enjoy the view of the sheep and horses grazing in the valley. Judy and Jerry will direct you to fine dining, rail excursions, a dozen golf courses, parks, museums (including the Harley-Davidson Motorcycle Museum, only minutes away), farm markets, wineries, antiques, and historic areas. The Dietz home is on the bicycle crossroad and near the York County Rail Trail, which extends into Maryland.

The Jam N Jelly Inn Bed and Breakfast
1310 INDIAN RIDGE ROAD, JOHNSON CITY, TENNESSEE 37604

Tel: **(423) 929-0039**; fax: **(423) 929-9026**	Open: **All year**
	Reduced Rates: **Available**
Best Time to Call: **9 AM–11 PM**	Breakfast: **Full**
Hosts: **Bud and Carol Kidner**	Credit Cards: **AMEX, DISC, MC, VISA**
Location: **5 mi. SW of I-81, Exit 35**	Pets: **No**
No. of Rooms: **1**	Smoking: **No**
No. of Private Baths: **1**	Social Drinking: **Permitted**
Double/pb: **$65**	Minimum Stay: **2 nights special weekend events**
Single/pb: **$55**	Airport Pickup: **Yes**
Suite: **$75**	

The Jam N Jelly is centrally located and presents a unique lodging experience. The inn is a custom-built log home that offers comfort and privacy to guests. The decor is a tasteful blend of country casual elegance in a home-like atmosphere. The accessible room has a TV and is furnished with antique reproductions and a queen bed. Amenities include a well-stocked book and video library, 52-inch-screen TV/VCR, 8–10-person hot tub, spacious front porch, and a large covered rear deck for quiet reflection. The inn has smoke detectors and a sprinkler system throughout for your safety. Inside you'll find a copy and fax machine, central heat, and air conditioning. The inn's main entrance is accessible by ramp from the well-lit off-street parking lot. Snacks and complimentary beverages are provided in the evenings.

Seven Wives Inn ✪
217 NORTH 100 WEST, ST. GEORGE, UTAH 84770

Tel: **(435) 628-3737; (800) 600-3737**	Open: **All year**
Best Time to Call: **After 9 AM**	Reduced Rates: **Available**
Hosts: **Jay and Donna Curtis**	Breakfast: **Full**
Location: **125 mi. NE of Las Vegas**	Credit Cards: **AMEX, DC, MC, VISA**
No. of Rooms: **1**	Children: **By arrangement**
No. of Private Baths: **1**	Smoking: **No**
Double/pb: **$100**	Social Drinking: **Permitted**

This delightful inn is featured on the walking tour of St. George; it is just across from the Brigham Young home and two blocks from the historic Washington County Court House. Your hosts offer traditional Western hospitality. Their home is decorated with antiques collected in America and Europe. Bedrooms are named after some of the seven wives of Donna's polygamous great-grandfather. A gourmet breakfast is served in the elegant dining room that will give you a hint of the past. St. George is located near Zion and Bryce national parks, boasts eight golf courses, and is noted for its mild winters. Dixie College is nearby. There's a swimming pool for your pleasure.

The Iris Inn ✪
191 CHINQUAPIN DRIVE, WAYNESBORO, VIRGINIA 22980

Tel: **(540) 943-1991**	Reduced Rates: **Corporate; Sun.–Thurs.**
Best Time to Call: **10 AM–8 PM**	Breakfast: **Full**
Hosts: **Wayne and Iris Karl**	Credit Cards: **MC, VISA**
Location: **25 mi. W of Charlottesville**	Pets: **No**
No. of Rooms: **1**	Children: **Welcome, by arrangement**
No. of Private Baths: **1**	Smoking: **No**
Double/pb: **$80–$140**	Social Drinking: **Permitted**
Single/pb: **$65**	Minimum Stay: **2 nights weekends**
Open: **All year**	Airport Pickup: **Yes**

Southern charm and grace in a totally modern facility overlooking the historic Shenandoah Valley from the Blue Ridge Mountains' wooded western slope—that's what awaits you at The Iris Inn. It's ideal for a weekend retreat, a refreshing change for the business traveler, and a tranquil spot for tourists to spend a night or more. The wheelchair-accessible room is comfortably furnished and delightfully decorated with nature and wildlife motifs. The bathroom has a lavatory without a vanity, for easier use. There are grab bars at the toilet and on the sides of the shower, which also has a seat. A pocket door connects the bathroom and bedroom. For your convenience, a ramp leads from the parking lot level to the porch. Eight other rooms are available.

Connors Bed & Breakfast ✪
ROUTE 1, BOX 255, CABLE, WISCONSIN 54821

Tel: **(715) 798-3661; (800) 848-3932**	Breakfast: **Full**
Hosts: **Alex and Mona Connors**	Credit Cards: **MC, VISA**
Location: **1.7 mi. N of Cable**	Pets: **No**
No. of Rooms: **1**	Children: **Welcome**
No. of Private Baths: **1**	Smoking: **No**
Suites: **$85**	Social Drinking: **Permitted**
Open: **All year**	Airport/Station Pickup: **Yes**

Located 40 miles south of Lake Superior, Connors Bed & Breakfast offers one wheelchair-accessible room with a private bath. The room is spacious and has a gas fireplace, wood floors for easy mobility, king-size bed, pedestal table with plenty of space to accommodate a wheelchair, a large sofa, and an armoire that can be reached from a seated position. The bath features a Kohler shower with a bench and built-in grab bars, a wall-mounted sink, and a taller toilet with adjacent grab bars. Next to your room is the parlor with hardwood floors, a piano, chess set, and fireplace—a perfect spot for a chat with other guests. From this room it's easy access to the dining area and the ramp leading outside. The region boasts many activities; in particular, the Cable-Hayward area hosts a fishing weekend called "Fishing Has No Boundaries" for the disabled in mid-May at the Chippewa Campground.

5

State-by-State Listings

ALABAMA

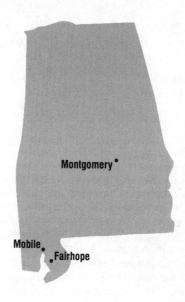

Montgomery •

Mobile•
  •Fairhope

Bay Breeze Guest House ✪
P.O. BOX 526, 742 SOUTH MOBILE STREET, FAIRHOPE, ALABAMA 36532

Tel: **(334) 928-8976**
Best Time to Call: **9 AM–9 PM**
Hosts: **Bill and Becky Jones**
Location: **20 mi. E of Mobile**
No. of Rooms: **4**
No. of Private Baths: **4**
Double/pb: **$95**
Guest Cottage Suite: **$105**
Open: **All year**

Breakfast: **Full**
Credit Cards: **AMEX, MC, VISA**
Pets: **Sometimes**
Children: **By arrangement**
Smoking: **No**
Social Drinking: **Permitted**
Minimum Stay: **2 nights weekends Apr.–Oct.**
Airport/Station Pickup: **Yes**

This unique bay-front stucco was built in the early 1930s and has been lovingly restored throughout the years. The house is decorated with family heirlooms, wicker, stained glass, hooked and oriental rugs, and period antiques that date back five generations. The guest rooms all have queen beds. The cottage suite features a living room and a minikitchen. Within walking distance you will find excellent restaurants, shops, and a sidewalk that follows the beach for an afternoon or evening stroll. Bill and Becky have their quarters upstairs, but are always available to cater to your needs or answer any questions you may have about the area.

Towle House ✪

1104 MONTAUK AVENUE, MOBILE, ALABAMA 36604

Tel: **(334) 432-6440**	Open: **All year**
Best Time to Call: **8 AM–8 PM**	Breakfast: **Full**
Hosts: **Felix and Carolyn Vereen**	Credit Cards: **MC, VISA**
No. of Rooms: **3**	Pets: **No**
No. of Private Baths: **1**	Children: **No**
Max. No. Sharing Baths: **4**	Smoking: **No**
Double/pb: **$70–$85**	Social Drinking: **Permitted**
Double/sb: **$70–$85**	Airport/Station Pickup: **Yes**

Towle House, circa 1874, is located in the heart of the historic district. This Italianate-style home is constructed of heart pine and cypress, and sits on a large lot surrounded by azaleas, dogwoods, and seasonal flowers. The house, originally used as a boys' school, has been recently restored and is furnished with turn-of-the-century antiques. Towle House is only 10 minutes away from the Convention Center, Mobile Auditorium, historic homes, antique shopping, and the revitalized downtown area. The Vereens' location is within easy access to the City of Mobile Museum, Fort Conde, and the USS *Alabama*.

Red Bluff Cottage ✪

551 CLAY STREET, MONTGOMERY, ALABAMA
(MAILING ADDRESS: P.O. BOX 1026, MONTGOMERY,
ALABAMA 36101)
redblufbnb@aol.com; www.bbonline.com/al/redbluff

Tel: **(334) 264-0056; fax: (334) 263-3054**	Suite: **$85**
	Open: **All year**
Best Time to Call: **9 AM–10 PM**	Breakfast: **Full**
Hosts: **Anne and Mark Waldo**	Pets: **No**
No. of Rooms: **4**	Children: **Welcome (crib)**
No. of Private Baths: **4**	Smoking: **No**
Double/pb: **$75**	Social Drinking: **Permitted**
Single/pb: **$65**	Airport/Station Pickup: **Yes**

This raised cottage is high above the Alabama River in Montgomery's historic Cottage Hill District, close to the State Capitol, Dexter Avenue King Memorial Baptist Church, the First White House of the Confederacy, the Civil Rights Memorial, and Old Alabama Town. The Alabama Shakespeare Festival Theatre, the Museum of Fine Arts, and the expanded zoo are also nearby. The bedrooms are downstairs. Guests come upstairs to read or relax in the living rooms, to enjoy the front porch view, and to have breakfast in the dining room. Many interesting antiques and a music room, complete with harpsichord, add to the charm of this home.

For key to listings, see inside front or back cover.

✪ This star means that rates are guaranteed through December 31, 1999, to any guest making a reservation as a result of reading about the B&B in *Bed & Breakfast U.S.A.*—1999 edition.

Important! To avoid misunderstandings, always ask about cancellation policies when booking.

Please enclose a self-addressed, stamped, business-size envelope when contacting reservation services.

For more details on what you can expect in a B&B, see Chapter 1.

Always mention *Bed & Breakfast U.S.A.* when making reservations!

We want to hear from you! Use the form on page 593.

ALASKA

Fairbanks

Chuglak

Anchorage

Alaska Private Lodgings ✪
P.O. BOX 200047, ANCHORAGE, ALASKA 99520–0047

Tel: **(907) 258-1717**; fax: **(907) 258-6613**
Best Time to Call: **9 AM–6 PM**
Coordinator: **Mercy Dennis**
States/Regions Covered: **Anchorage, Denali, Fairbanks, Girdwood, Homer, Hope, Kenai, Palmer, Seward, Southeast Regions, Talkeetna, Valdez, Wasilla, Willow, Yukon**

Descriptive Directory of B&Bs: **$5**
Rates (Single/Double):
 Modest: **$55–$65**
 Average: **$66–$85**
 Luxury: **$86 up**
Credit Cards: **AMEX, MC, VISA**

Alaskan hosts are this state's warmest resource! Mercy's accommodations range from an original log house of a pioneer's homestead, where the host is in the antique-doll business, to a one-bedroom apartment with a view of Mt. Denali. Many are convenient to the University of Alaska and Alaska Pacific University.

Elderberry B&B ✪
8340 ELDERBERRY STREET, ANCHORAGE, ALASKA 99502

Tel: **(907) 243-6968**
Hosts: **Norm and Linda Seitz**
No. of Rooms: **3**
No. of Private Baths: **2**
Max. No. Sharing Bath: **4**
Double/pb: **$80**
Double/sb: **$60**
Open: **All year**

Reduced Rates: **10% seniors; Sept. 15–Apr. 15 all rooms $50**
Breakfast: **Full**
Credit Cards: **MC, VISA**
Pets: **Sometimes**
Children: **Welcome**
Smoking: **No**
Social Drinking: **Permitted**

Elderberry B&B is the perfect place to stay while visiting Anchorage—it's located close to the airport, bike and walking trails, and the bus route, and within a short walking distance to many local restaurants. The Seitz home is a yellow two-story tastefully decorated with oak furnishings using Alaskan accents. Each guest room has matching furnishings, one with a queen, one with a double, and one with twin beds. Guests can enjoy two common rooms. One is for reading and relaxing, and the other has a big-screen TV and many videos to choose from. Linda considers Norm one of their best amenities, as he loves to tell guests all about Alaska. They both take special pride in their beautiful summer flowers, which have won blue ribbons at the state fair.

The Green Bough ✪
3832 YOUNG STREET, ANCHORAGE, ALASKA 99508
greenbough@compuserve.com

Tel: **(907) 562-4636; fax: (907) 562-0445**
Best Time to Call: **1 PM–9 PM**
Hosts: **Jerry and Phyllis Jost**
Location: **15 min. from airport/train**
No. of Rooms: **5**
Max. No. Sharing Bath: **4**
Double/pb: **$75–$85**
Single/pb: **$50**

Double/sb: **$65**
Open: **All year**
Reduced Rates: **Families; off-season**
Breakfast: **Continental, plus**
Pets: **No**
Children: **Welcome**
Smoking: **No**
Social Drinking: **No**

Since 1981, Anchorage's oldest bed and breakfast has been offering a special blend of gracious, unpretentious hospitality. Guest rooms are spacious and reflect a country atmosphere, featuring freshly ironed sheets, king, full, or twin beds, phones and TV's in some rooms. The aromas of coffee and cinnamon will start you off to a full day of sightseeing, shopping, fishing, or hiking. You can expect to meet guests from around the world, including the backyards of Alaska. The Green Bough is centrally located, near buses, hospitals, universities, and bike trails. Freezer and storage are available for your fish and extra gear. Jerry and Phyllis have been transplanted Alaskans since 1967, and want to share their experience and enthusiasm about the area with you.

"K" Street Bed & Breakfast ✪

1443 "K" STREET, ANCHORAGE, ALASKA 99501
Kstbb@Alaska.net

Tel: **(907) 279-1443**
Best Time to Call: **After 8 AM**
Host: **Kate Warrick**
No. of Rooms: **3**
No. of Private Baths: **1**
Max. No. Sharing Bath: **4**
Double/sb: **$85**
Suite: **$90**

Open: **All year**
Reduced Rates: **Available**
Breakfast: **Full**
Pets: **No**
Children: **Welcome, over 12**
Smoking: **No**
Social Drinking: **No**

This contemporary cedar home is located in downtown Anchorage. Guests can walk to restaurants, shopping, the Natural History Museum, or a Saturday market/deli. Drive a short distance to Chugach State Park, the airport, or the mountains. The interior of the bed and breakfast features hardwood floors, tile, and Alaskan art, plus a solarium. Outside you'll find large trees and a garden. Breakfast is made from natural wholesome foods, accompanied by gourmet coffee.

Peters Creek Bed & Breakfast ✪

22626 CHAMBERS LANE, CHUGIAK, ALASKA 99567

Tel: **(907) 688-3465; (888) 688-3465;**
   fax: **(907) 688-3466**
Best Time to Call: **After 10 AM**
Hosts: **Bob and Lucy Moody**
Location: **17 mi. N of Anchorage**
No. of Rooms: **4**
No. of Private Baths: **4**
Double/pb: **$85**
Single/pb: **$75**

Open: **All year**
Reduced Rates: **10% seniors**
Breakfast: **Full**
Credit Cards: **AMEX, DISC, MC, VISA**
Pets: **No**
Children: **Welcome, crib**
Smoking: **No**
Social Drinking: **No**
Foreign Languages: **Spanish**

Newly built Peters Creek Bed & Breakfast is located on the north shore of Peters Creek, in the middle of two and a half acres of wooded terrain. The decor is predominantly Victorian antiques; each guest room has cable TV, VCR, and refrigerator. After a hearty Alaskan breakfast, take a hike at the nearby Thunderbird Falls, fish at Fire Lake, or swim at Mirror Lake. Boating, canoeing, kayaking, dogsled rides, horseshoes, horseback riding, and skiing are just a few of the other activities you can enjoy.

A Bed & Breakfast on Minnie ✪

345 MINNIE STREET, FAIRBANKS, ALASKA 99701
minniebb@mosquitonet.com; www.AlaskaOne.com/minniestreet

Tel: **(888) 456-1849; (907) 456-1802;**
   fax: **(907) 451-1751**

Hosts: **Marnie and Lambert Hazelaar**
Location: **In Fairbanks**

No. of Rooms: **10**
No. of Private Baths: **6**
Max. No. Sharing Bath: **4**
Double/pb: **$100–$120**
Double/sb: **$75–$90**
Suites: **$125–$175**
Open: **All year**

Reduced Rates: **Sept. 16–May 14**
Breakfast: **Full**
Credit Cards: **AMEX, MC, VISA**
Pets: **No**
Children: **Welcome**
Smoking: **No**
Social Drinking: **Permitted**

This bed and breakfast is located within walking distance of the train depot and only five minutes from downtown, where you will find the post office, banks, gift shops, and restaurants. En route you will cross the beautiful Chena River. The cozy, comfortably decorated guest rooms have queen-size beds, cable TVs and phones. Ample parking is provided; rental cars are available. Marnie's sumptuous breakfasts include homemade breads, omelettes, and fruit salad.

7 Gables Inn ✪

P. O. BOX 80488, FAIRBANKS, ALASKA 99708

Tel: **(907) 479-0751; fax: (907) 479-2229**
Best Time to Call: **8 AM–5 PM**
Hosts: **Paul and Leicha Welton**
Location: **2 mi. W of Fairbanks**
No. of Rooms: **9**
No. of Private Baths: **9**
Double/pb: **$50–$120**
Single/pb: **$50–$110**
Suites: **$75–$180**
Open: **All year**

Reduced Rates: **50%, Oct.–Apr.**
Breakfast: **Full**
Other Meals: **Available**
Credit Cards: **AMEX, DC, DISC, MC, VISA**
Pets: **Sometimes**
Children: **Welcome**
Smoking: **No**
Social Drinking: **Permitted**
Airport/Station Pickup: **Yes**
Foreign Languages: **Spanish**

The Weltons' large Tudor-style home is central to many city attractions—Riverboat Discovery, Cripple Creek Resort, University Museum, Alaskaland, Gold Dredge #8—and within walking distance of the University of Alaska's Fairbanks campus. Paul designed and built the house, a worthy destination in its own right. You'll enter through a floral solarium, which leads to a foyer with antique stained glass and indoor waterfall. Party planners take note: 7 Gables has a wine cellar and a wedding chapel. Guests can use the laundry facilities, library, Jacuzzis, canoe, and bikes. All rooms have telephones, cable TV, and VCR, and 8 rooms have private Jacuzzi baths. Ample breakfasts feature dishes like salmon quiche, crab casserole, and peachy pecan crepes.

ARIZONA

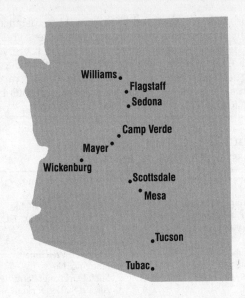

Arizona Trails Bed & Breakfast Reservation Service ✪
P.O. BOX 18998, FOUNTAIN HILLS, ARIZONA 85269
www.arizonatrails.com; aztrails@arizonatrails.com

Tel: **(602) 837-4284**
Best Time to Call: **8 AM–6 PM MST**
Coordinator: **Roxanne C. Boryezki**
States/Regions Covered: **Bisbee,
Flagstaff, Grand Canyon, Payson,
Phoenix, Prescott, Scottsdale,
Sedona, Tucson**

Rates (Single/Double):
  Modest: **$65–$85**
  Average: **$85–$135**
  Luxury: **$175–$250**
Credit Cards: AMEX, MC, VISA
Descriptive Directory of B&Bs: **Free**

Arizona Trails Bed & Breakfast Reservation Service has over 80 inspected properties statewide. Choices include traditional homestays, country inns, and historic properties. Full details for all properties are listed on Arizona Travels' web site. Leisure and corporate travel programs are available. Ask about special packages.

Mi Casa–Su Casa/Old Pueblo Bed and Breakfast ✪
RESERVATION SERVICE—ARIZONA
P.O. BOX 950, TEMPE, ARIZONA 85280-0950
www.mi-casa.org

Tel: **(602) 990-0682; (800) 456-0682;**
  fax: **(602) 990-3390**
Best Time to Call: **8 AM–8 PM**
Coordinator: **Ruth T. Young**
States/Regions Covered: **Ajo, Bisbee,**
  Cave Creek, Flagstaff, Fountain Hills,
  Mesa, Page, Phoenix, Prescott,
  Scottsdale, Sedona, Tempe, Tucson,
  Wickenburg

Rates (Single/Double):
  Modest: **$45–$65**
  Average: **$75–$125**
  Luxury: **$125–$340**
Credit Cards: **AMEX, MC, VISA**
Descriptive Directory of B&Bs: **$9.50**

Since 1981 Ruth has listed host homes and inns in Arizona; she has over 200 B&Bs in the state. Many offer easy access to national parks, historic towns, universities, water recreation areas, birding, hiking, tennis, golf, skiing, and the Mexican border. From scenic Lake Powell on the northern Arizona border to Ajo near Organ Pipe National Monument, this beautiful state has a vast expanse of scenic wonders to explore. There's a $5 surcharge for one-night stays.

B's B&B ✪
94 COPPINGER STREET, P.O. BOX 2019, CAMP VERDE,
ARIZONA 86322

Tel: **(520) 567-1988**
Host: **Beatrice Richmond**
Location: **90 mi. N of Phoenix**
No. of Rooms: **2**
No. of Private Baths: **2**
Double/pb: **$60**
Single/pb: **$50**

Open: **All year**
Breakfast: **Full**
Pets: **No**
Children: **Welcome**
Smoking: **No**
Social Drinking: **Permitted**
Foreign Languages: **French, Spanish**

B's B&B sits on a hillside; a huge redwood deck has a panoramic view. Set on an acre of natural landscaping, this bed and breakfast seems isolated, but is very close to the center of town. Things to do include excursions to Fort Verde State Park, Captain King's boat rides, outback tours, horseback riding, and much more. Breakfast may feature B's blintzes, homemade granola, and yogurt. Beatrice is a retired elementary school teacher and teaches English as a second language one evening a week. She also enjoys foreign languages and travel.

Dierker House
423 WEST CHERRY, FLAGSTAFF, ARIZONA 86001

Tel: **(520) 774-3249**
Host: **Dorothea Dierker**
No. of Rooms: **3**

Max. No. Sharing Bath: **4**
Double/sb: **$50**
Open: **All year**

Breakfast: **Full**
Pets: **No**
Children: **Welcome, over 12**

Smoking: **No**
Social Drinking: **Permitted**

This lovely old home in Flagstaff's historic section is located high in the mountains, at an elevation of 7000 feet. Flagstaff is the hub of wonderful day trips to the Grand Canyon, Native American ruins and reservations, Lake Powell, Monument Valley, and many more sites. The second-floor accommodations are extremely comfortable and include many amenities. In the morning, Dorothea serves an excellent and sociable breakfast in the dining room.

Boyd's Bunkhouse Bed & Breakfast ✪

15709 MAVERICK-CORDES JUNCTION, MAYER, ARIZONA 86333
www.prescottlink.com/boyds/index.html

Tel: **(800) 930-4545**
Hosts: **Nancy and Ken Boyd**
Location: **49 mi. N of Phoenix**
Guest Houses: **$69–$85, sleeps 1–6;**
  $255 weekly; $850 monthly
Open: **All year**
Breakfast: **Full**

Other Meals: **Available**
Credit Cards: **MC, VISA**
Pets: **Sometimes**
Children: **Welcome**
Smoking: **No**
Social Drinking: **Permitted**

Boyd's Bunkhouse is a modern B&B located in a quiet rural community. Decorated in southwestern style, each guest house includes a private entrance, two bedrooms, fully furnished kitchen, laundry facilities, phone, satellite TV and VCR, covered patio and parking, picnic table and barbecue grill. A country breakfast is provided either on the patio or in the guest house. Special features include local area history books and framed historical photos, as well as detailed descriptions of places to go and things to see nearby. Boyd's is within 33 miles of Prescott, 39 miles of Sedona, 78 miles from Flagstaff, and 158 miles from the South Rim of the Grand Canyon.

Serenity House Bed & Breakfast ✪

P.O. BOX 1254, 3RD STREET AND MAIN, MAYER, ARIZONA 86333
hether@primenet.com

Tel: **(520) 632-4430; (800) 484-2366,**
  ext. 0839
Hosts: **Sue and Bob Hetherington**
Location: **65 mi. N of Phoenix**
No. of Rooms: **2**
Max. No. Sharing Bath: **4**
Double/sb: **$55**

Open: **All year**
Reduced Rates: **After 2nd night**
Breakfast: **Continental, Plus**
Pets: **No**
Children: **Welcome, over 12**
Smoking: **No**
Social Drinking: **Permitted**

Located in the heart of Arizona in an old mining town, this country Victorian farmhouse is convenient to Prescott, Sedona, Jerome, Grand

Canyon, Flagstaff, and Phoenix. One guest room leads to the patio and pool, which is open May through September. The TV room has a movie library and a wood stove for chilly winter nights. The house is decorated with antiques, lace, teddy bears, and oak woodwork as well as hardwood floors and leaded and stained glass. Guests are invited to see Bob's model car collection or sit on the front porch swing and escape all the stress. This area has four mild seasons. Things to see and do include antiquing, arts and crafts fairs, horse racing in Prescott, gold panning, hiking, horseback riding, and sightseeing.

Casa Del Sol ✪
6951 E. HOBART, MESA, ARIZONA 85207

Tel: **(602) 985-5956**	Open: **All year**
Hosts: **Ray and Barb Leo**	Reduced Rates: **Available**
Location: **20 mi. E of Phoenix**	Breakfast: **Full**
No. of Rooms: **2**	Pets: **Sometimes**
Max. No. Sharing Bath: **4**	Children: **Welcome**
Double/sb: **$55–$65**	Smoking: **No**
Single/sb: **$45**	Social Drinking: **Permitted**

This luxurious Southwestern home sits on an acre of property with desert landscaping, fruit trees, and a solar-heated swimming pool. The guest rooms emphasize comfort, with queen-size beds and Southwest decor. The word for breakfast is fresh, from ground coffee and fresh-squeezed juice to home-baked breads, muffins and croissants, special omelettes, and waffles. Guests are welcome to enjoy the pool, Jacuzzi, fireplace, and VCR. Nearby attractions include beautiful state parks, the Salt River recreation area, Cactus League spring training, great shopping, golf, and restaurants.

Bed & Breakfast Southwest Reservation Service—Arizona ✪
2916 NORTH 70TH STREET, SCOTTSDALE, ARIZONA 85251
b&bsw@juno.com

Tel: **(602) 947-9704; (800) 762-9704;** fax: **(602) 874-1316**	Descriptive Directory: **Free**
Best Time to Call: **8 AM–8 PM**	Rates (Single/Double):
Coordinators: **Jo Cummings and Joan Petersen**	Modest: **$40–$75**
States/Regions Covered: **Arizona, New Mexico, Southern Colorado, Southern California**	Average: **$80–$100**
	Luxury: **$105–up**

This service offers Southwestern travelers unique homestays in suites, guesthouses, ranches, and inns. All host facilities are personally inspected and provide the three C's of bed and breakfasts: cleanliness, cordiality, and convenience. Jo and Joan's specialty is finding the perfect B&B for you. They can plan your trip to include many of the historical and natural wonders in the great Southwest, such as the San Diego Zoo, Durango Historic Railroad, Scottsdale golf courses, Sedona's Red Rock formations, and the Santa Fe opera. You will be awed by the spectacular scenic beauty and legendary Western hospitality.

Valley o' the Sun Bed & Breakfast ✪
P.O. BOX 2214, SCOTTSDALE, ARIZONA 85252

Tel: **(602) 941-1281; (800) 689-1281**	Open: **All year**
Best Time to Call: **After 5:30 PM**	Reduced Rates: **Seniors; weekly**
Host: **Kay Curtis**	Breakfast: **Continental, plus**
Location: **Tempe**	Pets: **No**
No. of Rooms: **3**	Children: **Welcome, over 10**
No. of Private Baths: **1**	Smoking: **Restricted**
Max. No. Sharing Bath: **4**	Social Drinking: **Permitted**
Double/pb: **$50**	Minimum Stay: **2 nights**
Double/sb: **$40**	Airport/Station Pickup: **Yes**
Single/sb: **$30**	

The house is ideally located in the college area of Tempe, but is close enough to Scottsdale for guests to enjoy its fine shops and restaurants. From the patio, you can enjoy a beautiful view of the Papago Buttes and McDowell Mountains. Local attractions include swimming at Big Surf, the Phoenix Zoo, and the Scottsdale Center for the Arts.

Cathedral Rock Lodge
61 LOS AMIGOS LANE, SEDONA, ARIZONA 86336

Tel: **(520) 282-7608; fax: (520) 282-4505**	Open: **All year**
	Reduced Rates: **Available**
Hosts: **Samyo and Carol Shannon**	Breakfast: **Full; Continental**
Location: **2.8 mi. from Rte. 89A**	Credit Cards: **DISC, MC, VISA**
No. of Rooms: **2**	Pets: **No**
No. of Private Baths: **2**	Children: **Welcome (crib)**
Double/pb: **$80–$90**	Smoking: **No**
Guest Cottage: **$130**	Social Drinking: **Permitted**
Suite: **$140**	

Set in rock terrace gardens surrounded by tall shade trees, this rambling country home boasts spectacular views of the surrounding mountains. The suite has its own deck, built against a giant pine tree. Guest bedrooms feature family treasures and handmade quilts. Each day starts with Samyo's and Carol's hot breads and homemade jams; fresh fruits from local orchards are summertime treats. Lovers of the great outdoors will delight in the natural scenic beauty of the area, and browsers will enjoy the many galleries and shops. In the evening, curl up in front of the fireplace, borrow a book, or select a videotape from your host's collection. Guest cottage breakfast is Continental.

Moestly Wood Bed & Breakfast ✪
2085 UPPER RED ROCK LOOP ROAD, SEDONA, ARIZONA 86336

Tel: **(520) 204-1461**	Breakfast: **Full**
Best Time to Call: **8 AM–8 PM**	Other Meals: **Available**
Hosts: **Roger and Carolyn Moe**	Credit Cards: **MC, VISA**
Location: **110 mi. N of Phoenix**	Pets: **No**
No. of Rooms: **2**	Children: **Welcome**
No. of Private Baths: **2**	Smoking: **No**
Suite: **$85–$95**	Social Drinking: **Permitted**
Open: **All year**	Minimum Stay: **2 nights on weekends**

This contemporary home is located in the beautiful Arizona red rock country. Just 4 miles out of town you can enjoy spectacular views of Cathedral Rock and the surrounding area, or take a short hike to Red Rock Crossing, one of the state's most photographed sites. Roger and Carolyn enjoy visitors and are happy to help with touring plans, hiking, golfing, or just browsing through Sedona's many shops and galleries. Their large redwood deck is very inviting. Relaxing by the fire is also a comfy, cozy way to spend the evening.

Tubac Country Inn ✪
13 BURRUEL STREET, P.O. BOX 1540, TUBAC, ARIZONA 85646

Tel: **(520) 398-3178**	Open: **All year**
Best Time to Call: **Anytime**	Breakfast: **Continental**
Hosts: **Ruth and Jim Goebel**	Pets: **No**
Location: **41 mi. S of Tucson**	Children: **Welcome, over 3**
No. of Rooms: **4**	Smoking: **No**
Suites: **$80–$90**	Social Drinking: **Permitted**

This adorable two-story Inn located in the center of Tubac will steal your heart away. Choose a one- or two-bedroom suite; two units have full kitchens for longer stays. Tubac, founded in 1752, is the oldest European settlement in Arizona. Today Tubac is the place where art and history meet. Visit galleries, boutiques, and restaurants all within walking distance of the Inn. Within a few minutes you can drive to shopping in Old Mexico, or see missions, museums, and national parks. The area boasts six outstanding golf courses.

Casa Tierra Adobe Bed and Breakfast Inn
11155 WEST CALLE PIMA, TUCSON, ARIZONA 85743

Tel: **(520) 578-3058; fax: (520) 578-3058**	Best Time to Call: **Mornings**
	Hosts: **Karen and Lyle Hymer-Thompson**

Location: **15 mi. W of Tucson**	Pets: **No**
No. of Rooms: **3**	Children: **Welcome, over 3**
No. of Private Baths: **3**	Smoking: **No**
Double/pb: **$75–$105**	Social Drinking: **Permitted**
Open: **Sept.–May**	Minimum Stay: **2 nights**
Reduced Rates: **10% after 7 days**	Foreign Languages: **Spanish**
Breakfast: **Full**	

Casa Tierra is located on five acres of beautiful Sonoran desert thirty minutes from downtown Tucson. This secluded desert area has hundreds of saguaro cactus, spectacular mountain views, and brilliant sunsets. Built and designed by owners Lyle and Karen, the all-adobe house features entryways with vaulted brick ceilings, an interior arched courtyard, Mexican furnishings, and a Jacuzzi. Each guest room has a private bath, queen-size bed, microwave, small refrigerator, and private patio and entrance. Nearby attractions include the Desert Museum, the Saguaro National Park, and Old Tucson. Karen is an artist/photographer; Lyle is a designer/builder who takes tours into Mexico.

Ford's Bed & Breakfast ✪
1202 NORTH AVENIDA MARLENE, TUCSON, ARIZONA 85715

Tel: **(520) 885-1202**	Suite: **$100–$120; sleeps 4**
Hosts: **Sheila and Tom Ford**	Open: **All year**
Location: **In Tucson**	Breakfast: **Full**
No. of Rooms: **2**	Pets: **No**
No. of Private Baths: **1**	Children: **No**
Double/pb: **$60**	Smoking: **No**
Single/pb: **$45**	Social Drinking: **Permitted**

A warm welcome awaits you at Ford's affordable B&B, located in a quiet residential cul-de-sac. Each room has its own entrance and garden patio, with a bird's-eye view of the mountains. Sheila, a retired nanny and dog breeder, has lived here since 1957 and will be happy to direct you to the many attractions in the area, including Sabino Canyon, Mount Lemmon, Saguaro Monument East, Colossal Cave, and hiking trails. A microwave, refrigerator, TV, and sitting room are available for guests' use.

Hideaway B&B ✪
4344 EAST POE STREET, TUCSON, ARIZONA 85711

Tel: **(520) 323-8067**	Reduced Rates: **Weekly**
Best Time to Call: **After 5 PM**	Breakfast: **Continental**
Hosts: **Dwight and Ola Parker**	Pets: **No**
No. of Rooms: **1**	Children: **No**
No. of Private Baths: **1**	Smoking: **No**
Guest Cottage: **$50–$60**	Minimum Stay: **3 nights**
Open: **Oct.–June; special arrangements**	Airport/Station Pickup: **Yes**
for the rest of year	

A cozy bungalow with its own entrance, Hideaway B&B is located in the hosts' backyard in central Tucson, just minutes from two major shopping centers. One mile away, a city park provides lots of diversions, with two golf courses, a driving range, tennis courts, and a zoo. Pima Air Museum, Davis Monthan Air Force Base, the University of Arizona, Colossal Cave, the Old Tucson movie set, and Mt. Lemmon Ski Resort are among the many sites of interest. The air-conditioned accommodations include a private bath, a bedroom, and a sitting room equipped with a TV and VCR.

Katy's Hacienda ✪
5841 EAST 9TH STREET, TUCSON, ARIZONA 85711

Tel: **(520) 745-5695**	Single/sb: **$45**
Host: **Katy Gage**	Open: **All year**
Location: **8 mi. from Rte. 10, Grant or**	Reduced Rates: **10% weekly**
Kolb exit	Breakfast: **Full**
No. of Rooms: **2**	Pets: **No**
No. of Private Baths: **1**	Children: **Welcome, over 8**
Max. No. Sharing Bath: **3**	Smoking: **Permitted**
Double/pb: **$55**	Social Drinking: **Permitted**
Single/pb: **$45**	Minimum Stay: **2 nights**
Double/sb: **$55**	Airport/Station Pickup: **Yes**

An ornamental iron guard protects this adobe brick house filled with charming antiques and glass. Guests can unwind in the backyard and the patio area, or come inside and enjoy the living room and television room. Katy's Hacienda is within walking distance of the bus line, fine restaurants, theaters, and a hospital. The El Con shopping area, the Randolph Golf Course, and the zoo are three miles away.

Natural Bed and Breakfast ✪

3150 EAST PRESIDIO ROAD, TUCSON, ARIZONA 85716
www.tbliz.com/naturalbb.htm

Tel: **(520) 881-4582**	Open: **All year**
Best Time to Call: **7 AM–8 PM**	Reduced Rates: **5% seniors**
Host: **Marc Haberman**	Breakfast: **Full**
No. of Rooms: **4**	Other Meals: **Available**
No. of Private Baths: **2**	Pets: **Sometimes**
Max. No. Sharing Bath: **2**	Children: **Welcome**
Double/pb: **$65**	Smoking: **No**
Single/pb: **$55**	Social Drinking: **Permitted**
Double/sb: **$65**	

Marc Haberman is a holistic health practitioner, and his B&B is natural in all senses of the word: it's a simply furnished, water-cooled home that provides a nontoxic, nonallergenic environment. The grounds are landscaped with palm and pine trees. Only whole-grain and natural foods are served here and the drinking water is purified. Soothing professional massages are available by request.

Quail's Vista Bed & Breakfast ✪

826 EAST PALISADES DRIVE, TUCSON, ARIZONA 85737

Tel: **(520) 297-5980**	Reduced Rates: **10% weekly**
Hosts: **Barbara and Dick Bauer**	Breakfast: **Continental, Plus**
Location: **10 mi. NW of Tucson**	Pets: **No**
No. of Rooms: **3**	Children: **Welcome**
No. of Private Baths: **2**	Smoking: **No**
Double/pb: **$65–$85**	Social Drinking: **Permitted**
Open: **All year**	Airport/Station Pickup: **Yes**

Native American artifacts and Mexican tile make this modern, solar-heated adobe on 2 acres of desert an attractive blend of the local cultures. Fiestaware dishes and grandmother's furniture in the guest room evoke memories of an older generation. From a seat on the redwood deck you can watch the gorgeous sunset and stargaze in the evening. The swim-stream hot tub is available for swimming or soaking. Breakfasts include a cereal buffet with several toppings, coffee, tea, juices, and baked goods. Light snacks may be put in the refrigerator. Your hostess, a professional Tucson tour guide, can help you discover the area's highlights, and maps, brochures, and restaurant menus are always on hand. The new Nest Room has a private entrance, refrigerator, microwave, cable TV, and a Jacuzzi bath.

Historic Sombrero Ranch ✪

31910 WEST BRALLIAR ROAD, WICKENBURG, ARIZONA 85390
www.wick-web.com/sombrero

Tel: **(520) 684-0222**
Hosts: **Peter Nufea and Betty Shute**
Location: **50 NW of Phoenix**
No. of Rooms: **4**
No. of Private Baths: **4**
Double/pb: **$75**
Suite: **$95, sleeps 4**
Open: **All year**

Breakfast: **Continental, Plus**
Credit Cards: **MC, VISA**
Pets: **No**
Children: **Welcome**
Smoking: **No**
Social Drinking: **No**
Foreign Languages: **German, French**

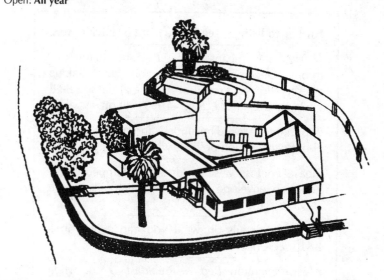

Historic Sombrero Ranch has offered the flavor of the west in comfort and style since 1937. This Mission-style, 5,000-square-foot home sits on top of a hill with 360-degree views surrounded by 50 acres of the Sonoran Desert. The ranch is within walking distance to town. Activities include horseback riding, jeep tours, golf, tennis, shopping, and dining. Guests may also enjoy day trips to Sedona, Grand Canyon, Lake Pleasant, and other historical sites. Whatever your pleasure, allow time for a most relaxing and enjoyable vacation.

The Johnstonian B&B ✪

321 WEST SHERIDAN AVENUE, WILLIAMS, ARIZONA 86046

Tel: **(520) 635-2178**
Best Time to Call: **Anytime**
Hosts: **Bill and Pidge Johnston**
Location: **55 mi. S of Grand Canyon National Park**

No. of Rooms: **4**
Max. No. Sharing Bath: **4**
Double/pb: **$70**
Single/pb: **$65**
Double/sb: **$55–$60**

Single/sb: **$50–$55**

Suites: **$115**

Open: **All year**

Breakfast: **Full**

Pets: **No**

Children: **Welcome**

Smoking: **No**

Social Drinking: **Permitted**

As old as the century, this two-story Victorian has been carefully restored and decorated in period style. You'll admire the antique oak furniture and the lovely floral wallpapers. In the winter, guests cluster around the wood-burning stove. Pidge's breakfast specialties include Ukrainian potato cakes, blueberry pancakes, and homemade breads.

For key to listings, see inside front or back cover.

✪ This star means that rates are guaranteed through December 31, 1999, to any guest making a reservation as a result of reading about the B&B in *Bed & Breakfast U.S.A.*—1999 edition.

Important! To avoid misunderstandings, always ask about cancellation policies when booking.

Please enclose a self-addressed, stamped, business-size envelope when contacting reservation services.

For more details on what you can expect in a B&B, see Chapter 1.

Always mention *Bed & Breakfast U.S.A.* when making reservations!

We want to hear from you! Use the form on page 593.

ARKANSAS

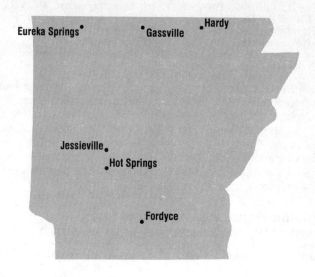

Eureka Springs • Gassville • Hardy

Jessieville •
Hot Springs

Fordyce

Crescent Cottage Inn
211 SPRING STREET, EUREKA SPRINGS, ARKANSAS 72632
raphael@ipa.net

Tel: (501) 253-6022; (800) 223-3246
   reservations only
Best Time to Call: 9:30 AM–9 PM
Hosts: Ralph and Phyllis Becker
Location: On Rte. 62B, Historic Loop
No. of Rooms: 4
No. of Private Baths: 4

Double/pb: $94–$132
Open: All year
Breakfast: Full
Credit Cards: DISC, MC, VISA
Pets: No
Children: Welcome, under 1, over 13
Social Drinking: Permitted

Crescent Cottage Inn, built in 1881, is the most historic and photo-graphed guest house of the region. Listed on the National Registry of Historic Places, this celebrated inn has the best views of the mountains. Rooms are furnished with antiques, Jacuzzis, TV, and VCR; two have fireplaces. Ralph and Phyllis serve a superb breakfast in the dining room or on the veranda overlooking the mountains and gardens. Complimentary soft drinks are available. Take a short walk along parks and springs or ride the trolley to old downtown on the Historic Loop.

Harvest House ✪
104 WALL STREET, EUREKA SPRINGS, ARKANSAS 72632

Tel: **(501) 253-9363; (800) 293-5665**	Breakfast: **Full**
Best Time to Call: **9 AM–9 PM**	Credit Cards: **DISC, MC, VISA**
Hosts: **Bill and Patt Carmichael**	Pets: **Sometimes**
No. of Rooms: **4**	Children: **Welcome, over 12**
No. of Private Baths: **4**	Smoking: **No**
Double/pb: **$89–$129**	Social Drinking: **Permitted**
Open: **All year**	

Located in the historic district of Eureka Springs, Harvest House is a step off the beaten path, yet close to the bustle of downtown. This turn-of-the-century Victorian house is filled with antiques, collectibles, and family favorites. All guest rooms have private entrances. Breakfast is served in the dining room or, weather permitting, in the screened-in gazebo overlooking pine and oak trees. Bill is a native Arkansan and knows all the hidden treasures of the area. Patt is a shopper with a particular interest in antiques and the local attractions.

Singleton House Bed and Breakfast ✪
11 SINGLETON, EUREKA SPRINGS, ARKANSAS 72632

Tel: **(501) 253-9111; (800) 833-3394**	Reduced Rates: **Midweek**
Host: **Barbara Gavron**	Breakfast: **Full**
No. of Rooms: **5**	Credit Cards: **AMEX, DISC, MC, VISA**
No. of Private Baths: **5**	Pets: **No**
Double/pb: **$69–$85**	Children: **Welcome**
Single/pb: **$65–$75**	Smoking: **No**
Suites: **$85–$105**	Social Drinking: **Permitted**
Open: **All year**	

You'll find a hidden garden, winding stone paths, and more than fifty birdhouses at this "old-fashioned place with a touch of magic." This historic district Victorian inn with its light and airy rooms is whimsically decorated with antiques, folk art, and eclectic treasures. Breakfast is served on a balcony that overlooks the fantasy wildflower garden and lily-filled goldfish pond. After breakfast take a one-block scenic walk or ride the old-time trolley to Eureka's shops and galleries.

Wynne Phillips House ✪
412 WEST FOURTH STREET, FORDYCE, ARKANSAS 71742

Tel: **(501) 352-7202**
Best Time to Call: **Morning**
Hosts: **Colonel and Mrs. James H. Phillips**
Location: **60 mi. S of Little Rock**
No. of Rooms: **4**
No. of Private Baths: **4**
Double/pb: **$62.50**

Open: **All year**
Breakfast: **Full**
Credit Cards: **MC, VISA**
Pets: **No**
Children: **Welcome**
Smoking: **No**
Social Drinking: **Permitted**

This is a gracious Colonial Revival, turn-of-the-century family home listed on the National Register of Historic Places, furnished with antiques and family heirlooms. Watch the sunset from the wraparound front porch, stroll through the arbors and gardens, or take a dip in the swimming pool. A country breakfast is served in the dining room.

Lithia Springs Bed & Breakfast Lodge ✪
593 HIGHWAY 126 NORTH, GASSVILLE, ARKANSAS 72635

Tel: **(870) 435-6100**
Best Time to Call: **After 1 PM**
Hosts: **Paul and Reita Johnson**
No. of Rooms: **5**
No. of Private Baths: **3**
Max. No. Sharing Bath: **4**
Double/pb: **$55–$70**

Double/sb: **$55–$70**
Open: **All year**
Breakfast: **Full**
Pets: **No**
Children: **Welcome, over 7**
Smoking: **No**

This 100-year-old former health lodge has been lovingly restored with an additional gift shop featuring many of the hosts' own fine handcrafts. The rooms are furnished with many antiques and period furniture. Breakfast is served in the dining room or on the large screened front porch. Lithia Springs is on 39 acres of meadows and woods. It is near the White and Buffalo Rivers, famous for fishing and canoeing, and between Bull Shoals and Norfork Lakes. It's 10 minutes from Mountain Home and a scenic drive to Blanchard Spring Caverns and Mountain View Folk Center.

Olde Stonehouse Bed & Breakfast Inn ✪
511 MAIN STREET, HARDY, ARKANSAS 72542

Tel: **(870) 856-2983; (800) 514-2983;**
 fax: **(870) 856-4036**
Best Time to Call: **10 AM–8 PM**

Host: **Peggy Volland**
No. of Rooms: **9**
No. of Private Baths: **9**

Double/pb: **$69**
Suites: **$99**
Open: **All year**
Reduced Rates: **10% Sun.–Thur.**
Breakfast: **Full**
Credit Cards: **AMEX, DISC, MC, VISA**
Pets: **No**

Children: **Welcome, over 13**
Smoking: **No**
Social Drinking: **Permitted**
Minimum Stay: **2 nights, holiday weekends and special events**
Station Pickup: **Yes**

Recapture the romance of times past at the Olde Stonehouse. Unwind in lovely air-conditioned rooms decorated with period antiques, quilts, and old lace, plus a ceiling fan and queen-size bed. Curl up in the large rocking chairs on the front porch or take a walk to Old Hardy Town's antique and crafts shops. Stroll along the river or join other guests for conversation and games. Awaken to the aroma of freshly brewed coffee and bread baking. After breakfast, canoeing, golfing, shopping, and horseback riding are among the many activities to choose from. The Inn is listed on the National Register of Historic Places.

Stillmeadow Farm ✪
111 STILLMEADOW LANE, HOT SPRINGS, ARKANSAS 71913

Tel: **(501) 525-9994**
Hosts: **Gene and Jody Sparling**
Location: **4 mi. S of Hot Springs**
No. of Rooms: **4**
No. of Private Baths: **2**
Max. No. Sharing Bath: **4**
Double/pb: **$70**
Single/pb: **$60**

Suites: **$90**
Open: **All year**
Breakfast: **Full**
Pets: **No**
Children: **Welcome, over 12**
Smoking: **No**
Social Drinking: **Permitted**

Stillmeadow Farm is a reproduction of an 18th-century New England saltbox, set in 75 acres of pine forest with walking trails and an herb garden. The decor is of early country antiques. Your hosts provide homemade snacks and fruit in the guest rooms. For breakfast, freshly baked pastries and breads are served. Hot Springs National Park, Lake Hamilton, the Mid-America Museum, and a racetrack are nearby.

Vintage Comfort B&B Inn ✪

303 QUAPAW AVENUE, HOT SPRINGS, ARKANSAS 71901
www.bbonline.com/ar/vintagecomfomfort

Tel: **(501) 623-3258; (800) 608-4682**	Breakfast: **Full**
Host: **Helen Bartlett**	Credit Cards: **AMEX, MC, VISA**
No. of Rooms: **4**	Pets: **No**
No. of Private Baths: **4**	Children: **Welcome, over 6**
Double/pb: **$70–$90**	Smoking: **No**
Single/pb: **$60–$75**	Social Drinking: **Permitted**
Open: **All year**	Airport/Station Pickup: **Yes**

This handsome turn-of-the-century Queen Anne–style home has been faithfully restored, attractively appointed, and air-conditioned. The theme here is comfort and Southern hospitality. Breakfast treats include biscuits and sausage gravy, grits, and regional hot breads. Afterwards, enjoy a short stroll to the famed Bath House Row or a brisk walk to the park, where miles of hiking trails will keep you in shape. Helen will be happy to direct you to the studios and shops of local artists and craftspeople. You are welcome to relax in the old-world sitting room and parlor or on the lovely veranda shaded by magnolia trees.

Mountain Thyme Bed & Breakfast Inn ✪

10860 SCENIC BYWAY 7 NORTH, JESSIEVILLE, ARKANSAS 71949

Tel: **(501) 984-5428; (888) 820-5424**	Reduced Rates: **$10 less after 3rd night**
Best Time to Call: **10 AM–10 PM**	Breakfast: **Full**
Hosts: **Rhonda and Michael Hicks, Polly Felker**	Credit Cards: **MC, VISA**
No. of Rooms: **8**	Pets: **No**
No. of Private Baths: **8**	Children: **Welcome, over 10**
Double/pb: **$80–$150**	Smoking: **No**
Open: **All year**	Social Drinking: **Permitted**

Mountain Thyme Bed & Breakfast Inn was built from the ground up by innkeepers who are B&B travelers. They know from experience what makes a comfortable and luxurious inn: great beds, expensive linens, ample light, individual temperature control, fireplaces, whirlpool tubs, and varied, delicious breakfasts served in the dining room. Mountain Thyme Bed & Breakfast Inn is the perfect spot for a romantic weekend or an extended stay in the Hot Springs area. Rhonda and Michael welcome you to their little bit of heaven, and look forward to helping you plan the vacation of your dreams.

CALIFORNIA

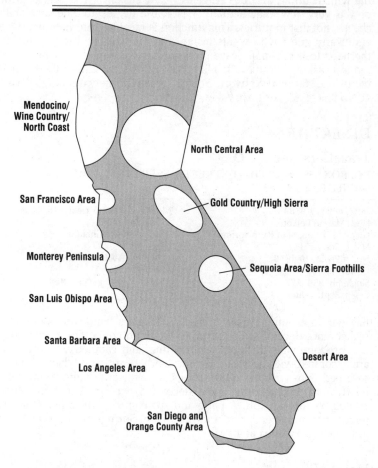

Mendocino/
Wine Country/
North Coast

North Central Area

San Francisco Area

Gold Country/High Sierra

Monterey Peninsula

Sequoia Area/Sierra Foothills

San Luis Obispo Area

Santa Barbara Area

Desert Area

Los Angeles Area

San Diego and
Orange County Area

Bed & Breakfast California ✪
P.O. BOX 282910, SAN FRANCISCO, CALIFORNIA 94128-2910
info@bbintl.com; www.bbintl.com

Tel: **(650) 696-1690; (800) 872-4500;**
  fax: (650) 696-1699
Best Time to Call: **9 AM–4 PM Mon.–Fri.**
Coordinator: **Susan L. Ross**
States/Regions Covered: **California
  statewide**

Rates (Single/Double):
  Modest: **$60 / $75**
  Average: **$76 / $105**
  Luxury: **$106–Up**

Bed & Breakfast California, one of the oldest services in the U.S., represents over 300 B&Bs, private homes, inns, separate units, and long-term stays throughout California, with emphasis on San Francisco, Berkeley, the wine country, and Los Angeles. The website for this service is one of the very few that actually has real-time, up-to-date availability checks, not just inquiries. This function is ideal for international travelers or any guest who wants instant information because it eliminates the need to fax, e-mail, leave messages on voice mail, or send written requests asking about availability. Bed & Breakfast California is a member of The National Network. You can reach this network at (888) TNN-4BNB [866-4262], or http://www.tnn4bnb.com.

DESERT AREA

Travellers Repose ✪
P.O. BOX 655, 66920 FIRST STREET, DESERT HOT SPRINGS, CALIFORNIA 92240

Tel: **(760) 329-9584**
Host: **Marian Relkoff**
Location: **12 mi. N of Palm Springs**
No. of Rooms: **3**
No. of Private Baths: **3**
Double/pb: **$65–$85**
Single/pb: **$59–$77**
Open: **Sept. 1–June 30**

Reduced Rates: **Weekly; 10% families on 2nd room**
Breakfast: **Continental**
Pets: **No**
Children: **Welcome, over 12**
Smoking: **No**
Social Drinking: **Permitted**

Bay windows, gingerbread trim, stained glass windows, and a white picket fence decorate this charming Victorian home. The warm look of oak predominates in floors, wainscoting, and cabinetry. Guest rooms are decorated with hearts, dolls, and teddy bears everywhere. There's a rose bedroom with antiques and lace, a blue-and-white room with a heart motif, and a green room decorated with pine furniture handcrafted by Sam Relkoff. A patio and spa complete the amenities. Golf, tennis, museums, galleries, and posh Palm Springs are nearby. Marian graciously serves tea at 4 PM.

Hotel Nipton ✪
72 NIPTON ROAD, NIPTON, CALIFORNIA 92364

Tel: **(760) 856-2335**
Best Time to Call: **8 AM–6 PM**
Hosts: **Jerry and Roxanne Freeman**
Location: **10 mi. from I-15**
No. of Rooms: **4**
Max. No. Sharing Bath: **4**
Double/sb: **$55**
Open: **All year**
Reduced Rates: **Group**

Breakfast: **Continental**
Other Meals: **Available**
Credit Cards: **DISC, MC, VISA**
Pets: **No**
Children: **Welcome**
Smoking: **No**
Social Drinking: **Permitted**
Foreign Languages: **Spanish**

TED JENSEN

The population of Nipton is 30! The restored hotel, with its foot-thick adobe walls, was built in 1904 and is located in the Mojave National Preserve. Nipton is in the heart of gold-mining territory, 30 minutes from Lake Mojave's Cottonwood Cove. You are welcome to relax on the porch or in the outdoor Jacuzzi. Continental breakfast is served in the parlor at your convenience.

GOLD COUNTRY/HIGH SIERRA

Silver Spur Bed & Breakfast ✪
44625 SILVER SPUR TRAIL, AHWAHNEE, CALIFORNIA 93601

Tel: **(559) 683-2896**	Reduced Rates: **Available**
Hosts: **Patty and Bryan Hays**	Breakfast: **Continental**
Location: **50 mi. N of Fresno**	Credit Cards: **DISC, MC, VISA**
No. of Rooms: **2**	Pets: **Sometimes**
No. of Private Baths: **2**	Children: **Welcome**
Double/pb: **$60**	Smoking: **No**
Open: **All year**	Social Drinking: **Permitted**

Silver Spur Bed & Breakfast is nestled in the Sierra Nevadas, just off historic Highway 49—key to the California Gold Country near the south and west gates of Yosemite National Park and minutes from many outdoor sports. This contemporary log home was built by Bryan and features beautiful clean rooms with private entrances, comfortable beds, and tasteful Southwestern decor. Outdoor resting and dining areas boast outstanding Sierra views. A healthy Continental breakfast is served daily. Patty is a part-time paralegal and gardening enthusiast and Bryan is a builder. Come enjoy Yosemite, and be treated to old-fashioned hospitality.

Tin Roof Bed & Breakfast ✪
24741 FORESTHILL ROAD, FORESTHILL, CALIFORNIA 95631

Tel: **(916) 367-4466**
Hosts: **Clyde and Judith Larrew**
No. of Rooms: **3**
No. of Private Baths: **3**
Double/pb: **$65–$85**
Double/sb: **$75–$85**
Open: **All year**
Reduced Rates: **Available**

Breakfast: **Full**
Credit Cards: **AMEX, MC, VISA**
Pets: **Sometimes**
Children: **By arrangement**
Smoking: **No**
Social Drinking: **Permitted**
Airport/Station Pickup: **Yes**

Visit the Tin Roof Bed & Breakfast and experience the mountain air and friendly people. Enjoy white-water rafting, fishing at a nearby mountain lake, hiking, gold-panning tours with Clyde, or relax in the oak rocking chairs on the porch. Winter sports include snowmobiling, cross-country skiing, snowshoeing, and snowplay at the China Wall Recreation Area. The house was built in 1875 and the charm of days gone by is still evident from the tin roof, wraparound porch, and creaky stairs. Inside, you'll find a wood stove in the kitchen, knotty pine walls, antique furniture, and interesting memorabilia throughout.

The Heirloom ✪
P.O. BOX 322, 214 SHAKELEY LANE, IONE, CALIFORNIA 95640
www.wpd-plus.com/theheirloom

Tel: **(209) 274-4468; (888) 628-7896**
Hosts: **Melisande Hubbs and Patricia Cross**
Location: **35 mi. E of Sacramento**
No. of Rooms: **6**
No. of Private Baths: **4**
Max. No. Sharing Bath: **2**
Double/pb: **$75–$102**
Single/pb: **$65–$92**
Double/sb: **$65–$95**

Single/sb: **$55–$75**
Open: **All year**
Reduced Rates: **Weekly**
Breakfast: **Full**
Credit Cards: **AMEX, MC, VISA**
Pets: **No**
Children: **Welcome, over 10**
Smoking: **No**
Social Drinking: **Permitted**
Airport/Station Pickup: **Yes**

Nestled in the Sierra foothills, yet close to the historic gold mines, wineries, antique shops, and museums, this 1863 mansion, with its lovely balconies and fireplaces, is a classic example of antebellum architecture. It is furnished with a combination of family treasures and period pieces. Patricia and Melisande's hearty breakfast includes such delights as quiche, crepes, soufflé, and fresh fruits. Afternoon refreshments are always offered.

Clementine's ✪
200 HANFORD STREET, P.O. BOX 1537, SUTTER CREEK, CALIFORNIA 95685

Tel: **(209) 267-9384**	Breakfast: **Full**
Hosts: **Sharon F. and Kit L. Meitinger**	Other Meals: **Available**
Location: **42 mi. E of Sacramento**	Credit Cards: **AMEX, MC, VISA**
No. of Rooms: **1**	Pets: **Yes**
No. of Private Baths: **1**	Children: **Welcome**
Double/pb: **$75**	Smoking: **No**
Single/pb: **$70**	Social Drinking: **Permitted**
Open: **All year**	Airport/Station Pickup: **Yes**
Reduced Rates: **10% 5 days**	

Clementine's is located near the Gold Country in northern California. This B&B is 1 hour from Kirkwood, a popular skiing area, and 1½ hours from Lake Tahoe. This Mediterranean-style house was built in 1939. The interior is tastefully decorated with stenciling, pictures, antiques, and memorabilia. Guests have their own private entrance and sitting room. The town has many boutiques and antique stores to explore. Amador County's excellent wineries offer tours and private tastings. There are enough restaurants to satisfy many a palate. Other things to see include Daffodill Hill, museums, mine sites, and summer festivals. Sharon and Kit do woodworking and sewing in their spare time; some of their handiwork is for sale.

LOS ANGELES AREA

El Camino Real Bed & Breakfast ✪
P.O. BOX 5598, SHERMAN OAKS, CALIFORNIA 91403-5598

Tel: **(818) 787-6862**	Rates (Single/Double):
Best Time to Call: **Evenings**	Average: **$55–$75 / $60–$100**
Coordinator: **Lisa Reinstein**	Luxury: **$60 / $115**
States/Regions Covered: **Beverly Hills,**	Credit Cards: **No**
Burbank, Hollywood, Malibu, San	Minimum Stay: **2 nights**
Diego, San Fernando Valley; Studio	
City; Sun Valley, ID; Zion, UT	

This service brings the tradition of California hospitality begun with the Franciscan missions to the present-day traveler. Homes are in beach communities conveniently located to such attractions as Disneyland, Knotts Berry Farm, and the movie studios. Average accommodations are in upper-middle-class homes with swimming pools/spas, except in hilly areas. Lisa offers modest apartments with simple furnishings and a luxurious private guesthouse on an estate with a hot tub and swimming pool. All hosts are longtime residents of California, familiar with the restaurants, tourist attractions, and the best ways of getting to them.

Marina del Rey Bed & Breakfast ✪
753 OXFORD AVENUE, MARINA DEL REY, CALIFORNIA 90292

Tel: **(310) 821-9862**
Best Time to Call: **5 PM–10 PM**
Hosts: **Peter and Carolyn Griswold**
Location: **15 min. N of Los Angeles International Airport**
No. of Rooms: **1**
No. of Private Baths: **1**
Suite: **$50–$80**

Open: **All year**
Reduced Rates: **Weekly**
Breakfast: **Continental**
Pets: **No**
Children: **Welcome, over 12**
Smoking: **No**
Social Drinking: **Permitted**
Minimum Stay: **2 nights**

Peter and Carolyn's two-story house has a spacious studio with a separate entrance, full kitchen, color TV, and queen-size bed. Have a leisurely breakfast in your room or on the large rooftop yard, then stroll across the street to admire the thousands of boats and yachts moored in the marina. Nearby, Fisherman's Village offers fine dining, shopping, and harbor cruises. Or you can borrow your hosts' bicycles and strike out for the bike path that runs from Malibu Beach in the north all the way down to San Pedro Harbor some 35 miles away.

Hideaway House ✪
8441 MELVIN AVENUE, NORTHRIDGE, CALIFORNIA 91324

Tel: **(818) 349-5421**
Best Time to Call: **6–10 PM**
Hosts: **Dean and Dorothy Dennis**
Location: **20 mi. NW of Los Angeles**
No. of Rooms: **1**
No. of Private Baths: **1**
Double/pb: **$55–$60**

Open: **All year**
Breakfast: **Full**
Pets: **Sometimes**
Children: **No**
Smoking: **No**
Social Drinking: **Permitted**
Airport/Station Pickup: **Yes**

Located in a beautiful Los Angeles suburb, this country ranch home on over an acre in the San Fernando Valley is a good base for exploring southern California. It's 30 minutes to the beach, and 50 minutes to Disneyland. Freeways, shops, and restaurants are nearby. Dean and Dorothy welcome you to their art- and antique-filled home, and will provide local guide service by prior arrangement.

The Whites' House ✪
17122 FAYSMITH AVENUE, TORRANCE, CALIFORNIA 90504

Tel: **(310) 324-6164**
Host: **Margaret White**
Location: **5 mi. S of Los Angeles International Airport**
No. of Rooms: **2**
No. of Private Baths: **2**
Double/pb: **$35–$40**
Single/pb: **$30**

Open: **All year**
Reduced Rates: **Weekly, monthly**
Breakfast: **Continental**
Pets: **No**
Children: **No**
Smoking: **No**
Social Drinking: **Permitted**

This modern home with fireplaces, deck, and patio is located on a cul-de-sac in a very quiet area. The airport is 15 minutes away and the Pacific Ocean, with its lovely beaches, can be reached in only 10 minutes. Disneyland, Universal Studios, Knotts Berry Farm, and Hollywood are 30 minutes from the door. Many of Margaret's guests return many times and become good friends. Each guest room has a TV and telephone.

MENDOCINO/WINE COUNTRY/NORTH COAST

Hillcrest B&B ✪
3225 LAKE COUNTY HIGHWAY, CALISTOGA, CALIFORNIA 94515

Tel: **(707) 942-6334**	Double/sb: **$50–$75**
Best Time to Call: **After 8 PM**	Open: **All year**
Host: **Debbie O'Gorman**	Breakfast: **Continental**
Location: **2 mi. N of Calistoga**	Pets: **Welcome**
No. of Rooms: **6**	Children: **No**
No. of Private Baths: **4**	Smoking: **No**
Max. No. Sharing Bath: **4**	Social Drinking: **Permitted**
Double/pb: **$65–$98**	

Hillcrest has a breathtaking valley view of Mt. St. Helena, in an area famed for its wineries and spas. Without leaving the B&B's 36-acre property, guests can hike, swim, use the outdoor spa, fish, or stay indoors and play the Steinway grand piano and enjoy the cherished family heirlooms at every turn. The original house was built by Debbie's great-great-grandfather and burned to the ground in 1964. An elegant Continental breakfast of juice, coffee, fresh fruit, and baked goods is served on antique china and silver. For those of you who do not mind paying a higher rate, 6 rooms are available.

Sterling House ✪
1604 HARLEY STREET, CALISTOGA, CALIFORNIA 94515

Tel: **(707) 942-8402**	Open: **All year**
Host: **Jewell Sterling**	Breakfast: **Full**
Location: **75 mi. N of San Francisco**	Pets: **No**
No. of Rooms: **1**	Children: **No**
No. of Private Baths: **1**	Smoking: **No**
Double/pb: **$85**	Social Drinking: **Permitted**
Single/pb: **$85**	Minimum Stay: **2 nights**

Calistoga is known worldwide for its spas, mineral waters, award-winning restaurants, delightful shopping, and, of course, its wineries. Sterling House, located in a quiet residential neighborhood, is surrounded by flowers and trees. A fountain graces a spacious private terrace and welcomes guests to enjoy the tranquil outdoors: The guest room is furnished with antiques, wicker, a ceiling fan, and a New Orleans–style king-size bed. The house has central heat and air-condition-ing. Jewell caters to special diets and preferences, such as vegetarian and health foods. Specialties may include pineapple pancakes, glorious granola, whole-grain breads, and muffins. Nearby activities include hiking, biking, golf, tennis, gliding, and hot-air ballooning. There is a $15 surcharge for one-night stays.

Muktip Manor ✪

12540 LAKESHORE DRIVE, CLEARLAKE, CALIFORNIA 95422

Tel: **(707) 994-9571**
Hosts: **Jerry and Nadine Schiffman**
Location: **101 mi. N of San Francisco**
No. of Rooms: **1 suite**
No. of Private Baths: **1**
Suite: **$65**

Open: **All year**
Breakfast: **Full**
Pets: **Welcome**
Children: **Sometimes**
Smoking: **Permitted**
Social Drinking: **Permitted**

Nadine and Jerry traded the often-frenzied San Francisco lifestyle for an uncomplicated existence by the largest lake in the state. They do not offer Victoriana, priceless antiques, or gourmet food. They do provide comfortable accommodations in an unpretentious beach house, a place to relax on the deck, and the use of their private beach and bicycles. They enjoy windsurfing and canoeing, and have been known to give instruction to interested guests. The motto of Muktip Manor is, "If you wish company, we are conversationalists; if you wish privacy, we're invisible."

Inn Oz ✪

13311 LAKESHORE DRIVE, P.O. BOX 1046, CLEARLAKE PARK, CALIFORNIA 95424

Tel: **(707) 995-0853**
Best Time to Call: **Between 8 AM and 6 PM PST**
Hosts: **Pauline and Charley Stephanski**
Location: **100 mi. N of San Francisco**
No. of Rooms: **1**
No. of Private Baths: **1**
Double/pb: **$60**

Open: **All year**
Reduced Rates: **10% seniors**
Breakfast: **Full, Continental**
Pets: **Yes**
Children: **Welcome**
Smoking: **Permitted**
Social Drinking: **Permitted**

On the shores of California's largest freshwater lake, two hours north of San Francisco by automobile (and faster by house in a cyclone), you'll find country so beautiful it could have inspired L. Frank Baum's tales of the land of Oz. Savor unsurpassed sunsets, full moons, and starry heavens over Clear Lake from your bed or on your private patio. Your spacious chamber has a private entrance, a wood-burning fireplace, and a fully equipped kitchenette; the bathroom has a shower and a tub with a portable whirlpool. Pianists are encouraged to tickle the ivories of the upright Steinway. For additional fun, ask your hosts to show you the doll's house Pauline's grandfather built in 1938.

Campbell Ranch Inn ✪
1475 CANYON ROAD, GEYSERVILLE, CALIFORNIA 95441
www.campbellranchinn.com

Tel: **(707) 857-3476; (800) 959-3878;** fax: **(707) 857-3239**	Open: **All year**
Best Time to Call: **8 AM–8 PM**	Breakfast: **Full**
Hosts: **Mary Jane and Jerry Campbell**	Credit Cards: **AMEX, MC, VISA**
Location: **1.6 mi. from Rte. 101, Canyon Road exit**	Pets: **No**
No. of Rooms: **5**	Children: **Welcome, over 10**
No. of Private Baths: **5**	Smoking: **No**
Double/pb: **$125–$165**	Social Drinking: **Permitted**
Guest Cottage: **$225**	Minimum Stay: **2 nights weekends**
	Airport/Station Pickup: **Yes**

"Spectacular!" and "Charming!" are expressions most often used when guests describe their stay at this picture-perfect hilltop home surrounded by 35 acres in the heart of the Sonoma County wine country. The spacious bedrooms, each with a king-size bed, are handsomely furnished; several have balconies where views of mountains and vineyards are a backdrop to the colorful flower gardens. Breakfast, beautifully served, features a selection of fresh fruit, choice of gourmet egg dishes, homemade breads and cakes, and a variety of beverages. You can burn off the calories on the Campbells' tennis court or in their swimming pool, or borrow a bike to tour the wineries. Water sports and fishing are less than four miles away. Jerry will be happy to make your dinner reservations at one of the area's fine restaurants, but leave room for Mary Jane's dessert, always served "at home." The romantic cottage has a fireplace, hot tub on the deck overlooking the vineyards, and a bathtub for two.

MONTEREY PENINSULA

Happy Landing Inn ✪
P.O. BOX 2619, CARMEL, CALIFORNIA 93921

Tel: **(408) 624-7917**	Credit Cards: **MC, VISA**
Best Time to Call: **8:30 AM–9 PM**	Pets: **No**
Hosts: **Robert Ballard and Dick Stewart**	Children: **Welcome, over 12**
Location: **120 mi. S of San Francisco**	Smoking: **No**
No. of Rooms: **7**	Social Drinking: **Permitted**
No. of Private Baths: **7**	Minimum Stay: **2 nights weekends**
Double/pb: **$90–$165**	Foreign Languages: **Japanese,**
Open: **All year**	**Portuguese, Spanish**
Breakfast: **Continental**	

Located on Monte Verde between 5th and 6th Streets, this Hansel and Gretel-style Inn is a charming and romantic place to stay. Rooms with cathedral ceilings open onto a beautiful garden with gazebo, pond, and flagstone paths. Lovely antiques and personal touches, including breakfast served in your room, make your stay special.

Inn Laguna Creek ✪

2727 SMITH GRADE, SANTA CRUZ, CALIFORNIA 95060
inncreek@aol.com; www.infopoint.com/sc/lodging/laguna_creek

Tel: **(408) 425-0692; (800) 730-5398;** fax: **(408) 426-9331**	Suite: **$185–$235**
Best Time to Call: **9 AM–8 PM**	Open: **All year**
Hosts: **Jim and Gay Holley**	Breakfast: **Full**
Location: **8 mi. N of Santa Cruz**	Credit Cards: **AMEX, DISC, MC, VISA**
No. of Rooms: **2**	Pets: **No**
No. of Private Baths: **2**	Children: **Welcome**
Double/pb: **$95–$105**	Smoking: **No**
	Social Drinking: **Permitted**

Surrounded by coastal redwoods and sheltered from the outside world, this contemporary retreat sits on three acres beside a peaceful mountain stream. The lawn and gardens are abundant with wildlife and are perfect for a picnic or just relaxing. Rooms are large and comfortable, each with queen bed, down comforters, robes, VCR, and a private deck overlooking the creek. The sitting room boasts a wet bar, videos, books, and games, with a hot tub just outside. Flexibility allows making a private suite for 2–5 people. There are lots of things to do, from hiking, biking, and surfing to beachcombing, whale watching, wine tasting, and antiquing. A country-style breakfast is served with special attention to dietary restrictions. Inn Laguna Creek is a stress-free environment where memories are made.

Redwood Croft ✪

275 NORTHWEST DRIVE, BONNY DOON, SANTA CRUZ, CALIFORNIA 95060

Tel: **(408) 458-1939**	Reduced Rates: **Available**
Best Time to Call: **8 AM–8 PM PST**	Breakfast: **Full**
Hosts: **Sitah, Dale, and Zoë Cummings**	Other Meals: **Available**
Location: **9 mi. N of Santa Cruz**	Pets: **Sometimes**
No. of Rooms: **2**	Children: **Welcome**
No. of Private Baths: **2**	Smoking: **No**
Double/pb: **$85–$125**	Social Drinking: **Permitted**
Open: **All year**	Foreign Languages: **Spanish, French**

The sentiment at Redwood Croft is quality for guests; no shortcuts are taken in the kitchen or amenities. Guest rooms are designed with an artist's eye and a grandmother's heart, complete with snuggly goose down, line-dried linen, fireplaces, and large tubs. The Garden Room has its own entrance, private deck, and a seven-foot spa under the country stars. The West Room has a king-size bed and a large tiled bathroom with a Roman tub and bidet. Breakfasts are lavish, with the freshest Croft ingredients. Special dietary needs can be accommodated. Afternoon tea is a cherished tradition. The guidebooks bring you to Santa Cruz; Redwood Croft's hospitality brings you back.

Redwood Reflections ○

4600 SMITH GRADE, SANTA CRUZ, CALIFORNIA 95060

Tel: **(408) 423-7221**	Open: **All year**
Best Time to Call: **8–9 AM; 3–8 PM**	Reduced Rates: **Available**
Hosts: **Ed and Dory Strong**	Breakfast: **Full**
Location: **70 mi. S of San Francisco**	Pets: **No**
No. of Rooms: **3**	Children: **Welcome**
No. of Private Baths: **3**	Smoking: **No**
Double/pb: **$80–$90**	Social Drinking: **Permitted**
Suite: **$100**	

Nestled in the Santa Cruz Mountains, Redwood Reflections offers ten unspoiled acres of giant redwoods and trails. The rambling, rustic home is paneled throughout, with lots of windows, and furnished in country antiques. Each secluded room provides a sitting area, private bath, TV, queen-size bed, down comforters, and a romantic fountain and fireplace. Guests may enjoy the swimming pool and spa and fulfill childhood fantasies concocting delicious treats from the antique soda fountain. Things to do include hiking, wine tasting, and exploring nearby beaches and numerous state parks in the area. A country-style breakfast is prepared on an antique wood stove. Waffles piled high with fresh berries and country hash browns are favorites of guests.

NORTH CENTRAL AREA

The Inn at Shallow Creek Farm ○

4712 ROAD DD, ORLAND, CALIFORNIA 95963

Tel: **(530) 865-4093; (800) 865-4093**	Open: **All year**
Best Time to Call: **Evenings**	Reduced Rates: **$10 less after 3rd night**
Hosts: **Mary and Kurt Glaeseman**	Breakfast: **Continental, Plus**
Location: **3 mi. from I-5**	Pets: **No**
No. of Rooms: **4**	Children: **Sometimes**
No. of Private Baths: **2**	Smoking: **No**
Max. No. Sharing Bath: **4**	Social Drinking: **Permitted**
Double/pb: **$75**	Airport/Station Pickup: **Yes**
Double/sb: **$65**	Foreign Languages: **French, German,**
Guest Cottage: **$85; sleeps 2–4**	**Spanish**

The orchards of Shallow Creek Farm are known for mandarin and navel oranges and sweet grapefruit. Luscious berries, fresh garden produce, and a collection of exotic poultry, including rare silver guinea hens and African geese, are quite extraordinary. The Inn, a gracious turn-of-the-century farmhouse, offers airy, spacious rooms furnished with carefully chosen antiques and family heirlooms, combining nostalgia with country comfort. Breakfast features homemade baked goods and jams, and a generous assortment of fresh fruits or juices and hot beverages.

Palisades Paradise B&B ✪
1200 PALISADES AVENUE, REDDING, CALIFORNIA 96003

Tel: **(530) 223-5305**
Best Time to Call: **10 AM–2 PM**
Host: **Gail Goetz**
Location: **1¹⁄₄ mi. from Rte. I-5 exit Hilltop Dr.**
No. of Rooms: **2**
Max. No. Sharing Bath: **4**
Double/sb: **$70–$90**
Single/sb: **$65–$75**

Open: **All year**
Reduced Rates: **Available**
Breakfast: **Continental, plus**
Credit Cards: **AMEX, MC, VISA**
Pets: **No**
Children: **Welcome, by arrangement**
Smoking: **No**
Social Drinking: **Permitted**

Enjoy breathtakingly beautiful views from the patio and spa deck of this contemporary riverside home near Shasta College and Simpson College. Stay in either the Cozy Retreat or the Sunset Suite, both aptly named. In the morning, Gail serves ample breakfasts, with gourmet coffee, pastries, and her own Palisades fruit puffs.

SAN DIEGO AND ORANGE COUNTY AREA

Bed & Breakfast Southwest Reservation Service—Southern California ✪
2916 NORTH 70TH STREET, SCOTTSDALE, ARIZONA 85251
b&bsw@juno.com

Tel: **(602) 947-9704; (800) 762-9704; fax: (602) 874-1316**
Best Time to Call: **8 AM–8 PM**
Coordinators: **Jo Cummings and Joan Petersen**
States/Regions Covered: **Arizona, New Mexico, Southern California, Southern Colorado**

Descriptive Directory: **Free**
Rates (Single/Double):
   Modest: **$40–$75**
   Average: **$80–$100**
   Luxury: **$105–up**

This service offers travelers unique homestays in suites, guesthouses, ranches, and inns. All host facilities are personally inspected and provide the three C's of bed and breakfasts: cleanliness, cordiality, and convenience. Jo and Joan's specialty is finding the perfect B&B for you. They can plan your trip to include many of the historical and natural wonders of the great Southwest, such as the San Diego Zoo, Durango Historic Railroad, Scottsdale golf courses, Sedona's Red Rock formations, and the Santa Fe opera. You will be awed by the spectacular scenic beauty and legendary Western hospitality.

The Blue Door ✪

13707 DURANGO DRIVE, DEL MAR, CALIFORNIA 92014

Tel: **(619) 755-3819**	Open: **All year**
Best Time to Call: **Anytime**	Breakfast: **Full**
Hosts: **Bob and Anna Belle Schock**	Pets: **No**
Location: **20 mi. N of San Diego**	Children: **Welcome, over 16**
No. of Rooms: **1 suite**	Smoking: **No**
No. of Private Baths: **1**	Social Drinking: **Permitted**
Suite: **$60–$70**	

Enjoy New England charm in a quiet southern California setting overlooking exclusive Torrey Pines State Reserve. A garden-level two-room suite with wicker accessories and king or twin beds is yours. The sitting room has a couch, a desk, and a color TV. Breakfast is served in the spacious country kitchen or in the dining room warmed by the fire on chilly days. Anna Belle prides herself on creative breakfast menus featuring homemade baked goods. Breakfast specialties include blueberry muffins, Swedish oatmeal pancakes, and Blue Door orange French toast. Your hosts will gladly direct you to the nearby racetrack, beach, zoo, or University of California at San Diego. There is a $10 surcharge for one-night stays.

At Your Leisure Bed and Breakfast ✪

525 SOUTH THIRD STREET, EL CAJON, CALIFORNIA 92019

Tel: **(619) 444-3124**	Open: **All year**
Best Time to Call: **Evenings**	Reduced Rates: **10% seniors; weekly**
Hosts: **Ron and Joan Leasure**	Breakfast: **Continental**
Location: **18 mi. E of San Diego Airport**	Credit Cards: **MC, VISA**
No. of Rooms: **2**	Pets: **No**
Max. No. Sharing Bath: **4**	Children: **Welcome**
Double/sb: **$68**	Smoking: **No**
Single/sb: **$65**	Social Drinking: **Permitted**

A warm welcome awaits you at this comfortable and historic 1928 home, decorated with antiques and vintage clothing. Guests can enjoy a glass of iced tea or a cup of hot chocolate in the game room, by the swimming pool, or on the front porch or patio. At Your Leisure Bed and Breakfast is located on the bus route, only one mile from the major freeways, and just minutes from the airport and train station. Places of interest include San Diego Zoo, Balboa Park, universities, golf courses, convention centers, stadium, beaches, mountains, deserts, and many sites in between, including fine restaurants and shopping.

Sea Breeze B&B ✪

121 NORTH VULCAN, ENCINITAS, CALIFORNIA 92024
www.compuvar.com/internet/seabreeze

Tel: **(760) 944-0318**	Open: **All year**
Host: **Kirsten Richter**	Reduced Rates: **10% weekly; seniors;** **families**
Location: **23 mi. N of San Diego**	
No. of Rooms: **5**	Breakfast: **Continental**
No. of Private Baths: **5**	Pets: **No**
Double/pb: **$75–$150**	Children: **Welcome (playpen)**
Double/sb: **$90**	Smoking: **Permitted**
Suite: **$150**	Social Drinking: **Permitted**

Choose among a separate apartment, three queen bedrooms, and a penthouse with a private spa, whirlpool tub, and shower in this contemporary two-story home filled with custom, one-of-a-kind furnishings. Sunbathe in privacy on the deck overlooking the Pacific, or stroll down to Moonlight Beach for a refreshing ocean dip. It's a short walk to downtown Encinitas, which boasts many fine restaurants. Mt. Palomar Observatory, Sea World, Del Mar Race Track, and the Mexican border are about a half hour away by car. Guests have use of a kitchenette. Continental breakfasts consist of muffins, fresh fruit, yogurt, and coffee, tea, or hot chocolate.

Betty S. Bed & Breakfast ✪

3742 ARIZONA STREET, SAN DIEGO, CALIFORNIA 92104-3327

Tel: **(619) 692-1385**	Guest Cottage: **$30–35, sleeps 2**
Host: **Betty Spiva Simpson**	Open: **All year**
Location: **1½ mi. NE of San Diego**	Reduced Rates: **10% weekly, seniors,** **families**
No. of Rooms: **2**	
No. of Private Baths: **1**	Breakfast: **Full**
Max. No. Sharing Bath: **3**	Pets: **Sometimes**
Double/pb: **$35**	Children: **Welcome, infants only**
Single/pb: **$30**	Smoking: **Restricted**
Double/sb: **$30**	Social Drinking: **Permitted**
Single/sb: **$25**	

This attractively furnished Craftsman bungalow is located three blocks from the north edge of Balboa Park, where there is a year-round swimming pool, tennis courts, golf course, and walking trails. A zoo and museums are within one mile. Downtown San Diego and Mission Valley and Fashion Valley shopping centers are within five to 10 minutes by car, or you may choose the excellent bus service. Beaches are within 20–25 minutes. Mercy and University hospitals, restaurants, banks, post office, and churches are also nearby. The cottage has a microwave and a small refrigerator. Laundry facilities are available for a small charge. Gift certificates are available.

The Cottage ✪
3829 ALBATROSS STREET, SAN DIEGO, CALIFORNIA 92103

Tel: **(619) 299-1564**
Best Time to Call: **9 AM–5 PM**
Hosts: **Robert and Carol Emerick**
Location: **1 mi. from Rte. 5**
No. of Rooms: **2**
No. of Private Baths: **2**
Double/pb: **$59–$80**
Guest Cottage: **$85–$95**

Open: **All year**
Breakfast: **Continental**
Credit Cards: **AMEX, MC, VISA**
Pets: **No**
Children: **Welcome**
Smoking: **No**
Social Drinking: **Permitted**

Located in the Hillcrest section, where canyons and old houses dot the landscape, this private hideaway offers a cottage with a king-size bed, full bath, and fully equipped kitchen. Decorated with turn-of-the-century furniture, the wood-burning stove and oak pump organ evoke memories of long ago. It's two miles to the zoo, less to Balboa Park, and it is within easy walking distance of restaurants, shops, and theater. The University of California, University of San Diego, and San Diego State University are nearby.

SAN FRANCISCO AREA

Bed and Breakfast San Francisco ✪
P.O. BOX 420009, SAN FRANCISCO, CALIFORNIA 94142

Tel: **(415) 479-1913**
Best Time to Call: **9:30 AM–5 PM**
 Mon.–Fri.

Coordinators: **Susan and Richard Kreibich**
States/Regions Covered: **Carmel, Marin**

County, Monterey, Napa, San
Francisco, Sonoma (wine country)
Descriptive Directory: **$2**
Rates (Double):
Modest: **$55–$65**

Average: **$75–$95**
Luxury: **$100–$175**
Credit Cards: **AMEX, DC, MC, VISA**
Minimum Stay: **2 nights**

The San Francisco locations are near all of the famous sights, such as
Fisherman's Wharf and Chinatown. Many are historic Victorian houses.
Some homes offer hot tubs and sundecks; a few are on yachts and
houseboats.

Burlingame B&B ✪
1021 BALBOA AVENUE, BURLINGAME, CALIFORNIA 94010

Tel: **(650) 344-5815**
Hosts: **Joe and Elnora Fernandez**
Location: **¹/₂ mi. from Rte. 101**
No. of Rooms: **1**
No. of Private Baths: **1**
Double/pb: **$60**
Single/pb: **$50**
Open: **All year**

Breakfast: **Continental**
Pets: **No**
Children: **Welcome**
Smoking: **No**
Social Drinking: **No**
Airport/Station Pickup: **Yes**
Foreign Languages: **Italian, Spanish**

Located in a pleasantly quiet neighborhood, with San Francisco only
minutes away by good public transportation, the house offers the privacy of upstairs guest quarters with a view of a creek and native flora
and fauna. It's all very clean and cheerfully decorated. Joe and Elnora
will direct you to restaurants and shops to suit your budget.

Goose & Turrets B&B ✪
835 GEORGE STREET, P.O. BOX 937, MONTARA, CALIFORNIA 94037-0937

Tel: **(650) 728-5451**
Best Time to Call: **10 AM–9 PM**
Hosts: **Raymond and Emily Hoche-
Mong**
Location: **23 mi. SW of San Francisco**
No. of Rooms: **5**
No. of Private Baths: **5**
Double/pb: **$85–$130**
Open: **All year**

Reduced Rates: **Available**
Breakfast: **Full**
Credit Cards: **AMEX, DC, DISC, MC,
VISA**
Pets: **No**
Children: **Welcome**
Smoking: **No**
Social Drinking: **Permitted**
Foreign Languages: **French**

Located only 20 minutes from San Francisco Airport and half a mile
from the beach, Goose & Turrets B&B is a convenient headquarters for
day excursions to San Francisco, Silicon Valley, Berkeley, Monterey
Aquarium, and Carmel. Nearby are restaurants, galleries, tidepools,
fishing, golf, hiking, horseback riding, shops, and remnants of the area's
lurid past during Prohibition. Enjoy delicious four-course breakfasts,
comfortable beds, quiet gardens with courting swing, hammock, foun-

tains, bocce ball court, and meet the mascot geese. English tea and tasty snacks are served every afternoon. Raymond and Emily are well-traveled pilots who have lived in the South and in Europe, at places whose customs and cuisines are reflected in the food and the hospitality provided at the inn.

Adella Villa B&B ✪
P.O. BOX 4528, PALO ALTO, CALIFORNIA 94309

Tel: **(650) 321-5195**; fax: **(650) 325-5121**	Breakfast: **Full**
Host: **Tricia Young**	Credit Cards: **AMEX, DC, MC, VISA**
Location: **30 mi. S of San Francisco**	Pets: **No**
No. of Rooms: **5**	Children: **Welcome, over 12**
No. of Private Baths: **5**	Smoking: **No**
Double/pb: **$115–$155**	Social Drinking: **Permitted**
Open: **All year**	Airport/Station Pickup: **Yes**
	Foreign Languages: **German, Spanish**

This gorgeous, restored 1920s Italian villa is located in an exclusive area near Stanford University and Silicon Valley. The B&B, a pink stucco mansion with white trim, stands on an acre of lush park-like grounds with a Japanese koi pond, an aviary, and a swimming pool. The music foyer boasts a Steinway grand piano crafted in the 1930s. Fans of antiques will find much to admire, including an English dining room set, a five-foot 19th-century Imari vase, and a French marble commode. But there's nothing old-fashioned about the guest room amenities, such as bathrobes, down comforters, cable TV, sherry and wine, and cooked-to-order breakfasts.

Casa Arguello ✪
225 ARGUELLO BOULEVARD, SAN FRANCISCO, CALIFORNIA 94118
103221.3126@Compuserve

Tel: **(415) 752-9482**; fax: **(415) 681-1400**	Open: **All year**
Best Time to Call: **8 AM–noon**	Breakfast: **Continental, plus**
Host: **William McKenzie**	Pets: **No**
No. of Rooms: **5**	Children: **Welcome, over 7**
No. of Private Baths: **3**	Smoking: **No**
Max. No. Sharing Bath: **4**	Social Drinking: **Permitted**
Double/pb: **$79.50–$87.50**	Minimum Stay: **2 nights**
Double/sb: **$58.95–$59.95**	Foreign Languages: **Spanish**

This spacious duplex has an elegant living room, dining room, and cheerful bedrooms that overlook neighboring gardens. Tastefully decorated with modern and antique furnishings, it is convenient to Golden Gate Park, Golden Gate Bridge, Union Square, and fine shops and restaurants. The University of California Medical School is nearby. Excellent public transportation is close by.

Rancho San Gregorio ✪

ROUTE 1, BOX 54, SAN GREGORIO, CALIFORNIA 94074

rsgleebud@aol.com

Tel: **(650) 747-0810; fax: (650) 747-0184**	Open: **All year**
Hosts: **Bud and Lee Raynor**	Reduced Rates: **Available**
Location: **35 mi. S of San Francisco**	Breakfast: **Full**
No. of Rooms: **3**	Pets: **No**
No. of Private Baths: **3**	Children: **Welcome**
Double/pb: **$85–$105**	Smoking: **No**
Suite: **$145**	Social Drinking: **Permitted**

Graceful arches and bright stucco characterize this Spanish Mission home set on 15 wooded acres. Rooms are decorated with American antiques and family pieces. Your hosts, Bud and Lee, are glad to share a snack and a beverage. A full feast features eggs or pancakes, fresh fruit and breads, and a variety of meats. The atmosphere is relaxing, and guests are welcome to borrow a book from the library, or play the organ. Rancho San Gregorio is close to the beach, horseback riding, and golf. San Francisco, Half Moon Bay, and a variety of state parks and recreational areas are within an hour's drive. For those of you who don't mind paying a higher rate, 2 rooms are available.

SAN LUIS OBISPO AREA

Baywood Bed & Breakfast Inn ✪

1370 SECOND STREET, BAYWOOD PARK, CALIFORNIA 93402

Tel: **(805) 528-8888**	Breakfast: **Full**
Best Time to Call: **8 AM–8 PM**	Other Meals: **Available**
Host: **Margaret Bennett**	Credit Cards: **MC, VISA**
Location: **12 mi. W of San Luis Obispo**	Pets: **No**
No. of Rooms: **15**	Children: **Welcome**
No. of Private Baths: **15**	Smoking: **No**
Double/pb: **$80–$150**	Social Drinking: **Permitted**
Suites: **$120–$160**	Minimum Stay: **2 days on holiday**
Open: **All year**	**weekends**

This waterfront establishment lies on a tiny peninsula that projects into Morro Bay. Outdoor types will find plenty to do here; the options include kayaking, golfing, hiking, bicycling, and picnicking. Several shops and restaurants are right in town, and Montano De Oro State Park, San Luis Obispo, and Hearst Castle are only minutes away. Each Baywood suite has bay views, cozy seating areas, and a wood-burning fireplace. Guests are treated to afternoon wine and cheese, room tours, and breakfast in bed.

SANTA BARBARA AREA

Carpinteria Beach Condo ✪

1825 CRAVENS LANE, CARPINTERIA, CALIFORNIA 93013

Tel: **(805) 684-1579**	Reduced Rates: **Available**
Best Time to Call: **7 AM–9 PM**	Breakfast: **Continental**
Hosts: **Bev and Don Schroeder**	Pets: **No**
Location: **11 mi. SE of Santa Barbara**	Children: **Welcome**
Guest Condo: **$75–$90**	Smoking: **No**
Open: **All year**	Social Drinking: **Permitted**

You may view majestic mountains from this one-bedroom condo across the street from the beach. If you tire of the ocean, there is also a spa and swimming pool. Play a set of tennis at the local Polo and Racquet Club, visit your hosts' fruit and flower ranch four miles away, or take a ten-minute drive into Santa Barbara. Breakfast is a do-it-yourself affair in the condo's complete minikitchen. The Amtrak station is located two blocks away.

Long's Seaview Bed & Breakfast ✪

317 PIEDMONT ROAD, SANTA BARBARA, CALIFORNIA 93105

Tel: **(805) 687-2947**	Open: **All year**
Best Time to Call: **Before 6 PM**	Breakfast: **Full**
Host: **LaVerne Long**	Pets: **No**
Location: **1 1/2 mi. from Hwy. 101**	Children: **No**
No. of Rooms: **1**	Smoking: **No**
No. of Private Baths: **1**	Social Drinking: **Permitted**
Double/pb: **$80**	Airport/Station Pickup: **Yes**
Single/pb: **$75**	

Overlooking Santa Barbara's prestigious north side, this ranch-style home is in a quiet, residential neighborhood. Breakfast is usually served on the patio, where you can see the ocean, Channel Islands, and the small family citrus orchard and garden. Convenient to the beach, Solvang, and Santa Ynez Valley, the large, airy bedroom is cheerfully furnished with antiques and king-size bed. The breakfast menu varies from Southern dishes to Mexican specialties.

SEQUOIA AREA/SIERRA FOOTHILLS

Kern River Inn Bed & Breakfast ✪

**P.O. BOX 1725, 119 KERN RIVER DRIVE, KERNVILLE,
CALIFORNIA 93238**

Tel: **(760) 376-6750; (800) 986-4382**	Location: **50 mi. NE of Bakersfield**
Best Time to Call: **10 AM–9 PM**	No. of Rooms: **6**
Hosts: **Jack and Carita Prestwich**	No. of Private Baths: **6**

Double/pb: **$89–$99**	Credit Cards: **AMEX, MC, VISA**
Single/pb: **$79–$89**	Pets: **No**
Open: **All year**	Children: **Welcome**
Reduced Rates: **Available**	Smoking: **No**
Breakfast: **Full**	Social Drinking: **Permitted**

Stay in a charming riverfront B&B in a quaint Western town within Sequoia National Forest. Carita and Jack specialize in romantic, relaxing getaways. Nearby activities include golf, hiking, biking, white-water rafting, downhill skiing, and year-round fishing in front of the Inn. It's an easy stroll to shops, restaurants, and parks, and a short drive to the giant redwood trees.

Cort Cottage ✪
P.O. BOX 245, THREE RIVERS, CALIFORNIA 93271

Tel: **(209) 561-4671**	Breakfast: **Continental**
Best Time to Call: **Before 9 PM**	Pets: **No**
Host: **Elsah Cort**	Children: **Welcome**
Location: **5 mi. W of Sequoia National Park**	Smoking: **No**
	Social Drinking: **Permitted**
Guest Cottage: **$85; sleeps 2**	Minimum Stay: **2 nights**
Open: **All year**	

Hidden in this Sierra Nevada foothill village you will find this secluded guest cottage, ten minutes away from the entrance to Sequoia National Park. Built as a home for Elsah's grandma in 1986, the cottage fits snugly into the hillside and herb garden with a panoramic view of the mountain. Amenities include an outdoor hot tub, a fully equipped kitchen, and a full bath with step-down tile tub. Elsah works at home, creating collages and poetry for her greeting card company, and as an R.N., offering craniosacral therapy.

COLORADO

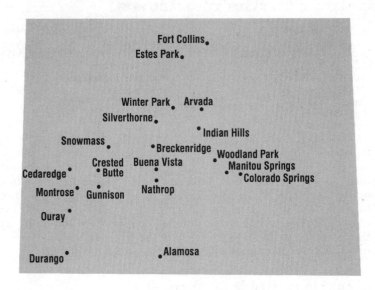

Fort Collins.
Estes Park.

Winter Park. Arvada
Silverthorne.
.Indian Hills
Snowmass.
.Breckenridge Woodland Park
Crested Buena Vista .Manitou Springs
Cedaredge. .Butte .Colorado Springs
Montrose. Gunnison Nathrop
Ouray.

Durango. .Alamosa

Cottonwood Inn B&B
123 SAN JUAN AVENUE, ALAMOSA, COLORADO 81101

Tel: **(719) 589-3882; (800) 955-2623**	Breakfast: **Full**
Host: **Julie Mordecai**	Credit Cards: **AMEX, DC, DISC, MC,**
Location: **150 mi. SW of Colorado**	**VISA**
Springs	Pets: **Sometimes**
No. of Rooms: **9**	Children: **Welcome**
No. of Private Baths: **7**	Smoking: **No**
Double/pb: **$85–$105**	Social Drinking: **Permitted**
Single/pb: **$71–$104**	Minimum Stay: **2 nights on special**
Suites: **$89–$93**	**weekends**
Open: **All year**	Airport/Station Pickup: **Yes**
Reduced Rates: **10–15% off season**	Foreign Languages: **Spanish**

The Cottonwood Inn B&B is centrally located for guests visiting southern Colorado and northern New Mexico. The Inn is furnished with antiques and reproductions. Nearby are Adams State College, the Great Sand Dunes National Monument, wildlife sanctuaries, Cumbres Toltec

Railway, three golf courses and horseback riding. Golf and train packages are available. Julie is an ex-schoolteacher, avid outdoor person, and enthusiastic baker. The inn is on the way to Santa Fe, Durango, and Denver.

On Golden Pond Bed & Breakfast
7831 ELDRIDGE, ARVADA, COLORADO 80005

Tel: **(303) 424-2296**	Reduced Rates: **10% weekly; seniors**
Host: **Kathy Kula**	Breakfast: **Full**
Location: **15 mi. W of Denver**	Credit Cards: **AMEX, DISC, MC, VISA**
No. of Rooms: **5**	Pets: **1 room only**
No. of Private Baths: **5**	Children: **1 room only**
Double/pb: **$60–$70**	Smoking: **No**
Single/pb: **$50–$60**	Social Drinking: **Permitted**
Suites: **$100–$120**	Foreign Languages: **German**
Open: **All year**	

A secluded retreat tucked into the Rocky Mountain foothills, this custom-built, two-story brick home has dramatic views of mountains, prairies, and downtown Denver. Birds and other wildlife are drawn to the ten-acre grounds, which have a fishing pond and hiking trails. After a full breakfast, stroll along the garden path, bicycle by the creek, swim laps in the pool, or ride horses into the foothills. Then join Kathy for a late afternoon kaffeeklatsch. Conclude the day with a soak in the hot tub. There are three suites with hot tub or Jacuzzi tub and fireplaces.

Evans House Bed & Breakfast ✪
102 SOUTH FRENCH STREET, P.O. BOX 387, BRECKENRIDGE, COLORADO 80424
www.colorado-bnb.com/evanshse

Tel: **(970) 453-5509**	Open: **All year**
Hosts: **Peter and Georgette Contos**	Breakfast: **Full**
Location: **85 mi. W of Denver**	Other Meals: **Available**
No. of Rooms: **4**	Pets: **No**
No. of Private Baths: **4**	Children: **Welcome**
Double/pb: **$73–$109**	Smoking: **No**
Double/sb: **$63–$90**	Social Drinking: **Permitted**
Suite: **$86–$127**	Foreign Languages: **Greek, French**

Get the feel of Breckenridge's mining days in this restored 1886 Victorian listed on the National Historic Register. Peter and Georgette can tell you about their town's past with the help of period photographs mounted on their walls. The common room—with a mountain view, books, and games—is a favorite gathering place, but shopping, restaurants, and evening entertainments will lure you to Main Street, two blocks away. Breckenridge's stunning mountain setting is appealing throughout the year. Admire wildflowers in the spring, attend special summer events, see the aspens change color in the fall; higher rates apply in the winter, when you have access to cold weather activities from the free shuttle bus that stops at the B&B's front door. A unique hot tub setting in our historic shed is offered with stained glass windows and a view.

Trout City Bed & Breakfast ✪
BOX 431, BUENA VISTA, COLORADO 81211

Tel: **(719) 495-0348**	Open: **June 1–Sept. 1**
Best Time to Call: **After 6 PM**	Breakfast: **Full**
Hosts: **Juel and Irene Kjeldsen**	Other Meals: **Available**
Location: **5 mi. E of Buena Vista on Hwy. 24**	Credit Cards: **MC, VISA**
	Pets: **No**
No. of Rooms: **4**	Children: **Welcome, over 10**
No. of Private Baths: **4**	Smoking: **No**
Double/pb: **$50**	Social Drinking: **Permitted**

Trout City Inn is a historic site on the famous South Park Narrow Gauge Railroad, and is located at the edge of a trout stream. It is an accurate reconstruction of a mountain railroad depot, with authentic private rail cars containing Pullman berths. The depot rooms feature Victorian decor, high ceilings, and four-poster or brass beds. Glass doors open onto a deck with views of the 14,000-foot peaks of the Continental Divide. Hiking, biking, panning for gold, and fly-fishing are within steps of the front door; white-water rafting is minutes away.

Cedars' Edge Llamas Bed and Breakfast ✪
2169 HIGHWAY 65, CEDAREDGE, COLORADO 81413
www.llamabandb.com

Tel: **(970) 856-6836**	Open: **All year**
Hosts: **Ray and Gail Record**	Breakfast: **Full**
Location: **50 mi. E of Grand Junction**	Pets: **No**
No. of Rooms: **4**	Children: **Welcome**
No. of Private Baths: **4**	Smoking: **No**
Double/pb: **$60–$85**	Social Drinking: **Permitted**
Single/pb: **$50–$75**	Airport/Station Pickup: **Yes**

Nestled on the southern slope of the Grand Mesa, this modern cedar home offers a panoramic view of several mountain ranges, plus the unique opportunity to share life on a llama-breeding ranch. The accommodations are immaculate. Cheerful rooms are tastefully decorated in pastel shades, with exposed beams, hanging plants, and light streaming in from many windows. Sportsmen and sportswomen can fish for trout, hunt deer and elk, or go cross-country and downhill skiing. After a filling breakfast, guests can join Ray and Gail in feeding or grooming well-behaved four-footed friends—a rewarding experience for all.

Timberline Bed & Breakfast ✪
2457 U50 ROAD, CEDAREDGE, COLORADO 81413

Tel: **(970) 856-7379**	Open: **All year**
Best Time to Call: **Mornings or evenings**	Breakfast: **Continental**
Hosts: **Al and Shirley Richardson**	Pets: **Yes**
Location: **60 mi. E of Grand Junction**	Children: **Welcome**
No. of Rooms: **1**	Smoking: **No**
No. of Private Baths: **1**	Social Drinking: **Permitted**
Double/pb: **$40**	Airport/Station Pickup: **Yes**
Single/pb: **$30**	

Set on a hillside at the foot of Grand Mesa, this B&B occupies the ground floor of a country home surrounded by pinyon, oak, and juniper trees. The three-room suite has a queen-size bed, living room, woodburning stove, and a fully equipped kitchen. Guests may while away the hours with fishing, hiking, boating, and cross-country and downhill skiing. Timberline lies within easy driving distance of Powderhorn Ski Resort, Black Canyon of the Gunnison, Colorado National Monument, and Curecanti National Recreation Area.

Holden House—1902 Victorian Bed & Breakfast Inn
1102 WEST PIKES PEAK AVENUE, COLORADO SPRINGS, COLORADO 80904
HoldenHouse@worldnet.att.net; www.bbonline.com/co/holden

Tel: **(719) 471-3980**	Breakfast: **Full**
Best Time to Call: **9 AM–9 PM**	Credit Cards: **AMEX, DC, DISC, MC,**
Hosts: **Sallie and Welling Clark**	**VISA**
No. of Rooms: **5**	Pets: **No**
No. of Private Baths: **5**	Children: **No**
Suites: **$115–$130**	Smoking: **No**
Open: **All year**	Social Drinking: **Permitted**

Built by Isabel Holden, this 1902 storybook Victorian, 1906 carriage house, and adjacent 1898 Victorian are centrally located near historic Old Colorado City. The Inn, lovingly restored by the Clarks in 1985, is filled with antiques and family heirlooms. Named for mining towns, guest rooms are furnished with queen beds, period furnishings, and down pillows. The Inn boasts five romantic suites with tubs for two, mountain views, fireplaces, and more! Gourmet breakfasts, served in the elegant formal dining room, might include carob chip muffins, Sallie's famous Southwestern Eggs Fiesta, fresh fruit, gourmet coffee, tea, and juice. Complimentary refreshments, homemade cookies, and turndown service are just some of Holden House's special touches, along with in-room phones and fax capability. Sallie and Welling will be happy to help in planning your itinerary around the many activities in the Pikes Peak region. Friendly resident cats Mingtoy and Muffin will greet you.

The Elizabeth Anne B&B ✪
P.O. BOX 3150, CRESTED BUTTE, COLORADO 81224

Tel: **(888) 745-4620**	Breakfast: **Full**
Hosts: **Karen and Kirk Smith**	Credit Cards: **AMEX, MC, VISA**
Location: **225 mi. SW of Denver**	Pets: **No**
No. of Rooms: **4**	Children: **Welcome (large room only)**
No. of Private Baths: **4**	Smoking: **No**
Double/pb: **$89–$120**	Social Drinking: **Permitted**
Open: **May 25–Oct. 10; Nov. 15–**	Minimum Stay: **2 days winter weekends**
Apr. 20	Airport Pickup: **Yes**

The Elizabeth Anne is in the National Historic District of Crested Butte, an 1880s mining town. This new Victorian home echoes the warmth and charm of Crested Butte's past. The common areas are decorated with Queen Anne furniture, and the bedrooms have a Victorian appeal of their own. Other amenities are a soothing hot tub, guest refrigerator, and bicycle and ski storage. Recreational opportunities abound, with Nordic and Alpine skiing in the winter. Summer offers mountain biking, hiking, fishing, golfing, and horseback riding. Crested Butte also has a myriad of shops and gourmet restaurants.

Apple Orchard Inn ✪
7758 COUNTY ROAD 203, DURANGO, COLORADO 81301

Tel: **(800) 426-0751**	Double/pb: **$85–$125**
Hosts: **Celeste and John Gardiner**	Guest Cottages: **$100–$150**
Location: **8 mi. N of Durango**	Open: **All year**
No. of Rooms: **10**	Reduced Rates: **10% AAA; after 3rd**
No. of Private Baths: **10**	**night; seniors**

Breakfast: **Full**
Other Meals: **Available**
Credit Cards: **AMEX, DISC, MC, VISA**
Pets: **No**
Children: **Welcome**

Smoking: **Restricted**
Social Drinking: **Permitted**
Airport/Station Pickup: **Yes**
Foreign Languages: **Portuguese**

The Apple Orchard Inn is a newly constructed two-story farmhouse with six cottages on four-and-a-half acres of orchards and gardens surrounded by mountains and cliffs. The Inn has beautiful wood trim, cherrywood floors, and elegant country furniture, including featherbeds, armoires, and vanities. Each cottage has a special feature such as a fireplace and Jacuzzi tub, French doors leading to a private patio, or a cozy bay window. Enjoy a scrumptious breakfast while watching the Durango-Silverton Narrow Gauge Train pass by. Gourmet lunches and dinners are prepared by Celeste, who has European training.

Country Sunshine B&B ✪
35130 HIGHWAY 550 NORTH, DURANGO, COLORADO 81301

Tel: **(970) 247-2853; (800) 383-2853**
Best Time to Call: **9 AM–6 PM**
Hosts: **Beanie and Gary Archie**
No. of Rooms: **6**
No. of Private Baths: **6**
Double/pb: **$85**
Open: **All year**

Breakfast: **Full**
Credit Cards: **AMEX, DC, DISC, MC, VISA**
Pets: **No**
Children: **Welcome, over 5**
Smoking: **No**
Social Drinking: **Permitted**

Enjoy southwest Colorado's splendor and beauty while staying at this spacious ranch-style home. Indulge your senses and spirit with mountain views, river songs, abundant wildlife, and the aroma of the ponderosa pines. Awaken to the smell of a country breakfast. Nearby is Mesa Verde National Park, Durango-Silverton Narrow Gauge Train, and Purgatory Ski Area. After a busy day, relax in the hot tub under the star-filled sky.

The Leland House Bed & Breakfast Suites ✪
721 EAST SECOND AVENUE, DURANGO, COLORADO 81301

Tel: **(970) 385-1920; (800) 664-1920**
Best Time to Call: **8 AM–5 PM**
Host: **Kirk Komick**
Location: **350 mi. SW of Denver**
No. of Rooms: **10**
No. of Private Baths: **10**
Double/pb: **$95–$105**
Suites: **$125–$175**
Open: **All year**

Reduced Rates: **Available**
Breakfast: **Full**
Other Meals: **Available**
Credit Cards: **AMEX, MC, VISA**
Pets: **No**
Children: **Welcome**
Smoking: **No**
Social Drinking: **Permitted**

Originally built in 1927 as an apartment house, the Leland House was restored by the Komicks as a B&B in 1993. All rooms have cable TV and telephone service. Six suites have separate living rooms, bedrooms, and full service kitchens; four studios have kitchenettes. The interior is decorated with rustic antiques, accented by photos, memorabilia, and biographies of historic figures associated with the property. Leland House is steps away from Durango's historic downtown district and the Durango-Silverton Narrow Gauge Railroad Station. Gourmet breakfasts consist of fresh-baked goods, homemade granola, and may include fruit-filled French toast or a Southwestern breakfast burrito.

Lightner Creek Inn Bed and Breakfast ✪
999 C.R. 207, DURANGO, COLORADO 81301
lci@frontier.net; www.lightnercreekinn.com

Tel: **(970) 259-1226; (800) 268-9804;** fax: **(970) 259-9526**	Reduced Rates: **20% Nov. 1–Apr. 30** Breakfast: **Full**
Best Time to Call: **9 AM–9 PM**	Credit Cards: **AMEX, DC, DISC, MC,**
Hosts: **Richard and Julie Houston**	**VISA**
Location: **4 mi W of Durango**	Pets: **No**
No. of Rooms: **9**	Children: **Welcome**
No. of Private Baths: **9**	Smoking: **No**
Double/pb: **$85–$165**	Social Drinking: **Permitted**
Open: **All year**	

Discover the Rocky Mountains' best-kept secret of French countryside elegance at the Lightner Creek Inn. The inn combines charming Victorian detail with antique furnishings and cozy fireplaces. Play the baby grand piano. Enjoy the tranquility of the pond, stream, and views from the gazebo. And don't forget about the gourmet breakfast. Activities include snowmobiling, river rafting, and trout fishing. Ride the Durango-Silverton Narrow Gauge train, explore the ancient Indian ruins at Mesa Verde, ski Purgatory, or take your appetite on a dinner sleigh.

Logwood—The Verheyden Inn ✪
35060 HIGHWAY 550, DURANGO, COLORADO 81301

Tel: **(970) 259-4396; (800) 369-4082**	Reduced Rates: **$10 less winter**
Best Time to Call: **After 10 AM**	**single occupancy**
Hosts: **Debby and Greg Verheyden**	Breakfast: **Full**
Location: **212 mi. NW of Albuquerque,**	Credit Cards: **MC, VISA**
NM	Pets: **No**
No. of Rooms: **8**	Children: **Welcome, over 7**
No. of Private Baths: **8**	Smoking: **No**
Double/pb: **$75–$130**	Social Drinking: **Permitted**
Single/pb: **$55–$120**	Minimum Stay: **2 nights holidays**
Open: **All year**	

This award-winning luxurious red cedar log home sits on 15 acres amid the beautiful San Juan Mountains and beside the Animas River. Southwest decor, fabulous views, rooms with TVs and fireplaces, and prize-winning desserts are only a part of what Logwood offers. Nearby activities include Purgatory downhill skiing, cross-country sleigh rides, hiking, horseback riding, and jeeping. Take in the Bar D show and dinner and Mesa Verde Park and hop aboard the Durango-Silverton Narrow Gauge train.

Scrubby Oaks Bed & Breakfast ✪
P.O. BOX 1047, DURANGO, COLORADO 81302
www.southwesterninns.com/scrubby.htm

Tel: **(970) 247-2176**	Single/pb: **$65**
Best Time to Call: **Early mornings;** **evenings**	Double/sb: **$70**
	Single/sb: **$55**
Host: **Mary Ann Craig**	Open: **Apr. 30–Oct. 31**
Location: **4 mi. from junction 160 and** **550**	Breakfast: **Full**
	Pets: **No**
No. of Rooms: **7**	Children: **Welcome**
No. of Private Baths: **3**	Smoking: **No**
Max. No. Sharing Bath: **4**	Social Drinking: **Permitted**
Double/pb: **$80**	

There's a quiet country feeling to this two-story home set on 10 acres overlooking the spectacular Animas Valley and surrounding mountains. Trees and gardens frame the patios where breakfast is apt to be served. All breads and preserves are homemade, and strawberry Belgian waffles are a specialty. On chilly mornings, the kitchen fireplace is the cozy backdrop for your wake-up cup of coffee or cocoa. You are made to feel part of the family and are welcome to play pool, take a sauna, read a book, watch a VCR movie, or simply take in the crisp air.

Eagle Cliff House
BOX 4312, ESTES PARK, COLORADO 80517

Tel: **(970) 586-5425; (800) 414-0922**	Open: **All year**
Best Time to Call: **Early morning**	Breakfast: **Full**
Hosts: **Nancy and Mike Conrin**	Pets: **No**
Location: **2½ mi. W of Estes Park**	Children: **Welcome**
No. of Rooms: **3**	Smoking: **No**
No. of Private Baths: **3**	Social Drinking: **Permitted**
Double/pb: **$80**	Minimum Stay: **2 nights, weekends**
Guest Cottage: **$115**	Airport/Station Pickup: **Yes**

Nancy and Mike are dedicated hikers who live within walking distance of Rocky Mountain National Park, so don't be surprised if they invite you for an afternoon's exploration of their favorite "backyard" trails. Saturday evening get-togethers are commonplace, especially in the summer. Recreational opportunities abound throughout the year, from golf, tennis, and horseback riding to cross-country and downhill skiing. One guest room of this woodsy retreat is decorated with mementos of Mexico and the American Southwest; the cottage and the second guest room are furnished in Victorian style.

Elizabeth Street Guest House ✪
202 EAST ELIZABETH, FORT COLLINS, COLORADO 80524

Tel: **(970) 493-BEDS [2337]**	Single/sb: **$45–$50**
Best Time to Call: **8–10 AM; 5–7 PM**	Open: **All year**
Hosts: **John and Sheryl Clark**	Breakfast: **Full**
Location: **65 mi. N of Denver**	Credit Cards: **AMEX, MC, VISA (for**
No. of Rooms: **3**	**deposits only)**
Max. No. Sharing Bath: **4**	Pets: **No**
Double/pb: **$85–$90**	Children: **Welcome, over 8**
Single/pb: **$65–$70**	Smoking: **No**
Double/sb: **$65–$70**	Social Drinking: **Permitted**

This completely renovated and restored 1905 brick American Four-square has leaded windows and oak woodwork. Family antiques, plants, old quilts, and handmade touches add to its charm. Of special interest is the unique 3-story miniature house in the entry hall. All of the bedrooms have sinks. It is close to historic Old Town Square, Estes Park, Rocky Mountain National Park, and a block away from Colorado State University. John and Sheryl will spoil you with their special brand of hospitality and homemade treats.

Eagle's Nest Bed and Breakfast ✪
206 NORTH COLORADO, GUNNISON, COLORADO 81230

Tel: **(970) 641-4457**
Best Time to Call: **10 AM–5 PM**
Hosts: **Jane and Hugh McGee**
No. of Rooms: **1**
No. of Private Baths: **1**
Double/pb: **$45**

Open: **All year**
Breakfast: **Full, Continental**
Pets: **No**
Children: **By arrangement**
Smoking: **No**
Social Drinking: **Permitted**

Built in 1923, this early American former judge's home features stained glass and interior maple woodwork. The spacious guest room has a private entrance, queen-size bed, and a cheery reading and breakfast room. Gunnison is a beautiful place to visit in all four seasons. Nearby is skiing at Crested Butte, hunting in the fall, and fishing at Blue Mesa Lake or the Gunnison River. During the summer the attractions include the Gunnison Rodeo, the Crested Butte Wildflower Festival, rafting, and much more.

Mary Lawrence Inn
601 NORTH TAYLOR, GUNNISON, COLORADO 81230
www.gunnison.co.com/main/lodging/maryl.htm

Tel: **(970) 641-3343**
Best Time to Call: **10 AM–10 PM**
Hosts: **Doug and Beth Parker**
Location: **195 mi. W and S of Denver**
No. of Rooms: **7**
No. of Private Baths: **7**
Double/pb: **$69–$85**
Single/pb: **$69–$85**
Suites: **$99–$139; sleep 2–4**

Open: **All year**
Breakfast: **Full**
Credit Cards: **MC, VISA**
Pets: **No**
Children: **Welcome**
Smoking: **No**
Social Drinking: **Permitted**
Airport/Station Pickup: **Yes**

An Italianate frame house with spacious, antique-filled guest rooms, comfortable common areas, and a large outdoor hot tub, the Mary Lawrence Inn is located in a well-kept neighborhood inside Gunnison's city limits. Surrounded by wilderness and Forest Service land, this B&B is a haven for sportspeople of all types; the Black Canyon of the Gunnison, the Alpine Tunnel, the town of Crested Butte, and many spectacular mountain vistas are all within an hour's drive.

Mountain View Bed & Breakfast ✪
4754 PICUTIS ROAD, P.O. BOX 631, INDIAN HILLS, COLORADO 80454

Tel: **(303) 697-6896**
Best Time to Call: **11 AM–3 PM**
Hosts: **Graham and Ortrud Richardson**
Location: **20 mi. W of Denver**
No. of Rooms: **4**

No. of Private Baths: **4**
Double/pb: **$80**
Guest Cabin: **$135, sleeps 4**
Suite: **$105, sleeps 4**
Open: **All year**

Reduced Rates: **10% seniors**
Breakfast: **Full**
Credit Cards: **AMEX, MC, VISA**
Pets: **No**

Children: **Welcome**
Smoking: **No**
Social Drinking: **Permitted**
Foreign Languages: **German**

Built in the 1920s as a writer's retreat, the Mountain View Bed & Breakfast is situated on $2^{1}/_{2}$ acres and offers a perfect romantic getaway. Guests can choose from three unique rooms or a private cabin, all with queen-size beds. Mountain View is located near Evergreen, which offers easy access to several mountain parks boasting many hiking trails and breathtaking views. Each afternoon, enjoy a cup of tea in the English tradition while sampling some Old Country delicacies. In the morning, wake to the aroma of freshly brewed coffee and a gourmet meal served by your European hosts.

Two Sisters Inn
TEN OTOE PLACE, MANITOU SPRINGS, COLORADO 80829

Tel: **(719) 685-9684; (800) 2 SIS-INN [274-7466]**
Best Time to Call: **Evenings**
Hosts: **Sharon Smith and Wendy Goldstein**
Location: **4 mi. W of Colorado Springs**
No. of Rooms: **5**
No. of Private Baths: **3**
Max. No. Sharing Bath: **4**
Double/pb: **$85**

Double/sb: **$69**
Guest Cottage: **$105**
Open: **All year**
Breakfast: **Full**
Credit Cards: **DISC, MC, VISA**
Pets: **No**
Children: **Welcome, over 10**
Smoking: **No**
Social Drinking: **Permitted**

This award-winning rose-colored Victorian Bungalow was built in 1919 as a boardinghouse and has been lovingly restored, with four bedrooms and a cozy honeymoon cottage in the back garden. The sunny rooms are filled with fresh flowers, family collectibles, and antiques. Sharon and Wendy are schooled chefs and prepare a three-course gourmet breakfast, accommodating special dietary needs. The inn is located at the base of Pikes Peak in the center of Manitou's historic district, within walking distance of the Mineral Springs. Nearby attractions include the Pikes Peak cog railway, the Garden of the Gods, and the United States Air Force Academy.

Maria's Bed & Breakfast ✪
20538 HIGHWAY 550 SOUTH, MONTROSE, COLORADO 81401

Tel: **(970) 249-8288; fax: (970) 240-8281**	Open: **Mar. 15–Dec. 31**
	Breakfast: **Full**
Best Time to Call: **8 AM–6 PM**	Pets: **No**
Host: **Harold LaMar**	Children: **Welcome**
Location: **5 mi. S of Montrose**	Smoking: **No**
No. of Rooms: **4**	Social Drinking: **No**
No. of Private Baths: **4**	Airport/Station Pickup: **Yes**
Double/pb: **$50**	

Colorful flowers, trees, and a beautifully groomed yard surround this gambrel-roofed home. Summer evenings can be spent on the large comfortable porches enjoying the majestic views of the San Juan Mountains while indulging in one of Harold's homemade pies. A few things to do and see include hunting, hiking, fishing, and skiing. Black Canyon National Monument, Ouray Hot Springs, Ridgeway Recreational Area, and Telluride are famous for their summer festivals and skiing. Harold gives all guests special attention and pampers them with home-cooked specialties, such as Belgian waffles with strawberries and whipped topping, eggs Benedict, Quiche Lorraine, blueberry muffins, breads, and jams.

Claveau's Streamside Bed and Breakfast ✪
18820 C.R. 162, NATHROP, COLORADO 81236

Tel: **(719) 395-2553**	Open: **All year**
Best Time to Call: **Anytime**	Breakfast: **Full**
Hosts: **Denny and Kathy Claveau**	Pets: **No**
Location: **130 mi. SW of Denver**	Smoking: **No**
No. of Rooms: **3**	Social Drinking: **Permitted**
No. of Private Baths: **3**	Minimum Stay: **Holiday weekends**
Double/pb: **$71–$76**	

Located within San Isabel National Forest, Claveau's Streamside Bed and Breakfast is in the shadow of the Rockies' Collegiate Peaks. Mt. Princeton, Mt. Yale, Mt. Harvard, Mt. Oxford, and other challenging

peaks beckon all to climb their glistening summits. Wildlife abounds here; deer, elk, bighorn sheep, and mountain goats are your hosts' neighbors. Winter offers downhill and cross-country skiing. Summer offers fishing, hiking, white-water rafting, horseback riding, or just relaxing by their stream. Kathy and Denny are environmentally active outdoor advocates. They look forward to helping guests plan their daily adventures. This is a Rocky Mountain paradise.

Ouray 1898 House ✪
322 MAIN STREET, P.O. BOX 641, OURAY, COLORADO 81427

Tel: **(970) 325-4871**	Open: **May 25–Sept. 25**
Best Time to Call: **After 5 PM**	Breakfast: **Full**
Hosts: **Lee and Kathy Bates**	Credit Cards: **AMEX, MC, VISA**
Location: **On Hwy. 550**	Pets: **No**
No. of Rooms: **3**	Children: **Welcome**
No. of Private Baths: **3**	Smoking: **No**
Double/pb: **$68–$85**	Social Drinking: **Permitted**

This 100-year-old house has been renovated to combine old-time elegance with modern amenities. Each guest room features antique furnishings, cable TV, and a deck where you can enjoy the view of the San Juan Mountains. You are also invited to use the hot tub and gazebo. A variety of foods are served at breakfast to tempt any appetite; coffee and tea are served at all times. Ouray, known as the "Jeep Capital of the World," is also famed for its natural hot springs and hiking trails.

Mountain Vista Bed & Breakfast ✪
P.O. BOX 1398, 358 LAGOON LANE, SILVERTHORNE,
COLORADO 80498

Tel: **(970) 468-7700**	Double/sb: **$65–$95**
Best Time to Call: **Evening**	Open: **All year**
Host: **Sandy Ruggaber**	Reduced Rates: **10% seniors**
Location: **60 mi. W of Denver**	Breakfast: **Full, Continental**
No. of Rooms: **3**	Pets: **No**
No. of Private Baths: **1**	Children: **Welcome, over 6**
Max. No. Sharing Bath: **4**	Smoking: **No**
Double/pb: **$70–$100**	Social Drinking: **Permitted**

Mountain Vista offers something for everyone. Since it's surrounded by fine resorts like Keystone, Arapahoe Basin, Copper Mountain, Brecken-ridge, and Vail, guests can enjoy downhill skiing at its best. In the summer, try hiking, kayaking, cycling, golf, tennis, rafting, and fishing (an outdoor grill is available for you to cook your catch). Visit the factory outlet stores or go to the many concerts, festivals, and cultural events offered throughout Summit County. After a busy day, relax by the fireplace with your favorite drink, watch TV, read, do a puzzle, or retire to a warm comfortable room. You will awaken in the morning to the smell of a hearty homemade breakfast.

Starry Pines ✪
2262 SNOWMASS CREEK ROAD, SNOWMASS, COLORADO 81654

Tel: **(970) 927-4202; (800) 527-4202**	Apartment: **$100–$120, for two**
Best Time to Call: **7 AM–9 AM,**	Open: **All year**
4 PM–9 PM	Reduced Rates: **Available**
Host: **Shelley Burke**	Breakfast: **Continental**
Location: **200 mi. W of Denver**	Children: **Welcome, over 6**
No. of Rooms: **2**	Smoking: **No**
Max. No. Sharing Bath: **4**	Social Drinking: **Permitted**
Double/sb: **$80–$95**	Minimum Stay: **2 nights ski season and**
Single/sb: **$75–$90**	**weekends**

On 70 private acres with its own trout stream and a panoramic view of the Rockies, Starry Pines offers you year-round activities and hospitality. Enjoy the Aspen summer music festival, ballet, and theater. Try hot-air balloon rides landing in the B&B's fields, or biking, hiking, jeeping, and riding in the back country. For quieter moments, there's a secluded picnic site with horseshoes and a hammock by the stream. Fall unveils spectacular aspen foliage. Winter and spring bring world-renowned skiing at four mountains only 25 minutes away, plus snowshoeing and cross-country skiing at Starry Pines's own door. At the end of the day, relax in the hot tub on the patio, then sit around the living room fireplace or watch a movie on the VCR.

Engelmann Pines ✪
P.O. BOX 1305, WINTER PARK, COLORADO 80482

Tel: **(970) 726-4632; (800) 992-9512**	Open: **May–Dec.**
Hosts: **Heinz and Margaret Engel**	Breakfast: **Full**
Location: **67 mi. W of Denver**	Credit Cards: **AMEX, DISC, MC, VISA**
No. of Rooms: **7**	Pets: **No**
No. of Private Baths: **5**	Children: **Welcome**
Max. No. Sharing Bath: **4**	Smoking: **No**
Double/pb: **$75–$115**	Social Drinking: **Permitted**
Single/pb: **$65–$105**	Station Pickup: **Yes**
Double/sb: **$55–$75**	Foreign Languages: **German**
Single/sb: **$45–$65**	

From its Rocky Mountain perch, this spacious modern lodge offers spectacular views of the Continental Divide. Bathrooms are equipped with Jacuzzis, and there is a complete kitchen for guests' use. A free bus ferries skiers from the front door to some of Colorado's best ski slopes; cross-country ski aficionados will find a trail just across the road. When the snow melts, it's time to go golfing, hiking, fishing, and horseback riding. In the morning, eager sportsmen and -women can fill up on marzipan cake, muesli, and fresh fruit crepes.

Woodland Inn Bed & Breakfast
159 TRULL ROAD, WOODLAND PARK, COLORADO 80863

Tel: **(800) 226-9565; (719) 687-8209**	Reduced Rates: **10% seniors; weekly;**
Best Time to Call: **8 AM–9 PM**	**groups booking 3 or more rooms**
Hosts: **Frank and Nancy O'Neil**	Breakfast: **Full**
Location: **18 mi. W of Colorado Springs**	Other Meals: **Available**
No. of Rooms: **6**	Credit Cards: **AMEX, DISC, MC, VISA**
No. of Private Baths: **6**	Pets: **No**
Double/pb: **$60–$80**	Children: **Welcome**
Suite: **$80–$120**	Smoking: **No**
Open: **All year**	Social Drinking: **Permitted**

Relax in the homelike atmosphere of this cozy country Inn located in the Colorado Rocky Mountains. Guest rooms are comfortably decorated, and some have spectacular views of Pikes Peak. A hearty breakfast is served in the dining room beside a warm fire or on the patio. Woodland Inn sits peacefully on twelve secluded acres, complete with a llama and a miniature donkey. On-site sports include badminton, volleyball, and ice skating. Or take a ride in a hot-air balloon with your host. Within minutes of the Inn, enjoy hiking, biking, cross-country skiing, trail riding, fishing, boating, golf, and many other tourist attractions in the Pikes Peak region.

CONNECTICUT

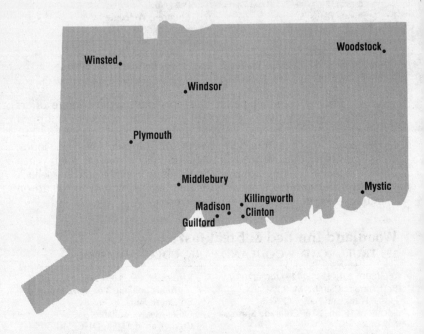

Covered Bridge Bed & Breakfast ✪
69 MAPLE AVENUE, NORFOLK, CONNECTICUT 06058

Tel: **(860) 542-5944**
Best Time to Call: **9 AM–6 PM**
Coordinators: **Hank and Diane Tremblay**
States/Regions Covered:
**Connecticut—Statewide; New
York—Amenia, Cherry Plains, Dover
Plains; Massachusetts—The
Berkshires**

Descriptive Directory: **$3**
Rates (Single/Double):
  Modest: **$85–$95**
  Average: **$95–$120**
  Luxury: **$120–$250**
Credit Cards: **AMEX, MC, VISA**
Minimum Stay: **2 nights holidays,
  weekends**

If you enjoy historic homes, charming farmhouses, Victorian estates,
picture-postcard New England scenery, unsurpassed fall foliage, music
festivals, theater, antiquing, auto racing, skiing, white-water rafting, or
hiking, call Diane.

Nutmeg Bed & Breakfast Agency ✪
P.O. BOX 271117, WEST HARTFORD, CONNECTICUT 06127

Tel: **(800) 727-7592; fax: (860) 232-7680**
Best Time to Call: **9:30 AM–5 PM**
Coordinator: **Michelle Souza**
States/Regions Covered:
  Connecticut—Statewide; Coventry, Hartford, Litchfield, Madison, Mystic, New Haven, Salisbury, Simsbury, Stamford, Woodbury

Rates (Single/Double):
  Modest: **$60–$75**
  Average: **$75–$95**
  Luxury: **$95–$210**
Credit Cards: **AMEX, MC, VISA**
Minimum Stay: **2 nights, holiday weekends**

Nutmeg Bed & Breakfast Agency is an exclusive member of Bed & Breakfast: The National Network, and has been serving travelers since 1981. With more than 105 B&Bs on her roster, Michelle can accommodate those traveling through the state, help to arrange a romantic getaway, house the business traveler, and assist those on a temporary assignment who may need a longer stay. Attractions include Mystic Seaport and Aquarium, two casinos, wonderful theaters and museums in all cities, the beautiful coastline and fine beaches, and magnificent fall foliage.

Captain Dibbell House ✪
21 COMMERCE STREET, CLINTON, CONNECTICUT 06413

Tel: **(860) 669-1646; fax: (860) 669-2300**
Hosts: **Ellis and Helen Adams**
Location: **21 mi. E of New Haven**
No. of Rooms: **4**
No. of Private Baths: **4**

Double/pb: **$75–$95**
Single/pb: **$65–$85**
Open: **Apr.–Dec.**
Reduced Rates: **Weekly; 10% seniors; 3 or more nights**
Breakfast: **Full**

Credit Cards: **AMEX, MC, VISA**
Pets: **No**
Children: **Welcome, over 14**

Smoking: **No**
Social Drinking: **Permitted**
Airport/Station Pickup: **Yes**

Ellis and Helen fell in love with this piece of Connecticut shore years ago when they used to come from their home in New York to spend the weekend sailing. They liked it so much, in fact, that they bought this sea captain's home, located just one-half mile from the shore and marinas and a short drive from the town beach, and converted it into a B&B. Clinton is ideally situated for exploring the Connecticut coast; not far away you'll find Hammonasset State Beach, Mystic Seaport and Aquarium, Gillette Castle, the Goodspeed Opera House, the Essex Steam Train, Long Wharf Theater, Clinton Crossing Premium Outlet Center, and Yale. In order to help you enjoy the Connecticut shore they love so much, the Adamses are happy to lend you their bicycles and beach chairs.

B.&B. at B ✪
279 BOSTON STREET, GUILFORD, CONNECTICUT 06437

Tel/fax: **(203) 453-6490**
Hosts: **Cecilia Marteb and Helen Boyce**
Location: **10 mi. N of New Haven**
No. of Rooms: **2**
No. of Private Baths: **1**
Max. No. Sharing Bath: **3**
Double/pb: **$95**
Single/pb: **$75**
Double/sb: **$85**

Suite: **$140**
Open: **All year**
Breakfast: **Full**
Pets: **Sometimes**
Children: **Welcome, over 12**
Smoking: **Permitted**
Social Drinking: **Permitted**
Airport/Station Pickup: **Yes**
Foreign Languages: **Spanish**

Cecilia and Helen offer guests a quiet atmosphere and complete privacy. Guest rooms have king-size beds and central air. There's a private TV sitting room with free HBO. For your convenience and privacy, a screened deck with a separate entrance is provided. Guilford offers the fantastic Westwood walking trails; biking is another local pasttime. B.&B. at B is 5 miles from Hammonasset State Park and beach and 15 miles north of Yale University. Don't forget to visit the 12 galleries, antique shops, and museums on the Guilford Green.

Acorn Bed & Breakfast ✪
628 ROUTE 148, KILLINGWORTH, CONNECTICUT 06419
acorn@connix.com; www.conix.com~acorn

Tel: **(860) 663-2214**
Hosts: **Carole and Richard Pleines**
Location: **8 mi. S/SE of Middletown**
No. of Rooms: **2**
No. of Private Baths: **2**
Double/pb: **$95–$105**
Open: **All year**

Breakfast: **Full**
Credit Cards: **DC, DISC, MC, VISA**
Pets: **No**
Children: **No**
Smoking: **No**
Social Drinking: **Permitted**
Airport/Station Pickup: **Yes**

Acorn Bed & Breakfast offers a setting that is rural, yet convenient to fine restaurants, antique shops, summer and winter theater, biking, hiking, skiing, fishing, and beaches. Your hosts have an inground pool, two porches where you can sit and enjoy the wonderful array of birds, and a living room with a fireplace. Carole and Richard will do their best to ensure you a peaceful, relaxing, stress-free stay. Breakfast may consist of muffins, fresh fruit, cereal, toast, jams, and eggs donated by the resident chickens. Tea, coffee, and juice are available for early risers. Acorn is 30 to 40 minutes from New Haven and New London, one hour from Foxwoods Casino. The shoreline bustles with art, craft, and antique shows, shops, and art galleries. A cruise on the Connecticut River is a great way to spend the day.

Honeysuckle Hill B&B ✪
116 YANKEE PEDDLER PATH, MADISON, CONNECTICUT 06443

Tel: **(203) 245-4574**
Best Time to Call: **12 noon–7 PM**
Host: **Linda Von Blon**
Location: **20 mi. E of New Haven**
No. of Rooms: **2**
No. of Private Baths: **2**
Double/pb: **$75**
Single/pb: **$65**
Suite: **$100**

Open: **All year**
Reduced Rates: **Available**
Breakfast: **Full**
Pets: **No**
Children: **Welcome, over 6**
Smoking: **No**
Social Drinking: **Permitted**
Minimum Stay: **On holiday weekends**
Airport/Station Pickup: **Yes**

Honeysuckle Hill is a large raised ranch located midway between New Haven and Old Saybrook. This quiet shoreline retreat is close to a variety of activities. The suite has a fireplace, queen-size bed, cable TV, VCR, and a large sitting area. The twin room will accommodate one or two. A short walk takes you to the village boutiques, art or antiques shows on the green, and beaches. If you venture farther you can cruise the Connecticut River, tour the Thimble Islands, take in a musical at Goodspeed, or shop at the Westbrook Factory Stores and Clinton Crossing.

Tucker Hill Inn ✪
96 TUCKER HILL ROAD, MIDDLEBURY, CONNECTICUT 06762

Tel: **(203) 758-8334; fax (203) 598-0652**
Best Time to Call: **9 AM–noon; after 4 PM**
Hosts: **Richard and Susan Cebelenski**
Location: **5 mi. W of Waterbury**
No. of Rooms: **4**
No. of Private Baths: **2**
Max. No. Sharing Bath: **4**
Double/pb: **$85–$120**

Double/sb: **$70–$85**
Open: **All year**
Reduced Rates: **Weekly**
Breakfast: **Full**
Credit Cards: **MC, VISA**
Pets: **No**
Children: **Welcome**
Smoking: **No**
Social Drinking: **Permitted**

Built in 1920, this large Colonial-style home, just down from the village green, exemplifies warm hospitality and charm. The spacious guest rooms are bright and airy, decorated with fine linens and pretty accessories. Breakfast features such caloric creations as pancakes, waffles, and omelettes. Facilities for antiquing, music, theater, golf, tennis, water sports, and cross-country skiing are nearby.

Pequot Hotel Bed and Breakfast
711 COW HILL ROAD, MYSTIC, CONNECTICUT 06355

Tel: **(860) 572-0390**	Reduced Rates: **10% Jan.–Mar.**
Best Time to Call: **8 AM–8 PM**	Breakfast: **Full**
Host: **Nancy Mitchell**	Other Meals: **Available**
Location: **135 mi. NE of New York**	Pets: **No**
No. of Rooms: **3**	Children: **Welcome, over 8**
No. of Private Baths: **3**	Smoking: **No**
Double/pb: **$95–$145**	Social Drinking: **Permitted**
Suites: **$95–$135; sleeps 4**	Airport/Station Pickup: **Yes**
Open: **All year**	

The Pequot Hotel is an authentically restored 1840 stagecoach stop, in the center of the Burnett's Corners Historic District, just 2½ miles from the charming New England seacoast village of Mystic, Connecticut. This large, comfortable Greek Revival–style inn is situated on 23 wooded acres convenient to the Mystic Seaport Museum, the Mystic Marinelife Aquarium, Foxwoods and Mohegan Sun Casinos, and Nautilus Submarine Memorial Museum. At the end of a busy day, guests are free to relax on the large screened porch or in one of the elegant fireplaced parlors. Recommendations and reservations for dinner at one of the area's fine restaurants are provided by the innkeeper. Nancy, a resident of Mystic since 1974, is a retired international flight attendant and dedicated preservationist.

Shelton House Bed & Breakfast ✪
663 MAIN STREET, ROUTE 6, PLYMOUTH, CONNECTICUT 06782
sheltonHBB@aol.com

Tel: **(860) 283-4616**	Double/sb: **$75**
Best Time to Call: **Evening**	Single/sb: **$65**
Hosts: **Pat and Bill Doherty**	Open: **All year**
Location: **10 mi. N of Waterbury**	Breakfast: **Full**
No. of Rooms: **4**	Pets: **No**
No. of Private Baths: **2**	Children: **No**
Max. No. Sharing Bath: **4**	Smoking: **No**
Double/pb: **$85–$95**	Social Drinking: **No**
Single/pb: **$75**	

Enjoy a step back in time in this 1825 Greek Revival, elegantly furnished with antiques and period furniture. The grounds boast perennial gar-

dens and a fountain. After a full day of shopping and sightseeing, enjoy afternoon tea and relax in the spacious parlor, complete with fireplace and TV. Shelton House is convenient to I-84, one mile to Route 8, 20 minutes to historic Litchfield, 30 minutes to Hartford. Nearby are antique centers, vineyards, nature preserves, and skiing. There's a $5 surcharge for one-night stays.

The Charles R. Hart House ✪

1046 WINDSOR AVENUE, WINDSOR, CONNECTICUT 06095
harthous@ntplx.net; www.ntplx.net/~harthous

Tel: **(860) 688-5555**	Open: **All year**
Best Time to Call: **8 AM–6 PM**	Breakfast: **Full**
Hosts: **Dorothy and Bob McAllister**	Pets: **No**
Location: **6 mi. N of Hartford**	Children: **Welcome, over 12**
No. of Rooms: **4**	Smoking: **No**
No. of Private Baths: **4**	Social Drinking: **Permitted**
Double/pb: **$75–$85**	Station Pickup: **Yes**
Single/pb: **$65–$75**	

In 1896 Charles Hart, a prominent Hartford merchant, added Colonial Revival flavor to this Queen Anne-style Victorian home. The house has original Lincrusta wall coverings and ceramic-tiled fireplaces, and is fully restored and furnished with period pieces. This B&B offers a warm atmosphere, with gourmet breakfasts served in an elegant dining room. This inn is centrally located with easy access to the interstate, rail, bus, and airport. A room-by-room tour of the house and trip planning are available by accessing the McAllisters' web site.

B&B by the Lake ✪
19 DILLON BEACH ROAD, WINSTED, CONNECTICUT 06098

Tel: **(860) 738-0230 May 15–Oct. 25;**
   (914) 232-6864 Oct. 25–May 15
Hosts: **Gayle Holt and Anastasio Rossi**
Location: **25 mi. W of Hartford**
No. of Rooms: **4**
Max. No. Sharing Bath: **4**

Double/sb: **$85**
Open: **May 15–Oct. 25**
Breakfast: **Continental, Plus**
Pets: **No**
Smoking: **No**
Social Drinking: **Permitted**

Guests will feel at home in this turn-of-the-century rustic lodge overlooking Litchfield County's West Hill Lake. Guests can take a nap on one of the rockers on the wraparound porch or enjoy the view of the encircling woods and Connecticut's cleanest spring-fed lake. Breakfast can be served on the porch or in the music room and features homemade blueberry and apple muffins, as well as a fresh fruit platter. After breakfast the choices are a woodsy walk, a cool clear lake, a sandy beach, a sunny dock, or a canoe for two. In the evenings there are moon glimmerings, fireside movies on the VCR, or Chopin on an antique grand piano.

Taylor's Corner Bed & Breakfast ✪
880 ROUTE 171, WOODSTOCK, CONNECTICUT 06281-2930
taylors@neca.com; www.neguide.com/taylors

Tel: **(860) 974-0490; fax: (860) 974-**
   0498
Hosts: **Peggy and Doug Tracy**
Location: **50 mi. NE of Hartford**

No. of Rooms: **3**
No. of Private Baths: **3**
Double/pb: **$85–$90**
Single/pb: **$80–$85**

Open: **All year**
Reduced Rates: **10% weekly**
Breakfast: **Full (weekends), Continental (weekdays)**

Pets: **No**
Children: **Welcome, over 12**
Smoking: **No**
Social Drinking: **Permitted**

This 18th-century Colonial is listed on the National Register of Historic Places and features eight working fireplaces. Common areas and spacious air-conditioned guest rooms are furnished with antiques. Originally a farmhouse, Taylor's Corner maintains a rustic setting surrounded by gardens, pastures, and towering trees. After experiencing a hint of Denmark at the breakfast table, guests are invited to meet Jessie Brown, the resident Scotch Highland cow. Nearby you can visit the Bowen House Museum on Woodstock's common, or do some antique shopping in Putnam. Old Sturbridge Village is 20 minutes away. Peggy is a full-time innkeeper and Doug pursues a marketing career.

For key to listings, see inside front or back cover.

✪ This star means that rates are guaranteed through December 31, 1999, to any guest making a reservation as a result of reading about the B&B in *Bed & Breakfast U.S.A.*—1999 edition.

Important! To avoid misunderstandings, always ask about cancellation policies when booking.

Please enclose a self-addressed, stamped, business-size envelope when contacting reservation services.

For more details on what you can expect in a B&B, see Chapter 1.

Always mention *Bed & Breakfast U.S.A.* when making reservations!

We want to hear from you! Use the form on page 593.

DELAWARE

Wilmington

New Castle

Dagsboro

Becky's Country Inn ✪
401 MAIN STREET, DAGSBORO, DELAWARE 19939

Tel: **(302) 732-3953**
Best Time to Call: **Evenings**
Hosts: **Bill and Becky Madden**
Location: **9 mi. W of Bethany Beach**
No. of Rooms: **3**
No. of Private Baths: **3**
Double/pb: **$75–$85**
Single/pb: **$65**

Open: **All year**
Reduced Rates: **10% seniors**
Breakfast: **Continental, plus**
Pets: **No**
Children: **No**
Smoking: **No**
Social Drinking: **Permitted**

The oldest home in Dagsboro, this Colonial house sits on the main street, just nine miles from the beaches—close enough to enjoy all the beach activities and just far enough away to enjoy country quiet. The library is a great place to be if you need to relax by the fireplace with a good book. In the summer, relax by the pool or on the fifty-foot deck. All the bedrooms are done in a warm, country atmosphere. Breakfast is served in the dining room, on the deck, or by the pool. Your hosts can direct you to outlet stores, antiquing spots, and fine restaurants.

William Penn Guest House ✪
206 DELAWARE STREET, NEW CASTLE, DELAWARE 19720

Tel: **(302) 328-7736**	Single/sb: **$50**
Best Time to Call: **Anytime**	Open: **All year**
Hosts: **Mr. and Mrs. Richard Burwell**	Breakfast: **Continental**
Location: **2 mi. from I-95**	Pets: **No**
No. of Rooms: **4**	Children: **Welcome, over 10**
Max. No. Sharing Bath: **4**	Smoking: **No**
Double/pb: **$60–$90**	Social Drinking: **Permitted**
Double/sb: **$60–$90**	Foreign Languages: **Italian**

If you're a history buff, perhaps a stay in a 1682 house named for William Penn is what you've been seeking. Located in the heart of New Castle's historic district, the accommodations here are most comfortable. A lovely park for strolling and for the children to play in borders the Delaware shore, just two blocks away. The University of Delaware is 15 minutes from the house.

The Boulevard Bed & Breakfast ✪
1909 BAYNARD BOULEVARD, WILMINGTON, DELAWARE 19802
blvdbb@wserv.com

Tel: **(302) 656-9700; fax: (302) 656-9701**	Single/sb: **$65**
	Open: **All year**
Hosts: **Charles and Judy Powell**	Reduced Rates: **Corporate**
Location: **½ mi. from I-95, Exit 8**	Breakfast: **Full**
No. of Rooms: **6**	Credit Cards: **AMEX, MC, VISA**
No. of Private Baths: **4**	Pets: **No**
Max. No. Sharing Bath: **3**	Children: **Welcome**
Double/pb: **$80–$85**	Smoking: **No**
Single/pb: **$75–$80**	Social Drinking: **Permitted**
Double/sb: **$70**	

This beautifully restored city mansion was built in 1913 and has earned a place on the National Register of Historic Places. Upon entering, you'll be struck by the impressive foyer and magnificent staircase, leading to a landing complete with a window seat and large leaded-glass windows flanked by 15-foot-tall fluted columns. Breakfast is served in the formal dining room or on the screened-in porch. Although Baynard Boulevard is a quiet and peaceful street, it's just a short walk away from the downtown business district. Parks are close by, and it's just a short drive to Hagley, Winterthur, the Delaware Natural History Museum or the Art Museum; or head for nearby Chadds Ford, Pennsylvania, and the famous Brandywine River Museum.

Darley Manor Inn B&B ✪
3701 PHILADELPHIA PIKE, WILMINGTON, DELAWARE 19703

Tel: **(302) 792-2127; (800) 824-4703**
Best Time to Call: **11 AM–10 PM**
Hosts: **Ray and Judith Hester**
Location: **7 mi. N of Wilmington**
No. of Rooms: **6**
No. of Private Baths: **6**
Double/pb: **$89**
Suites: **$99–$139**
Open: **All year**
Reduced Rates: **Available**

Breakfast: **Full**
Credit Cards: **AMEX, DC, DISC, MC, VISA**
Pets: **No**
Children: **Welcome, over 9**
Smoking: **No**
Social Drinking: **Permitted**
Minimum Stay: **2 nights, weekends Apr., May, Oct., Nov., major holidays**

This 1790s National Register Colonial manor house was home to Victorian America's most famous illustrator, F.O.C. Darley. His work accompanied the writing of Hawthorne, Cooper, Irving, Poe, Longfellow, Charles Dickens, and others. The seventeen rooms, including three parlors, are decorated in 1850s antiques and reproductions. All rooms have air-conditioning, TV/VCR, full or wall-canopied queen-size beds, and phones; two suites have a working fireplace. Breakfast is served in the dining room or on the large porch. The Victorian azalea garden, with small fountains, is great for relaxation. All Brandywine Valley attractions are nearby, including Winterthur, Longwood, Brandywine River Museum, Hagley, and historic Philadelphia. Many good restaurants are within five to ten minutes.

DISTRICT OF COLUMBIA

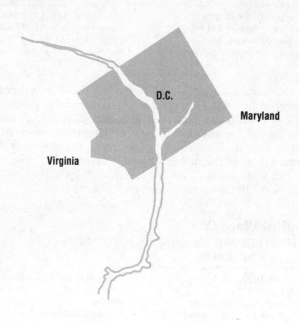

Bed & Breakfast Accommodations, Ltd.
P.O. BOX 12011, WASHINGTON, D.C. 20005
bnbaccom@aol.com

Tel: **(202) 328-3510; fax (202) 332-3885**
Best Time to Call: **10 AM–5 PM Mon.–Fri.**
Coordinator: **Wendy Serpan**
States/Regions Covered: **Washington, D.C.; Virginia and Maryland suburbs**

Rates: (Single/Double):
  Average: **$45–$150 / $55–$150**
Credit Cards: **AMEX, DISC, DC, MC, VISA**

This service has a network of 80 homes, apartments, guesthouses, and inns. Most of the accommodations are convenient to public transportation. Several of the homes are historic properties. There is a wide range of accommodations, from budget to luxury.

Bed & Breakfast League/Sweet Dreams and Toast ✪
P.O. BOX 9490, WASHINGTON, D.C. 20016
bedandbreakfast-washingtondc@erols.com

Tel: **(202) 363-7767; fax: (202) 363-8396**
Best Time to Call: **9 AM–5 PM Mon.–Thurs., 9 AM–1 PM Fri.**
Coordinator: **Millie Groobey**
States/Regions Covered: **Washington, D.C.**

Rates (Single/Double):
  Modest: **$48–$58 / $58–$68**
  Average: **$58–$73 / $68–$90**
  Luxury: **$78–$120 / $88–$150**
Credit Cards: **AMEX, DC, MC, VISA**
Minimum Stay: **2 nights**

Bed & Breakfast League/Sweet Dreams and Toast reservation services were merged in 1988. They offer accommodations in privately owned homes and apartments. Many are in historic districts; all are in good, safe sections of the city within easy walking distance of an excellent public transportation system. Gracious hosts will cheerfully direct you to points of interest, monuments, museums, shops, and restaurants. The office of this service is closed on federal holidays, Thanksgiving, and Christmas. A $10 fee is charged for each reservation.

A Capitol Place ✪
134 12TH STREET SE, WASHINGTON, D.C. 20003
acapitolplace@erols.com

Tel: **(202) 543-1020;**
  fax: **(202) 543-1734**
Hosts: **Jim and Mary Pellettieri**
Location: **½ mi. E of U.S. Capitol Building**
Suite: **$95–$145; sleeps 1–4**
Open: **All year**

Reduced Rates: **10% after 7th night**
Breakfast: **Full**
Pets: **No**
Children: **Welcome**
Smoking: **No**
Social Drinking: **Permitted**
Minimum Stay: **2 nights**

Stay in this newly renovated, private five-room "English Basement" apartment—the entire lower level of a 100-year-old Victorian Rowhouse in the historic Capitol Hill district. The light, sunny guest apartment gives you your own entrance to the bay-fronted living/dining room, with cable, color TV, and telephone. The sitting room has a library bed and writing desk; the separate master bedroom has a queen-size bed. The suite includes a modern bath and fully equipped kitchen stocked with breakfast makings, as well as sodas and snacks. Homemade brownies greet you on your arrival. Your hosts enjoy sharing time and ideas with you, and encourage visits to the main house whenever you wish. It's only a 10-minute walk to historic Eastern Market, the Metro, cafes and shops, and a 15-minute walk to the U.S. Capitol, the Library of Congress, and the Supreme Court.

Hereford House Bed & Breakfast ✪
604 SOUTH CAROLINA AVENUE SE, WASHINGTON, D.C. 20003

Tel: **(202) 543-0102**
Host: **Ann Edwards**
Location: **8 blocks from U.S. Capitol Building**
No. of Rooms: **4**
Max. No. Sharing Bath: **4**
Double/sb: **$65–$73**
Single/sb: **$50–$63**

Open: **All year**
Reduced Rates: **10% seniors 65 + ; $5 less after 7 nights**
Breakfast: **Full, Continental**
Children: **Welcome, over 12**
Smoking: **No**
Social Drinking: **Permitted**

Hereford House is a 1915 brick townhouse situated on a pretty tree-lined street on historic Capitol Hill, one block from the Eastern Market Metro Station. The U.S. Capitol, the Mall (home of the Smithsonian Institution), Supreme Court, and Congressional Library are a 10-minute walk from the house. Restaurants, cafes, banks, antique stores, and the historic Eastern Market are all within walking distance, making Hereford House the perfect location for visitors to the nation's capital. Bountiful cooked English breakfasts are served by your full-time British hostess. Guests share the company of newly made friends (and resident dog) in the living room. Two additional guest rooms are available at a second location five minutes away. Ask Ann for details.

FLORIDA

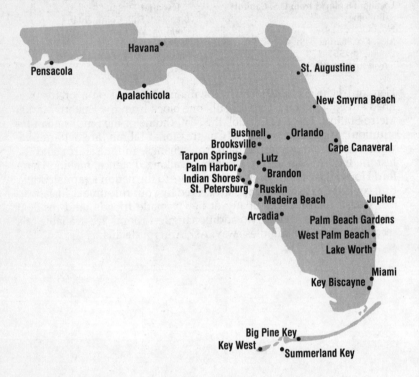

Havana •
Pensacola •
Apalachicola •
St. Augustine •
New Smyrna Beach •
Bushnell • • Orlando
Brooksville •
Tarpon Springs • • Lutz
Palm Harbor • • Brandon
Indian Shores •
St. Petersburg • • Ruskin
• Madeira Beach
Arcadia •
Cape Canaveral •
Jupiter •
Palm Beach Gardens •
West Palm Beach •
Lake Worth •
Miami •
Key Biscayne •
Big Pine Key •
Key West • • Summerland Key

Coombs House Inn ✪
80 SIXTH STREET, APALACHICOLA, FLORIDA 32320

Tel: **(850) 653-9199**
Best Time to Call: **Anytime**
Hosts: **Marilyn and Charles Schubert**
Location: **75 mi. SW of Tallahassee**
No. of Rooms: **15**
No. of Private Baths: **15**
Double/pb: **$89–$129**
Single/pb: **$69–$89**

Suites: **$109–$129**
Open: **All year**
Breakfast: **Continental**
Credit Cards: **AMEX, MC, VISA**
Pets: **Sometimes**
Children: **Welcome**
Smoking: **No**
Social Drinking: **Permitted**

Elegantly restored, this 1905 Victorian mansion welcomes those special guests who appreciate the charm and historical authenticity of another era and an intimate homey atmosphere. The three-story mansion features high ceilings and nine fireplaces. Inside you'll admire antique fur-

niture of the period, paintings, historical photographs, imported English chintz draperies that frame the large bay windows, and oriental carpets. Each guest room has a private bath and cable TV. Located only minutes from fishing, boating, the Apalachicola River, and the white beaches of St. George Island.

Historic Parker House ✪
427 WEST HICKORY STREET, ARCADIA, FLORIDA 34266

Tel: **(941) 494-2499; (800) 969-2499**	Single/sb: **$60**
Best Time to Call: **8 AM–10 PM**	Open: **All year**
Hosts: **Bob and Shelly Baumann**	Reduced Rates: **10%**
Location: **45 mi. E of Sarasota**	Breakfast: **Continental**
No. of Rooms: **4**	Credit Cards: **AMEX, MC, VISA**
No. of Private Baths: **2**	Pets: **No**
Max. No. Sharing Bath: **4**	Children: **Welcome, over 10**
Double/pb: **$75**	Smoking: **No**
Single/pb: **$75**	Social Drinking: **Permitted**
Double/sb: **$60**	

Once you step inside the Historic Parker House you become acquainted with a much grander, yet simpler life. The 6000-square-foot home is chock full of antiques, old clocks, and Florida's past. The original section of the home dates to the mid-1890s; a large addition was put in in 1914 by the original owners, the Parkers, Florida cattle barons. Located in historic downtown Arcadia, recently named one of the one hundred best small towns in America, the home is close to antique and gift shopping and the Peace River for canoeing. Nearby are all of South Central Florida's attractions.

The Barnacle ✪
1557 LONG BEACH DRIVE, BIG PINE KEY, FLORIDA 33043

Tel: **(305) 872-3298; (800) 465-9100;**
  fax: **(305) 872-3863**
Best Time to Call: **10 AM–8 PM**
Hosts: **Jane and Tim Marquis**
Location: **Mile marker 33**
No. of Rooms: **4**
No. of Private Baths: **4**

Double/pb: **$105–$140**
Open: **All year**
Breakfast: **Full**
Pets: **No**
Children: **Welcome, over 16**
Smoking: **No**

Tim and Jane welcome you to their Caribbean-style home, where tranquility and leisurely breezes prevail. Enjoy the private beach, where you can scuba dive, snorkel, and swim. Then take a nature walk, soak in the hot tub, ride a bicycle or paddle boat, or nap in the hammock between the palms. Here, your time is your own. The ultimate in privacy is the self-contained cottage, a tropical treehouse with stained glass windows and a private terrace. The rooms overlook the ocean or open to the atrium, with a hot tub, waterfall, and lush plants. The Ocean room has a private entrance and opens to the patio on the beach. Special attention is given to the detail of the villa, decorated with artistic flair. The Barnacle puts emphasis on the sun and sea with warm hospitality.

Bed & Breakfast-on-the-Ocean "Casa Grande" ✪
P.O. BOX 378, BIG PINE KEY, FLORIDA 33043

Tel: **(305) 872-2878**
Host: **Kathleen Threlkeld**

Location: **30 mi. E of Key West**
No. of Rooms: **3**

No. of Private Baths: **3**
Double/pb: **$85–$110**
Open: **All year**
Breakfast: **Full**

Pets: **No**
Children: **No**
Smoking: **Permitted**
Social Drinking: **Permitted**

This spectacular Spanish-style home, facing the ocean, was custom-designed to suit the natural beauty of the Keys. The large landscaped garden patio, with panoramic beach views, is where you'll enjoy Kathleen's bountiful breakfast. It is also the site of the hot tub/Jacuzzi for relaxing by day or under a moonlit sky. The large and airy guest rooms are comfortably cooled by Bahama fans or air-conditioning. Key deer and birds abound. From the private beach, you'll enjoy swimming, fishing, snorkeling, bicycling, and jogging. There's a picnic table, gas grill, hammock, and Windsurfer for guests to use, compliments of the gracious host.

Paradise Lodging ✪

31316 AVENUE J, BIG PINE KEY, FLORIDA 33043-4657

Tel: **(305) 872-9009**
Host: **Joan Thoman**
Location: **30 mi. E of Key West**
Guest Cottage: **$85, for two**
Open: **All year**

Breakfast: **Continental**
Pets: **Sometimes**
Children: **Welcome**
Smoking: **Permitted**
Social Drinking: **Permitted**

Paradise Lodging is located on a tropical canal in a residential setting 6 miles from Bahia Honda State Park (one of the best beaches in the country) and the famed Looe Key Reef. This spacious two-bedroom unit sleeps six and has a large kitchen and living room, telephone, two cable TVs, and air conditioning. Joan offers free boat docking twenty feet from your door, a barbecue grill for cooking your dinner, and bicycles for your exercise. Other things to do include fishing, scuba diving, snorkeling, and sharing in the night life in Key West.

Behind the Fence ✪

1400 VIOLA DRIVE AT COUNTRYSIDE, BRANDON, FLORIDA 33511

Tel: **(813) 685-8201**
Best Time to Call: **2–8 PM**
Hosts: **Larry and Carolyn Yoss**
Location: **15 mi. E of Tampa**
No. of Rooms: **5**
No. of Private Baths: **3**
Max. No. Sharing Bath: **4**
Double/pb: **$69–$72**
Double/sb: **$59–$69**
Single/sb: **$49–$59**

Suites: **$72–$79**
Open: **All year**
Reduced Rates: **10% seniors;
   June–Aug.; weekly**
Breakfast: **Continental, plus**
Pets: **Sometimes**
Children: **Welcome**
Smoking: **No**
Social Drinking: **Permitted**
Airport/Station Pickup: **Yes**

As the name suggests, this inn is nestled in the trees behind a fence on a quiet secluded lot. The ambiance of another era is reflected in the authentic country furnishings from the 1800s—you will feel as if you have entered another world. The house was built in 1976 in early saltbox style. The interior was finished in county salvage material from before the turn of the century. Art League tours of the house for groups interested in early lifestyles or antiques began in 1978 and are still available today. Nearby are restaurants, canoeing, fishing, horseback riding, golf, and Florida's largest mall. Within driving distance is downtown Tampa, the Florida Aquarium, Florida State Fairgrounds, Busch Gardens, Adventure Island, Museum of Science and Industry, University of South Florida, west coast beaches, and Disney World.

Verona House ✪

201 SOUTH MAIN STREET, BROOKSVILLE, FLORIDA 34601
www.bbhost.com/veronabb

Tel: **(352) 796-4001**	Open: **All year**
Hosts: **Bob and Jan Boyd**	Reduced Rates: **Available**
Location: **50 mi. N of Tampa**	Breakfast: **Full, Continental**
No. of Rooms: **4**	Credit Cards: **AMEX, DISC, MC, VISA**
No. of Private Baths: **4**	Pets: **No**
Double/pb: **$65**	Smoking: **No**
Single/pb: **$55**	Social Drinking: **Permitted**
Suites: **$80–$100**	Airport/Station Pickup: **Yes**

The Verona House is a unique 1925 Sears & Roebuck catalog house. The B&B is located among the rolling hills and oak tree–lined streets of this historical town, established in 1856. Guest rooms have queen-size beds and are furnished with antiques and collectible pieces. You'll enjoy true Southern hospitality at breakfast, which may include Jan's baked casseroles, muffins, nut bread, or quiche.

Cypress House Bed and Breakfast ✪

5175 SOUTHWEST 90 BOULEVARD, C.R. 476B, BUSHNELL, FLORIDA 33513

Tel: **(352) 568-0909; (888) 568-1666**	Suite: **$85**
Best Time to Call: **8 AM–10 PM**	Open: **All year**
Hosts: **Jan Fessler and Thelma Schaum**	Reduced Rates: **Available**
Location: **50 mi. N of Tampa**	Breakfast: **Continental, buffet**
No. of Rooms: **6**	Pets: **Horses ($10 per night)**
No. of Private Baths: **3**	Children: **Welcome, over 5**
Max. No. Sharing Bath: **4**	Smoking: **Restricted**
Double/pb: **$70**	Social Drinking: **Permitted**
Double/sb: **$50**	

A new log home built in the gracious old Florida style, Cypress House is set on wooded farmland. From the oak rockers on the wide wraparound veranda, you can see oak trees draped with moss. The Webster Flea Market (Mondays only) and Brooksville's Christmas House are nearby, and Disney World and Busch Gardens are an hour away. You won't have to travel far to browse for antiques, fish, hike, or go canoeing. To bolster your energy, your hosts offer a generous breakfast buffet and evening dessert. Your hosts have seven horses and offer one- to six-hour trail rides. There's a pool 15 × 40 feet, long enough for lap swimming.

Beachside Bed & Breakfast ✪

629 ADAMS AVENUE, CAPE CANAVERAL, FLORIDA 32920

Tel: **(407) 799-4320**	Open: **All year**
Best Time to Call: **8 AM–Noon;**	Breakfast: **Continental**
5 PM–10 PM	Pets: **No**
Hosts: **Tony and Dorothy Dean Saccaro**	Children: **Welcome**
Location: **47 mi. E of Orlando**	Smoking: **No**
Suite: **$65**	Social Drinking: **Permitted**

At Beachside Bed & Breakfast you can watch a space launch from the beach. The ocean is only a few yards from the guest suite, with private entrance, twin beds, living room, and kitchen stocked for breakfast to enjoy at your leisure. Cape Canaveral and Kennedy Space Center are minutes away. Walt Disney World and Orlando are just an hour's drive. Orlando International Airport is 45 minutes away, a shuttle service is available.

Historic Havana House Bed & Breakfast ○

301 EAST SIXTH AVENUE, HAVANA, FLORIDA 32333

Tel: **(850) 539-5611**
Hosts: **Shirley and Bruce Gaver**
Location: **12 mi. N of Tallahassee**
No. of Rooms: **2**
No. of Private Baths: **2**
Double/pb: **$75**

Open: **All year**
Breakfast: **Full**
Pets: **No**
Children: **Welcome, over 8**
Smoking: **No**
Social Drinking: **Permitted**

This B&B, situated on a quiet residential street two blocks from the center of town, is a likely stop for collectors—at last count, Havana had thirty antique shops plus many related businesses. Tallahassee, the state capital and home of Florida State University, is only fifteen minutes away by car. A restored 1907 frame house, Historic Havana House has a large screened porch, and guests are welcome to watch cable TV in the common area. For breakfast, your hosts will design a menu to suit your preferences.

Meeks B&B on the Gulf Beaches ○

19418 GULF BOULEVARD, #408, INDIAN SHORES, FLORIDA 33785
okgreta@aol.com; www.beachdirectory.com/meeks

Tel: **(813) 596-5424; fax: (813) 593-0065**
Best Time to Call: **7 AM–10 PM**
Hosts: **Greta and Bob Meeks**
Location: **35 min. from Tampa Airport**
No. of Rooms: **7**
No. of Private Baths: **5**
Double/pb: **$60–$75**

Single/pb: **$50–$60**
Suites: **$75–$125**
Open: **All year**
Breakfast: **Continental, full**
Pets: **No**
Children: **Welcome**
Smoking: **No**
Social Drinking: **Permitted**

Beach! Pool! Sunsets! Enjoy your stay in this beach condo overlooking the Gulf of Mexico. A beach cottage is sometimes available. Choose your breakfast, then bask in the sun, swim in the gulf, and catch spectacular sunsets from your balcony. Dine at nearby seafood restaurants and visit the local seabird sanctuary, sunken gardens, and the Dali Museum. Other nearby attractions are Busch Gardens in Tampa and sponge diving in Tarpon Springs. This B&B is located between Clearwater and St. Petersburg Beach, only two hours from Walt Disney World. Your hostess is a real estate broker.

Innisfail ○

17576 BRIDLE COURT, JUPITER, FLORIDA 33478
Kathie@vannoorden.com; www.vannoorden.com

Tel: **(561) 744-5902; fax: (561) 744-3387**
Hosts: **Katherine and Luke VanNoorden**

Location: **20 mi. N of Palm Beach**
No. of Rooms: **2**
No. of Private Baths: **2**

Double/pb: **$75–$85**
Open: **All year**
Reduced Rates: **10% weekly**
Breakfast: **Continental**
Other Meals: **Available**

Pets: **Welcome**
Children: **Welcome, over 7**
Smoking: **No**
Social Drinking: **Permitted**

Innisfail is located in the farm area of Jupiter. This gracious new home is framed with royal palms and palmettos. Start your day with a dip in the heated pool. As the sun peeps through towering pines, enjoy a leisurely, expanded Continental breakfast on the lanai. Browse through the VanNoorden home gallery or stroll out to the studio to observe the sculpture studio in action. While you don't have to be an art lover, it does help to be an animal lover, as Innisfail has three royal standard poodles and three cats. At day's end, take in the vivid sunsets while relaxing at the pool. Your host will direct you to the local sights and good eating places in the area.

Hibiscus House ✪
345 WEST ENID DRIVE, KEY BISCAYNE, FLORIDA 33149

Tel: **(305) 361-2456**
Best Time to Call: **9 AM–5 PM**
Hosts: **Bernice and Earl Duffy**
Location: **10 mi. SE of Miami**
No. of Rooms: **2**
No. of Private Baths: **2**
Double/pb: **$65**
Single/pb: **$60**

Open: **All year**
Reduced Rates: **May 1–Dec. 15**
Breakfast: **Full**
Pets: **No**
Children: **No**
Smoking: **No**
Social Drinking: **Permitted**
Minimum Stay: **2 nights**

Welcome to an island paradise only 15 minutes from downtown Miami and 20 minutes from Miami International Airport. Key Biscayne features two lushly landscaped parks, a championship golf course, and miles of white sandy beaches; your hosts offer private beach privileges. Tennis courts and bicycle paths are in plentiful supply. Add to this the famous Miami Seaquarium and easy access to Greater Miami's many attractions and you have all of the ingredients for a very pleasant visit.

Center Court Historic Inn & Cottages ✪
916 CENTER STREET, KEY WEST, FLORIDA 33040

Tel: **(305) 296-9292; (800) 797-8787**
Best Time to Call: **9 AM–6 PM**
Host: **Naomi Van Steelandt**
Location: **120 mi. S of Miami**
No. of Rooms: **14**
No. of Private Baths: **14**
Double/pb: **$128–$148**
Guest Cottage: **$168–$298, sleeps 2–6**
Suites: **$178**
Open: **All year**

Reduced Rates: **May 1–Dec. 15**
Breakfast: **Continental, plus**
Credit Cards: **AMEX, DISC, MC, VISA**
Pets: **Welcome in cottages**
Children: **Welcome in cottages**
Smoking: **Restricted**
Social Drinking: **Permitted**
Minimum Stay: **3 nights weekends, cottages**

Center Court is located one half-block off Duval street and U.S. 1, within walking distance to every major attraction. All rooms and cottages have been recently renovated with loving care and have lightweight comforters, feather pillows, hair dryers, TV, telephones, fans and air-conditioning. Amenities include private sundecks, an eight-person Jacuzzi, heated pool, exercise room, and lush tropical gardens. In the morning, enjoy breakfast at your leisure.

Mango Inn Bed and Breakfast ✪
128 NORTH LAKESIDE DRIVE, LAKE WORTH, FLORIDA 33460

Tel: **(561) 533-6900; (888) MANGO-19**
Hosts: **Erin and Bo Allen**
Location: **5 mi. S of West Palm Beach**
No. of Rooms: **8**
No. of Private Baths: **8**
Double/pb: **$75–$120**
Open: **All year**
Reduced Rates: **10% seniors; weekly**
Breakfast: **Full (weekends), Continental (weekdays)**

Credit Cards: **AMEX, DC, DISC, MC, VISA**
Pets: **No**
Children: **No**
Smoking: **No**
Social Drinking: **Permitted**
Minimum Stay: **2 nights, weekends**

Built in 1915, this stucco home is nestled among the majestic Queen Palms shading the foot of the bridge that leads to the white sandy beaches of the Atlantic Ocean. The Inn is furnished with a mixture of antiques and updated pieces. Each guest room boasts down pillows, monogrammed designer bed linens, and central air. Breakfast can be served poolside or by the coral stone fireplace. The menu may consist of fresh-baked breads—such as mango-cashew muffins or orange scones with homemade blackberry butter—fresh-squeezed juices, and tropical fruit. Guests can enjoy the beach, water sports, golfing, parks, and shopping downtown in the Arts & Antiques District. Lunch or dine at eclectic restaurants and upscale coffeehouses, or take a day excursion to South Beach, Palm Beach, the Bahamas, and more.

The Country Place ✪
20617 COUNTY LINE DRIVE, LUTZ, FLORIDA 33549

Tel: **(813) 948-1016**
Best Time to Call: **9 AM–5 PM**
Hosts: **The DeHaans**
Location: **15 mi. N of Tampa**
No. of Rooms: **4**
No. of Private Baths: **4**
Double/pb: **$45**
Suites: **$65**

Open: **All year**
Reduced Rates: **Available**
Breakfast: **Full**
Pets: **No**
Children: **Welcome, over 12**
Smoking: **No**
Social Drinking: **Permitted**

Located on a palm tree grove, The Country Place is a farm-style house. Amenities include a fishing lake, pool, and game room. Nearby attractions range from Busch Gardens, the beaches, and Tarpon Springs to Tampa, which has many festivals and places of interest. Breakfast may feature fresh fruit, quiche, French toast, omelettes, and homemade coffee cake. Group rates are available.

Lighthouse Bed & Breakfast ❂
13355 2ND STREET, MADEIRA BEACH, FLORIDA 33708

Tel: **(813) 391-0015; (800) 241-0334**
Hosts: **Joyce and John Dickinson**
Location: **4 mi. W of St. Petersburg**
No. of Rooms: **5**
No. of Private Baths: **5**
Double/pb: **$45–$110**
Open: **All year**
Breakfast: **Full (winter), Continental (summer)**

Credit Cards: **MC, VISA**
Pets: **Sometimes**
Children: **Welcome, over 5**
Smoking: **Permitted**
Social Drinking: **Permitted**
Airport Pickup: **Yes**

Lighthouse Bed & Breakfast is located only 50 steps from the Intracoastal Waterway and 300 steps from white sand on the Gulf of Mexico's beaches. Guests enjoy the comfort of the Key West–style surroundings with a palm-filled courtyard, a gazebo for dining or relaxing, and a sundeck atop the lighthouse—for lying in the sun or watching the sunrise or sunset. If you want to cook your own supper, there's a barbecue grill. It's an easy walk to the famous John's Pass Boardwalk and village where shopping, restaurants, jet skiing, parasailing, chartered fishing boats, and casino cruises are available. St. Petersburg Pier, Dali Museum, and the Florida International Museum are within ten minutes. Busch Gardens in Tampa is approximately thirty minutes away. In 1995 St. Petersburg was awarded a major league baseball team. The Lighthouse is a quiet retreat from the city's traffic and commercial buildings, yet close enough to join in the rush if you want to. Breakfast specialties include pancakes, waffles, and omelettes. For those flying in, airport door-to-door service is available.

Redland's Bed and Breakfast ❂
19521 SOUTHWEST 128 COURT, MIAMI, FLORIDA 33177

Tel: **(305) 238-5285**
Hosts: **Tim and Marianne Hamilton**
Location: **18 mi. S of Miami**
No. of Rooms: **1**
No. of Private Baths: **1**
Guest Cottage: **$50**
Open: **All year**

Reduced Rates: **10% seniors**
Breakfast: **Continental**
Pets: **Sometimes**
Children: **Welcome**
Smoking: **No**
Social Drinking: **Permitted**

This romantic tropical guest house has a private entrance, kitchen, living room, TV, air-conditioning, pool, and Jacuzzi. Enjoy breakfast at your leisure by the pool or at the gazebo. Bicycles are available for the nearby bike trails. Centrally located near Miami's farming community, Redland's is twenty-five minutes from the Miami airport, Florida Keys, and Everglades National Park.

Night Swan Intracoastal Bed & Breakfast ✪
512 SOUTH RIVERSIDE DRIVE, NEW SMYRNA BEACH, FLORIDA 32168
www.nightswan.com

Tel: **(904) 423-4940; (800) 465-4261**	Open: **All year**
Best Time to Call: **9 AM–9 PM**	Reduced Rates: **Available**
Hosts: **Martha and Charles** **Nighswonger**	Breakfast: **Continental, full**
	Credit Cards: **AMEX, DISC, MC, VISA**
Location: **15 mi. S of Daytona Beach**	Pets: **No**
No. of Rooms: **15**	Children: **Welcome**
No. of Private Baths: **15**	Smoking: **No**
Double/pb: **$80–$95**	Social Drinking: **Permitted**
Suites: **$115–$150; sleeps 4**	Airport/Station Pickup: **Yes**

Come sit on Night Swan's wraparound porch or by its windows and watch pelicans, dolphins, sailboats, and yachts ply the Atlantic Intracoastal Waterway. Then enjoy the waterfront yourself: surf, swim, fish, drive, or bicycle along the bathing beach two miles to the east. This spacious three-story home in New Smyrna's historic district has a central fireplace and intricate, natural woodwork in every room, and some rooms overlook the Indian River. Breakfast is served in the dining room; low-cholesterol dishes are a house specialty.

PerriHouse Bed & Breakfast Inn
10417 CENTURION COURT, ORLANDO, FLORIDA 32836
Perrihse@iag.net; www.perrihouse.com

Tel: **(407) 876-4830; (800) 780-4830;** fax: **(407) 876-0241**	Open: **All year**
	Reduced Rates: **Seniors; weekly**
Best Time to Call: **9 AM–9 PM**	Breakfast: **Continental**
Hosts: **Nick and Angi Perretti**	Credit Cards: **AMEX, DC, DISC, MC,** **VISA**
Location: **3 mi. N of I-4 Exit 27, Lake** **Buena Vista, on SR 535N**	Pets: **No**
No. of Rooms: **8**	Children: **Welcome (crib)**
No. of Private Baths: **8**	Smoking: **No**
Double/pb: **$89–$129**	Social Drinking: **Permitted**
Single/pb: **$79–$129**	Airport/Station Pickup: **Yes**

PerriHouse is a quiet, private country estate Inn secluded on 3 acres of land adjacent to the Walt Disney World Resort complex. Because of its outstanding location, downtown Disney and Pleasure Island are only 3 minutes away; EPCOT center is only 5 minutes. It's the perfect vacation setting for families who desire a unique travel experience with a comfortable, convenient home away from home. An upscale Continental

breakfast awaits you each morning, and a refreshing pool and spa relaxes you after a full day of activities. Each guest room features its own private bath, entrance, TV, telephone, ceiling fan, and central air/heat. The PerriHouse grounds are being developed and landscaped to create a future bird sanctuary and wildlife preserve. Come bird-watch on the peaceful, tranquil grounds of the PerriHouse estate and wake up to bird songs outside your window. Your hosts, Nick and Angi, instinctively offer their guests a unique blend of cordial hospitality, comfort, and friendship!

Heron Cay ✪

15106 PALMWOOD ROAD, PALM BEACH GARDENS, FLORIDA 33410
heroncay@magg.net

Tel: **(561) 744-6315; fax (561) 744-0943**	Double/pb: **$105–$180**
Best Time to Call: **After 10 AM**	Suites: **$155–$165**
Hosts: **Randy and Margie Salyer**	Open: **All year**
Location: **15 mi. N of Palm Beach International Airport**	Reduced Rates: **Available**
	Breakfast: **Full**
No. of Rooms: **9**	Pets: **Borzoi dogs only**
No. of Private Baths: **7**	Children: **By arrangement**
Max. No. Sharing Bath: **4**	Smoking: **Restricted**
	Social Drinking: **Permitted**

At Heron Cay you'll think you're in Key West. This island-style home is quietly nestled on two tropical acres overlooking the Intracoastal Waterway. Randy and Margie's private half-acre island is fun to explore—it protects their harbor, which accommodates boats to 55 feet, plus a boat ramp for smaller water toys. All guest rooms open to a balcony leading to the sundeck and several patio areas for relaxation beside the 10-foot-deep pool or heated spa. Guests are provided with refrigerators in rooms and may use the recreation room and barbecue area poolside. Fine restaurants, major shopping, and miles of natural ocean beaches are just minutes away. Margie and Randy are avid boaters who regularly invite longer-staying guests aboard their 48-foot sportsfisherman, *Waterfront Lady*, for Palm Beach area cruises.

Bed & Breakfast of Tampa Bay ✪
126 OLD OAK CIRCLE, OAK TRAIL, PALM HARBOR, FLORIDA 34683

Tel: **(813) 785-2342**
Best Time to Call: **7–9 AM; 6–10 PM**
Hosts: **Vivian and David Grimm**
Location: **18 mi. W of Tampa**
No. of Rooms: **4**
No. of Private Baths: **2**
Max. No. Sharing Bath: **4**
Double/pb: **$60**
Single/pb: **$40**

Double/sb: **$45**
Single/sb: **$30**
Suite: **$75**
Open: **All year**
Breakfast: **Full**
Pets: **Sometimes**
Children: **Welcome**
Smoking: **No**
Social Drinking: **Permitted**

A premier facility in a premier location: this new Art Deco residence is 1¹⁄₂ miles from the Gulf of Mexico and 25 minutes from Busch Gardens, Dali Museum, and Weeki-Wachee Springs. Shopping, restaurants, churches, and public transportation are within easy walking distance. The Grimms' home has an ivory stucco exterior, with front pillars, a tile roof, and stained glass doors. Inside, artifacts from their world travels are shown to advantage under 12-foot ceilings. Amenities include a pool and Jacuzzi, a grand piano, and bicycles for local excursions.

Gulf Beach Inn ✪
10655 GULF BEACH HIGHWAY, PENSACOLA, FLORIDA 32507

Tel: **(850) 492-4501**
Hosts: **Fred and Lisa Krause**
Location: **Near Perdido Key**
No. of Rooms: **2**

Guest Cottage: **$75**
Open: **All year**
Reduced Rates: **After 3rd night**
Breakfast: **Full**

Pets: **Sometimes**
Children: **Welcome**
Smoking: **No**

Social Drinking: **Permitted**
Airport/Station Pickup: **Yes**
Foreign Languages: **German**

The Gulf Beach Inn is a traditional B&B located on Big Lagoon. The Krauses offer a family-friendly atmosphere, private beach, and dock great for swimming. Nearby, visit the National Naval Aviation Museum, state and national parks, excellent restaurants, and an outlet mall.

Ruskin House Bed and Breakfast ◐
120 DICKMAN DRIVE SOUTHWEST, RUSKIN, FLORIDA 33570

Tel: **(813) 645-3842**
Hosts: **Melanie Hubbard and Mac Miller**
Location: **20 mi. S of Tampa**
No. of Rooms: **3**
No. of Private Baths: **3**
Double/pb: **$75**
Suite: **$110**
Open: **All year**

Breakfast: **Continental**
Credit Cards: **AMEX, MC, VISA**
Pets: **No**
Children: **Welcome**
Smoking: **No**
Social Drinking: **Permitted**
Foreign Languages: **French**

Located in rural Hillsborough County, within easy driving distance of Tampa, St. Petersburg, and Sarasota, this landmarked Victorian house features columned verandas and a tower. The interior boasts a massive dogleg staircase, fireplace, hardwood floors, high ceilings, and original wall coloring. Rooms are furnished with period antiques and Oriental rugs. Rocking chairs and hammocks grace the upper veranda. The house looks over the Ruskin Inlet, which winds around three acres of lawn, tropical glades, and flower gardens. Your hosts teach literature and have interests in local history, archeology, and ecology.

Kenwood Inn
38 MARINE STREET, ST. AUGUSTINE, FLORIDA 32084

Tel: **(904) 824-2116**
Best Time to Call: **10 AM–10 PM**
Hosts: **Mark, Kerrianne, and Caitlin Constant**
Location: **40 mi. S of Jacksonville**
No. of Rooms: **14**
No. of Private Baths: **14**
Double/pb: **$85–$175**
Suite: **$115–$150**

Open: **All year**
Reduced Rates: **Midweek**
Breakfast: **Continental**
Credit Cards: **DISC, MC, VISA**
Pets: **No**
Children: **Welcome, over 8**
Smoking: **No**
Social Drinking: **Permitted**

If you are to discover a Victorian building in Florida, how appropriate that it should be in the historic section of St. Augustine, one of the oldest cities in the U.S. This New England–style inn is a rarity in the South; this one has old-fashioned beds with color-coordinated touches right down to the sheets and linens. Breakfast may be taken in your room, in the courtyard surrounded by trees, or by the swimming pool. Tour trains, waterfront shops, restaurants, and museums are within walking distance. Flagler College is three blocks away.

Bayboro House on Old Tampa Bay ✪
1719 BEACH DRIVE SOUTHEAST, ST. PETERSBURG, FLORIDA 33701
bayborohouse@juno.com

Tel: **(813) 823-4955**	Breakfast: **Continental**
Hosts: **Gordon and Antonia Powers**	Credit Cards: **MC, VISA**
Location: **1/2 mi. from I-275, Exit 9**	Pets: **No**
No. of Rooms: **4**	Children: **No**
No. of Private Baths: **4**	Smoking: **No**
Double/pb: **$85–$145**	Social Drinking: **Permitted**
Open: **All year**	

Richly appointed in antiques and collectibles, the historic Bayboro House is what you would expect in a luxury waterfront bed and breakfast. All rooms have a water view, air-conditioning, TV and VCR, a morning paper is delivered to your door, and there's a pool and spa for guest enjoyment. Breakfast includes fresh fruits, juice, rolls, muffins, homemade breads, cereal, coffee and tea served in the formal dining room.

Florida Keys House ✪
P.O. BOX 41, SUMMERLAND KEY, FLORIDA 33042

Tel: **(305) 872-4680**	Pets: **No**
Best Time to Call: **8 AM–8 PM**	Children: **Welcome, over 10**
Hosts: **Capt. Dave and Camille Wiley**	Smoking: **Restricted**
Location: **27 mi. E of Key West**	Social Drinking: **Permitted**
Suites: **$89–$150**	Minimum Stay: **2 nights**
Open: **All year**	Foreign Languages: **French, Spanish**
Breakfast: **Continental**	

Key West and the Lower Keys offer some of the finest tarpon and flats fishing in the world. Captain Dave specializes in light tackle "sight casting" (fly or spin) along the shallow back country flats for tarpon and bonefish. While fishing with the Wileys, guests enjoy dockside accommodations consisting of two bedrooms, bath, living room, central air, and kitchen stocked with breakfast selections to prepare at your leisure. After a busy day, relax in the hammock beneath the coconut tree.

Knightswood ✪
P.O. BOX 151, SUMMERLAND KEY, FLORIDA 33042

Tel: **(305) 872-2246; (800) 437-5402**
Hosts: **Chris and Herb Pontin**
Location: **26 mi. E of Key West**
No. of Rooms: **2**
No. of Private Baths: **2**
Double/pb: **$85**
Single/pb: **$70**

Open: **All year**
Breakfast: **Continental, plus**
Pets: **No**
Children: **No**
Smoking: **No**
Social Drinking: **Permitted**
Minimum Stay: **2 nights**

Knightswood boasts one of the loveliest water views in the Keys. The guest apartment is self-contained and very private. Snorkeling, fishing, and boating can be enjoyed right from the Pontins' dock. You are welcome to swim in the freshwater pool, relax in the spa, or sunbathe on the white sand beach. Trips to protected Looe Key Coral Reef can be arranged. Fine dining and Key West nightlife are within easy reach.

B&B on the Bayou ✪
P.O. BOX 1545, TARPON SPRINGS, FLORIDA 34688
bbbayou@gte.net

Tel: **(813) 942-4468**
Hosts: **Al and Chris Stark**
Location: **15–20 min. NW of Tampa**
No. of Rooms: **3**
No. of Private Baths: **1**
Max. No. Sharing Bath: **2**
Double/pb: **$55**
Single/pb: **$50**
Double/sb: **$55**
Single/sb: **$50**

Suite: **$99**
Open: **All year**
Reduced Rates: **Available**
Breakfast: **Continental**
Pets: **No**
Children: **Welcome, over 7**
Smoking: **No**
Social Drinking: **Permitted**
Airport Pickup: **Yes**

Come stay at this beautiful, contemporary home situated on a quiet bayou. Fish for a big red or watch the blue herons and pelicans nesting in a bird sanctuary behind the B&B. Go for a swim in your host's solar-heated pool or soak your cares away in a whirlpool spa. Then take a stroll through the famous sponge docks and do some antiquing in town. The Inn is located just minutes from a white sandy beach with breathtaking sunsets. Busch Gardens and Adventure Islands are close by. Private tours with transportation are available.

East Lake Bed & Breakfast ✪
421 OLD EAST LAKE ROAD, TARPON SPRINGS, FLORIDA 34689
littleflower@prodigy.com

Tel: **(727) 937-5487**
Best Time to Call: **8 AM–9 PM**
Hosts: **Dick and Marie Fiorito**

Location: **2 mi. E of US 19**
No. of Rooms: **1**
No. of Private Baths: **1**

Double/pb: **$40**
Single/pb: **$35**
Open: **All year**
Breakfast: **Full**
Pets: **No**

Children: **No**
Smoking: **Restricted**
Social Drinking: **Permitted**
Airport/Station Pickup: **Yes**

Just off a quiet road that runs along Lake Tarpon's horse country, this meticulously maintained home on two-and-a-half acres offers respite for the visitor. The guest room and bath are decorated in tones of blue, enhanced with beautiful accessories. Fresh fruit, cheese omelette, home-made bread and jam, and a choice of beverage is the Fioritos' idea of breakfast. It is beautifully served on the tree-shaded, screened terrace. They'll be happy to direct you to the Greek Sponge Docks, deep-sea fishing opportunities, golf courses, beaches, and great restaurants.

Heartsease ☻
272 OLD EAST LAKE ROAD, TARPON SPRINGS, FLORIDA 34689

Tel: **(813) 934-0994**
Best Time to Call: **After 7 PM**
Hosts: **Gerald and Sharon Goulish**
Suite: **$55–$60**
Open: **All year**
Reduced Rates: **Available**

Breakfast: **Continental**
Pets: **No**
Children: **No**
Smoking: **No**
Social Drinking: **Permitted**
Airport Pickup: **Yes**

You'll find plenty of "heartsease," meaning peace of mind and tranquility, at Gerald and Sharon's guest cottage. Wicker and pine furniture and a green and mauve color scheme create a light, airy feeling. Amenities include a private entrance, a mini-kitchen stocked with a microwave and breakfast fixings, cable TV, private bath, tennis court, and a deck overlooking the in-ground pool. Pluck an orange or a grapefruit from one of the many fruit trees and then settle in the gazebo, an ideal place for observing the bald eagles that nest nearby. Golf courses, Tampa's Old Hyde Park, Harbour Island, and Tarpon Springs' famed sponge docks are all within a short drive.

The Royal Palm House ☻
3215 SPRUCE AVENUE, WEST PALM BEACH, FLORIDA 33407

Tel: **(561) 863-9836**
Best Time to Call: **After 8 AM**
Hosts: **Joe Pulvino and Kathie Mattson**
No. of Rooms: **5**
No. of Private Baths: **5**
Double/pb: **$75–$95**
Single/pb: **$70–$90**
Suites: **$105–$125**
Open: **All year**

Breakfast: **Continental**
Other Meals: **Available**
Credit Cards: **DISC, MC, VISA**
Pets: **Sometimes**
Children: **No**
Smoking: **No**
Social Drinking: **Permitted**
Airport Pickup: **Yes**

Built in 1925 during the Florida land boom by a local doctor, this rare Dutch Colonial was constructed using tropical techniques that introduce constant cooling breezes off the Atlantic Ocean. The house has been completely renovated and decorated with eclectic furnishings, including items from Kathie's extensive world travels. Joe's former occupation as a bakery owner is evident in the fresh breads and muffins baked every morning for breakfast. Royal Palm House is located in the heart of the Old Northwood Historic District and just minutes from Palm Beach, downtown West Palm Beach, the legendary shops of Worth Avenue, Fravis Cultural Center, Singer Island, West Palm Airport, and the Tri-Rail commuter train to Fort Lauderdale and Miami.

For key to listings, see inside front or back cover.

✪ This star means that rates are guaranteed through December 31, 1999, to any guest making a reservation as a result of reading about the B&B in *Bed & Breakfast U.S.A.—1999* edition.

Important! To avoid misunderstandings, always ask about cancellation policies when booking.

Please enclose a self-addressed, stamped, business-size envelope when contacting reservation services.

For more details on what you can expect in a B&B, see Chapter 1.

Always mention *Bed & Breakfast U.S.A.* when making reservations!

We want to hear from you! Use the form on page 593.

GEORGIA

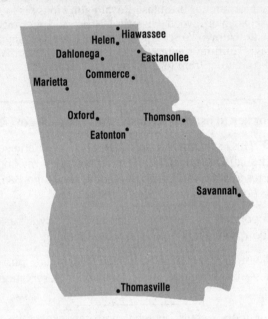

Hiawassee
Helen
Dahlonega
Eastanollee
Commerce
Marietta
Oxford
Thomson
Eatonton
Savannah
Thomasville

Magnolia Inn ✪
206 CHERRY STREET, COMMERCE, GEORGIA 30529

Tel: **(706) 335-7257**
Best Time to Call: **8 AM–8 PM**
Hosts: **Annette and Jerry Potter**
Location: **60 mi. N of Atlanta**
No. of Rooms: **4**
No. of Private Baths: **4**
Double/pb: **$60–$85**
Single/pb: **$50–$75**
Open: **All year**

Reduced Rates: **10% seniors; Dec.–Feb.**
Breakfast: **Full**
Credit Cards: **MC, VISA**
Pets: **No**
Children: **Welcome, over 10; under 10
 by arrangement**
Smoking: **No**
Social Drinking: **Permitted**
Airport/Station Pickup: **Yes**

Built in 1909, this restored Queen Anne Victorian is decorated with antiques and collectibles. In historic Commerce, you can browse through an antique mall, enjoy an old-fashioned soda at the local drugstore, or visit the crafts and gift shops. Magnolia Inn is only minutes away from the outlet malls, Atlanta Dragway, and Road Atlanta. It's twenty minutes to the University of Georgia and one hour to Atlanta. Take part in a thrilling Murder Mystery Weekend or just relax in the porch swing and rockers on the front veranda.

Lily Creek Lodge ✪
2608 AURARIA ROAD, DAHLONEGA, GEORGIA 30533
www.lilycreeklodge.com

Tel: **(706) 864-6848**	Open: **All year**
Best Time to Call: **Noon–6 PM**	Reduced Rates: **7th night free**
Hosts: **Dan and Sharon Bacek**	Breakfast: **Continental**
Location: **60 mi. N of Atlanta**	Credit Cards: **AMEX, MC, VISA**
No. of Rooms: **12**	Pets: **No**
No. of Private Baths: **12**	Children: **Welcome**
Double/pb: **$75–$95**	Smoking: **Restricted**
Suites: **$95–$135**	Social Drinking: **Permitted**

Lily Creek Lodge is located four miles south of Dahlonega's historic town square. This scenic area is nestled in a valley in the foothills of the Blue Ridge Mountains. Amenities include memorable views, a pool with waterfall, hot tub, gazebo, rocking chair deck, and a tree house where you can enjoy your breakfast (by appointment) or birdwatch. Lily Creek's rooms and common areas are furnished with antiques, art, fine linens, and feather comforters.

Royal Guard Inn
65 PARK STREET SOUTH, DAHLONEGA, GEORGIA 30533

Tel: **(706) 864-1713**	Reduced Rates: **$5 seniors; corporate rates Sun.–Thurs.**
Best Time to Call: **10 AM–9 PM**	
Hosts: **John and Farris Vanderhoff**	Breakfast: **Full**
Location: **50 mi. N of Atlanta**	Credit Cards: **AMEX, MC, VISA**
No. of Rooms: **5**	Pets: **No**
No. of Private Baths: **5**	Children: **By arrangement**
Double/pb: **$70–$85**	Smoking: **No**
Open: **All year**	Social Drinking: **Permitted**

Located in the northeast Georgia mountains, Dahlonega is where the first major U.S. gold rush occurred in 1828. Dahlonega Gold Museum, Price Memorial Hall—on the site of one of the first U.S. branch mints—and gold-panning areas are all in the heart of the historic downtown. Royal Guard Inn, a half-block from the old town square, is a restored and enlarged old home. John and Farris serve complimentary wine and cheese on the great wraparound porch. Breakfast, served on fine china and silver on crisp white linen, includes a casserole, pastries, or hotcakes from an old family recipe, and fresh fruit and whipped cream.

Apple Orchard Country Inn ✪
ROUTE 2, BOX 353, LIBERTY HILL ROAD, EASTANOLLEE, GEORGIA 30538

Tel: **(706) 779-7292; fax: (706) 779-7705**
Hosts: **Wade M. and Lu Loraine Lambert**
Location: **90 mi. E of Atlanta**
No. of Rooms: **4**
No. of Private Baths: **4**
Double/pb: **$75–$95**
Single/pb: **$75**
Suites: **$125**

Open: **All year**
Breakfast: **Full**
Other Meals: **Available**
Credit Cards: **AMEX, MC, VISA**
Pets: **No**
Smoking: **No**
Social Drinking: **Permitted**
Station Pickup: **Yes**

Apple Orchard Country Inn is located sixty-five miles west of Greenville and Spartanburg, and thirty minutes from scenic Alpine Helen. Cleveland, home of the Cabbage Patch Dolls, is one hour away. There's gold mining in Dahlonega as well as quaint shops and antiques. Water sports are available at Lakes Hanier and Hartwell; golf, tennis, horseback riding, and other outdoor activities are at state and federal parks. Apple Orchard Country Inn's own attractions include a producing apple orchard, a pre–Civil War cemetery, and an old baptismal. This two-story home sits on twenty acres of wooded parklike land. The interior is furnished with a mixture of Oriental and traditional antiques. Amenities include an 18 × 36 pool, TV and VCRs in all rooms.

The Crockett House—"A Traditional Bed and Breakfast" ✪
671 MADISON ROAD, EATONTON, GEORGIA 31024
www.bbonline.com/ga/crocketthouse/

Tel: **(706) 485-2248**
Hosts: **Christa and Peter Crockett**
Location: **73 mi. E of Atlanta**
No. of Rooms: **6**
No. of Private Baths: **4**
Double/pb: **$85–$95**
Single/pb: **$65**
Double/sb: **$65**

Open: **All year**
Breakfast: **Full**
Credit Cards: **MC, VISA**
Pets: **No**
Children: **Welcome, over 10**
Smoking: **No**
Social Drinking: **Permitted**

The Crockett House, circa 1895, is nestled among hundred-year-old pecan, oak, pine, and magnolia trees and is gracefully adorned by its beautiful weeping willows. Experience a new adventure as you step back in time to luxurious accommodations, fine dining, and a slower pace at this perfect place for a rendezvous. Features include eleven fireplaces, large wraparound porch, antique-filled guest rooms with double, queen, or king beds, claw-footed tubs, and refreshments upon arrival. Christa's memorable gourmet breakfast is served in elegant style. The Crockett House is located on Georgia's historic antebellum

trail, approximately one hour and fifteen minutes from Atlanta, one hour and thirty minutes from Augusta, fifty minutes from Athens, and forty minutes from Macon.

Hilltop Haus ✪
P. O. BOX 154, 362 CHATTAHOOCHEE STREET, HELEN, GEORGIA 30545

Tel: **(706) 878-2388**	Suites: **$80–$135**
Best Time to Call: **9 AM–10 PM**	Open: **All year**
Hosts: **Frankie Allen and Barbara Nichols**	Breakfast: **Full**
	Credit Cards: **MC, VISA**
Location: **60 mi. from I-85**	Pets: **No**
No. of Rooms: **4**	Children: **Welcome**
No. of Private Baths: **4**	Smoking: **Restricted**
Double/pb: **$60–$90**	Social Drinking: **Permitted**
Single/pb: **$50–$80**	

This split-level overlooks the Alpine town of Helen and the Chattahoochee River. It is near the foothills of the Smoky Mountains, six miles from the Appalachian Trail. Rich wood paneling and rooms with fireplaces create a homey atmosphere for the traveler. Guests may choose a private room or the efficiency with a separate entrance. A full breakfast is served in the bright, plant-filled sunroom. Your hostess will be happy to direct you to the many outdoor activities and sights.

Henson Cove Place ✪
3840 CAR MILES ROAD, HIAWASSEE, GEORGIA 30546-9585
www.yhc.edu/users/nle

Tel: **(800) 714-5542; (706) 896-6195**	Hosts: **Bill and Nancy Leffingwell**
Best Time to Call: **After 10 AM**	Location: **2 hrs. N of Atlanta**

No. of Rooms: **2**
No. of Private Baths: **2**
Double/pb: **$60**
Suites: **$60**
Open: **All year**
Breakfast: **Full**

Credit Cards: **MC, VISA**
Pets: **No**
Children: **Welcome, over 10**
Smoking: **No**
Social Drinking: **Permitted**

Henson Cove Place has a warm, homey atmosphere that will envelop you as you head for your room. The furniture and decorations are from Bill and Nancy's families and have stories behind them. You can browse through the magazine collection, read any of 2000 books, watch TV in the sitting room, and relax on the front porch. Or attend a festival, country music show, or hike or stop in the many small shops in the area. In the morning you'll be greeted with hot coffee and breakfast. A typical menu might be fruit cup, juice, muffins, pecan waffles, apple French toast with baby sausages, or fruit-filled crêpes. Bill is a furniture maker specializing in reproductions. Nancy operates a business service above his workshop. Both like talking to guests and making their stay an enjoyable one.

Whitlock Inn Bed & Breakfast ✪

57 WHITLOCK AVENUE, MARIETTA, GEORGIA 30064
www.mindspring.com/~whitlockinn/

Tel: **(770) 428-1495**
Best Time to Call: **9 AM–5 PM**
Host: **Alexis Edwards**
Location: **20 mi. NW of Atlanta**

No. of Rooms: **5**
No. of Private Baths: **5**
Double/pb: **$100**
Open: **All year**

Breakfast: **Continental**
Credit Cards: **AMEX, DISC, MC, VISA**
Pets: **No**

Children: **Welcome, over 12**
Smoking: **No**
Social Drinking: **Permitted**

Built in the 1900s by wealthy Mariettans, this Victorian mansion is in a National Register District of some of the South's finest antebellum homes. Purchased in 1994 by the Edwards family, the property was restored and turned into one of Georgia's most beautiful bed and breakfasts. After graduating from college, their daughter Alexis moved into the inn's carriage house and became the innkeeper. The Whitlock is located one block from the historic town square, with antique shops, restaurants, carriage rides, and live theater. Whitlock Inn Bed & Breakfast is frequently busy with weddings and receptions.

The Hopkins House Bed & Breakfast ✪
1111 WESLEY STREET, OXFORD, GEORGIA 30054

Tel: **(770) 784-1010**
Best Time to Call: **8 AM–9 PM**
Hosts: **Ralph and Nancy Brian**
Location: **35 mi. SE of Atlanta**
No. of Rooms: **5**
No. of Private Baths: **5**
Double/pb: **$85–$100**
Suites: **$150**
Open: **All year**

Reduced Rates: **10% seniors**
Breakfast: **Full (weekends), Continental (weekdays)**
Credit Cards: **AMEX, DISC, MC, VISA**
Pets: **Sometimes**
Children: **Welcome**
Smoking: **No**
Social Drinking: **Permitted**

The Hopkins House Bed & Breakfast is in the historic district—the birthplace of Emory University, Georgia Tech, and a Methodist shrine. Built in 1847, this Greek Revival–style home was spared during the Civil War on "Sherman's march to the sea." Guest rooms are exquisitely decorated in warm prints and handmade country quilts, set off by antiques, plates, dolls, and whimsicals. You are invited to enjoy the expansive screened porch with rocking chairs, overlooking acres of green and gardens. To cool off from the warm Georgia days, take a dip in the pool.

R.S.V.P. Savannah—B&B Reservation Service ✪
611 EAST 56TH STREET, SAVANNAH, GEORGIA 31406

Tel: **(912) 232-7787; (800) 729-7787**
Best Time to Call: **9:30 AM–5:30 PM**
  Mon.–Fri.
Coordinator: **Sonja Lazzaro**
States/Regions Covered: **Brunswick,**

**Savannah, St. Simons Island; South
Carolina—Beaufort, Charleston**
Rates (Single/Double): **$80–$350**
Credit Cards: **AMEX, DISC, MC, VISA**

Accommodations include elegantly restored inns, guesthouses, and private homes. They're located in the best historic districts as well as along the coast, from South Carolina's Low Country to Georgia's Sea Islands. A special blend of cordial hospitality, comfort, and services is provided. All are air-conditioned in the summer. Facilities for children and the disabled are often available. Please note that while some hosts accept credit cards, some do not. Sonja is closed on Wednesday.

Joan's on Jones ✪
17 WEST JONES STREET, SAVANNAH, GEORGIA 31401

Tel: **(912) 234-3863; (800) 407-3863;**
  fax: **(912) 234-1455**
Hosts: **Joan and Gary Levy**
Location: **140 mi. N of Jacksonville, FL**
Suites: **$115–$130; sleeps 2–4**
Open: **All year**
Reduced Rates: **Weekly**

Breakfast: **Continental**
Pets: **Sometimes**
Children: **Welcome**
Smoking: **No**
Social Drinking: **Permitted**
Minimum Stay: **3 days for St. Patrick's
  Day week only**

Clip-clopping along the brick streets of the city's historic district, horse-drawn carriages take you back to a more serene and elegant era. This bed and breakfast maintains the old-fashioned mood, with its original heart-pine floors, antique furnishings, and Savannah gray brick walls. (Note the late-19th-century documents that slipped behind one of the fireplace mantels.) All the historic places of interest, including the famous squares, are a short walk away. Joan and Gary, former restaurateurs, live upstairs and invite you to tour their home if you're staying at least two nights.

Lion's Head Inn ✪
120 EAST GASTON STREET, SAVANNAH, GEORGIA 31401

Tel: **(912) 232-4580**
Host: **Christy Dell'orco**
Location: **Downtown Savannah**
No. of Rooms: **6**
No. of Private Baths: **5**
Double/pb: **$95–$150**
Single/pb: **$85–$140**
Suites: **$140–$190**

Open: **All year**
Reduced Rates: **Available**
Breakfast: **Continental**
Credit Cards: **AMEX, DISC, MC, VISA**
Pets: **No**
Children: **Welcome**
Smoking: **No**
Social Drinking: **Permitted**

This elegant 19th-century mansion is tastefully adorned with pristine Empire furniture and accessories. A collection of European and American art, Italian marble, and French bronze sculptures and 19th-century lighting beautify each room. The Inn is located on Gaston Street, the prime residential street in the historic district. Stroll across the street to picturesque Forsyth Park and enjoy all the historic attractions and amenities within walking distance. Enjoy gracious living at its best and experience true 19th-century grandeur at the Lion's Head Inn.

Serendipity Cottage Bed & Breakfast ❂
339 EAST JEFFERSON STREET, THOMASVILLE, GEORGIA 31792

Tel: **(912) 226-8111; (800) 383-7377**
   for reservations
Hosts: **Kathy and Ed Middleton**
Location: **35 mi. N of Tallahassee,**
   Florida
No. of Rooms: **3**
No. of Private Baths: **3**
Double/pb: **$80**

Single/pb: **$75**
Open: **All year**
Breakfast: **Full**
Credit Cards: **AMEX, DISC, MC, VISA**
Pets: **No**
Children: **Welcome, over 12**
Smoking: **No**
Social Drinking: **Permitted**

While it's only a 40-minute drive from Florida State University, Serendipity Cottage is located in a Victorian town, where a slower pace is the norm. Built in 1906, the house is decorated with a tasteful mix of Victorian antiques and comfortable country surroundings. Freshly starched and ironed bed linens greet you when you retire, and at wake-up call your choice of beverage is delivered to your room in the morning. People Hill Plantation, recently featured on A&E's *America's Castles*, is just south of town. Ed, a retired naval architect, and Kathy, a retired retail shop owner, share an interest in antiques, preservation of old homes, and counted cross-stitch.

Four Chimneys B&B
2316 WIRE ROAD SOUTHEAST, THOMSON, GEORGIA 30824

Tel: **(706) 597-0220**
Best Time to Call: **9 AM–10 PM**
Hosts: **Maggie and Ralph Zieger**
Location: **35 mi. W of Augusta**
No. of Rooms: **4**
No. of Private Baths: **3**
Double/pb: **$50–$75**
Single/pb: **$40–$65**

Open: **All year**
Breakfast: **Continental, plus**
Credit Cards: **MC, VISA**
Pets: **No**
Children: **Welcome, over 12**
Smoking: **Restricted**
Social Drinking: **Permitted**
Foreign Languages: **German**

Escape from the modern world at this early 1800s country house with a rocking-chair porch. The old-fashioned landscape features a large herb garden and heirloom flowers. Antique and reproduction furniture complement the original heart-pine interior. A small library and a cozy parlor invite you to relax at your leisure. Guest rooms have four-poster beds and working fireplaces. Restaurants, golf courses, and antique shops are nearby. Fox hunts and other equestrian events take place throughout the year.

HAWAII

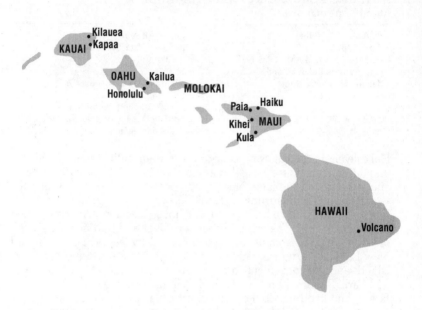

Bed & Breakfast Honolulu Statewide ✪
3242 KAOHINANI DRIVE, HONOLULU, HAWAII 96817
bnbshi@aloha=bnb.com; www.aloha.bnb.com

Tel: **(800) 288-4666; (808) 595-7533;**
  fax: **(808) 595-2030**
Best Time to Call: **8 AM–5 PM**
  Mon.–Fri., 8 AM–noon Sat.
Coordinator: **Mary Lee**
States/Regions Covered:
  Hawaii—statewide

Rates (Single/Double):
  Modest: **$45–$55 / $45–$60**
  Average: **$55–$70 / $55–$75**
  Luxury: **$75 up / $75 up**
Credit Cards: **DISC, MC, VISA**

This home-based family service, started in 1982, pays careful attention
to visitors who want to be more than tourists. That's made it Hawaii's
largest statewide agency, listing more than 1000 rooms, on all islands.
Many agencies have membership fees and directories; this one doesn't!
When you call the 800 number, use the e-mail address, or fax Bed &

Breakfast Honolulu, Mary Lee can match your needs, desires, and pocketbook to her computerized listings.

Haikuleana B&B, Plantation House ✪
555 HAIKU ROAD, HAIKU, MAUI, HAWAII 96708
blumblum@maui.net

Tel: **(808) 575-2890**; fax: **(808) 575-9177**	Open: **All year**
Best Time to Call: **8 AM–8 PM HST**	Reduced Rates: **Weekly**
Hosts: **Authors Ralph H. and Jeanne Elizabeth Blum**	Breakfast: **Full**
No. of Rooms: **4**	Pets: **No**
No. of Private Baths: **4**	Children: **Welcome, over 7**
Double/pb: **$95–$125**	Smoking: **No**
Single/pb: **$85–$125**	Social Drinking: **Permitted**
	Foreign Languages: **French, Italian, Russian, Spanish, German**

Haikuleana is the gateway to upcountry Maui. Built in the 1850s, this plantation-style house is nestled among 100-year-old Cook Island pines and lush tropical foliage. Nearby are pools, secluded waterfalls, the world-famous windsurfing at Hookipa Beach, golfing, horseback riding, restaurants, and a health club. The house was completely renovated from 1990 to 1992. The original 12-foot ceilings and traditional fretwork of early Colonial architecture are enhanced by period Hawaiian and New England furniture. This is a perfect place for exploring the entire island, and it's convenient to the town of Hana and Haleakala Crater and Park. Rooms are furnished with ceiling fans, phones, and designer fabrics and bedding; dual-control electric blankets are provided for the winter months. Ralph and Jeanne can accommodate weddings and reunions.

Bev & Monty's Bed & Breakfast ✪
4571 UKALI STREET, HONOLULU, OAHU, HAWAII 96818

Tel: **(808) 422-9873**	Open: **All year**
Best Time to Call: **7 AM–9 PM HST**	Reduced Rates: **Weekly**
Hosts: **Bev and Monty Neese**	Breakfast: **Continental**
Location: **4¹/₂ mi. from airport**	Pets: **No**
No. of Rooms: **2**	Children: **Welcome**
Max. No. Sharing Bath: **4**	Smoking: **Permitted**
Double/sb: **$55**	Social Drinking: **Permitted**
Single/sb: **$45**	Airport/Station Pickup: **Yes**

This typical Hawaiian home is convenient to many of Hawaii's most popular attractions. Bev and Monty are just a mile above historic Pearl Harbor, and the Arizona Memorial can be seen from their veranda. They enjoy sharing a Hawaiian aloha for a convenient overnight stay or a long vacation when they can share their favorite places with you. This comfortable home is just off the access road leading east to Honolulu and Waikiki, or west to the North Shore beaches and pineapple fields.

Good hiking country as well as city entertainment and shopping centers are located nearby.

Akamai Bed & Breakfast ✪
172 KUUMELE PLACE, KAILUA, OAHU, HAWAII 96734

Tel: **(808) 261-2227; (800) 642-5366**	Open: **All year**
Best Time to Call: **8 AM–8 PM**	Breakfast: **Full**
Host: **Diane Van Ryzin**	Pets: **No**
No. of Rooms: **2**	Children: **No**
No. of Private Baths: **2**	Smoking: **No**
Double/pb: **$75**	Social Drinking: **Permitted**
Single/pb: **$75**	Minimum Stay: **3 nights**

Guests at Akamai stay in a separate wing of the house; each studio has a private entrance, bath, kitchenette, private phone, cable TV, and radio. Honolulu and Waikiki are within a half-hour drive, but you may prefer to lounge by your host's pool or take the eight-minute stroll to the beach. No meals are served here, but your refrigerator is stocked with breakfast foods and the kitchen area is equipped with light cooking appliances, dishes, and flatware. Laundry facilities are also available.

Papaya Paradise ✪
395 AUWINALA ROAD, KAILUA, OAHU, HAWAII 96734
bnbweb.com/papaya.html

Tel: **(808) 261-0316; fax: (808) 261-0316**	Open: **All year**
	Breakfast: **Continental**
Best Time to Call: **7 AM–8 PM (HST)**	Pets: **No**
Hosts: **Bob and Jeanette Martz**	Children: **Welcome, over 6**
Location: **10 mi. E of Honolulu**	Smoking: **Permitted**
No. of Rooms: **2**	Social Drinking: **Permitted**
No. of Private Baths: **2**	Minimum Stay: **3 nights**
Double/pb: **$75–$80**	

The Martz paradise is located on the windward side of Oahu, 20 miles from Waikiki/Honolulu airport and a short walk from Kailua Beach. Each B&B unit has its own private entrance and is furnished in tropical rattan and wicker, with two beds, two comfortable lounge chairs, air conditioning, ceiling fan, cable TV, and telephone. Guest rooms open onto a 20 × 40-foot swimming pool and Jacuzzi surrounded by tropical plants, trees, and Hawaiian flowers. Breakfast includes fresh-baked muffins or breads, and is served on the lanai, where a small library and comfortable reading chairs are provided.

Hale Aloha of Kauai ✪

1400 KANEPOONUI ROAD, KAPAA, HAWAII 96746
www.haleyaloha.com

Tel: **(800) 822-2328; (808) 822-2323**	Breakfast: **Continental**
Best Time to Call: **4–9 PM (EST)**	Credit Cards: **MC, VISA**
Hosts: **Jimmy and Solange Latif**	Pets: **No**
Location: **14 mi. N of Lihue, Kauai**	Children: **Welcome**
Guest Floor: **$85–$185, sleeps 2–6**	Smoking: **No**
Open: **All year**	Social Drinking: **Permitted**
Reduced Rates: **Seniors 10%, group**	Foreign Languages: **Italian, French,**
discounts	**Arabic**

Kauai, the oldest of the islands, was the first to be inhabited because it is the only island that has navigable rivers. It is also home to Waimea Canyon, the only canyon on any of the islands, known as the Grand Canyon of Kauai. There are endless sights and things to do, including hiking, horseback riding, helicopter rides, snorkeling, whale watching, boating, sailing, and deep sea fishing. Go to the north shore to see the spectacular Na Pali coast. Famous movies have been made here, such as *King Kong, Raiders of the Lost Ark,* and *Jurassic Park.* Jimmy is a retired photojournalist and world traveler and Solange is a retired nurse. Amenities include a full outdoor kitchen, TV in the library room, washing machine, and pool.

Eva Villa ✪

815 KUMULANI DRIVE, KIHEI, MAUI, HAWAII 96753
Pounder@maui.net

Tel: **(800) 884-1845;**	Open: **All year**
fax: **(808) 874-6407**	Reduced Rates: **Summer**
Hosts: **Rick and Dale Pounds**	Breakfast: **Continental**
Location: **5 mi. S of Kahalui**	Pets: **No**
No. of Rooms: **4**	Children: **Welcome, over 13**
No. of Private Baths: **4**	Smoking: **No**
Double/pb: **$95**	Social Drinking: **Permitted**
Guest Apartment: **$95**	Minimum Stay: **3 nights**
Cottage: **$100**	

Eva Villa is located at the top of Maui Meadows, just above Wailea on the dry side of the island. The islands of Lanai, Molokini, and Kahoolawe can be viewed from the rooftop deck. The grounds include many fruit and tropical trees and plants; there is also a koi pond with frogs, fish, and beautiful lilies. Amenities include a pool, Jacuzzi, barbecue facilities, outside table and chairs, and cable TV. Eva Villa has three guest sections. The main house has a studio that looks out on the pool and Jacuzzi. It contains a queen bed, kitchen, counter bar, and eating area. Also in the main house is the apartment, containing two bedrooms—one queen, one twin—living room, and kitchenette with a microwave oven and a two-burner hot plate. The cottage is separate from the house and has a kitchen, living room, queen-size bed, and a wrap-around lanai with a barbecue.

Whale Watch House ✪
726 KUMULANI DRIVE, KIHEI, MAUI, HAWAII 96753

Tel: **(808) 879-0570; fax: (808) 874-8102**
Best Time to Call: **8 AM–8 PM**
Hosts: **Patricia and Patrick Lowry**
No. of Rooms: **4**
No. of Private Baths: **4**
Double/pb: **$65**
Single/pb: **$60**
Guest Cottage: **$95, sleeps 2; studio, $85**

Open: **All year**
Reduced Rates: **10% less June, July, Sept., Oct.**
Breakfast: **Continental**
Pets: **No**
Children: **No**
Smoking: **No**
Social Drinking: **Permitted**
Minimum Stay: **2 nights**

Whale Watch House is located at the very edge of Ulupalakua Ranch on Haleakala, Maui's 10,228-foot dormant volcano. At every turn there are wonderful views of the ocean, the mountains, and the neighboring islands, Lanai and Kahoolawe. Your hosts' lush tropical garden is filled with fruits and flowers, and the swimming pool is large enough for laps. Sunbathe on the large decks around the house, cottage, and pool, or drive down to the beach—you'll be there in five minutes.

Hale Ho'o Maha ✪
P.O. BOX 422, KILAUEA, KAUAI, HAWAII 96754
hoomaha@aloha.net; www.aloha.net/~hoomaha

Tel: **(800) 851-0291; (808) 828-1341; fax: (808) 828-2046**
Best Time to Call: **7 AM–7 PM**
Hosts: **Kirby B. Guyer and Toby Searles**
Location: **23 mi. N of Lihue Airport**
No. of Rooms: **4**
No. of Private Baths: **2**
Max. No. Sharing Bath: **4**
Double/pb: **$75–$80**

Double/sb: **$55–$65**
Open: **All year**
Reduced Rates: **10% after 5th night**
Breakfast: **Continental**
Pets: **No**
Children: **Welcome, over 10**
Smoking: **No**
Social Drinking: **Permitted**
Foreign Languages: **Spanish**

Escape to a B&B that lives up to its name, which means "house of rest" in Hawaiian. This single-story home is perched on the cliffs along Kauai's north shore. Sandy beaches, rivers, waterfalls, and riding stables are five minutes away. Ask your hosts to direct you to "Queens Bath"—a natural saltwater whirlpool. Guests have full use of the kitchen, gas grill, cable TV, and boogie boards. When in Rome, do as the Romans: Kirby will teach you to dance the hula and make leis, and Toby will instruct you in scuba diving.

Kula Cottage ✪
206 PUAKEA PLACE, KULA, MAUI, HAWAII 96790

Tel: **(808) 871-6230, 878-2043**	Pets: **No**
Best Time to Call: **8 AM–5 PM**	Children: **Welcome, over 12**
Hosts: **Larry and Cecilia Gilbert**	Smoking: **Permitted**
Location: **16 mi. SE of Kahului**	Social Drinking: **Permitted**
Guest Cottage: **$85, sleeps 2**	Minimum Stay: **2 nights**
Open: **All year**	Foreign Languages: **Spanish**
Breakfast: **Continental**	

Flowers and fruit-bearing trees surround this new, fully equipped one-bedroom bungalow. There are wonderful views of the ocean and the West Maui Mountains, plus loads of amenities: a wood-burning fireplace, washer and dryer, patio furniture, barbecue, cooler, beach towels, and more. Nearby are restaurants, the beach, a national park, gardens, and a winery. Your hosts can arrange sailing, snorkeling, and helicopter trips for you. The Continental breakfast features home-baked breads, fresh fruit, juice, and coffee or tea.

Kula View Bed and Breakfast ✪
140 HOLOPUNI ROAD (MAILING ADDRESS: P.O. BOX 322), KULA, MAUI, HAWAII 96790

Tel: **(808) 878-6736**	Open: **All year**
Best Time to Call: **8 AM–6 PM**	Reduced Rates: **10% weekly**
Host: **Susan Kauai**	Breakfast: **Continental**
Location: **16 mi. E of Kahului**	Pets: **No**
No. of Rooms: **1**	Children: **No**
No. of Private Baths: **1**	Smoking: **No**
Double/pb: **$85**	Social Drinking: **Permitted**
Single/pb: **$85**	Minimum Stay: **2 nights**

The fragrances of island fruits and flowers fill the fresh mountain air at this B&B 2000 feet above sea level, on the slopes of the dormant volcano Haleakala. The upper-level guest room has its own private entrance and a spacious deck that faces majestic Haleakala Crater, where the sunrises are nothing short of magical. Breakfast is served at a sun-warmed wicker table overlooking a flower and herb garden. Kula View is surrounded by two acres of lush greenery, yet it is close to Kahului Airport, shopping centers, parks, and beaches.

Kuau Cove Plantation ✪
2 WAA PLACE, PAIA, HAWAII 96779

Tel: **(808) 579-8988;**	Location: **7 mi. E of Kahului Airport**
fax: **(808) 579-8710**	No. of Rooms: **4**
Best Time to Call: **10 AM–8 PM**	No. of Private Baths: **4**
Hosts: **Russell and Jane Mori**	Double/pb: **$85**

Single/pb: **$85**
Suites: **$95**
Open: **All year**
Reduced Rates: **Available**
Breakfast: **Continental**
Credit Cards: **MC, VISA**

Pets: **No**
Children: **Welcome, over 6; under 12 free**
Smoking: **No**
Social Drinking: **Permitted**
Minimum Stay: **2 nights**

Nestled near a tropical ocean bay on the north shore of Maui, Kuau Cove has the charm of an old Hawaiian plantation home. Nearby are sandy beaches, Mama's Fish House, Kuau Food Mart and Deli, a world-class surfing and windsurfing beach, restaurants, entertainment, antique shops, and art and clothing boutiques. Kahului Airport, shopping malls, and the Maui Arts and Cultural Center are ten minutes away, en route to the town of Hana and Haleakala Crater, Maui's two top destinations. There are two large guest rooms in the main house with queen beds and ceiling fans. In addition, there are two studio apartments; one has an ocean view, the other overlooks a lovely shaded garden. The ocean studio has a private lanai.

Hale Kilauea ✪
P.O. BOX 28, VOLCANO, HAWAII 96785

Tel: **(808) 967-7591; (800) 733-3839; fax: (808) 985-7008**
Best Time to Call: **8 AM–10 PM**
Hosts: **Maurice Thomas and Jiranan**
Location: **28 mi. NE of Hilo**
No. of Rooms: **5**
No. of Private Baths: **5**
Double/pb: **$55–$75**

Open: **All year**
Breakfast: **Continental**
Credit Cards: **AMEX, MC, VISA**
Pets: **Sometimes**
Children: **Welcome**
Smoking: **No**
Social Drinking: **Permitted**

Hale Kilauea is a quiet place near the heart of Volcano Village, just outside Hawaii Volcanoes National Park, the world's only "drive-in volcano." Colorful, exotic native birds live in the towering pines and ohia trees that surround this B&B. After a day of climbing mountains and peering into craters, enjoy an evening of conversation around the living room fireplace. Your host Maurice, a lifelong Volcano resident, has neighbors and friends who know about volcano geology and the history and tradition of old Hawaii. Cottages available.

IDAHO

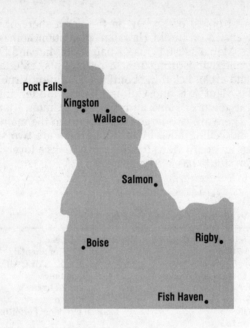

Idaho Heritage Inn ✪
109 WEST IDAHO, BOISE, IDAHO 83702

Tel: **(208) 342-8066**
Best Time to Call: **9 AM–8 PM**
Hosts: **Phyllis and Tom Lupher**
No. of Rooms: **6**
No. of Private Baths: **6**
Double/pb: **$60–$80**
Suites: **$85–$105**

Open: **All year**
Breakfast: **Full**
Credit Cards: **AMEX, DISC, MC, VISA**
Pets: **No**
Children: **Welcome, over 5**
Smoking: **No**
Social Drinking: **Permitted**

The Idaho Heritage Inn is a traditional bed and breakfast located just six blocks from downtown Boise and a short walk from Boise's beautiful greenbelt, a paved river path leading to nature trails, historic museums, art galleries, and Zoo Boise. Many of the city's finest restaurants, shops, and movie theaters are just blocks away. The Inn's guest rooms are gracefully and comfortably appointed with antique furniture, giving each one its own special atmosphere in which to relax and enjoy. This

1904 Inn served as a former governor's mansion and home to the late Senator Frank Church and continues to host guests of political prominence, such as former First Lady Barbara Bush.

Bear Lake Bed and Breakfast ✪
500 LOVELAND LANE, FISH HAVEN, IDAHO 83287

Tel: **(208) 945-2688**	Double/sb: **$69**
Best Time to Call: **Anytime**	Open: **All year**
Host: **Esther Harrison**	Breakfast: **Full**
Location: **125 mi. N of Salt Lake City, Utah, on Bear Lake**	Credit Cards: **MC, VISA**
	Pets: **Sometimes**
No. of Rooms: **4**	Children: **Welcome, over 12**
No. of Private Baths: **1**	Smoking: **No**
Max. No. Sharing Bath: **4**	Social Drinking: **Permitted**
Double/pb: **$79**	

Make yourselves at home in this spacious secluded log home, hand-built and designed by the owners. Sitting on the deck you can absorb the peace and beauty of the turquoise blue lake below. The national forest is half a mile behind the B&B and the colors are a sight to behold in the fall with the yellow aspens and red and orange maples mixed with the green pines. You will find total hospitality here. Each guest room is decorated in a different style, and yummy aromas come from the kitchen each morning. Take part in all lake activities, including boat rentals. Apart from the waterfront, there is a tour-guided cave, horseback riding, chuck wagon dinners, and mountain biking. Esther subs at local schools and makes items for the B&B gift shop. She has horses and loves the out-of-doors.

Kingston 5 Ranch Bed & Breakfast ✪

P.O. BOX 130, 42297 SILVER VALLEY ROAD, KINGSTON,
IDAHO 83839
k5ranch@nidlink.com; www.nidlink.com/~k5ranch

Tel: **(208) 682-4862; (800) 254-1852;**	Single/sb: **$55**
fax: **(208) 682-9445**	Suites: **$85**
Best Time to Call: **8 AM–8 PM**	Open: **All year**
Hosts: **Walt and Pat Gentry**	Breakfast: **Full**
Location: **20 mi. E of Coeur d'Alene; 60**	Credit Cards: **MC, VISA**
mi. E of Spokane, WA	Pets: **By arrangement (outdoors only)**
No. of Rooms: **3**	Children: **Welcome, over 12**
No. of Private Baths: **2**	Smoking: **No**
Max. No. Sharing Bath: **4**	Social Drinking: **Permitted**
Double/sb: **$65**	Minimum Stay: **3 nights, suites**

Kingston 5 Ranch is located in the heart of the Coeur d'Alene Mountains. Two luxurious suites have spectacular views of the surrounding
mountains and valleys, in-room private baths with jetted tubs, fireplaces, and private outdoor spas. This area is an outdoor paradise. In
winter enjoy skiing and snowmobiling. In summertime, choose from
Silver Mountain outdoor concerts, mountain biking, tennis, golf, hiking,
fishing, canoeing, and river float trips, all within minutes of the property. Guests' horses can be accommodated on site. A recently retired
health administrator, Walt is an expert horseman who truly enjoys the
outdoors. Pat continues to work as a health care administrator. They
invite you to "come home to the country."

River Cove ✪

P.O. BOX 1862, POST FALLS, IDAHO 83854
www.nidlink.com/~rivercove

Tel: **(208) 773-9190**	Open: **All year**
Best Time to Call: **After 5 PM**	Reduced Rates: **Available**
Hosts: **Eric and Rosalynd Wurmlinger**	Breakfast: **Full**
Location: **20 mi. E of Spokane**	Pets: **Sometimes**
No. of Rooms: **3**	Children: **No**
No. of Private Baths: **3**	Smoking: **No**
Double/pb: **$99**	Social Drinking: **Permitted**
Suites: **$139**	Airport Pickup: **Yes**

Eric and Rosalynd invite you to experience the elegant waterfront setting of their contemporary home. Nestled among the wooded foothills
of the Spokane River and five boat miles from beautiful Lake Coeur
d'Alene in northern Idaho, River Cove is the perfect choice for a wonderful getaway or a private wedding. Enjoy a refreshing stroll along the
river or perhaps a moonlight swim. You may even be invited to join the
innkeepers for a boat cruise to one of the many fine waterfront restaurants. In the winter, enjoy one of the several world-class ski resorts.

BlackSmith Inn ✪
227 NORTH 3900 EAST, RIGBY, IDAHO 83442

Tel: **(208) 745-6208; fax: (208) 745-0602**
Best Time to Call: **Before noon**
Hosts: **Mike and Karla Black**
Location: **20 mi. N of Idaho Falls**
No. of Rooms: **4**
No. of Private Baths: **4**
Double/pb: **$65–$75**
Single/pb: **$60–$70**
Open: **All year**

Reduced Rates: **20% Oct.–Mar., weekly; 10% seniors**
Breakfast: **Full**
Credit Cards: **MC, VISA**
Pets: **No**
Children: **Welcome**
Smoking: **No**
Social Drinking: **Permitted**
Airport/Station Pickup: **Yes**

The BlackSmith Inn is a contemporary round Eagle's Nest home, cedar-sided for a unique Western flavor. Guest rooms feature Western murals and quilts; local artwork can be found in the common areas. Decking and patio areas allow you to enjoy pleasant cool evenings. The Inn is 85 miles from West Yellowstone, 20 miles from I-15, 2 miles from the local golf course, and within a short distance of distinctive shops, galleries, antique stores, and museums. Nearby, Ricks College offers plays and other activities throughout the year. There is plenty of winter and summer fun, including skiing, fly fishing, and much more. Mike and Karla are registered nurses. In their spare time, they raise and train Tennessee Walking horses shown locally, and are in the process of building a greenhouse that will use hydroponics.

Heritage Inn ✪
510 LENA STREET, SALMON, IDAHO 83467

Tel: **(208) 756-3174**
Best Time to Call: **8 AM–8 PM**
Host: **Audrey Nichols**
Location: **½ mi. from Hwy. 93**
No. of Rooms: **4**
Max. No. Sharing Bath: **3**
Double/sb: **$40–$45**
Single/sb: **$30–$35**

Cottage: **$45**
Open: **Apr.–Oct.**
Breakfast: **Continental, plus**
Credit Cards: **MC, VISA**
Pets: **No**
Children: **Welcome**
Smoking: **Restricted**
Social Drinking: **Permitted**

Built by a prominent businessman, who later became the first governor of Idaho in 1890, this two-story brick farmhouse is more than 100 years old. Heritage Inn is located in a quiet neighborhood two blocks from a shopping center and five blocks from the Salmon River, where you can take a stroll along the river-of-no-return. Rooms are large and comfortable, adorned with antiques and wallpaper that sets off the large windows. Breakfast is served in the dining room; while you wait you are invited to enjoy a cup of coffee and a magazine from the history library on the glassed-in sunporch. Audrey has enjoyed running the inn for twelve years and working in her many flower gardens. As a native of

Salmon, she will be happy to point you to the many attractions. Glacier Mountain Park in Montana and Yellowstone National Park are a day's drive away.

Beale House
107 CEDAR STREET, WALLACE, IDAHO 83873

Tel: **(208) 752-7151**
Hosts: **Jim and Linda See**
Location: **90 mi. E of Spokane, Washington**
No. of Rooms: **5**
No. of Private Baths: **1**
Max. No. Sharing Bath: **4**
Double/pb: **$75–$95**
Double/sb: **$75–$95**

Open: **All year**
Reduced Rates: **3 nights or more; multiple room booking**
Breakfast: **Full**
Pets: **No**
Children: **No**
Smoking: **No**
Social Drinking: **Permitted**

Listed on the National Register of Historic Places, as is the entire town of Wallace, the Beale House is just four blocks from downtown. This 1904 Colonial Revival home offers an atmosphere of comfortable elegance that is enhanced by antique furnishings and parquet floors. Local attractions include tours of a silver mine and bordello, mining and railroad museums, an art center, and melodrama performances. Visitors can enjoy golf, tennis, mountain biking, hiking, rafting, canoeing, fishing, hunting, bird watching, snowmobiling, alpine or cross-country skiing, or simply take in mountain views from the hot tub or front porch wicker. Jim and Linda are educators and travelers who like to share photographs and stories of former owners. They promise to turn each guest's stay into an unforgettable experience.

For key to listings, see inside front or back cover.

✪ This star means that rates are guaranteed through December 31, 1999, to any guest making a reservation as a result of reading about the B&B in *Bed & Breakfast U.S.A.—1999* edition.

Important! To avoid misunderstandings, always ask about cancellation policies when booking.

Please enclose a self-addressed, stamped, business-size envelope when contacting reservation services.

For more details on what you can expect in a B&B, see Chapter 1.

Always mention *Bed & Breakfast U.S.A.* when making reservations!

We want to hear from you! Use the form on page 593.

ILLINOIS

Galena
Mundelein
Sycamore
Chicago
Rock Island
Mossville
Nauvoo
Bloomington
Quincy
Champaign
Rochester
Jerseyville
Arcola
Mt. Carmel
Maeystown

Curly's Corner ✪
425 EAST CR, 200 N, ARCOLA, ILLINOIS 61910

Tel: **(217) 268-3352**
Best Time to Call: **Anytime**
Hosts: **Warren and Maxine Arthur**
Location: **35 mi. S of Champaign; 5 mi.**
  from I-57
No. of Rooms: **4**
No. of Private Baths: **2**
Max. No. Sharing Bath: **3**
Double/pb: **$55–$60**

Single/sb: **$40**
Open: **All year**
Breakfast: **Full**
Pets: **No**
Children: **Welcome, over 10**
Smoking: **No**
Social Drinking: **No**
Airport/Station Pickup: **Yes**

This ranch-style farmhouse is located in a quiet Amish community. Your hosts are dedicated to cordial hospitality and will gladly share information about the area. They offer comfortable bedrooms with king- or queen-size beds. In the morning, enjoy a wonderful breakfast of homemade biscuits, apple fried, fresh country bacon, and eggs. Curly's Corner is a half mile from beautiful Rockome Gardens.

Vrooman Mansion—A Bed & Breakfast Hospitality Establishment

701 EAST TAYLOR, BLOOMINGTON, ILLINOIS 61701

Tel: **(309) 828-8816**
Best Time to Call: **Evening**
Hosts: **John and Nanako McEntire**
Location: **150 mi. S of Chicago**
No. of Rooms: **5**
No. of Private Baths: **1**
Max. No. Sharing Bath: **4**
Double/pb: **$95**
Single/pb: **$85**
Double/sb: **$80**
Single/sb: **$70**

Open: **All year**
Reduced Rates: **5% seniors; 10% families**
Breakfast: **Continental, plus**
Credit Cards: **MC, VISA**
Pets: **No**
Children: **Welcome, over 10**
Smoking: **No**
Social Drinking: **No**
Airport/Station Pickup: **Yes**
Foreign Languages: **Japanese**

Built in 1869, Vrooman Mansion is listed on the National Register of Historic Places. It has 35 rooms and over 10,000 square feet of living space. The mansion's one-acre parklike setting will help you relax from the cares of modern life. Guest rooms are tastefully decorated with antique and period furniture. Each room has its own theme, drawn from the history of the prominent family that graced the home in years gone by. Breakfast is served in the red dining room on the same hand-carved table where former First Lady Eleanor Roosevelt, playwright Rachel Crothers, and many other famous dignitaries have dined.

The Golds

2065 COUNTY ROAD, 525 E, CHAMPAIGN, ILLINOIS 61821

Tel: **(217) 586-4345**
Best Time to Call: **Evenings**
Hosts: **Bob and Rita Gold**
Location: **6 mi. W of Champaign**
No. of Rooms: **3**
Max. No. Sharing Bath: **4**

Double/sb: **$50**
Single/sb: **$45**
Open: **All year**
Reduced Rates: **15% weekly**
Breakfast: **Continental**
Pets: **No**

Children: **Welcome**   Social Drinking: **Permitted**
Smoking: **No**

One of the most beautiful views in Champaign County is yours from the deck of this restored farmhouse. The house is set on six acres surrounded by prime central Illinois farmland. Inside you'll find country antiques, complemented by beautiful wainscoting. An open walnut stairway leads to bedrooms decorated with queen-size beds, handmade quilts, and oriental rugs. Guests can relax by the living room wood stove or enjoy a beverage on the deck. Bob and Rita offer garden fruits and cider for breakfast, served with homemade jams, muffins, and coffee cakes. The Golds is two miles from Lake of the Woods, and 20 minutes from the University of Illinois campus. Shopping and restaurants are also within easy reach.

A City Bed & Breakfast ✪
2150 NORTH LINCOLN PARK WEST, CHICAGO, ILLINOIS 60614

Tel: **(773) 472-0027**   Reduced Rates: **Available**
Host: **Susan Barton**   Breakfast: **Continental**
No. of Rooms: **1**   Pets: **No**
No. of Private Baths: **1**   Children: **Welcome, over 6**
Double/pb: **$70**   Smoking: **No**
Single/pb: **$60**   Social Drinking: **Permitted**
Open: **All year**

Nestled in a vintage apartment building in the heart of Lincoln Park, this bed and breakfast offers a charming yet sophisticated ambiance. Accommodations are spacious and comfortable. Guests are welcomed with a panoramic view of Lincoln Park, Lake Michigan, and Chicago's skyline. A breakfast buffet is Susan's specialty, with a selection of fruit juices, fresh-baked goods, fine jams, and the best coffee. Within walking distance guests can enjoy Lincoln Park's famous zoo, flower conservatory and gardens, jogging and cycling paths, and beaches. Shopping at Water Tower Place, a visit to the John Hancock Center Observatory, or a tour of the Art Institute are only a short bus ride away. Ask Susan about dinner, theater, or the Chicago Symphony.

Lake Shore Drive Bed and Breakfast ✪
P.O. BOX 148643, CHICAGO, ILLINOIS 60614

Tel: **(773) 404-5500**   Single/pb: **$80**
Best Time to Call: **9 AM–11 PM,**   Open: **All year**
   weekdays   Breakfast: **Continental, plus**
Host: **Barbara**   Pets: **No**
Location: **2 mi. N of center Chicago**   Children: **No**
No. of Rooms: **1**   Smoking: **No**
No. of Private Baths: **1**   Social Drinking: **Permitted**
Double/pb: **$90**   Minimum Stay: **3 nights**

Barbara welcomes you to her lovely home in the sky, featuring spectacular wraparound views of Lake Michigan, Lincoln Park, and the Chicago skyline. The romantic guest room features cable TV, air-conditioning, and a dazzling view of the city and the sailboats on Lake Michigan. Lake Michigan's beaches, Lincoln Park Zoo, Wrigley Field, jogging and cycling paths, fine dining, jazz and blues clubs, theaters, and great shopping are all within walking distance of this neighborhood. Excellent public transportation at the corner provides easy access to downtown, Orchestra Hall, the Art Institute, architectural walking tours, Lake Michigan cruises, Northwestern Memorial Hospital, and McCormick Convention Center. Having hosted guests from all over the world, Barbara gives an extra-special welcome to visitors from abroad. Your gracious and charming hostess can update you on all there is to do and see in Chicago.

Old Town Bed & Breakfast
1451 NORTH NORTH PARK AVENUE, CHICAGO, ILLINOIS 60610

Tel: **(312) 440-9268**
Best Time to Call: **Anytime**
Host: **Michael Serritella**
No. of Rooms: **2**
Max. No. Sharing Bath: **4**
Double/sb: **$90**
Open: **All year**

Breakfast: **Continental**
Credit Cards: **AMEX, MC, VISA**
Pets: **No**
Children: **No**
Smoking: **No**
Social Drinking: **Permitted**

This modern town house is furnished with fine art and old family photographs. Each guest room has air-conditioning, a phone, and fully cabled TV. For your convenience there is both on-street and off-street parking. Restaurants, major museums, and public transportation are within walking distance. Enjoy breakfast indoors or, weather permitting, in the private, walled garden. Michael, a former teacher and university administrator, is knowledgeable about the city and surrounding countryside, and is eager to help guests make the most of their trip.

Avery Guest House ✪
606 SOUTH PROSPECT STREET, GALENA, ILLINOIS 61036

Tel: **(815) 777-3883**
Best Time to Call: **9 AM–9 PM**
Hosts: **Gerry and Armon Lamparelli**
Location: **15 mi. E of Dubuque, Iowa**
No. of Rooms: **3**
Max. No. Sharing Bath: **4**
Double/pb: **$90**
Double/sb: **$75**

Open: **All year**
Reduced Rates: **10% Sun.–Thur.**
Breakfast: **Full**
Credit Cards: **DISC, MC, VISA**
Pets: **No**
Children: **Welcome, over 12**
Smoking: **Restricted**
Social Drinking: **Permitted**

Built before the Civil War days and remodeled in the 1920s, the Avery Guest House is located within a few blocks of Galena's main shopping center and historical buildings. After a day of exploring, Avery Guest House is a homey refuge where you can share your experiences with your hosts or other guests. Enjoy the view from our porch swing, watch TV, or join in on a table game. Sleep will come easily on a comfortable queen-size bed in one of our three guest rooms. Breakfast is served in a sunny dining room with a bay window overlooking the Galena River Valley.

The Homeridge Bed and Breakfast
1470 NORTH STATE STREET, JERSEYVILLE, ILLINOIS 62052

Tel: **(618) 498-3442**	Reduced Rates: **Corporate rate $10 less**
Best Time to Call: **Anytime**	**Sun.–Thurs.**
Hosts: **Sue and Howard Landon**	Breakfast: **Full**
Location: **45 mi. N of St. Louis, Mo.**	Credit Cards: **MC, VISA**
No. of Rooms: **4**	Pets: **No**
No. of Private Baths: **4**	Children: **Welcome, over 14**
Double/pb: **$95**	Smoking: **No**
Single/pb: **$85**	Social Drinking: **No**
Open: **All year**	Airport/Station Pickup: **Yes**

The Homeridge, built in 1867, is a beautiful, warm, 14-room Italianate Victorian private home on 18 acres in a comfortable country atmosphere. You'll admire the original woodwork, 12-foot ceilings, and crown molding; a hand-carved, curved stairway leads to the third floor with its 12 × 12-foot cupola or watchtower room. Other details include a 20 × 40-foot swimming pool and an expansive, pillared front porch. Once the estate of Senator Theodore S. Chapman (1891–1960), this B&B is being reviewed for listing in the National Historic Registry. Homeridge is conveniently located between Springfield, Illinois, and St. Louis, Missouri.

Corner George Inn ✪
CORNER OF MAIN AND MILL, P.O. BOX 103, MAEYSTOWN, ILLINOIS 62256

Tel: (618) 458-6660; (800) 458-6020; fax: (618) 458-7770	Open: **All year**
Best Time to Call: **9 AM–9 PM**	Breakfast: **Full**
Hosts: **David and Marcia Braswell**	Credit Cards: **AMEX, DISC, MC, VISA**
Location: **45 min. S of St. Louis**	Pets: **No**
No. of Rooms: 7	Children: **Welcome, over 12**
No. of Private Baths: 7	Smoking: **No**
Double/pb: **$77–$145**	Social Drinking: **Permitted**
	Foreign Languages: **German**

A frontier Victorian structure built in 1884—when it was known as the Maeystown Hotel and Saloon—the Corner George Inn has been painstakingly restored. In addition to the seven antique-filled guest rooms, there are two sitting rooms, a wine cellar, and an elegant ballroom, where David and Marcia serve breakfast. Maeystown is a quaint 19th-century village; guests can tour it on a bicycle built for two or aboard a horse-drawn carriage. Nearby are St. Louis, Fort de Chartres, Fort Kaskaskia, and the scenic bluff road that hugs the Mississippi.

The Poor Farm Bed & Breakfast ✪
POOR FARM ROAD, MOUNT CARMEL, ILLINOIS 62863
poorfarm@midwest.net

Tel: **(800) 646-3276; (618) 262-4663;** fax: **(618) 262-8199**	Reduced Rates: **Available**
Hosts: **Liz and John Stelzer**	Breakfast: **Full**
Location: **1 mi. N of Mount Carmel**	Other Meals: **Available**
No. of Rooms: 5	Credit Cards: **AMEX, DISC, MC, VISA**
No. of Private Baths: 5	Pets: **No**
Double/pb: **$45–$55**	Children: **Welcome**
Single/pb: **$45–$55**	Smoking: **Restricted**
Suites: **$85–$95**	Social Drinking: **Permitted**
Open: **All year**	Airport Pickup: **Yes**

Named for its previous use—as a 19th-century shelter for the homeless—this stately, 35-room brick landmark offers you a gracious glimpse of yesteryear with its quiet, country charm. The Poor Farm is adjacent to a 25-acre county park and within sight of an 18-hole golf course. Red Hill State Park, Beall Woods Conservation Area and Nature Preserve, a swimming pool, driving range, tennis courts, boating, and fishing are only minutes away. Historic old New Harmony and Riverboat gaming in Evansville, Indiana, are a 45-minute drive away. These amenities, plus your hosts' Midwestern hospitality, make this B&B the "inn" place to stay.

Old Church House Inn B&B ✪

1416 EAST MOSSVILLE ROAD, MOSSVILLE (PEORIA), ILLINOIS 61552

Tel: **(309) 579-2300**	Open: **All year**
Best Time to Call: **9 AM–9 PM CST**	Reduced Rates: **Weekly**
Hosts: **Dean and Holly Ramseyer**	Breakfast: **Continental, Plus**
Location: **On Peoria's Northside**	Other Meals: **Available**
No. of Rooms: **2**	Credit Cards: **DISC, MC, VISA**
No. of Private Baths: **1**	Pets: **No**
Max. No. Sharing Bath: **4**	Children: **By arrangement**
Double/pb: **$109**	Smoking: **No**
Double/sb: **$69**	Social Drinking: **No**

Nestled in the scenic Illinois River Valley on Peoria's Northside, Old Church House Inn welcomes you to the plush warmth of the Victorian era. Curl up to a crackling fire, take tea in the flower garden, sink deep into the queen-size featherbeds, and enjoy being pampered. Listed on the National Historic American Building Survey, this 1869 church still boasts soaring 18-foot ceilings, tall arched windows, and an "elevated library." Victorian antiques, period furnishings, pedestal sinks, colorful quilts, terry robes, and fine soaps allow guests to relax in luxury. Swiss chocolates, a house specialty, are placed on pillows during chamber service. Bicycling and cross-country skiing on the Rock Island Trail are just five minutes away, while nearby Peoria features riverboat cruises, cultural attractions, antiquing, and a full range of dining choices to suit your taste!

Round-Robin Guesthouse ✪

231 EAST MAPLE AVENUE, MUNDELEIN, ILLINOIS 60060
members.aol.com/rndrobin

Tel: **(800) 301-7664**	Open: **All year**
Hosts: **George and Laura Loffredo**	Reduced Rates: **10% seniors, families**
Location: **38 mi. NW of Chicago**	Breakfast: **Full**
No. of Rooms: **6**	Credit Cards: **AMEX, MC, VISA**
No. of Private Baths: **3**	Pets: **No**
Max. No. Sharing Bath: **4**	Children: **Welcome**
Double/pb: **$65**	Smoking: **No**
Double/sb: **$50–$65**	Social Drinking: **Permitted**
Suite: **$130**	

This handsome red Victorian with white trim takes its name from the letters circulated by your hosts' relatives for more than 70 years; to encourage you to write friends and family, George and Laura will provide you with paper, pen, and stamps. The many local diversions ensure that you'll have plenty to write about. Six Flags Great America, the Volo Auto Museum, and the antique village of Long Grove are barely fifteen minutes away by car, and you're never far from golf, swimming, and horseback riding. During the summer, the Chicago Symphony is in residence at nearby Ravinia Park. Or you can enjoy Laura's renditions of classical and ragtime music on the piano. You'll wake up to the aroma of fresh-brewed coffee; coffee cake, muffins, and homemade jam are served between 7:30 and 9 AM.

The Ancient Pines Bed & Breakfast ✪
2015 PARLEY STREET, NAUVOO, ILLINOIS 62354

Tel: **(217) 453-2767**	Open: **All year**
Best Time to Call: **9 AM–9 PM**	Reduced Rates: **15% weekly**
Host: **Genevieve Simmens**	Breakfast: **Full**
Location: **225 mi. SW of Chicago**	Pets: **Sometimes**
No. of Rooms: **3**	Children: **Welcome**
Max. No. Sharing Bath: **3**	Smoking: **No**
Double/sb: **$49**	Social Drinking: **Permitted**
Single/sb: **$45**	

This turn-of-the-century brick home is rich in detail inside and out, from the stained glass windows and etched-glass front door to the tin ceilings, open staircase, and carved woodwork. Wander through herb and flower gardens, play croquet on the lawn, or enjoy music or chess in the library. Local attractions include wineries (Nauvoo holds its own grape festival), Civil War reenactments, historic Mormon homes, and Nauvoo State Park. Whatever your itinerary, you'll wake to the aroma of baking bread, served with eggs and sausage or ham. Special low-cholesterol menus are available upon request.

The Kaufmann House ✪
1641 HAMPSHIRE, QUINCY, ILLINOIS 62301

Tel: **(217) 223-2502**	Reduced Rates: **After 4th night**
Hosts: **Emery and Bettie Kaufmann**	Breakfast: **Continental, Plus**
Location: **100 mi. W of Springfield**	Pets: **No**
No. of Rooms: **3**	Children: **Welcome (crib)**
No. of Private Baths: **3**	Smoking: **No**
Double/pb: **$70**	Social Drinking: **No**
Single/pb: **$65**	Airport/Station Pickup: **Yes**
Open: **All year**	

History buffs will remember Quincy, set right on the Mississippi River, as the scene of the famous Lincoln–Douglas debates, while architecture buffs will be attracted to the town's feast of Victorian styles—Greek Revival, Gothic Revival, Italianate, and Richardsonian. The Kaufmann House, built over 100 years ago, sits under huge maples, housing antiques and welcoming guests to the Robin Green Room, the Gray Antique Room, and the Patriot Country Suite. The suite has a sitting room, trundle bed, bath, and balcony. Guests may enjoy breakfast in the Ancestor's Room, on a stone patio, or at a picnic table under the trees.

They are invited to play the piano, watch TV, or enjoy popcorn by the fire. The Kaufmanns describe themselves as "Christians who have love for God, people, nature, and life."

Country Dreams Bed & Breakfast ✪
3410 PARK LANE, ROCHESTER, ILLINOIS 62563
muhsl@fgi.net; www.softfoundry.com/countrydreams

Tel: **(217) 498-9210**
Hosts: **Ralph and Kay Muhs**
Location: **10 mi. E of Springfield**
No. of Rooms: **4**
No. of Private Baths: **4**
Double/pb: **$75**
Suite: **$130**
Open: **All year**
Reduced Rates: **Available**

Breakfast: **Full, weekends; Continental, weekdays**
Other Meals: **Available**
Credit Cards: **AMEX, MC, VISA**
Pets: **No**
Children: **Welcome, over 12**
Smoking: **No**
Social Drinking: **Permitted**

Built in 1997 and located on 16 pristine acres, Country Dreams Bed & Breakfast is more than a cozy comfortable hideaway. Guests can stroll around the small lake and watch the swans, geese, and ducks, or just relax on the huge deck and savor the sights, sounds, and smells of the unpolluted rural countryside. There are acres of green grass, fruit trees, flowers by the thousands, and your hosts' own century-old cemetery. Country Dreams is conveniently close to Springfield, the capital city, yet rural in all the best ways. All of the guest rooms are different. Two have TV/VCR combinations, one has a fireplace and whirlpool bath, and three have phones. Ralph and Kay built the house from the ground up. Kay is a dietitian and Ralph is a retired elementary school teacher turned building contractor.

Top o' the Morning ✪
1505 19TH AVENUE, ROCK ISLAND, ILLINOIS 61201

Tel: **(309) 786-3513**
Best Time to Call: **After 5 PM**
Hosts: **Sam and Peggy Doak**
Location: **1½ mi. from Rte. 92, 18th Ave. exit**
No. of Rooms: **3**
No. of Private Baths: **3**

Double/pb: **$60–$80**
Open: **All year**
Breakfast: **Full**
Pets: **No**
Children: **Welcome**
Smoking: **Permitted**
Social Drinking: **Permitted**

Sam and Peggy welcome you to their country estate, set on a bluff overlooking the Mississippi River, near the center of the Quad Cities area. The 18-room mansion is situated at the end of a winding drive on three acres of lawn, orchards, and gardens. The guest rooms, graced with lovely chandeliers and oriental rugs, command a spectacular view of the cities and river. The parlor, with its grand piano and fireplace, is an inviting place to relax. Local attractions are Mississippi River boat rides, riverboat casinos, Rock Island Arsenal, Black Hawk State Park, Augustana College, and St. Ambrose University.

Country Charm Inn ✪
15165 QUIGLEY ROAD, SYCAMORE, ILLINOIS 60178

Tel: **(815) 895-4797**
Best Time to Call: **Anytime**
Hosts: **Howard and Donna Petersen**
Location: **55 mi. W of Chicago**
No. of Rooms: **3**
No. of Private Baths: **3**
Double/pb: **$55–$75**
Open: **All year**
Reduced Rates: **On a weekly basis**

Breakfast: **Continental, weekdays; full, weekends**
Pets: **No**
Children: **Welcome**
Smoking: **No**
Social Drinking: **No**
Minimum Stay: **Only for local weekend events**

On a tree-topped knoll in rich farming country stands this rambling, turn-of-the-century stucco home. Howard and Donna's comfortable accommodations blend understated elegance with casual warmth and friendliness. Enjoy a full country breakfast on the cozy front porch; house specialties range from egg-cheese dishes and designer pancakes to peach cobblers and pecan roll rings. Then lounge around the sunken fireplace, watch a movie on the large-screen TV with surround sound, borrow a book from the loft library, or roam around the farm. Champ, the trick horse, sends personal note cards to children telling about his barnyard pals, including llamas and another horse. For those planning to exchange vows, the Petersens have built a charming wedding chapel on the property.

INDIANA

Chesterton

Marion

Rockville

Indianapolis

Paoli

Gray Goose Inn
350 INDIAN BOUNDARY ROAD, CHESTERTON, INDIANA 46304

Tel: **(800) 521-5127; (219) 926-5781**
Best Time to Call: **9 AM–9 PM**
Hosts: **Tim Wilk and Charles Ramsey**
Location: **60 mi. E of Chicago**
No. of Rooms: **8**
No. of Private Baths: **8**
Double/pb: **$80–$156**
Suites: **$138–$156**

Open: **All year**
Reduced Rates: **10% seniors**
Breakfast: **Full**
Credit Cards: **AMEX, DISC, MC, VISA**
Pets: **No**
Children: **Welcome, over 12**
Smoking: **Restricted**
Social Drinking: **Permitted**

Elegant accommodations await you in this English country-style house overlooking a 30-acre lake. Guest rooms feature four-poster beds, fine linens, and thick, fluffy towels. Some rooms are decorated in Williamsburg style, some have fireplaces and Jacuzzi. Enjoy a quiet moment in the common rooms, or relax with a cup of coffee in the scenic wicker room. Take long walks beside shady oaks, feed the Canada geese and wild ducks. The Gray Goose is five minutes from Dunes State and National Lakeshore Parks. Swimming, hiking, and fishing sites on Lake Michigan are all within easy reach. Dining and weekend entertainment are within walking distance.

The Tranquil Cherub ✪
2164 NORTH CAPITOL AVENUE, INDIANAPOLIS, INDIANA 46202-1251

Tel: **(317) 923-9036**	Reduced Rates: **Weekly**
Best Time to Call: **Evenings**	Breakfast: **Full**
Hosts: **Thom and Barbara Feit**	Credit Cards: **AMEX, MC, VISA**
Location: **¹/₂ mi. from I-65 Exit 115**	Pets: **No**
No. of Rooms: **4**	Children: **Welcome, over 14**
No. of Private Baths: **4**	Smoking: **Restricted**
Double/pb: **$65–$75**	Social Drinking: **Permitted**
Suite: **$80–$85**	Airport Pickup: **Yes**
Open: **All year**	

From the central location of this B&B, you are only minutes from downtown and all the exciting things Indianapolis has to offer. As you enter the foyer, the beautifully crafted oak staircase and pier mirror will draw your eye. Lace curtains, Beardsley prints, Art Deco and Mission-style furniture decorate the rooms. Guest rooms are professionally decorated and offer their own personalities. In the morning the aroma of freshly brewed coffee, breakfast breads, and offerings such as French toast or a strata will waft to your room. Breakfast is served in the dining room, where beveled glass accents the oak paneling and fireplace. Weather permitting, breakfast is served on the back deck. Outside, the perennial gardens and lily ponds enhance this secluded nook in the midst of an urban setting.

Golden Oak Bed & Breakfast
809 WEST FOURTH STREET, MARION, INDIANA 46952

Tel: **(765) 651-9950**	Open: **All year**
Best Time to Call: **9 AM–9 PM**	Breakfast: **Full**
Hosts: **Lois and Dave Lutes**	Credit Cards: **AMEX, MC, VISA**
Location: **60 mi. N of Indianapolis**	Pets: **No**
No. of Rooms: **4**	Children: **Welcome**
No. of Private Baths: **4**	Smoking: **No**
Double/sb: **$65**	Social Drinking: **Permitted**
Single/sb: **$60**	

Enjoy the elegance of this beautifully restored two-story home built in the 1890s. Inside, the rooms glow with the rich oak woodwork that inspires this B&B's name. Throughout the house, you'll see hand-crocheted items; similar ones are for sale in your hosts' gift shop. The James Dean Gallery and Historical Museum, the Mississinewa Battlefield, beaches, golf courses, and antique shops are among the area's attractions. For your dining pleasure, the Hostess House of Marion is within walking distance.

Big Locust Farm ✪
3295 WEST COUNTY ROAD 25 SOUTH, PAOLI, INDIANA 47454

Tel: **(812) 723-4856**	Open: **All year**
Best Time to Call: **8 PM**	Reduced Rates: **$5 after first night**
Hosts: **Joe and Glenda Lindley**	Breakfast: **Full**
Location: **50 mi. NW of Louisville,**	Credit Cards: **MC, VISA**
Kentucky	Pets: **No**
No. of Rooms: **2**	Children: **By arrangement**
No. of Private Baths: **2**	Smoking: **No**
Double/pb: **$70**	Social Drinking: **Permitted**
Single/pb: **$60**	

A warm country welcome awaits you at Big Locust Farm, a new brick country Victorian home that sits on 60 acres. Inside, the flooring and woodwork are made of oak, and central heat and air assure guests' comfort. The rooms are decorated with lace curtains, comfortable beds, and antiques. Your day will begin with a hearty breakfast that may include egg and meat dishes, breads or muffins, fruit, juice, and coffee. Enjoy a stroll in the herb, rose, and perennial gardens or rest on the large front porch while the world goes by. Wander along the limestone bottom creek or through the woods. Local attractions include antique shops, Frenck Lick Railroad and Winery, West Baden Dome, Patoka Lake, and much more.

Suits Us ✪
514 NORTH COLLEGE, ROCKVILLE, INDIANA 47872

Tel: **(765) 569-5660; (888) 4SUITS-US**	Open: **All year**
Hosts: **Marty and Bev Rose**	Breakfast: **Full**
Location: **50 mi. W of Indianapolis**	Pets: **No**
No. of Rooms: **4**	Children: **Welcome**
No. of Private Baths: **4**	Smoking: **No**
Double/pb: **$55–$75**	Social Drinking: **Permitted**
Suites: **$125, sleeps 2–6**	

This classic plantation-style home, with its widow's walk and generous front porch, dates to the early 1880s. The Strausses, a locally prominent family, bought the house about 20 years later; their overnight guests included Woodrow Wilson, Annie Oakley, James Whitcomb Riley, and John Lewis. Today Marty and Bev extend their hospitality to you. All guest rooms have a TV and VCR. Guests are invited to choose a movie from the video library, or use one of the bikes to explore the area. Turkey Run Park is 10 miles away, while five universities—Indiana State, DePauw, Wabash, St. Mary-of-the-Woods, and Rose-Hulman—are within a 30-mile radius. Also, Rockville sponsors its own annual event, the Covered Bridge Festival.

For key to listings, see inside front or back cover.

✪ This star means that rates are guaranteed through December 31, 1999, to any guest making a reservation as a result of reading about the B&B in *Bed & Breakfast U.S.A.*—1999 edition.

Important! To avoid misunderstandings, always ask about cancellation policies when booking.

Please enclose a self-addressed, stamped, business-size envelope when contacting reservation services.

For more details on what you can expect in a B&B, see Chapter 1.

Always mention *Bed & Breakfast U.S.A.* when making reservations!

We want to hear from you! Use the form on page 593.

IOWA

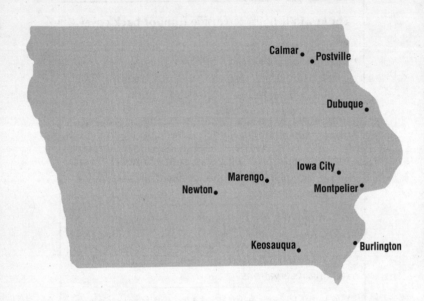

The Schramm House Bed & Breakfast ✪
616 COLUMBIA STREET, BURLINGTON, IOWA 52601

Tel: **(800) 683-7117; fax: (319) 754-0373**
Hosts: **Sandy and Bruce Morrison**
No. of Rooms: **3**
No. of Private Baths: **3**
Double p/b: **$65–$75**
Open: **All year**
Reduced Rates: **10% seniors**

Breakfast: **Full**
Credit Cards: **AMEX, DISC, MC, VISA**
Pets: **No**
Children: **Welcome**
Smoking: **No**
Social Drinking: **Permitted**
Airport/Station Pickup: **Yes**

Step into the past when you enter this restored 1870s Victorian home located in the heart of the historical district. Unique architectural features and antique furnishings create the mood of a bygone era. Experience Burlington hospitality while having lemonade on the porch or tea by the fire with your hosts. Walk to the Mississippi River, antique shops, restaurants, and more. A formal breakfast is served in the dining room. Weather permitting, the sunporch offers a bright and cheerful alternative for your morning meal.

Calmar Guesthouse
103 NORTH STREET, R.R. 1, BOX 206, CALMAR, IOWA 52132

Tel: **(319) 562-3851**
Host: **Lucille Kruse**
Location: **10 mi. S of Decorah**
No. of Rooms: **5**
Max. No. Sharing Bath: **5**
Double/sb: **$40–$45**
Open: **All year**

Breakfast: **Full**
Pets: **No**
Children: **Welcome**
Smoking: **No**
Social Drinking: **Permitted**
Airport/Station Pickup: **Yes**

A recent guest reports that "The Calmar Guesthouse is a spacious, lovely, newly remodeled Victorian home located on the edge of town. The atmosphere is enhanced by the friendly, charming manner of Lucille, who made us feel right at home. The rooms were comfortable, private, and pretty. After a peaceful night's sleep, we were served a delicious breakfast of fresh farm eggs with ham and cheeses, croissants with butter and jam, homemade cinnamon rolls, and coffee. I would recommend it to anyone visiting the area." Nearby points of interest include Lake Meyer, the world's smallest church, and Spillville, home of hand-carved Bily Bros. Clocks.

Juniper Hill Farm Bed & Breakfast Inn ✪
15325 BUDD ROAD, DUBUQUE, IOWA 52002
JHBandB@aol.com

Tel: **(319) 582-4405; (800) 572-1449**
Best Time to Call: **8 AM–10 PM**

Hosts: **Bill and Ruth McEllhiney**
Location: **3.75 mi. NW of Dubuque**

No. of Rooms: **3**
No. of Private Baths: **3**
Double/pb: **$70**
Suites: **$90–$130**
Open: **All year**
Reduced Rates: **Available**
Breakfast: **Full**

Credit Cards: **MC, VISA**
Pets: **No**
Children: **Welcome, over 6**
Smoking: **No**
Social Drinking: **Permitted**
Minimum Stay: **2 nights, weekends**

Juniper Hill Farm Bed & Breakfast Inn is nestled in the Mississippi River Hills on 40 acres of woods, meadows, and hiking trails, with a fishing pond and a spectacular valley view enjoyed from the year-round outdoor hot tub. The shake-sided cottage has a modified country decor with white-painted wood walls showcasing the soft colors throughout. The Inn is near Heritage Train—a rails-to-trails path used for biking or cross-country skiing—and adjacent to Sundown ski area, making it the only Iowa B&B where you can ski to the front door. Ruth and Bill will gladly help plan your exploration of surrounding areas.

The Richards House
1492 LOCUST STREET, DUBUQUE, IOWA 52001

Tel: **(319) 557-1492**
Best Time to Call: **Anytime**
Host: **Michelle Delaney**
No. of Rooms: **6**
No. of Private Baths: **4**
Max. No. Sharing Bath: **2**

Double/pb: **$45–$85**
Double/sb: **$40–$65**
Suites: **$50–$95**
Open: **All year**
Reduced Rates: **40% Sun.–Thurs.**
Breakfast: **Full**

Credit Cards: **AMEX, DC, DISC, MC, VISA**
Pets: **Sometimes**
Children: **Welcome (crib)**

Smoking: **Restricted**
Social Drinking: **Permitted**
Airport/Station Pickup: **Yes**

Inside and out, this four-story Victorian is a feast for the eyes, with its gabled roof, stained glass windows, gingerbread trim, and elaborate woodwork. Rooms are furnished in period style. Guests can continue their journey back in time with a ride on the Fenelon Place Cable Car, the shortest inclined railway in the country. Then it's time to pay respects to another form of transportation at the Woodward Riverboat Museum. You're welcome to use the kitchen for light snacks; in the morning, Michelle takes over, setting out fresh fruit, waffles, pancakes, sausage, and homemade breads.

Two Bella Vista Place Bed & Breakfast ✪
2 BELLA VISTA PLACE, IOWA CITY, IOWA 52245

Tel: **(319) 338-4129**
Host: **Daissy P. Owen**
Location: **1 mi. from Highway 80, Exit 244**
No. of Rooms: **4**
Max. No. Sharing Bath: **4**
Double/pb: **$85–$95**
Double/sb: **$60**

Single/sb: **$45–$55**
Open: **All year**
Reduced Rates: **Available**
Breakfast: **Full**
Pets: **No**
Smoking: **No**
Social Drinking: **Permitted**
Foreign Languages: **Spanish**

This lovely, air-conditioned 1920s home is tastefully decorated with antiques and artifacts Daissy has collected on her travels to Latin America and Europe. Accommodations include two suites with TVs, one with a kitchen, and two rooms that share a bath. Guests can relax in the comfort of their rooms or join the company of other guests in the living room, on the front porch, or enjoying the view of the river from the deck. You will be impressed with Daissy's hospitality, hearty breakfast, and famous coffee. Located close to downtown, the University of Iowa, Amana Colonies, Kalona, and the Hoover Library.

The Golden Haug ✪
517 EAST WASHINGTON, IOWA CITY, IOWA 52240

Tel: **(319) 338-6452; 354-4284**
Hosts: **Nila Haug and Dennis Nowotny**
Location: **2 mi. from I-80, Exit 244**
No. of Rooms: **4**
No. of Private Baths: **4**
Double/pb: **$70–$95**
Single/pb: **$68–$95**
Double/sb: **$85–100**

Open: **All year**
Reduced Rates: **Available**
Breakfast: **Full**
Pets: **No**
Children: **Welcome**
Smoking: **No**
Social Drinking: **Permitted**
Airport Pickup: **Yes**

Built in the 1920s, this Arts and Crafts house has been restored and updated to provide comfortable accommodations and modern conveniences such as central air and whirlpool tubs. Visitors can retreat to the privacy of their rooms or enjoy camaraderie with others. Guests have commented that "the location is ideal, the beds comfortable, and the food fantastic." The convenient downtown location is within walking distance of the University of Iowa, shopping, restaurants, and houses of worship.

Mason House Inn of Bentonsport ✪

ROUTE 2, BOX 237, KEOSAUQUA, IOWA 52565

Tel: **(319) 592-3133; (800) 592-3133**
Hosts: **Sheral and William McDermet**
Location: **40 mi. SE of Ottumwa**
No. of Rooms: **9**
No. of Private Baths: **5**
Max. No. Sharing Bath: **3**
Double/pb: **$74**
Single/pb: **$54**
Double/sb: **$54–$59**

Single/sb: **$44–$49**
Open: **All year**
Breakfast: **Full**
Other Meals: **Available**
Credit Cards: **MC, VISA**
Pets: **Sometimes**
Children: **Welcome**
Smoking: **No**
Social Drinking: **Permitted**

Mason House Inn was built next to the Des Moines River by Mormon artisans en route to Salt Lake City. The three-story Georgian house contains 26 rooms. It is the only steamboat inn, built as such, still hosting persons in Iowa. The Inn has the only fold-down copper bathtub in the state. Sheral and Bill purchased the Inn in 1989 and have done extensive remodeling, allowing for ground-level rooms with private baths. Guests will find a full cookie jar in every room. The entire village is on the National Register of Historic Places. Iowa's oldest courthouse is six miles to the east. Bill served as a pastor for local congregations for 29 years, and Sheral was a manager for a deli before moving to Bentonsport.

Loy's Farm Bed & Breakfast ○
2077 KK AVENUE, MARENGO, IOWA 52301

Tel: **(319) 642-7787**	Double/sb: **$55–$65**
Best Time to Call: **7 AM–9:30 PM**	Single/sb: **$45**
Hosts: **Loy and Robert Walker**	Open: **All year**
Location: **3 mi. from I-80, Exit 216 N**	Breakfast: **Full**
No. of Rooms: **3**	Other Meals: **Available**
No. of Private Baths: **1**	Pets: **If caged**
Max. No. Sharing Bath: **4**	Children: **Welcome**
Double/pb: **$55–$65**	Smoking: **No**
Single/pb: **$45**	Social Drinking: **Permitted**

The Walkers invite you to visit their contemporary farm home in the heartland of rural Iowa. Enjoy the peaceful surroundings of a large lawn, gardens, and patio. The rooms are furnished in modern and refinished pieces. Guests are welcome to relax in the family room by the fire or to stop by the recreation room for a game of shuffleboard or pool and a treat from the snack bar. A farm tour gives you the chance to see the farm facilities and operations. Each morning enjoy a typical farm breakfast with a gourmet touch. Visit the historic villages of the Amana Colonies, originally developed as a communal system. The Amana Colonies are Iowa's largest tourist attraction. Tanger Mall, 64 designer outlet stores, and twelve restaurants (six that serve German food) are all located nearby. Herbert Hoover's birthplace, the Kalona Amish, Brucemore Mansion, and Iowa City are all just a short drive away.

Varners' Caboose Bed & Breakfast ○
204 EAST SECOND STREET, P.O. BOX 10, MONTPELIER, IOWA 52759

Tel: **(319) 381-3652**	Open: **All year**
Best Time to Call: **Afternoons**	Breakfast: **Full**
Hosts: **Bob and Nancy Varner**	Pets: **Sometimes**
Location: **11 mi. W of Davenport**	Children: **Welcome**
No. of Rooms: **1**	Smoking: **No**
No. of Private Baths: **1**	Social Drinking: **Permitted**
Double/pb: **$60**	Airport/Station Pickup: **Yes**

Bob and Nancy offer their guests the unique experience of staying in a genuine Rock Island Line caboose. Their home, located close to the Mississippi, was the original Montpelier Depot, and the caboose is a self-contained unit with bath, shower, and kitchen set on its own track behind the house. It sleeps four, with a queen-size bed and two singles in the cupola. The rate is increased to $70 when more than two occupy the caboose. A fully prepared egg casserole, fruit, homemade breads, juice, and coffee or tea are left in the kitchen to be enjoyed at your leisure. Enjoy this quiet town while being a few minutes downstream from the heart of the Quad Cities.

LaCorsette Maison Inn ✪
629 FIRST AVENUE EAST, NEWTON, IOWA 50208

Tel: **(515) 792-6833**
Host: **Kay Owen**
Location: **25 mi. E of Des Moines**
No. of Rooms: **7**
No. of Private Baths: **7**
Double/pb: **$70–$185**
Suites: **$85–$185**
Open: **All year**

Breakfast: **Full**
Other Meals: **Available**
Pets: **Sometimes**
Children: **By arrangement**
Smoking: **No**
Social Drinking: **Permitted**
Airport/Station Pickup: **Yes**

Bringing a touch of Spanish architecture to the American heartland, this 21-room mansion has all the hallmarks of the Mission style, from its stucco walls and red-tiled roof to its interior oak woodwork. Certain nights of the week, Kay doubles as a chef, preparing elaborate five-course dinners for as many as 57 scheduled guests; the first caller to make reservations selects the entree, and a house tour precedes the meal. Overnight guests wake up to a full breakfast accented by the herbs and vegetables Kay grows in the backyard. If you want to work off the calories, tennis courts and a pool are in the area.

Old Shepherd House ✪
256 W. TILDEN STREET, BOX 251, POSTVILLE, IOWA 52162

Tel: **(319) 864-3452**
Best Time to Call: **10 AM–10 PM**
Host: **Rosalyn Krambeer**
Location: **25 mi. SE of Decorah**
No. of Rooms: **4**
No. of Private Baths: **4**
Double/pb: **$50**

Single/sb: **$40**
Open: **All year**
Breakfast: **Full**
Pets: **Sometimes**
Children: **Welcome**
Smoking: **Restricted**
Social Drinking: **Permitted**

Postville, a town of 1500 with four quaint crafts shops and a fabulous antique emporium, is in northeast Iowa in an area known as the state's

Little Switzerland. Within a thirty-mile radius you can canoe the Iowa
River, or visit sites like the Vesterheim Museum, Effigy Mounds, Villa
Louis, Spook Cave, and Bily Brothers clock museum. Shepherd House,
built in the early 1880s, is furnished entirely with antique and Victorian
pieces. Your hostess is an interior decorator, and she's filled her home
with unusual window treatments, restored trunks, and crafts work.

For key to listings, see inside front or back cover.

✪ This star means that rates are guaranteed
through December 31, 1999, to any guest making
a reservation as a result of reading about the B&B
in *Bed & Breakfast U.S.A.*—1999 edition.

Important! To avoid misunderstandings, always ask
about cancellation policies when booking.

Please enclose a self-addressed, stamped, business-size envelope when contacting reservation
services.

For more details on what you can expect in a
B&B, see Chapter 1.

Always mention *Bed & Breakfast U.S.A.* when making reservations!

We want to hear from you! Use the form on page
593.

KANSAS

Wakeeney •

Abilene •

Tonganoxie •

Balfours' House
940 1900 AVENUE, ABILENE, KANSAS 67410
www.abileneks.com

Tel: **(785) 263-4262**
Hosts: **Gilbert and Marie Balfour**
Location: **2¼ mi. S of Abilene**
Suites: **$75–$180**
Open: **All year**
Breakfast: **Full**

Credit Cards: **AMEX, MC, VISA**
Pets: **By arrangement**
Children: **By arrangement**
Smoking: **No**
Social Drinking: **Permitted**

Stay in a relaxing contemporary country home landscaped into the hillside just outside of town, with breathtaking views from horizon to horizon. Enjoy flower beds and a grapevine-covered patio. Amenities include private entrance, patios, TV, VCR, stereo, fireplace, indoor pool, and spa.

Almeda's Bed and Breakfast Inn ✪
220 SOUTH MAIN, TONGANOXIE, KANSAS 66086

Tel: **(913) 845-2295**	Double/sb: **$30**
Best Time to Call: **Before 9 AM;**	Single/sb: **$25**
evenings	Suite: **$65**
Hosts: **Almeda and Richard Tinberg**	Open: **All year**
Location: **20 mi. W of Kansas City**	Breakfast: **Continental, plus**
No. of Rooms: **6**	Pets: **No**
No. of Private Baths: **2**	Children: **Welcome**
Max. No. Sharing Bath: **4**	Smoking: **Restricted**
Double/pb: **$40**	Social Drinking: **Permitted**
Single/pb: **$35**	

This small-town B&B has a tranquil, friendly atmosphere. An inn for decades—during World War I it attained coast-to-coast fame as the Myers Hotel—it was designated a historic landmark in 1983. The rooms are decorated with country flair, accented by antiques from Almeda's collection. Guests may sip a cup of coffee by the stone bar in the room used as a bus stop in the thirties; the movie *Bus Stop* was inspired by this site. A plaque outside the dining room tells the story of the hotel.

Thistle Hill Bed & Breakfast ✪
ROUTE 1, BOX 93, WAKEENEY, KANSAS 67672
www.bbonline.com/ks/thistlehill/

Tel: **(785) 743-2644**	Breakfast: **Full**
Hosts: **Dave and Mary Hendricks**	Credit Cards: **MC, VISA**
Location: **1½ mi. from I-70, Exit 120**	Pets: **No**
No. of Rooms: **3**	Children: **Welcome**
No. of Private Baths: **3**	Smoking: **Restricted**
Double/pb: **$59–$75**	Social Drinking: **Permitted**
Single/pb: **$45–$49**	Airport/Station Pickup: **Yes**
Open: **All year**	

Secluded and rustic, Thistle Hill is a cedar farm home, centrally located between Kansas City and Denver. Guests will enjoy the peaceful Western Kansas prairie that surrounds them. Spring and summer visitors are invited to explore the many cottage-style flower and herb gardens or stroll the walking trails in the 60 acres of prairie grasses and wildflowers. In the fall you may want to go antiquing, bird watch, or relax in the hot tub. Our central location allows you to tour Sternberg Museum, Cottonwood Ranch, Castle Rock, and Cedar Bluff Reservoir. During the holiday season, you'll certainly want to include a trip into Wakeeney to view the large display of Christmas lights.

KENTUCKY

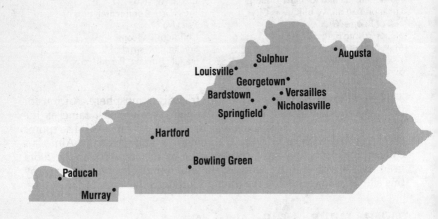

Augusta White House Inn B&B ✪
307 MAIN STREET, AUGUSTA, KENTUCKY 41002

Tel: **(606) 756-2004**
Best Time to Call: **6–10 PM**
Host: **Rebecca Spencer**
Location: **50 mi. SE of Cincinnati, Ohio**
No. of Rooms: **5**
Max. No. Sharing Bath: **4**
Double/sb: **$79**
Single/sb: **$59**
Guest Cottage: **$75**

Open: **All year**
Reduced Rates: **Available**
Breakfast: **Full**
Credit Cards: **AMEX, DISC, MC, VISA**
Pets: **No**
Children: **No**
Smoking: **No**
Social Drinking: **No**
Airport/Station Pickup: **Yes**

AWHIBB is located in the downtown section of historic Augusta, in a beautifully restored, two-story brick structure (the Buerger Tin Shop, circa 1840) that combines Victorian elegance and Southern hospitality. Comfortably sized rooms with flowered wallpaper and high, crown-molded ceilings may well remind you of your grandparents' home, albeit with all modern conveniences. In addition to their own room, guests have use of the parlor, formal dining and living rooms, and sheltered porch. Breakfast includes fresh-baked bread with an array of gourmet entrees and side dishes to please even the most discriminating palates. Antique shops and excellent restaurants are a short stroll away.

Beautiful Dreamer
EAST STEPHEN FOSTER AVENUE, BARDSTOWN, KENTUCKY 40004

Tel: **(800) 811-8312**	Open: **All year**
Host: **Lynell Ginter**	Breakfast: **Full**
Location: **30 mi. SE of Louisville**	Credit Cards: **MC, VISA**
No. of Rooms: **4**	Pets: **No**
No. of Private Baths: **4**	Children: **Welcome, over 8**
Double/pb: **$85**	Smoking: **No**

Decorated with antiques and cherry furniture, this Federal-style home, circa 1895, is located in the historic district. Relax on the porch and enjoy a breathtaking view of My Old Kentucky Home, or show off your talent on the baby grand piano. The Beautiful Dreamer Room has a double Jacuzzi, the Captain's Room has a fireplace and a single Jacuzzi, and the Stephen Foster Room is wheelchair accessible, featuring a shower with rails and a double sink that can accommodate a wheelchair. All rooms are air-conditioned, have queen-size beds, and include a hearty breakfast. Music lovers will be happy to know that this B&B is within walking distance of *The Stephen Foster Story*.

Jailer's Inn ✪
111 WEST STEPHEN FOSTER AVENUE, BARDSTOWN, KENTUCKY 40004

Tel: **(502) 348-5551; (800) 948-5551**	Reduced Rates: **Available**
Best Time to Call: **10 AM–5 PM**	Breakfast: **Full**
Host: **C. Paul McCoy**	Credit Cards: **AMEX, DISC, MC, VISA**
Location: **35 mi. S of Louisville**	Pets: **No**
No. of Rooms: **6**	Children: **Welcome**
No. of Private Baths: **6**	Smoking: **No**
Double/pb: **$65–$100**	Social Drinking: **Permitted**
Open: **Mar.–Dec.**	Station pickup: **Yes**

For the ultimate in unusual experiences, spend the night in "jail" without having committed a crime. Built in 1819, this former jail originally housed prisoners upstairs, and has been completely remodeled and furnished with fine antiques and oriental rugs. An adjacent building, once used as the women's cell, has been transformed into a charming suite, where bunk beds are suspended from a brick wall and the decor is black-and-white checks instead of stripes. The town is famous for *The Stephen Foster Story*, an outdoor musical production. Take time to visit the Getz Museum of Whiskey History and a Civil War museum, and take a tour of My Old Kentucky Home conducted by guides in antebellum costumes. Two guest rooms have Jacuzzi tubs.

Alpine Lodge ✪
5310 MORGANTOWN ROAD, BOWLING GREEN, KENTUCKY 42101

Tel: **(502) 843-4846; (888) 444-3791, #6293**	Guest Cottage: **$150, sleeps 6**
Best Time to Call: **9 AM–9 PM**	Suites: **$75–$95**
Hosts: **Dr. and Mrs. David Livingston**	Open: **All year**
Location: **60 mi. N of Nashville, Tenn.**	Reduced Rates: **Weekly**
No. of Rooms: **5**	Breakfast: **Full**
No. of Private Baths: **3**	Other Meals: **Available**
Max. No. Sharing Bath: **4**	Pets: **Dogs welcome**
Double/pb: **$65**	Children: **Welcome**
Single/pb: **$45**	Smoking: **Permitted**
Double/sb: **$55**	Social Drinking: **Permitted**
Single/sb: **$38**	Airport/Station Pickup: **Yes**
	Foreign Languages: **Spanish**

The lush Bluegrass Region of Kentucky is the setting for this spacious Swiss chalet–style home that's situated on four lovely acres and furnished with many antiques. A typical Southern breakfast of eggs, sausage, biscuits and gravy, fried apples, grits, coffee cake, and beverage starts your day. If you can manage to get up from the table, stroll the grounds complete with nature trails and gardens, enjoy the hot tub, or take a swim in the pool. Afterwards, take in the sights and sounds of Opryland, Mammoth Cave, or the battlefields of historic Bowling Green. In the evening, relax in the living room, where Dr. Livingston, a music professor, may entertain you with selections played on the grand piano.

Jordan Farm Bed & Breakfast ✪
4091 NEWTOWN PIKE, GEORGETOWN, KENTUCKY 40324

Tel: **(502) 863-1944, 868-9002**	Pets: **No**
Best Time to Call: **Anytime**	Children: **Welcome**
Hosts: **Harold and Becky Jordan**	Smoking: **No**
Location: **8 mi. N of Lexington**	Social Drinking: **Permitted**
Suites: **$75–$85**	Minimum Stay: **2 nights weekends Apr. and Oct.**
Open: **All year**	
Breakfast: **Continental**	Airport/Station Pickup: **Yes**

Derby fans will want to stay on this 100-acre thoroughbred farm in the middle of Kentucky's legendary horse country. Indeed, the Kentucky Horse Park is only five minutes away. From the guest room's private deck, you can watch the Jordans' horses cavort in the fields. Or drop a line into the fishing pond and try your luck. Separate guesthouse with two large Jacuzzi suites and mini-kitchens and two-bedroom guest cottage, with fireplace, Jacuzzi, and much more.

Ranney Porch Bed & Breakfast ✪
3810 HIGHWAY 231 NORTH, HARTFORD, KENTUCKY 42347

Tel: **(502) 298-7976**
Best Time to Call: **After 4 PM**
Hosts: **Peggy Jo and Rance Ranney**
Location: **17.7 mi. S of Owensboro**
No. of Rooms: **1**
No. of Private Baths: **1**
Double/pb: **$50**

Single/pb: **$40**
Open: **All year**
Breakfast: **Full**
Pets: **No**
Children: **Welcome**
Smoking: **No**
Social Drinking: **No**

One of the unique features of this country B&B is the 57-foot porch spanning the length of the building, which is modeled after a Georgia tenant house. The exterior has blue trim, black shutters, and a candy apple red door. Inside, a Story and Clark piano sits on the foyer's red brick floor tiles, which came from the roof of a train depot. In the living room, cherry furniture complements the cherry wood floor. The bedroom's antique quilts and firm mattress assure you a good night's sleep. Numerous special events throughout the year, such as the Bar-be-que Festival, Yellow Banks Dulcimer Festival, and Bluegrass Music Festival, make this a place to visit often. Traditional and vegetarian meals are offered.

Ashton's Victorian Secret Bed & Breakfast ✪
1132 SOUTH FIRST STREET, LOUISVILLE, KENTUCKY 40203

Tel: **(502) 581-1914; (800) 449-4691,**
   Pin 0604
Hosts: **Nan and Steve Roosa**

Location: **1 mi. S of downtown**
   Louisville
No. of Rooms: **3**

No. of Private Baths: **1**
Max. No. Sharing Bath: **3**
Double/pb: **$68–$89**
Double/sb: **$58–$68**
Open: **All year**
Reduced Rates: **Weekly**

Breakfast: **Continental**
Pets: **No**
Children: **Welcome**
Smoking: **Permitted**
Social Drinking: **Permitted**

An elegant brick Victorian with lavish woodwork, this B&B has modern amenities like an exercise room with a bench press and a rowing machine, and color TVs in guest rooms. The Louisville area is rich in historic homes. Railbirds and would-be jockeys will want to make pilgrimages to the famous tracks at Churchill Downs (site of the Kentucky Derby) and Louisville Downs (home of harness races).

Diuguid House Bed & Breakfast ✪
603 MAIN STREET, MURRAY, KENTUCKY 42071

Tel: **(502) 753-5470; (888) 261-3028**
Best Time to Call: **4–10 PM**
Hosts: **Karen and George Chapman**
Location: **45 mi. S of Paducah**
No. of Rooms: **3**
Max. No. Sharing Bath: **5**
Double/sb: **$45**
Open: **All year**

Reduced Rates: **Seventh night free**
Breakfast: **Full**
Credit Cards: **MC, VISA**
Pets: **No**
Children: **Welcome**
Smoking: **No**
Social Drinking: **Permitted**
Airport/Station Pickup: **Yes**

Upon walking into this 1890s Queen Anne, listed on the National Register of Historic Places, guests see an impressive sweeping oak staircase and unusual hallway fretwork. In addition to their rooms, visitors have use of the parlor, TV lounge, and dining room. Murray State University houses a local history museum, an art gallery, and the National Boy Scout Museum. The town, a top-rated retirement community, offers lots of theatrical and musical events. For outdoor activities, take the twenty-minute drive to Land Between the Lakes, where you can hike, hunt, fish, admire the resident buffalo herd, or see a working historical farm.

Sandusky House & O'Neal Log Cabin Bed & Breakfast ✪
1626 DELANY FERRY ROAD, NICHOLASVILLE, KENTUCKY 40356

Tel: **(606) 223-4730**
Best Time to Call: **8 AM–10 PM**
Hosts: **Jim and Linda Humphrey**
Location: **6 mi. SW of Lexington**
No. of Rooms: **3**
No. of Private Baths: **3**
Double/pb: **$79**
Guest Cabin: **$99**
Open: **All year**
Reduced Rates: **Available**

Breakfast: **Full; Continental plus in cabin**
Credit Cards: **MC, VISA**
Pets: **No**
Children: **Welcome, over 12 in house; no age restriction in cabin**
Smoking: **No**
Social Drinking: **Permitted**
Airport/Station Pickup: **Yes**

A tree-lined drive to the Sandusky House is just a prelude to the handsome Greek Revival residence built about 1850 with bricks fired on the premises. Once the property was a 1000-acre farm owned by Revolutionary War veteran Jacob Sandusky—he acquired the site in a 1780 land grant from Patrick Henry, then the governor of Virginia. Today the B&B sits on a ten-acre estate amid horse farms, yet is close to downtown Lexington, Keeneland Race Track, Kentucky Horse Park, and many other attractions. The 180-year-old authentic log cabin has been reconstructed and has two bedrooms, kitchen, living room with a fireplace, whirlpool tub, and air-conditioning.

Ehrhardt's B&B ✪
285 SPRINGWELL LANE, PADUCAH, KENTUCKY 42001

Tel: **(502) 554-0644**	Reduced Rates: **10% seniors**
Best Time to Call: **9 AM–10 PM**	Breakfast: **Full**
Hosts: **Eileen and Phil Ehrhardt**	Other Meals: **Available**
Location: **1 mi. from I-24**	Pets: **No**
No. of Rooms: **2**	Children: **Welcome, over 12**
Max. No. Sharing Bath: **4**	Smoking: **No**
Double/sb: **$50**	Social Drinking: **No**
Single/sb: **$45**	Airport/Station Pickup: **Yes**
Open: **All year**	

Eileen and Phil offer warm, friendly hospitality in a relaxed atmosphere. Their B&B is located ten minutes from downtown Paducah, home of the National Quilt Museum, quaint shops, a beautiful riverfront, and excellent restaurants. Guest rooms are decorated with family antiques. Breakfast is served in the dining room or on the screened porch overlooking a quiet wooded area.

Trinity Hills Farm B&B—Stained Glass Studio ✪
10455 OLD LOVELACEVILLE ROAD, PADUCAH, KENTUCKY 42001

Tel: **(800) 488-3998**	Open: **All year**
Best Time to Call: **10 AM–10 PM**	Reduced Rates: **Available**
Hosts: **Mike and Ann Driver, Jim and**	Breakfast: **Full**
Nancy Driver	Credit Cards: **DISC, MC, VISA**
Location: **12 mi. W of Paducah**	Pets: **Sometimes**
No. of Rooms: **5**	Children: **Welcome**
No. of Private Baths: **5**	Smoking: **No**
Double/pb: **$70**	Social Drinking: **Permitted**
Suite: **$80–$105**	Airport Pickup: **Yes**

Share the serenity of the Drivers' 17-acre country retreat. This three-story home features romantic upstairs suites. Amenities include private whirlpools or spas in upstairs suites, queen beds in all rooms, a treadmill, spacious common areas, and guest rooms ideal for family gatherings. You'll enjoy extras such as robes, soft music, and evening refreshments. Your hosts love to share the beauty of Nancy's stained glass windows and other unique creations. Things to do include fishing, hiking, boating, and bird-watching. Or just unwind in the large spa on the patio by the flower and water gardens. Kentucky and Barkley lakes, Columbus Belmont State Park, the National Quilt Museum, antiques, and shopping are all nearby. Trinity Hills is centrally located between Nashville, St. Louis, and Memphis.

Maple Hill Manor B&B ✪
2941 PERRYVILLE ROAD, SPRINGFIELD, KENTUCKY 40069

Tel: **(606) 336-3075; (800) 886-7546**	Reduced Rates: **Available**
Hosts: **Bob and Kay Carroll**	Breakfast: **Full**
No. of Rooms: **7**	Credit Cards: **MC, VISA**
No. of Private Baths: **7**	Pets: **No**
Double/pb: **$65–$90**	Children: **Welcome (crib)**
Single/pb: **$55–$80**	Smoking: **No**
Open: **All year**	Social Drinking: **Permitted**

This hilltop manor house built in 1851 is situated on 14 tranquil acres in the scenic Bluegrass Region of Kentucky. Listed on the National Register of Historic Places, its Italianate design features 13-foot ceilings, 9-foot windows and doors, a profusion of fireplaces, and a solid cherry spiral staircase. The bedrooms are large, airy, and beautifully decorated with carefully chosen antique furnishings. The romantic honeymoon bed chamber has a canopy bed and Jacuzzi bath. In the evening, Bob and Kay graciously offer complimentary beverages and homemade dessert. Within an hour of Lexington and Louisville, you can visit Perryville Battlefield and Shaker Village and take a tour of distilleries. Murder mystery packages and gift certificates are available.

Sulphur Trace Farm B&B ✪
P.O. BOX 127, 8499 HIGHWAY 157, SULPHUR, KENTUCKY 40070

Tel: **(502) 743-5956**
Best Time to Call: **After 6 PM**
Hosts: **Penney Sanders and**
  Francis Thiemann
Location: **32 mi. E of Louisville**
No. of Rooms: **2**
No. of Private Baths: **2**
Double/pb: **$70**
Single/pb: **$55**

Open: **Mar. 1–Oct. 31**
Reduced Rates: **10% seniors**
Breakfast: **Full**
Pets: **No**
Children: **Welcome**
Smoking: **No**
Social Drinking: **Permitted**
Airport/Station Pickup: **Yes**

Located at the edge of bluegrass country, Sulphur Trace Farm is 35 minutes from Louisville and 55 minutes from Cincinnati. Access either city or stay in the countryside to enjoy nearby antique shopping in Shelbyville, LaGrange, or Frankfort. Then visit the casino riverboat in Rising Sun, Indiana. Francis designed and built the contemporary house out of stone and wood. Breakfast is served in the great room, where you will look out over the farm. Birds are abundant, as are the sheep and goats who won't be far from the back door.

Shepherd Place ✪
31 HERITAGE ROAD (U.S. 60), VERSAILLES, KENTUCKY 40383

Tel: **(606) 873-7843; (800) 278-0864**
Hosts: **Marlin and Sylvia Yawn**
Location: **10 mi. W of Lexington**
No. of Rooms: **3**
No. of Private Baths: **3**
Double/pb: **$75**
Single/pb: **$65**

Open: **All year**
Breakfast: **Full**
Pets: **No**
Children: **Welcome, over 12**
Smoking: **No**
Social Drinking: **Permitted**
Airport/Station Pickup: **Yes**

Marlin and Sylvia encourage you to make yourself comfortable in their pre–Civil War home, built around 1815. Rest in a spacious, beautifully decorated bedroom or relax in the parlor. Enjoy the lovely scenery while sitting on the patio or the porch swing. You might even want to pet the resident ewes, Abigail and Victoria. Brochures, menus, and plenty of ideas will be available to help you plan the rest of your stay.

LOUISIANA

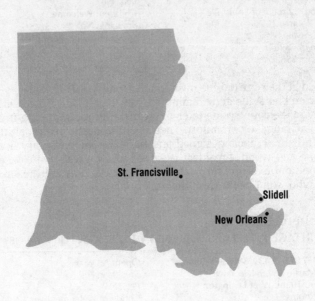

St. Francisville

Slidell

New Orleans

Bed & Breakfast, Inc.—New Orleans ✪
1021 MOSS STREET, BOX 52257, NEW ORLEANS, LOUISIANA 70152-2257

Tel: **(504) 488-4640; (800) 729-4640;**
  fax: **(504) 488-4639**
Coordinator: **Hazell Boyce**
States/Regions Covered: **New Orleans**
Descriptive Directory: **Free**

Rates (Single/Double):
Modest: **$36–$46 / $41–$51**
Average: **$41–$76 / $41–$76**
Luxury: **$71–$101 / $76–$101**
Credit Cards: **No**

New Orleans is called The City That Care Forgot. You are certain to be carefree, visiting the French Quarter, taking Mississippi riverboat rides, taking plantation tours, as well as dining in fine restaurants and attending jazz concerts. Hazell's hosts, many with historic properties along the streetcar line and in the French Quarter, will help you get the most out of your stay.

New Orleans Bed & Breakfast and Accommodations ✪
P.O. BOX 8163, NEW ORLEANS, LOUISIANA 70182-8163
neworleansbandb.com; smb@neworleansbandb.com

Tel: **(504) 838-0071; (504) 838-0072;** **fax: (504) 838-0140**	Rates (Single/Double):
Best Time to Call: **8:30 AM–4:30 PM**	Modest: **$55–$65**
Coordinator: **Sarah Margaret Brown**	Average: **$65–$75**
States/Regions Covered:	Luxury: **$75–$85**
Louisiana—Covington, Jeanerette,	Credit Cards: **AMEX, DISC, MC, VISA**
Lafayette, Mandeville, New Iberia,	**(for deposit only)**
New Orleans	

For over twenty years, Sarah Margaret Brown, a knowledgeable reservationist, has successfully matched guests and hosts. Her roster is filled with antebellum mansions, furnished houses suitable for reunions and small business groups, apartments, condos, time shares, and one- to four-bedroom homes. All accommodations have been inspected. Discount tickets are available for some attractions, three-day bus/streetcar tickets can be purchased for $8. All breakfasts are continental. The staff has visited many of the country homes and attractions and will be happy to assist you with tours of the city or any part of Louisiana.

Beau Séjour ✪
1930 NAPOLEON AVENUE, NEW ORLEANS, LOUISIANA 70115

Tel: **(504) 897-3746**	Breakfast: **Continental**
Best Time to Call: **10 AM–8 PM**	Pets: **No**
Hosts: **Gilles and Kim Gagnon**	Children: **Welcome**
No. of Rooms: **5**	Smoking: **Permitted**
No. of Private Baths: **5**	Social Drinking: **Permitted**
Double/pb: **$99**	Minimum Stay: **2 nights special events**
Single/pb: **$90**	**and holidays**
Suites: **$150**	Foreign Languages: **French**
Open: **All year**	

Kim and Gilles recently restored their 1906 Beau Séjour house to its original character, with beautiful detailing and wood floors. It is decorated in the best New Orleans style, blending country and European antiques with Louisiana and New Orleans touches. Located in one of the most picturesque neighborhoods of New Orleans, surrounded by lush tropical plantings, and on the Mardi Gras parade route, the mansion is convenient to convention and tourist attractions. Kim and Gilles are dedicated to New Orleans preservation and enjoy sharing their knowledge of local restaurants, excursions, and the culture of the "Big Easy."

The Chimes Bed & Breakfast ✪

CONSTANTINOPLE AT COLISEUM, BOX 52257, NEW ORLEANS, LOUISIANA 70152-2257

Tel: **(504) 488-4640; (800) 729-4640**
Best Time to Call: **10 AM–5 PM**
   Mon.–Fri.
Hosts: **Jill and Charles Abbyad and**
   Susan Smith
Location: **In New Orleans**
No. of Rooms: **5**
No. of Private Baths: **5**
Double/pb: **$66–$89**

Suites: **$86–$129**
Open: **All year**
Reduced Rates: **Available**
Breakfast: **Continental, plus**
Pets: **Sometimes**
Children: **Welcome**
Social Drinking: **Permitted**
Minimum Stay: **Special events**
Foreign Languages: **French**

These quaint guest quarters sit behind a Victorian uptown home.
Stained and leaded glass windows, French doors, cypress staircases,
and a brick courtyard enhance the friendly, relaxed atmosphere here.
Caring for a property of this magnitude is an ongoing commitment and
truly a labor of love. Your hosts, who are coming to the end of a two-
year renovation, typify Southern hospitality. Three blocks from St.
Charles Avenue, the Chimes cottages are minutes away from major New
Orleans attractions including the French Quarter, convention centers,
Audubon Zoological Gardens with the walk-through Louisiana Swamp
Exhibit, the Mississippi River, and universities. The historic St. Charles
Avenue streetcar makes the famous restaurants, jazz clubs, art galleries,
and antique shops accessible without an auto. Your hosts live on the
second floor of the main house—their door is always open! They will-
ingly share their vast knowledge of New Orleans, offering suggestions

for tours and restaurants. For your convenience, each suite has a tele-phone, tea/coffeepot, television set, and stereo. Laundry facilities and use of a refrigerator are available.

Essem's House—New Orleans First Bed & Breakfast

3658 GENTILLY BOULEVARD, NEW ORLEANS, LOUISIANA 70182-8163

smb@neworleansbandb.com

Tel: **(504) 947-3401; (504) 838-0071;** **fax: (504) 838-0140**	Double/sb: **$55–$60**
Best Time to Call: **8:30 AM–4:30 PM**	Guest Cottage: **$65–$75**
Host: **Sarah Margaret Brown**	Open: **All year**
Location: **3 mi. from the French Quarter**	Reduced Rates: **Available**
No. of Rooms: **3**	Breakfast: **Continental**
No. of Private Baths: **2**	Pets: **No**
Max. No. Sharing Bath: **4**	Children: **Welcome, over 10**
Double/pb: **$60–$75**	Smoking: **No**
	Minimum Stay: **2 nights, Special events**

In the 1930s, when New Orleans was first developed, the prime loca-tions were along the route of the Old Gentilly Bayou, the highest point of the city. These lots are large and have a country atmosphere with oak-lined streets. Because builders went to California to see new de-signs, many of the homes are California Spanish-style, including this B&B. Essem's House is a one-of-a-kind, 10-room brick home. Built in the 1930s by a bootlegger, the house has a secret basement and an inter-esting history. Guest rooms are large and airy. One has a king bed and private bath, the other two have double beds and share a bath. You will enjoy the continental breakfast and the suggestions of Sarah Margaret every morning.

The Glimmer Inn ✪

1631 SEVENTH STREET, NEW ORLEANS, LOUISIANA 70115

Tel: **(504) 897-1895**	Single/sb: **$60**
Best Time to Call: **9 AM–9 PM**	Open: **All year**
Hosts: **Sharon Agiewich and** **Cathy Andros**	Breakfast: **Continental, plus**
	Pets: **By arrangement**
No. of Rooms: **6**	Children: **Welcome**
No. of Private Baths: **1**	Smoking: **Permitted**
Max. No. Sharing Bath: **4**	Social Drinking: **Permitted**
Double/pb: **$85**	Minimum Stay: **2 nights**
Double/sb: **$70**	

This restored 1891 Victorian home has wonderful period elements: twelve-foot cove ceilings, cypress woodwork, side and front galleries, a wraparound front porch, and an enclosed brick patio. Public rooms are comfortably furnished for reading, TV viewing, and musical enjoy-ment. The main house's guest rooms are beautifully appointed, with antiques, ceiling fans, and individually controlled air-conditioning and heat. Also offered is a private carriage house with bath, refrigerator, and central air-conditioning and heating. The Glimmer Inn is across the street from the historic Garden District, a block from the trolley line and Mardi Gras parade route, and fifteen minutes from the French Quarter. Let Cathy and Sharon know your interests; they pride themselves on meeting guests' travel needs in a relaxed but attentive atmosphere.

Sun & Moon Bed & Breakfast

1037 NORTH RAMPART STREET, NEW ORLEANS, LOUISIANA 70116

Tel: **(504) 529-4652**
Best Time to Call: **Mornings**
Hosts: **Mary Pat Van Tine, owner;**
  Kathleen Barrow, mngr.
No. of Rooms: **2**
No. of Private Baths: **2**
Double/pb: **$75**

Open: **All year**
Breakfast: **Continental**
Pets: **No**
Children: **Welcome**
Smoking: **No**
Social Drinking: **Permitted**
Minimum Stay: **2 nights**

Sun & Moon Bed & Breakfast is located in the French Quarter and provides a warm homelike atmosphere to guests. Each guest room has a TV and a small refrigerator for midnight snacking, and all are air conditioned. Kathleen will make your stay a memorable one, and she can fill you in on all the local happenings, clubs, restaurants, and points of interest.

Butler Greenwood ✪

8345 U.S. HIGHWAY 61, ST. FRANCISVILLE, LOUISIANA 70775

Tel: **(504) 635-6312**
Best Time to Call: **Anytime**
Host: **Anne Butler**
Location: **25 mi. N of Baton Rouge**
Guest Cottages: **$100–$110, sleeps 2–6**
Open: **All year**
Reduced Rates: **Families**

Breakfast: **Continental, plus**
Credit Cards: **AMEX, MC, VISA**
Pets: **Sometimes**
Children: **Welcome**
Smoking: **Permitted**
Social Drinking: **Permitted**

Butler Greenwood offers six cottages on picturesque plantation grounds. Choose from the 1796 kitchen, with exposed beams and skylights; the nineteenth-century cook's cottage, with a fireplace and porch swing; the romantic gazebo with antique stained glass windows; the treehouse at the edge of a steep wooded ravine, with a wonderful 3-level deck and fireplace; the dovecote, three stories, sleeps six, with a fireplace and Jacuzzi; or the pond house on its own pond. All sites have private baths, partial kitchens, and cable TV. Rates include a tour of the main house—listed on the National Register of Historic Places—and the extensive grounds. A tour book is available, describing the area's history and attractions. Continental-plus breakfast is served; other amenities include a pool, nature walks, and ballooning.

Salmen-Fritchie House Circa 1895 ✪
127 CLEVELAND AVENUE, SLIDELL, LOUISIANA 70458

Tel: **(504) 643-1405; (800) 235-4168,** **for reservations**	Suites: **$115–$125**
Best Time to Call: **8 AM–9 PM**	Open: **All year**
Hosts: **Homer and Sharon Fritchie**	Reduced Rates: **Available**
Location: **30 mi. N of New Orleans**	Breakfast: **Full**
No. of Rooms: **5**	Credit Cards: **AMEX, DISC, MC, VISA**
No. of Private Baths: **5**	Pets: **No**
Double/pb: **$85–$95**	Children: **Welcome, over 10**
Single/pb: **$75–$85**	Smoking: **No**
Cottage: **$150 for 2**	Social Drinking: **Permitted**
	Station Pickup: **Yes**

You'll feel the sense of history as you step inside this magnificent sixteen-room house listed on the National Register of Historic Places. From the front door to the back, the great hall measures twenty feet wide and eighty-five feet long! All the rooms are filled with beautiful antiques, reminiscent of days gone by. Hospitality is a way of life here. Arrive by 4 PM and you can join your hosts for tea in the parlor and afterward, a tour of the house and grounds. In the morning, you'll receive fresh hot coffee in your room. Then you'll enjoy a full Southern breakfast in the bright, cheery breakfast room. A cottage has been added, with a screened-in porch, living room, kitchen, bedroom, and marble tub Jacuzzi.

MAINE

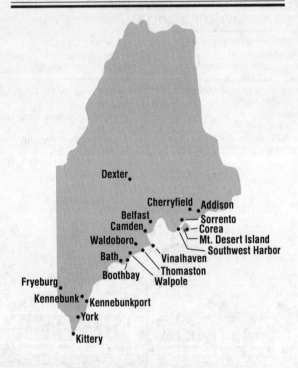

Dexter

Cherryfield · Addison
Belfast · Sorrento
Camden · Corea
Waldoboro · Mt. Desert Island
Southwest Harbor
Bath · Vinalhaven
Boothbay · Thomaston
Walpole
Fryeburg ·
Kennebunk · · Kennebunkport
· York
· Kittery

Pleasant Bay Bed and Breakfast ✪
BOX 222 WEST SIDE ROAD, ADDISON, MAINE 04606
Pleasantbay@nemaine.com

Tel: **(207) 483-4490; fax: (207) 483-4653**
Hosts: **Leon and Joan Yeaton**
Location: **42 mi. N of Ellsworth**
No. of Rooms: **3**
No. of Private Baths: **1**
Max. No. Sharing Bath: **4**
Double/pb: **$70**
Single/pb: **$60**

Double/sb: **$55**
Single/sb: **$45–$50**
Open: **All year**
Breakfast: **Full**
Credit Cards: **MC, VISA**
Pets: **No**
Children: **Welcome**
Smoking: **No**
Social Drinking: **Permitted**

The Yeatons' 110-acre llama farm rests on a knoll by the shores of Pleasant Bay and the Pleasant River. Watch shorebirds and seals play in the rising and falling tides. Explore the shoreline in seclusion or meander along rustic trails, accompanied by a gentle llama. Relax before the hearth at sunset. In the morning, you'll wake up to a full Down East breakfast made with farm-fresh eggs laid by your hosts' own chickens.

Elizabeth's Bed and Breakfast ✪
360 FRONT STREET, BATH, MAINE 04530

Tel: **(207) 443-1146**	Single/sb: **$45**
Host: **Elizabeth Lindsay**	Open: **Apr. 15–Jan. 1**
Location: **40 mi. up the coast from**	Breakfast: **Continental**
Portland	Pets: **No**
No. of Rooms: **4**	Children: **Welcome, over 12**
Max. No. Sharing Bath: **4**	Smoking: **Restricted**
Double/sb: **$55–$65**	Social Drinking: **Permitted**

Elizabeth's Bed & Breakfast is a fine old Federalist house overlooking the Kennebec River. Guests enjoy the country antiques and collectibles throughout the house. Located within easy walking distance to historic downtown Bath, where excellent restaurants and shops abound. Breakfast may include French toast, pancakes, eggs, muffins, fruit, or cereal. Elizabeth frequently serves brunch on Sunday.

Fairhaven Inn ✪
RR 2, BOX 85, NORTH BATH ROAD, BATH, MAINE 04530

Tel: **(207) 443-4391; (888) 443-4391**	Double/sb: **$70–$80**
Hosts: **Susie and David Reed**	Single/sb: **$50–$60**
Location: **35 mi. N of Portland**	Open: **All year**
No. of Rooms: **8**	Breakfast: **Full**
No. of Private Baths: **7**	Pets: **No**
Max. No. Sharing Bath: **4**	Children: **Yes**
Double/pb: **$80–$120**	Smoking: **No**
Single/pb: **$50–$65**	Social Drinking: **Permitted**

An 18th-century Colonial mansion on a hill above the Kennebec River, Fairhaven Inn is furnished with antique and country pieces. Shaded by hemlock, birch, and pine trees, the 16-acre grounds lure cross-country skiers in the winter, and strollers year round. Around the bend, Bath Country Club is open to the public for golfing, and beaches are nearby. Bird-watchers can study migratory waterfowl at Merrymeeting Bay. You'll get stamina for the day's activities from ample breakfasts of juice, fruit crisps, hot cereal or homemade granola, and main courses such as baked eggs in crêpe cups, strawberry banana French toast, and blueberry pig.

The Galen C. Moses House ✪
1009 WASHINGTON STREET, BATH, MAINE 04530
galenmoses@clinic.net; www.bnbcity.com/inns/20028

Tel: **(207) 442-8771**	Location: **40 mi. N of Portland**
Hosts: **James Haught and Larry Kieft**	No. of Rooms: **4**

No. of Private Baths: **4**	Children: **Welcome, over 12**
Double/pb: **$69–$99**	Smoking: **No**
Open: **All year**	Social drinking: **Permitted**
Breakfast: **Full**	Minimum stay: **2 nights weekends**
Credit Cards: **MC, VISA**	**June–Oct.**
Pets: **No**	

Built in 1874 for Galen Clapp Moses, this Italianate structure has been draped in very vivid colors of plum, pink, and teal, and has been given the nickname "the Pink House." The large rooms are reminiscent of nineteenth-century Victorian style. There are many surprises throughout the house, including antiques, elegant gardens, and a full theater located on the third floor—during World War II, it was used to entertain officers from a nearby naval air station. The house also contains a number of assuredly friendly spirits, who make their presence known on a frequent basis. Breakfast varies according to the cook's mood, and may include blueberry pancakes, mushroom quiche, or sour cream chive omelettes. Coffee, juices, and muffins are available for early risers and late sleepers.

Belfast Bay Meadows Inn ✪
90 NORTHPORT AVENUE, BELFAST, MAINE 04915
bbmi@acadia.net

Tel: **(800) 335-2370**	Reduced Rates: **30% Nov.–April**
Best Time to Call: **7 AM–10 PM**	Breakfast: **Full**
Hosts: **John and Patty Lebowitz**	Credit Cards: **AMEX, MC, VISA**
Location: **100 mi. N of Portland**	Pets: **Welcome**
No. of Rooms: **12**	Children: **Welcome**
No. of Private Baths: **12**	Smoking: **No**
Double/pb: **$75–$125**	Social Drinking: **Permitted**
Open: **All year**	

Stroll winding, grassy paths through 17 bayside acres, flowered meadows, gardens, and forest to the cold blue waters of Penobscot Bay, where you'll see wheeling gulls, white-sailed schooners heeling to the breeze, and green-shadowed islands in bright morning mist. This breezy, bright blue bay is shaded by whispering, mottled forest. Experience cool summer mornings on the spacious breakfast deck with big green umbrellas. Enjoy sweet, fresh local fruit, fancy muffins, creamy eggs with tender lobster, and tasty sweet peppers. This exemplary, very large, shingled Down East cottage and renovated post-and-beam barn boasts wonderful international antique decor: fine paintings, colorful Persian carpets, and comfortable furnishings. Rooms have air-conditioning, phones, TV. Belfast Bay is a lot like grandma's house, not so much lavish as lived in and dearly loved.

Kenniston Hill Inn ✪
ROUTE 27, P.O. BOX 125, BOOTHBAY, MAINE 04537

Tel: **(207) 633-2159; (800) 992-2915**
Best Time to Call: **10 AM–10 PM**
Hosts: **Susan and David Straight**
Location: **50 mi. N of Portland**
No. of Rooms: **10**
No. of Private Baths: **10**
Double/pb: **$69–$120**

Open: **All year**
Breakfast: **Full**
Credit Cards: **DISC, MC, VISA**
Pets: **No**
Children: **Welcome, over 8**
Smoking: **No**
Social Drinking: **Permitted**

Boothbay's oldest inn, Kenniston Hill has welcomed wayfarers since the late 1790s when David Kenniston built this handsome, center-chimney Georgian Colonial. This local landmark is just a five-minute drive to all of Boothbay Harbor's attractions and activities, yet its shady knoll, wildflower gardens, and picket-fence patio seem far from the bustle. Guest rooms are decorated with antiques and five have fireplaces. Perennial gardens provide seasonal fresh flowers. The rocking chairs on the front porch and wing chairs by the authentic open-hearth fireplace are perfect for relaxing. David and Susan's sumptuous breakfast specialties include early New England dishes such as blueberry pot pie, as well as peaches and cream French toast, zucchini walnut pancakes with Maine maple syrup, or hash brown potato pie.

Blue Harbor House, A Village Inn
67 ELM STREET, ROUTE 1, CAMDEN, MAINE 04843-1904
www.blueharborhouse.com; balidog@midcoast.com

Tel: **(207) 236-3196; (800) 248-3196;**
fax: (207) 236-6523
Best Time to Call: **9:30 AM–9:30 PM**

Hosts: **Jody Schmoll and Dennis Hayden**
Location: **85 mi. NE of Portland**
No. of Rooms: **10**

No. of Private Baths: **10**
Double/pb: **$85–$145**
Open: **All year**
Breakfast: **Full**
Credit Cards: **AMEX, DISC, MC, VISA**

Pets: **By arrangement**
Children: **By arrangement**
Smoking: **No**
Social Drinking: **Permitted**

A classic village inn on the Maine coast, Blue Harbor House welcomes guests to relax in a restored 1810 Cape where yesterday's charms blend perfectly with today's comforts. The beautiful village of Camden, renowned for its spectacular setting where the mountains meet the sea, is just outside the door. The inn's inviting guest rooms are bright with country antiques and hand-fashioned quilts. Some rooms have canopy beds and whirlpool tubs. Breakfast and dinner showcase regional specialties. Jody and Dennis look forward to welcoming you!

Hawthorn Inn ✪
9 HIGH STREET, CAMDEN, MAINE 04843
www.midcoast.com/~hawthorn

Tel: **(207) 236-8842; fax: (207) 236-6181**
Best Time to Call: **9 AM–9 PM**
Hosts: **Nick and Patty Wharton**
Location: **On Rte. 1, 190 mi. N of Boston**
No. of Rooms: **10**
No. of Private Baths: **10**
Double/pb: **$100–$195**

Reduced Rates: **$20 less daily Nov. 1–May 1**
Breakfast: **Full**
Credit Cards: **AMEX, MC, VISA**
Pets: **No**
Children: **Welcome, over 12**
Smoking: **No**
Social Drinking: **Permitted**

The airy rooms of this Victorian inn are an elegant mixture of the old and the new. Guests enjoy breakfast while relaxing on the deck or getting warm by the fire. All rooms overlook either Mt. Battie or Camden Harbor. A score of sports can be enjoyed in the area, and shops and restaurants are a short walk away. Rooms with fireplaces, specialty Jacuzzis, TVs, and VCRs are available.

Ricker House ✪
PARK STREET, P.O. BOX 256, CHERRYFIELD, MAINE 04622

Tel: **(207) 546-2780**
Hosts: **Bill and Jean Conway**
Location: **32 mi. E of Ellsworth**
No. of Rooms: **2**
Max. No. Sharing Bath: **4**
Double/sb: **$60**
Single/sb: **$50**
Open: **May–Nov.**

Reduced Rates: **Available**
Breakfast: **Full**
Pets: **No**
Children: **Welcome (crib)**
Smoking: **No**
Social Drinking: **Permitted**
Airport/Station Pickup: **Yes**

This comfortable 1803 Federal Colonial, listed on the National Register of Historic Places, borders the Narraguagus River. Eastern Maine offers the scenic coastal area and many activities for guests such as swimming, canoeing, hiking, and fishing. The village is historic and fun to tour. William and Jean provide brochures and other information on the area.

The Black Duck Inn on Corea Harbor
P.O. BOX 39, CROWLEY ISLAND ROAD, COREA, MAINE 04624
bduck@acadia.net; www.blackduck.com

Tel: **(207) 963-2689**	Open: **All year**
Best Time to Call: **8 AM–9 PM**	Reduced Rates: **$10 less Oct. 15–May 15**
Hosts: **Barry C. Canner and Robert Travers**	Breakfast: **Full**
Location: **300 mi. NE of Boston, MA**	Pets: **No**
No. of Rooms: **4**	Children: **Welcome, under 1, over 7**
No. of Private Baths: **2**	Smoking: **No**
Max. No. Sharing Bath: **4**	Social Drinking: **Permitted**
Double/pb: **$90**	Minimum Stay: **3 nights cottage**
Double/sb: **$70–$85**	Foreign Languages: **Danish**
Guest Cottage: **$99–$145**	

Guests enjoy casual elegance in this 100-year-old New England fisherman's home overlooking one of the most spectacular working harbors in Maine, the outer islands, and the open ocean. The rooms are filled with antiques, contemporary art, and the hosts' eclectic collections. You'll also meet their dog, two cats, and potbelly pig. There are a variety of common areas with a fireplace, TV, and a library. Outside is a large deck, over 12 acres of woods, harbor frontage, salt marshes, sub-Arctic plant species, and granite rock outcrops and ledge. Located nearby are the Schoodic section of the Acadia National Park, several beaches, wildlife areas, Bar Harbor, Campobello, restaurants, antique shops, and other attractions.

The Brewster Inn ✪
37 ZION'S HILL ROAD, DEXTER, MAINE 04930

Tel: **(207) 924-3130**	Breakfast: **Full**
Best Time to Call: **9 AM–9 PM**	Other Meals: **Available**
Hosts: **Michael and Ivy Brooks**	Credit Cards: **MC, VISA**
Location: **40 mi. NW of Bangor**	Pets: **No**
No. of Rooms: **7**	Children: **Welcome**
No. of Private Baths: **7**	Smoking: **No**
Double/pb: **$59–$89**	Social Drinking: **Permitted**
Single/pb: **$49–$79**	Airport/Station Pickup: **Yes**
Open: **All year**	
Reduced Rates: **7th night free; 10% seniors**	

Built for Governor Owen Brewster, this 1930s home is listed on the National Register of Historic Places, and embodies classic, comfortable elegance. Guests are invited to use the dining room, living room, and sunroom, which are furnished with a variety of antiques, reproductions, and family heirlooms. Books, arts and crafts, and an antique radio collection spill over to many of the rooms. Guest rooms feature original tile baths, fireplaces, or window seats, plus cozy quilts and special bath amenities. The Inn is close to Maine's coasts, mountains, and lake regions. Ivy is a graphic designer and former university professor and Michael is an expert in process control photography and guitars.

Acres of Austria ✪

RR1, BOX 177, ROUTE 5, FIRELANE 48, FRYEBURG, MAINE 04037

Tel: **(800) 988-4391**	Breakfast: **Full**
Hosts: **Candice and Franz Redl**	Other Meals: **Available**
Location: **60 mi. W of Portland**	Credit Cards: **MC, VISA**
No. of Rooms: **4**	Pets: **No**
No. of Private Baths: **4**	Children: **Welcome**
Double/pb: **$65–$125**	Smoking: **No**
Single/pb: **$59**	Social Drinking: **Permitted**
Open: **All year**	Airport/Station Pickup: **Yes**
Reduced Rates: **Available**	Foreign Languages: **German, French**

Make yourself at home on the Redls' 65 acres. View the old Saco River, the White Mountains, or acres of forest from any room in the house. Browse through the library, test your billiard skills with a game of Carombol on a 1920s table from Vienna, or use a canoe to paddle the romantic river. Nearby, visit the outlet and antique shops, or enjoy golfing, scenic plane rides, skiing, or many other outdoor activities. Breakfast is served on the screen porch or by the warmth of a crackling fire. Make arrangements to try one of Franz's Austrian dinner specialties, including Kas'nockn, Wiener schnitzel, Sacher torte, and many more. Get a taste of Europe for a fraction of the price.

The Alewife House ✪

1917 ALEWIVE ROAD, KENNEBUNK, MAINE 04043-9739
alewifehouse@lamere.net
www.virtualcities.com/ons/me/k/mek9502.htm

Tel: **(207) 985-2118**	Open: **All year**
Best Time to Call: **8 AM–11 PM**	Breakfast: **Continental, Plus**
Hosts: **Maryellen and Tom Foley**	Credit Cards: **MC, VISA**
Location: **25 mi. S of Portland**	Pets: **No**
No. of Rooms: **2**	Children: **Welcome, over 12**
No. of Private Baths: **2**	Smoking: **No**
Double/pb: **$95**	Social Drinking: **Permitted**

Step back in time as you enter this 1756 farmhouse, located in horse country with rolling hills and gardens. Inside, the house is decorated with antiques; more are sold in the on-site shop. Awaken to the aroma of hot muffins, fresh fruit, and fresh-perked coffee served on the sun-porch each morning. Then explore the area's coastline or the many nearby lakes.

Arundel Meadows Inn ✪
P.O. BOX 1129, KENNEBUNK, MAINE 04043
www.biddeford.com/arundel-meadows-inn

Tel: **(207) 985-3770**
Best Time to Call: **9 AM–9 PM**
Hosts: **Mark Bachelder and Murray Yaeger**
Location: **2 mi. N of Kennebunk**
No. of Rooms: **7**
No. of Private Baths: **7**
Double/pb: **$75–$95**

Suites: **$100–$125**
Open: **All year**
Breakfast: **Full**
Pets: **Sometimes**
Children: **Welcome, over 11**
Smoking: **No**
Social Drinking: **Permitted**

The Arundel Meadows Inn is situated on three and a half acres next to the Kennebunk River. Murray, a retired professor, and Mark, a professional chef, have always loved this area, and it is a dream come true for them to watch others enjoy it. They renovated this 165-year-old house themselves, and meticulously planned the decor. Several guest rooms have fireplaces and two suites sleep four. Mark's beautifully prepared breakfast specialties are the perfect start for your day. It's just three minutes to the center of town, and about ten to Kennebunk Beach. In the afternoon, come back to the Inn for tea and enjoy homemade sweets and beverages.

Lake Brook Bed & Breakfast ✪
P.O. BOX 762, KENNEBUNKPORT, MAINE 04046

Tel: **(207) 967-4069**
Best Time to Call: **9 AM–9 PM**
Host: **Carolyn A. McAdams**
Location: **25 mi. S of Portland**
No. of Rooms: **4**
No. of Private Baths: **4**
Double/pb: **$85–$100**
Single/pb: **$70**
Suite: **$120**

Open: **All year**
Breakfast: **Full**
Credit Cards: **MC, VISA**
Pets: **No**
Children: **Welcome**
Smoking: **No**
Social Drinking: **Permitted**
Foreign Languages: **Spanish**

Lake Brook is an appealing turn-of-the-century New England farm-house. Its wraparound porch is equipped with comfortable rocking chairs, and flower gardens stretch right down to the tidal brook that feeds the property. The shops and restaurants of Dock Square are within easy walking distance, and Kennebunk Beach is a little more than one mile away. Breakfasts include such main dishes as quiche, baked French toast, and Mexican chili eggs and cheese.

Gundalow Inn ✪
6 WATER STREET, KITTERY, MAINE 03904

Tel: **(207) 439-4040**
Hosts: **Cevia and George Rosol**
Location: **50 mi. N of Boston**
No. of Rooms: **6**
No. of Private Baths: **6**
Double/pb: **$80–$125**
Single/pb: **$80–$125**

Open: **All year**
Breakfast: **Full**
Credit Cards: **DISC, MC, VISA**
Pets: **No**
Children: **Welcome, over 16**
Smoking: **No**
Social Drinking: **Permitted**

Gundalow Inn is a wonderful brick Victorian overlooking Portsmouth harbor. Guest rooms are comfortably furnished with antiques; most have water views. Savor a hearty home-cooked breakfast by the fireplace or on the patio. Stroll over to Colonial Portsmouth, a town noted for its museums, theaters, restaurants, cafes, gardens, festivals, boat tours, and antique and craft shops. Strawbery Banke and Prescott Park are within walking distance. It's a ten-minute drive to beaches and factory outlets, and the White Mountains are two hours away. Of course, you can always relax with a book on the porch or patio or in the parlor.

Bed & Breakfast Year 'Round—the MacDonalds ✪
P.O. BOX 52, MT. DESERT, MAINE 04660

Tel: **(207) 244-3316**
Best Time to Call: **Anytime**
Hosts: **Stan and Binnie MacDonald**
Location: **45 mi. S of Bangor**
No. of Rooms: **3**

No. of Private Baths: **3**
Double/pb: **$75–$85**
Open: **All year**
Reduced Rates: **$15 less Oct. 16–June 14**

Breakfast: **Full**
Credit Cards: **MC, VISA**
Pets: **No**
Children: **Welcome, over 6**

Smoking: **No**
Social Drinking: **Permitted**
Minimum Stay: **2 nights**

Built in 1850 in Somesville, Mt. Desert's first permanent settlement, this B&B is listed on the National Register of Historic Places. The beautifully furnished home has views of the water and mountains from almost every window. In addition to having full use of the living and music rooms, guests may lounge on the screened porch, in the garden court-yard, or in the backyard. At this location, you'll have the pleasure of village living apart from summer crowds. There's much to enjoy on foot, notably Somes Harbor, historic Brookside Cemetery, a bookstore, a museum, and a summer theater. Somesville is surrounded by Acadia National Park and is nearly equidistant from the larger towns of North-east Harbor, Southwest Harbor, and Bar Harbor. You'll be ready to go exploring after breakfasting on fresh fruit, blueberry pancakes or crepes, and homemade breads and muffins. Stan and Binnie enjoy read-ing and music—Stan plays a mean banjo!

Black Friar Inn
10 SUMMER STREET, BAR HARBOR, MT. DESERT ISLAND, MAINE 04609

Tel: **(207) 288-5091**
Best Time to Call: **12–3 PM; evenings**
Hosts: **Perry and Sharon Risley and Falke**
No. of Rooms: **7**

No. of Private Baths: **7**
Double/pb: **$90–$140**
Single/pb: **$85–$135**
Open: **May 1–Nov. 30**
Reduced Rates: **Mid Oct.–mid June**

Breakfast: **Full**
Credit Cards: **DISC, MC, VISA**
Pets: **No**
Children: **Welcome, over 11**
Smoking: **No**

Social Drinking: **Permitted**
Minimum Stay: **2 nights June 15–**
Columbus Day
Airport/Station Pickup: **Yes**

This uniquely restored Victorian incorporates beautiful woodwork, mantels, and tin from area churches and homes. Afternoon refreshments are served in the sunroom, which is paneled in cypress and embossed tin, or by the fireside in the intimate English pub. Full breakfasts include fresh fruit, juice, eggs, Belgian waffles, and home-baked breads, rolls, and muffins, served in the dining area, featured on the back cover of the 1992 edition of *Bed & Breakfast U.S.A.* Guests have a short walk to shops, restaurants, and the waterfront; it's an easy drive to Acadia National Park.

Hearthside B&B ✪

7 HIGH STREET, BAR HARBOR, MT. DESERT ISLAND, MAINE 04609
hearth@acadia.net; www.hearthsideinn.com

Tel: **(207) 288-4533**
Best Time to Call: **8 AM–10 PM**
Hosts: **Susan and Barry Schwartz**
No. of Rooms: **9**
No. of Private Baths: **9**
Double/pb: **$90–$135**
Open: **All year**

Reduced Rates: **Before June 15**
Breakfast: **Full**
Credit Cards: **DISC, MC, VISA**
Pets: **No**
Children: **Welcome, over 10**
Smoking: **No**
Social Drinking: **Permitted**

After a day in the National Park, relax in front of a crackling fireplace in a Victorian B&B, located in town on a quiet side street. Begin your day with a fantastic full breakfast buffet and end in afternoon tea/lemonade and homemade cookies. Each room has antique furniture, queen-size bed, and air conditioning. Some have a balcony or fireplace or a whirlpool bath.

The Kingsleigh Inn 1904 ✪

P.O. BOX 1426, MAIN STREET, SOUTHWEST HARBOR,
MT. DESERT ISLAND, MAINE 04679

Tel: **(207) 244-5302**
Hosts: **Ken and Cyd Champagne Collins**
Location: **45 mi. E of Bangor**
No. of Rooms: **8**
No. of Private Baths: **8**
Double/pb: **$90–$120**
Suite: **$105–$175**
Open: **All year**

Reduced Rates: **Available**
Breakfast: **Full**
Credit Cards: **MC, VISA**
Pets: **No**
Children: **Welcome, over 12**
Smoking: **No**
Social Drinking: **Permitted**

Built at the turn of the century, the Kingsleigh Inn is a shingled and pebble-dash Colonial revival. The house overlooks Southwest Harbor, where generations of boatbuilders and fishermen have earned their living. For that special occasion, try our secluded turret suite, three rooms with a working fireplace, king bed, and panoramic views of the harbor. All guest rooms are tastefully decorated and many have beautiful harbor views. Afternoon refreshments are served on a wraparound porch overlooking the harbor or, on cooler days, by a crackling fire. For breakfast your hosts serve freshly brewed coffee, teas, juices, home-baked muffins and breads, fresh fruit, and a daily specialty, such as omelettes, blueberry buttermilk pancakes, or lemon French toast. Cyd and Ken take pleasure in welcoming you to Mt. Desert Island and will gladly direct you to swimming, hiking, fishing expeditions, whale-watching, restaurants, museums, and shopping.

The Lamb's Ear Inn ○

P.O. BOX 30, 60 CLARK POINT ROAD, SOUTHWEST HARBOR, MT. DESERT ISLAND, MAINE 04679
www.acadia.net/lambsear

Tel: **(207) 244-9828**	Open: **May–Nov.**
Host: **Elizabeth Hoke**	Breakfast: **Full**
Location: **45 mi. E of Bangor**	Credit Cards: **DISC, MC, VISA**
No. of Rooms: **6**	Pets: **No**
No. of Private Baths: **6**	Children: **Welcome, over 10**
Double/pb: **$85–$165**	Smoking: **No**
Suite: **$135**	Social Drinking: **Permitted**

A stately home that dates to the mid-19th century, The Lamb's Ear overlooks the waterfront of Southwest Harbor, a quaint fishing village. While swimming, sailing, and fishing are the primary activities here, you'll want to set aside time to explore nearby galleries, museums, and Acadia National Park. After a full breakfast of eggs, Belgian waffles, fresh fruit, and muffins, you'll be ready for the day's adventures.

Lindenwood Inn

P.O. BOX 1328, SOUTHWEST HARBOR, MT. DESERT ISLAND, MAINE 04679

Tel: **(207) 244-5335; (800) 307-5335**
Host: **James King**
No. of Rooms: **15**
No. of Private Baths: **15**
Double/pb: **$85–$145**
Suites: **$165–$195**
Cottages and Apartments: **$125–$195**
Open: **All year**

Reduced Rates: **Nov. 1–June 30**
Breakfast: **Full**
Pets: **No**
Children: **Welcome, over 12 in Inn, any age cottages and apartments**
Smoking: **No**
Social Drinking: **Permitted**

Built at the turn of the century as a sea captain's home, the Inn derives its name from the stately linden trees that line the front lawn. Each room is individually decorated and many enjoy harbor views from sun-drenched private balconies. On cool mornings you'll be greeted by glowing fireplaces and a hearty full breakfast. Relax and unwind in one of the Inn's elegant sitting rooms or on the large shaded front porch, where you can hear the sounds of the working harbor. Acadia National Park and all the island's activities are only minutes away.

Penury Hall ✪

BOX 68, MAIN STREET, SOUTHWEST HARBOR, MT. DESERT ISLAND, MAINE 04679
www.acadia.net/penury-n

Tel: **(207) 244-7102; fax: (207) 244-5651**
Hosts: **Gretchen and Toby Strong**
No. of Rooms: **3**
Max. No. Sharing Bath: **3**
Double/sb: **$70**
Single/sb: **$65**
Open: **All year**
Reduced Rates: **Nov. 1–April 30**

Breakfast: **Full**
Pets: **No**
Children: **Welcome, over 16**
Smoking: **No**
Social Drinking: **Permitted**
Minimum Stay: **2 nights June 1– Oct. 30**
Airport/Station Pickup: **Yes**

This gray frame house is on the quiet side of Mt. Desert Island. Built in 1830, it is comfortably furnished with traditional pieces, antiques, and original art. Gretchen and Toby are cosmopolitan and cordial. Their motto is: "Each guest is an honorary member of the family," and you'll soon feel at home. Knowledgeable about the area's highlights, they'll direct you to special shops and restaurants and all of the best things to see and do. Breakfast often features eggs Benedict and blueberry pancakes or cinnamon waffles. You are welcome to use the canoe. After a day of hiking or skiing, relax in the sauna. There's a $10 surcharge for one-night stays.

Pointy Head Inn ✪

H.C.R. 33 BOX 2A, BASS HARBOR, MT. DESERT ISLAND, MAINE 04653

Tel: **(207) 244-7261**
Best Time to Call: **9:30 AM–3 PM**
Hosts: **Doris and Warren Townsend**
Location: **18 mi. S of Bar Harbor**
No. of Rooms: **6**
No. of Private Baths: **2**
Max. No. Sharing Bath: **4**
Double/pb: **$95**
Double/sb: **$70**

Single/sb: **$45**
Open: **May 15–Oct.**
Breakfast: **Full**
Pets: **No**
Children: **Welcome, over 10**
Smoking: **No**
Social Drinking: **Permitted**
Airport/Station Pickup: **Yes**

In Colonial times a sea captain made his home here, overlooking beautiful Bass Harbor. Today, this sprawling Inn is a haven for artists and photographers who appreciate the quiet side of Mount Desert Island. The house is decorated with nautical accents and homey furnishings. One of its special qualities is the beautiful sunsets that can be enjoyed from your room or the comfortable porch. The Inn is set in a quaint fishing village bordering Acadia National Park. Swimming, canoeing, nature trails, fishing, and mountain climbing are just a few of the activities that can be enjoyed locally. A variety of restaurants, shops, and galleries are within walking distance.

Bass Cove Farm B&B ✪

H.C. 32, BOX 132, ROUTE 185, SORRENTO, MAINE 04677
basscove@downeast.net; www.downeast.net/com/basscove

Tel: **(207) 422-3564**	Open: **All year**
Hosts: **Mary Ann Solet and Michael Tansey**	Reduced Rates: **10% less Nov.–Apr.; suite, weekly**
Location: **30 mi. NE of Bar Harbor**	Breakfast: **Full**
No. of Rooms: **3**	Credit Cards: **MC, VISA**
No. of Private Baths: **1**	Pets: **Sometimes**
Max. No. Sharing Bath: **4**	Children: **Welcome, over 12**
Double/sb: **$50**	Smoking: **No**
Single/sb: **$45**	Social Drinking: **No**
Suites: **$70–$80**	Minimum Stay: **2 nights for suite**

This 1840s farmhouse is located in a small coastal village—Bass Cove can be seen from the dining room. Outdoor enthusiasts can hike, bike, swim, boat, follow a nature trail, or visit the nearby shops and flea markets for antiques and treasures from local attics. Talk to the artists and craftspeople in their gallery/studio, or attend concerts by local and visiting musicians. Mary Ann does editorial work in her electronic cottage; she is a fiber craftsperson and herb and flower gardener. Mike, group home counselor and photographer, is a Harry S. Truman Manure Pitchoff champion at Maine's Common Ground Country Fair. He oversees the small greenhouse/rabbitry.

Harbour Woods Mount Desert Island ✪

P.O. BOX 1214, ROUTE 102, SOUTHWEST HARBOR, MAINE 04679
www.acadia.net/harbourwoods/

Tel: **(207) 244-5388**	Guest Cottage: **$69–$115**
Best Time to Call: **After 10 AM**	Open: **All year**
Hosts: **Joseph and Christine Titka**	Breakfast: **Continental, plus**
Location: **20 mi. S of Ellsworth**	Pets: **No**
No. of Rooms: **3**	Children: **Welcome, over 12**
No. of Private Baths: **3**	Smoking: **No**
Double/pb: **$75–$115**	Social Drinking: **Permitted**

This 1800s Maine home retains all the charm and character celebrating a bygone era. Warm tones and subtle wall coverings create an atmosphere of casual elegance. Guest rooms are attractively decorated with distinctive personalities. All boast queen beds piled with plump pillows, cozy crackling fireplaces, TVs, candy, and telephones with free local calls. While listening to soft music, enjoy a variety of coffees, teas, juices, home-baked breads, muffins, bagels, and hot and cold cereals. A refrigerator, tea, and cookies are provided on the house. Take a leisurely swim in the Titkas' heated pool or privately reserve the indoor hot tub.

The Island House ✪

CLARK POINT ROAD, P.O. BOX 1006, SOUTHWEST HARBOR, MAINE 04679

Tel: **(207) 244-5180**	Carriage House: **$95–$165**
Best Time to Call: **AM**	Suite: **$140, sleeps 4**
Hosts: **Ann and Charles Bradford**	Open: **All year**
Location: **21 mi. S of Ellsworth**	Reduced Rates: **Available**
No. of Rooms: **4**	Breakfast: **Full**
No. of Private Baths: **2**	Pets: **No**
Max. No. Sharing Bath: **4**	Children: **Welcome, over 10**
Double/pb: **$60–$75**	Smoking: **No**
Single/pb: **$60–$65**	Social Drinking: **Permitted**
Double/sb: **$50–$70**	Minimum Stay: **2 nights in August**
Single/sb: **$50–$65**	

Launched in the mid-1800s as Mt. Desert Island's first summer hotel, The Island House retains its old-time charm as a gracious seacoast family home. Furnishings collected from Ann's childhood in Southeast Asia blend beautifully with the spacious, simply decorated rooms. Breakfasts, served in the dining room, may include eggs Florentine, blueberry coffee cake, and a sausage or cheese casserole. Your hosts know the island well and will be happy to help you plan your day. Acadia National Park is two miles away and Bar Harbor is 15 miles away.

Serenity on the Oyster ✪

ROUTE 1, BOX 5915, THOMASTON, MAINE 04861
www.midcoast.com/~serene/

Tel: **(207) 354-2063; (888) SERENE 1**	Single/sb: **$65**
Best Time to Call: **9 AM**	Open: **All year**
Hosts: **Chuck and Terry Fleming**	Breakfast: **Full**
Location: **1½ hrs. NE of Portland**	Credit Cards: **MC, VISA**
No. of Rooms: **4**	Pets: **No**
No. of Private Baths: **1**	Children: **Welcome, over 12**
Max. No. Sharing Bath: **4**	Smoking: **No**
Double/pb: **$85**	Social Drinking: **Permitted**
Double/sb: **$75**	Airport/Station Pickup: **Yes**

Serenity overlooks the Oyster River from five acres of wooded land, including a quarter-acre pond. Guests will experience total relaxation in the spacious rooms. A New England-style breakfast is served in the formal dining room and may consist of fresh-baked breads, cakes, and ethnic delights. This B&B is conveniently located on Route 1, just before the historic town of Thomaston.

Fox Island Inn ✪
P.O. BOX 451, VINALHAVEN, MAINE 04863

Tel: **(207) 863-2122, Oct.–May;**
   (850) 425-5059
Best Time to Call: **Evenings**
Host: **Gail Reinertsen**
Location: **70 mi. N of Portland**
No. of Rooms: **6**
Max. No. Sharing Bath: **4**
Double/sb: **$50–$75**

Single/sb: **$40**
Open: **June–Sept.**
Breakfast: **Continental**
Pets: **No**
Children: **Welcome, over 8**
Smoking: **No**
Social Drinking: **Permitted**

This midcoast Maine island is the perfect getaway from tourist traffic and crowds. To get to the Inn, leave your car in the ferry parking lot in Rockland and enjoy the hour-plus cruise across island-dotted Penobscot Bay. Once there it's a short walk to the Inn. Guest rooms are simply decorated with quilts and flowers. In the morning enjoy a hearty home-made Continental breakfast. Things to do include hiking, biking, swimming in the ocean or spring-fed quarries, and enjoying the great little restaurants located a few blocks away.

Broad Bay Inn & Gallery ✪
1014 MAIN STREET, P.O. BOX 607, WALDOBORO, MAINE 04572
brdbayin@midcoast.com

Tel: **(207) 832-6668; (800) 736-6769**
Host: **Libby Hopkins**
Location: **80 mi. N of Portland**
No. of Rooms: **5**
Max. No. Sharing Bath: **4**
Double/sb: **$40–$75**
Single/sb: **$35–$60**
Open: **All year**

Breakfast: **Full**
Credit Cards: **MC, VISA**
Pets: **No**
Children: **Welcome, over 12**
Smoking: **No**
Social Drinking: **Permitted**
Foreign Languages: **French**

The Inn, set in a charming midcoast village, is a classic Colonial, circa 1830, with light, airy, handsomely decorated rooms. Some guest rooms have canopy beds, and all have Victorian furnishings. There's a large deck on which to sip afternoon tea or sherry, and Libby's garden is lovely enough to be included in local Garden Club tours. This is a convenient base from which to enjoy the quaint fishing villages, the lighthouse, and the Audubon Sanctuary. Guests can swim at Damariscotta Lake, and morning or evening sailboat cruises are easily arranged. A sumptuous breakfast often includes crepes and herbed cheese omelettes. Libby is a theater buff and retired commercial artist; she has a gallery, which is located in the two-story barn behind the Inn. Three watercolor workshops are offered in the summer, with excursions to the new Andrew Wyeth wing at Farnsworth Museum.

Brannon-Bunker Inn ○
349L STATE ROUTE 129, (DAMARISCOTTA) WALPOLE, MAINE 04543

Tel: **(207) 563-5941; (800) 563-9225**
Best Time to Call: **9 AM–9 PM**
Hosts: **Jeanne and Joseph Hovance**
No. of Rooms: **7**
No. of Private Baths: **5**
Max. No. Sharing Bath: **2**
Double/pb: **$70–$75**
Single/pb: **$65–$70**
Double/sb: **$65–$70**

Single/sb: **$55–$60**
Suites: **$85–$125**
Open: **Apr.–Dec.**
Breakfast: **Continental, plus**
Credit Cards: **AMEX, MC, VISA**
Pets: **No**
Children: **Welcome**
Smoking: **No**
Social Drinking: **Permitted**

The Brannon-Bunker Inn is an informal, relaxing inn, ideally situated in rural, coastal Maine. Guests may choose from accommodations in the 1900 converted barn or the carriage house across the stream. Each room is individually decorated in styles ranging from Colonial to Victorian. Hosts Jeanne and Joseph Hovance will help you plan your days over breakfast. Nearby activities include golf, ocean swimming at Pemaquid Beach Park, and fishing on the Damariscotta River.

The Cape Neddick House
1300 ROUTE 1, P.O. BOX 70, CAPE NEDDICK (YORK), MAINE 03902

Tel: **(207) 363-2500; fax (207) 363-4499**
Hosts: **John and Dianne Goodwin**
Location: **12 mi. N of Portsmouth, New Hampshire**
No. of Rooms: **5**
No. of Private Baths: **5**
Double/pb: **$70–$120**
Single/pb: **$65–$110**

Suites: **$100–$130**
Open: **All year**
Reduced Rates: **Weekly**
Breakfast: **Full**
Pets: **No**
Children: **Welcome, over 5**
Smoking: **No**
Social Drinking: **Permitted**

Replete with family treasures, this inherited 1885 Victorian farmhouse is located in the historic coastal town of York. Relax by a fireplace in the living room in fall or winter, or cool off on the deck overlooking gardens and woods in spring and summer. Shop till you drop at nearby factory outlets, boutiques, and antique shops, or observe Mother Nature's creations on rural roads, in wildlife sanctuaries, and on the beaches. Sleep in antique-filled bedrooms under handmade quilts and air-conditioning. The two-room suite has a fireplace. Awake to the scent of cinnamon popovers, strawberry scones, peach almond torte, or ham and apple biscuits—enough to sustain you for another day of exploring the Maine coast.

For key to listings, see inside front or back cover.

✪ This star means that rates are guaranteed through December 31, 1999, to any guest making a reservation as a result of reading about the B&B in *Bed & Breakfast U.S.A.*—1999 edition.

Important! To avoid misunderstandings, always ask about cancellation policies when booking.

Please enclose a self-addressed, stamped, business-size envelope when contacting reservation services.

For more details on what you can expect in a B&B, see Chapter 1.

Always mention *Bed & Breakfast U.S.A.* when making reservations!

We want to hear from you! Use the form on page 593.

MARYLAND

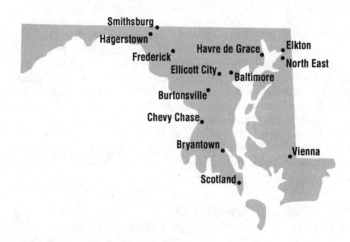

Amanda's B&B Reservation Service ✪
1428 PARK AVENUE, BALTIMORE, MARYLAND 21217

Tel: **(410) 225-0001; (800) 899-7533;**
  fax (410) 728-8957
Best Time to Call: **8:30 AM–5:30 PM**
  Mon.–Fri.; 8:30 AM–noon Sat.
Coordinator: **Betsy Grater**
States/Regions Covered: **Delaware,**
  District of Columbia, Maryland, New

Jersey, Pennsylvania, Virginia, West
Virginia
Descriptive Directory of B&Bs: **$5**
Rates (Single/Double):
  Modest: **$60–$65**
  Luxury: **$85–$150**
Credit Cards: **AMEX, DISC, MC, VISA**

Amanda's is a regional reservation service for private homes, small inns, cottages, and yachts. This service represents almost 200 properties throughout Maryland and the six surrounding states. Accommodations include everything from economical to luxury rooms with Jacuzzis and private baths.

Betsy's Bed and Breakfast ✪
1428 PARK AVENUE, BALTIMORE, MARYLAND 21217

Tel: **(410) 383-1274**	Open: **All year**
Best Time to Call: **9:30 AM–10 PM**	Breakfast: **Full**
Host: **Betsy Grater**	Credit Cards: **AMEX, MC, VISA**
No. of Rooms: **3**	Pets: **No**
No. of Private Baths: **3**	Children: **Welcome**
Double/pb: **$85–$125**	Smoking: **No**
Single/pb: **$65**	Social Drinking: **Permitted**

A petite estate, this four-story row house is in Bolton Hill, a historic Baltimore neighborhood listed on the National Registry. The interior features 12-foot ceilings with center medallions, a hall floor inlaid with oak and walnut, crown moldings, and carved marble fireplaces. This charming old house is uniquely decorated with a large collection of original brass rubbings, heirloom quilts, and interesting wall groupings. Modern amenities include a hot tub. Betsy's B&B is just a few blocks from a new light-rail stop at "Cultural Station," and steps away from Meyerhoff Symphony Hall, the Lyric Opera House, Antique Row, and the Maryland Institute of Art. The Inner Harbor is seven minutes away by car.

Shady Oaks of Serenity ✪
P.O. BOX 842, BRYANTOWN, MARYLAND 20617-0842

Tel: **(800) 597-0924**	Breakfast: **Continental**
Best Time to Call: **4–11 PM**	Pets: **No**
Hosts: **Kathy and Gene Kazimer**	Children: **Welcome, over 14**
Location: **35 mi. from Washington, D.C.**	Smoking: **No**
Suites: **$65**	Social Drinking: **Permitted**
Open: **All year**	

Shady Oaks of Serenity is a new Georgian Victorian situated on three acres and surrounded by trees. This secluded home is off the beaten path, yet within a 45-minute drive of the nation's capital and Annapolis, home of the U.S. Naval Academy. Just down the road is Amish country with antiques and unique shops, historic churches, the renowned Dr. Mudd Home, and Gilbert Run Park, a favorite county stop. Also, this retreat may be of interest to those visiting patients at the Charlotte Hall Veterans Home, only minutes away. Guest rooms are decorated in various themes; each has a private bath. Visitors are welcome to gather in the sitting room and the front porch or enjoy an evening on the deck. Kathy and Gene cordially invite you to be a guest in their home and visit historic Charles County. The morning brings fresh coffee, homemade muffins or breads, and a fresh variety of fruits.

The Taylors' B&B ✪
P.O. BOX 238, BURTONSVILLE, MARYLAND 20866-0238

Tel: **(301) 236-4318**	Open: **All year**
Best Time to Call: **9–11 AM; 7–9 PM**	Breakfast: **Continental**
Hosts: **Ruth and Fred Taylor**	Pets: **No**
Location: **30 min. from Washington,**	Children: **No**
D.C., and the Inner Harbor	Smoking: **No**
No. of Rooms: **1**	Social Drinking: **Permitted**
No. of Private Baths: **1**	Foreign Languages: **French**
Double/pb: **$60**	

This gracious two-story Colonial home offers a breath of fresh country air just 30 minutes from Washington, D.C., and Baltimore's Inner Harbor district. Guests can enjoy the grand piano, the extensive collection of books in the library, and Ruth's paintings. In warm weather, cool drinks are served in the gazebo; in winter, guests gather by the fireplace in the family room. Both of your hosts are retired. Ruth likes to read, sew, paint, and cook; Fred enjoys reading, writing, history, and music. They've traveled extensively and know how to make guests feel welcome. Tennis courts, horseback riding, and nature trails are nearby.

Chevy Chase Bed & Breakfast ✪
6815 CONNECTICUT AVENUE, CHEVY CHASE, MARYLAND 20815

Tel: **(301) 656-5867; fax (301)**	Single/pb: **$60–$65**
656-5867	Open: **All year**
Best Time to Call: **Anytime**	Reduced Rates: **Families**
Host: **S. C. Gotbaum**	Breakfast: **Continental, plus**
Location: **1 mi. N of Washington, D.C.**	Pets: **No**
No. of rooms: **2**	Children: **Welcome**
No. of Private Baths: **2**	Smoking: **No**
Double/pb: **$70–$75**	Social Drinking: **Permitted**

Enjoy the convenience of being close to the transportation and sights of Washington, D.C., and Maryland's Montgomery County while staying at a relaxing, turn-of-the century, country-style house. Rooms have beamed ceilings and are filled with rare tapestries, oriental rugs, baskets, copperware, and native crafts from Mexico to the Mideast. The garden room has a cathedral ceiling and private deck. The gabled skylight room has a king-size bed. Your host is a sociologist with a private consulting business. Breakfast items include homemade breads, jams, pancakes, French toast, and a special blend of Louisiana coffee. When you want to take a break from touring, the lovely garden is there for you. There is a $5 surcharge for one-night stays.

The Garden Cottage at Sinking Springs Herb Farm ✪
234 BLAIR SHORE ROAD, ELKTON, MARYLAND 21921

Tel: **(410) 398-5566**
Best Time to Call: **9 AM–9 PM**
Hosts: **Ann and Bill Stubbs**
Location: **4¹/₂ mi. from Rte. 40**
No. of Rooms: **1**
No. of Private Baths: **1**
Guest Cottage: **$93 for 2; sleeps 3**
Open: **All year**
Reduced Rates: **5% seniors**

Breakfast: **Full**
Credit Cards: **MC, VISA**
Other Meals: **Available**
Pets: **No**
Children: **Welcome**
Smoking: **No**
Social Drinking: **Permitted**
Airport/Station Pickup: **Yes**

Guests frequently comment on the peaceful beauty of this 128-acre historic farm. The garden cottage has a sitting room and fireplace adjoining the bedroom. Breakfast features coffee ground from organically grown beans, herbal teas, homemade buns, fruit, and juice. A full country breakfast prepared with unprocessed food fresh from the farm is available at no extra charge. Lectures on herbs and craft classes are available, and a gift shop is on the premises. Longwood Gardens and the famed Winterthur Museum are close by. Historic Chesapeake City, with excellent restaurants, is five minutes away.

Hayland Farm ✪
5000 SHEPPARD LANE, ELLICOTT CITY, MARYLAND 21042

Tel: **(410) 531-5593**
Host: **Dorothy Mobley**
Location: **Bet. Baltimore and D.C.**
No. of Rooms: **3**
No. of Private Baths: **1**
Max. No. Sharing Bath: **4**
Double/pb: **$60**
Single/pb: **$40**

Double/sb: **$40**
Single/sb: **$25**
Open: **All year**
Breakfast: **Full**
Pets: **No**
Children: **No**
Smoking: **No**
Social Drinking: **Permitted**

When you breathe the country-fresh air, it may surprise you that Baltimore and Washington, D.C., are only a short drive away. At Hayland Farm you will find gracious living in a large manor house furnished in a handsome, yet comfortable, style. Dorothy is retired and has traveled extensively. She enjoys sharing conversation with her guests. In warm weather, the 20- by 50-foot swimming pool is a joy.

Middle Plantation Inn ✪
9549 LIBERTY ROAD, FREDERICK, MARYLAND 21701
bandb@MPInn.com; http://www.MPInn.com

Tel: **(301) 898-7128**
Best Time to Call: **6–10 PM**
Hosts: **Shirley and Dwight Mullican**

Location: **5 mi. E of Frederick**
No. of Rooms: **4**
No. of Private Baths: **4**

Double/pb: **$95–$110**
Open: **All year**
Breakfast: **Continental**
Credit Cards: **MC, VISA**

Pets: **No**
Children: **Welcome, over 15**
Smoking: **No**
Social Drinking: **Permitted**

Dwight and Shirley have furnished their handsome stone and log home with antiques collected on their travels. Their charming B&B will appeal to Civil War buffs, since Gettysburg, Pennsylvania, Sharpsburg, Maryland, and Harpers Ferry, West Virginia, are all 40 minutes away by car. Closer to home, Frederick's 33-block historic district boasts a fascinating mix of museums, galleries, antique shops, and eateries. And for more antiquing, guests should head to nearby New Market.

Lewrene Farm B&B ✪
9738 DOWNSVILLE PIKE, HAGERSTOWN, MARYLAND 21740

Tel: **(301) 582-1735**
Hosts: **Lewis and Irene Lehman**
Location: **3½ mi. from I-70 and I-81**
No. of Rooms: **6**
No. of Private Baths: **3**
Max. No. Sharing Bath: **4**
Double/pb: **$79–$115**
Double/sb: **$62–$68**

Suites: **$115**
Open: **All year**
Breakfast: **Full**
Children: **Welcome**
Smoking: **No**
Social Drinking: **No**
Foreign Languages: **Spanish**

Lewis and Irene will help you discover the peaceful beauty of their 125-acre farm located in a historic area near the Antietam Battlefield. Guests are treated like old friends and are welcome to lounge in front of the fireplace or to play the piano in the Colonial-style living room. You're invited to enjoy snacks and a video in the evening. Harpers Ferry, Fort Frederick, the C&O Canal, and Gettysburg are nearby. Irene sells antiques and collectibles on the premises.

Sunday's Bed & Breakfast ✪
39 BROADWAY, HAGERSTOWN, MARYLAND 21740

Tel: **(800) 221-4828; (301) 797-4331**
Best Time to Call: **Anytime**
Host: **Bob Ferrino**
Location: **70 mi. NW of Washington, D.C.**
No. of Rooms: **4**
No. of Private Baths: **4**
Double/pb: **$75–$115**
Single/pb: **$55–$95**

Open: **All year**
Reduced Rates: **Available**
Breakfast: **Full**
Credit Cards: **DC, MC, VISA**
Pets: **Sometimes**
Children: **Welcome, over 10**
Smoking: **No**
Social Drinking: **Permitted**
Airport Pickup: **Yes**

Built in 1890, this elegant Queen Anne Victorian is located in Hagerstown's historic north end, on a street lined with other grand old homes. Relax in your room or in the many public areas and porches. You may want to visit the area's numerous attractions, such as the National Historical Parks of Antietam, Harpers Ferry, Whitetails Ski Resort, and the C&O Canal. Or choose among the myriad other historic sites, antique shops, fishing areas, golf courses, museums, shopping outlets, and theaters.

The Wingrove Manor Inn ✪

635 OAK HILL AVENUE, HAGERSTOWN, MARYLAND 21740
www.interaccess.com/wingrove manor/index.html

Tel: **(301) 797-7769; fax (301) 797-8659**
Host: **Winnie Price**
Location: **70 mi. NW of Washington, D.C.**
Suites: **$85–$125**
Open: **All year**
Reduced Rates: **Available**

Breakfast: **Continental**
Credit Cards: **MC, VISA**
Pets: **No**
Children: **Welcome, off-season**
Smoking: **No**
Social Drinking: **Permitted**
Minimum Stay: **2 nights peak season**
Airport Pickup: **Yes**

The Wingrove Manor is a beautifully restored bed and breakfast on a street lined with Victorian mansions. Relax in the wicker rockers stretched across a large Southern porch surrounded by 23 white columns, ceramic tiled floors, and breathtaking beauty. Inside you will find magnificent turn-of-the-century craftsmanship, marble fireplaces, a winding staircase, oriental rugs, crystal chandeliers, and towering white columns—all reflecting the home's lineage. The common rooms are elegant. Featured on the first floor is the Canopy Suite with a queen-size bed, marble fireplace, private entrance, TV, VCR, and a full bath with a Jacuzzi, ideally suited for honeymooners. On the second floor are three spacious rooms all with TV, VCR, telephone, double-thick towels, fragrant sprays, sweet soaps, and queen beds that bid travelers welcome and promise a good night's sleep.

Currier House ✪
800 SOUTH MARKET STREET, HAVRE de GRACE, MARYLAND 21078

Tel: (800) 827-2889; (410) 939-7886
Best Time to Call: 8 AM–8 PM
Hosts: Jane and Paul Belbot
Location: 35 mi. NE of Baltimore
No. of Rooms: 4
No. of Private Baths: 4
Double/pb: $85–$95
Single/pb: $75–$85

Open: All year
Reduced Rates: No
Breakfast: Full
Credit Cards: AMEX, DISC, MC, VISA
Pets: No
Children: No
Smoking: No
Social Drinking: Permitted

Currier House, located in Havre de Grace's historic residential district at the top of the Chesapeake Bay, has been occupied by the Currier family since 1861. The B&B is furnished with antiques, family heirlooms, and mementos that have been passed from generation to generation. Just one block from the Currier House are the Decoy and Maritime museums and the Concord Point Lighthouse, the oldest lighthouse in continuous operation in this country. Numerous antique shops, galleries, boutiques, and restaurants are within walking distance; a water taxi operates from one end of town to the other. Currier House was always a waterman's home, and keeping the tradition alive, a waterman's breakfast is served in the morning.

The Mill House B&B ✪
102 MILL LANE, NORTH EAST, MARYLAND 21901

Tel: (410) 287-3532
Best Time to Call: Before 9 AM; after 4 PM
Hosts: Lucia and Nick Demond
Location: 40 mi. NE of Baltimore
No. of Rooms: 2
Max. No. Sharing Bath: 4
Double/sb: $65–$75

Single/sb: $60–$70
Open: Mar. 1–Dec. 1
Breakfast: Full
Credit Cards: MC, VISA
Pets: No
Children: Welcome, over 12
Smoking: No
Social Drinking: Permitted

A genuine mill house that dates to the early 18th century, this B&B is furnished entirely in antiques. You'll see picturesque mill ruins and wildflowers on the grounds, but you won't see the parlor's original Queen Anne paneling; that was purchased by Henry Francis Du Pont and installed in his Winterthur estate bedroom. The Winterthur Museum and the Brandywine River Museum are less than an hour's drive away, as is Baltimore's Inner Harbor. Sightseers will be sustained with a full breakfast, including homemade breads fresh from the oven.

St. Michael's Manor B&B
ST. MICHAEL'S MANOR, SCOTLAND, MARYLAND 20687

Tel: **(301) 872-4025**
Hosts: **Joe and Nancy Dick**
Location: **9 mi. S of St. Marys City**
No. of Rooms: **4**
Max. No. Sharing Bath: **4**
Double/sb: **$70**
Single/sb: **$50**

Open: **All year**
Breakfast: **Full**
Pets: **No**
Children: **By arrangement**
Smoking: **Downstairs**
Social Drinking: **Permitted**

St. Michael's Manor was built in 1805 on land patented to Leonard Calvert during the 17th century. Today, the white stucco manor home on picturesque Long Neck Creek is included in the state's Pilgrimage Tour. The beautiful handcrafted woodwork has been preserved and is complemented by antiques and handcrafts. Your hosts offer you the use of a canoe, paddleboat, bikes, spa, and swimming pool. Estate wine tasting is also available. The manor house is near Point Lookout State Park, the Chesapeake Bay, and historic St. Marys City.

Blue Bear Bed & Breakfast ✪
13810 FRANK'S RUN ROAD, SMITHSBURG, MARYLAND 21783

Tel: **(800) 381-2292**
Best Time to Call: **After 4 PM**
Hosts: **Ellen Panchula and Marilyn Motter**
Location: **6 mi. from I-70, exit 35**
No. of Rooms: **2**
No. of Private Baths: **2**
Double/pb: **$60–$65**

Single/pb: **$50–$55**
Open: **All year**
Breakfast: **Continental**
Pets: **No**
Children: **Welcome, over 12**
Smoking: **No**
Social Drinking: **Permitted**

Ellen, a full-time schoolteacher, and her sister Marilyn, a professional dog groomer, have joined together at the Blue Bear Bed & Breakfast to offer guests year-round hospitality. Their home is decorated in an informal country mode, with several antiques and a charming collection of friendly-faced teddy bears throughout the house. Guests can relax and enjoy beautiful views from the front porch or tour nearby battlefields. Breakfast consists of fresh fruits, homemade breads, pastries, and coffee cake. Snacks are offered in the evening.

The Tavern House ✪

111 WATER STREET, P.O. BOX 98, VIENNA, MARYLAND 21869

Tel: **(410) 376-3347**
Hosts: **Harvey and Elise Altergott**
Location: **15 mi. NW of Salisbury**
No. of Rooms: **4**
Max. No. Sharing Bath: **4**
Double/sb: **$70–$75**
Single/sb: **$65–$70**

Open: **All year**
Breakfast: **Full**
Credit Cards: **MC, VISA**
Pets: **No**
Children: **Welcome, over 12**
Smoking: **Permitted**
Social Drinking: **Permitted**

Vienna is a quiet little town on the Nanticoke River, where one can escape the stress of the 20th century. Careful restoration has brought back the simple purity of this Colonial tavern. The stark white "lime, sand, and hair" plaster accents the authentic furnishings. This is a place for those who enjoy looking at the river and marshes, watching an osprey in flight, or taking a leisurely walk. Days begin with a special full breakfast that is always a social event. For the sports minded, there's tennis, boating, and flat roads for bicycling, all within easy reach. This is an excellent base for exploring the Eastern Shore, interesting small towns, and Blackwater National Wildlife Refuge.

MASSACHUSETTS

Buckland, South Deerfield
Cummington,
North New Salem   Weston•
Amherst•
Ware•
•Auburn

Lynn, Swampscott

Scituate,
Norwell•

Cummaquid
Yarmouthport
Plymouth,   Orleans
Brewster •E. Orleans
Rehoboth•   Sandwich,•   Cape
Wareham, ••Dennis   Cod
New Bedford,   South Dennis| •Chatham
Woods Hole• Falmouth   Harwich Port
Vineyard Haven• Oak Bluffs
Nantucket

Bed & Breakfast Associates—Bay Colony, Ltd. ✪
P.O. BOX 57166, BABSON PARK, BOSTON,
MASSACHUSETTS 02157-0166
info@bnbboston.com; www.bnbboston.com

Tel: (781) 449-5302; (800) 347-5088;
  fax: (781) 449-5958
Best Time to Call: 9:30 AM—5 PM
  Mon.–Fri.
Coordinators: Arline Kardasis and
  Marilyn Mitchell
States/Regions Covered: Boston,
  Brookline, Cambridge, Cape Cod,
  Concord, Framingham, Gloucester,

Martha's Vineyard, Nantucket,
  Newton, North Shore, South Shore
Rates (Single/Double):
  Modest: $50–$65/$60–$75
  Average: $65–$100/$75–$100
  Luxury: $100–$150/$100–$175
Credit Cards: AMEX, CB, DC, MC, VISA
Minimum Stay: 2 nights

Bed & Breakfast Associates—Bay Colony is one of the original reservation services. Founded in 1981 by Marilyn and Arline, they provide a
highly personalized service with a staff of six who together have accumulated 70 years of experience. Guest requests for specific amenities

are carefully matched with over 150 B&B inns, homes, or unhosted apartments. Accommodations range from elegant Victorian brownstones and inns, located in the heart of Boston's best and most convenient neighborhoods, to suburban homes in 35 towns, including Cambridge and Brookline. Properties are fully inspected and are also available throughout Cape Cod and on the romantic islands of Martha's Vineyard and Nantucket. Most B&Bs are non-smoking. Requests for TV, phone, air-conditioning, canopy bed, Jacuzzi, or fireplaces can usually be met. They even offer swimming pools, oceanside settings, one kosher home, and an Arabian horse farm. Photos of B&Bs can be sent by e-mail.

Bed & Breakfast Cambridge & Greater Boston
P.O. BOX 1344, CAMBRIDGE, MASSACHUSETTS 02238-1344

Tel: **(617) 262-1155; (800) 888-0178**
Best Time to Call: **10 AM–5 PM**
  Mon.–Fri, 10 AM–3 PM Sat.
Coordinator: **Pamela Carruthers**
States/Regions Covered: **Boston, Cambridge, Lexington, and surrounding areas**

Rates (Single/Double):
  Average: **$60–$90**
  Luxury: **$90–$125**
Credit Cards: **AMEX, MC, VISA**
Minimum Stay: **2 nights**

Tally and Pamela can place you in host homes convenient to historic Lexington and Concord, downtown Boston, or in Cambridge. Many are close to Harvard and MIT, Lahey Clinic, historic Wright Tavern, Emerson's home, Walden Pond, and the Charles River. Unusual restaurants, specialty shops, and cultural happenings abound. Just tell your host about your interests and you will be assured of excellent advice. There's a $10 surcharge for one-night stays.

Bed & Breakfast Reservations—North Shore ✪
P.O. BOX 600035, GREATER BOSTON BRANCH, NEWTONVILLE, MASSACHUSETTS 02160-0001
bnbinc@ix.netcom.com; www.bnbinc.com

Tel: **(617) 964-1606; fax (617) 332-8572; (outside Massachusetts) (800) 832-2632**
Best Time to Call: **9 AM–5 PM Mon.–Fri. In-season: Sun. 7–8:30 PM; weekend messages monitored**
Coordinator: **Sheryl Felleman**
States/Regions Covered:
  Massachusetts—North Shore; Gloucester, Marblehead,

Newburyport, Rockport, Salem; Coastal Maine, New England fall foliage ski areas
Rates (Single/Double):
  Modest: **$50–$65 / $65–$70**
  Average: **$65–$75 / $75–$95**
  Luxury: **$100–$135 / $115–$200**
Credit Cards: **AMEX, MC, VISA**
Minimum Stay: **2 nights**

Explore the city and the many tourist attractions this region offers, then escape to the beautiful beaches of Cape Cod. Choose an antique Victorian, renovated brick townhouse, historic inn, classic Colonial, private suite, or deck house on the beach with ocean views. Guests are assured of carefully inspected accommodations and the finest New England hospitality. Greater Boston locations are close to area colleges and public transportation. The roster includes selected bed and breakfasts elsewhere on the Massachusetts North Shore, coastal Maine, and New England fall foliage/ski areas. Short-term relocation and weekly vacation rentals are available in selected locations. For tourists, families with children, business travelers, romantic getaways, special events, and extended travel itineraries, call today and let the staff plan a wonderful stay for you.

Bed and Breakfast Cape Cod, Nantucket and Martha's Vineyard ✪

Orleans Bed and Breakfast Associates Inc.
P.O. BOX 1312, ORLEANS, MASSACHUSETTS 02553
bedandb@ccapecod.net; orleansbnb@capecod.net
www.bandbcapecod.com; www.capecod.net/bb

Tel: **(800) 541-6226; (508) 255-3824;** fax: **(508) 240-0599**	**Martha's Vineyard, Nantucket, Plymouth**
Best Time to Call: **8 AM–8 PM**	Descriptive Directory of B&Bs: **Free**
Coordinators: **Gilles and Susanne Thibault**	Rates: **$65–$195**
	Credit Cards: **AMEX, DISC, MC, VISA**
States/Regions Covered: **Cape Cod,**	Minimum Stay: **2 nights in season**

Gilles and Susanne offer a great variety of historical sites, waterfront homes and cottages where you can walk on Cape Cod and the islands. Gilles and Susanne represent approximately 180 bed and breakfasts and inns. The Thibaults believe that all homes reflect on each other. All houses are inspected yearly. An exciting bridal reservation service caters to wedding guests. As of January 1999 Orleans Bed and Breakfast Associates and Bed and Breakfast Cape Cod will become one.

BOSTON AREA
B&B Host Homes of Boston
P.O. BOX 117, WABAN BRANCH, BOSTON, MASSACHUSETTS 02168

Tel: **(617) 244-1308; (800) 600-1308;** fax: **(617) 244-5156**	Descriptive Directory: **Free** Rates (Single/Double):
Best Time to Call: **9 AM–noon; 1:30–4:30 PM weekdays**	Modest: **$68–$75 / $75–$81** Average: **$75–$81 / $81–$95**
Coordinator: **Marcia Whittington**	Luxury: **$105–$150 / $105–$175**
States/Regions Covered: **Boston, Brookline, Cambridge, Hamilton, Lincoln, Milton, Needham, Newton, Scituate, Southborough, Sudbury, Waltham, Weymouth**	Credit Cards: **AMEX, MC, VISA** Minimum Stay: **2–3 nights**

Since 1982 Marcia has culled a variety of historic townhouses and Victorian and Colonial homes from Boston's best areas and surrounding suburbs. You'll find sites near major hotels and institutions, Haynes Convention Center, historic sites, and public transportation. Hosts offer free parking (except downtown), hearty continental breakfasts, and a cordial welcome to their bustling city of colleges, museums, and cultural life. To fax your reservation request, complete the form in the Host Homes of Boston brochure. A credit card is necessary to make reservations.

Bed & Breakfast Associates—Bay Colony, Ltd. ✪

P.O. BOX 57166, BABSON PARK, BOSTON,
MASSACHUSETTS 02157-0166
info@bnbboston.com; www.bnbboston.com

Tel: (781) 449-5302; (800) 347-5088;
fax: (781) 449-5958
Best Time to Call: 9:30 AM–5 PM
Mon.–Fri.
Coordinators: Arline Kardasis and
Marilyn Mitchell
States/Regions Covered: Boston,
Brookline, Cambridge, Cape Cod,
Concord, Framingham, Gloucester,

Martha's Vineyard, Nantucket,
Newton, North Shore, South Shore
Rates (Single/Double):
Modest: $50–$65 / $60–$75
Average: $65–$100 / $75–$100
Luxury: $100–$150 / $100–$175
Credit Cards: AMEX, CB, DC, MC, VISA
Minimum Stay: 2 nights

Bed & Breakfast Associates—Bay Colony is one of the original reservation services. Founded in 1981 by Marilyn and Arline, they provide a highly personalized service with a staff of six who together have accumulated 70 years of experience. Guest requests for specific amenities are carefully matched with over 150 B&B inns, homes, or unhosted apartments. Accommodations range from elegant Victorian brownstones and inns, located in the heart of Boston's best and most convenient neighborhoods, to suburban homes in 35 towns, including Cambridge and Brookline. Properties are fully inspected and are also available throughout Cape Cod and on the romantic islands of Martha's Vineyard and Nantucket. Most B&Bs are non-smoking. Requests for TV, phone, air-conditioning, canopy bed, Jacuzzi, or fireplaces can usually be met. They even offer swimming pools, oceanside settings, one kosher home, and an Arabian horse farm. Photos of our bed and breakfasts can be sent by mail.

Bed & Breakfast Reservations Greater Boston/ Cape Cod ✪

P.O. BOX 600035, GREATER BOSTON BRANCH, NEWTONVILLE, MASSACHUSETTS 02160-0001
bnbinc@ix.netcom.com; www.bnbinc.com

Tel: **(617) 964-1606; fax (617) 332-8572; (outside Massachusetts) (800) 832-2632**
Best Time to Call: **9 AM–5 PM Mon.–Fri. In season: Sun. 7–8:30 PM; weekend messages monitored**
Coordinator: **Suzanne Ross**
States/Regions Covered: **Boston, Brookline, Cambridge, Chestnut Hill,**

Concord, Newton, South Shore, Plymouth, Sturbridge, Cape Cod
Rates (Single/Double):
Modest: **$50–$65 / $65–$70**
Average: **$65–$75 / $75–$95**
Luxury: **$100–$135 / $115–$200**
Credit Cards: **AMEX, MC, VISA**
Minimum Stay: **2 nights**

Explore the city and the many tourist attractions this region offers, then escape to the beautiful beaches of Cape Cod. Choose an antique Victorian, renovated brick townhouse, historic inn, classic Colonial, private suite, or deck house on the beach with ocean views. Guests are assured of carefully inspected accommodations and the finest New England hospitality. Greater Boston locations are close to area colleges and public transportation. The roster includes selected bed and breakfasts elsewhere on the Massachusetts North Shore, coastal Maine, and New England fall foliage/ski areas. Short-term relocation and weekly vacation rentals are available in selected locations. For tourists, families with children, business travelers, romantic getaways, special events, and extended travel itineraries, call today and let the staff plan a wonderful stay for you.

George Fuller House

148 MAIN STREET, ESSEX, MASSACHUSETTS 01929

Tel: **(978) 768-7766; (800) 477-0148**
Best Time to Call: **10 AM–10 PM**
Hosts: **Cindy and Bob Cameron**
Location: **3 mi. off Rte. 128, Exit 15**
No. of Rooms: **7**
No. of Private Baths: **7**
Double/pb: **$100–$125**
Suites: **$145–$155**
Open: **All year**

Reduced Rates: **10% less Nov. 1–May 31**
Breakfast: **Full**
Credit Cards: **AMEX, DISC, MC, VISA**
Pets: **No**
Children: **Welcome, over 6**
Smoking: **No**
Social Drinking: **Permitted**
Airport/Station Pickup: **Yes**

This handsome Federalist home retains much of its 19th-century paneling and woodwork; four of the guest rooms have working fireplaces. The Camerons have decorated the house with antique beds, handmade quilts, braided rugs, and caned Boston rockers. Three hundred years ago, Essex was a shipbuilding center. Among landlubbers, Essex's main claim to fame is its antique shops. Whether you venture out on sea or on land, you'll be fortified by Cindy's versions of breakfast classics, such as her French toast drizzled with brandied lemon butter.

Williams Guest House ✪

136 BASS AVENUE, GLOUCESTER, MASSACHUSETTS 01930

Tel: **(508) 283-4931**	Guest Cottage: **$550 weekly for 2**
Best Time to Call: **8 AM–8 PM**	Open: **May 1–Nov. 1**
Host: **Betty Williams**	Reduced Rates: **Off-season, before June**
Location: **30 mi. N of Boston**	**17 and after Labor Day**
No. of Rooms: **7**	Breakfast: **Continental**
No. of Private Baths: **5**	Pets: **No**
Max. No. Sharing Bath: **4**	Children: **Welcome, in cottage**
Double/pb: **$65**	Smoking: **No**
Double/sb: **$56**	Social Drinking: **Permitted**

Located five miles from Rockport, and one and a half miles from Rocky Neck, Gloucester is a quaint fishing village on the North Shore. Betty's Colonial Revival house borders the finest beach, Good Harbor. The guest rooms are furnished with comfort in mind. Betty will be happy to suggest many interesting things to do, such as boat tours, sport fishing, whale-watching trips, sightseeing cruises around Cape Ann, the Hammond Castle Museum, and the shops and galleries of the artist colony.

Diamond District Breakfast Inn

142 OCEAN STREET, LYNN, MASSACHUSETTS 01902-2007

Tel: **(781) 599-4470; (800) 666-3076;**	Suites: **$185–$225**
(781) 599-5122	Open: **All year**
Best Time to Call: **9 AM–5 PM**	Reduced Rates: **Available**
Hosts: **Sandra and Jerry Caron**	Breakfast: **Full**
Location: **8 mi. NE of Boston**	Credit Cards: **AMEX, DC, MC, VISA**
No. of Rooms: **11**	Pets: **No**
No. of Private Baths: **7**	Children: **Welcome**
Double/pb: **$95–$140**	Smoking: **No**
Double/sb: **$80–$115**	

This 17-room Georgian mansion was built in 1911 by a Lynn shoe manufacturer. The architect's design includes a foyer, a grand staircase that winds up three floors, and a spacious living room with a fireplace, an ocean view, and French doors leading to a large verandah that overlooks the gardens and ocean. Antiques and Oriental rugs fill the house. Among the other furnishings you'll see are an 1895 rosewood Knabe concert grand piano and a Chippendale dining room table and chairs. Guest rooms offer down comforters, some fireplaces, ocean views, TV, telephone, air conditioning, modem jacks, and voice mail. Two deluxe suites boast ocean views, fireplaces, whirlpool, and deck. A candlelight breakfast is served in the dining room or on the verandah. Stroll the three-mile sandy beach with a walking promenade or dine in local res-

taurants. Located on a tree-lined street close enough to hear the surf. Public transportation stops nearby.

1810 House Bed & Breakfast ✪

**147 OLD OAKEN BUCKET ROAD, NORWELL,
MASSACHUSETTS 02061**
tuttle1810@aol.com

Tel: **(781) 659-1810**
Best Time to Call: **8 AM–9 PM**
Hosts: **Susanne and Harold Tuttle**
Location: **20 mi. S of Boston**
No. of Rooms: **3**
No. of Private Baths: **2**
Max. No. Sharing Bath: **4**

Double/pb: **$75–$85**
Open: **All year**
Breakfast: **Full**
Pets: **No**
Children: **Welcome, over 6**
Smoking: **No**
Social Drinking: **No**

The 1810 House is located in Norwell, a beautiful historic town halfway between Plymouth and Boston. The antique half-Cape with original beamed ceilings, three working fireplaces, wide pine floors, and hand-stenciled walls is furnished with Oriental rugs and interesting collectibles accumulated over the years. Guest rooms are bright, cheery, and air-conditioned. Norwell is an ideal location for day trips to Cape Cod, Concord, Lexington, the North Shore, and Newport, Rhode Island. Public transportation by subway or commuter boat is nearby. Weather permitting, enjoy a ride in Harold's Model T depot hack. There is a $10 surcharge for one-night stays.

The Allen House
18 ALLEN PLACE, SCITUATE, MASSACHUSETTS 02066

Tel: **(781) 545-8221**
Best Time to Call: **Mornings; evenings**
Hosts: **Christine and Iain Gilmour**
Location: **32 mi. SE of Boston**
No. of Rooms: **6**
No. of Private Baths: **6**
Double/pb: **$69–$149**

Open: **All year**
Breakfast: **Full**
Pets: **No**
Children: **Welcome, over 12**
Smoking: **No**
Social Drinking: **Permitted**
Airport/Station Pickup: **Yes**

With views of the village center, this white gabled Victorian overlooks the yacht harbor. When the Gilmours came to the United States in 1976, they brought along the lovely furniture of their native Great Britain. English antiques fill the house. They also imported British rituals: tea is a frequent celebration. For breakfast, Christine, a professional caterer, offers standards such as waffles and pancakes, as well as gourmet treats. The Allen House is distinguished by good music and good food. Iain, an accomplished musician, cheerfully shares the large library of classical music.

Marshall House ✪
11 EASTERN AVENUE, SWAMPSCOTT, MASSACHUSETTS 01907

Tel: **(781) 595-6544**
Hosts: **Pat and Al Marshall**
Location: **10 mi. N of Boston**
No. of Rooms: **3**
Max. No. Sharing Bath: **4**
Double/sb: **$85**
Single/sb: **$75**
Open: **All year**
Reduced Rates: **10% seniors**

Breakfast: **Continental**
Credit Cards: **AMEX, MC, VISA**
Pets: **No**
Children: **Welcome, over 6**
Smoking: **No**
Social Drinking: **Permitted**
Minimum Stay: **2 nights, weekends**
Airport/Station Pickup: **Yes**

Marshall House, built circa 1900, is located just a short walk from the beaches of the North Shore. The many porches of this spacious home offer salty breezes and an ocean view. Inside, the rooms are decorated with country furnishings, some cherished antiques, and accents of wood and stained glass. The bedrooms have modern amenities such as color televisions and refrigerators. Guests are welcome to relax in the common room and warm up beside the wood stove. This B&B is located ten miles from Logan International Airport. Pat and Al will gladly direct you to nearby restaurants, historic seacoast villages, and popular bicycle touring routes.

Webb-Bigelow House

863 BOSTON POST ROAD, WESTON, MASSACHUSETTS 02193

Tel: **(781) 899-2444**	Double/sb: **$95**
Hosts: **Mr. and Mrs. Robert C. Webb**	Open: **Apr.–Nov. 30**
Location: **4 mi. from Rte. 90, Exit 15**	Breakfast: **Full**
No. of Rooms: **3**	Pets: **No**
No. of Private Baths: **2**	Children: **Welcome, over 10**
Max. No. Sharing Bath: **1**	Smoking: **Restricted**
Double/pb: **$99**	Social Drinking: **Permitted**
Single/pb: **$95**	Minimum Stay: **2 nights Sept.–Oct.**

Experience old New England in this historic 1827 house built by Alphaeus Bigelow Jr. The Webbs added to its charm, surrounding it with lawns and flowers. Today it sits on three acres in Weston's National Registered Historic District and remains one of the finest preserved residences on the Post Road. Explore a wooded trail, relax by the pool, admire the fall foliage, or just read by a cozy fire. Hearty breakfasts, featuring fruit from the Webbs' orchards, are served in the formal dining room or on the pool deck. This B&B is twenty minutes from Radcliffe, Harvard, Wellesley, MIT, Boston University, and Boston College. Area attractions include Longfellow's Wayside Inn, Faneuil Hall Market Place, Plymouth, Salem, and Concord.

CAPE COD/MARTHA'S VINEYARD

Bed & Breakfast Cape Cod, Inc. ✪

P.O. BOX 341, WEST HYANNISPORT, MASSACHUSETTS 02672-0341
www.bandbcapecod.com; bedand@capecod.net

Tel: **(508) 775-2772**; fax: **(508) 775-2884**; **(800) 686-5252** for reservations	Descriptive Directory: **Free**
	Rates (Single/Double):
	Modest: **$65 / $75**
Best Time to Call: **8:30 AM–6 PM**	Average: **$75 / $95**
Coordinator: **Clark Diehl**	Luxury: **$95 / $195**
States/Regions Covered: **Cape Cod, Martha's Vineyard, Nantucket; South of Boston at Plymouth and Scituate**	Credit Cards: **AMEX, DISC, MC, VISA**
	Minimum Stay: **2 nights in season**

It's a little over an hour's drive from Boston to the charm, history, and relaxation of Cape Cod and the islands. Choose from more than 115 of Clark's inspected and approved restored sea captains' houses, host homes, or small inns. Enjoy the warm-water beaches on Nantucket Sound, golf, biking, and other recreational activities. Don't miss the discount shopping. Your hosts can direct you to attractions, including whale watches and antiques, seafood restaurants, and pleasant evening entertainment at a wonderful summer theater. There is a $10 surcharge for one-night stays, subject to availability. Brochures are available upon request.

Bed and Breakfast Cape Cod, Nantucket and Martha's Vineyard
Orleans Bed & Breakfast Associates, Inc. ✪
P.O. BOX 1312, ORLEANS, MASSACHUSETTS 02553
bedandb@ccapecod.net; Orleansbnb@capecod.net
www.bandbcapecod.com; www.capecod.net/bb

Tel: **(800) 541-6226; (508) 255-3824;** fax: **(508) 240-0599**	**Martha's Vineyard, Nantucket, Plymouth**
Best Time to Call: **8 AM–8 PM**	Descriptive Directory: **Free**
Coordinators: **Gilles and Susanne Thibault**	Rates: **$65–$195**
	Credit Cards: **AMEX, DISC, MC, VISA**
States/Regions Covered: **Cape Cod,**	Minimum Stay: **2 nights in season**

Gilles and Susan offer a great variety of historical sites, waterfront homes and cottages, and homes where you can walk on Cape Cod and the islands. Gilles and Susanne represent approximately 180 bed and breakfasts and inns. The Thibaults believe that all homes reflect on each other. All houses are inspected yearly, and an exciting bridal reservation service caters to wedding guests. As of January 1999, Orleans Bed and Breakfast Associates and Bed and Breakfast Cape Cod will become one.

On School House Pond ✪
1580 OLD KINGS HIGHWAY, BREWSTER, MASSACHUSETTS 02631

Tel: **(508) 896-7341**	Open: **All year**
Hosts: **Pat and Bill Busch**	Breakfast: **Continental**
Location: **2 mi. from Rte. 6, Exit 10**	Pets: **No**
No. of Rooms: **1**	Children: **Welcome**
No. of Private Baths: **1**	Smoking: **No**
Double/pb: **$68**	Social Drinking: **Permitted**

Lovingly furnished with collectibles and antiques, this home was built in the late 1700s and owned at one time by two sea captains. On School House Pond features a large, sunny guest room with a sitting area and screened porch. Centrally located between Hyannis and Provincetown, this B&B is just minutes from antique shops, theaters, specialty shops, the bike trail, National Seashore, and many wonderful restaurants. Breakfast includes fresh-ground coffee, homemade coffee cakes, breads, and jams. Pat does professional estate sales, enjoys old-fashioned crafts, and is actively involved with the town historic district commission board. Bill is a home inspector and enjoys gardening.

Blowin' a Gale ✪
219 OLD HARBOR ROAD, ROUTE 28, CHATHAM, MASSACHUSETTS 02633

Tel: **(508) 945-9716**	Reduced Rates: **Available**
Best Time to Call: **After 10 AM**	Breakfast: **Continental, plus**
Hosts: **Nancy and Bob Petrus**	Credit Cards: **MC, VISA**
Location: **90 mi. SE of Boston**	Pets: **No**
No. of Rooms: **2**	Children: **Welcome, over 12**
Max. No. Sharing Bath: **4**	Smoking: **No**
Double/sb: **$85**	Social Drinking: **Permitted**
Single/sb: **$75**	Minimum Stay: **2 nights**
Open: **June 15–Oct. 15**	Airport/Station Pickup: **Yes, prearranged**

If you are looking for restful, old-fashioned accommodations in a small homey atmosphere, Bob and Nancy invite you to this 1888 historic Victorian home. Blowin' a Gale is a charming guesthouse located one half-mile north of the downtown rotary on Route 28 and within walking distance of beaches, restaurants, and shops. Breakfast is served in the dining area or outside on the deck. A sitting area is provided for guests to enjoy TV. A phone and refrigerator are provided.

The Acworth Inn ✪

**4352 MAIN STREET, P.O. BOX 256, CUMMAQUID,
MASSACHUSETTS 02637**

Tel: **(800) 362-6363; (508) 362-3330**
Best Time to Call: **8 AM–10 PM**
Hosts: **Cheryl and Jack Ferrell**
Location: **5 mi. N of Hyannis**
No. of Rooms: **6**
No. of Private Baths: **6**
Double/pb: **$85–$125**
Open: **All year**
Reduced Rates: **Nov.–Apr.**

Breakfast: **Full**
Credit Cards: **AMEX, DISC, MC, VISA**
Pets: **No**
Children: **Welcome, over 12**
Smoking: **No**
Social Drinking: **Permitted**
Minimum Stay: **2 nights holidays**
Foreign Language: **German**

Acworth Inn sits quietly alongside the Old Kings Highway that winds through the historic, unspoiled north side of Cape Cod. Located near the town of Barnstable, Acworth Inn offers guests an opportunity to experience the gracious lifestyle of a bygone era. The Inn, circa 1860, is especially noted for the many hand-painted furnishings that decorate each of the bright, airy guest rooms. From its central location, day trips to Martha's Vineyard, Nantucket, and all points on the Cape are easily accomplished.

Isaiah Hall B&B Inn ✪

152 WHIG STREET, P.O. BOX 1007, DENNIS, MASSACHUSETTS 02638

Tel: **(508) 385-9928; (800) 736-0160**
Best Time to Call: **8 AM–10 PM**
Host: **Marie Brophy**
Location: **7 mi. E of Hyannis**
No. of Rooms: **10**
No. of Private Baths: **10**
Double/pb: **$85–$128**
Single/pb: **$75–$117**

Suite: **$142–$156**
Open: **Apr. 15–mid-Oct.**
Breakfast: **Continental, plus**
Credit Cards: **AMEX, MC, VISA**
Pets: **No**
Children: **Welcome, over 7**
Smoking: **No**
Social Drinking: **Permitted**

This Cape Cod farmhouse built in 1857 offers casual country living on the quiet, historic north side. The house is decorated in true New England style with quilts, antiques, and oriental rugs. Four rooms have balconies and one has a fireplace. Within walking distance are the beach, good restaurants, the Cape Playhouse, and countless antique and craft shops. It is also close to freshwater swimming, bike paths, and golf. All guest rooms have air-conditioning.

The Parsonage Inn ✪

**202 MAIN STREET, P.O. BOX 1501, EAST ORLEANS,
MASSACHUSETTS 02643**

Tel: **(508) 255-8217**
Best Time to Call: **10 AM–9 PM**

Hosts: **Ian and Elizabeth Browne**
Location: **90 mi. SE of Boston**

No. of Rooms: **8**
No. of Private Baths: **8**
Double/pb: **$90–$115**
Suites: **$125**
Open: **All year**
Reduced Rates: **Oct.–May**

Breakfast: **Full**
Credit Cards: **AMEX, MC, VISA**
Pets: **No**
Children: **Welcome, over 6**
Smoking: **No**
Social Drinking: **Permitted**

This quiet, romantic inn is housed in a charming 18th-century parsonage just one and a half miles from the sparkling waters at Nauset Beach. Bike trails, lakes, galleries, fine stores, and restaurants are all nearby. Delicious breakfasts are served in the morning; in the evening, your hosts set out complimentary hors d'oeuvres in the parlor. And fresh floral arrangements add a special touch to the comfortable, tastefully decorated rooms.

Captain Tom Lawrence House—1861 ✪
75 LOCUST STREET, FALMOUTH, MASSACHUSETTS 02540
www.sunsol.com/captaintom/

Tel: **(508) 540-1445; (800) 266-8139;**
   fax: **(508) 457-1790**
Best Time to Call: **8 AM–noon**
Host: **Barbara Sabo**
Location: **67 mi. S of Boston**
No. of Rooms: **6**
No. of Private Baths: **6**
Double/pb: **$85–$165**
Open: **All year**

Reduced Rates: **Off-season**
Breakfast: **Full**
Credit Cards: **MC, VISA**
Pets: **No**
Children: **Welcome, over 11**
Smoking: **No**
Social Drinking: **Permitted**
Foreign Languages: **German**

Captain Lawrence was a successful whaler in the 1800s. When he retired from the sea, he built himself a town residence on Locust Street. Today, the house remains much as he left it, including the original hardwood floors, circular stairwell, high ceilings, and antique furnishings; central air-conditioning has been added. In the morning, Barbara serves a hearty breakfast of fruit and creative entrees. Her Black Forest bread and Belgian waffles are truly special. She grinds her own flour from organically grown grain. She will gladly help you get around town—it's half a mile to the beach, a short walk to downtown Falmouth, and four miles to Woods Hole Seaport.

Hewins House Bed & Breakfast ✪
20 HEWINS STREET, FALMOUTH, MASSACHUSETTS 02540

Tel: **(800) 555-4363; (508) 457-4363**
Best Time to Call: **9 AM–5 PM**
Host: **Virginia Price**
Location: **In Falmouth Village of Cape Cod**
No. of Rooms: **3**
No. of Private Baths: **3**

Double/pb: **$85–$95**
Single/pb: **$75–$85**
Open: **Apr. 15–Nov. 1**
Reduced Rates: **10% after 4 nights or off-season**
Breakfast: **Full**
Pets: **No**

Children: **Welcome**   Minimum Stay: **2 nights**
Smoking: **No**   Station Pickup: **Yes**
Social Drinking: **Permitted**

This gracious 1820 Federal Colonial is located on Falmouth's Village Green. The well-preserved interior is decorated with antiques and period reproductions, giving the house a true nineteenth-century ambiance. Feel free to play the Steinway or relax with a book in the living room or on the porch, which overlooks the lovely gardens. Breakfast always includes fresh-ground coffee or tea, juice, fruit, and a hot entree such as Belgian waffles or gingerbread pancakes. If you have any diet restrictions, let your host know and she'll be happy to accommodate you. Enjoy the attractions of Falmouth or use Hewins House as a base from which to explore Cape Cod, Martha's Vineyard, and the surrounding area.

Palmer House Inn

81 PALMER AVENUE, FALMOUTH, MASSACHUSETTS 02540-2857
palmerhse@aol.com; www.palmerhouseinn.com

Tel: **(508) 548-1230; (800) 472-2632;**
  fax: (508) 540-1878
Best Time to Call: **10 AM–10 PM**
Hosts: **Ken and Joanne Baker**
Location: **Historic area, Falmouth**
  Village
No. of Rooms: **13**
No. of Private Baths: **13**

Double/pb: **$78–$160**
Single/pb: **$68–$150**
Suite: **$150–$185**
Open: **All year**
Reduced Rates: **Nov.–Apr.**
Breakfast: **Full**
Credit Cards: **AMEX, DC, DISC, MC,**
  VISA

Pets: **No**
Children: **Welcome, over 10**

Smoking: **No**
Social Drinking: **Permitted**

Built at the turn of the century, the main inn and adjacent guest house reflect the gentility and charm of the Victorian era. Stained glass windows, rich woodwork, hardwood floors, and antique furnishings create an overall sense of warmth and harmony. Beautiful beaches, quaint shops, ferry shuttles, and excellent restaurants are only a short stroll from the inn. Breakfast at the inn is an event. Guests rave about entrees such as Swiss eggs in puff pastry, chocolate-stuffed French toast with crème Anglaise, and pain perdu with orange cream. Late afternoon is the perfect time to enjoy a frosty glass of iced tea and freshly baked cookies while rocking on the porch. In cooler weather, curl up by the fire with a good book and a cup of hot chocolate. In the evening, unwind in a whirlpool tub.

Dunscroft-by-the-Sea ✪
24 PILGRIM ROAD, HARWICH PORT, MASSACHUSETTS 02646

Tel: **(508) 432-0810; (800) 432-4345**
Hosts: **Alyce and Wally Cunningham**
Location: **10 mi. E of Hyannis**
No. of Rooms: **9**
No. of Private Baths: **9**
Double/pb: **$95–$185**
Honeymoon Cottage: **$175–$235**

Open: **All year**
Breakfast: **Full**
Credit Cards: **AMEX, MC, VISA**
Pets: **No**
Children: **Welcome, over 14**
Smoking: **No**
Social Drinking: **Permitted**

With its breathtaking, private mile-long beach, this romantic 14-room Colonial inn, its cedar shingles weathered a traditional waterfront gray, offers everything you'd expect from a Cape Cod bed and breakfast. The many amenities include flower gardens, spacious grounds, an enclosed sunporch, a piano in the living room, library, a king suite with a fireplace, a Jacuzzi for two, king and queen canopied and fourposter beds, and robes for lounging or for the beach. Located within easy walking distance are Harwich Port's shops, galleries, and restaurants. You'll awaken to the aroma of freshly ground coffee as Alyce prepares a generous breakfast.

1875 House ✪
36 SEVENTH STREET, NEW BEDFORD, MASSACHUSETTS 02740

Tel: **(508) 997-6433**
Best Time to Call: **After 7 PM**
Hosts: **Cynthia Poyant and
Steven Saint-Aubin**
Location: **55 mi. S of Boston**
No. of Rooms: **3**
No. of Private Baths: **3**
Double/pb: **$55–$70**
Single/pb: **$35–$45**

Open: **All year**
Reduced Rates: **10% family, seniors**
Breakfast: **Continental**
Pets: **Sometimes**
Children: **Welcome**
Smoking: **Permitted**
Social Drinking: **Permitted**
Airport/Station Pickup: **Yes**

Located in the historic district, this 1875 Victorian home is within walking distance of downtown. Some of the local attractions include the Whaling Museum, art museum, Rotch Jones Duff Museum, and beaches. Cape Cod and Newport, R.I., are only 30 minutes away. The home has undergone thoughtful restoration, reflected in the tasteful decor throughout. Family photographs, books, and curio pieces are displayed in the sitting and dining rooms. Your hosts enjoy active exercise and sports. Cynthia is a social worker and Steven is an anesthetist. They welcome you to relax with them.

The Beach Rose ✪
74 COLOMBIAN AVENUE, BOX 2352, OAK BLUFFS, MASSACHUSETTS 02557

Tel: **(508) 693-6135**
Best Time to Call: **9 AM–9 PM**
Hosts: **Gloria and Russ Everett**
Location: **70 mi. SE of Boston**
No. of Rooms: **3**
Max. No. Sharing Bath: **4**
Double/sb: **$60–$100**
Single/sb: **$60**
Open: **May–Oct.**

Reduced Rates: **Off-season**
Breakfast: **Continental, plus**
Pets: **No**
Children: **Welcome, over 5**
Smoking: **No**
Social Drinking: **Permitted**
Minimum Stay: **3 nights holiday weekends; 2 nights summer weekends**

The Beach Rose is named for the colorful island plant, *Rosa rugosa*, whose pink flowers and bright red rose hips punctuate the island dunes. This charming home, nestled in an oak and pine woodland on Martha's Vineyard, is decorated in country antique style. Greet the morning with a breakfast of fresh fruit, a delicious entree du jour, homemade muffins and jams, and freshly brewed beverages. Your hosts provide warm hospitality and personal attention. Guests will want to see the gingerbread cottages of the Martha's Vineyard camp-meeting grounds, the Gay Head cliffs, and the historic whaling homes of Edgartown. The Vineyard has a myriad of sightseeing and other activities to offer visitors: biking, sailing, nature trails, fishing, picturesque beaches, and much more.

Academy Place Bed & Breakfast ✪
8 ACADEMY PLACE, P.O. BOX 1407, ORLEANS, MASSACHUSETTS 02653

Tel: **(508) 255-3181**
Hosts: **Sandy and Charles Terrell**
Location: **25 mi. E of Hyannis**
No. of Rooms: **5**
No. of Private Baths: **3**
Max. No. Sharing Bath: **4**
Double/pb: **$85–$95**
Double/sb: **$75**
Open: **Late May–mid Oct.**

Reduced Rates: **Available**
Breakfast: **Continental, Plus**
Credit Cards: **MC, VISA**
Pets: **No**
Children: **Welcome, over 6**
Minimum stay: **2 nights all holidays and weekends July–Aug.**
Smoking: **No**
Station Pickup: **Yes**

A quaint Cape Cod home on the village green with comfortable beds awaits you. This 1752 sea captain's house with many antique charms and period antiques is on the edge of Orleans's shopping district. Many fine retail stores and restaurants are a short walk away. For swimming, sunbathing, and fishing, the Atlantic Ocean and Cape Cod Bay beaches are within $2^1/2$ miles. The Cape Cod National Seashore is 4 miles by car or can be reached by a paved bike path, which is $^1/4$ mile from the house. An expanded Continental breakfast of homemade hot tasty muffins and breads with chilled juices and fresh fruits, freshly brewed coffee, teas, or hot chocolate is served daily. All rooms are air conditioned.

Morgan's Way Bed and Breakfast ✪

NINE MORGAN'S WAY, ORLEANS, CAPE COD, MASSACHUSETTS 02653
morgnway@capecod.net; www.capecodaccess.com/morgansway

Tel: **(508) 255-0831**
Best Time to Call: **11:30 AM–9 PM**
Hosts: **Page McMahan and Will Joy**
Location: **90 mi. SE of Boston**
No. of Rooms: **1**
No. of Private Baths: **1**
Double/pb: **$90–$115**
Single/pb: **$90–$115**
Guest Cottage: **$600–$805 weekly; sleeps 3**

Open: **All year**
Breakfast: **Full**
Pets: **No**
Children: **Welcome, over 12**
Smoking: **No**
Social Drinking: **Permitted**
Minimum Stay: **2 nights; 1 week for cottage; 3 nights holiday weekends**

This dramatic contemporary home, overlooking five acres of gardens and wooded land, offers guests a peaceful, romantic getaway. Soaring cathedral ceilings, oak beams, arched windows with panoramic views, oriental carpets, and porcelains give a feeling of luxury throughout. Specially appointed bedrooms have queen-size beds; those desiring extra privacy may prefer to stay in the poolside guest cottage. Relax on the massive, flower-filled deck or lounge by the large heated pool after a refreshing swim. Page's memorable breakfasts include creative fruit courses, delicious entrees, and homemade breads; she always has low-fat and low-cholesterol alternatives on hand. Morgan's Way is located just one mile from Orleans center and two miles from Nauset Beach; golf courses, lakes, bike trails, galleries, shops, and restaurants are all nearby. Page, an avid gardener, has a background in health administration, and Will is a civil engineer; they love sharing their property and Cape Cod, and will treat you as their special houseguest. For those of you who do not mind a higher rate, 1 room is available.

Foxglove Cottage Bed & Breakfast ✪
101 SANDWICH ROAD, PLYMOUTH, MASSACHUSETTS 02360

Tel: **(800) 479-4746; (508) 747-6576;** fax: **(508) 747-7622**	Breakfast: **Full**
Hosts: **Mr. and Mrs. Charles K. Cowan**	Pets: **No**
Location: **40 mi. S of Boston**	Children: **Welcome, over 12**
No. of Rooms: **3**	Smoking: **No**
No. of Private Baths: **3**	Social Drinking: **Permitted**
Double/pb: **$85–$90**	Minimum Stay: **2 nights weekends June–Oct.**
Open: **All year**	Station Pickup: **Yes**

Foxglove Cottage offers elegant and romantic lodging for the discerning traveler. This charming, restored Cape-style home is located around the corner from Plimoth Plantation and beaches. Guest rooms are tastefully furnished in American and English antiques, with original working fireplaces, wide pineboard floors, and air conditioning. Relax in the common room and watch cable TV, or read by the fireplace. The room opens onto a deck overlooking rolling fields and pastures filled with nature's wonders, including deer, coyotes, and red fox. Enjoy breakfast on the deck while planning your day's activities over a cup of gourmet coffee. Floxglove is conveniently located for day trips to Boston, Newport, Cape Cod, Nantucket, Martha's Vineyard, and Plymouth's famous whale watching trips, all less than an hour's drive away.

Plymouth Bay Manor B&B ✪
259 COURT STREET, PLYMOUTH, MASSACHUSETTS 02360

Tel: **(800) 492-1828**	Location: **40 mi. S of Boston**
Best Time to Call: **Afternoon**	No. of Rooms: **3**
Hosts: **Larry and Cindi Hamlin**	No. of Private Baths: **3**

Double/pb: **$85–$110**
Open: **Feb.–Nov.**
Reduced Rates: **Available**
Breakfast: **Full**
Credit Cards: **MC, VISA**

Pets: **No**
Children: **Welcome, over 12**
Smoking: **No**
Social Drinking: **Permitted**
Station Pickup: **Yes**

Guests will enjoy spectacular views of Plymouth Bay from each of the antique-furnished guest rooms. Plymouth Bay Manor B & B is a grand, three-story, shingle-style New England home built in 1903. This romantic retreat is situated on one acre of beautiful grounds. A beautifully presented and bountiful breakfast, fresh from your hosts' gardens, is served each morning.

The Captain Ezra Nye House ✪
152 MAIN STREET, SANDWICH, MASSACHUSETTS 02563

Tel: **(800) 388-2278;** fax: **(508) 833-2897**
Best Time to Call: **10 AM–6 PM**
Hosts: **Elaine and Harry Dickson**
Location: **60 mi. SE of Boston**
No. of Rooms: **6**
No. of Private Baths: **6**
Double/pb: **$85–$110**
Single/pb: **$75–$100**
Suites: **$100–$110**

Open: **All year**
Reduced Rates: **Off season**
Breakfast: **Full**
Credit Cards: **AMEX, DISC, MC, VISA**
Pets: **No**
Children: **Welcome, over 10**
Smoking: **No**
Social Drinking: **Permitted**
Airport/Station Pickup: **Yes**
Foreign Languages: **Spanish**

The Captain Ezra Nye House is a stately 1829 Federal home built by a seafarer noted for his record-breaking North Atlantic crossings and daring ocean rescues. The house sits in the heart of Sandwich, the oldest town on Cape Cod, and is within walking distance of museums, shops, and fine restaurants. Guests rooms are tastefully decorated in soft pastel tones, antiques, and an eclectic art collection. Hearty homemade breakfasts are served in the dining room. A cozy den and parlor with fireplaces complete the common areas.

Dillingham House ✪
71 MAIN STREET, SANDWICH, MASSACHUSETTS 02563

Tel: **(508) 833-0065**
Best Time to Call: **6–8 PM**
Host: **Kathleen Kenney**
Location: **60 mi. S of Boston**
No. of Rooms: **3**
No. of Private Baths: **3**
Double/pb: **$85**
Open: **All year**

Reduced Rates: **$10 less Nov.–Mar.**
Breakfast: **Continental**
Pets: **Sometimes**
Children: **Welcome**
Smoking: **Permitted**
Social Drinking: **Permitted**
Minimum Stay: **2 nights off-season**

Dillingham House is named for its first owner, who helped to found Sandwich, Cape Cod's oldest town. The house has many of the hallmarks of 17th-century construction, such as wide pine floors, exposed beams and rafters, and cozy brick hearths. Kathy is a Cape native and loves to discuss local lore. A Continental breakfast of juice, fresh fruit, muffins, and coffee or tea will fortify you for your excursions, whether they occur on land or on sea.

Captain Nickerson Inn ✪
333 MAIN STREET, SOUTH DENNIS, MASSACHUSETTS 02660

Tel: **(508) 398-5966**
Best Time to Call: **2 PM–6 PM Mon.–Fri.**
Hosts: **Pat and Dave York**
Location: **90 mi. SE of Boston**
No. of Rooms: **5**
No. of Private Baths: **3**
Max. No. Sharing Bath: **4**
Double/pb: **$82–$95**
Single/pb: **$77–$90**
Double/sb: **$65–$80**
Single/sb: **$65–$75**

Open: **Mar. 1–Dec. 21**
Reduced Rates: **Off season 15–20%,
    10% after fifth night**
Breakfast: **Full**
Credit Cards: **DISC, MC, VISA**
Pets: **No**
Children: **Welcome**
Smoking: **No**
Social Drinking: **Permitted**
Minimum Stay: **2 nights July–Aug.,
    3 nights July fourth weekend**

This delightful sea captain's home was built in 1828 and changed to its present Queen Anne style in 1879. Guest rooms are decorated with period four-poster or white iron queen beds and oriental or handwoven rugs. Relax in the fireplaced living room complete with a TV and VCR, a small selection of video movies, and popular board games. The Inn is situated on a bike path and bicycles are available for a small fee. Breakfast is served in the dining room, which has a fireplace and stained glass windows. Area attractions include championship public golf courses, world-class beaches, paddleboats, horseback riding, museums, fishing, crafts and antique shops, and a local church which has the oldest work-

ing pipe organ in the country. Cape Cod's 20-plus-mile bike trail is only a half mile away.

Nancy's Auberge ✪
98 MAIN STREET, P.O. BOX 4433, VINEYARD HAVEN, MARTHA'S VINEYARD, MASSACHUSETTS 02568

Tel: **(508) 693-4434**	Reduced Rates: **Available**
Best Time to Call: **Evenings**	Breakfast: **Continental**
Host: **Nancy Hurd**	Credit Cards: **MC, VISA**
Location: **7 mi. SE of Woods Hole**	Pets: **No**
No. of Rooms: **3**	Children: **Welcome**
No. of Private Baths: **1**	Smoking: **No**
Max. No. Sharing Bath: **4**	Social Drinking: **Permitted**
Double/pb: **$118**	Minimum Stay: **Summer season; holiday**
Double/sb: **$88–$98**	**weekends**
Open: **All year**	

Nancy's Auberge is a 150-year-old island home with a harbor view, convenient location, and three fireplaces. Comfortable and inviting whatever the season, the antique-filled B&B offers as much privacy as you seek. One guest remarked, "It's so picturesque. It's like living on a postcard." Since it's just a block and a half from the ferry, a car is not necessary. However, off-street parking is available. Within a few blocks are some of the island's finest restaurants, the Vineyard Playhouse, the Katherine Cornell Theatre, artisans' shops, windsurfing, sailing, and tennis. Nearby are excellent golf courses, horseback riding, and world-famous beaches. The town beach is a block away. Nancy's passions are travel, music, sports, and cooking.

The 1720 House

130 MAIN STREET, VINEYARD HAVEN, MASSACHUSETTS 02568
abbyquinn@aol.com

Tel: **(508) 693-6407**
Best Time to Call: **7:30 AM–9 PM**
Host: **Abby Hirsch**
No. of Rooms: **6**
No. of Private Baths: **3**
Max. No. Sharing Bath: **4**
Double/pb: **$85–$150**
Single/pb: **$85–$135**
Double/pb: **$85–$145**
Suites: **$175**
Open: **All year**
Reduced Rates: **Available**

Breakfast: **Continental**
Credit Cards: **MC, VISA**
Pets: **No**
Children: **Welcome, over 6**
Smoking: **Restricted**
Social Drinking: **Permitted**
Minimum Stay: **3 nights holiday weekends**
Airport Pickup: **Yes**
Foreign Languages: **Dutch, French, German**

The 1720 House is located one and a half blocks from the beach, three blocks from the ferry, and three blocks from the town of Vineyard Haven, which is filled with quaint stores, restaurants, and a movie house. Rooms are tastefully decorated in Colonial style and offer the comfort of days gone by. Outside, the house is surrounded by landscaped flower gardens allowing for peaceful and private afternoons. Activities include deep-sea fishing, horseback riding, boating, biking, swimming, theater, and arts. Breakfast specialties include fresh-baked muffins, cakes, and breads. Abby is a writer and TV producer. The house provides bikes and afternoon tea or sherry.

Mulberry Bed and Breakfast ✪
257 HIGH STREET, WAREHAM, MASSACHUSETTS 02571

Tel: **(508) 295-0684**	Open: **All year**
Best Time to Call: **Before 9 AM,**	Reduced Rates: **15% weekly**
after 4 PM	Breakfast: **Full**
Host: **Frances Murphy**	Pets: **No**
Location: **52 mi. S of Boston**	Children: **Welcome, over 10**
No. of Rooms: **3**	Smoking: **No**
Max. No. Sharing Bath: **4**	Social Drinking: **Permitted**
Double/sb: **$60–$70**	Airport/Station Pickup: **Yes**
Single/sb: **$50–$55**	

Frances Murphy welcomes you to her vintage Cape Cod home, built in 1847. The house is one and a half stories and is painted white with red shutters. It is named for the mulberry tree in the yard that attracts many birds and provides shade from the summer sun. Frances has created a home-away-from-home atmosphere, where guests can relax in a small living room with a piano, or join her in a larger living-dining area with fireplace. Spend the night in an Early American–style bedroom and have breakfast on the spacious private deck. Home-baked breads and muffins, casseroles, and fresh fruit are served with jams and jellies made from Frances's fruit trees. In the afternoon, snacks and cool drinks are served. Mulberry Bed and Breakfast is located in the historic part of town, ten minutes from the beach.

The Marlborough ✪
320 WOODS HOLE ROAD, FALMOUTH, WOODS HOLE, MASSACHUSETTS 02543

Tel: **(508) 548-6218**	Open: **All year**
Best Time to Call: **10 AM–9 PM**	Breakfast: **Full**
Host: **Al Hammond**	Credit Cards: **AMEX, MC, VISA**
Location: **2½ mi. from Rte. 28**	Pets: **No**
No. of Rooms: **6**	Children: **Welcome, over 2**
No. of Private Baths: **6**	Smoking: **No**
Double/pb: **$90–$135**	Social Drinking: **Permitted**
Single/pb: **$90–$130**	

This faithful reproduction of a full Cape house is beautifully decorated with antiques, collectibles, fabric wall coverings, and matching bed linens. It is situated on a shaded half-acre with a paddle tennis court, swimming pool, and hammock. It's 1 mile to a private beach. Ferries to Martha's Vineyard are a mile away. Al serves a full gourmet breakfast year round.

One Centre Street Inn ✪
ONE CENTRE STREET, YARMOUTHPORT, MASSACHUSETTS 02675

Tel: (888) 407-1653; (508) 362-8910
Best Time to Call: 10 AM–8 PM
Host: Karen Iannello
No. of Rooms: 6
No. of Private Baths: 4
Max. No. Sharing Bath: 4
Double/pb: $85–$95
Double/sb: $75
Suites: $120
Open: All year

Reduced Rates: $10 Oct. 15–May 15
Breakfast: Full
Credit Cards: MC, VISA
Pets: No
Children: Welcome, over 8
Smoking: No
Social Drinking: Permitted
Minimum Stay: 2 nights, weekends in summer

This 1824 parsonage offers understated elegance on the historic north side of Cape Cod. The Inn's walls are adorned with original prints and paintings by a local artist. Enjoy the piano in the parlor or take a ride to the beach on a bicycle provided by the Inn. A gourmet breakfast is served daily, including fruit, scones, muffins, yogurt, juice, freshly ground coffee, and such entrees as orange French toast with strawberry Grand Marnier sauce, the house specialty.

CENTRAL/WESTERN/SOUTHERN MASSACHUSETTS

Folkstone Bed & Breakfast Reservation Service ✪
P.O. BOX 211, WILLIAMSBURG, MASSACHUSETTS 01096-0211

Tel: (800) 762-2751; (508) 480-0380
Best Time to Call: 9 AM–5 PM,
    Mon.–Fri.
Coordinator: Eleanor M. Hebert
States/Regions Covered: Auburn, Barre,
    Concord, Groton, Lancaster, Palmer,
    Southboro, Stowe, Sturbridge,
    Thompson, Worcester

Descriptive Directory: Free
Rates (Single/Double):
    Modest: $55–$60
    Average: $70–$75
    Luxury: $90 / $95–$120
Credit Cards: AMEX, MC, VISA

Eleanor's service offers comfortable relaxed lodging in a wide variety of host homes, including convenient in-town locations and country hideaways throughout central Massachusetts and northeast Connecticut. Experience the wealth of cultural entertainment and recreational opportunities this area has to offer.

Allen House Victorian Inn ✪
599 MAIN STREET, AMHERST, MASSACHUSETTS 01002
www.allenhouse.com

Tel: (413) 253-5000
Hosts: Alan and Ann Zieminski
Location: 5 mi. from Rte. 91, Exit 19
No. of Rooms: 7

No. of Private Baths: 7
Double/pb: $55–$125
Single/pb: $45–$105
Open: All year

Millikan

Breakfast: **Full**
Pets: **No**
Children: **Welcome, over 7**
Smoking: **No**

Social Drinking: **Permitted**
Minimum Stay: **College and fall foliage weekends**

This 1886 Queen Anne Stick–style Victorian features period antiques, art, decor, and art wall coverings by designers from the Aesthetic movement, which emphasized art in interior decoration; Charles Eastlake, Walter Crane, and William Morris are represented. Allen House Victorian Inn is located on three scenic acres in the heart of Amherst, within walking distance of Emily Dickinson House, Amherst College, the University of Massachusetts, and innumerable galleries, museums, theaters, shops, and restaurants. Free busing is available throughout the five-college area. A full formal breakfast is served. Afternoon, evening tea and refreshments are served. There are private phones and central air.

Captain Samuel Eddy House ✪
609 OXFORD STREET SOUTH, AUBURN, MASSACHUSETTS 01501

Tel: **(508) 832-7282**
Best Time to Call: **10 AM–9 PM**
Hosts: **Diedre and Mike Meddaugh**
Location: **5 mi. S of Worcester**
No. of Rooms: **3**
No. of Private Baths: **3**
Double/pb: **$70**
Single/pb: **$55**

Suites: **$90–$120; sleeps 2–5**
Open: **All year**
Reduced Rates: **Available**
Breakfast: **Full**
Pets: **No**
Children: **Welcome, over 5**
Smoking: **No**
Social Drinking: **Permitted**

The Captain Samuel Eddy House, circa 1765, is a typical New England design. The center chimney Colonial home has three fireplaces, one in each parlor, and a Sturbridge fireplace in the keeping room—which now serves as a dining room. The house is decorated in period style with antiques, four-poster beds, Windsor and wing-back chairs, beautiful draperies, original wide-board floors, and hand-stenciled walls. The sunroom, circa 1980, lets guests enjoy a view of the woods, garden, and Eddy Pond. The inn is conveniently located near the Mass Pike, Exit 10, south of Worcester and east of Sturbridge.

1797 House ✪
UPPER STREET, BUCKLAND, MASSACHUSETTS 01338

Tel: **(413) 625-2975**
Best Time to Call: **5 PM–9 PM**
Host: **Janet Turley**
Location: **13 mi. from Rte. 91, Exit 26**
No. of Rooms: **3**
No. of Private Baths: **3**
Double/pb: **$65–$80**

Single/pb: **$58**
Open: **Jan. 2–Oct. 31**
Breakfast: **Full**
Pets: **No**
Children: **No**
Smoking: **No**
Social Drinking: **Permitted**

This white, center-hall Colonial, circa 1797, has a lovely screened-in porch for summer enjoyment and four fireplaces and down quilts for cozy winter pleasure. Prestigious Deerfield Academy, Old Deerfield, Sturbridge Village, and the historic sights of Pioneer Valley are all close by. The University of Massachusetts, Smith, Amherst, and Williams are convenient to Janet's home. Sensational breakfast treats include stuffed croissants, French toast, and special casseroles, along with fresh fruit and breakfast meats.

Windfields Farm ✪
154 WINDSOR BUSH ROAD, CUMMINGTON, MASSACHUSETTS 01026

Tel: **(413) 684-3786**
Best Time to Call: **Before 9 PM**
Hosts: **Carolyn and Arnold Westwood**
Location: **20 mi. E of Pittsfield**
No. of Rooms: **2**
Max. No. Sharing Bath: **4**
Double/sb: **$70**
Single/sb: **$50**

Open: **May 1–Mar. 1**
Reduced Rates: **10% midweek**
Breakfast: **Full**
Pets: **No**
Children: **Welcome, over 12**
Smoking: **No**
Social Drinking: **Permitted**
Minimum Stay: **2 nights most weekends**

Since 1983, the Westwoods have been welcoming guests to their secluded 19th-century homestead in the rolling Berkshire countryside. The hundred-acre estate includes organic gardens, flower beds, wild blueberry fields, and a brook and a pond. Hiking and skiing trails, a state forest, and the Audubon Wildlife Sanctuary are within walking distance. Arnold, a retired Unitarian minister, built his own sugarhouse and greenhouse and doubles as publisher of a local monthly newspaper. Carolyn is an award-winning gardener. Both are active in community affairs and conservation, and, during the late winter mud season, they make maple syrup from their property's 500 taps.

Bullard Farm Bed & Breakfast ✪
89 ELM STREET, NORTH NEW SALEM, MASSACHUSETTS 01364

Tel: **(978) 544-6959**	Reduced Rates: **Available**
Host: **Janet Kraft**	Breakfast: **Full**
Location: **75 mi. W of Boston**	Credit Cards: **MC, VISA**
No. of Rooms: **4**	Pets: **Sometimes**
Max. No. Sharing Bath: **4**	Children: **Welcome, over 3**
Double/sb: **$75**	Smoking: **No**
Single/sb: **$65**	Social Drinking: **Permitted**
Suite: **$90, sleeps 4**	Airport/Station Pickup: **Yes**
Open: **All year**	

Just half an hour from Amherst and historic Deerfield, you'll find this 200-year-old restored Colonial home with all the trimmings, like six working fireplaces, exposed beams, and treasured family antiques. Allow plenty of time for surveying the 300-acre property, with its rhododendron gardens, cultivated blueberries, hiking and cross-country ski trails, old swimming hole, and 18th-century mill sites. The renovated barn with an upper-level dance floor serves as a conference center offering occasional nature programs, jazz concerts, and other events. Sleigh rides and hayrides are available upon request.

Five Bridge Inn B&B ✪
154 PINE STREET, REHOBOTH, MASSACHUSETTS 02769

Tel: **(508) 252-3190**	Breakfast: **Full**
Hosts: **Ann and Harold Messenger**	Other Meals: **Available**
Location: **35 mi. S of Boston**	Credit Cards: **AMEX, DC, DISC, MC,**
No. of Rooms: **5**	**VISA**
No. of Private Baths: **3**	Pets: **Sometimes**
Max. No. Sharing Bath: **4**	Children: **Welcome**
Double/pb: **$85**	Smoking: **No**
Single/pb: **$75**	Social Drinking: **Permitted**
Double/sb: **$65**	Minimum Stay: **2 nights, weekends**
Suites: **$95, sleeps 5**	Airport/Station Pickup: **Yes**
Open: **All year**	
Reduced Rates: **$10 less Sun.–Thurs.,**	
Jan.–Feb.; 10% seniors, families	

Five Bridge B&B Inn is a unique Georgian Colonial secluded on 60 acres of forest and field. Enjoy the private tennis court, lap pool, jogging track, and hiking trails all on the property. Nearby are golf courses, restaurants, and a riding stable next door to the inn. Homemade breads, mushroom quiche, French toast, and farm-raised sausage are just a few breakfast treats you may be served in the dining room that overlooks open pastures, wooded trails and Duffy, the resident llama. Ann and Harold offer local attraction information and brochures upon request.

Deerfield's Yellow Gabled House ✪

111 NORTH MAIN STREET SOUTH DEERFIELD, MASSACHUSETTS 01373

Tel: **(413) 665-4922**
Best Time to Call: **9 AM–9 PM**
Hosts: **Edna Julia Stahelek**
Location: **30 mi. N of Springfield**
No. of Rooms: **2**
Max. No. Sharing Bath: **4**
Double/sb: **$75–$110**
Suite: **$85–$125**
Open: **All year**

Reduced Rates: **Available**
Breakfast: **Full**
Pets: **No**
Children: **Welcome, over 14**
Smoking: **No**
Social Drinking: **Permitted**
Minimum Stay: 2 nights weekends
   Apr.–Nov.
Station Pickup: **Yes**

This Gothic-Country house is a picturesque structure, yellow with black shutters. Period antiques and hardwood floors lend an elegant, relaxed atmosphere to your stay. The inviting living and dining rooms are for your use and comfort. Deerfield's Yellow Gabled House offers air conditioning, colorful gardens, sitting areas in the summer, and many amenities, including bathrobes. The inn is close to hiking, golf, and historic sites.

The Wildwood Inn
121 CHURCH STREET, WARE, MASSACHUSETTS 01082

Tel: **(413) 967-7798; (800) 860-8098**
Best Time to Call: **After 10 AM**
Hosts: **Fraidell Fenster and Richard Watson**
Location: **8 mi. N of Mass. Pike (I-90), Exit 8**
No. of Rooms: **9**
No. of Private Baths: **7**
Max. No. Sharing Bath: **4**
Double/pb: **$60–$90**
Double/sb: **$50–$70**

Open: **All year**
Reduced Rates: **10%, weekly; 50%, monthly**
Breakfast: **Full**
Credit Cards: **AMEX, DC, DISC, MC, VISA**
Pets: **No**
Children: **Welcome, over 6**
Smoking: **No**
Social Drinking: **Permitted**

Everything about this old-fashioned country home, with its rambling two acres, is designed to help you unwind. There's a swing on the porch, a hammock under the firs, a blazing fire in the winter, and a Norman Rockwell-esque brook-fed swimming hole in the summer. Your host Fraidell has furnished guest rooms with early cradles, heirloom quilts, and American primitive antiques, all of which work to spell welcome. Homemade muffins, Wildwood's own peach butter, and "country yummies" are a part of the "no-lunch" breakfast. Wildwood is centrally located to attractions and activities in five New England states, including Old Sturbridge Village, Basketball and Volleyball Halls of Fame, Old Deerfield, and the Five College area. Popular pastimes include tennis or canoeing in a park behind the inn, cross-country or downhill skiing, or engaging in lively conversation with other guests from around the world.

NANTUCKET

Lynda Watts Bed & Breakfast ✪
30 VESTAL STREET, BOX 478, NANTUCKET, MASSACHUSETTS 02554

Tel: **(508) 228-3828; fax (508) 228-4162**
Hosts: **Lynda and David Watts**
No. of Rooms: **2**
Max. No. Sharing Bath: **4**
Double/sb: **$80**
Open: **All year**
Reduced Rates: **20% Jan. 1–Apr. 15**

Breakfast: **Continental**
Credit Cards: **MC, VISA**
Pets: **No**
Children: **Welcome**
Smoking: **Permitted**
Social Drinking: **Permitted**
Minimum Stay: **2 nights**

Lynda and David's 20-year-old saltbox house is located on a quiet street in a residential neighborhood, only a seven-minute walk to town. It is simply furnished and guest rooms are equipped with TVs. Weather permitting, breakfast is served on the sunny patio.

MICHIGAN

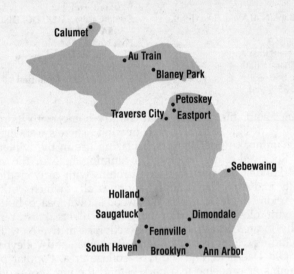

Calumet

Au Train

Blaney Park

Petoskey

Traverse City • Eastport

Sebewaing

Holland

Saugatuck

Dimondale

Fennville

South Haven

Brooklyn • Ann Arbor

The Urban Retreat Bed & Breakfast ✪
2759 CANTERBURY ROAD, ANN ARBOR, MICHIGAN 48104

Tel: **(734) 971-8110**
Best Time to Call: **5–10 PM**
Hosts: **Andre Rosalik and Gloria Krys**
Location: **40 mi. W of Detroit**
No. of Rooms: **2**
Max. No. Sharing Bath: **4**
Double/pb: **$60–$65**
Single/pb: **$50**

Double/sb: **$55–$60**
Single/sb: **$45**
Open: **All year**
Breakfast: **Full**
Pets: **No, cats on premises**
Children: **No**
Smoking: **Restricted**
Social Drinking: **Permitted**

This 1950s ranch-style house is located on a quiet, tree-lined street, 10 minutes from downtown and the University of Michigan campus. The home is decorated with antiques and collectibles from the early 1900s, with an abundance of bird's-eye maple furniture. Adjacent to the property is the County Farm Park, 127 acres of meadowland with walking and jogging paths and a 13-box bluebird trail. The Retreat has been designated as a Backyard Wildlife Habitat by the National Wildlife Federation. Andre and Gloria emphasize a quiet, relaxed atmosphere and assure their guests a peaceful visit and personal attention.

Pinewood Lodge ✪
P.O. BOX 176, M28 WEST, AU TRAIN, MICHIGAN 49806

Tel: **(906) 892-8300**	Single/sb: **$65**
Best Time to Call: **9 AM–9 PM**	Open: **All year**
Hosts: **Jerry and Jenny Krieg**	Breakfast: **Full**
Location: **24 mi. E of Marquette**	Credit Cards: **DISC, MC, VISA**
No. of Rooms: **7**	Pets: **No**
No. of Private Baths: **5**	Children: **No**
Max. No. Sharing Bath: **4**	Smoking: **No**
Double/pb: **$95–$125**	Social Drinking: **Permitted**
Double/sb: **$75**	Airport/Station Pickup: **Yes**

This B&B is a pine log home on the shores of Lake Superior. Pictured Rocks National Shoreline is right down the highway, and you can see the Grand Islands from the living room. Guests can enjoy activities year-round, from swimming, diving, and boating to ice fishing, snowmobiling, and downhill and cross-country skiing.

Celibeth House ✪
ROUTE 1, BOX 58A, M-77 BLANEY PARK ROAD, BLANEY PARK, MICHIGAN 49836

Tel: **(906) 283-3409**	Reduced Rates: **10% after 2nd night**
Host: **Elsa Strom**	Breakfast: **Continental**
Location: **60 mi. W of Mackinac Bridge**	Credit Cards: **MC, VISA**
No. of Rooms: **7**	Pets: **No**
No. of Private Baths: **7**	Children: **Welcome**
Double/pb: **$50–$55**	Smoking: **No**
Single/pb: **$45–$50**	Social Drinking: **Permitted**
Open: **May 1–Dec. 1**	

This lovely house, built in 1895, is situated on 85 acres overlooking a small lake. Many of the scenic attractions of Michigan's upper peninsula lie within an hour's drive. Guests may enjoy a cozy living room, a quiet reading room, a card/game room, a comfortably furnished porch, or an outdoor deck and lots of nature trails. Elsa is a retired personnel manager who enjoys reading, gardening, traveling, and collecting antiques.

Dewey Lake Manor Bed & Breakfast ✪
11811 LAIRD ROAD, BROOKLYN, MICHIGAN 49230

Tel: **(517) 467-7122**	Hosts: **Joe and Barb Phillips**
Best Time to Call: **Before 10 PM**	Location: **45 mi. SW of Ann Arbor**

No. of Rooms: **6**
No. of Private Baths: **6**
Double/pb: **$60–$115**
Single/pb: **$55–$110**
Open: **All year**
Reduced Rates: **Available**
Breakfast: **Full**
Other Meals: **Picnic baskets for special events**

Credit Cards: **MC, VISA**
Pets: **No**
Children: **Welcome**
Smoking: **No**
Social Drinking: **Permitted**
Minimum Stay: **3 nights on race weekends, 2 nights holiday weekends**

Sitting atop a knoll on Dewey Lake, this country retreat in the Irish Hills awaits Manor guests. Joe and Barb's 1870 Italianate home has spacious, airy rooms furnished with antiques, five fireplaces, central air, and original kerosene chandeliers. Guests may linger over breakfast in the formal dining room, or on the porch or deck overlooking the lake. Picnics, bonfires, volleyball, or croquet may be enjoyed on the large lawn. A paddleboat and canoe are provided for guests. Golf courses, quaint towns, and many antique shops are nearby. Come experience the country with the Phillips family.

The Calumet House ✪
1159 CALUMET AVENUE, P.O. BOX 126, CALUMET, MICHIGAN 49913

Tel: **(906) 337-1936**
Hosts: **George and Rose Chivses**
Location: **10 mi. N of Hancock-Houghton**
No. of Rooms: **2**
Max. No. Sharing Bath: **4**
Double/sb: **$35**
Single/sb: **$30**

Open: **All year**
Breakfast: **Full**
Pets: **No**
Children: **No**
Smoking: **No**
Social Drinking: **Permitted**
Airport/Station Pickup: **Yes**
Foreign Languages: **Finnish**

The Calumet House is set in a historic old mining town known for its clean air and scenic vistas. Built in 1895, the house boasts its original woodwork and is filled with local antique furnishings. In the morning, you're in for a treat with Rose's home cooking. Breakfast specialties include English scones, pancakes, local berries in season, and homemade jam. Calumet House is within walking distance of the village, with its opera house, museum, and antique shops. Your hosts will also direct you to local hunting and fishing, as well as to places that any botanist would call paradise. It's 10 miles north of Michigan Technological University and Suomi College.

Bannicks B&B ✪
4608 MICHIGAN ROAD, M-99, DIMONDALE, MICHIGAN 48821

Tel: **(517) 646-0224**
Hosts: **Pat and Jim Bannick**
Location: **5 mi. SW of Lansing**
No. of Rooms: **2**

Max. No. Sharing Bath: **3**
Double/sb: **$40**
Single/sb: **$25**
Open: **All year**

Breakfast: **Full**
Pets: **No**
Children: **Welcome**

Smoking: **No**
Social Drinking: **Permitted**

This large ranch-style home features a stained glass entry, nautical-style basement, and a Mona Lisa bathroom. Guest accommodations consist of comfortable bedrooms and a den-TV room. Your hosts invite you to share a cup of coffee anytime. They will be happy to advise on the sights of Michigan's capital city, just five minutes away. Michigan State University is eight miles away.

Torch Lake Sunrise Bed and Breakfast ✪
BOX 52, 3644 BLASEN SHORES, EASTPORT, MICHIGAN 49627

Tel: **(616) 599-2706**
Host: **Betty A. Collins**
Location: **35 mi. N of Traverse City**
No. of Rooms: **3**
No. of Private Baths: **3**
Double/pb: **$85–$125**

Open: **May 15–Dec. 15**
Breakfast: **Full**
Pets: **Sometimes**
Children: **Welcome**
Smoking: **No**
Social Drinking: **Permitted**

This B&B overlooks what *National Geographic* calls the third most beautiful lake in the world. All rooms are furnished with antiques and have decks and private baths. Close at hand are several golf courses, tennis courts, gourmet restaurants, and ski resorts. For summer activities, a canoe, a rowboat, and paddleboards are available. In winter, cross-country skiing awaits you just outside. Wake up seeing the sunrise over the lake and smelling the wonderful aroma of fresh muffins baking! Perhaps you'll be served a frittata, or strawberry pancakes, or eggs Benedict, but always fresh fruit of the season.

The Kingsley House
626 WEST MAIN STREET, FENNVILLE, MICHIGAN 49408

Tel: **(616) 561-6425**
Hosts: **Gary and Kari King**
Location: **8 mi. SE of Saugatuck**
No. of Rooms: **8**
No. of Private Baths: **8**
Double/pb: **$80–$105**
Suites: **$110–$165**
Open: **All year**

Reduced Rates: **10% seniors; AARP**
Breakfast: **Full weekends, Continental, plus, weekdays**
Pets: **No**
Smoking: **No**
Social Drinking: **Permitted**
Airport/Station Pickup: **Yes**

This elegant Queen Anne Victorian takes its name from the locally prominent family who built it in 1886. Furnished and decorated in period style, the inn reflects the warmth and charm of a bygone era. Full family-style breakfasts are served in the formal dining room. Honeymoon suites with whirlpool baths and fireplaces are available. Saugatuck, Holland, and the sandy beaches of Lake Michigan are only minutes away.

The Brick Inn ✪
74 WEST 24TH STREET, HOLLAND, MICHIGAN 49423

Tel: **(616) 396-0401**
Hosts: **Ed and Freda Mott**
Location: **35 mi. W of Grand Rapids**
No. of Rooms: **2**
Max. No. Sharing Bath: **4**
Double/sb: **$70**
Open: **Apr. 1–Dec. 31**

Breakfast: **Full**
Pets: **No**
Children: **Welcome**
Smoking: **No**
Social Drinking: **Permitted**
Airport/Station Pickup: **Yes**

The Brick Inn is located in a unique neighborhood of homes in the city of Holland, famous for its Tulip Gardens, Wooden Shoe Factory, Dutch Village, Windmill Island, and Veldeer's Delft Factory. Guests will be within walking distance of Hope College and downtown Holland. Rooms are spacious, decorated with antiques and beautiful antique linens; each has a sitting area with a TV. Breakfast is served in the formal dining room and might include homemade muffins, apple dumplings, or chocolate crepes. After a busy day of sightseeing, you may want to enjoy the private patio garden or relax in the living room by the fireplace. Ed and Freda are retired and enjoy gardening and spending time with their guests.

Montgomery Place ✪
618 EAST LAKE STREET, PETOSKEY, MICHIGAN 49770

Tel: **(616) 347-1338**
Best Time to Call: **After 10 AM**
Hosts: **Ruth Bellissimo and Diane Gillette**

No. of Rooms: **3**
No. of Private Baths: **3**
Double/pb: **$95–$105**
Suite: **$135**

Open: **All year**
Breakfast: **Full**
Credit Cards: **DISC, MC, VISA**
Pets: **No**

Children: **Welcome, over 6**
Smoking: **No**
Social Drinking: **Permitted**
Airport/Station Pickup: **Yes**

From the beautiful veranda of Montgomery Place, you can admire Lake Michigan's Little Traverse Bay, just as guests did in 1878 when this Victorian inn first opened its doors. Petoskey is in the heart of Michigan's Little New England; the town's Gaslight District offers excellent shopping and dining. Mackinac Island is just a short drive away, as are numerous beaches, lakes, and other points of interest. The area's scenic roads wind through forests, valleys, and upland meadows. Five major ski resorts provide the Midwest's best downhill and cross-country skiing. For those of you who don't mind paying a higher rate, one other room is available.

Serenity—A Bed & Breakfast ✪
504 RUSH STREET, PETOSKEY, MICHIGAN 49770

Tel: **(616) 347-6171**
Best Time to Call: **After 10 AM**
Hosts: **Ralph and Sherry Gillett**
No. of Rooms: **3**
No. of Private Baths: **3**
Double/pb: **$85**
Open: **All year**

Reduced Rates: **Jan. 1–May 1**
Breakfast: **Full**
Credit Cards: **MC, VISA**
Pets: **No**
Children: **Welcome, over 12**
Smoking: **No**
Social Drinking: **Permitted**

Serenity is a lovely Victorian home with two glass-enclosed porches, natural oak hardwood floors, antiques, lace, and soft music that create an ambience of tranquil beauty. This B&B lies within walking distance of the historic Gaslight District, where you can enjoy a special shopping experience and many fine restaurants overlooking Little Traverse Bay. Mackinac Island is only 35 miles from Petoskey. Also featured are three major ski resorts, lovely beaches, golfing, and breathtaking sunsets.

Sherwood Forest Bed & Breakfast ✪
938 CENTER STREET, P.O. BOX 315, SAUGATUCK, MICHIGAN 49453

Tel: **(800) 838-1246**
Best Time to Call: **9 AM–9 PM**
Hosts: **Keith and Sue Charak**
Location: **40 mi. SW of Grand Rapids**
No. of Rooms: **5**
No. of Private Baths: **5**
Double/pb: **$85–$165**
Guest Cottage: **$140 Sept.–May; $850 weekly Jun.–Aug.**
Suites: **$145–$165**

Open: **All year**
Breakfast: **Continental**
Other Meals: **Available**
Credit Cards: **DC, DISC, MC, VISA**
Pets: **No**
Children: **Welcome, over 12**
Smoking: **No**
Social Drinking: **Permitted**
Minimum Stay: **2 nights, weekends; May 1–Oct. 31**

This beautiful Victorian home offers inviting elegance in a wooded setting. Guest rooms are furnished with antiques, cozy wing chairs, Oriental rugs, and air conditioning. There are two suites available. One reproduces the serenity of the north woods with a replica of the inside of a log cabin, including a stone-mantel gas fireplace, viewed from either the two-person Jacuzzi or the comfort of the bedroom. The second suite features the same amenities, decorated in the flair of the 19th century. Another room boasts a hand-painted mural that transforms the room into a canopied tree loft, complemented by a gas fireplace. In the summer, swim in the pool adorned with dolphins riding the ocean waves. Or walk one-half block to a Lake Michigan public beach to enjoy spectacular sunsets.

Rummel's Tree Haven ✪
41 NORTH BECK STREET, M-25, SEBEWAING, MICHIGAN 48759

Tel: **(517) 883-2450**
Best Time to Call: **Afternoons; evenings**
Hosts: **Carl and Erma Rummel**
Location: **28 mi. NE of Bay City**
No. of Rooms: **2**
Double/pb: **$50**
Single/pb: **$35**

Open: **All year**
Breakfast: **Full**
Pets: **Sometimes**
Children: **Welcome (crib)**
Smoking: **Permitted**
Social Drinking: **Permitted**
Airport/Station Pickup: **Yes**

A tree grows right through the porch and roof of this charming old home that was built by the Beck family in 1878. Guests can relax in large, airy rooms furnished with twin beds and comfortable family pieces. City dwellers are sure to enjoy the small-town friendliness and the quiet of the countryside. Saginaw Bay offers fine fishing, hunting, boating, bird-watching, or just plain relaxing. Carl and Erma offer color

TV, videocassettes, and the use of the barbecue and refrigerator. They love having company and will do all they can to make you feel welcome and relaxed.

The Seymour House ☯

1248 BLUE STAR HIGHWAY, SOUTH HAVEN, MICHIGAN 49090
seymour@cybersol.com

Tel: **(616) 227-3918;** fax: **(616) 227-3010**	Breakfast: **Full**
Best Time to Call: **8 AM–10 PM**	Other Meals: **Available**
Hosts: **Tom and Gwen Paton**	Credit Cards: **MC, VISA**
Location: **10 mi. S of Saugatuck**	Pets: **No**
No. of Rooms: **5**	Children: **Welcome, in cabin**
No. of Private Baths: **5**	Smoking: **No**
Double/pb: **$80–$155**	Social Drinking: **Permitted**
Guest Cabin: **$100–$130; $495–$625 weekly**	Minimum Stay: **2–3 nights weekends May 1–Nov. 1 main house; 2 nights most weekends, 3–4 nights holidays in cabin**
Open: **All year**	
Reduced Rates: **Available**	

The Seymour House is a stately brick Italianate-style Victorian featuring original pocket doors and intricate carved wood trim on doors and windows. You will enjoy nature and ultimate relaxation on the Patons' 11 acres. The grounds feature maintained nature trails and a stocked one-acre pond. Relax on white wicker in the garden patio beneath giant oaks and weeping willows. The B&B is located half a mile from Lake Michigan; it's only minutes to the popular resort towns of Saugatuck and South Haven. Gwen's pottery and photography are featured in the gift shop.

Linden Lea, A B&B on Long Lake

279 SOUTH LONG LAKE ROAD, TRAVERSE CITY, MICHIGAN 49684
lindenlea@aol.com

Tel: **(616) 943-9182**	Breakfast: **Full**
Hosts: **Jim and Vicky McDonnell**	Pets: **No**
Location: **9 mi. W of Traverse City**	Children: **Welcome, by arrangement**
No. of Rooms: **2**	Smoking: **No**
No. of Private Baths: **2**	Social Drinking: **Permitted**
Double/pb: **$95**	Minimum Stay: **Holiday weekends**
Open: **All year**	Airport/Station Pickup: **Yes**
Reduced Rates: **$80 Nov.–Apr.**	

This inn is in an enchanting spot on a crystal clear lake. Lakeside rooms are comfortably furnished with window seats, antiques, treasures, and central air. Guests are invited to relax by the fire and listen for loons, take a walk on the peaceful sandy beach, or enjoy the rowboat and paddleboat. Guests say this B&B is one of the best.

MINNESOTA

Fergus Falls

Stacy

Minneapolis/St. Paul

Round Lake   Sherburn

Bergerud B's ✪
ROUTE 5, BOX 61, FERGUS FALLS, MINNESOTA 56537

Tel: **(218) 736-4720; (800) 557-4720**
Hosts: **James and Sylvia Bergerud**
Location: **12 mi. S of Fergus Falls**
No. of Rooms: **3**
Max. No. Sharing Bath: **4**
Double/pb: **$75**
Double/sb: **$45–$50**
Single/sb: **$35**

Open: **All year**
Breakfast: **Full**
Other Meals: **Available**
Pets: **No**
Children: **Welcome, over 8**
Smoking: **No**
Social Drinking: **Permitted**
Foreign Languages: **Norwegian**

This home was built by the host's grandfather in 1895, on the century farm homesteaded in 1881. Jim and Sylvia have modernized the house, but the original structure remains much the same. Located twelve miles from the city, Bergerud B's offers a peaceful night of rest and relaxation. Take a walk in the country, play a game of pool, or just sit by one of the two fireplaces on a cool night with a good book and a cup of hot cider.

Awake to the smell of flavored coffee and a sumptuous hearty breakfast. Upon your departure Jim and Sylvia will fill your thermos and send you on your way with a baked goody. Your hosts enjoy meeting new people and will make your stay at Bergerud's a memorable experience.

Shingle Creek Bed & Breakfast ✪
5206 NORTH VINCENT AVENUE, MINNEAPOLIS, MINNESOTA 55430

Tel: **(612) 529-7063**	Open: **June 1–Oct. 31**
Hosts: **Dick and Wilma Sweere**	Reduced Rates: **Weekly**
Location: **5 mi. NW of Minneapolis**	Breakfast: **Continental**
No. of Rooms: **1**	Pets: **No**
No. of Private Baths: **1**	Children: **Welcome, over 4**
Double/pb: **$65**	Smoking: **No**
Single/pb: **$55**	Social Drinking: **Permitted**

This one-and-a-half-story Cape Cod Colonial home is located in a safe residential neighborhood within walking distance to a major shopping center, Metro bike trail, walking nature trail, and the Metro bus. Major sports facilities and downtown Minneapolis are 10 minutes away, the Mall of America 20 minutes, and the Minneapolis Zoo 30 minutes.

The Prairie House on Round Lake ✪
RR 1, BOX 105, ROUND LAKE, MINNESOTA 56167

Tel: **(507) 945-8934**	Single/sb: **$45**
Hosts: **Ralph and Virginia Schenck**	Open: **All year**
No. of Rooms: **4**	Breakfast: **Full**
No. of Private Baths: **1**	Pets: **Welcome**
Max. No. Sharing Bath: **4**	Children: **Welcome**
Double/pb: **$55**	Smoking: **No**
Single/pb: **$55**	Social Drinking: **Permitted**
Double/sb: **$45**	Airport/Station Pickup: **Yes**

Built in 1879 by a prominent Chicago businessman, this farmhouse is a retreat from the bustle of city life. It's a working horse farm: American paint horses roam the pasture, and three barns house both young stock in training and show horses that are exhibited all over the world. A cupola rising from the central stairway is circled by four dormer bedrooms on the second floor. Antique furniture accented with equine touches reflects the spirit of the farm. Fishing, hiking, swimming, boating, and tennis are at the doorstep.

The Garden Gate ✪
925 GOODRICH AVENUE, ST. PAUL, MINNESOTA 55105

Tel: **(612) 227-8430; (800) 967-2703**	Location: **1 mi. from I-94 exit Lexington Parkway**
Hosts: **Mary and Miles Conway**	

No. of Rooms: **3**
Max. No. Sharing Bath: **4**
Double/sb: **$65–$75**
Single/sb: **$55**
Open: **All year**
Breakfast: **Continental**

Credit Cards: **AMEX, DISC, MC, VISA**
Pets: **Sometimes**
Children: **Welcome**
Smoking: **No**
Social Drinking: **Permitted**

A garden of delights awaits you at this Victorian duplex in the heart of St. Paul's Victoria Crossing neighborhood, within easy reach of downtown, the airport, the capitol, and the Mall of America. The Gladiola, Rose, and Delphinium rooms are as beautiful as their namesakes. A typical breakfast may include fresh fruit, baked pastries, cereal, and yogurt. To pamper the body as well as the palate, guests may arrange to have a therapeutic massage.

Four Columns Inn ✪
668 140TH STREET, SHERBURN, MINNESOTA 56171

Tel: **(507) 764-8861**
Hosts: **Norman and Pennie Kittleson**
Location: **150 mi. SW of Minneapolis**
No. of Rooms: **4**
No. of Private Baths: **4**
Double/pb: **$55–$75**
Suite: **$75**

Open: **All year**
Breakfast: **Full**
Pets: **No**
Children: **By arrangement**
Smoking: **No**
Social Drinking: **Permitted**

Built as a guesthouse in 1884, this former stagecoach stop now welcomes the modern-day traveler. Lovingly remodeled by the Kittlesons, this Victorian mansion offers four rooms, including a bridal suite. The house is filled with antiques and musical instruments, including a player piano, a 1950s jukebox, and a grand piano. A walnut-paneled den, two fireplaces, a circular stairway, a library, and a redwood hot tub in a greenhouse full of flowers complete your home away from home. Breakfast is served with a warm hospitality that will round out your stay in the country. Four Columns is located in South Central Minnesota, just two miles from I-90, exit 87.

Kings Oakdale Park Guest House ✪
6933 232 AVENUE NORTHEAST, STACY, MINNESOTA 55079

Tel: **(612) 462-5598**
Hosts: **Donna and Charles Solem**
Location: **38 mi. N of St. Paul**
No. of Rooms: **3**
No. of Private Baths: **2**
Double/pb: **$32**
Single/pb: **$26**
Double/sb: **$30**
Single/sb: **$25**

Suites: **$35**
Open: **All year**
Breakfast: **Continental**
Pets: **Sometimes**
Children: **No**
Smoking: **Permitted**
Social Drinking: **Permitted**
Foreign Languages: **French**

This comfortable home is situated on four landscaped acres on the banks of Typo Creek. The picnic tables, volleyball net, and horseshoe game are sure signs of a hospitable country place. It is a serene retreat for people on business trips to the Twin Cities. The Wisconsin border and the scenic St. Croix River, where boat trips are offered, are minutes from the house. Charles and Donna will direct you to the most reasonable restaurants in town. For late snacks, refrigerators in the bedrooms are provided.

For key to listings, see inside front or back cover.

✪ This star means that rates are guaranteed through December 31, 1999, to any guest making a reservation as a result of reading about the B&B in *Bed & Breakfast U.S.A.*—1999 edition.

Important! To avoid misunderstandings, always ask about cancellation policies when booking.

Please enclose a self-addressed, stamped, business-size envelope when contacting reservation services.

For more details on what you can expect in a B&B, see Chapter 1.

Always mention *Bed & Breakfast U.S.A.* when making reservations!

We want to hear from you! Use the form on page 593.

MISSISSIPPI

Corinth
Iuka
West
Port Gibson

Lincoln, Ltd. Bed & Breakfast—Mississippi Reservation Service ✪
P.O. BOX 3479, 2303 23RD AVENUE, MERIDIAN, MISSISSIPPI 39303

Tel: **(601) 482-5483; resv. only: (800) 633-MISS [6477]; fax: (601) 693-7447**
Best Time to Call: **9 AM–5 PM**
Coordinator: **Barbara Lincoln Hall**
States/Regions Covered:
  Mississippi—Natchez to Memphis, Alabama

Descriptive Directory: **$3.50**
Rates (Single/Double):
  Average: **$65–$75 / $75–$85**
  Luxury: **$85–$125 / $95–$165**
Credit Cards: **AMEX, MC, VISA**

For the traveling businessperson or for the vacationer, a stay with one of Barbara's hosts offers a personal taste of the finest Southern hospitality. All rooms have private baths. Mississippi abounds with historic-house tours, called "pilgrimages," in March and April, and Natchez and Vicksburg have similar pilgrimages in autumn. In May, Meridian is host to the Jimmie Rodgers Festival. Accommodations range from a cozy, historic log cabin to an elegant antebellum mansion.

The Samuel D. Bramlitt House ○
1125 CRUISE STREET, CORINTH, MISSISSIPPI 38834

Tel: **(601) 286-5370; (800) 484-1107 (7645)**	Breakfast: **Full**
Hosts: **Cindy and Kevin Thomas**	Other Meals: **Available**
Location: **80 mi. SE of Memphis, Tennessee**	Credit Cards: **AMEX, MC, VISA**
No. of Rooms: **5**	Pets: **No**
No. of Private Baths: **5**	Children: **Welcome**
Double/pb: **$75**	Smoking: **No**
Open: **All year**	Social Drinking: **Permitted**
	Airport/Station Pickup: **Yes**

Starry skies, soft summer breezes, the fragrance of magnolia and roses, a good book, and the smell of fresh-baked bread are only a few of the pleasures you will enjoy at the Samuel D. Bramlitt House, circa 1892. This gracious and warm Victorian mansion is filled with antiques and is located in the historic district of Corinth. Guests are invited to sip iced tea on one of the four verandas or walk to one of Mississippi's oldest drugstores complete with soda fountain. Explore the historic homes and churches, attend one of the many colorful festivals and battle reenactments, or visit nearby Shiloh National Military Park and Natchez Trace Parkway.

Eastport Inn Bed & Breakfast ○
100 SOUTH PEARL STREET, IUKA, MISSISSIPPI 38852

Tel: **(601) 423-2511**	Reduced Rates: **Available**
Best Time to Call: **8 AM–5 PM**	Breakfast: **Continental**
Host: **Betty Watson**	Other Meals: **Available**
No. of Rooms: **7**	Credit Cards: **AMEX, DC, DISC, MC, VISA**
No. of Private Baths: **7**	
Double/pb: **$50**	Pets: **No**
Single/pb: **$40**	Children: **Welcome**
Suites: **$50**	Smoking: **No**
Open: **All year**	Social Drinking: **Permitted**

This gracious home was built in 1864 and is decorated in period style, with four-poster beds and floral bedspreads. For swimming and boating, Pickwick Lake is six miles away; Shiloh National Park, Tishomingo State Park, Coleman State Park, and the Natchez Trace Drive are also nearby.

Oak Square Plantation ✪
1207 CHURCH STREET, PORT GIBSON, MISSISSIPPI 39150

Tel: **(601) 437-4350; (800) 729-0240**
Best Time to Call: **Anytime**
Hosts: **Mr. and Mrs. William D. Lum**
Location: **On Hwy. 61 between**
   Natchez and Vicksburg
No. of Rooms: **12**
No. of Private Baths: **12**
Double/pb: **$85–$95**

Single/pb: **$70–$75**
Open: **All year**
Breakfast: **Full**
Credit Cards: **AMEX, DISC, MC, VISA**
Pets: **No**
Children: **Welcome**
Smoking: **No**
Social Drinking: **Permitted**

Port Gibson is the town that Union General Ulysses S. Grant said was "too beautiful to burn." Oak Square is the largest and most palatial antebellum mansion, circa 1850, in Port Gibson, and is listed on the National Register of Historic Places. The guest rooms are all furnished with family heirlooms, and all have canopied beds. Guests will enjoy the courtyard, gazebo, and beautiful grounds. A chairlift for upstairs rooms is available. You will enjoy the delightful Southern breakfast and tour of the mansion. Your hosts offer complimentary wine, tea, or coffee, and will enlighten you on the many historic attractions in the area.

The Alexander House ✪
210 GREEN STREET, P.O. BOX 187, WEST, MISSISSIPPI 39192

Tel: **(800) 350-8034**
Hosts: **Ruth Ray and Woody Dinstel**
Location: **70 mi. N of Jackson**
No. of Rooms: **5**
No. of Private Baths: **3**
Max. No. Sharing Bath: **4**
Double/pb: **$65**
Double/sb: **$65**

Suites: **$110**
Open: **All year**
Breakfast: **Full**
Other Meals: **Available**
Pets: **Sometimes**
Children: **Welcome, over 10**
Smoking: **No**
Social Drinking: **Permitted**

The Alexander House, which has been dated to the 1880s, opened as a bed and breakfast in March 1994. Located in the town historic district, the house has been carefully restored with authentic decor, but with added conveniences. A full breakfast is served each morning and may include hot biscuits, fruit compote, grits, eggs, or casseroles. The two-story home has three bedrooms and a suite.

For key to listings, see inside front or back cover.

✪ This star means that rates are guaranteed through December 31, 1999, to any guest making a reservation as a result of reading about the B&B in *Bed & Breakfast U.S.A.*—1999 edition.

Important! To avoid misunderstandings, always ask about cancellation policies when booking.

Please enclose a self-addressed, stamped, business-size envelope when contacting reservation services.

For more details on what you can expect in a B&B, see Chapter 1.

Always mention *Bed & Breakfast U.S.A.* when making reservations!

We want to hear from you! Use the form on page 593.

MISSOURI

Bed & Breakfast Kansas City—Missouri & Kansas
P.O. BOX 14781, LENEXA, KANSAS 66285

Tel: **(913) 888-3636**
Coordinator: **Edwina Monroe**
States/Regions Covered:
  Kansas—Lenexa, Overland Park;
  Missouri—Independence, Kansas
  City, Lee's Summit, Parkville,

St. Joseph, Springfield, Warrensburg,
Weston
Rates (Double):
  Average: **$60–$90**
  Luxury: **$95–$160**
Credit Cards: **No**

You will enjoy visiting such places as the Truman Library and home, Crown Center, Country Club Plaza, Arrowhead Stadium, Royals Stadium, Kemper Arena, the Missouri Repertory Theatre, the American Heartland Theater, Nelson Art Gallery, New Theatre Restaurant, and Toy & Miniature Museum.

Borgman's Bed & Breakfast ✪
ARROW ROCK, MISSOURI 65320
kborgman@mid-mo.net

Tel: **(660) 837-3350**	Open: **All year**
Best Time to Call: **7–9 AM**	Reduced Rates: **10% 3 nights**
Hosts: **Helen and Kathy Borgman**	Breakfast: **Continental**
Location: **100 mi. E of Kansas City**	Pets: **Sometimes**
No. of Rooms: **4**	Children: **Welcome**
Max. No. Sharing Bath: **4**	Smoking: **No**
Double/sb: **$50–$55**	Social Drinking: **Permitted**
Single/sb: **$40**	

This 1860 home is spacious and comfortable, and it is furnished with cherished family pieces. Helen is a seamstress, artisan, and baker. Wait till you taste her fresh breads! Daughter Kathy is a town tour guide, so you will get firsthand information on this National Historic Landmark town at the beginning of the Santa Fe Trail. A fine repertory theater, the Lyceum, is open in summer. Crafts shops, antique stalls, and the old country store are fun places to browse in. Good restaurants are within walking distance.

Caverly Farm & Orchard
100 CEDAR RIDGE ROAD, BLAND, MISSOURI 65014

Tel: **(573) 646-3732**	Location: **85 mi. WSW of St. Louis**
Best Time to Call: **8 AM–10 PM**	No. of Rooms: **3**
Hosts: **David and Nancy Caverly**	No. of Private Baths: **3**

Double/pb: **$50**
Single/pb: **$45**
Open: **All year**
Breakfast: **Full**
Other Meals: **Available**

Pets: **Sometimes**
Children: **Welcome, crib**
Smoking: **No**
Social Drinking: **Permitted**

Caverly Farm & Orchard bed and breakfast is located on a 57-acre farm in central Missouri. The farm is in a colorful valley of grazing land, hay fields, and wooded hillsides. The renovated 1850 farmhouse has a new roof and siding and completely new bedrooms, decorated with a collection of antiques gathered over 35 years. Guests can enjoy fishing and hiking on the farm or floating on nearby rivers. Antique and craft shops, farm auctions, and five major Missouri wineries are within 30 to 45 minutes.

The Wildflower Inn ✪
2739 HIGHWAY D, BOURBON, MISSOURI 65441

Tel: **(573) 468-7975**
Best Time to Call: **4–7 PM**
Hosts: **Mary Lou and Jerry Hubble**
Location: **65 mi. from St. Louis**
No. of Rooms: **4**
No. of Private Baths: **4**
Double/pb: **$75–$85**

Open: **All year**
Breakfast: **Full**
Pets: **No**
Children: **No**
Smoking: **No**
Social Drinking: **Permitted**

The Wildflower Inn sits graciously on forty-two acres in the foothills of the Ozarks, surrounded by natural springs, Missouri woodlands, wildflowers, and native birds. Guest rooms are tastefully furnished with queen-size beds and color TVs. You're invited to relax in the great room in front of an old-fashioned fireplace. A candlelight breakfast is served in the dining area. The antique china and Mary Lou's specialties all add up to a gourmet treat. Just outside the back door you can enjoy a one-of-a-kind rejuvenating spa nestled at the edge of the woods, in a custom-crafted gazebo and adjoining deck. Area attractions include Meramec State Park, canoeing, Meramec Caverns, wineries, antiquing, and Six Flags.

Ozark Mountain Country B&B Service
BOX 295, BRANSON, MISSOURI 65615

Tel: **(417) 334-4720; (800) 695-1546**
Best Time to Call: **10 AM–4 PM;**
   7–10 PM
Coordinator: **Kay Cameron**
States/Regions Covered:
  Missouri—Branson, Camdenton,
  Carthage, Hollister, Kimberling City,
  Marionville, Osage Beach, Shell

Knob, Springfield, West Plains;
Arkansas—Eureka Springs
Rates (Single/Double):
  Modest: **$35–$55**
  Average: **$60–$75**
  Luxury: **$80–$150**
Credit Cards: **AMEX, DISC, MC, VISA**

After receiving a stamped, self-addressed legal envelope, Kay will send you a complimentary copy of her descriptive listings of more than one hundred carefully selected small inns, private cottages, and luxurious suites. She will also include coupons. Discounts are available for groups and stays of more than three nights.

Cameron's Crag ✪
P.O. BOX 295, BRANSON, MISSOURI 65613

Tel: **(417) 335-8134; (800) 933-8529**	Breakfast: **Full**
Host: **Glen Cameron**	Other Meals: **Available**
Location: **3 mi. S of Branson**	Pets: **No**
Suites: **$75–$95; sleeps 2**	Children: **Welcome, infants, and over 6**
Open: **All year**	Smoking: **No**
Reduced Rates: **$10 less Jan.–Mar., after 1st night**	Social Drinking: **Permitted**
	Airport Pickup: **Yes**

Enjoy your choice of three delightful accommodations in this striking contemporary home perched high on a bluff overlooking Lake Taney-como. All three suites have private entrances, king-size beds, and a deck with a private spa. You'll savor one of your host's hearty breakfasts before you explore area attractions like Silver Dollar City, Table Rock State Park, and Mutton Hollow Craft Village.

Bellevue Bed & Breakfast ✪
312 BELLEVUE, CAPE GIRARDEAU, MISSOURI 63701

Tel: **(800) 768-6822; (573) 335–3302**	Breakfast: **Full**
Hosts: **Fred and Jackie Hoelscher**	Credit Cards: **MC, VISA**
Location: **100 mi. S of St. Louis**	Pets: **No**
No. of Rooms: **4**	Children: **Welcome**
No. of Private Baths: **4**	Smoking: **No**
Double/pb: **$65–$95**	Social Drinking: **Permitted**
Single/pb: **$60–$90**	Airport/Station Pickup: **Yes**
Open: **All year**	

Built in 1891, this Second Empire Victorian home has been faithfully returned to its turn-of-the-century elegance. The original ceiling stencils have been restored in the dining room and parlor. Guest rooms are furnished in antiques, have queen-size beds and private baths, one with a whirlpool tub for two. A full breakfast served in the formal dining room features fresh breads and seasonal fruits. Guests may enjoy a lei-surely stroll to the nearby riverfront and shopping at the many nearby antique and specialty shops. Fred is a retired salesman who will make you feel at home and tell you all you want to know about the area.

Garth Woodside Mansion
RR3, BOX 578, HANNIBAL, MISSOURI 63401

Tel: **(573) 221-2789**
Best Time to Call: **10 AM–7 PM**
Hosts: **Irv and Diane Feinberg**
Location: **99 mi. N of St. Louis**
No. of Rooms: **8**
No. of Private Baths: **8**
Double/pb: **$67–$107**

Open: **All year**
Breakfast: **Full**
Credit Cards: **MC, VISA**
Pets: **No**
Children: **Welcome, over 12**
Smoking: **No**
Social Drinking: **Permitted**

This Second Empire Victorian, built in 1871, has a three-story flying staircase, 14-foot ceilings, and eight hand-carved marble fireplaces. Many of the room furnishings date back to the original owners. Stroll the 39 country acres, then sit down for a leisurely afternoon beverage. Breakfast, served in the formal dining room, features peach French toast, fluted quiche cups, and eggs picante. This location is ideal for touring Mark Twain country or for a romantic getaway. What's more, your hosts will pamper you with wonderful extras like nightshirts and turn-down service.

Pridewell ✪
600 WEST 50TH STREET, KANSAS CITY, MISSOURI 64112

Tel: **(816) 931-1642**
Best Time to Call: **4–9 PM**
Hosts: **Edwin and Louann White**
No. of Rooms: **2**
No. of Private Baths: **1**
Double/pb: **$80**
Single/pb: **$75**

Open: **All year**
Breakfast: **Full**
Pets: **No**
Children: **Welcome**
Smoking: **No**
Social Drinking: **Permitted**

This fine Tudor residence is situated in a wooded residential area on the battlefield of the Civil War's Battle of Westport. The Nelson Art Gallery, the University of Missouri at Kansas City, and the Missouri Repertory Theatre are close by. It is adjacent to the Country Club Plaza shopping district, which includes several four-star restaurants, tennis courts, and a park.

The Dickey House Bed & Breakfast Inn ✪
331 SOUTH CLAY STREET, MARSHFIELD, MISSOURI 65706

Tel: **(417) 468-3000**	Breakfast: **Full**
Hosts: **William and Dorothy Buesgen**	Credit Cards: **DISC, MC, VISA**
Location: **22 mi. NE of Springfield**	Pets: **No**
No. of Rooms: **6**	Children: **Welcome, over 12**
No. of Private Baths: **6**	Smoking: **No**
Double/pb: **$60–$115**	Social Drinking: **Permitted**
Open: **All year**	Airport Pickup: **Yes**
Reduced Rates: **Available**	Foreign Languages: **German**

As you approach this lovely Greek Revival mansion, named for the prominent lawyer who built it in 1913, the Ionic columns, widow's walk, and front entrance with beveled glass will transport you to a by-gone era. Each bedroom is furnished with antiques and reproductions. Outside, oak trees and benches punctuate the lawns and gardens. An Amish settlement, the Buena Vista Exotic Animal Park, Laura Ingalls Wilder Museum, and Bass Pro Shop are among the nearby points of interest. Branson and Silver Dollar City are one hour to the south. To revive you after the day's activities, your hosts offer complimentary beverages and snacks.

Gramma's House
1105 HIGHWAY D, MARTHASVILLE, MISSOURI 63357
www.grammashouse.com

Tel: **(314) 433-2675**	Suites: **$105**
Best Time to Call: **9 AM–9 PM**	Open: **All year**
Hosts: **Judy and Jim Jones**	Breakfast: **Full**
Location: **50 mi. W of St. Louis**	Credit Cards: **MC, VISA**
No. of Rooms: **4**	Pets: **No**
No. of Private Baths: **4**	Smoking: **No**
Double/pb: **$75**	Social Drinking: **Permitted**
Guest Cottage: **$115**	

At this romantic, 160-year-old farmhouse, morning starts with a hearty breakfast, like grandma used to make. You can relax and maybe hear a bobwhite's call. Accommodations include two rooms in the main house, plus two cottages, each with fireplaces. The area boasts many unique shops, five wineries, the Daniel Boone home, and a wide variety of res-

taurants. Nearby is the Katy Trail State Park, a 185-mile hiking and biking trail. Bike rentals and repairs are available in town.

Dear's Rest B&B ✪

1408 CAPP HILL RANCH ROAD, OZARK, MISSOURI 65721
info@dearsrest.com; www.dearsrest.com

Tel: **(800) 588-2262; (417) 581-3839**
Best Time to Call: **Before 10:30 PM**

Hosts: **Linda and Allan Schilter**
Location: **10 mi. S of Ozark**

Suite: **$85**	Pets: **No**
Open: **All year**	Children: **Welcome, crib**
Breakfast: **Full**	Smoking: **No**
Credit Cards: **DISC, MC, VISA**	Social Drinking: **Permitted**

When was the last time you walked through a forest, saw wildlife, over 150 species of birds, wildflowers, explored the crystal-clear waters of a spring-fed creek, or relaxed in a hot tub surrounded by the natural beauty of the Ozark Hills? Dear's Rest makes it all a reality when you stay in this new rustic Amish-built home, decorated with a fireplace and family antiques that give guests a comfortable homey feeling. This B&B is located adjoining the Mark Twain National Forest, 45 minutes from Branson, Springfield, the famous Bass Pro Shops and Museum, and a major Civil War battlefield. Downtown Ozark is an antique shoppers' heaven. A breakfast of simple country fare—often described as the "no lunch breakfast"—is served in the sunroom or on the deck. Linda and Allan entertain one party at a time, consisting of one through six people, to ensure your comfort and privacy.

Charlotte's Apple Blossom Inn ✪
200 WEST BROADWAY, PLATTSBURG, MISSOURI 64477

Tel: **(816) 930-3243**	Open: **Mar.–Dec.**
Hosts: **Darrell and Charlotte Apple**	Breakfast: **Full**
Location: **30 mi. N of Kansas City**	Pets: **No**
No. of Rooms: **3**	Children: **By arrangement**
No. of Private Baths: **3**	Smoking: **No**
Double/pb: **$55**	

Darrell and Charlotte lovingly restored this 1910 home with lighting, color, and a warm interior that says "welcome." After a day of exploring the Pony Express and Jesse James attractions or the Amish settlement, relax in their comfortable parlor with an evening apple dessert. In the morning enjoy a full breakfast consisting of an apple specialty with freshly ground coffee from a local shop and home-baked breads and muffins. For early risers, coffee is served upstairs. Each room's decor has a distinctive personality, with antique wicker, claw-footed tub, or handmade quilts. Visit local shops for antiques and specialty gifts. Restaurants are within walking distance. Afterward, enjoy a stroll down the quiet tree-lined streets to see other period homes.

Lafayette House
2156 LAFAYETTE AVENUE, ST. LOUIS, MISSOURI 63104
www.bbonline.com/mo/lafaytte

Tel: **(314) 772-4429; (800) 641-8965**	No. of Private Baths: **3**
Best Time to Call: **8 AM–5 PM**	Max. No. Sharing Bath: **3**
Hosts: **Nancy Hammersmith and Anna Millét**	Double/pb: **$85–$150**
	Double/sb: **$60**
No. of Rooms: **6**	Suite: **$95**

Open: **All year**
Breakfast: **Full**
Pets: **Sometimes**

Children: **Welcome**
Smoking: **No**
Social Drinking: **Permitted**

This 1876 Queen Anne mansion is located in historic Lafayette Square. Lafayette House is only minutes from downtown St. Louis. Attend a baseball or football game, shop historic Union Station, visit the St. Louis Arch, Science Center, zoo, or simply stroll through the lovely Lafayette Square Park. A gourmet breakfast will be a memorable treat. Anna's menu may consist of homemade breads, muffins, crab-stuffed quiche, or Belgian waffles with warm blueberry compote, just to name a few of her culinary delights. The house is furnished with antiques and traditional furniture. The suite can accommodate six and has a kitchen. For a romantic getaway, try the room with a fireplace and Jacuzzi. For business guests, this B&B offers a fax, in-room phones, and flexible breakfast hours.

Napoleon's Retreat ✪
1815 LAFAYETTE AVENUE, ST. LOUIS, MISSOURI 63104

Tel: **(314) 772-6979; (800) 700-9980**
Best Time to Call: **8 AM–9 PM**
Hosts: **Michael Lance and Jeff Archuleta**
Location: **1 mi. SW of downtown**
No. of Rooms: **4**
No. of Private Baths: **4**
Double/pb: **$75–$85**
Single/pb: **$65–$75**
Suite: **$95**

Open: **All year**
Reduced Rates: **10% families; multiple nights, Dec.–Feb.**
Breakfast: **Full**
Credit Cards: **AMEX, MC, VISA**
Pets: **No**
Children: **Welcome, over 6**
Smoking: **No**
Social Drinking: **Permitted**

"Meet me in St. Louis" begins with your arrival at Napoleon's Retreat, an elegant Second French Empire Victorian located in the historic district of Lafayette Square, one mile from the Arch. This architectural gem combines today's modern comforts with traditional St. Louis charm. Guest rooms are furnished with European and American antiques and paintings, queen-size beds, telephones, and TV. Napoleon's Retreat is within 3 miles of the world-famous Botanical Gardens, St. Louis Cathedral, zoo, Forest Park, and Washington University. Breakfast includes the house blend of coffees, juice, fruit, and an entree. For pleasure or business, this is the perfect retreat.

The Winter House ✪
3522 ARSENAL STREET, ST. LOUIS, MISSOURI 63118
kmwinter@swbell.net

Tel: **(314) 664-4399**	Open: **All year**
Hosts: **Kendall and Sarah Winter**	Reduced Rates: **After 2nd night**
Location: **1 mi. S of I-44; 1 mi. W of I-55**	Breakfast: **Full**
	Credit Cards: **AMEX, DC, MC, VISA**
No. of Rooms: **3**	Pets: **No**
No. of Private Baths: **3**	Children: **Welcome**
Double/pb: **$85–$100**	Smoking: **No**
Single/pb: **$65–$85**	Social Drinking: **Permitted**
Suite: **$80–100 for 2**	

This ten-room Victorian, built in 1897, features a first-floor bedroom with a pressed-tin ceiling, a second-floor suite with a balcony and decorative fireplace, and the Rose Room with king bed, roses motif, and a fireplace. Breakfast, served in the dining room on crystal and antique Wedgwood, always includes fresh-squeezed orange juice. Fruit, candy, and fresh flowers are provided in bedrooms; live piano is available by reservation. Nearby attractions include the Missouri Botanical Garden, which adjoins Tower Grove Park, a Victorian walking park on the National Register of Historic Places. The Arch, Busch Baseball Stadium, the zoo, the symphony, Irans World Dome, and Union Station are all within four miles, and fine dining is in walking distance. There is a $20 surcharge for one night stays.

The Schwegmann House B&B Inn ✪
438 WEST FRONT STREET, WASHINGTON, MISSOURI 63090
www.usmo.com/~schwghse

Tel: **(800) 949-2262**	Open: **All year**
Hosts: **Cathy and Bill Nagel**	Breakfast: **Full**
Location: **50 mi. W of St. Louis**	Credit Cards: **MC, VISA**
No. of Rooms: **9**	Pets: **No**
No. of Private Baths: **9**	Children: **Welcome, weekdays**
Double/pb: **$75–$95**	Smoking: **No**
Suite: **$120–$150**	Social Drinking: **Permitted**

Located in the heart of the Missouri River wine country, this three-story, Federal-style brick home overlooks the river in the historic district of

Washington. Tall ceilings, a graceful staircase, and fine antiques create an air of country elegance. Each guest room is tastefully decorated and features custom-designed handmade quilts. Schwegmann House is listed on the National Register of Historic Places. There is much for guests to enjoy, including 11 nearby wineries, biking, hiking, antique shops, historic sites, unique gift shops, and excellent restaurants. A bountiful breakfast of freshly baked specialties is served daily.

For key to listings, see inside front or back cover.

✪ This star means that rates are guaranteed through December 31, 1999, to any guest making a reservation as a result of reading about the B&B in *Bed & Breakfast U.S.A.*—1999 edition.

Important! To avoid misunderstandings, always ask about cancellation policies when booking.

Please enclose a self-addressed, stamped, business-size envelope when contacting reservation services.

For more details on what you can expect in a B&B, see Chapter 1.

Always mention *Bed & Breakfast U.S.A.* when making reservations!

We want to hear from you! Use the form on page 593.

MONTANA

Whitefish. .Coram
Kalispell.

Poison⦁.
⦁Ronan

Glendive.

.Stevensville .Helena
.Hamilton

.Bozeman .Billings
⦁Livingston

Red Lodge.

The Josephine Bed & Breakfast ✪
514 NORTH 29TH STREET, BILLINGS, MONTANA 59101
josephine@imt.net; www.thejosephine.com

Tel: **(406) 248-5898; (800) 552-5898**
Best Time to Call: **Anytime**
Hosts: **Doug and Becky Taylor**
No. of Rooms: **5**
No. of Private Baths: **3**
Max. No. Sharing Bath: **4**
Double/pb: **$68–$78**
Single/pb: **$58–$68**
Double/sb: **$58**
Single/sb: **$48**

Open: **All year**
Reduced Rates: **Medical and extended stays**
Breakfast: **Full**
Credit Cards: **AMEX, MC, VISA**
Pets: **No**
Children: **Welcome, over 12**
Smoking: **No**
Social Drinking: **Permitted**
Airport Pickup: **Yes**

This lovely, historic home is comfortably elegant. The porch, with its swing and quaint seating, offers the ideal place for breakfast or relaxing. Charming picket fences, shade trees, and flowers take you back in time. Each room is individually decorated with antiques, collectibles, and old photographs. Doug, a Billings native, enjoys cooking and travel, Becky enjoys crafts and antiques, and both are knowledgeable about the area. The B&B is within walking distance of downtown's museums, galleries, theaters, and shopping. It's only minutes to the airport, horse-racing rodeos, golf courses, and historic attractions. Skiing and Little Big Horn (Custer) Battlefield are an hour away; Yellowstone National Park is a beautiful 3-hour drive via scenic Beartooth Pass.

Chokecherry House ✪

1233 STORYMILL ROAD, BOZEMAN, MONTANA 59715
rpope@montana.campus.mci.net

Tel: **(406) 587-2657**	Breakfast: **Continental**
Hosts: **Rick and Kimberly Pope**	Pets: **No**
Location: **2 mi. N of Bozeman**	Children: **Welcome**
Guesthouse: **$140; sleeps 6**	Smoking: **No**
Open: **All year**	Social Drinking: **Permitted**
Reduced Rates: **10% after 6th night,**	Minimum Stay: **2 nights**
seniors	Airport/Station Pickup: **Yes**

Restored and spacious, Chokecherry House is situated on an acre at the foothills of the Bridger Mountains on Bridger Creek Golf Course. Rick and Kimberly offer a private hot tub, phone, VCR, TV, fully equipped kitchen, and great views. Both hosts are artists; Rick is a university professor and a licensed fishing guide.

Millers of Montana Bed & Breakfast Inn ✪

1002 ZACHARIA LANE, BOZEMAN, MONTANA 59715

Tel: **(406) 763-4102**	Single/sb: **$45**
Hosts: **Doug and Joyce Miller**	Open: **All year**
Location: **12 mi. SW of Bozeman**	Reduced Rates: **7th day free**
No. of Rooms: **4**	Breakfast: **Full**
No. of Private Baths: **2**	Pets: **Sometimes**
Max. No. Sharing Bath: **4**	Children: **Welcome**
Double/pb: **$60–$70**	Smoking: **No**
Double/sb: **$50**	Social Drinking: **Permitted**

This Cape Cod–style house is on a secluded 20-acre ranch, with breath-taking views of the Spanish Peaks and the Bridger Mountains. Quiet and comfortable, the B&B is furnished with country pieces and antiques. Yellowstone National Park is one hour away, and it's only 30 minutes to the Madison, Jefferson, and Yellowstone Rivers. For blue-ribbon trout fishing, walk over to the Gallatin River. Bozeman itself, home of Montana State University and the Museum of the Rockies, is worth visiting. Doug is in construction, and ranching, softball, and fishing are his hobbies. Joyce, a full-time hostess who retired from a culinary career, is interested in cooking, sewing, and crafts.

Torch and Toes B&B

309 SOUTH THIRD AVENUE, BOZEMAN, MONTANA 59715

Tel: **(406) 586-7285; (800) 446-2138**	Open: **All year**
Best Time to Call: **8 AM–noon**	Reduced Rates: **Government employees**
Hosts: **Ronald and Judy Hess**	Breakfast: **Full**
Location: **100 mi. SE of Helena**	Pets: **No**
No. of Rooms: **4**	Children: **Welcome**
No. of Private Baths: **4**	Smoking: **No**
Double/pb: **$80–$90**	Social Drinking: **Permitted**
Single/pb: **$70**	Airport/Station Pickup: **Yes**

Set back from the street, this Colonial Revival house is centrally located in the Bon Ton Historic District. Lace curtains, leaded glass windows, and period pieces remind one that this is a house with a past. Ron is a professor of architecture at nearby Montana State University; Judy is a weaver interested in historic preservation. Their home is furnished in a charming blend of nostalgic antiques, humorous collectibles, and fine furnishings. Breakfast always includes a special egg dish, fresh fruit, and muffins. Afterward, relax on the redwood deck in summer, or by a cozy fire in winter. Nearby attractions include blue-ribbon trout streams, hiking, skiing, and the Museum of the Rockies. Yellowstone National Park is one and a half hours away.

Voss Inn ○

319 SOUTH WILLSON, BOZEMAN, MONTANA 59715

Tel: **(406) 587-0982; fax: (406) 585-2964**	Single/pb: **$75–$85**
	Open: **All year**
Best Time to Call: **9:30 AM–9:30 PM**	Breakfast: **Full**
Hosts: **Bruce and Frankee Muller**	Credit Cards: **AMEX, MC, VISA**
Location: **3 mi. from I-90**	Pets: **No**
No. of Rooms: **6**	Children: **Sometimes**
No. of Private Baths: **6**	Smoking: **No**
Double/pb: **$85–$95**	Social Drinking: **Permitted**

This handsome 100-year-old brick mansion, flanked by Victorian gingerbread porches, is set like a gem on a tree-lined street in historic Bozeman. The bedrooms are elegantly wallpapered and furnished with brass and iron beds, ornate lighting, oriental throw rugs over polished hardwood floors—a perfect spot for a first or second honeymoon. The parlor has a good selection of books, as well as a chess set for your pleasure. It's north of Yellowstone, on the way to Glacier, with trout fishing, mountain lakes, and skiing within easy reach. Don't miss the Museum of the Rockies on the Montana State University campus ten blocks away.

Wild Rose Bed and Breakfast ✪

10280 HIGHWAY 2 EAST, P.O. BOX 130396, CORAM,
MONTANA 59913-0396
www.cyberport.net/wildrose

Tel: **(406) 387-4900**	Reduced Rates: **Available**
Hosts: **Joseph and Brenda Mihalko**	Breakfast: **Full**
No. of Rooms: **4**	Other Meals: **Available**
No. of Private Baths: **3**	Credit Cards: **MC, NOVUS, VISA**
Max. No. Sharing Bath: **4**	Pets: **No**
Double/pb: **$90–$125**	Children: **Welcome, over 12**
Double/sb: **$90**	Smoking: **No**
Open: **All year**	Social Drinking: **Permitted**

A Wild Rose is located six miles from Glacier National Park and within ten minutes of hiking, biking, rafting, horseback riding, boat tours, golfing, skiing, and sightseeing. Guest rooms are beautifully decorated in Victorian flair with deluxe mattresses, natural linens, and lavish amenities. Accommodations include an elegant Whirlpool Suite. Guests can explore the seven acres and enjoy fantastic views, unwind in the outdoor therapeutic spa, or indulge in a relaxing massage. A hearty gourmet breakfast is served along with A Wild Rose's blend of freshly ground coffee.

The Hostetler House Bed & Breakfast ✪

113 NORTH DOUGLAS STREET, GLENDIVE, MONTANA 59330

Tel: **(406) 365-4505; (800) 965-8456**	Reduced Rates: **Weekly, seniors**
Best Time to Call: **Anytime**	Breakfast: **Full**
Hosts: **Craig and Dea Hostetler**	Credit Cards: **DISC, MC, VISA**
No. of Rooms: **2**	Pets: **No**
Max. No. Sharing Bath: **4**	Children: **Welcome, over 16**
Double/sb: **$50**	Smoking: **No**
Single/sb: **$45**	Social Drinking: **Permitted**
Open: **All year**	Airport/Station Pickup: **Yes**

Located one block from the Yellowstone River and two blocks from downtown shopping and restaurants, the Hostetler House is a charming 1912 historic home with two comfortable guest rooms done in casual country decor. Nearby are parks, a swimming pool, tennis courts, antique shops, churches, a golf course, a museum, Dawson Community College, fishing, hunting, and hiking. Guests may relax in the hot tub, sitting room, enclosed sunporch, or on the deck. Wake up to the smell of freshly ground gourmet coffee, tea, and homemade bread. A full breakfast is served on Grandma's china in the dining room, sunporch, or on the deck. Dea is an interior decorator who grew up on a nearby wheat farm, and Craig is a mechanical engineer, pilot, and avid outdoorsman.

Deer Crossing ○

396 HAYES CREEK ROAD, HAMILTON, MONTANA 59840
www.net/go/deercrossing; deercros@bitterroot.net

Tel: **(406) 363-2232; (800) 763-2232**
Best Time to Call: **8 AM**
Host: **Mary Lynch**
Location: **45 mi. S of Missoula**
No. of Rooms: **5**
No. of Private Baths: **5**
Double/pb: **$75–$110**
Bunk House: **$110, sleeps 2–5**
Suites: **$110**
Open: **All year**

Reduced Rates: **5% seniors**
Breakfast: **Full**
Other Meals: **Available**
Credit Cards: **AMEX, MC, VISA**
Pets: **Horses**
Children: **Welcome**
Smoking: **No**
Social Drinking: **Permitted**
Airport/Station Pickup: **Yes**

Experience old western charm and hospitality at its best. Deer Crossing is located along the Lewis and Clark Trail amidst 25 acres of tall pines and a pasture overlooking Bitterroot Valley. Mornings start with a savory cup of freshly ground coffee and a hearty ranch breakfast. Afterward guests may enjoy a horseback ride, mountain hike, or world-class fly-fishing. The Charlie Russell Suite is decorated in Western art and memorabilia, plus a double Jacuzzi tub. The Big Sky Suite has panoramic views and two gracious guest rooms. For larger parties, consider the Bunk House, reminiscent of yesteryear. Kick off your boots, hang your hat, and make yourself at home!

Appleton Inn Bed and Breakfast ○

1999 EUCLID AVENUE, HIGHWAY 12 WEST, HELENA,
MONTANA 59601
appleton@ixi.net; www.appletoninn.com

Tel: **(406) 449-7492; (800) 956-1999;**
fax: **(406) 449-1261**

Hosts: **Cheryl Boid and Tom Woodall**
Location: **5 mi. W of I-15**

No. of Rooms: **5**
No. of Private Baths: **5**
Double/pb: **$75–$95**
Suites: **$85–$125**
Open: **All year**
Breakfast: **Full**
Credit Cards: **AMEX, DC, DISC, MC, VISA**

Pets: **Sometimes**
Children: **Welcome, over 8**
Smoking: **No**
Social Drinking: **Permitted**
Airport Pickup: **Yes**

Relax in the splendor of this beautiful Victorian built in 1890 by George Appleton and listed on the National Register of Historic Places. Guest rooms are individually decorated with antique and handcrafted furnishings and telephones. Wild rice quiche, huckleberry blintzes, or apple pancakes are breakfast favorites, served on antique Franciscan appleware and fine linens. Enjoy afternoon refreshments in one of the two parlors or in the perennial gardens. The Inn is close to hiking trails, golf courses, and a lake—mountain bikes are available. You'll be minutes from historic Last Chance Gulch, the state capitol, museums, restaurants, and specialty shops.

Creston Country Inn ✪
70 CRESTON ROAD, KALISPELL, MONTANA 59901

Tel: **(800) 257-7517; (406) 755-7517**
Best Time to Call: **8 AM–9 PM**
Hosts: **Ginger Lockner and Rick Malloch**
Location: **East Kalispell**
No. of Rooms: **4**
No. of Private Baths: **4**
Double/pb: **$80–$95**
Single/pb: **$65–$80**

Open: **May–Oct.**
Reduced Rates: **Available, seniors**
Breakfast: **Full**
Credit Cards: **MC, VISA**
Pets: **No**
Children: **Welcome, over 10**
Smoking: **No**
Social Drinking: **Permitted**

The Creston Country Inn, a 1920s farmhouse furnished with antiques, provides guests with majestic mountain views and rural serenity. Located near Glacier National Park and Flathead Lake, the inn's visitors have some of Montana's most beautiful country near their doorstep. The inn sits on four-and-one-half acres, and includes two picturesque red barns, large pasture, and gardens. Guests can stroll the grounds along the meandering creek, sit under the willow trees, or just relax on the porch. During the evenings, gather in the living room by the woodburning stove and enjoy the library, TV, or parlor games. A gourmet breakfast is served each morning; special diets are met upon request.

The River Inn on the Yellowstone✪
4950 HIGHWAY 89 SOUTH, LIVINGSTON, MONTANA 59047
www.wtp.net/go/riverinn

Tel: **(406) 222-2429**
Best Time to Call: **1–7 PM**

Hosts: **Dee Dee Van Zyl and Ursula Neese**

Location: **4 mi. S. of Livingston**
No. of Rooms: **3**
No. of Private Baths: **3**
Double/pb: **$70–$90**
Single/pb: **$60–$80**
Open: **Mar.–Oct.**
Reduced Rates: **$5 after 3rd night; off-season**

Breakfast: **Full**
Other Meals: **Available**
Credit Cards: **MC, VISA**
Pets: **Sometimes**
Children: **Welcome, over 9**
Smoking: **No**
Social Drinking: **Permitted**
Airport Pickup: **Yes**

Restored in 1995, this lovely one-hundred-year-old farmhouse is located 20 feet from the west bank of the Yellowstone River, with approximately 5 acres and 500 feet of riverfront for meandering or fishing. Guest rooms offer superb views of the Absaroka Mountains, the river, the islands, and the canyon. The dining room is large, with bookcases, leaded glass windows, and a window seat. French doors open onto a rock patio, where on the warmest of mornings breakfast is served. Hosts guide hiking, biking, and canoeing trips. Yellowstone Park is less than 50 miles away, Historical Livingston just minutes away. Also available are a rustic cabin, Calamity Jane's, $60 double, $50 single, and a turn-of-the-century sheepherder's wagon, double $40, single $30.

Hawthorne House ✪

304 THIRD AVENUE, EAST, POLSON, MONTANA 59860

Tel: **(406) 883-2723; (800) 290-1345**
Best Time to Call: **After 5 PM, weekends**
Hosts: **Gerry and Karen Lenz**
Location: **70 mi. N of Missoula**
No. of Rooms: **4**
Max. No. Sharing Bath: **4**
Double/sb: **$50**

Single/sb: **$45**
Open: **All year**
Breakfast: **Full**
Pets: **No**
Children: **Welcome, over 12**
Smoking: **No**
Social Drinking: **No**

In the small western Montana town of Polson, at the foot of Flathead Lake, you'll find Hawthorne House, an English Tudor home on a quiet shady street. In summer, cheerful window boxes welcome the weary traveler. The house is furnished with antiques from Karen's grandparents. There are plate collections, Indian artifacts, and glassware. The kitchen has some interesting collections. Breakfast is always special, with something baked fresh each morning. Nearby attractions include Glacier National Park, the National Bison Range, Kerr Dam, and great scenic beauty. Golf abounds. There are always activities on the lake and river.

Willows Inn ✪

224 SOUTH PLATT AVENUE, RED LODGE, MONTANA 59068
bbhost.com/willowsinn

Tel: **(406) 446-3913**
Best Time to Call: **8 AM–10 PM**

Hosts: **Elven, Kerry, and Carolyn Boggio**
Location: **60 mi. SW of Billings**

No. of Rooms: **5**
No. of Private Baths: **3**
Max. No. Sharing Bath: **4**
Double/pb: **$55–$75**
Double/sb: **$60**
Single/sb: **$50**
Guest Cottages: **$80 for 2**
Open: **All year**
Reduced Rates: **10% after 4th night;
    10% seniors**

Breakfast: **Continental**
Credit Cards: **DISC, MC, VISA**
Pets: **No**
Children: **Welcome**
Smoking: **No**
Social Drinking: **Permitted**
Minimum Stay: **2 nights in cottage**

Tucked beneath the majestic Beartooth Mountains in the northern Rockies, the historic town of Red Lodge provides an ideal setting for this charming three-story Queen Anne. Flanked by giant evergreens and colorful flower beds, the Inn is reminiscent of a bygone age, complete with white picket fence, gingerbread trim, and front porch swing. Overstuffed sofas and wicker pieces complement the warm and cheerful decor. Delicious home-baked pastries are Elven's specialty—she uses her own Finnish recipes for these mouth-watering treats. Championship rodeos, excellent cross-country and downhill skiing, opportunities to hike, golf, and fish abound in this special area, still unspoiled by commercial progress. Yellowstone National Park is only 65 miles away.

The Timbers Bed and Breakfast ✪

1184 TIMBERLANE ROAD, RONAN, MONTANA 59864
timbers@ronan.net

Tel: **(406) 676-4373; (800) 775-4373;
    fax: (406) 676-4370**
Best Time to Call: **9 AM–9 PM**
Hosts: **Doris and Leonard McCravey**
Location: **52 mi. N of Missoula**
Suites: **$75–$155**
Open: **All year**

Breakfast: **Full, Continental**
Credit Cards: **MC, VISA**
Pets: **Sometimes**
Children: **Welcome**
Smoking: **No**
Social Drinking: **Permitted**

This bed & breakfast hideaway sits on twenty-one secluded acres, with a view of the Rocky Mountain Mission Range. The house borders the Mission Wilderness area; a glassed-in wraparound deck provides unparalleled views of the mountains. Cathedral ceilings, hand-hewn beams, and a barn-wood dining area give the home a sophisticated yet warm country feel. Accommodations include a two-room suite with a private bath located on the lower level of the house. Flathead Lake, National Bison Range, Glacier Park, Native-American Cultural Center, horseback riding, whitewater rafting, golf, fishing, art galleries, local rodeos, and pow-wows are among the nearby attractions.

Country Caboose ✪
852 WILLOUGHBY ROAD, STEVENSVILLE, MONTANA 59870

Tel: **(406) 777-3145**
Host: **Lisa Thompson**
Location: **35 mi. S of Missoula**
No. of Rooms: **1**
No. of Private Baths: **1**
Double/pb: **$59**
Single/pb: **$59**

Open: **May–Sept.**
Breakfast: **Full**
Pets: **No**
Children: **Welcome**
Smoking: **No**
Social Drinking: **Permitted**

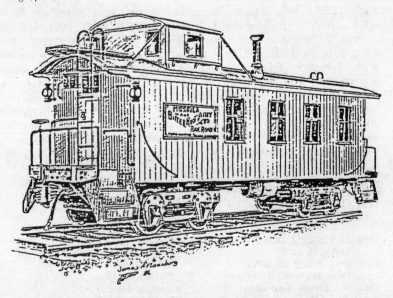

If you enjoy romantic train rides, why not spend the night in an authentic caboose? This one dates back to 1923, is made of wood, and is painted red, of course. It is set on real rails in the middle of the countryside. The caboose sleeps two and offers a spectacular view of the Bitterroot Mountains, right from your pillow. In the morning, breakfast is served at a table for two. Specialties include huckleberry pancakes, quiche, and strawberries in season. Local activities include touring St. Mary's Mission, hiking the mountain trails, fishing, and hunting.

Haus Rustika Bed and Breakfast ✪
396 DRY GULCH ROAD, STEVENSVILLE, MONTANA 59870
rustika@marsweb.com

Tel: **(406) 777-2291**
Best Time to Call: **8 AM–9 PM**
Hosts: **Grace and Werner Will**
Location: **26 mi. S of Missoula**

No. of Rooms: **4**
Max. No. Sharing Bath: **4**
Double/sb: **$50**
Single/sb: **$35**

Open: **All year**
Reduced Rates: **7th night free; families
  10–20%**
Breakfast: **Full**
Other Meals: **Available**

Pets: **Sometimes**
Children: **Welcome**
Smoking: **No**
Social Drinking: **Permitted**

Haus Rustika is located near historic Stevensville in the Bitterroot Valley of western Montana. Nearby activities include a wildlife refuge, outdoor sports, small-town entertainment, shopping, and restaurants. The use of wood and old barn boards in this Dutch Colonial house gives it a rustic charm and complements the antique furniture. All guest bedrooms are accessible by a separate entrance. A mile-long nature trail is located behind the house and winds through the pine forest, the sage brush, and along the creek. Grace and Werner are retired teachers of special education and German. They love entertaining, gourmet cooking, and gardening. Their love of traveling is reflected in the guest bedrooms, where the decor of each typifies a different continent.

Good Medicine Lodge ✪
537 WISCONSIN AVENUE, WHITEFISH, MONTANA 59937
www.wtp.net/go/goodrx

Tel: **(800) 860-5488**
Hosts: **Christopher and Susan Ridder**
Location: **¹/₂ mi. N of Whitefish**
No. of Rooms: **9**
No. of Private Baths: **9**
Double/pb: **$105**
Single/pb: **$95**
Suites: **$135–$195**
Open: **Dec. 15–Apr. 15, May 15–
  Oct. 31**

Reduced Rates: **$10 less Dec. 15–
  Apr. 15**
Breakfast: **Full**
Credit Cards: **AMEX, DISC, MC, VISA**
Pets: **No**
Children: **Welcome**
Smoking: **No**
Social Drinking: **Permitted**
Airport/Station Pickup: **Yes**
Foreign Languages: **French, German**

Good Medicine Lodge is a classic Montana getaway hewn from solid cedar timbers and decorated in a Western motif with fabrics influenced by Native American textiles. Guest rooms have vaulted ceilings and telephones; most have balconies with mountain views. One room is wheelchair accessible. The lodge features crackling fireplaces, an outdoor spa, guest laundry, and a ski room complete with boot and glove dryers. The Ridders' B&B is located minutes from skiing, golfing, skating, Glacier Park, shopping, and dining. Downtown Whitefish and the Amtrak station are one-half mile away. The lodge is 9 miles from Glacier International Airport, 24 miles from Glacier Park, and 60 miles from the Canadian border.

NEBRASKA

Oakland.
Gretna.
.Lincoln
.Crete

The Parson's House ✪
638 FOREST AVENUE, CRETE, NEBRASKA 68333

Tel: **(402) 826-2634**
Hosts: **Harold and Sandy Richardson**
Location: **25 mi. SW of Lincoln**
No. of Rooms: **2**
Max. No. Sharing Bath: **4**
Double/sb: **$45**
Single/sb: **$35**

Open: **All year**
Breakfast: **Full**
Pets: **No**
Children: **No**
Smoking: **No**
Social Drinking: **No**
Airport/Station Pickup: **Yes**

Enjoy warm hospitality in this newly refinished, turn-of-the-century home tastefully decorated with antiques. Doane College lies one block away; the beautiful campus is just the place for a leisurely afternoon stroll. It's just a short drive to Lincoln, the state capital and home of the University of Nebraska. Harold, a Baptist minister with the local U.C.C. church, runs a remodeling business while Sandy runs the bed and breakfast. After a day's activity, they invite you to relax in their modern whirlpool tub and make their home yours for the duration of your stay.

Bundy's Bed and Breakfast ✪
16906 SOUTH 255, GRETNA, NEBRASKA 68028

Tel: **(402) 332-3616**	Single/sb: **$20**
Best Time to Call: **7 AM–9 PM**	Open: **All year**
Hosts: **Bob and Dee Bundy**	Breakfast: **Full**
Location: **30 mi. S of Omaha**	Pets: **Sometimes**
No. of Rooms: **4**	Children: **No**
Max. No. Sharing Bath: **4**	Smoking: **No**
Double/sb: **$35**	Social Drinking: **No**

The Bundys have a pretty farmhouse painted white with black trim. Here you can enjoy country living just 30 minutes from downtown Lincoln and Omaha. The rooms are decorated with antiques, attractive wallpapers, and collectibles. In the morning, wake up to farm-fresh eggs and homemade breads. The house is just a short walk from a swimming lake, and is three miles from a ski lodge.

The F. M. Hall House ✪
1039 SOUTH 11TH STREET, LINCOLN, NEBRASKA 68508

Tel: **(402) 475-4255**	Suites: **$85–$115**
Hosts: **Ed and Yana Beranek**	Open: **All year**
Location: **1 mi. from Rte. I-80**	Reduced Rates: **10% seniors**
No. of Rooms: **2**	Breakfast: **Continental, Plus**
No. of Private Baths: **2**	Credit Cards: **MC, VISA**

Pets: **No**
Children: **Welcome, over 12**

Smoking: **No**
Social Drinking: **Permitted**

This 1884 Victorian features elaborate woodwork, five fireplaces, and beautiful stained glass windows. The home has been painstakingly restored from an apartment building to a single-family floor plan with two suites for guests. The Belvedere Suite has all the amenities of a penthouse apartment, with full kitchen, private bath, and comfortable furnishings. The Empire Suite has a beautiful tiled bathroom, sunny sitting room, and a wet bar. The grounds include landscaped gardens with a brick gazebo and reflective pond. Yana and Ed delight in sharing the house's history as well as insiders' tips on attractions, events, and dining in Lincoln.

Benson Bed and Breakfast ✪
402 NORTH OAKLAND AVENUE, OAKLAND, NEBRASKA 68045-1135

Tel: **(402) 685-6051**
Hosts: **Stan and Norma Anderson**
Location: **58 mi. NW of Omaha**
No. of Rooms: **3**
Max. No. Sharing Bath: **4**
Double/sb: **$50–$55**
Single/sb: **$42**

Open: **All year**
Reduced Rates: **After 3rd day**
Breakfast: **Full**
Pets: **No**
Children: **Welcome, over 10**
Smoking: **No**
Social Drinking: **Permitted**

Once used as a rooming house, this B&B was built in 1905 with brick walls nearly one foot thick, and renovated in 1990. There is a common area of five beautifully decorated rooms for your relaxation; one is a new garden room featuring many plants and a picket fence on the wall. On the main floor there is a crafts and gift shop. Nearby is the Swedish Heritage Center and an eighteen-hole golf course. Norma serves a huge breakfast and collects things from various soft drink companies, which are displayed in the family room.

For key to listings, see inside front or back cover.

✪ This star means that rates are guaranteed through December 31, 1999, to any guest making a reservation as a result of reading about the B&B in *Bed & Breakfast U.S.A.*—1999 edition.

Important! To avoid misunderstandings, always ask about cancellation policies when booking.

Please enclose a self-addressed, stamped, business-size envelope when contacting reservation services.

For more details on what you can expect in a B&B, see Chapter 1.

Always mention *Bed & Breakfast U.S.A.* when making reservations!

We want to hear from you! Use the form on page 593.

NEVADA

Carson City. •Silver Springs   •East Ely

Mi Casa–Su Casa/Old Pueblo Bed and Breakfast ✪
RESERVATION SERVICE—NEVADA
P.O. BOX 950, TEMPE, ARIZONA 85280-0950
www.micasa.org

Tel: **(602) 990-0682; (800) 456-0682;**
   fax: **(602) 990-3390**
Best Time to Call: **8 AM–8 PM**
Coordinator: **Ruth T. Young**
Descriptive Directory of B&Bs: **$9.50**

States/Regions Covered:
   Nevada—Henderson, Las Vegas;
   Arizona; Utah; New Mexico
Rates (Single/Double): **$60–$75**
Credit Cards: **AMEX, MC, VISA**

This service offers travelers unique accommodations in Nevada, from individual homes in quiet neighborhoods two miles from "the Strip" to a contemporary two-story house in Henderson, near Boulder Dam.

Steptoe Valley Inn ✪

**P.O. BOX 151110, 220 EAST 11TH STREET, EAST ELY,
NEVADA 89315-1110**
www.nevadaweb.com/steptoe

Tel: **(702) 289-8687 June–Sept.;** **(702) 435-1196 Oct.–May**	Open: **June–Sept.**
Hosts: **Jane and Norman Lindley**	Breakfast: **Full**
Location: **70 mi. W of Great Basin National Park**	Credit Cards: **AMEX, MC, VISA**
No. of Rooms: **5**	Pets: **No**
No. of Private Baths: **5**	Children: **By arrangement**
Double/pb: **$84**	Smoking: **No**
Single/pb: **$73**	Social Drinking: **Permitted**
	Foreign Languages: **Spanish**

This Inn opened in July 1991 after major reconstruction. Located near the Nevada Northern Railway Museum, it was originally Ely City Grocery of 1907. The five second-floor rooms have country decor and private balconies, and the elegant Victorian dining room and library are downstairs. The large yard has mature trees, a gazebo, and rose garden. Norman is an airline captain and ex-rancher and Jane is a retired stewardess and local tour guide. Their guests can enjoy cool nights, scenic countryside, the "Ghost Train of Old Ely," the Great Basin National Park, and Cave Lake State Park, or just relax on the veranda!

A Secret Garden ✪

P.O. BOX 1150, SILVER SPRINGS, NEVADA 89429-1150

Tel: **(702) 577-0837**	Open: **All year**
Best Time to Call: **8 AM–9 PM**	Breakfast: **Full**
Hosts: **Tom and Gail Wilson**	Credit Cards: **VISA**
Location: **45 mi. SE of Reno**	Pets: **Sometimes**
No. of Rooms: **1**	Children: **By arrangement**
No. of Private Baths: **1**	Smoking: **No**
Double/pb: **$65**	Social Drinking: **Permitted**
Single/pb: **$55**	Airport/Station Pickup: **Yes**

In the sparsely populated Mountain View area of south Silver Springs, a tall fence shelters this freshly remodeled hacienda from the surrounding desert. Visitors will find shade trees and a wide verandah for summer afternoons and a cozy guest room for chilly nights. Breakfast time can be a surprise or guests can help with their menus. Tom and Gail cheerfully attempt to accommodate special menu requests when arranged at the time of your reservation. Within hiking or cycling distance are two state parks, Lake Lahontan and Fort Churchill. Also nearby are excellent restaurants and entertainment.

Deer Run Ranch Bed and Breakfast
5440 EASTLAKE BOULEVARD, WASHOE VALLEY, CARSON CITY, NEVADA 89704

Tel: **(702) 882-3643**	Breakfast: **Full**
Best Time to Call: **7 AM–8 PM**	Credit Cards: **AMEX, DISC, MC, VISA**
Hosts: **David and Muffy Vhay**	Pets: **No**
Location: **8 mi. N of Carson City**	Children: **Welcome, over 12**
No. of Rooms: **2**	Smoking: **No**
No. of Private Baths: **2**	Social Drinking: **Permitted**
Double/pb: **$80–$95**	Minimum Stay: **2 nights, holidays and**
Open: **All year**	**special events weekends**
Reduced Rates: **$10 less Mon.–Thurs.**	

Deer Run Ranch, a working alfalfa farm, overlooks Washoe Lake and the Sierra Nevada Mountains. A private entry leads to a private wing of the house, which includes a sitting room with fireplace, phone, TV, VCR, guest refrigerator, and two guest rooms with window seats. The decor includes Navajo rugs and old photographs, and paintings by well-known local artists grace the comfortable guest areas, lending Western ambience to this house designed and built by your host, who is an architect. Your hosts also have a pottery studio, woodshop, and large garden on the premises. Guests can enjoy the aboveground pool, pond, and boat. Things to do in the area include skiing, biking, hiking, and hang gliding; Washoe Lake State Park is next door. For fine dining, casino hopping, and entertainment, Lake Tahoe, Reno, Virginia City, and Carson City are only minutes away.

NEW HAMPSHIRE

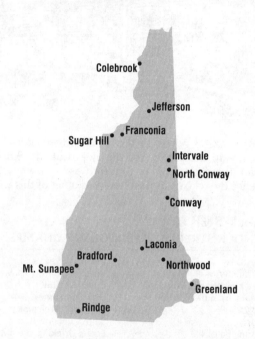

Colebrook

Jefferson

Franconia

Sugar Hill

Intervale

North Conway

Conway

Laconia

Bradford

Mt. Sunapee

Northwood

Greenland

Rindge

Candlelite Inn Bed and Breakfast ✪
5 GREENHOUSE LANE, BRADFORD,
NEW HAMPSHIRE 03221

Tel: **(888) 812-5571; (603) 938-5571;**
  fax: **(603) 938-2564**
Hosts: **Les and Marilyn Gordon**
Location: **20 mi. W of Concord**
No. of Rooms: **6**
No. of Private Baths: **6**
Double/pb: **$65–$95**
Open: **All year**

Reduced Rates: **Available**
Breakfast: **Full**
Credit Cards: **AMEX, DISC, MC, VISA**
Pets: **No**
Children: **Welcome**
Smoking: **No**
Social Drinking: **Permitted**

Candlelite is an 1897 Victorian inn nestled on three acres in the Lake
Sunapee region. A gourmet breakfast complete with dessert is served
in the sun room overlooking the pond. On a lazy summer day, sip lem-

onade on the gazebo porch; in the winter, drink hot chocolate by a warm cozy fire in the parlor. Ski the slopes of Mt. Sunapee or Pat's Peak, or walk the back roads of Bradford as the leaves change. Come and experience the relaxed atmosphere and quiet of this all-seasons inn.

Monadnock B&B ✪
1 MONADNOCK STREET, COLEBROOK, NEW HAMPSHIRE 03576

Tel: **(603) 237-8216**
Best Time to Call: **8 AM–9 PM**
Hosts: **Barbara and Wendell Woodard**
Location: **1 block from the junction of Rtes. 3 and 26**
No. of Rooms: **7**
Max. No. Sharing Bath: **4**
Double/sb: **$50–$60**
Single/sb: **$35**

Open: **All year**
Reduced Rates: **15% weekly**
Breakfast: **Full**
Pets: **Sometimes**
Children: **Welcome**
Smoking: **Permitted**
Social Drinking: **Permitted**
Airport/Station Pickup: **Yes**

Located one block off Main Street, in a quiet picturesque country community of 2,500 people, Monadnock B&B offers easy access to shops and restaurants. This 1916 house has a natural fieldstone porch, chimney, and foundation. Inside there is gorgeous woodwork. Hiking, biking, canoeing, fishing, golfing, and bird-watching are minutes away. In winter you can snowmobile over 200 miles of groomed trails from the front door. Alpine and cross-country skiing are nearby. An added attraction is watching birds close up, thanks to an in-window bird feeder. A country breakfast is served each morning.

The Foothills Farm ✪
P.O. BOX 1368, CONWAY, NEW HAMPSHIRE 03818

Tel: **(207) 935-3799**
Best Time to Call: **Early evenings**

Hosts: **Kevin and Theresa Early**
Location: **10 mi. SE of Conway Village**

No. of Rooms: **5**
No. of Private Baths: **1**
Max. No. Sharing Bath: **4**
Double/pb: **$85**
Single/pb: **$85**
Double/sb: **$45–$50**
Single/sb: **$42**
Guest Cottage: **$85–$95**
Open: **All year**
Reduced Rates: **Available**

Breakfast: **Full**
Credit Cards: **AMEX, MC, VISA**
Pets: **Sometimes**
Children: **By arrangement**
Smoking: **No**
Social Drinking: **Permitted**
Minimum Stay: **2 nights weekends
    during fall foliage and holidays**
Airport/Station Pickup: **Yes**

This restored 1850s clapboard farmhouse is located on a quiet back road in the foothills of the White Mountains. The house is surrounded by gardens of flowers, vegetables, and herbs. The fifty-acre farm has a new stable to accommodate equine guests, a trout stream, and numerous trails for cross-country skiing, hiking, and mountain biking. You're welcome to feed the chickens and pet the horses. Guest rooms are furnished in period antiques; one has a fireplace. Relax in the den, where you will find a crackling fire, or in warmer weather, on the screened porch overlooking gardens and paddocks. Breakfast specialties include eggs Benedict with home fries and blueberry pancakes with sausage, served in a country kitchen that has an antique stove and pine paneling. Kevin and Theresa have bicycles to lend and can direct you to the less-traveled areas of this scenic region. Scores of restaurants, factory outlets, and antique shops are also nearby.

Bungay Jar Bed & Breakfast ✪
EASTON VALLEY ROAD, P.O. BOX 15, FRANCONIA, NEW HAMPSHIRE 03580

Tel: **(603) 823-7775; fax: (603) 444-0100**	Open: **All year**
Hosts: **Kate Kerivan and Lee Strimbeck, owners**	Breakfast: **Full**
	Credit Cards: **AMEX, DISC, MC, VISA**
Location: **6 mi. from Rte. I-93, Exit 38**	Pets: **No**
No. of Rooms: **6**	Children: **Welcome, over 6**
No. of Private Baths: **6**	Smoking: **No**
Double/pb: **$75–$150**	Social Drinking: **Permitted**
Suite: **$150–$195**	Minimum Stay: **2 nights foliage season, holiday weekends**

Built in 1969 from an 18th-century barn, this post-and-beam house is nestled among fifteen acres of woodland bounded by a river, forest, and spectacular mountain views. In winter, guests are greeted by a crackling fire and the aroma of mulled cider in the two-story living room reminiscent of a hayloft. Antique country furnishings enhance the decor. Apple pancakes served with local maple syrup are a specialty, as are homemade breads, preserves, fruit compotes, granola, and imaginative egg dishes. Refreshments of cider and cheese are served each afternoon. Your hosts are avid hikers and skiers, so you are sure to benefit from their expert knowledge. Guests can enjoy the flower and herb gardens, the water lily pond, and the view of the pastures, llamas, and horses from the porches. A garden shop and nursery are on premises.

The Inn at Forest Hills
P.O. BOX 783, ROUTE 142, FRANCONIA, NEW HAMPSHIRE 03580
www.innatforesthills.com; bbusa@fhills.com

Tel: **(603) 823-9550; (800) 280-9550** reservations only	Breakfast: **Full**
	Other Meals: **Sometimes**
Best Time to Call: **10 AM–9 PM**	Credit Cards: **MC, VISA**
Hosts: **Gordon and Joanne Haym**	Pets: **No**
Location: **150 mi. N of Boston**	Children: **Welcome, over 12**
No. of Rooms: **7**	Smoking: **No**
No. of Private Baths: **7**	Social Drinking: **Permitted**
Double/pb: **$85–$145**	Minimum Stay: **2 nights fall foliage and most weekends**
Suite: **$105–$145**	
Open: **All year**	Station Pickup: **Yes**
Reduced Rates: **Available**	

Formerly part of the Forest Hills Hotel, this Tudor-style Inn was built in 1890 to accommodate social events and large families. In 1961 the building was donated to Franconia College and became the home of its president. Gordon and Joanne purchased the Inn in 1992 and began their bed and breakfast venture. Eighteen charming historic rooms showcase the majestic scenery and year-round attractions of the White Mountains. The Inn is located near Cannon, Bretton Woods, and Loon. Guests can cross-country ski on the property or at nearby trails. Enjoy gracious hospitality and relax in country casualness in the sun-filled solarium or by the fireplaces in the living room or Alpine room. In the morning, savor a gourmet breakfast by the fireplace.

Ayres Homestead Bed & Breakfast ○
47 PARK AVENUE, GREENLAND, NEW HAMPSHIRE 03840

Tel: **(603) 436-5992**
Hosts: **David and Priscilla Engel**
Location: **3 mi. W of Portsmouth**
No. of Rooms: **4**
No. of Private Baths: **1**
Max. No. Sharing Bath: **4**
Double/pb: **$55**
Single/pb: **$50**
Double/sb: **$50**

Single/sb: **$45**
Suites: **$95**
Open: **All year**
Breakfast: **Full**
Pets: **Sometimes**
Children: **Welcome**
Smoking: **No**
Social Drinking: **Permitted**

The Thomas Ayres House, begun in 1737 as a two-room post-and-beam structure, has been enlarged and remodeled many times in its 250-year history. Priscilla and Dave will tell you of the famous people, including Paul Revere, George Washington, and John Adams, who passed by its doors. Set on six acres on the historic village green, its nine rooms have wainscoting, exposed beams, and wide board floors; seven have fireplaces. The bedrooms are made cozy with antiques, braided rugs, afghans, and rockers. Breakfast is served in the dining room on an antique table set in front of a brick fireplace with artfully displayed pewterware and ironware.

The Forest—A Country Inn ○
ROUTE 16A, P.O. BOX 37, INTERVALE, NEW HAMPSHIRE 03845
www.forest-inn.com

Tel: **(603) 356-9772; (800) 448-3534**
Hosts: **Lisa and Bill Guppy**
Location: **1½ m. from Rte. 16**
No. of Rooms: **11**
No. of Private Baths: **11**
Double/pb: **$69–$139**
Guest cottage: **$95–$169**
Open: **All year**

Reduced Rates: **May 1–June 30; Oct. 20–Dec. 13; mid-week Jan.**
Breakfast: **Full**
Credit Cards: **AMEX, DISC, MC, VISA**
Pets: **No**
Children: **Welcome, over 5**
Smoking: **No**
Social Drinking: **Permitted**

Located two miles north from North Conway Village and reigning over 25 acres in the White Mountains, this three-story Victorian Inn has been in operation since the late 1800s. As you enter the Inn, the warmth of a wood-burning fireplace and an oriental rug set the tone for a memorable stay. The stone cottage has a fireplace and is the favorite for honeymooners. The newly renovated Forest Cottage boasts a gas fireplace and a Jacuzzi tub. Relax by the garden-side pool or take advantage of all the recreational possibilities the valley has to offer, such as downhill and cross-country skiing, hiking, biking, canoeing, fishing, golfing, and much more. In the winter, enjoy cross-country trails that begin at the back door. Packages are available.

The Jefferson Inn ✪
ROUTE 2, RR1, BOX 68A, JEFFERSON, NEW HAMPSHIRE 03583

Tel: **(603) 586-7998; (800) 729-7908;**
  fax: **(603) 586-7808**
Hosts: **Marla Mason and Don Garretson**
No. of Rooms: **11**
No. of Private Baths: **11**
Double/pb: **$80–$120**
Single/pb: **$75–$100**
Suites: **$120–$175**
Open: **Dec.–Mar.; May–Oct.**

Reduced Rates: **Winter mid-week**
Breakfast: **Full**
Credit Cards: **AMEX, DISC, MC, VISA**
Pets: **No**
Children: **Welcome**
Smoking: **No**
Social Drinking: **Permitted**
Foreign Languages: **German**

Nestled in the foothills of the northern White Mountains near Mount Washington, this charming 1896 Victorian Inn offers spectacular views and outdoor adventures year-round. Bring your boots, binoculars, and bicycles for superb hiking, cycling, and sightseeing. Next to the Inn you'll find the trailhead to Mt. Starr King and Mt. Waumbek. Three of the best cycling trails start in the driveway. Tee off at the Waumbek, the oldest 18-hole championship golf course in New Hampshire, or take a dip in the spring-fed swimming pond. In the winter you can ski, ice skate, and snowmobile right outside the door. Antique shops, children's amusement parks, summer theater, and downhill skiing are nearby. The Inn is perfect for a private getaway or a family vacation. A delightful gourmet breakfast and afternoon tea with fresh baked goods are included.

Ferry Point House ✪
100 LOWER BAY ROAD, SANBORNTON, LACONIA,
NEW HAMPSHIRE 03269
ferrypt@together.net; www.tiac.net/users/berg

Tel: **(603) 524-0087; fax: (603) 524-**
  0087
Best Time to Call: **After 2 PM**
Hosts: **Diane and Joe Damato**
Location: **90 mi. N of Boston**
No. of Rooms: **5**
No. of Private Baths: **5**
Double/pb: **$85–$110**

Open: **All year**
Reduced Rates: **15% weekly**
Breakfast: **Full**
Pets: **No**
Children: **Welcome, over 10**
Social Drinking: **Permitted**
Airport/Station Pickup: **Yes**
Foreign Languages: **French**

New England's past is well preserved in this 150-year-old Victorian located on picturesque Lake Winnisquam. Enjoy breathtaking views of the water and the mountains from a 60-foot veranda. Of course, the view is even more enjoyable when you're sipping lemonade or the house blend of coffee. Guest rooms overlook the lake and are furnished with antiques, collectibles, and fresh flowers. Breakfast is served in a Victorian-style dining room, and your hosts take pride in offering unusual dishes, such as cheese baked apples, crepes, or Grand Marnier French toast. Ferry Point House is minutes from regional activities such as boating, skiing, dinner cruises, and a large selection of fine restaurants.

Rest Assured

47 LAIGHTON AVENUE SOUTH, LACONIA,
NEW HAMPSHIRE 03246

Tel: **(603) 524-9021**	Single/sb: **$75**
Best Time to Call: **After 6 PM**	Open: **All year**
Hosts: **Maurice and Helene Gouin**	Breakfast: **Full**
Location: **30 mi. N of Concord**	Pets: **Sometimes**
No. of Rooms: **3**	Children: **Welcome**
No. of Private Baths: **1**	Smoking: **No**
Max. No. Sharing Bath: **2**	Social Drinking: **Permitted**
Double/pb: **$100**	Airport/Station Pickup: **Yes**
Double/sb: **$85**	Foreign Languages: **French**

This contemporary home stands on the shore of Lake Winnisquam. Winnisquam in Indian translation means "Smiling Water," and the serenity of the lake, mountain, and surrounding woodlands can truly lift one's spirit. The lakefront ground-floor room has a queen-size bed, private bath, and patio forty-five degrees from the lake. The second-floor lakefront room has a queen-size bed, shared bath, and a deck that looks out at the lake and mountains. The Wood View room has twin beds that can be made into a king, and a shared bath. These two rooms are ideal for families traveling together. Your hosts offer two TV rooms, and a solarium with a lot of plants. Plants also dominate outside, both flowers and vegetables flourish. Seasonal activities include everything from boating to cross-country skiing. Weather and time permitting, a cruise on Lake Winnisquam in the Gouins' restored, solar-powered launch will add to your unforgettable memories.

Blue Goose Inn B&B ✪

24 ROUTE 103B, P.O. BOX 2117, MT. SUNAPEE,
NEW HAMPSHIRE 03255

Tel: **(603) 763-5519**	Single/pb: **$50**
Best Time to Call: **Before noon**	Double/sb: **$55**
Hosts: **Meryl and Ronald Caldwell**	Single/sb: **$41.50**
Location: **10 mi. from I-89**	Open: **All year**
No. of Rooms: **4**	Breakfast: **Full**
No. of Private Baths: **4**	Credit Cards: **MC, VISA**
Double/pb: **$60**	Pets: **No**

Children: **Welcome**	Social Drinking: **Permitted**
Smoking: **No**	Airport/Station Pickup: **Yes**

This well-restored, early 19th-century Colonial farmhouse is located on 3¹/₂ acres along Lake Sunapee, at the base of Mt. Sunapee. The cozy, comfortable guest rooms are furnished in a quaint, country style. Make yourself at home in any of the common areas. The living room has a fireplace, TV, VCR, and book and video library; the card and game room has plenty of diversions; there's refrigerator space in the kitchen, and the porch, weather permitting, is ideal for breakfast and snacks. Kids will have fun in the summer playhouse. The Mt. Sunapee area is a mini-resort for vacationers of all ages, offering boating, swimming, hiking, downhill and cross-country skiing, snowmobiling, crafts fairs, antiquing, and much more.

The Buttonwood Inn

**P.O. BOX 1817, MT. SURPRISE ROAD, NORTH CONWAY,
NEW HAMPSHIRE 03860
button-w@moose.ncia.net; www.buttonwoodinn.com**

Tel: **(800) 258-2625; (603) 356-2625;** fax: **(603) 356-3140**	Breakfast: **Full**
Hosts: **Claudia and Peter Needham**	Other Meals: **Available, for groups and President Day Weekend**
Location: **1¹/₂ mi. from Rte. 16**	Credit Cards: **AMEX, DISC, MC, VISA**
No. of Rooms: **10**	Pets: **No**
No. of Private Baths: **10**	Children: **Welcome, over 3**
Double/pb: **$80–$170**	Smoking: **No**
Single/pb: **$70–$160**	Social Drinking: **Permitted**
Open: **All year**	Minimum Stay: **2 nights weekends**
Reduced Rates: **Available; families**	

This 1820s farmhouse is set on seventeen secluded acres, two miles from North Conway Village. The interior is decorated with Shaker furniture, stenciling, and antiques. Rooms have gas fireplaces and Jacuzzis. Outside, admire the three-time award-winning gardens. Guests can hike or cross-country ski from the back door. The Needhams dish up fabulous breakfasts. The Buttonwood Inn offers a memorable blend of hospitality, laughter, and kindness.

The Victorian Harvest Inn, Circa 1850 ✪

**28 LOCUST LANE, P.O. BOX 1763, NORTH CONWAY,
NEW HAMPSHIRE 03860-1763**

Tel: **(603) 356-3548; (800) 642-0749**	Max. No. Sharing Bath: **4**
Best Time to Call: **10 AM–8 PM**	Double/pb: **$80–$120**
Hosts: **David and Judy Wooster**	Single/pb: **$65–$95**
Location: **140 mi. N of Boston**	Double/sb: **$55–$80**
No. of Rooms: **6**	Single/sb: **$45–$70**
No. of Private Baths: **4**	Open: **All year**

Reduced Rates: **Available**
Breakfast: **Full**
Credit Cards: **AMEX, DISC, MC, VISA**
Pets: **No**
Children: **Welcome, over 6**

Smoking: **No**
Social Drinking: **Permitted**
Minimum Stay: **2 days, foliage and holidays**
Airport/Station Pickup: **Yes**

This quiet Victorian inn has a four-season location nestled on a country lane in the heart of the Mount Washington Valley. Make yourself at home in the library with a gas fireplace, window seat with mountain views, soft music, good books, and favorite movies. An inviting breakfast from a varied gourmet menu is served in the dining room. Special dietary needs can be met with advance notice. A deck, picket-fenced pool, and landscaped grounds and gardens welcome you after a day of exploring all that the Mount Washington Valley has to offer.

Meadow Farm
JENNESS POND ROAD, NORTHWOOD, NEW HAMPSHIRE 03261

Tel: **(603) 942-8619**
Hosts: **Douglas and Janet Briggs**
Location: **18 mi. E of Concord**
No. of Rooms: **3**
Max. No. Sharing Bath: **4**
Double/sb: **$65**
Single/sb: **$45**
Guest Cottage: **$600 weekly**

Open: **All year**
Reduced Rates: **Families**
Breakfast: **Full**
Credit Cards: **AMEX, MC, VISA**
Pets: **Sometimes**
Children: **Welcome**
Smoking: **No**
Social Drinking: **Permitted**

Meadow Farm is set on 50 acres of quiet woods and horse pastures. The house is an authentic New England Colonial dating back to 1770, with wide-pine floors, beamed ceilings, and old fireplaces. In the morning, a hearty country breakfast of homemade breads, seasonal fruit, and local syrup is served in the keeping room. Guests are invited to swim and canoe at the private beach. The property also has plenty of wooded trails for long walks or cross-country skiing. Meadow Farm is an ideal location for those en route to Concord, the seacoast, or the mountains.

Grassy Pond House
RINDGE, NEW HAMPSHIRE 03461

Tel: **(603) 899-5166, 899-5167**
Best Time to Call: **Mornings**
Hosts: **Carmen Linares and Robert Multer**
Location: **60 mi. NW of Boston**
No. of Rooms: **3**
No. of Private Baths: **2**
Max. No. Sharing Bath: **4**
Double/pb: **$70**

Single/pb: **$60**
Double/sb: **$60**
Single/sb: **$50**
Open: **All year**
Breakfast: **Full**
Pets: **No**
Children: **Welcome, over 14**
Smoking: **No**
Social Drinking: **Permitted**

This secluded 19th-century farmhouse is set among 150 acres of woods and fields. The house has been restored, enlarged, and decorated in period pieces. Guest quarters, overlooking the gardens and lake, feature a private entrance and a living room with fireplace. Breakfast specialties include pancakes with local maple syrup, fresh eggs and bacon, and plenty of good Colombian coffee. This setting, high in the Monadnock region, is perfect for hiking, skiing, boating, fishing, and swimming.

The Hilltop Inn
SUGAR HILL, NEW HAMPSHIRE 03585
bb@hilltopinn.com; www.hilltopinn.com

Tel: **(603) 823-5695; (800) 770-5695**
Hosts: **Mike and Meri Hern**
Location: **2¹/₂ mi. W of Franconia**
No. of Rooms: **6**
No. of Private Baths: **6**
Double/pb: **$80–$130**
Single/pb: **$60–$85**
Guest Cottage: **$175–$250**

Suites: **$100–$175**
Open: **All year**
Breakfast: **Full**
Pets: **Welcome**
Children: **No**
Smoking: **Restricted**
Social Drinking: **Permitted**
Airport/Station Pickup: **Yes**

The Hilltop Inn is a sprawling, 19th-century Victorian located in a small, friendly village. Inside, you'll find a warm, cozy atmosphere, comfortable furnishings, and lots of antiques. The kitchen is the heart of the house in more ways than one. In the morning, homemade muffins are served fresh from the old-fashioned Garland stove. Local attractions include Franconia Notch, White Mountain National Forest, North Conway, great skiing, and spectacular foliage. Enjoy lovely sunset views, stroll along the quiet country roads; read in porch rockers, or enjoy conversation by the fire. All guest rooms have handmade quilts and antiques.

NEW JERSEY

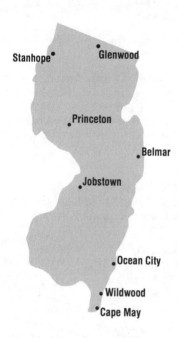

Bed & Breakfast of Princeton—A Reservation Service ✪
P.O. BOX 571, PRINCETON, NEW JERSEY 08542
bbop@compuserve.com

Tel: **(609) 924-3189;**
  fax: **(609) 921-6271**
Coordinator: **John W. Hurley**

States/Regions Covered: **Princeton**
Rates (Single/Double):
  Average: **$40–$55 / $50–$65**

Bed & Breakfast of Princeton offers homestay accommodations in a small group of private homes located within a 1¹/₄-mile radius of the center of Princeton. A few homes are within walking distance of the town center. Others are convenient to public transportation, or a few minutes away by automobile. There is a two-night minimum stay, and a continental breakfast is provided. Most homes are nonsmoking. Personal checks are accepted for deposit or total payment; cash or travelers checks are required for any balance due.

Delaware Valley Excursions ✪

P.O. BOX 459, STOCKTON, NEW JERSEY 08559
www.innreservations.com

Tel: **(800) 981-4667; (609) 397-9494**	Rates (Double):
Best Time to Call: **8 AM–10 PM**	Modest: **$65–$115**
Coordinator: **Tracey Fredandall**	Average: **$115–$175**
States/Regions Covered:	Luxury: **$175–$250**
Pennsylvania—Bucks County; New	Credit Cards: **AMEX, MC, VISA**
Jersey—Hunterdon County	

Tracey has lived in Bucks County for more than twenty-seven years. Combining her love of the area as well as eleven years in the hospitality industry, she can share her expertise to create the perfect getaway, business meeting, or wedding for you. After helping you find a place to stay, Delaware Valley Excursions will show you where to go and what to do.

Down the Shore B&B ✪

201 SEVENTH AVENUE, BELMAR, NEW JERSEY 07719
lodgings@cris.com; www.belmar.com/downtheshore

Tel: **(732) 681-9023**	Open: **All year**
Best Time to Call: **Before noon**	Reduced Rates: **Available**
Hosts: **Annette and Al Bergins**	Breakfast: **Full**
Location: **1 block from ocean**	Pets: **Sometimes**
No. of Rooms: **3**	Smoking: **No**
No. of Private Baths: **1**	Social Drinking: **Permitted**
Max. No. Sharing Bath: **4**	Minimum Stay: **2 nights/weekends in**
Double/pb: **$90**	**season**
Double/sb: **$80**	Station Pickup: **Yes**

Down the Shore's name couldn't be more appropriate—this B&B is located one block from the boardwalk and the beach. When you want to get out of the sun, rest up in your comfortable, air-conditioned room, read, play games on the shaded porch, or watch TV in the parlor. Racing fans can choose between the thoroughbreds at Monmouth Park and the trotters at Freehold Raceway, while the culturally inclined can catch world-class entertainment at the Garden State Arts Center. A complete breakfast is served each morning, including fresh fruit, juices, baked casseroles, and homemade granola.

Barnard-Good House ✪

238 PERRY STREET, CAPE MAY, NEW JERSEY 08204

Tel: **(609) 884-5381**	No. of Private Baths: **5**
Best Time to Call: **9 AM–9 PM**	Double/pb: **$95–$155**
Hosts: **Nan and Tom Hawkins**	Single/pb: **$85.50–$139.50**
No. of Rooms: **5**	Suite: **$145–$150**

Open: **Apr.–Nov.**
Breakfast: **Full**
Credit Cards: **MC, VISA**
Pets: **No**
Children: **Welcome, over 14**

Smoking: **No**
Social Drinking: **Permitted**
Minimum Stay: **2 nights spring and fall;
    3 nights summer**

Nan and Tom cordially invite you to their Second Empire Victorian cottage, circa 1865, just a five-minute walk from the beach and all tours, restaurants, and activities. They love antiques and continually add to their collection, using them to create a warm and comfortable atmosphere. Nan's breakfast is a four-course gourmet treat with everything made from scratch. It's touted as one of the best in New Jersey—Nan and Tom have been written up by many important publications. A typical morning repast could be strawberry-apple juice, chilled peach soup, shrimp and spinach roulade, tomato flan, three-grain wild rice bread, and walnut fudge tart. Many evening treats are served and iced tea is always available in the warm weather months.

Apple Valley Inn ✪

P.O. BOX 302, CORNER OF ROUTES 517 AND 565, GLENWOOD, NEW JERSEY 07418

Tel: **(973) 764-3735**
Best Time to Call: **5–8 PM**
Hosts: **Mitzi and John Durham**
Location: **45 mi. NW of New York City**

No. of Rooms: **7**
No. of Private Baths: **2**
Max. No. Sharing Bath: **4**
Double/pb: **$90–$110**

Single/pb: **$90**
Double/sb: **$70–$80**
Single/sb: **$70**
Open: **All year**
Reduced Rates: **10% seniors midweek**

Breakfast: **Full**
Pets: **No**
Children: **Welcome, over 13**
Smoking: **Permitted**
Social Drinking: **Permitted**

Apple Valley Inn, a rustic 19th-century mansion with exposed beams, red brick chimneys, and hand-painted fire screens, takes its name from the fruit farms that used to dominate the area. Bedrooms are named for apples—Granny Smith, Jonathan, Yellow Delicious—and are furnished in Colonial style. Guests can stroll in an apple orchard, swim in a pool, and fish for river trout without leaving the property. Local recreational options include skiing and horseback riding. The Inn is located on the Appalachian Trail. Breakfasts feature ham-cheese dandy or Dutch baby pancakes, accompanied by fresh fruit and homemade breads, muffins, and jams.

Belle Springs Farm ✪
2770 MONMOUTH ROAD, JOBSTOWN, NEW JERSEY 08041

Tel: **(609) 723-5364**
Host: **Lyd Sudler**
Location: **5 miles from N.J. Tpke., Exit 7**
No. of Rooms: **2**
Max. No. Sharing Bath: **4**
Double/sb: **$50**

Open: **All year**
Breakfast: **Full**
Other Meals: **Available**
Pets: **No**
Children: **Welcome**
Smoking: **Permitted**
Social Drinking: **Permitted**

This spacious, contemporary farmhouse was built in 1961 and is attractively furnished with family heirlooms. Central air conditioning, a fireplace, and a Steinway add to comfort and ambiance. From the porch, there's a spectacular view of the pastures and deer that come out of the woods at dusk. It's situated in the heart of Burlington County, where every little town, including Burlington, Bordentown, and Mt. Holly, is a pre-Revolutionary gem. It is a half hour to Philadelphia or Princeton. Lyd enjoys music, gardening, and pampering her guests. If you want to bring your horse, there's a $10 charge for the turnout in the pasture.

Northwood Inn
401 WESLEY AVENUE, OCEAN CITY, NEW JERSEY 08226
nwoodinn@bellatlantic.net; www.northwoodinn.com

Tel: **(609) 399-6071**
Best Time to Call: **11 AM–10 PM**
Hosts: **Marj and John Loeper**
Location: **8 mi. S of Atlantic City**
No. of Rooms: **7**
No. of Private Baths: **7**

Double/pb: **$90–$160**
Single/pb: **$85–$155**
Suites: **$135–$150; sleeps 4**
Open: **All year**
Breakfast: **Full**
Credit Cards: **AMEX, MC, VISA**

Pets: **No**
Children: **Welcome, over 10**
Smoking: **No**

Social Drinking: **Permitted**
Minimum Stay: **Holiday weekends**
Airport/Station Pickup: **Yes**

This award-winning, elegantly restored Victorian has 19th-century charm with 20th-century comforts. Distinctively decorated rooms include private baths (one with a Jacuzzi), central air conditioning, and TV. The main floor common space consists of a parlor, fully stocked library, billiard room, and dining room with cafe tables. Along with two porches, the guests have the use of the rooftop deck with a whirlpool spa year-round. The inn offers complimentary beach tags, bicycles, morning papers, and a bountiful breakfast. Northwood Inn is ideally located three blocks from the beach, boardwalk, shops, and restaurants in the heart of the Ocean City Historic District.

Serendipity Bed & Breakfast ✪
712 NINTH STREET, OCEAN CITY, NEW JERSEY 08226

Tel: **(609) 399-1554; (800) 842-8544;**
  fax: (609) 399-1527
Best Time to Call: **Mornings**
Hosts: **Clara and Bill Plowfield**
Location: **8 mi. S of Atlantic City**
No. of Rooms: **6**
No. of Private Baths: **4**
Max. No. Sharing Bath: **4**

Double/pb: **$85–$129**
Double/sb: **$75–$95**
Open: **All year**
Breakfast: **Full**
Other Meals: **Available, Oct.–May**
Credit Cards: **AMEX, DISC, MC, VISA**
Pets: **No**
Children: **Welcome, over 10**

Smoking: **No**   Minimum Stay: **2 nights weekends**
Social Drinking: **Permitted**

Welcome to Serendipity! Like its name, Serendipity is a delightfully unique, fully air-conditioned, and immaculately maintained seashore inn. Warm hospitality and beautifully decorated airy rooms with TV, wicker, and pastels are blended into a memorable getaway for you. A delicious healthy breakfast is served each morning; vegetarian, heart-healthy, and macrobiotic diets are accommodated. This B&B stands one half-block from the beach, and the boardwalk is open all year. Clara and Bill offer cooking and muffin-baking classes, special occasion packages, and a vegetarian Thanksgiving dinner.

Red Maple Farm

R.D. 4, RAYMOND ROAD, PRINCETON, NEW JERSEY 08540

Tel: **(732) 329-3821**
Best Time to Call: **Evenings**
Hosts: **Roberta and Lindsey Churchill**
Location: **1 hour from New York**
No. of Rooms: **3**
Max. No. Sharing Bath: **4**
Double/sb: **$58–$78**
Single/sb: **$48–$68**

Open: **All year**
Reduced Rates: **10% weekly**
Breakfast: **Full**
Credit Cards: **AMEX, DISC, MC, VISA**
Pets: **No**
Children: **Welcome, over 8**
Smoking: **No**
Social Drinking: **Permitted**

Roberta is a former chef who owned one of New Jersey's best restaurants; today she's a passionate gardener, reader, and political activist. Lindsey is a sociology professor. Their house, built between 1740 and 1820, has five working fireplaces, latched doors and, reportedly, a resident Hessian ghost. The grounds include a 1740 smokehouse, an 1850 barn whose cellar hid runaway slaves on the underground railroad, and the stone ruins of an older barn, which make a great backdrop for the modern swimming pool. The gates of Princeton University are four miles distant, and New York City, Philadelphia, and New Hope, Pennsylvania, are all about an hour away by car.

Whistling Swan Inn ✪

110 MAIN STREET, STANHOPE, NEW JERSEY 07874
wswan@worldnet.att.net; www.bbianj.com/whistlingswan

Tel: **(973) 347-6369**
Best Time to Call: **9 AM–6 PM**
Hosts: **Paula Williams and Joe Mulay**
Location: **45 mi. W of New York City**
No. of Rooms: **10**
No. of Private Baths: **10**
Double/pb: **$95–$150**
Open: **All year**
Reduced Rates: **Weekly**

Breakfast: **Full**
Credit Cards: **AMEX, DISC, MC, VISA**
Pets: **No**
Children: **Welcome, over 12**
Smoking: **No**
Social Drinking: **Permitted**
Airport/Station Pickup: **Yes, by
    arrangement**

You'll feel like you're back in grandmother's house when you visit this lovely Queen Anne Victorian located in a small, historic village. The massive limestone wraparound porch leads to comfortable rooms filled with family antiques. Your hosts have labored tirelessly to make the ornate woodwork, large fireplaces, old-fashioned fixtures, and even the banister light look like new. Take a bubble bath in a claw-footed tub and then wrap yourself in a fluffy robe before retiring. Your room will be individually decorated in varying period motifs. Breakfast includes homemade muffins, breads, and fruit, along with a hot egg, cheese, or fruit dish. Special arrangements are easily made for corporate guests who need to eat early or require the data port hookups, copy service, or meeting room. The Inn is close to the International Trade Zone, Waterloo Village, Lake Musconetcong, restaurants, and state parks and forests.

The Sea Gypsy ✪

209 EAST MAGNOLIA AVENUE, WILDWOOD, NEW JERSEY 08260
www.angelfire.com/nj/SeaGypsy

Tel: **(609) 522-0690**	Open: **All year**
Hosts: **Natalie and Todd Kieninger,**	Reduced Rates: **Oct. 1–June 1**
Anna and Keith Grimm	Breakfast: **Full**
Location: **75 mil. SE of Philadelphia, Pa.;**	Credit Cards: **MC, VISA**
30 mi. S of Atlantic City	Pets: **No**
No. of Rooms: 5	Children: **Welcome**
No. of Private Baths: 5	Smoking: **No**
Double/pb: **$60–$85**	Social Drinking: **Permitted**
Suite: **$120**	Airport/Station Pickup: **Yes**

This impressive turn-of-the-century Queen Anne-style inn is located in a primary historic district, just blocks from the beach, boardwalk, amusement piers, and walking mall. Interior and exterior detailing make this charming bed and breakfast a pure delight. Turrets, dormers, and spacious porches recall memories of a special time in America's history. Antique furnishings, Jacuzzi, TV, VCR, video library, bicycles, and an old-fashioned candy cupboard add to the many extras. The surrounding region offers many attractions to birders, dolphin and whale watchers, water sports enthusiasts, and sunbathers.

NEW MEXICO

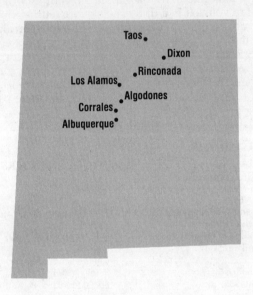

Bed & Breakfast Southwest Reservation Service—New Mexico ✪
2916 NORTH 70TH STREET, SCOTTSDALE, ARIZONA 85251
b&bsw@juno.com

Tel: **(602) 947-9704; (800) 762-9704;**
  fax: **(602) 874-1316**
Best Time to Call: **8 AM–8 PM**
Coordinators: **Jo Cummings and Joan Petersen**
States/Regions Covered: **Arizona, New Mexico, Southern Colorado, Southern California**

Descriptive Directory: **Free w/SASE**
Rates (Single/Double):
  Modest: **$40–$75**
  Average: **$80–$100**
  Luxury: **$105–up**

This service offers travelers unique homestays in suites, guesthouses, ranches, and inns. All host facilities are personally inspected and provide the three C's of bed and breakfasts: cleanliness, cordiality, and convenience. Jo and Joan's specialty is finding the perfect B&B for you.

They can plan your trip to include many of the historical and natural wonders of the great Southwest, such as the San Diego Zoo, Durango Historic Railroad, Scottsdale golf courses, Sedona's Red Rock formations and the Santa Fe opera. You will be awed by the spectacular scenic beauty and legendary Western hospitality.

Mi Casa–Su Casa/Old Pueblo Bed and Breakfast ✪

Reservation Service—New Mexico
P.O. BOX 950, TEMPE, ARIZONA 85280-0950

Tel: **(602) 990-0682; (800) 456-0682;**
fax: **(602) 990-3390**
Best Time to Call: **8 AM–8 PM**
Coordinator: **Ruth T. Young**
States/Regions Covered: **New Mexico:**
Albuquerque, Bernalillo, Chimayo,
Corrales, Espanola, Las Cruces,
Lincoln, Los Ojos, Santa Fe, Taos;
Arizona; Utah; Nevada

Descriptive Directory of B&Bs: **$9.50**
Rates (Single/Double):
Modest: **$65–$75**
Average: **$75–$85**
Luxury: **$85–up**
Credit Cards: **AMEX, MC, VISA**

This service offers travelers unique accommodations, from an award-winning inn built in 1772 with some original adobe walls, to host homes and inns near the Rio Grande River, pueblos, and skiing. All have been inspected and offer a warm Southwestern welcome.

Anderson's Victorian House ✪

11600 MODESTO AVENUE NORTHEAST, ALBUQUERQUE,
NEW MEXICO 87122

Tel: **(505) 856-6211**
Best Time to Call: **7–8:30 AM;**
4–9 PM
Host: **Judy Anderson**
Location: **3.3 mi. E from Rte. I-25**
No. of Rooms: **3**
No. of Private Baths: **1**
Max. No. Sharing Bath: **4**
Double/pb: **$50–$70**
Single/pb: **$40**
Double/sb: **$35**

Single/sb: **$30**
Open: **All year**
Reduced Rates: **10% families; weekly**
Breakfast: **Full**
Other Meals: **Available**
Pets: **Sometimes**
Children: **Welcome, over 4**
Smoking: **No**
Social Drinking: **Permitted**
Airport Pickup: **Yes**

Anderson's Victorian House is a newly constructed, two-story house on a one-acre tract with spectacular views. Guest rooms are decorated with antiques and pieces your hosts collected in their world travels. Horseback riding, skiing, hiking, and golf are available nearby. Judy will gladly direct you to the Sandia Ski Area, Albuquerque's Old Town, Sante Fe, the Indian Cultural Center, and other points of interest. Prize-winning coffee cake, muffins, and more are breakfast delights. Cheese and wine or coffee, tea, and cookies are served in the evening.

Canyon Crest ✪
5804 CANYON CREST NORTHEAST, ALBUQUERQUE, NEW MEXICO 87111

Tel: **(505) 821-4898**
Best Time to Call: **7 AM–10 PM**
Hosts: **Jan and Chip Mansure**
Location: **7 mi. NE of Albuquerque**
No. of Rooms: **2**
Max. No. Sharing Bath: **4**
Double/pb: **$65–$75**

Double/sb: **$60**
Open: **All year**
Breakfast: **Continental**
Pets: **No**
Children: **Welcome**
Smoking: **No**
Social Drinking: **No**

Warm hospitality awaits you upon entering this two-story contemporary home furnished in Southwestern decor. Enjoy the splash of color from the hosts' prize-winning batik pictures and floral arrangements, as well as antiques and collectibles from their teaching and travels in Africa. After a great day of skiing, hiking, ballooning, antiquing, visiting galleries and museums, exploring Indian pueblos or golfing, come home to a cup of coffee or tea and good conversation with Jan and Chip. Indulge in a quiet night's sleep and awaken to a hearty breakfast of cereal, muffins, and fresh fruit.

The Corner House ✪
9121 JAMES PLACE NORTHEAST, ALBUQUERQUE, NEW MEXICO 87111

Tel: **(505) 298-5800**
Host: **Jean Thompson**
Location: **4 mi. N of I-40**
No. of Rooms: **4**
No. of Private Baths: **2**
Max. No. Sharing Bath: **3**
Double/pb: **$45–$50**
Double/sb: **$40–$50**
Single/sb: **$30–$35**

Open: **All year**
Reduced Rates: **10% families, seniors**
Breakfast: **Full**
Other Meals: **Available**
Pets: **Sometimes**
Children: **Welcome (crib)**
Smoking: **No**
Social Drinking: **Permitted**

Jean welcomes you to her handsome Southwestern-style home decorated in a delightful mix of antiques and collectibles. Breakfast specialties include Jean's homemade muffins. The Corner House is located in a quiet residential neighborhood within view of the magnificent Sandia Mountains. It is convenient to Old Town Albuquerque, Santa Fe, many Indian pueblos, and the launch site for the Kodak Albuquerque International Balloon Fiesta.

The Ranchette B&B ✪

2329 LAKEVIEW ROAD SOUTHWEST, ALBUQUERQUE, NEW MEXICO 87105
www.viva.com/nm/ranchette/

Tel: **(505) 877-5140;**
  fax: **(505) 873-8274**
Best Time to Call: **After 4 PM**
Host: **Reverend Janis Hildebrand**
Location: **5 mi. SW of Albuquerque**
No. of Rooms: **2**
No. of Private Baths: **1**
Max. No. Sharing Bath: **3**
Double/pb: **$85**
Double/sb: **$65**
Open: **All year**

Reduced Rates: **Jan.–Mar.; 10% seniors;
  20% families**
Breakfast: **Full**
Other Meals: **Available**
Credit Cards: **AMEX, DC, DISC, MC,
  VISA**
Pets: **Sometimes**
Children: **Welcome**
Smoking: **No**
Social Drinking: **No**

Enjoy vistas of mountains at sunrise and sunset in restful spiritual surroundings in this adobe-style home, complete with an Arabian horse. Accommodations inside and outside include a fireplace, grand piano, hot tub, swings, walking paths, terry robes, original art, antiques, and in-room phones. Gourmet vegetarian meals are served; breakfast is included with the room, dinner upon request for an additional fee. Ranchette is located 10 minutes from downtown and Historic Old Town, 30 minutes from the Balloon Fiesta Park, and one hour from Santa Fe and Acoma Pueblo Sky City. Janis is a nondenominational minister, licensed marriage and family therapist, and licensed school counselor. A pianist and gourmet cook, she aspires to compete at dressage and hunter jumper events.

Rio Grande House ✪

3100 RIO GRANDE BOULEVARD NORTHWEST, ALBUQUERQUE, NEW MEXICO 87107

Tel: **(505) 345-0120**
Best Time to Call: **Anytime**

Hosts: **James Hughes**

Location: **4 mi. N of Rte. I-40, Exit Rio Grande Blvd.**
No. of Rooms: **5**
No. of Private Baths: **5**
Double/pb: **$75–$85**
Single/pb: **$55–$65**

Open: **All year**
Breakfast: **Full**
Pets: **Sometimes**
Children: **Welcome**
Smoking: **Permitted**
Social Drinking: **Permitted**

This landmark white adobe residence is close to historic Old Town, major museums, Rio Grande Nature Center, and the International Balloon Fiesta launch site. Southwestern charm is reflected through the beamed ceilings, brick floors, and kiva fireplaces. Museum-quality antiques and collectibles from East Africa, Nepal, Yemen, and Pakistan are used to decorate each room. Jim, a college professor, writer, and actor, will be happy to relate their history.

Hacienda Vargas ✪

1431 EL CAMINO REAL, P.O. BOX 307, ALGODONES, NEW MEXICO 87001

Tel: **(505) 867-9115; (800) 261-0006**
Best Time to Call: **8:30 AM–9 PM**
Hosts: **Paul and Julie DeVargas**
Location: **22 mi. S of Santa Fe, 25 mi. N of Albuquerque**
No. of Rooms: **8**
No. of Private Baths: **8**
Double/pb: **$69–$89**
Suites: **$89–$139**
Open: **All year**

Reduced Rates: **Available**
Breakfast: **Full**
Credit Cards: **MC, VISA**
Pets: **No**
Children: **Welcome, over 12**
Smoking: **No**
Social Drinking: **Permitted**
Minimum Stay: **Balloon Fiesta, Christmas, Indian Market**
Foreign Languages: **Spanish, German**

Hacienda Vargas is a romantic hideaway in a historic old adobe hacienda, completely restored and elegantly decorated with antiques. The beautiful rooms have fireplaces and private entrances; four suites have Jacuzzi tubs. Golf, fishing, snow skiing, horseback riding, and hiking are nearby. This B&B is conveniently located south of Santa Fe and north of Albuquerque. Romance packages are available. Paul and Julie are ex-bankers who love history and have traveled extensively.

Chocolate Turtle B&B ✪

1098 WEST MEADOWLARK LANE, CORRALES, NEW MEXICO 87048

Tel: **(505) 898-1800; (800) 898-1842; fax: (505) 898-5328**
Best Time to Call: **After 9 AM**
Host: **Carole Morgan**
Location: **4 mi. N of Albuquerque**
No. of Rooms: **4**
No. of Private Baths: **4**
Double/pb: **$79**
Single/pb: **$55–$60**

Suites: **$90–$95**
Open: **All year**
Reduced Rates: **Available**
Breakfast: **Full**
Credit Cards: **AMEX, DISC, MC, VISA**
Pets: **No**
Children: **Welcome, over 5**
Smoking: **No**
Social Drinking: **Permitted**

The Chocolate Turtle B&B is a refurbished Territorial located on the northern boundary of Albuquerque. It's a short drive to the Sandia Tram, Old Town Albuquerque, Rio Grande Zoo, the Indian Pueblo Cultural Center, the Petroglyphs, several golf courses, and the Kodak Albuquerque Balloon Fiesta Park. Santa Fe is 45 minutes away. Guests have the main house to themselves, with its large room that offers views of the Sandia Mountains, TV, VCR, and dining room. Snacks and cold drinks are available at all times in the refrigerator. The decor is Southwestern, there is a spa, and in your room you will find the scrumptious handmade chocolates that give this B&B its name.

La Casita Guesthouse ✪
P.O. BOX 103, DIXON, NEW MEXICO 87527

Tel: **(505) 579-4297**
Hosts: **Sara Pene and Celeste Miller**
Location: **25 mi. S of Taos**
Guest Cottage: **$75–$115, sleeps 2–4**
Open: **All year**
Breakfast: **Continental**

Pets: **No**
Children: **Welcome**
Smoking: **No**
Social Drinking: **Permitted**
Foreign Languages: **Spanish**

The rural mountain village of Dixon is home to many artists and craftspeople. La Casita is a traditional New Mexico adobe with *vigas, latillas,* and Mexican tile floors. Guests enjoy use of the living room, fully equipped kitchen, two bedrooms, one bath, and a lovely patio. It is a perfect spot for relaxing and is just minutes from the Rio Grande, river rafting, hiking, and cross-country skiing. Indian pueblos, ancient Anasazi ruins, museums, art galleries, horseback-riding ranches, and alpine skiing are within an hour's drive. Sara and Celeste are weavers.

Casa del Rey Bed & Breakfast
305 ROVER, LOS ALAMOS, NEW MEXICO 87544

Tel: **(505) 672-9401**
Best Time to Call: **After 5 PM**
Host: **Virginia L. King**
No. of Rooms: **2**
Max. No. Sharing Bath: **4**
Double/sb: **$45**
Single/sb: **$35**

Open: **All year**
Reduced Rates: **Weekly; families**
Breakfast: **Continental, plus**
Pets: **No**
Children: **Welcome, over 5**
Smoking: **No**
Social Drinking: **Permitted**

This adobe contemporary home is located in the quiet residential area of White Rock, and is situated in the Jemez Mountains with a view of Santa Fe across the valley. The surroundings are rich in Spanish and Indian history. Pueblos, museums, Bandelier National Monument, skiing, hiking trails, tennis, and golf are all within easy reach. Virginia is rightfully proud of her beautifully kept house, with its pretty flower gardens. In summer, her breakfast of granola, home-baked rolls and muffins, along with fruits and beverages, is served on the sunporch, where you can enjoy the lovely scenery.

Casa Rinconada del Rio Guest Houses✪
BOX 10A, TAOS HIGHWAY 68, RINCONADA, NEW MEXICO 87531

Tel: **(505) 579-4466**
Host: **JoAnne Gladin-de la Fuente**
Location: **20 mi. S of Taos; 45 mi. N. of Santa Fe**
Guest Houses: **$55–$130; sleep 5–6**
Open: **All year**

Breakfast: **Continental**
Pets: **Small**
Children: **Welcome**
Smoking: **Permitted**
Social Drinking: **Permitted**

Casa Rinconada is nestled in the canyon of the Sangre de Cristo Mountains, with their weather-carved cliffs. The colors of the high mesas continuously evolve with the light of day and time of season. Imagine yourself in the privacy of your own adobe home. The backyard is an orchard where you may enjoy the fruits of the season, or go to the legendary Rio Grande to fish, relax, enjoy a bonfire, bask in the sun, or take in a peaceful evening under the diamond bright stars. The many attractions include Indian Pueblos, fishing, rafting, skiing, opera, galleries, local artists, museums, historic churches, and much more. Casa Rinconada is a convenient locale with pleasurable travels to Taos, Santa Fe, Los Alamos, and many small villages of historical interest.

American Artists Gallery House Bed & Breakfast ○
132 FRONTIER ROAD, P.O. BOX 584, TAOS, NEW MEXICO 87571
aagh@taos.newmex.com; www.taoswebb.com/hotel/artistshouse

Tel: **(800) 532-2041; (505) 758-4446**	Double/pb: **$75–$150**
Best Time to Call: **7 AM–9 PM**	Guest Cottage: **$75–$115**
Hosts: **LeAn and Charles Clamurro**	Suites: **$150**
Location: **Less than 1 mi. from historic Taos Plaza**	Open: **All year**
	Breakfast: **Full**
No. of Rooms: **10**	Pets: **No**
No. of Private Baths: **10**	Smoking: **No**

"Step into our world and re-create with us at the American Artists Gallery House." Adorning the walls throughout the inn is artwork of three cultures that have come together at this charming hacienda. Enjoy unobstructed vistas of Taos Mountain, an outdoor hot tub, and woodburning kiva fireplaces. From La Cocina enjoy a satisfying gourmet breakfast specially created by Charles. If it's romance you want, you'll want to stay in one of our double-tub Jacuzzi suites with a wet bar, antique vigas, skylights for stargazing, and kiva fireplaces. "Stay with us. We're part of the beauty and magic of Taos."

La Posada de Taos ○
309 JUANITA LANE, P.O. BOX 1118, TAOS, NEW MEXICO 87571
www.taosnet.com/laposada/

Tel: **(505) 758-8164; (800) 645-4803**	Reduced Rates: **10% Nov.–Jan., Apr.–May**
Best Time to Call: **Before 9 PM**	Breakfast: **Full**
Hosts: **Bill and Nancy Swan**	Pets: **No**
Location: **70 mi. N of Santa Fe**	Children: **Welcome, over 12**
No. of Rooms: **6**	Smoking: **No**
No. of Private Baths: **6**	Minimum Stay: **2 nights holidays**
Double/pb: **$85–$120**	Airport/Station Pickup: **Yes**
Single/pb: **$75–$110**	
Open: **All year**	

Escape to another world, to the warmth and serenity of northern New Mexico. La Posada is nestled in the heart of the historic district, just two-and-a-half blocks from the Taos Plaza, and is the first bed and breakfast in Taos. La Posada is within walking distance to galleries, museums, restaurants, and shops. After a busy day, return to casual elegance, country pine antiques, fireplaces, and tastefully decorated guest rooms with handmade quilts, local art, and attention to detail. A separate honeymoon house is available.

Touchstone Bed & Breakfast Inn ✪

**110 MABEL DODGE LANE, P.O. BOX 2896, TAOS,
NEW MEXICO 87571-2896**
www.taoswebb.com/touchstone

Tel: **(505) 758-0192; (800) 758-0192;**
  fax: **(505) 758-3498**
Best Time to Call: **11 AM–2 PM**
Host: **Bren Price**
Location: **1 mi. N of Taos Plaza**
No. of Rooms: **8**
No. of Private Baths: **8**
Double/pb: **$85–$150**

Reduced Rates: **10% seniors**
Breakfast: **Full**
Credit Cards: **MC, VISA**
Pets: **No**
Children: **Welcome, over 12**
Smoking: **No**
Social Drinking: **Permitted**

Situated on two acres bordering Pueblo lands, Touchstone Bed & Breakfast Inn offers a quiet ambiance. The property boasts full mountain views, towering cottonwoods, evergreens, wildflower gardens, a trout stream, and an impressive apple orchard. Antiques, kiva fireplaces, *viga* ceilings, fine art, oriental rugs, down pillows and comforters, and custom-designed baths—some with Jacuzzis—complete the most luxurious accommodations. A gourmet breakfast is served each morning in an atrium that has a fireplace designed by Tony Luhan and overlooks the courtyard. Guests may use the video collection and cassette library as well as an outdoor hot tub. All rooms have cable TV, VCR, and phones.

NEW YORK

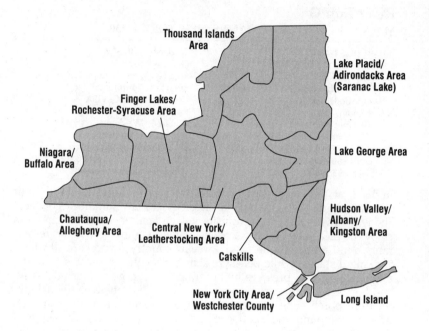

Thousand Islands
Area

Lake Placid/
Adirondacks Area
(Saranac Lake)

Finger Lakes/
Rochester-Syracuse Area

Niagara/
Buffalo Area

Lake George Area

Chautauqua/
Allegheny Area

Central New York/
Leatherstocking Area

Catskills

Hudson Valley/
Albany/
Kingston Area

New York City Area/
Westchester County

Long Island

CATSKILLS

Maplewood ✪
PARK ROAD, P.O. BOX 40, CHICHESTER, NEW YORK 12416

Tel: **(914) 688-5433**
Best Time to Call: **After 7 PM**
Host: **Nancy Parsons**
Location: **25 mi. NW of Kingston**
No. of Rooms: **4**
Max. No. Sharing Bath: **4**
Double/sb: **$55–$65**

Single/sb: **$40**
Open: **All year**
Breakfast: **Full**
Pets: **No**
Children: **Welcome**
Smoking: **No**
Social Drinking: **Permitted**

A Colonial manor on a quiet country lane, and nestled among stately maples, this is a charming B&B. Each spacious bedroom has a view of the Catskills. In summer, you can swim in the in-ground pool, or play badminton, croquet, or horseshoes. In winter, ski Belleayre, Hunter, and Cortina, all only 12 miles away. In any season, enjoy the art galleries, boutiques, great restaurants, and theater at Woodstock, 20 minutes away. After a great day outdoors, come home to a glass of wine and good conversation. After a good night's sleep, you'll enjoy freshly squeezed orange juice, homemade breads and pastries, and freshly ground coffee.

River Run ○

MAIN STREET, FLEISCHMANNS, NEW YORK 12430

Tel: **(914) 254-4884**
Best Time to Call: **10 AM–10 PM**
Host: **Larry Miller**
Location: **2¹/₂ hrs from NYC; 35 mins.
  W of Woodstock**
No. of Rooms: **10**
No. of Private Baths: **6**
Max. No. Sharing Bath: **2**
Double/pb: **$75–$105**
Single/pb: **$68–$95**
Double/sb: **$55–$80**

Single/sb: **$50–$72**
Open: **All year**
Reduced Rates: **Groups; longer stays**
Breakfast: **Continental, Plus**
Credit Cards: **MC, VISA**
Pets: **Welcome**
Children: **Welcome**
Smoking: **Restricted**
Social Drinking: **Permitted**
Minimum Stay: **2 nights peak seasons; 3
  nights holiday weekends**

In 1887, at the confluence of the Bushkill and Little Red Kill trout streams, Addison Scott built a classic Victorian summer "cottage." Today, as River Run, this exquisite village landmark invites guests to enjoy the pleasures of every season. Tennis, swimming, theater, restaurants, a museum, antiques, and a weekly country auction are all within walking distance, while Belleayre skiing (downhill and cross-country), magnificent forest preserve hiking trails, fishing, golf, river float trips, and horseback riding are just minutes away. Rejuvenate on the delightful front porch or in the book-filled parlor, complete with piano and fireplace. Step into the oak-floored dining room, bathed in the colors of the inn's signature stained glass windows, and enjoy hearty, homemade breakfasts and refreshments. The bus from New York City stops right at the front door!

The Eggery Inn ○

COUNTY ROAD 16, TANNERSVILLE, NEW YORK 12485

Tel: **(518) 589-5363; fax (518)
  589-5774**
Best Time to Call: **10 AM–8 PM**
Hosts: **Julie and Abe Abramczyk**
No. of Rooms: **15**
No. of Private Baths: **15**
Double/pb: **$80–$110**
Open: **All year**
Reduced Rates: **Off-season**

Breakfast: **Full**
Credit Cards: **AMEX, MC, VISA**
Pets: **No**
Children: **Welcome**
Smoking: **Restricted**
Social Drinking: **Permitted; full liquor
  license**
Minimum Stay: **2 nights weekends; 3
  nights holiday weekends**

This Dutch Colonial farmhouse, built circa 1900, is nestled in the northern Catskills at an elevation of 2,200 feet. Guest rooms, decorated in a country motif, have carpeting, color TV, phones, and comforters or spreads. Queen-size and two-bed accommodations are available, and six first-floor rooms are accessible to guests in wheelchairs. The public room's oak balustrade, Franklin stove, player piano, Mission Oak furniture, and panoramic views invite guests to relax. Breakfast selections include omelettes, fruit-filled hotcakes, and heart-smart entrees. The Inn is ideal for small groups. Hiking trails, scenic waterfalls, the famous Woodstock colony, and the alpine ski areas of Hunter and Windham mountains are nearby. A freshly prepared dinner is served for groups by prior arrangement.

CENTRAL NEW YORK/LEATHERSTOCKING AREA

Pickle Hill Bed and Breakfast ✪

795 CHENANGO STREET, BINGHAMTON, NEW YORK 13901

Tel: **(607) 723-0259**	Reduced Rates: **On long stays**
Best Time to Call: **Anytime**	Breakfast: **Full**
Hosts: **Leslie and Tom Rossi**	Credit Cards: **No**
Location: **185 mi. NW of New York City**	Pets: **No**
No. of Rooms: **2**	Children: **Welcome**
Max. No. Sharing Bath: **4**	Smoking: **Yes, area available**
Double/sb: **$50**	Social Drinking: **Permitted**
Single/sb: **$40**	Airport/Station Pickup: **Yes**
Open: **All year**	

Make yourself comfortable at Pickle Hill, built more than 100 years ago. Read, listen to music, and play board games in the lounge, then rally around the living room piano for a songfest, or join your hosts in the family room for conversation. Sports lovers can play bocci, basketball, or badminton on the side lawn; baseball fields, tennis courts, golf courses, bike paths, and cross-country ski trails are all nearby. Mark Twain's Elmira home, the Farmer's Museum, and the Baseball Hall of Fame in Cooperstown are all within driving distance. Closer to home, Binghamton's Performing Arts Center supplies top-notch entertainment, and the Tri-Cities Opera Company features some of the nation's most promising young singers.

Chalet Waldheim ✪

RD 1, BOX 51-G-2, BURLINGTON FLATS, NEW YORK 13315
fkuhne@aol.com

Tel: **(800) 654-8571; (607) 965-8803**	Breakfast: **Continental, Plus**
Hosts: **Franzi and Heinz Kuhne**	Pets: **No**
Location: **15 minutes W of Cooperstown**	Children: **No**
Suite: **$160**	Smoking: **No**
Open: **All year**	Social Drinking: **Permitted**
Reduced Rates: **15% seniors; 3-day stays**	Minimum Stay: **Holidays and special events**
	Foreign Languages: **German**

Share the quiet seclusion of this very special hilltop setting amid 75 acres of forest and field. An adult retreat, this finely crafted chalet is molded in the age-old Black Forest style. It's the perfect hideaway, yet close enough to the village of Cooperstown, which offers museums, lakes, and opera. Come and enjoy a European country atmosphere, and relax in the warmth of classic antique furnishings and abundant artwork. Breakfast is a bountiful Continental buffet that includes freshly baked breads and house specialties.

Creekside Bed & Breakfast ✪

RD 1, BOX 206, COOPERSTOWN, NEW YORK 13326

Tel: **(607) 547-8203**	Open: **All year**
Best Time to Call: **Anytime**	Breakfast: **Full**
Hosts: **Fred and Gwen Ermlich**	Pets: **No**
Location: **2 mi. S of Cooperstown**	Children: **Welcome (crib)**
No. of Rooms: **6**	Smoking: **No**
No. of Private Baths: **6**	Social Drinking: **Permitted**
Double/pb: **$80–$95**	Minimum Stay: **2 nights seasonal**
Guest Cottage: **$135–$150; sleeps 2**	**weekends; 3 nights holiday weekends**
Suites: **$95–$150**	Foreign Languages: **French, German**

This nationally renowned B&B offers beautiful furnishings in an elegant atmosphere. All rooms have private baths, queen-size beds, color TV, and HBO. The Bridal Suite, Penthouse Suite, and Honeymoon Cottage are ideal for newlyweds and other romantics. You can amble through the flower gardens and lawns, and fish or take a dip in the creek. Gwen and Fred, who perform with the Glimmerglass Opera, serve a full breakfast, catering to guests who are looking for something special.

Litco Farms Bed & Breakfast ✪

P.O. BOX 1048, COOPERSTOWN, NEW YORK 13326-1048
hrtworks@telenet.net

Tel: **(607) 547-2501**	Open: **Apr.–Nov.**
Hosts: **Margaret and Jim Wolff**	Breakfast: **Full**
Location: **2 mi. NW of Cooperstown**	Pets: **No**
No. of Rooms: **4**	Children: **Welcome**
No. of Private Baths: **4**	Smoking: **No**
Double/sb: **$69–$99**	Social Drinking: **Permitted**
Suites: **$99–$119**	Airport/Station Pickup: **Yes**

Seventy acres of unspoiled meadows, woodlands, and an eight-acre beaver pond are yours to explore at Litco Farms. An on-site quilt shop attracts many visitors interested in Quilt-Inn hands-on workshops. After spending the day at the Baseball Hall of Fame, the Farmers Museum, and the Fenimore House Museum, guests may relax and unwind around the large in-ground pool. Some may prefer a day of fishing on

Canadarago Lake or the Glimmerglass, the lake made famous by James Fenimore Cooper. You can always explore the many antique and specialty shops in this most picturesque area of central New York.

Sunrise Farm ✪
RD 3, BOX 95, NEW BERLIN, NEW YORK 13411-9614

Tel: **(607) 847-9380**	Reduced Rates: **Families; weekly**
Hosts: **Janet and Fred Schmelzer**	Breakfast: **Full**
Location: **30 mi. from I-87**	Other Meals: **Available**
No. of Rooms: **1**	Pets: **No**
No. of Private Baths: **1**	Children: **Welcome**
Double/pb: **$55**	Smoking: **No**
Single/pb: **$40**	Social Drinking: **Permitted**
Open: **All year**	

Scottish Highland cattle are raised on this 80-acre organic farm about 20 miles from both Oneonta and Cooperstown. This peaceful farm has spectacular views of sunsets, and sunrises for early risers. The spacious guest room is on the second floor, and on a clear night stars can be seen through the skylight. Breakfast may include homemade breads, muffins, preserves, honey from the farm's hives, fresh fruit, eggs, and bacon. In winter a woodstove keeps the house cozy. Hartwick, Colgate, and SUCO are all within easy driving distance, as are two state parks. Activities include swimming, golfing, boating, horseback riding, ice skating, cross-country skiing, and antiquing. Hunters are welcome.

Country Spread Bed & Breakfast ✪
P.O. BOX 1863, 23 PROSPECT STREET, RICHFIELD SPRINGS, NEW YORK 13439

Tel: **(315) 858-1870**	Suites: **$80**
Best Time to Call: **4–8 PM**	Open: **All year**
Hosts: **Karen and Bruce Watson**	Breakfast: **Full**
Location: **20 mi. SE of Utica on**	Credit Cards: **MC, VISA**
Rte. 28; Cooperstown vicinity	Pets: **No**
No. of Rooms: **2**	Children: **Welcome (crib)**
Max. No. Sharing Bath: **4**	Smoking: **No**
Double/pb: **$55**	Social Drinking: **Permitted**
Single/pb: **$45**	Minimum Stay: **Sometimes**
Double/sb: **$50**	Airport/Station Pickup: **Yes**
Single/sb: **$40**	

Longtime area residents Karen and Bruce have restored their 1893 cozy home into a wonderful retreat, tastefully decorated in country style. Your day will start with warm muffins, homemade preserves, pancakes with pure maple syrup, fresh eggs, granola, and chilled juice. Relax on the deck with the newspaper, and then visit some of the area's attractions, including Cooperstown, museums, summer theater, Glimmerglass Opera, fine dining, antique and specialty shops, and small-town happenings. Nearby Canadarago and Otsego lakes offer excellent boating, fishing, and swimming.

CHAUTAUQUA/ALLEGHENY AREA

Brookside Manor Bed & Breakfast ✪
3728 ROUTE 83, FREDONIA, NEW YORK 14063-9740

Tel: **(716) 672-7721; (800) 929-7599**	Open: **All year**
Best Time to Call: **After noon**	Reduced Rates: **Available**
Hosts: **Andrea Andrews and Dale Mirth**	Breakfast: **Full**
Location: **42 mi. SW of Buffalo**	Credit Cards: **MC, VISA**
No. of Rooms: **3**	Pets: **Sometimes**
No. of Private Baths: **3**	Children: **Welcome**
Double/pb: **$69**	Smoking: **No**
Single/pb: **$59**	Social Drinking: **Permitted**

Situated on five and a half partially wooded acres, this brick Victorian manor, circa 1875, is only six minutes from historic Fredonia and the State University of New York campus there. Guest rooms feature air conditioners, queen-size beds, large windows with antique interior shutters, ceiling fans, hardwood floors, two-seated showers, and unique family heirlooms. Outside, a covered patio, woods, a meadow, and a spring-fed brook offer a relaxing atmosphere. Lily Dale Spiritualist Center and Lake Erie are ten minutes away. Andrea is a New England native and experienced caterer, Dale is a native and former research scientist. Both enjoy sharing their home and knowledge of the area with guests. Eight cats are in residence, but are permitted only in Andrea and Dale's private area.

FINGER LAKES/ROCHESTER/SYRACUSE AREA

Adventures Bed & Breakfast Reservation Service ✪
P.O. BOX 83, SCOTTSVILLE, NEW YORK 14546

Tel: **(716) 768-2699; (800) 724-1932**	Rates (Single/Double):
Best Time to Call: **9 AM–5 PM**	Modest: **$55–$65**
Coordinator: **Rita Filowick**	Average: **$75–$95**
States/Regions Covered: **Finger Lakes,**	Luxury: **$100–$195**
Genesee Valley Area, Rochester	

Adventures is more than a reservation service representing B&Bs in the Finger Lakes and Genesee Valley regions. Adventures can plan an exciting visit for you, whether it's cross-country skiing, fishing, hiking, a business meeting, a small retreat, or a wedding. Travel the country roads, hills, and velvet green vineyards. Stroll the path of history in a working Colonial village, take a hot-air balloon ride, spend the day antiquing, or hike along the Sea Way Trail. Visit the museums, planetarium, and theaters Rochester has to offer. Enjoy fun-filled festivals throughout the Finger Lakes and Rochester areas. All accommodations are within a few hours of Niagara Falls, Corning, Syracuse, and Toronto.

Addison Rose Bed & Breakfast ✪
37 MAPLE STREET, ADDISON, NEW YORK 14801

Tel: **(607) 359-4650**	Open: **All year**
Hosts: **Bill and Mary Ann Peters**	Breakfast: **Full**
No. of Rooms: **3**	Pets: **No**
No. of Private Baths: **3**	Children: **No**
Double/pb: **$65–$85**	Smoking: **No**
Single/pb: **$65–$85**	Social Drinking: **Permitted**

Warmth, friendliness, and hospitality characterize this bed and breakfast, which combines elegance and country charm. Built in 1892, this magnificent Queen Anne home has been painstakingly restored by the Peters family and furnished with period antiques to recapture the ambience of the Victorian age. Guest rooms, named for the original owners and other local personalities, suggest a bygone era. The city of Corning, museums, and Finger Lake wineries are just minutes away.

Pandora's Getaway ✪
83 OSWEGO STREET, BALDWINSVILLE, NEW YORK 13027

Tel: **(315) 635-9571; (888) 638-8668**	Single/sb: **$50**
Best Time to Call: **Anytime**	Open: **All year**
Host: **Sandy Wheeler**	Reduced Rates: **Available**
Location: **3 mi. from Route 90 Exit 90**	Breakfast: **Full**
No. of Rooms: **4**	Credit Cards: **MC, VISA**
No. of Private Baths: **2**	Pets: **No**
Max. No. Sharing Bath: **2**	Children: **Welcome (crib)**
Double/pb: **$85**	Smoking: **Restricted**
Single/pb: **$70**	Social Drinking: **Permitted**
Double/sb: **$60**	Airport Pickup: **Yes**

Standing on an imposing hill with lawns sloping to the street, Pandora's Getaway, an 1845 Greek Revival home, is a local landmark listed on the National Register of Historic Places. The stately trees sheltering the house add to its grandeur. Let Sandy show you upstate hospitality at its best. Guests are welcome to enjoy the entire B&B, including the front porch with rockers and the large living room with a fireplace. Rooms are furnished with interesting antiques, collectibles, and crafts, some of them for sale. Breakfast, served in the formal dining room with pieces drawn from Sandy's collection of colorful Depression glass, features specialties like quiche, homemade breads, and fresh fruit.

Roberts-Cameron House ✪
68 NORTH STREET, CALEDONIA, NEW YORK 14423

Tel: **(716) 538-6316**
Best Time to Call: **Evenings**
Hosts: **Elizabeth and Robert Wilcox**
Location: **12 mi. SW of Rochester**
No. of Rooms: **2**
Max. No. Sharing Bath: **4**
Double/pb: **$70**
Single/pb: **$55**
Double/sb: **$60**

Single/sb: **$45**
Open: **All year**
Breakfast: **Full**
Pets: **Sometimes**
Children: **Welcome**
Smoking: **Permitted (downstairs)**
Social Drinking: **Permitted**
Airport/Station Pickup: **Yes**

A clapboard farmhouse built in 1886 by William Roberts, a descendant of an early Scottish settler, this B&B is furnished with family antiques and collectibles from western New York. If you want to acquire some antiques of your own, the surrounding countryside is prime browsing territory, and Elizabeth runs her own antique and crafts shop. Just five minutes from the front door, the Genesee Country Museum lets visitors spend a day strolling through a re-created 19th-century hamlet; costumed villagers and craftspeople go about their daily chores May through October. Your hosts serve a generous country breakfast featuring New York maple syrup.

1865 White Birch Bed & Breakfast
69 EAST FIRST STREET, CORNING, NEW YORK 14830

Tel: **(607) 962-6355**
Hosts: **Kathy and Joe Donahue**
Location: **Off Rte. 17**
No. of Rooms: **4**
No. of Private Baths: **2**
Max. No. Sharing Bath: **4**
Double/pb: **$75**
Single/pb: **$60**
Double/sb: **$65**

Single/sb: **$55**
Open: **All year**
Breakfast: **Full**
Credit Cards: **AMEX, MC, VISA**
Pets: **No**
Children: **Welcome**
Smoking: **No**
Social Drinking: **Permitted**
Airport/Station Pickup: **Yes**

Kathy and Joe invite you to visit this 1865 Victorian home, restored to bring out the beauty of the winding staircase and hardwood floors. Cozy rooms await you, decorated in country and family antiques. Guests are invited to linger over breakfast and enjoy delights such as sauteed apples and cinnamon, egg and cheese souffle, blueberry muffins, and plenty of hot coffee. The White Birch is located in a residential historic section of Corning, yet is within walking distance of the Corning and Rockwell museums, restored Market Street, and fine dining.

Fox Ridge Farm B&B ✪
4786 FOSTER ROAD, ELBRIDGE, NEW YORK 13060
foxridge@dreamscape.com

Tel: **(315) 673-4881**	Single/sb: **$50**
Best Time to Call: **8 AM–9 PM**	Open: **All year**
Hosts: **Marge and Bob Sykes**	Reduced Rates: **Available**
Location: **17 mi. SW of Syracuse**	Breakfast: **Full**
No. of Rooms: **3**	Credit Cards: **AMEX, DISC, MC, VISA**
No. of Private Baths: **1**	Pets: **No**
Max. No. Sharing Bath: **3**	Children: **Welcome, over 6**
Double/pb: **$75**	Smoking: **No**
Single/pb: **$60**	Social Drinking: **Permitted**
Double/sb: **$65**	Airport Pickup: **Yes**

Fox Ridge Farm B&B is located on a quiet rural road surrounded by woods. Hiking trails wander through the 120 acres of woodlands, stately pines, and sparkling streams—a paradise for birders. These same trails are also used for cross-country skiing or snowshoeing in the winter. Stroll around the expansive lawns and flower gardens or kick off your shoes in the spacious family room, which has wood paneling, hardwood floors, a wood-burning stove, a TV, stereo, and reading library. Each guest room is individually decorated with floral wallpaper, handmade quilts, hardwood floors or carpeting, and in some cases, four-poster beds. One room, overlooking the flower garden, has both double and queen beds. Hearty breakfasts are served in the large country kitchen, with its stone fireplace.

Just a "Plane" Bed & Breakfast ✪
RD 2, BOX 40, ROUTE 19A, FILLMORE, NEW YORK 14735

Tel: **(716) 567-8338**	Reduced Rates: **10% seniors**
Hosts: **Craig and Audrey Smith**	Breakfast: **Full**
Location: **50 mi. S of Rochester**	Credit Cards: **AMEX, MC, VISA**
No. of Rooms: **4**	Pets: **Sometimes**
No. of Private Baths: **4**	Children: **Welcome**
Double/pb: **$57**	Smoking: **No**
Single/pb: **$45**	Social Drinking: **Permitted**
Open: **All year**	Airport Pickup: **Yes**

A stay at Just a "Plane" Bed & Breakfast is anything but plain. This three-story Dutch Colonial was built in 1926 by Craig's grandparents, and has been well maintained with very few changes other than added bathrooms. Audrey's love of crafting, decorating, and baking is very noticeable. Breakfast is served in the sunroom and consists of fresh-baked muffins, bread, or waffles served with fresh fruit and jams. Craig's love for flying offers a special flair to your stay. He offers plane rides over the seventeen-mile gorge at Letchworth or a trip around beautiful Rushford Lake. Located seven miles south of the beautiful

Grand Canyon of the East—Letchworth State Park—on an operating crop farm, this B&B offers a relaxing and enjoyable stay.

The Gorham House ✪

P.O. BOX 43, 4752 EAST SWAMP ROAD, GORHAM,
NEW YORK 14461-0043
gorham.house@juno.com; www.angelfire.com/biz/gorhamhouse/

Tel: **(716) 526-4402**	Open: **All year**
Hosts: **Nancy and Al Rebmann**	Reduced Rates: **Available**
Location: **9 mi. SE of Canandaigua**	Breakfast: **Full**
No. of Rooms: **3**	Pets: **No**
No. of Private Baths: **1**	Children: **Welcome, over 12**
Max. No. Sharing Bath: **4**	Smoking: **No**
Double/pb: **$100**	Social Drinking: **Permitted**
Double/sb: **$70**	Minimum Stay: **2 nights peak season**

Built before the turn of the century, this 14-room country Colonial-style farmhouse is decorated with family treasures and special finds. You will never forget the two elegant common rooms and the intimate library with its cozy parlor, divided by large pocket doors. Spacious, beautifully appointed guest rooms have seating and reading areas. The kitchen contains a large collection of advertising tins; the eat-in pantry features framed Cream of Wheat advertisements from the 1900s. Warm yourself by the woodstove after skiing. Walk the five acres and explore the many different wildflowers, berry bushes, fruit trees, and Nancy's herb garden. Or just relax on one of three porches.

Sandy Creek Manor House ✪

1960 REDMAN ROAD, HAMLIN, NEW YORK 14464
agreatbnb@aol.com; www.3zcom/sandycreekbnb

Tel: **(716) 964-7528; (800) 594-0400;**	Single/sb: **$60**
fax: **(716) 964-9244**	Open: **All year**
Best Time to Call: **9 AM–9 PM**	Reduced Rates: **Weekly**
Hosts: **Shirley Hollink and James**	Breakfast: **Full**
Krempasky	Credit Cards: **AMEX, DISC, MC, VISA**
Location: **20 mi. W of Rochester**	Pets: **Welcome**
No. of Rooms: **4**	Children: **Welcome, over 12**
Max. No. Sharing Bath: **4**	Smoking: **No**
Double/sb: **$75**	Social Drinking: **Permitted**

Escape to this quiet, comfortable, European-style bed & breakfast. Built in 1910, this English Tudor home is surrounded by six wooded acres, complete with a salmon stream in the back. It is located less than a half-hour's drive to downtown Rochester and about seventy minutes to the natural beauty of Niagara Falls and the heart of the fruit belt, with numerous farm markets and antique shops. Guest rooms have TVs, air-conditioning, radios, snuggly robes, slippers, and other amenities.

Unique packages range from sweetheart dinners, sleigh rides, and murder mysteries to massage treatments.

The Amity Rose B&B
8264 MAIN STREET, HAMMONDSPORT, NEW YORK 14840

Tel: **(607) 569-3408; (800) 982-8818**
Best Time to Call: **10 AM–9 PM**
Host: **Bucky Laufersweiler**
No. of Rooms: **4**
No. of Private Baths: **4**
Double/pb: **$85–$125**
Open: **Apr.–Dec.**

Breakfast: **Full**
Pets: **No**
Children: **Welcome, over 12**
Smoking: **No**
Social Drinking: **Permitted**
Minimum Stay: **2 nights, weekends**

Hammondsport is located in the heart of New York's wine country, at the southern end of the famed Finger Lakes region. Whether you spend your time driving, hiking, biking, or just plain relaxing, Amity Rose is the safe haven in which to end your day. The village square with its historic bandstand and park benches lends visitors the nuances of days gone by. During the summer months, the music flows from the bandstand on Thursday evenings. Guests can enjoy the shops, restaurants, or the Glen Curtiss Museum. Right next door, there is a track for running or walking; tennis courts and a trout stream are just down the street. Amity Rose is within walking distance to Village Square and Keuka Maid.

Blushing Rose B&B

11 WILLIAM STREET, HAMMONDSPORT, NEW YORK 14840

Tel: **(607) 569-3402; (800) 982-8818**
Best Time to Call: **10 AM–9 PM**
Hosts: **Ellen and Frank Laufersweiler**
Location: **20 mi. W of Corning**
No. of Rooms: **4**
No. of Private Baths: **4**
Double/pb: **$85–$105**

Open: **Apr.–Dec.**
Breakfast: **Full**
Pets: **No**
Children: **No**
Smoking: **No**
Social Drinking: **Permitted**
Minimum Stay: **2 nights, weekends**

The Blushing Rose is an Italianate Victorian home built in 1843 and painted the shade of pink that gives this B&B its name. Ellen and Bucky opened the inn in 1986, decorating it with Victorian antiques and country accents including handmade quilts, ruffled curtains, grapevine wreaths, braided rugs, and period oak furnishings. Guest enjoy a breakfast of fresh fruit, juice, homemade granola, jams and jellies, and a hot entree, perhaps French toast or cheese strada. Hammondsport is located at the southern end of the Finger Lakes region, and it's a short walk to Keuka Lake. Watkins Glenn, Corning, and famous Finger Lake wineries are all a short drive away.

Log Country Inn—B&B of Ithaca ✪

P.O. BOX 581, ITHACA, NEW YORK 14851

Tel: **(800) 274-4771**
Best Time to Call: **7 AM–11 PM**
Hosts: **Wanda and Slawomir Grunberg**
Location: **11 mi. S of Ithaca**
No. of Rooms: **5**

No. of Private Baths: **3**
Double/pb: **$65–$75**
Single/pb: **$55–$65**
Suites: **$110–150**
Open: **All year**

Reduced Rates: **Available**
Breakfast: **Full**
Credit Cards: **AMEX, MC, VISA**
Pets: **Sometimes**
Children: **Welcome**
Smoking: **No**

Social Drinking: **Permitted**
Minimum Stay: **During parents'
weekend, graduations, and reunions
at Cornell and Ithaca College**
Foreign Languages: **Polish, Russian**

Escape to the rustic charm of a log house located at the edge of a 7,000-acre state forest in the Finger Lakes region. Guests will enjoy modern accommodations provided in the spirit of international hospitality. You will wake up to the sound of birds and enjoy exploring the peaceful surroundings. A full European breakfast is served and might include blintzes or Russian pancakes. Your hosts offer afternoon tea and a sauna during the fall and winter months. Nearby, Cornell, Ithaca College, Corning Glass Center, wineries, and antique stores are just a few of the sites, and there is easy access to hiking and cross-country trails. Wanda is a former biologist and Slawomir is a documentary filmmaker.

Allan's Hill Bed and Breakfast
2513 SAND HILL ROAD, MT. MORRIS, NEW YORK 14510

Tel: **(716) 658-4591; (800) 431-5580**
Best Time to Call: **After 5 PM**

Hosts: **George and Joyce Swanson**
Location: **35 mi. S of Rochester**

No. of Rooms: **3**
Max. No. Sharing Bath: **4**
Double/pb: **$80**
Double/sb: **$55–$65**
Open: **All year**
Breakfast: **Full**

Credit Cards: **DISC, MC, VISA**
Pets: **No**
Children: **Welcome**
Smoking: **No**
Social Drinking: **Permitted**
Airport/Station Pickup: **Yes**

Sixteen acres of land surround this restored 1830 country home, giving guests the chance to stroll through stately walnut groves, sit by the pond, picnic, and go bird-watching and cross-country skiing. Nearby Letchworth State Park offers a spectacular, 17-mile drive along the gorge of the Genesee River. The area's wineries will lure you with tours and tastings, and Rochester, with its museums, shops, concerts, and theaters, is within easy driving distance.

Finton's Landing Bed and Breakfast ✪
661 EAST LAKE ROAD, PENN YAN, NEW YORK 14527-9421

Tel: **(315) 536-3146**
Best Time to Call: **7 AM–9 PM**
Hosts: **Doug and Arianne Tepper**
Location: **30 mi. S of NYS Thruway, exit 42; 30 mi. N of Rte. 17, exit 38**
No. of Rooms: **4**
No. of Private Baths: **4**
Double/pb: **$99**
Open: **All year**

Reduced Rates: **10% weekly**
Breakfast: **Full**
Credit Cards: **MC, VISA**
Pets: **No**
Children: **Welcome, over 10**
Smoking: **No**
Social Drinking: **Permitted**
Foreign Languages: **Dutch**

Finton's Landing, a historic steamboat landing on Keuka Lake, is known for its view of the Bluff, pristine water, and the 165-foot private cove. The Teppers' hammock defies anyone to stay awake while gazing into the evergreens. Artwork and murals add pure delight to this 1860 Victorian, while pine-plank floors and whimsical period pieces keep it casual. The parlor fireplace is a winter retreat. A luscious two-course breakfast is served on the porch, weather permitting, or in the dining room overlooking the wildflowers. Activities include nature walks, wine tastings, antiquing, Watkins Glen car races, Windmill Craft Market shopping, and relaxing at the beach.

The Wagener Estate Bed & Breakfast ✪
351 ELM STREET, PENN YAN, NEW YORK 14527

Tel: **(315) 536-4591**
Best Time to Call: **1–4 PM; 7–10 PM**
Hosts: **Joanne and Scott Murray**
Location: **20 mi. from NYS Thruway, Exit 42, Geneva**
No. of Rooms: **6**
No. of Private Baths: **4**
Max. No. Sharing Bath: **4**

Double/pb: **$85**
Single/pb: **$80**
Double/sb: **$70**
Single/sb: **$65**
Open: **All year**
Breakfast: **Full**
Credit Cards: **AMEX, DISC, MC, VISA**
Pets: **No**

Children: **Welcome, over 5**　　　　Social Drinking: **Permitted**
Smoking: **No**

Once the home of Abraham Wagener, the founder of Penn Yan, this lovely fifteen-room estate is furnished with antiques and charm. This bed and breakfast sits on four scenic acres, with shaded lawns, apple trees, and gentle breezes. The pillared veranda offers you a perfect spot for reflection, conversation, and refreshments. Things to see include wineries, Keuka and Seneca Lakes, the Corning Glass Museum, Watkins Glen, public beaches, parks, Outlet Trail, and the well-known Windmill Farm and Crafts Market. Joanne and Scott serve a sumptuous breakfast as part of your relaxing stay.

HUDSON VALLEY/ALBANY/KINGSTON AREA

Alexander Hamilton House ✪
49 VAN WYCK STREET, CROTON-ON-HUDSON, NEW YORK 10520

Tel: **(914) 271-6737**
Best Time to Call: **8 AM–6 PM**
Host: **Barbara Notarius**
Location: **30 mi. NW of New York City**
No. of Rooms: **7**
No. of Private Baths: **7**
Double/pb: **$95–$125**
Single/pb: **$75–$85**
Suites: **$135–$250**
Open: **All year**

Breakfast: **Full**
Credit Cards: **AMEX, DC, DISC, MC, VISA**
Pets: **No**
Children: **Welcome**
Smoking: **No**
Social Drinking: **Permitted**
Minimum Stay: **2 nights weekends**
Airport/Station Pickup: **Yes**
Foreign Languages: **French**

No, Hamilton didn't live here; this beautiful Victorian home was built some eight decades after his death. The home, with its 35-foot in-ground swimming pool and spectacular Hudson River views, would please even the most patrician lodgers. West Point, Van Cortlandt Manor, Boscobel, Kykuit, and Storm King Art Center are all nearby, and New York City is within striking distance. After sightseeing, relax in the large living room complete with fireplace, piano, and numerous antiques. Baby equipment is available for guests with small children. Five rooms have a fireplace and two have two-person Jacuzzis.

Hoosick Bed and Breakfast ✪
ROUTE 7 TROY-BENNINGTON ROAD, P.O. BOX 145, HOOSICK, NEW YORK 12089
www.bbonline.com/ny/hoosic

Tel: **(518) 686-5875; (888) 686-5875**
Hosts: **Maria and John Recco**
Location: **8 mi. W of Bennington, Vt.**
No. of Rooms: **3**
Max. No. Sharing Bath: **4**

Double/sb: **$50**
Single/sb: **$40**
Open: **All year**
Reduced Rates: **5% families**
Breakfast: **Full**

Pets: **Yes**
Children: **Welcome**
Smoking: **No**

Social Drinking: **Permitted**
Foreign Languages: **Greek, Spanish**

This recently restored 1840 Greek Revival farmhouse is located fifteen miles from Williamstown, Massachusetts, forty miles from Saratoga Springs, a half hour from the ski slopes of Vermont and the Berkshires, and minutes from local antique centers. Right on site there are barnyard animals to feed and an open field for relaxing, walking, or cross-country skiing. Breakfast specialties might include fresh-baked Texas-size muffins, blueberry pancakes, eggs, coffee, and juice, which you can enjoy privately or with your hosts. Maria and John also offer guests evening tea and the use of a full kitchen.

Mallard Manor ✪
345 LAKEVIEW DRIVE, MAHOPAC, NEW YORK 10541

Tel: **(914) 628-3595**
Hosts: **Jean and Joe Costello**
Location: **50 mi. N of New York**
No. of Rooms: **2**
Max. No. Sharing Bath: **4**
Double/sb: **$70**
Open: **All year**

Reduced Rates: **10% seniors**
Breakfast: **Full**
Pets: **No**
Children: **Welcome, over 10**
Smoking: **No**
Social Drinking: **Permitted**

This warm and cozy Dutch Colonial is the perfect spot if you are looking to get away from the hectic pace of city life. Nestled among the rolling hills and reservoirs of the lower Hudson Valley, it lets guests unwind in comfortable surroundings. The house features wide-planked floors, faux finished and stenciled walls, and a mural depicting the history of Mahopac, painted by a local artist. Informal gardens continue the relaxed mood outdoors. Whether you are in town for business or pleasure, Jean and Joe will make your visit a memorable one.

Morgan House ✪
12 POWELTON ROAD, NEWBURGH, NEW YORK 12550
www.hudval.com/morgan

Tel: **(914) 561-0326**
Best Time to Call: **4:30 PM weekdays**
Hosts: **Pat and Richard Morgan**
Location: **60 mi. N of New York City**
No. of rooms: **2**
Max. No. Sharing Bath: **4**
Double/pb: **$85**
Single/pb: **$75**
Open: **All year**

Reduced Rates: **Available**
Breakfast: **Full**
Credit Cards: **AMEX, MC, VISA**
Pets: **Sometimes**
Children: **Welcome, over 10**
Smoking: **No**
Social Drinking: **Permitted**
Airport Pickup: **Yes, weekends only**

Warm hospitality awaits you in this lovely home nestled in a quiet wooded setting with a perennial, herb, and "secret" garden. Breakfast is served by candlelight in the dining room or on the deck, where guests are invited to choose their own music. There are two charming guest rooms. The Heart Room is romantic and filled with touches of sweet sentiments; the Cottage Room is whimsical and enchanting. Guests can listen to music, enjoy the library, or play the piano in a private living room. Nearby are fine restaurants, West Point, wineries, hiking, Woodbury Commons, the New York State Thruway, and I-84. Your hosts both work in nearby school districts and enjoy welcoming guests into their home.

Empty Nest Bed and Breakfast
423 LAKE ROAD, NEW WINDSOR, NEW YORK 12553

Tel: **(914) 496-9263**	Open: **Jan. 16–Nov. 14**
Hosts: **Pat and Dick Coleman**	Breakfast: **Full**
Location: **12 mi. N of West Point; 60 mi.**	Pets: **No**
N of NYC	Smoking: **No**
No. of Rooms: **3**	Social Drinking: **Permitted**
Max. No. Sharing Bath: **4**	Minimum Stay: **2 nights holiday**
Double/sb: **$85**	**weekends, homecoming; 4 nights**
Single/sb: **$70**	**West Point graduation**

Situated on a pretty country road, surrounded by 165 acres of rolling hills and meadows, this property has been family-owned since the 1870s. The weathered barn and outside buildings are reminiscent of years gone by. Built in 1967, Empty Nest is a charming country home, decorated with pretty florals and prints, family antiques, quilts, and dolls. A gourmet breakfast, served on the screened porch, frequently stretches into lunch as guests linger over their food. A guest from Alabama comments: "I am accustomed to kind people and Southern hospitality and this surpasses any service I received at home."

The Milton Bull House ✪
1065 ROUTE 302, PINE BUSH, NEW YORK 12566

Tel: **(914) 361-4770**	Open: **All year**
Best Time to Call: **9 AM–9 PM**	Reduced Rates: **Weekly**
Hosts: **Ellen and Graham Jamison**	Breakfast: **Full**
Location: **75 mi. NW of New York City**	Pets: **No**
No. of Rooms: **2**	Children: **Welcome**
No. of Private Baths: **1**	Smoking: **No**
Max. No. Sharing Bath: **4**	Social Drinking: **Permitted**
Double/sb: **$65**	Airport/Station Pickup: **Yes**
Single/sb: **$54**	Foreign Languages: **French**

The Milton Bull House is a traditional bed and breakfast. The historic house has nine large rooms furnished with antiques. Part of the house dates to 1816 and is Federal in style. The two guest rooms share a full bath. The house is located in a lovely area of the Hudson Valley—in the foothills of the Shawangunk Mountain Ridge—which provides wonderful scenery as well as opportunities for hiking and rock climbing. Shopping malls, such as Woodbury Common, antique marts, and wineries are nearby. Although the area is rural, the Bull House is very close to Route 17, the NYS Thruway, and I-84. There are sixty acres of open farmland, lawns, gardens, orchards, and an in-ground swimming pool. Rates include an old-fashioned farm breakfast with home baking.

Maggie Towne's B&B ✪

PHILLIPS ROAD, PITTSTOWN, NEW YORK (MAILING ADDRESS: BOX 82, RD 2, VALLEY FALLS, NEW YORK 12185)

Tel: **(518) 663-8369; 686-7331**	Open: **All year**
Host: **Maggie Towne**	Breakfast: **Full**
Location: **14 mi. E of Troy**	Pets: **Sometimes**
No. of Rooms: **3**	Children: **Welcome (crib)**
Max. No. Sharing Bath: **4**	Smoking: **No**
Double/sb: **$45**	Social Drinking: **Permitted**
Single/sb: **$35**	

This lovely old Colonial is located amid beautiful lawns and trees. Enjoy a cup of tea or glass of wine before the huge fireplace in the family room. Use the music room or curl up with a book on the screened-in porch. Mornings, your host serves home-baked goodies. She will gladly prepare a lunch for you to take on tour or enjoy at the house. It's 20 miles to historic Bennington, Vermont, and 30 to Saratoga.

Lee's Deer Run Bed & Breakfast ✪

411 COUNTY ROAD #71, STILLWATER, NEW YORK 12170

Tel: **(518) 584-7722, 587-0921**	Breakfast: **Full**
Best Time to Call: **8 AM–8 PM**	Pets: **No**
Hosts: **Rose and Don Lee**	Children: **Welcome, over 12**
Location: **8 mi. SE of Saratoga Springs**	Smoking: **No**
Suites: **$85–$200**	Social Drinking: **Permitted**
Open: **All year**	Minimum Stay: **2 nights racing season**

Lee's Deer Run is located on 65 acres of rolling countryside adjacent to Saratoga National Park and just ten minutes from the Saratoga Race Track, performing arts center, spa and mineral baths, Skidmore College, and historic Saratoga Springs. Rose and Don transformed a circa 1800 barn into an exquisite home. The two suites have king-size poster beds, comfortable sofas, easy chairs, and air-conditioning. Rose and Don will offer plenty of suggestions on area restaurants and information on current events.

Sharon Fern's Bed & Breakfast ✪
8 ETHIER DRIVE, TROY, NEW YORK 12180

Tel: **(518) 279-1966**
Best Time to Call: **Mornings**
Hosts: **Bill and Sharon Ernst**
Location: **10 mi. from NYS Thruway**
No. of Rooms: **2**
Max. No. Sharing Bath: **3**
Double/sb: **$55**
Single/sb: **$50**

Open: **All year**
Reduced Rates: **10% seniors**
Breakfast: **Full**
Pets: **No**
Children: **Welcome (crib)**
Smoking: **No**
Social Drinking: **Permitted**

In the country on a quiet dead-end street, just outside of Albany, New York's capital, you'll find this tri-level contemporary home with flower boxes on the balcony. Enjoy spacious accommodations with a potpourri of memorabilia and a splash of antiques. Amenities include a separate entrance, a 20-foot × 40-foot in-ground pool, and a beautiful yard where guests are invited to enjoy a game of croquet or badminton. Skiers and hikers will locate mountains in nearly every direction: the Adirondacks, Catskills, and Green Mountains are all one-half hour away, as well as Saratoga Race Track.

Boulevard House Bed and Breakfast ✪
1017 ROUTE 52, WALDEN, NEW YORK 12586

Tel: **(914) 778-1602**
Best Time to Call: **8 AM–10 PM**
Hosts: **Larry and Jean Winum**
Location: **60 mi. NW of New York City**
No. of Rooms: **2**
No. of Private Baths: **1**
Double/pb: **$80**
Single/pb: **$65**
Open: **Jan. 11–Dec. 21**

Breakfast: **Full**
Other Meals: **Available**
Credit Cards: **DISC, MC, VISA**
Pets: **Sometimes**
Children: **Welcome, crib**
Smoking: **No**
Social Drinking: **Permitted**
Airport/Station Pickup: **Yes**

The Boulevard Bed and Breakfast is centrally located outside the village of Walden. The Winums live within a comfortable driving distance of golf courses, antique shops, wineries, West Point, Hudson River attractions, historic sites, and farmers' markets. A three-course breakfast is served every morning, beginning with fresh fruit and ending with a sweet treat often made from local apples. Raising a large family made it easy for Larry and Jean to extend their hospitality to guests.

Meadowlark Farm B&B ✪
180 UNION CORNERS ROAD, WARWICK, NEW YORK 10992

Tel: **(914) 651-4286**
Best Time to Call: **Evening**
Hosts: **Dorothy Haupt**

Location: **55 mi. NW of NYS**
No. of Rooms: **2**
Max. No. Sharing Bath: **4**

Double/sb: **$75**
Open: **All year**
Reduced Rates: **Available**
Breakfast: **Full**
Other Meals: **Available**
Pets: **Sometimes**

Children: **No**
Smoking: **No**
Social Drinking: **Permitted**
Minimum Stay: **2 nights weekends**
Airport/Station Pickup: **Yes**

Hand-hewn beamed ceilings add to the charm of this English-style farmhouse built in the late 1880s. Guest rooms have queen-size beds, cable TV, air conditioning, and phones. Guests are invited to walk the grounds, pet the horse, or just relax in the chaise longue while enjoying the tranquility of the surroundings. Breakfast, which can be served in your room, the dining room, or on the terrace overlooking the horse pasture, includes vegetables fresh from the garden. Meadowlark is located within minutes of West Point Military Academy, Sugar Loaf Craft Village, Warwick Valley Winery, Shawangunk Wine Trails, the outlet mall at Woodbury Commons, and the Renaissance Festival in Sterling Forest. The B&B is within easy driving distance to Vernon Valley/Great Gorge Ski Resort, hiking trails, Harriman State Park, Greenwood Lake, and equestrian activities. Ask about special tours.

LAKE GEORGE AREA

Hilltop Cottage ✪
4825 LAKESHORE DRIVE, BOLTON LANDING, NEW YORK 12814-0186

Tel: **(518) 644-2492**
Best Time to Call: **Anytime**
Hosts: **Anita and Charlie Richards**
Location: **8 mi. from I-87**
No. of Rooms: **3**
No. of Private Baths: **3**
Double/pb: **$65–$80**

Open: **All year**
Breakfast: **Full**
Credit Cards: **MC, VISA**
Children: **Welcome, over 4**
Smoking: **Restricted**
Social Drinking: **Permitted**
Foreign Languages: **German**

Hilltop Cottage is a clean, comfortable, renovated caretaker cottage in the beautiful Lake George–Eastern Adirondack region. You can walk to the beach, marinas, shops, and restaurants. Guests will enjoy the hearty breakfasts, homey atmosphere, helpful hosts, wood-burning stove, and fall foliage.

Country Life B&B
67 TABOR ROAD, GREENWICH, NEW YORK 12834

Tel: **(518) 692-7203; (888) 692-7203;**
    fax: **(518) 692-9203**
Best Time to Call: **4–9 PM**
Hosts: **Wendy and Richard Duvall**
Location: **Rte. 372 off Rte. 22, 14 mi. E**

of Saratoga Springs, 14 mi. W of
Arlington, Vt.
No. of Rooms: **3**
No. of Private Baths: **2**
Max. No. Sharing Bath: **4**

Double/pb: **$65–$75**
Double/sb: **$65–$75**
Open: **All year**
Reduced Rates: **Available**
Breakfast: **Full**
Pets: **No**

Children: **Welcome (crib)**
Smoking: **No**
Social Drinking: **Permitted**
Minimum Stay: **2 nights racing season**
Foreign Languages: **Spanish, German**

Guests feel right at home in this 1830 farmhouse, restored to retain its original charm. There are 100 quiet acres of brooks, fields, meadows, and trees for guests to roam. Nearby are galleries, museums, restaurants, antique shops, and athletic areas, including fishing, boating, skiing, hiking, horseback riding, and golfing. Albany, Saratoga Springs, Lake George, and Vermont are all within a 45-minute drive. Wendy and Richard bring 16 years of experience from their bed and breakfast on Long Island to this bucolic area of the capital region.

Crislip's Bed & Breakfast ✪

693 RIDGE ROAD, QUEENSBURY, NEW YORK 12804-9717

Tel: **(518) 793-6869**
Hosts: **Ned and Joyce Crislip**
Location: **20 mi. N of Saratoga Springs**
No. of Rooms: **4**
No. of Private Baths: **3**
Double/pb: **$55–$75**
Single/pb: **$45–$65**
Open: **All year**
Reduced Rates: **Over 3 nights**

Breakfast: **Full**
Credit Cards: **MC, VISA**
Pets: **Sometimes**
Children: **Welcome**
Smoking: **No**
Social Drinking: **Permitted**
Minimum Stay: **Major holiday weekends**
Airport/Station Pickup: **Yes**

Located between Saratoga Springs and Lake George, this Quaker-built Federal home provides spacious accommodations complete with period antiques, four-poster beds, down comforters, and private baths. The country breakfast menu features buttermilk pancakes, scrambled eggs, and sausages. Ned Crislip, a music teacher, and his wife, Joyce, invite you to enjoy the grounds surrounding their dwelling, which include nearly two acres of lawn and gardens, old stone walls, and mountain views of Vermont.

Six Sisters Bed and Breakfast

149 UNION AVENUE, SARATOGA SPRINGS, NEW YORK 12866
stay@sistersbandb.com; www.sistersbandb.com

Tel: **(518) 583-1173;**
  fax: **(518) 587-2470**
Hosts: **Kate Benton and Steve Ramirez**
Location: **30 mi. N of Albany**
No. of Rooms: **4**
No. of Private Baths: **4**
Double/pb: **$75–$100**
Single/pb: **$65–$85**

Suites: **$85–$150**
Open: **All year**
Reduced Rates: **10%–15% Sun.–Thurs.**
  Nov.–Mar.; 10% seniors; corporate,
  extended stays
Breakfast: **Full**
Credit Cards: **DISC, MC, VISA**
Pets: **No**

Children: **Welcome, over 8**	Minimum Stay: **Special weekends,**
Smoking: **No**	**racing season**
Social Drinking: **Permitted**	

Some people visit this town for its naturally carbonated mineral waters, other people for its racetracks. Bathers and railbirds will both be delighted by Kate and Steve's 1890 Victorian, named for Kate's sisters. All rooms have TVs, refrigerators, air-conditioning and either king- or queen-size beds; two have whirlpool tubs. After sampling one of Steve's mouth-watering breakfasts, guests are encouraged to take a mug of coffee, tea, or cider out to the veranda overlooking Saratoga's streets and racecourse. Then it's an easy walk to boutiques, antique shops, restaurants, and the National Museum of Racing.

LAKE PLACID/ADIRONDACKS AREA

Crown Point Bed & Breakfast (The Wyman House) ✪

P.O. BOX 490, MAIN STREET, ROUTE 9 N, CROWN POINT, NEW YORK 12928

Tel: **(518) 597-3651**	Reduced Rates: **10% seniors**
Best Time to Call: **10 AM–7 PM**	Breakfast: **Continental, plus**
Hosts: **Hugh and Sandy Johnson, owners**	Credit Cards: **MC, VISA**
Location: **7 mi. N of Ticonderoga**	Pets: **No**
No. of Rooms: **5**	Children: **Welcome**
No. of Private Baths: **5**	Smoking: **No**
Double/pb: **$60–$75**	Social Drinking: **Permitted**
Single/pb: **$55–$75**	Minimum Stay: **2 nights on holiday**
Suites: **$120, sleeps 4**	**weekends**
Open: **All year**	

Return to an era of stately Victorian elegance. Sleep in a hundred-year-old manor house graciously furnished with period antiques. The 18-room house, built in 1886 by Richard Wyman, a local banker, took three years to complete. It was designed by Witherbee and Sherman and constructed by an Italian craftsman. Six different kinds of paneled woodwork (oak, pine, chestnut, mahogany, cherry, and walnut), pocket doors, and four fireplaces grace the house. Enjoy a summer evening on one of the three porches, view the sunrise over the Green Mountains of Vermont, or experience the double rainbows of the Adirondack region.

Gatehouse Herbs Bed & Breakfast ✪

98 VAN BUREN STREET, DOLGEVILLE, NEW YORK 13329

Tel: **(315) 429-8366**	No. of Rooms: **3**
Best Time to Call: **5–9 PM**	No. of Private Baths: **3**
Hosts: **Carol and Kermit (Kerry) Gates**	Double/pb: **$75**
Location: **30 mi. E of Utica**	Single/pb: **$65**

Suite: **$85**	Pets: **No**
Open: **Apr.–Nov.**	Children: **Welcome, over 6**
Reduced Rates: **10% after 15th day**	Smoking: **No**
Breakfast: **Full**	Social Drinking: **Permitted**

Nestled in the Adirondack foothills and overlooking a lily pond in the village of Dolgeville, Gatehouse Herbs Bed & Breakfast is a romantic getaway. This National Register property includes a Queen Anne Victorian house, your host's ancestral home. The twelve-acre grounds contain perennial gardens, quiet woods, and a bubbling brook. Guest rooms are decorated with family antiques. Enjoy a bountiful breakfast in the dining room or on the breakfast porch. Specialties include pancakes with fresh maple syrup, omelets, blueberry muffins, and scones. Through the Mohawk Valley rolled the covered wagons and later the mule-drawn barges of the Erie Canal. Visiting nearby historic sites is like turning the pages of a story of the frontier age. Cooperstown and the oldest Russian monastery in the United States are within an hour's drive. Hiking, biking, and canoeing in the Adirondack Park are just minutes away.

The Book & Blanket Bed & Breakfast ✪
ROUTE 9N (P.O. BOX 164), JAY, NEW YORK 12941

Tel: **(518) 946-8323**	Single/pb: **$70**
Best Time to Call: **Anytime**	Double/sb: **$55–$60**
Hosts: **Kathy, Fred, Samuel, and Daisy the Basset Hound**	Single/sb: **$40**
Location: **17 mi. E of Lake Placid**	Open: **All year**
No. of Rooms: **3**	Breakfast: **Full**
No. of Private Baths: **1**	Pets: **Sometimes**
Max. No. Sharing Bath: **4**	Children: **Welcome**
Double/pb: **$75**	Smoking: **No**
	Social Drinking: **Permitted**

The Book & Blanket

This 125-year-old Greek revival residence is situated on the east branch of the Ausable River in Jay, N.Y.—an Adirondack hamlet complete with covered bridge and village green. Filled with antiques and books for borrowing and browsing, this house boasts three guest bedrooms honoring Jane Austen, F. Scott Fitzgerald, and Jack London. In winter, guests can relax before a fire; in summer the porch swing is just the thing. Whiteface Ski Mountain is seven miles away, and Lake Placid a mere 17. Ausable Chasm, Fort Ticonderoga, and ferries to Vermont are easy day trips. The owners enjoy baking, juggling, and their adorable basset hound.

Brook's Sunshine Cottage B&B and Annex ✪
6 MAPLE STREET, LAKE PLACID, NEW YORK 12946
Sunshine@Netheaven.com; www.helpco.com.80/Brooks

Tel: (518) 523-3661; fax: (518) 523-2331	Open: **All year**
Best Time to Call: **9 AM–8 PM**	Reduced Rates: **Available**
Hosts: **Bernadine and Joseph Brooks**	Breakfast: **Full**
Location: **150 mi. N of Albany**	Credit Cards: **MC, VISA**
No. of Rooms: **4**	Pets: **No**
Max. No. Sharing Bath: **4**	Children: **Welcome**
Double/pb: **$75**	Smoking: **No**
Double/sb: **$55–$60**	Social Drinking: **Permitted**
Single/sb: **$40**	Minimum Stay: **2 nights winter and summer, weekends**
Suites: **$75–$99; sleeps 4**	Airport/Station Pickup: **Yes**

This century-old B&B is located one block from Main Street in the center of the Olympic Village. The activities are endless, with something for every family member: skating, snowshoeing, cross country and downhill skiing, boating, biking, and hiking the forty-six peaks, to name a few. There are three rooms in the main house, as well as four apartment suites in the annex. There are fireplaces in the common areas for your relaxing pleasure. The suites have TV, VCR, air conditioning, fully equipped kitchens, living room, and private bath.

Fogarty's Bed and Breakfast ✪
37 RIVERSIDE DRIVE, SARANAC LAKE, NEW YORK 12983

Tel: (518) 891-3755; (800) 525-3755	Open: **All year**
Best Time to Call: **After 3 PM**	Breakfast: **Full**
Hosts: **Jack and Emily Fogarty**	Pets: **No**
Location: **150 mi. N of Albany**	Children: **Welcome**
No. of Rooms: **5**	Smoking: **Permitted**
Max. No. Sharing Bath: **3**	Social Drinking: **Permitted**
Double/sb: **$55**	Airport Pickup: **Yes**
Single/sb: **$40**	

High on a hill overlooking Lake Flower and Mts. Baker, McKenzie, and Pisgah—but only three minutes from the center of town—you'll find Fogarty's. The B&B's porches, wide doors, and call buttons attest to its past as a cure cottage. The living and dining rooms are decorated with handsome woodwork, and the bathrooms have the original 1910 fixtures. Swimmers and boaters can use Fogarty's dock, and cross-country skiers will find trails within a mile. More ambitious athletes should take a brief drive to Lake Placid's Olympic courses or the slopes of Whiteface and Big Tupper. Emily and Jack are Adirondack natives, so feel free to ask them for suggestions.

Mountain Shadows Guesthouse ✪
50 OLD MILITARY ROAD, SARANAC LAKE, NEW YORK 12983

Tel: **(518) 891-0327**	Suite: **$60–$110**
Best Time to Call: **Evenings**	Open: **All year**
Host: **Tricia Sullivan Bixler**	Reduced Rates: **10% seniors**
Location: **140 mi. N of Albany**	Breakfast: **Full**
No. of Rooms: **2**	Pets: **No**
Max. No. Sharing Bath: **4**	Children: **Welcome**
Double/sb: **$40–$50**	Smoking: **No**
Single/sb: **$30–$40**	Social Drinking: **Permitted**

Mountain Shadows Guesthouse is located in the heart of the Adirondack Mountains of upstate New York, just seven miles from Lake Placid, site of the 1980 Winter Olympic Games. Although Mountain Shadows is within walking distance of the village center, this charming home is in the most prestigious neighborhood. With its unusual architectural design and hidden stairways, you'll find this a unique, out-of-the-way retreat. Relax on the porch or deck, or climb the mountain just outside your window. Nearby activities include bird-watching, hiking, swimming, boating, golfing, fishing, and, in the winter, downhill or Nordic skiing. When you leave you will feel as though you've been in the country visiting friends.

LONG ISLAND

A Reasonable Alternative, Inc. ✪
117 SPRING STREET, PORT JEFFERSON, NEW YORK 11777

Tel: **(516) 928-4034**	Rates (Single/Double):
Best Time to Call: **Noon–5 PM**	Modest: **$44/$52**
Coordinator: **Kathleen Dexter**	Average: **$60/$68**
States/Regions Covered: **East Quoque,**	Luxury: **$78/$150**
Glen Cove, Long Beach, Miller Place,	Credit Cards: **MC, VISA**
Montauk, Port Jefferson, Setauket,	Minimum Stay: **2 nights weekends**
Southampton, Stony Brook, Syosset	**resort area, 3 nights holiday**
	weekends resort areas

Bounded by Long Island Sound and the Atlantic Ocean, from the New York City border to Montauk 100 miles to the east, the cream of host homes has been culled by Kathleen for you. There's much to see and do, from museums, historic homes, theater, and horse racing, to the famous beaches, including Jones Beach, Fire Island, Shelter Island, and the exclusive Hamptons. (The Hamptons require a two-day minimum stay in July and August.) Adelphi College, Hofstra University, C. W. Post, Stony Brook, and St. Joseph's are a few of the nearby schools.

Mainstay Bed & Breakfast ✪
579 HILL STREET, SOUTHAMPTON, NEW YORK 11968

Tel: **(516) 283-4375**	Open: **All year**
Best Time to Call: **AM**	Reduced Rates: **Available**
Host: **Elizabeth Main**	Breakfast: **Continental**
Location: **80 mi. E of New York City**	Credit Cards: **MC, VISA**
No. of Rooms: **8**	Pets: **No**
No. of Private Baths: **3**	Children: **Welcome**
Max. No. Sharing Bath: **4**	Smoking: **No**
Double/pb: **$50–$165**	Social Drinking: **Permitted**
Double/sb: **$50–$120**	Minimum Stay: **2 nights weekends**
Suite: **$150–$215**	**June–Labor Day**

This charmingly restored Colonial guesthouse was built in the 1870s. Once a country store, Mainstay now accommodates those looking for a cozy retreat where they can enjoy white sandy beaches, nature walks, sports, biking, and dining. Rooms are beautifully decorated with antique iron and brass beds. The large master suite has a fireplace, TV, and claw-footed tub. (If you fall in love with the furniture, you may be able to buy it—many of the antique and European country pieces are available for purchase.) Breakfast, typically including homemade muffins, cereals, fruit, juice, and coffee, is served in the dining room. The B&B is within walking distance of antique shops, other stores, galleries, and museums.

1880 Seafield House ✪
2 SEAFIELD LANE, WESTHAMPTON BEACH, NEW YORK 11978

Tel: **(800) 346-3290**	Open: **All year**
Best Time to Call: **9 AM–5 PM**	Reduced Rates: **$95, Oct. 15–May 15**
Host: **Elsie Collins**	Breakfast: **Full**
Location: **90 mi. E of New York City**	Pets: **No**
No. of Rooms: **3 suites**	Children: **No**
No. of Private Baths: **3**	Smoking: **No**
Suites: **$175–$200**	Social Drinking: **Permitted**

This 100-year-old home in posh Westhampton is five blocks from the beach, and boasts its own pool and tennis court. Victorian lounges, a caned rocker, piano, hurricane lamps, Shaker benches, and Chinese porcelain all combine to create the casual, country inn atmosphere. When the sea air chills Westhampton Beach, the parlor fire keeps the house toasty warm. The aromas of freshly brewing coffee and Mrs. Collins' breads and rolls baking in the oven are likely to wake you in time for breakfast. You'll leave this hideaway relaxed, carrying one of Mrs. Collins' homemade goodies.

NEW YORK CITY AREA/WESTCHESTER COUNTY

Abode, Ltd. ✪
P.O. BOX 20022, NEW YORK, NEW YORK 10021

Tel: **(212) 472-2000; (800) 835-8880**	States/Regions Covered: **Manhattan**
Best Time to Call: **Mon.–Fri., 9 AM–**	Rates (Single/Double): **$110–$400**
5 PM	Credit Cards: **AMEX**
Coordinator: **Shelli Leifer**	Minimum Stay: **4 nights**

Shelli is a friendly, savvy New Yorker with sensitive insight as to where a guest would be most comfortable. Her roster grows steadily with accommodations in safe neighborhoods that are "East Side, West Side, and all around the town." Private brownstones boasting a country inn ambience and private luxury apartments are especially attractive for couples traveling together. Prices range from $110 for a studio to $400 for 3 bedrooms. Reduced rates are available for extended stays. Theaters, museums, galleries, restaurants, and shopping are within easy reach of all accommodations.

Bed & Breakfast (& Books)
35 WEST 92ND STREET, NEW YORK, NEW YORK 10025

Tel: **(212) 865-8740**	Rates (Single/Double):
Best Time to Call: **10 AM–5 PM**	Average: **$75–$100 / $100–$110**
Mon.–Fri.	Credit Cards: **AMEX**
Coordinator: **Judith Goldberg**	Minimum Stay: **2 nights**
States/Regions Covered: **Manhattan**	

Accommodations are conveniently located in residential areas near transportation and within walking distance of many cultural attractions. Hosts are photographers, psychologists, lawyers, dancers, teachers, and artists. They are pleased to share their knowledge of fine shops, reasonable restaurants, galleries, theater, and bookstores. Unhosted apartments are $100 to $130 for two.

The New York Bed and Breakfast Reservation Center ✪
331 WEST 57TH STREET, SUITE 221, NEW YORK, NEW YORK 10019
smartsleep.aol; members.aol.com/~smartsleep

Tel: **(212) 977-3512**	Rates (Single/Double):
Coordinator: **Yann Gabriel**	Modest: **$60–$70**
States/Regions Covered: **New York City,**	Average: **$70–$80**
Southampton, New York; San	Luxury: **$80–$100**
Francisco; London; Paris, France	Credit Cards: **AMEX**
	Minimum Stay: **2 nights**

Yann has a wide range of bed and breakfast accommodations. Several are within a few blocks of major midtown hotels and theaters. As an ex–bed and breakfast host, Yann has insight on what travelers expect. Personal inspections and specific descriptions help guests and corporations trying to cut down on travel expenses. Yann can suggest reasonably priced airport pickups to facilitate getting into New York. Hosted and unhosted flats and apartments are available in Paris, as well as private chateaus in France.

The Bennett's ✪
226 READ AVENUE, CRESTWOOD, NEW YORK 10707

Tel: **(914) 779-8559**	Breakfast: **Continental**
Host: **Françoise Bennett**	Other Meals: **Available**
Location: **15 mi. N of New York City**	Pets: **No**
No. of Rooms: **1**	Children: **No**
No. of Private Baths: **1**	Smoking: **No**
Double/pb: **$50**	Social Drinking: **Permitted**
Single/pb: **$40**	Foreign Languages: **French**
Open: **All year**	

Located in beautiful Westchester County, and owned by an artistic couple, this private home offers one single room with two twin beds. Nearby are Sarah Lawrence College, Bronxville, and Scarsdale. The B&B is only 35 minutes by train to Grand Central Station in New York City, with a three-minute walk to Crestwood Station.

Kroghs Nest ✪
4 HILLCREST ROAD, HARTSDALE, NEW YORK 10530

Tel: **(914) 946-3479**	Open: **All year**
Best Time to Call: **7 AM–10 PM**	Reduced Rates: **15% weekly; students**
Hosts: **Claudia and James P. Krogh**	Breakfast: **Full**
Location: **21 mi. N of New York City's**	Credit Cards: **AMEX**
Grand Central Station	Pets: **No**
No. of Rooms: **2**	Children: **Welcome (crib & high chair)**
No. of Private Baths: **2**	Smoking: **No**
Max. No. Sharing Bath: **4**	Social Drinking: **Permitted**
Double/pb: **$75**	Airport/Station Pickup: **Yes**
Single/pb: **$65**	

Built in 1896, this Center Hall Victorian sits on a hillside acre, enclosed by greenery and beautiful flowers. You'll admire the authentic Colonial decor: breakfast is served on a large antique table surrounded by pine cupboards and porcelain ornaments. The bedrooms have air-conditioning, color TV, and clock radio. Washing machines and dryers are available for guests' use. The location couldn't be more convenient, since New York City's stores, historic sites, museums, restaurants, and theaters are easily accessible. Educational institutions within 10 miles include Sarah Lawrence College, Pace Westchester University, the State University of New York at Purchase, and New York Medical College.

NIAGARA/BUFFALO AREA

Eden Inn Bed & Breakfast ✪
8362 NORTH MAIN STREET, EDEN, NEW YORK 14057

Tel: **(716) 992-4814**
Hosts: **Chris and Betsy Walits**
Location: **17 mi. SW of Buffalo**
No. of Rooms: **5**
No. of Private Baths: **4**
Max. No. Sharing Bath: **4**
Double/pb: **$69–$82**
Single/pb: **$69–$82**
Double/sb: **$59–$69**
Single/sb: **$59–$69**
Suites: **$79–$92**

Open: **All year**
Reduced Rates: **Corporate, after 3rd night**
Breakfast: **Full, weekends; Continental, weekdays**
Credit Cards: **AMEX, DISC**
Pets: **No**
Children: **Welcome**
Smoking: **No**
Social Drinking: **Permitted**

Each room at the Eden Inn is tastefully appointed, with a theme in mind. The Rose suite features roses, brass, wicker, and a whirlpool tub. The Bluhmen suite has a double whirlpool tub. The Vineyard features grapes and a claw-footed tub. Standard room themes include trains and the Garden of Eden. Located in the center of Eden, the inn is six miles from Hamburg and forty miles from Niagara Falls. Nearby is the Erie Country Fair and Eden's Corn Festival. There are three cats on the premises.

The Teepee ✪
14396 FOUR MILE LEVEL ROAD, GOWANDA, NEW YORK 14070-9796

Tel: **(716) 532-2168**	Open: **All year**
Hosts: **Max and Phyllis Lay**	Breakfast: **Full**
Location: **30 mi. S of Buffalo**	Pets: **Sometimes**
No. of Rooms: **3**	Children: **Welcome (crib)**
Max. No. Sharing Bath: **3**	Smoking: **No**
Double/sb: **$50**	Social Drinking: **Permitted**
Single/sb: **$40**	Airport/Station Pickup: **Yes**

Max and Phyllis Lay are Seneca Indians living on the Cattaraugus Indian Reservation. Their airy four-bedroom home is clean, modern, and decorated with family Indian articles, many of them crafted by hand. The reservation offers country living and the opportunity of seeing firsthand the customs of a Native American community. A fall festival with arts, crafts, and exhibition dancing is held in September. Canoeing, fishing, rafting, cross-country and downhill skiing, and a sport called snowsnake are among the local activities. Your hosts will gladly arrange tours of the Amish community and hot-air balloon rides over the beautiful rolling hills.

The Cameo Inn
4710 LOWER RIVER ROAD, ROUTE 18F, LEWISTON, NEW YORK 14092
www.cameoinn.com

Tel: **(716) 754-2075**	Suites: **$115**
Best Time to Call: **9 AM–9 PM**	Open: **All year**
Hosts: **Gregory and Carolyn Fisher**	Breakfast: **Full**
Location: **5 mi. N of Niagara Falls**	Credit Cards: **DISC, MC, VISA**
No. of Rooms: **4**	Pets: **No**
No. of Private Baths: **2**	Children: **Welcome, over 10**
Max. No. Sharing Bath: **4**	Smoking: **No**
Double/pb: **$85**	Social Drinking: **Permitted**
Single/pb: **$80**	Minimum Stay: **2 nights holiday**
Double/sb: **$65**	**weekends, special events, and**
Single/sb: **$60**	**June–Sept.**

Gregory and Carolyn's authentically furnished Queen Anne Victorian home commands a majestic view of the lower Niagara River. Located just 25 miles north of Buffalo and 5 miles north of Niagara Falls, The Cameo is conveniently situated for sightseeing, antiquing, fishing and boating, golfing, bicycling, or shopping at local factory outlets and malls. History buffs will want to travel 5 miles north to Old Fort Niagara, which dates from the American Revolution; the bridge to Canada is minutes away. A full country breakfast is served in the dining room each morning.

Manchester House

653 MAIN STREET, NIAGARA FALLS, NEW YORK 14301
71210.65@compuserve.com; www.manchesterhouse.com

Tel: **(716) 285-5717, 282-2144; (800) 489-3009**	Reduced Rates: **Available**
Best Time to Call: **9 AM–6 PM**	Breakfast: **Full**
Hosts: **Lis and Carl Slenk**	Credit Cards: **MC, VISA**
No. of Rooms: **3**	Pets: **No**
No. of Private Baths: **3**	Children: **Welcome**
Double/pb: **$75**	Smoking: **No**
Single/pb: **$60**	Social Drinking: **Permitted**
Open: **All year**	Foreign Languages: **German**

Before it was incorporated, Niagara Falls was known as Manchester—hence the name for this tastefully renovated B&B, which was a doctor's office for more than sixty years. Lis and Carl collected ideas and furniture for their home during the ten years they spent in England and Germany. Manchester House is conveniently located near the falls, with easy access to Canada. (Spacious off-street parking is provided.) The bright, cheerful guest rooms offer a choice of queen-size or single beds. Breakfast features home-baked specialties.

THOUSAND ISLANDS AREA

Way Back In Bed & Breakfast ✪

247 PROCTOR AVENUE, OGDENSBURG, NEW YORK 13669
www.1000islands.com/wayback/

Tel: **(315) 393-3844**	Open: **All year**
Best Time to Call: **Before 9 PM**	Breakfast: **Full**
Hosts: **Rena and Milton Goldberg**	Pets: **No**
Location: **Minutes from 1000 Islands**	Children: **Welcome, over 5**
No. of Rooms: **2**	Smoking: **No**
Max. No. Sharing Bath: **4**	Social Drinking: **Permitted**
Double/sb: **$60**	Airport Pickup: **Yes**

Situated on just over three acres, this bed and breakfast sits "way back in" from the road and offers quiet, friendly surroundings away from street noises. Both attractively appointed guest rooms have a view of the St. Lawrence River and assure you a pleasant night's sleep. Breakfast, served either in the dining room or the Florida room, opens with a mug of fresh-brewed coffee or tea to provide a wonderful start to the day's activities. Your hosts will gladly assist you in choosing restaurants and keep you informed of any special events, such as antique and horse shows, fishing derbies, and the Ogdensburg Seaway Festival Days.

For key to listings, see inside front or back cover.

✪ This star means that rates are guaranteed through December 31, 1999, to any guest making a reservation as a result of reading about the B&B in *Bed & Breakfast U.S.A.*—1999 edition.

Important! To avoid misunderstandings, always ask about cancellation policies when booking.

Please enclose a self-addressed, stamped, business-size envelope when contacting reservation services.

For more details on what you can expect in a B&B, see Chapter 1.

Always mention *Bed & Breakfast U.S.A.* when making reservations!

We want to hear from you! Use the form on page 593.

NORTH CAROLINA

A Bed of Roses ✪
135 CUMBERLAND AVENUE, ASHEVILLE, NORTH CAROLINA 28801
info@abedofroses.com

Tel: **(704) 258-8700; (800) 471-4182**
Best Time to Call: **9 AM–9 PM**
Host: **Caroline Logie**
Location: **½ mi. N of Asheville**
No. of Rooms: **5**
No. of Private Baths: **5**
Double/pb: **$95–$125**
Suites: **$125–$145 for 2**
Open: **All year**
Reduced Rates: **Available**

Breakfast: **Full**
Credit Cards: **MC, VISA**
Pets: **No**
Children: **Welcome, over 10 main house, under 10 cottage**
Smoking: **Restricted**
Social Drinking: **Permitted**
Minimum Stay: **2 nights holidays; in-season weekends**

Styled after an English country cottage, this inn is a cheerful Queen Anne Victorian, circa 1897, listed on the Register of Historic Homes. Each guest room is uniquely decorated. Some include fireplaces, antique bath fixtures, Jacuzzi tubs, balcony, or deck. Breakfast consists of homemade granola, coffee cakes, seasonal fruits, quiche, or pancakes with maple syrup. Guests are invited to enjoy a cool glass of lemonade or iced tea and cookies in the summer on the front porch rockers. Gourmet coffees and teas are always available. Biltmore House and Gardens, the Thomas Wolfe Memorial, botanical gardens, and the Blue Ridge Parkway are all minutes away.

Acorn Cottage

**25 SAINT DUNSTANS CIRCLE, ASHEVILLE,
NORTH CAROLINA 28803**
acorncott@aol.com; www.bbonline.com/nc/acorn cottage

Tel: **(828) 253-0609; (800) 699-0609**	Open: **All year**
Best Time to Call: **10 AM–9 PM**	Breakfast: **Full**
Host: **Sharon Tabor**	Credit Cards: **AMEX, DISC, MC, VISA**
Location: **1¼ mi. from Route I-40, exit 50/50B**	Pets: **No**
	Smoking: **No**
No. of Rooms: **4**	Social Drinking: **Permitted**
No. of Private Baths: **4**	Minimum Stay: **2 nights weekends, March 15–Dec. 31**
Double/pb: **$80–$100**	
Single/pb: **$75**	

An English country cottage in the woodsy heart of Asheville, Acorn is built of local granite; the interior boasts maple floors and a granite fireplace. The guest rooms feature queen-size beds, fine linens, air-conditioning, TV, and baths stocked with special soaps. A delicious full breakfast is served each morning with fresh fruit, varied entrees, juice, coffee or tea, and an assortment of breads. Then you're ready for the quarter-mile trip to the Biltmore Estate. Add 10% for one-night weekend or holiday stays.

The Colby House

230 PEARSON DRIVE, ASHEVILLE, NORTH CAROLINA 28801

Tel: **(704) 253-5644; (800) 982-2118**	Breakfast: **Full**
Hosts: **Everett and Ann Colby**	Credit Cards: **MC, VISA**
No. of Rooms: **4**	Pets: **No**
No. of Private Baths: **4**	Children: **Welcome, over 12**
Double/pb: **$95–$135**	Smoking: **Restricted**
Open: **All year**	Social Drinking: **Permitted**

This elegant Dutch-Tudor house in the Montford Historic District is a special place, thanks to its porch, beautiful gardens, and inviting fireplaces. Each guest room has its own individual decor and queen-size beds. Refreshments are available at all times, and wine and cheese are served in the evening. Breakfasts vary daily, but are always served on fine china, with heirloom crystal and silver. Southern hospitality abounds in your hosts' personal attention to every guest's needs.

Corner Oak Manor ✪

53 ST. DUNSTANS ROAD, ASHEVILLE, NORTH CAROLINA 28803

Tel: **(704) 253-3525**	Cottage: **$130–$145**
Best Time to Call: **9 AM–9 PM**	Open: **All year**
Hosts: **Karen and Andy Spradley**	Breakfast: **Full**
Location: **1¼ mi. from Rte. 40, Exit 50**	Credit Cards: **AMEX, DISC, MC, VISA**
No. of Rooms: 4	Pets: **No**
No. of Private Baths: 4	Children: **Welcome, over 12**
Double/pb: **$90–$115**	Smoking: **No**
Single/pb: **$75–$85**	Social Drinking: **Permitted**

Surrounded by maple, oak, and evergreen trees, this lovely English Tudor home is located minutes away from the famed Biltmore Estate and Gardens. The rooms have queen-size beds beautifully covered in fine linen. The window treatments and coordinated wall coverings could easily grace the pages of a decorating magazine. Handmade wreaths, weavings, and stitchery complement the furnishings. Breakfast specialties include orange French toast, blueberry-ricotta pancakes, or four-cheese-herb quiche. A living room fireplace, baby grand piano, outdoor deck, and Jacuzzi are among the gracious amenities.

Flint Street Inns ✪

100 & 116 FLINT STREET, ASHEVILLE, NORTH CAROLINA 28801

Tel: **(704) 253-6723**	Open: **All year**
Best Time to Call: **9 AM–9 PM**	Breakfast: **Full**
Hosts: **Rick, Lynne, and Marion Vogel**	Credit Cards: **AMEX, DISC, MC, VISA**
Location: **¼ mi. from Rte. 240**	Pets: **No**
No. of Rooms: 8	Children: **No**
No. of Private Baths: 8	Smoking: **Permitted**
Double/pb: **$95**	Social Drinking: **Permitted**
Single/pb: **$75**	

These two early twentieth-century homes located on an acre of land with stately old trees, flower gardens, and a fish pond offer the best in bed & breakfast accommodations. Guest rooms are furnished with antiques, quilts, and colored wallpaper; some have working fireplaces. Each room has special touches such as fresh flowers and reading material. Flint Street lies within walking distance to the historic Art Deco downtown area, where you will find excellent restaurants, sidewalk cafes, bookstores, antique shops, and arts and craft galleries. Breakfast may include orange cinnamon French toast, cheese sausage balls, vegetable egg casserole, eggs to order, a variety of cereals, fresh fruit, and inn-baked breads. Also offered are complimentary beverages. For those who enjoy sweets, a selection of baked treats is always available.

The Banner Elk Inn Bed & Breakfast ✪

407 MAIN STREET EAST, HIGHWAY 194 NORTH, BANNER ELK, NORTH CAROLINA 28604

Tel: **(704) 898-6223**
Best Time to Call: **9 AM–10 PM**
Host: **Beverly Lait**
Location: **17 mi. W of Boone**
No. of Rooms: **5**
No. of Private Baths: **4**
Double/pb: **$80–$115**
Single/pb: **$70–$110**
Suites: **$140–$160; sleeps 4**
Open: **All year**
Reduced Rates: **Available**
Breakfast: **Full, weekend; continental, weekdays**

Credit Cards: **MC, VISA**
Pets: **Yes**
Children: **Welcome, Sun.–Thurs.; over 6, weekends**
Smoking: **No**
Social Drinking: **Permitted**
Minimum Stay: **Mid-July; first 2 weeks of Oct.; ski season Dec. 25–Mar. 30; 2 nights weekends**
Foreign Languages: **Spanish, German**

Your host, Beverly, spent years with the Foreign Service, and original tapestries, artwork, and antiques from around the world fill her stunningly renovated historic home. The Inn is located halfway between the Sugar Resort and Beech Mountain ski slopes, near such major tourist attractions as Grandfather Mountain and Natural Habitat, Linville Falls, Valle Crucis, and the Blue Ridge Parkway. You'll have energy to visit all these places after Beverly's full breakfasts of homemade breads, eggs, fruit, juice, and coffee or tea. We now have a third-floor loft with a private bath.

Delamar Inn ✪

217 TURNER STREET, BEAUFORT, NORTH CAROLINA 28516
www.bbonline.com/nc/ncbbi/

Tel: **(919) 728-4300; (800) 349-5823**	Open: **All year**
Best Time to Call: **Anytime**	Breakfast: **Continental, plus**
Hosts: **Tom and Mabel Steepy**	Credit Cards: **MC, VISA**
Location: **140 mi. SE of Raleigh**	Pets: **No**
No. of Rooms: **4**	Children: **Welcome, over 10**
No. of Private Baths: **4**	Smoking: **Restricted**
Double/pb: **$78–$108**	Social Drinking: **Permitted**
Single/pb: **$72–$104**	Airport/Station Pickup: **Yes**

The Delamar Inn, built in 1866, is located in historic Beaufort, North Carolina's third oldest town. The Inn offers four guest rooms furnished with antiques, each room with a private bath. After a delightful breakfast, stroll down to the historic restoration grounds, maritime museum, or the open-air bus, or browse in the waterfront specialty shops. Tom and Mabel, your hosts, can offer directions to local beaches for shell collecting, sunbathing, or fishing. Try a short ride to Fort Macon, Tryon Palace, or the ferry to the Outer Banks. The Inn was selected for the '95 historic homes tour.

Maple Lodge

P. O. BOX 1236, 152 SUNSET DRIVE, BLOWING ROCK, NORTH CAROLINA 28605
innkeeper@maplelodge.net; www.maplelodge.net

Tel: **(828) 295-3331**	Hosts: **Marilyn and David Bateman**
Best Time to Call: **10 AM–9 PM**	No. of Rooms: **11**

No. of Private Baths: **11**
Double/pb: **$85–$150**
Suites: **$140–$150**
Open: **Mar. 1–Jan. 5**
Reduced Rates: **Available**
Breakfast: **Full**
Credit Cards: **AMEX, DISC, MC, VISA**

Pets: **No**
Children: **Welcome, over 12**
Smoking: **No**
Social Drinking: **Permitted**
Minimum Stay: **2 nights weekends and
    special occasions**

This charming inn reflects the simplicity and grace of the '30s and '40s. Guest rooms are furnished with antiques, handmade quilts, and goose-down comforters. Two parlors offer guests a homey atmosphere, complete thanks to the stone fireplace, old-timey pump organ, books, and games. Breakfast features fruits, cereals, home-baked breads and muffins, and a different main dish each day. Maple Lodge is within a short stroll to craft shops, art galleries, antiques, fine restaurants, and the Blowing Rock Stage Company, which performs during the summer. Outside town is the Blue Ridge Parkway and the Moses Cone Park; nearby is Grandfather Mountain, golf, canoeing, and white-water rafting.

Estes Mountain Retreat ✪
ROUTE 10, BOX 500, BURNSVILLE, NORTH CAROLINA 28714

Tel: **(828) 682-7264; (888) 272-9885**
Best Time to Call: **After 7 PM**
Hosts: **Bruce and Maryallen Estes**
Location: **37 mi. NE of Asheville**
No. of Rooms: **2**
No. of Private Baths: **2**
Double/pb: **$65**
Single/pb: **$55**
Open: **All year**

Reduced Rates: **15% Jan.–May; 10%
    seniors**
Breakfast: **Full**
Pets: **No**
Children: **Welcome, over 3**
Smoking: **No**
Social Drinking: **Permitted**
Foreign Languages: **French**

Breathtaking mountain views await you at this three-level cedar log home with a rock chimney, fireplace, and porches. Because Burnsville is in Pisgah National Forest, you won't have to travel far to go rafting, fishing, hiking, and rock and gem hunting, and golfing. Mt. Mitchell, Linville Caverns, outdoor theater, the Biltmore Mansion, and the Carl Sandburg Home are all within an hour's drive.

Hamrick Inn ✪
7787 HIGHWAY 80 SOUTH, BURNSVILLE, NORTH CAROLINA 28714

Tel: **(704) 675-5251**
Best Time to Call: **Mornings**
Hosts: **Neal and June Jerome**
Location: **55 mi. NE of Asheville; 16 mi.
    from I-40, Exit 72**
No. of Rooms: **4**
No. of Private Baths: **4**
Double/pb: **$70–$80**

Single/pb: **$65–$75**
Open: **Apr. 2–Oct. 31**
Reduced Rates: **Weekly**
Breakfast: **Full**
Pets: **No**
Children: **Welcome**
Smoking: **Permitted**
Social Drinking: **Permitted**

This charming three-story Colonial-style stone Inn is nestled at the foot of Mt. Mitchell, the highest mountain east of the Mississippi River. Much of the lovely furniture was built by Neal and June. The den has a fine selection of books as well as a TV set for your enjoyment. There is a private porch off each bedroom, where you may take in the view and the cool mountain breezes. Golfing, hiking, fishing, rock hounding, crafts shopping, and fall foliage wandering are local activities. Pisgah National Park, Linville Caverns, Crabtree Meadows, and the Parkway Playhouse are area diversions.

Little Toe-Hold B&B ✪
873 SOUTH TOE RIVER ROAD, BURNSVILLE, NORTH CAROLINA 28714

Tel: **(828) 675-5036**	Open: **All year**
Best Time to Call: **10 AM–9 PM**	Reduced Rates: **Weekly, 10% seniors**
Hosts: **Ursula and Jay Morse**	Breakfast: **Full**
Location: **55 mi. NE of Asheville**	Pets: **No**
No. of Rooms: **1**	Children: **No**
No. of Private Baths: **1**	Smoking: **No**
Double/pb: **$75**	Social Drinking: **Permitted**
Single/pb: **$70**	Foreign Languages: **German, Spanish,**
Suites: **$90**	**French**
Guest Cottage: **$180–$325**	

Set among rhododendrons and 80-foot pines, this lovely chalet home features a Great Room with a cathedral ceiling, 2-person Jacuzzi in the suite, antiques, objets d'art and paintings, and a library of books for your enjoyment. South-Toe-Hold is surrounded by two national parks, scenic South Toe River, and the Blue Ridge Parkway. You are invited to hike, swim, fish, water-tube, or gem-mine at Little Switzerland. Mt. Mitchell Golf Course is within walking distance. Nearby attractions include the Biltmore Estate, Penland Art School, Mt. Mitchell, and Grandfather Mountain with its Biosphere and bear habitat.

The Elizabeth Bed & Breakfast ✪
2145 EAST 5TH STREET, CHARLOTTE, NORTH CAROLINA 28204

Tel: **(704) 358-1368**	Suite: **$100–$105**
Best Time to Call: **Evening**	Open: **All year**
Host: **Joan Mastny**	Breakfast: **Full**
Location: **3 mi. from Rte I-77, Exit 10B**	Credit Cards: **MC, VISA**
No. of Rooms: **4**	Pets: **No**
No. of Private Baths: **4**	Children: **Welcome, over 12**
Double/pb: **$75–$95**	Smoking: **No**
Single/pb: **$70–$90**	Social Drinking: **Permitted**

This 1923 lavender "lady" is in historic Elizabeth, Charlotte's second oldest neighborhood. Rooms are decorated in European country style and are beautifully appointed with antiques, ceiling fans, decorator lin-

ens, and unique collections. All rooms have central air-conditioning; some have TV and phone. Guests may relax in the garden courtyard complete with a charming gazebo or stroll beneath giant oak trees to convenient restaurants and shopping.

The Homeplace Bed & Breakfast
5901 SARDIS ROAD, CHARLOTTE, NORTH CAROLINA 28270

Tel: **(704) 365-1936; fax: (704) 366-2729**

Best Time to Call: **9 AM–9 PM**
Hosts: **Peggy and Frank Dearien**

Location: **10 mi. from I-77; I-85**
No. of Rooms: **3**
No. of Private Baths: **3**
Double/pb: **$118**
Single/pb: **$98**
Suite: **$135**
Open: **All year**

Breakfast: **Full**
Credit Cards: **AMEX, MC, VISA**
Pets: **No**
Children: **Welcome, over 10**
Smoking: **No**
Social Drinking: **No**

Peggy and Frank established The Homeplace in 1984. Their B&B is a restored 1902 country Victorian home situated on two and a half wooded acres. This beautiful setting is located six miles from uptown Charlotte and three miles from major shopping areas. The interior offers ten-foot ceilings, heart-of-pinewood floors, double stairways, and spacious bedrooms with elegant decor. Your hosts' warm hospitality and breakfast will make your stay a memorable one.

Still Waters ✪
6221 AMOS SMITH ROAD, CHARLOTTE, NORTH CAROLINA 28214

Tel: **(704) 399-6299**
Best Time to Call: **Evenings**
Hosts: **Janet and Rob Dyer**
Location: **3 mi. W of Charlotte**
No. of Rooms: **4**
No. of Private Baths: **4**
Double/pb: **$55–$90**
Open: **All year**

Reduced Rates: **Available**
Breakfast: **Full**
Credit Cards: **MC, VISA**
Pets: **No**
Children: **Welcome**
Smoking: **No**
Social Drinking: **Permitted**

Relax on the river just outside Charlotte city limits—only minutes away from downtown, the airport, or the interstates, but a world away from the bustle of everyday life. Visit this lakefront log home on two wooded acres. Enjoy the deck, garden, dock, and boat ramp, or play on the sport court. Guests stay in either of two large rooms or in a suite. Full breakfasts always feature homemade sourdough rolls and fresh-ground coffee.

The Blooming Garden Inn ✪
513 HOLLOWAY STREET, DURHAM, NORTH CAROLINA 27701

Tel: **(919) 687-0801; fax: (919) 688-1401**
Best Time to Call: **Evenings**
Hosts: **Frank and Dolly Pokrass**
Location: **Downtown Durham**
No. of Rooms: **5**
No. of Private Baths: **5**
Double/pb: **$95–$115**
Suites: **$150–$185**

Open: **All year**
Reduced Rates: **Corporate**
Breakfast: **Full**
Credit Cards: **AMEX, DC, DISC, MC, VISA**
Pets: **No**
Children: **Welcome**
Smoking: **No**
Social Drinking: **Permitted**

If you appreciate flowers—and who doesn't?—you'll love staying at this restored 1892 Victorian with glorious gardens at every turn. The house is handsome, too, with its gabled roof, beveled and stained glass windows, and wraparound porch supported by Tuscan columns. What's more, you're right in the center of Durham's historic Holloway District, just moments from shops, superb restaurants, galleries, theaters, Duke University, and the University of North Carolina. For the ultimate in pampering, luxury suites with Jacuzzis big enough for two are available. A big feature at Blooming Garden Inn is the gourmet breakfast. Guests are offered a brief local tour by hosts, as well as Dolly Dollars to use in the special shop directly across from the inn, in the Holly House, the other restored Victorian, now available for extended stays at very attractive rates.

Blaine House ✪

661 HARRISON AVENUE, HIGHWAY 28 NORTH, FRANKLIN, NORTH CAROLINA 28734
blainebb@dnet.net; www.intertekweb.com/blainebb/

Tel: **(888) 349-4230**
Best Time to Call: **10 AM–8 PM**
Hosts: **Suzy Chandler and Karin Gorboff**
Location: **65 mi. SW of Asheville**
No. of Rooms: **4**
No. of Private Baths: **3**
Double/pb: **$69–$85**
Single/pb: **$60–$80**
Suites: **$95**
Open: **All year**

Reduced Rates: **10% Nov. 15–May 31**
Breakfast: **Full, Continental**
Credit Cards: **MC, VISA**
Pets: **No**
Children: **Welcome, over 12**
Smoking: **No**
Social Drinking: **Permitted**
Minimum Stay: **2 nights holiday weekends and in Oct.**
Foreign Languages: **French**

Suzy and Karen welcome you to their gracious historic home, where you will enjoy peace and tranquility amidst the beautiful mountains of western North Carolina. Blaine House reflects the grace and serenity that is reminiscent of homes of yesteryear. A true bed & breakfast, this 1920 home has been restored to its original state, revealing beautiful oak floors and beadboard ceilings and walls. Guest rooms are well appointed and thoughtfully decorated with curios and relics to enhance their individual distinctiveness. Awake to the aroma of a chef's choice breakfast that promises to be a truly memorable experience. The fact that Blaine House is a small, intimate B&B allows Suzy and Karin to pamper guests and attend to their every need.

Buttonwood Inn ✪
50 ADMIRAL DRIVE, FRANKLIN, NORTH CAROLINA 28734

Tel: **(888) 368-8895; (704) 369-8985**
Best Time to Call: **After 5 PM**
Host: **Liz Oehser**
Location: **75 mi. SW of Asheville**
No. of Rooms: **4**
No. of Private Baths: **4**
Double/pb: **$65–$90**

Single/pb: **$60**
Open: **All year**
Breakfast: **Full**
Pets: **No**
Children: **Welcome, over 10**
Smoking: **Permitted**
Social Drinking: **Permitted**

Enhanced by a mountain skyline, this recently renovated inn awaits guests with a warm, cozy country welcome. Rooms are decorated with antiques, quilts made by your host's aunt, country pieces, collectibles, and crafts, many of which are offered for sale. The common room and guest room feature pinewide plank flooring. Breakfast may include delights such as puffy scrambled egg crêpes, stuffed French toast, egg souffles, apple sausage ring, homemade breads, muffins and scones, and house specialties—blintz soufflé or Dutch baby. At an altitude of 2150 feet, Franklin is a short drive from the Blue Ridge and Smokey Mountain Parkways, Biltmore Estate in Asheville, hiking, gem mining, horseback riding, white water rafting, and antique and craft shopping.

Heritage Inn ✪
43 HERITAGE HOLLOW, FRANKLIN, NORTH CAROLINA 28734

Tel: **(828) 524-4150; (888) 524-4150**
Best Time to Call: **3–9 PM**
Host: **Tina and Jim Bottomley**
Location: **135 mi. NE Atlanta, Georgia**
No. of Rooms: **6**
No. of Private Baths: **6**
Double/pb: **$65–$85**
Single/pb: **$55–$75**
Open: **All year**

Breakfast: **Full, Continental**
Pets: **No**
Children: **Welcome, over 14**
Smoking: **No**
Social Drinking: **Permitted**
Minimum Stay: **2 nights, holiday and October weekends**
Airport Pickup: **By arrangement**

Rocking on the veranda over a cascading waterfall is one of the favorite pastimes at this tin-roofed, in-town country inn. Nestled in the Smoky Mountains tall pines, it is close to gem mining, white-water rafting, hiking trails, and country auctions, within walking distance of museums, mountain crafts and antique shops. Each immaculate, tastefully furnished room has its own entrance and porch for added privacy. Kitchenettes are available. A full breakfast and evening dessert are served. Complimentary beverages are offered throughout the day and evening.

The Waverly Inn ✪

783 NORTH MAIN STREET, HENDERSONVILLE, NORTH CAROLINA 28792
jsheiry@aol.com

Tel: **(800) 537-8195; (704) 693-9193; fax: (704) 692-1010**	Open: **All year**
	Reduced Rates: **Off-season**
Best Time to Call: **9:30 AM–10 PM**	Breakfast: **Full**
Hosts: **John and Diane Sheiry**	Credit Cards: **AMEX, DISC, MC, VISA**
Location: **20 mi. S of Asheville**	Pets: **No**
No. of Rooms: **14**	Children: **Welcome**
No. of Private Baths: **14**	Smoking: **Restricted**
Double/pb: **$79–$149**	Social Drinking: **Permitted**
Single/pb: **$79**	

Built as a boardinghouse in 1898, the Waverly is distinguished by its handsome Eastlake staircase—a factor that earned the Inn a listing on the National Register of Historic Places. Furnishings like four-poster canopy beds and claw-footed tubs combine Victorian stateliness and Colonial Revival charm. You'll walk away sated from all-you-can-eat breakfasts of pancakes and French toast. Noteworthy local sites include the Biltmore Estate, the Carl Sandburg house, the Blue Ridge Parkway, and the Flat Rock Playhouse.

Colonial Pines Inn ✪

541 HICKORY STREET, HIGHLANDS, NORTH CAROLINA 28741

Tel: **(704) 526-2060**	Guest Cottages: **$105–$250; sleep 4–6**
Best Time to Call: **Afternoons**	Open: **All year**
Hosts: **Chris and Donna Alley**	Reduced Rates: **Winter**
Location: **80 mi. SW of Asheville**	Breakfast: **Full**
No. of Rooms: **7**	Credit Cards: **MC, VISA**
No. of Private Baths: **7**	Pets: **No**
Double/pb: **$80–$120**	Children: **Welcome, in cottage only**
Single/pb: **$70–$105**	Smoking: **No**
Suites: **$110–$140**	Social Drinking: **Permitted**

Located in a charming, uncommercial mountain resort town, this white Colonial is flanked by tall columns and is surrounded by two acres. The scenic view may be enjoyed from comfortable rocking chairs on the wide veranda. Donna, a former interior decorator, has furnished the Inn with antiques, art, and interesting accessories. Chris is a classical guitarist, woodworker, and great cook. The hearty breakfast includes a variety of homemade breads, and a guest pantry is stocked with afternoon refreshments.

The Guest House ✪
1436 NORTH 4TH STREET (HWYE 64), HIGHLANDS, NORTH CAROLINA 28741

Tel: **(704) 526-4536**
Best Time to Call: **9 AM–9 PM**
Host: **Juanita Hernandez**
Location: **100 mi. NE of Atlanta**
No. of Rooms: **4**
No. of Private Baths: **4**
Double/pb: **$85–$105**
Open: **All year**
Reduced Rates: **Available**

Breakfast: **Full**
Credit Cards: **MC, VISA**
Pets: **No**
Smoking: **No**
Social Drinking: **Permitted**
Minimum Stay: **Weekends July–Sept., holidays, and Oct.**
Foreign Languages: **Spanish, German**

A charming Alpine-style mountain chalet nestled among stately trees, this B&B is more ample than its compact looks suggest. Inside you'll admire the plush, cream-colored carpeting, chestnut paneling, light wall coverings, teakwood furniture, and native stone fireplace. Deep contemporary seats invite guests to slip off their shoes and relax. Partake of the spectacular view from the open deck, with its sun umbrella and rocking chairs. After a restful night in your tastefully decorated room—accented with Juanita's artistic touches—you'll wake up to one of her superb breakfasts.

Lakeside Inn ✪
1921 FRANKLIN ROAD, HIGHLANDS, NORTH CAROLINA 28741

Tel: **(828) 526-4498**
Best Time to Call: **After 6 PM**
Hosts: **Cathy and Hank Ross**
Location: **120 mi. NE of Atlanta**
No. of Rooms: **4**
No. of Private Baths: **4**

Double/pb: **$105–$115**
Single/pb: **$100–$110**
Open: **All year**
Breakfast: **Full, Continental**
Credit Cards: **MC, VISA**
Pets: **No**

Children: **Welcome**
Smoking: **No**
Social Drinking: **Permitted**

Minimum Stay: **June–Oct. 2 nights,
weekends**

Nestled among the oaks and hemlocks, Lakeside Inn has a lovely view of Lake Sequoyah and borders the Nantahala National Forest. You can enjoy the scenery from the patio of this restored 1930s lodge or use the canoe that is provided by your hosts for a leisurely ride. Lakeside Inn offers cozy rooms and has a common area with a fireplace, cable TV, books and games. Breakfast entrees include French toast, burritos, fresh fruits, and freshly baked muffins. Area activities range from hiking, horseback riding, mountain biking, fishing, rappelling, and white-water rafting to enjoying the quaint town of Highlands.

Ye Olde Stone House ✪
**1337 SOUTH FOURTH STREET, HIGHLANDS,
NORTH CAROLINA 28741**

Tel: **(828) 526-5911**
Best Time to Call: **Afternoon; evening**
Hosts: **Jim and Rene Ramsdell**
Location: **80 mi. SW of Asheville**
No. of Rooms: **4**
No. of Private Baths: **4**
Double/pb: **$80–$95**
Single/pb: **$70**
Chalet: **$105–$125, sleeps 4**
Guest Cabin: **$140–$190, sleeps 7**

Open: **All year**
Reduced Rates: **Available**
Breakfast: **Full**
Credit Cards: **MC, VISA**
Pets: **No**
Children: **Welcome**
Smoking: **Restricted**
Social Drinking: **Permitted**
Minimum Stay: **Holidays, peak
weekends**

Ye Olde Stone House is built of stones and hidden in a vale surrounded by giant hemlocks and native flowers. Enjoy a touch of yesterday as you relax and unwind from everyday cares. Amenities include a cozy glassed-in gazebo, two sitting rooms with fireplaces, rockers on the front deck that allow you to take in mountain views, a guest refrigerator, and snacks. Rooms are attractively furnished in an appealing blend of family treasures, antiques, and collectibles. Savor a delicious breakfast you'll long remember, including seasonal fruits, enticing entrees, and homemade breads.

The Pines Plantation Inn ✪
**1570 LILLY'S BRIDGE ROAD, MOUNT GILEAD,
NORTH CAROLINA 27306
www.bestinns.net/usa/NC/pines.html**

Tel: **(800) 711-1134; (910) 439-1894**
Hosts: **Carol and Don Day**
Location: **50 mi. E of Charlotte**
No. of Rooms: **5**
No. of Private Baths: **5**
Double/pb: **$60–$80**

Open: **All year**
Reduced Rates: **10% corporate,
multiple rooms; 5th night free**
Breakfast: **Full**
Credit Cards: **MC, VISA**
Pets: **Sometimes**

Children: **Welcome, over 8**   Social Drinking: **Permitted**
Smoking: **No**

On beautiful, unspoiled Lake Tillery on the western edge of the Uwharrie National Forest, you'll find this 1878 antique-filled mansion house, once the center of a 1500-acre working plantation. The house has 14-foot ceilings, an elegant staircase, and beautifully appointed guest rooms—most with fireplaces. Guests are invited to enjoy the sunroom, library, parlor, and dining room. Take a stroll on the beautiful grounds or relax on one of the quiet porches. Nearby attractions include Lake Tillery, Morrow Mountain State Park, Town Creek Indian Mounds, Reed Gold Mine, Charlotte Motor Speedway, and Seagrove pottery shops.

New Berne House Bed and Breakfast Inn ○

709 BROAD STREET, NEW BERN, NORTH CAROLINA 28560

Tel: **(919) 636-2250; (800) 842-7688**
Hosts: **Marcia Drum and**
  Howard Bronson
Location: **1 mi. from Hwy. 70**
No. of Rooms: **7**
No. of Private Baths: **7**
Double/pb: **$88**
Single/pb: **$68**
Open: **All year**

Reduced Rates: **AAA, AARP**
Breakfast: **Full**
Credit Cards: **AMEX, MC, VISA**
Pets: **No**
Children: **Welcome, over 12**
Smoking: **No**
Social Drinking: **Permitted**
Airport/Station Pickup: **Yes**

Located in the heart of New Bern's historic district, this brick Colonial is furnished in the style of an English country manor with a mixture of antiques, traditional pieces, and attic treasures. Guests are pampered with afternoon tea or coffee served in the parlor. A sweeping stairway leads upstairs to romantic bedchambers, one with a brass bed reportedly rescued in 1897 from a burning brothel. Breakfast specialties such as praline and cream waffles, honey-glazed ham, and homemade breads and muffins are served in the dining room. New Berne House is within walking distance of Tryon Palace, North Carolina's Colonial capitol, and the governor's mansion. Ask about the exciting Mystery Weekends.

Key Falls Inn ○

151 EVERETT ROAD, PISGAH FOREST, NORTH CAROLINA 28768

Tel: **(704) 884-7559**
Best Time to Call: **9 AM–9 PM**
Hosts: **Clark and Patricia Grosvenor,**
  and Janet Fogleman
No. of Rooms: **4**
No. of Private Baths: **4**
Double/pb: **$60–$85**
Single/pb: **$60–$75**

Suites: **$75–$95**
Open: **All year**
Breakfast: **Full**
Credit Cards: **AMEX, DC, MC, VISA**
Pets: **No**
Children: **Welcome, over 12**
Smoking: **No**
Social Drinking: **Permitted**

Visitors to this B&B will be able to make the most of western North Carolina's natural and cultural attractions. Key Falls Inn is situated on a 28-acre estate with its own tennis court, pond, and outdoor barbecue. For quieter moments, sit on one of the porches and enjoy the mountain views. Music lovers will want to get tickets to the acclaimed Brevard Festival, an annual summer event.

Breakfast Creek ✪
4361 OCEAN BREEZE AVENUE SW, SHALLOTTE, NORTH CAROLINA 28470

Tel: **(888) 754-3614**	Suite: **$75**
Best Time to Call: **Mornings**	Open: **All year**
Hosts: **Tim Tryon and Diana Turtle**	Breakfast: **Full**
Location: **35 mi. S of Wilmington**	Pets: **No**
No. of Rooms: **3**	Children: **Welcome**
No. of Private Baths: **2**	Smoking: **No**
Max. No. Sharing Bath: **4**	Social Drinking: **Permitted**
Double/pb: **$60**	

Breakfast Creek is a modest white brick house filled with sunlight and antiques. It overlooks the Atlantic Ocean, Shallotte Inlet, Intracoastal Waterway, and acres of living wetlands. Diana is a devoted gardener, Tim is a musician and woodworker; both love sailing and the beach. The B&B is located fifteen minutes from Ocean Isle, and twenty minutes from Holden Beach, Calabash, Southport, Fort Fisher, Wilmington, and the Grand Strand. None of these are reachable without passing at least one golf course. During his first visit, a guest said, "It's like staying with friends at the beach without the sand."

Turby Villa B&B ✪
2072 NC HIGHWAY 18 NORTH, SPARTA, NORTH CAROLINA 28675

Tel: **(336) 372-8490**	Open: **All year**
Host: **Mrs. Maybelline Turbiville**	Breakfast: **Full**
No. of Rooms: **3**	Pets: **No**
No. of Private Baths: **3**	Children: **Welcome**
Double/pb: **$50**	Smoking: **Permitted**
Single/pb: **$35**	Social Drinking: **Permitted**

At an altitude of 3000 feet, this contemporary two-story brick home is the centerpiece of a 20-acre farm. The house is surrounded by an acre of trees and manicured lawns, and the lovely views are of the scenic Blue Ridge Mountains. Breakfast is served either on the enclosed porch with its white wicker furnishings or in the more formal dining room with its Early American–style furnishings. Mrs. Turbiville takes justifiable pride in her attractive, well-maintained B&B.

Cedar Hill Farm B&B ✪
778 ELMWOOD ROAD, STATESVILLE, NORTH CAROLINA 28625

Tel: **(704) 873-4332; (800) 948-4423**
Hosts: **Brenda and Jim Vernon**
Location: **45 mi. N of Charlotte**
No. of Rooms: **3**
No. of Private Baths: **3**
Double/pb: **$70**
Guest Cottages: **$85–$95**

Open: **All year**
Breakfast: **Full**
Credit Cards: **AMEX, MC, VISA**
Pets: **Sometimes**
Children: **Welcome**
Smoking: **No**
Social Drinking: **Permitted**

A three-story Federal farmhouse furnished with antique and country pieces, Cedar Hill is surrounded by 32 acres of rolling green, the better to feed the Vernons' sheep. Brenda and Jim sell fleece coverlets and crafts from their own hand-spun wool; they also make furniture and cure turkey and ham in a smokehouse on site. Stay in the farmhouse or in the private cottages. Either way you'll have an air-conditioned room with a telephone and cable TV. The country breakfasts will leave you full. You can work off calories swimming in your hosts' pool or playing badminton, but you might want to relax in a porch rocker or hammock first. The cottages now have working fireplaces.

Scott's Keep ✪
308 WALNUT STREET, SWANSBORO, NORTH CAROLINA 28584

Tel: **(910) 326-1257; (800) 348-1257**
Best Time to Call: **Anytime**
Hosts: **Frank and Norma Scott**
Location: **150 mi. SE of Raleigh**
No. of Rooms: **3**
Max. No. Sharing Bath: **4**
Double/pb: **$60**
Double/sb: **$50**
Open: **All year**

Reduced Rates: **15% weekly**
Breakfast: **Full**
Credit Cards: **AMEX, DISC, MC, VISA**
Pets: **No**
Children: **Welcome, over 6**
Smoking: **No**
Social Drinking: **Permitted**
Minimum Stay: **2 nights, May 15–Sept. 15 weekends**

This simple contemporary is located on a quiet street two blocks from the waterfront. Your hosts want you to feel right at home in the bright, spacious living room and comfortable guest rooms. The larger bedroom is decorated with wicker and features an antique trunk, queen-size bed, and colorful quilts. The smaller bedroom is furnished in classic maple with twin beds and grandmother's quilts. For breakfast, Norma serves blueberry or apple spice muffins with fruit and homemade jellies. This historic seaside village is filled with inviting shops and waterside seafood restaurants. Your hosts will point the way to beautiful beaches, waterskiing, sailing, and windsurfing.

Four Rooster Inn ✪
**403 PIREWAY ROAD, ROUTE 904, TABOR CITY,
NORTH CAROLINA 28463**

Tel: **(910) 653-3878; (800) 653-5008**
Hosts: **Gloria and Bob Rogers**
Location: **24 mi. NW of Myrtle Beach,
South Carolina; 45 min. from I-95**
No. of Rooms: **4**
No. of Private Baths: **2**
Max. No. Sharing Bath: **4**
Double/pb: **$70–$80**
Single/pb: **$65–$75**
Double/sb: **$65**
Single/sb: **$55**

Open: **All year**
Reduced Rates: **Fifth night free**
Breakfast: **Full**
Credit Cards: **AMEX, DC, DISC, MC,
VISA**
Pets: **No**
Children: **Welcome, by arrangement**
Smoking: **No**
Social Drinking: **Permitted**
Airport/Station Pickup: **Yes**

Experience the warm, gracious hospitality of the old South in the charm of a country setting. The Inn has been restored to a comfortable elegance with china, crystal, antiques, beautiful fabrics and fine linens. Amenities include afternoon tea, evening turn-down service accented with chocolates, and coffee or tea at your door when you awake. A full breakfast is served in the dining room and may include yam bread, French toast, or eggs Benedict. The Four Rooster Inn is located forty-five minutes from Interstate 95 and a short drive from Myrtle Beach golf courses, Waccamaw Pottery shopping, Brookgreen Gardens, and historic Wilmington. The Inn provides a comfortable haven whether you are traveling for business or pleasure. Gloria and Bob are dedicated to the art of service for their guests.

Little Warren ✪
304 EAST PARK AVENUE, TARBORO, NORTH CAROLINA 27886

Tel: **(919) 823-1314; (800) 309-1314**
Hosts: **Patsy and Tom Miller**

Location: **Easy access from I-95**
No. of Rooms: **3**

No. of Private Baths: **3**
Double/pb: **$65**
Single/pb: **$58**
Open: **All year**
Reduced Rates: **Corporate, upon request**
Breakfast: **Full**

Credit Cards: **AMEX, DISC, MC, VISA**
Pets: **No**
Children: **Welcome, over 6**
Smoking: **Permitted**
Social Drinking: **Permitted**
Foreign Languages: **Spanish**

Established in 1984, Little Warren is actually a large and gracious family home built in 1913. It is located along the Albemarle Trail in Tarboro's historic district. The deeply set, wraparound porch overlooks one of the last originally chartered town commons still in existence. Inside, you'll find rooms of beautiful antiques from England, Africa, and America. In the morning, choose from a full English, Southern, or expanded Continental breakfast.

Acadian House Bed & Breakfast ✪

129 VAN NORDEN STREET, WASHINGTON, NORTH CAROLINA 27889

Tel: **(919) 975-3967**
Best Time to Call: **Mornings and evenings**
Hosts: **Johanna and Leonard Huber**
Location: **105 mi. E of Raleigh**
No. of Rooms: **4**
No. of Private Baths: **4**
Double/pb: **$55–$65**

Suites: **$100**
Open: **Feb. 1–Dec. 14**
Breakfast: **Full**
Credit Cards: **AMEX, DISC, MC, VISA**
Pets: **No**
Children: **Welcome, over 12**
Smoking: **No**
Social Drinking: **Permitted**

Acadian House Bed & Breakfast, a 1900 home located in Colonial Washington, features a unique herringbone-patterned brick porch. It is decorated throughout with antiques and local crafts. A Victorian staircase leads to guest rooms and the library, where books and games are provided. Johanna and Leonard, transplanted New Orleanians, serve a full breakfast featuring southern Louisiana Acadian specialties such as beignets and café au lait along with traditional breakfast foods. Acadian House is one block from the scenic Pamlico River; museums and antique shops are nearby. The business traveler will find a writing table, telephone, and fax available. Copying facilities are also nearby.

Pamlico House ✪

400 EAST MAIN STREET, WASHINGTON, NORTH CAROLINA 27889
pamlicohouse@coastalnet.com; www.bbonline.com/nc/pamlico/

Tel: **(919) 946-7184; fax: (919) 946-9944**
Hosts: **Jane and George Fields**
Location: **20 mi. E of Greenville**
No. of Rooms: **4**
No. of Private Baths: **4**

Double/pb: **$75–$85**
Single/pb: **$65–$75**
Open: **All year**
Breakfast: **Full**
Credit Cards: **AMEX, DISC, MC, VISA**
Pets: **No**

Children: **Welcome, over 6**   Social Drinking: **Permitted**
Smoking: **No**

Pamlico House is where tourists, sweethearts, and business travelers all relish their stay. Stroll along the waterfront; explore the historic district with houses dating from the 1790s, one still showing scars of the Civil War. Rock on the wrap-around front porch, or enjoy the wicker furniture in the room where Charles Kuralt slept. Explore the unique Estuarium and Goose Creek State Park, rent a kayak, go antiquing, or visit the other historic towns nearby. At breakfast indulge yourself with French toast, waffles with strawberries and cream, or Norwegian pancakes.

Belle Meade Inn ✪

**1534 SOUTH MAIN STREET, WAYNESVILLE,
NORTH CAROLINA 28786**

Tel: **(704) 456-3234**	Reduced Rates: **10% AARP; weekly**
Hosts: **Gloria and Al DiNofa**	Breakfast: **Full**
Location: **27 mi. W of Asheville**	Credit Cards: **DISC, MC, VISA**
No. of Rooms: **4**	Pets: **No**
No. of Private Baths: **4**	Children: **Welcome, over 6**
Double/pb: **$70–$75**	Smoking: **No**
Single/pb: **$60–$65**	Social Drinking: **Permitted**
Open: **All year**	

Nestled in the mountains, and within easy reach of the Great Smoky National Park, this elegant home is a frame dwelling built in the craftsman style popular in the early 1900s. The warm richness of the chestnut woodwork in the formal rooms and the large stone fireplace in the living room complement the appealing blend of antique and traditional furnishings. The friendly attention to guests' needs is exemplified in such thoughtful touches as "early bird" coffee brought to your door, complimentary refreshments on the veranda, and fresh flowers and mints in your room. Nearby attractions include Biltmore House, Catalooche Ski Slope, mountain art and crafts festivals, and white-water rafting and tubing.

Weldon Place Inn ✪
500 WASHINGTON AVENUE, WELDON, NORTH CAROLINA 27890

Tel: (252) 536-4582; (800) 831-4470	Open: All year
Best Time to Call: Before 9 PM	Reduced Rates: Available
Hosts: Angel and Andy Whitby	Breakfast: Full
Location: 2 mi. E of I-95, exit 173	Credit Cards: AMEX, MC, VISA
No. of Rooms: 4	Pets: No
No. of Private Baths: 4	Children: Welcome, over 12
Double/pb: $65–$99	Smoking: Restricted
Single/pb: $60–$70	Social Drinking: No

This home away from home is centrally located between New York and Florida. Sleep in a canopy bed and awake to the sound of singing sparrows; after breakfast, stroll through the National Registered Historic District. At Weldon Place Inn your peace of mind begins with personal attention to ensure you the ultimate in solitude and relaxation. Select the romantic retreat package and you'll enjoy sparkling cider, a whirlpool tub, and breakfast in bed. Local attractions include a state historic site, the early canal system, River Overlook of the rapids, and the railroad.

Anderson Guest House ✪
520 ORANGE STREET, WILMINGTON, NORTH CAROLINA 28401

Tel: (910) 343-8128	Open: All year
Best Time to Call: 8 AM–5 PM	Breakfast: Full
Hosts: Landon and Connie Anderson	Pets: Sometimes
No. of Rooms: 2	Children: Welcome
No. of Private Baths: 2	Smoking: No
Double/pb: $85	Social Drinking: Permitted
Single/pb: $65	Airport/Station Pickup: Yes

This 19th-century town house has a private guest house overlooking a garden. The bedrooms have ceiling fans, fireplaces, and air-conditioning. Enjoy cool drinks upon arrival and a liqueur before bed. Breakfast specialties are eggs Mornay, blueberry cobbler, and crepes. Your hosts can point out the sights of this historic town and direct you to the beaches.

Live Oaks Bed & Breakfast ✪

318 SOUTH 3RD STREET, WILMINGTON, NORTH CAROLINA 28401

Tel: **(910) 762-6733**
Best Time to Call: **9 AM–8 PM**
Hosts: **Margi and Doug Erickson**
Location: **98 mi. E of Raleigh**
No. of Rooms: **3**
No. of Private Baths: **3**
Double/pb: **$95–$115**
Open: **All year**
Reduced Rates: **Available**

Breakfast: **Full**
Credit Cards: **DC, DISC, MC, VISA**
Pets: **Sometimes**
Children: **Welcome, over 12**
Smoking: **No**
Social Drinking: **Permitted**
Minimum Stay: **2 nights Apr.–Oct.;
festival weekends**
Airport Pickup: **Yes**

Built in 1883, this lovely restored Carpenter Gothic home welcomes you with Victorian-era charm. Located in the heart of Wilmington's Historic District, this B&B puts unique stores, restaurants, museums, galleries, antique shops and the Battleship USS *North Carolina* within walking distance. All guest rooms have queen-size beds. The Victorian Room has romantic appeal, while the Blue Room has a four-poster rice bed and wall-to-wall carpeting. The Garden Room, with its own private entrance, is a cozy retreat. The first floor's twelve-foot ceilings boast original plaster molding, which has been restored. The grand Victorian parlor and dining room are finished with period pieces and antique reproductions. Breakfasts are sumptuous with fresh fruit, muffins, and a hot entree. Guest refrigerator and snacks are available.

Mickle House ✪

927 WEST FIFTH STREET, WINSTON-SALEM, NORTH CAROLINA 27101

Tel: **(336) 722-9045**
Best Time to Call: **10 AM–10 PM**
Host: **Barbara Garrison**

Location: **1 mi. from Rte. 40, Broad St.
exit**
No. of Rooms: **2**

No. of Private Baths: **2**
Double/pb: **$85–$95**
Single/pb: **$85–$95**
Open: **All year**
Breakfast: **Full**

Credit Cards: **MC, VISA**
Pets: **No**
Children: **No**
Smoking: **No**
Social Drinking: **Permitted**

Step back in time to visit a quaint Victorian cottage painted a soft yellow, with dark green shutters and gingerbread trim. The fully restored home, located in the National Historic District of West End, is furnished with lovely antiques, such as the canopy and poster beds in the guest rooms. Dessert is served in the afternoon or evening, and a full breakfast, with fresh fruit and freshly baked breads and muffins, awaits you in the morning. Old Salem, the Medical Center, and the Convention Center are five minutes away; fine restaurants, parks, shops, and the library are within easy walking distance.

For key to listings, see inside front or back cover.

✪ This star means that rates are guaranteed through December 31, 1999, to any guest making a reservation as a result of reading about the B&B in *Bed & Breakfast U.S.A.—*1999 edition.

Important! To avoid misunderstandings, always ask about cancellation policies when booking.

Please enclose a self-addressed, stamped, business-size envelope when contacting reservation services.

For more details on what you can expect in a B&B, see Chapter 1.

Always mention *Bed & Breakfast U.S.A.* when making reservations!

We want to hear from you! Use the form on page 593.

NORTH DAKOTA

.Stanley

The TTT Ranch ✪
93 TRIPLE T ROAD, STANLEY, NORTH DAKOTA 58784

Tel: **(701) 628-2418**
Hosts: **Joyce and Fred Evans**
Location: **60 mi. W of Minot**
No. of Rooms: **2**
Max. No. Sharing Bath: **4**
Double/sb: **$65**
Single/sb: **$40**

Open: **All year**
Reduced Rates: **Available**
Breakfast: **Full**
Pets: **No**
Children: **Welcome**
Smoking: **No**
Social Drinking: **No**

Get a taste of real country life at The TTT Ranch while enjoying the
sights and sounds of the natural world. The scenic vistas are unchanged
from those that lured explorers, ranchers, and homesteaders more than
a century ago. The ranch is nestled in the Little Knife River Valley. Its
waterway meanders through the broad valley, with spacious coulees
fanning out on either side. The valley provides abundant natural habitat for wildlife. The area is the outback of America, a paradise not only

for those who live here, but also for those who travel this way. This area enchanted members of the Lewis and Clark expedition. Lewis wrote in his journal on May 5, 1805, "The country is as yesterday, beautiful in the extreme."

For key to listings, see inside front or back cover.

✪ This star means that rates are guaranteed through December 31, 1999, to any guest making a reservation as a result of reading about the B&B in *Bed & Breakfast U.S.A.*—1999 edition.

Important! To avoid misunderstandings, always ask about cancellation policies when booking.

Please enclose a self-addressed, stamped, business-size envelope when contacting reservation services.

For more details on what you can expect in a B&B, see Chapter 1.

Always mention *Bed & Breakfast U.S.A.* when making reservations!

We want to hear from you! Use the form on page 593.

OHIO

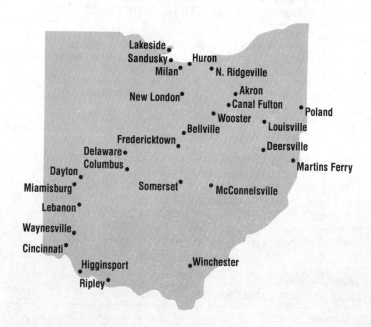

Helen's Hospitality House
1096 PALMETTO, AKRON, OHIO 44306

Tel: **(330) 724-7151; 724-3034**
Best Time to Call: **8 AM–11 PM**
Host: **Helen Claytor**
Location: **1 mi. from I-77 S, Exit 123B**
No. of Rooms: **2**
No. of Private Baths: **1**
Max. No. Sharing Bath: **4**
Double/pb: **$40**
Single/pb: **$35**
Double/sb: **$35**

Single/sb: **$30**
Open: **All year**
Reduced Rates: **Weekly**
Breakfast: **Full**
Pets: **No**
Children: **Welcome, over 10**
Smoking: **No**
Social Drinking: **Permitted**
Airport/Station Pickup: **Yes**

Located in a quiet neighborhood on a dead-end street, Helen's centrally air-conditioned house is a bit of country in the city. It is a renovated old farmhouse furnished with antiques and reproductions. On warm days, breakfast is served on the screened, glass-enclosed porch. Quaker Square, Akron University, the Firestone PGA, and Portage Lakes are just a few of the local attractions. Helen is a retired teacher who enjoys being a B&B hostess.

Portage House ✪
601 COPLEY ROAD, STATE ROUTE 162, AKRON, OHIO 44320

Tel: **(330) 535-1952**
Best Time to Call: **8 AM–11 PM**
Host: **Jeanne Pinnick**
Location: **2 mi. from I-77**
No. of Rooms: **4**
No. of Private Baths: **1**
Max. No. Sharing Bath: **3**
Double/pb: **$44**
Double/sb: **$36**

Single/sb: **$34**
Open: **Feb. 1–Nov. 30**
Reduced Rates: **$3 less after 1st night**
Breakfast: **Full**
Pets: **Restricted**
Children: **Welcome (crib)**
Smoking: **No**
Social Drinking: **Permitted**
Foreign Languages: **French, Spanish**

Steeped in history, this gracious Tudor home, nestled in a parklike setting, dates back to 1917. A stone wall down the street served as the western boundary of the United States in 1785. Jeanne and her late husband Harry, a physics professor at the nearby University of Akron, opened their B&B in 1982. Jeanne manages the B&B and has the coffeepot on with refreshments available for arriving guests. If bread is being baked, you'll be offered some hot out of the oven.

Pleasant Valley ✪
1226 HATHAWAY ROAD, BELLVILLE, OHIO 44813

Tel: **(419) 886-2366**
Hosts: **Dan and Antonia Reese**
Location: **60 mi. N of Columbus**
No. of Rooms: **5**
No. of Private Baths: **3**
Max. No. Sharing Bath: **4**
Double/pb: **$85**
Double/sb: **$75**
Suites: **$100–$140**

Open: **All year**
Breakfast: **Full**
Other Meals: **Available**
Credit Cards: **AMEX, MC, VISA**
Pets: **No**
Children: **Welcome, over 12**
Smoking: **No**
Social Drinking: **Permitted**

Enjoy the warmth and charm of Old World elegance with all the modern conveniences. The house is decorated with stained glass, oriental rugs, antiques, parquet floors, and art treasures collected from all over the world. Dan and Antonia own a landscaping business that is located on the premises. Guests will enjoy the beauty and variety of trees and shrubbery used for landscaping. You can enjoy relaxing in the privacy of your room, play croquet or badminton, swim in the pool, explore the forty acres of fields and woods, or browse in the Reeses' art- and antique-filled Castle Door Gallery. Breakfast is served in the dining area, around the pool, or on the screened porch.

Pleasant Hill—1845 ✪
451 EAST CHERRY STREET, CANAL FULTON, OHIO 44614

Tel: **(330) 854-0551**
Hosts: **Betty and Terry Stoffer**
Location: **15 mi. S of Akron**
No. of Rooms: **2**
Max. No. Sharing Bath: **4**
Double/sb: **$65**
Single/sb: **$55**

Open: **All year**
Reduced Rates: **10% after 3 nights**
Breakfast: **Full**
Credit Cards: **DISC, MC, VISA**
Pets: **No**
Children: **Welcome**
Smoking: **No**

Built in 1845 at the height of the canal era, Pleasant Hill provides a glimpse of an earlier time. Lovingly restored in 1993 and located in Canal Fulton's National Register Historic District, this Greek Revival home offers warm hospitality along with the comfort of air-conditioning and in-room color cable TV. Enjoy a walk around the village, visit the shops, ride the canal boat, see the museums, then relax with a glass of iced tea on the veranda. Breakfast includes juice, fruit, hearty main dishes, and home-baked breads and muffins.

Prospect Hill Bed and Breakfast
408 BOAL STREET, CINCINNATI, OHIO 45210

Tel: **(513) 421-4408**
Best Time to Call: **10 AM–8 PM**
Hosts: **Gary Hackney and Tony Jenkins**
Location: **Downtown**
No. of Rooms: **4**
No. of Private Baths: **2**

Max. No. Sharing Bath: **4**
Double/pb: **$99–$129**
Single/pb: **$99–$129**
Double/sb: **$89–$109**
Single/sb: **$89–$109**
Open: **All year**

Reduced Rates: **10% weekly**
Breakfast: **Full**
Pets: **No**

Children: **Welcome, over 10**
Smoking: **No**
Social Drinking: **Permitted**

This restored Italianate Victorian town house was built in 1867 on Prospect Hill, Cincinnati's first suburb, now a national historic district. The original woodwork, doors, hardware, and light fixtures remain intact—your hosts are interested in historic preservation. All the rooms have spectacular views, fireplaces, and period antique furniture. It's only a fifteen-minute walk from here to Fountain Square or the Ohio River. Mt. Adams, the University of Cincinnati, Playhouse in the Park, the Music Hall, Eden Park, the William Howard Taft Historic Site, and most area museums and hospitals are within a mile.

Shamrock B&B ✪
5657 SUNBURY ROAD, COLUMBUS, OHIO 43230

Tel: **(614) 337-9849**
Best Time to Call: **8 AM–10 PM**
Host: **Tom McLaughlin**
Location: **½ mi. from I-270 Exit 30B #161**
No. of Rooms: **2**
No. of Private Baths: **2**
Double/pb: **$60**
Single/pb: **$50**
Open: **All year**

Reduced Rates: **5% seniors; 10% over 4 days**
Breakfast: **Full**
Other meals: **Available**
Pets: **Sometimes**
Children: **Welcome, over 10**
Smoking: **No**
Social Drinking: **Permitted**
Airport Pickup: **Yes**

Shamrock B&B is situated on one and a quarter acres of woods in the northeastern Columbus area. A host of attractions lie nearby: shopping malls, cinemas, Hoover Dam, Inniswoods Botanical Gardens, Busch Brewery, Ohio Historical Village, Short North Gallery Hop, German Village, the Polaris Amphitheatre, and Ohio State University. Tom is a retired schoolteacher who loves gardening and travel, and his brick home is filled with 18th-century antiques and original art. Guest areas are on the first floor, so this B&B is wheelchair accessible.

Candlewick Bed & Breakfast ✪
4991 BATH ROAD, DAYTON, OHIO 45424

Tel: **(937) 233-9297**
Hosts: **George and Nancy Thompson**
Location: **10 mi. NE of Dayton**
No. of Rooms: **2**
Max. No. Sharing Bath: **4**
Double/sb: **$55–$60**
Single/sb: **$45**

Open: **All year**
Breakfast: **Full**
Pets: **No**
Children: **No**
Smoking: **No**
Social Drinking: **No**
Airport Pickup: **Yes**

This tranquil Dutch Colonial home sits atop a hill on five rolling acres. George, a retired engineer, and Nancy, a retired teacher, invite you to spend a quiet, restful night in comfortable rooms containing a charming blend of antiques and Colonial and country furnishings. A full breakfast includes fresh fruit and juice, choice homemade pastries, and freshly brewed coffee. Weather permitting, enjoy breakfast on the screened porch overlooking a large pond often visited by wild ducks and geese. Convenient to Wright-Patterson Air Force Base and Museum and two major universities, Candlewick is a peaceful retreat, perfect for either business or pleasure.

Mulberry Lane ✪
224 WEST MAIN STREET, P.O. BOX 61, DEERSVILLE, OHIO 44693

Tel: **(740) 922-0425**	Double/sb: **$60**
Best Time to Call: **9 AM–5 PM**	Single/sb: **$55**
Hosts: **Dick and Ferrel Zeimer**	Open: **All year**
Location: **90 mi. S of Cleveland**	Breakfast: **Full**
No. of Rooms: **3**	Pets: **No**
No. of Private Baths: **1**	Children: **No**
Max. No. Sharing Bath: **4**	Smoking: **No**
Double/pb: **$70**	Social Drinking: **Permitted**

Built in 1830, restored in 1989, and tastefully furnished with antiques and period pieces, Mulberry Lane is a great getaway place. Peaceful little Deersville lies between two large lakes where guests can go fishing and boating. Country auctions, antique shops, glass factories, the birthplaces of Clark Gable and General George Armstrong Custer, early Moravian settlements, and Amish country are all within reach. If you don't feel like touring, you're welcome to relax on the porch swing with a good book. Freshly baked muffins are always served at Dick and Ferrel's breakfasts in their country kitchen.

Welcome Home Inn ✪
6640 HOME ROAD, DELAWARE, OHIO 43015

Tel: **(740) 881-6588**	Single s/b: **$50–$60**
Best Time to Call: **Evenings**	Open: **All year**
Hosts: **Forrest and Brenda Williams**	Reduced Rates: **15% weekly**
No. of Rooms: **4**	Breakfast: **Full**
No. of Private Baths: **2**	Pets: **No**
Max. No. Sharing Bath: **4**	Children: **Welcome, over 10**
Double/pb: **$80–$95**	Smoking: **No**
Single/pb: **$70–$85**	Social Drinking: **No**
Double/sb: **$60–$70**	

Welcome Home Inn is a new Southern farmhouse, located on six wooded acres. Enjoy country tranquility, sit in a wicker chair, or swing on the big wraparound porch. Breakfast is served in the spacious dining room, accented by stained glass windows above a grand piano. Oak antiques accent much of the home. You might want to visit the nearby Columbus Zoo, Olentangy Indian Caverns, quaint Powell antique shops, and the Scioto River boat marina. Or drive to downtown Columbus, 30 minutes away, to see the State Capitol and surrounding attractions.

Heartland Country Resort ✪
2994 TOWNSHIP ROAD 190, FREDERICKTOWN, OHIO 43019

Tel: (800) 230-7030; (419) 768-9300
Best Time to Call: Day
Host: Dorene Henschen
Location: 40 mi. NE of Columbus
No. of Rooms: 7
No. of Private Baths: 7
Double/pb: $80–$175
Open: All year

Reduced Rates: 10% seniors, AAA, corporations, extended stays
Breakfast: Continental, plus
Other meals: Available
Credit Cards: DISC, MC, VISA
Children: Welcome
Smoking: No
Social Drinking: Permitted

At the Heartland Country Resort you can rent a horse, bring your own, or just watch others. The bed and breakfast is an inviting, restored 1878 farmhouse with a deck and screened porch. You will experience serenity in this 104-acre country setting with hills, streams, woods, wildlife, pastures, fields, and barns, which you can explore on foot or horseback. During every season, you can enjoy a petting zoo of farm animals and numerous recreation opportunities, both on and near the resort. The new log home suites have private Jacuzzis and glass-front stoves.

J. Dugan 1830 Ohio River House ✪
P.O. BOX 188, HIGGINSPORT, OHIO 45131

Tel: (937) 375-4395; fax: (937) 375-4394
Hosts: Andrew and Judy Lloyd
Location: 35 mi. E of Cincinnati, US Route 52
No. of Rooms: 5
No. of Private Baths: 3
Max. No. Sharing Bath: 4
Double/pb: $75
Single/pb: $65

Suites: $95
Open: All year
Reduced Rates: 10% seniors
Breakfast: Full
Credit Cards: MC, VISA
Pets: Welcome
Children: Welcome
Smoking: Restricted
Social Drinking: Permitted

J. Dugan 1830 Ohio River House Bed & Breakfast is surrounded by two acres of landscaped grounds with over 500 feet of private riverfront and a lovely terrace at the river's edge. This stately home boasts antique-filled guest and common rooms capturing the ambiance of the turn of the century. A family-style breakfast is served in the large, brick-floored kitchen. Guests can watch TV, read, or play cards in the spacious living room, decorated in a manner reminiscent of a riverboat casino.

Captain Montague's Bed & Breakfast ✪

229 CENTER STREET AT CLEVELAND ROAD, HURON, OHIO 44839
judytann@aol.com; www.innsandouts.com/inns/P208270.html

Tel: **(800) 276-4756; (419) 433-4756**
Hosts: **Judy and Mike Tann**
Location: **54 mi. W of Cleveland, 60 mi. E of Toledo**
No. of Rooms: **7**
No. of Private Baths: **7**
Double/pb: **$75–$140**
Suite: **Bridal $115–$150**
Open: **All year**

Reduced Rates: **Nov. 1–Mar. 31**
Breakfast: **Continental, plus**
Pets: **No**
Children: **No**
Smoking: **No**
Social Drinking: **Permitted**
Minimum Stay: **2 nights weekends, Memorial Day–Labor Day**

The Captain's is that perfect romantic retreat in a stately colonial manor that radiates Victorian charm. Experience a bygone era of lace, luster, and love. Nestled in the heart of Ohio's vacation land on the shores of Lake Erie, the Captain's is within minutes of golfing, nature preserves, boating, antiquing, Cedar Point Amusement Park, and the Lake Erie Islands. Enjoy the pool, latticed gazebo, and impeccable gardens. Discover the excitement of the Captain's themed weekends from November through March.

Idlewyld Bed & Breakfast ✪

350 WALNUT STREET, LAKESIDE, OHIO 43440 (MAILING ADDRESS: 17600 DETROIT #908, LAKEWOOD, OHIO 44107)

Tel: **(419) 798-4198; (216) 228-8168**
Hosts: **Dan and Joan Barris**
Location: **70 mi. W of Cleveland**
No. of Rooms: **14**
No. of Private Baths: **5**
Max. No. Sharing Bath: **3**
Double/pb: **$45–$65**
Double/sb: **$40–$50**

Open: **Mid May–Oct.**
Reduced Rates: **Available**
Breakfast: **Continental, plus**
Pets: **No**
Children: **Welcome**
Smoking: **No**
Social Drinking: **No**

A stay at Idlewyld is like visiting an era when life was uncomplicated by high tech. Nestled in a quaint Victorian community on the shore of Lake Erie, the house is newly decorated in a country antique style. Many rooms feature stenciling. Guests gather in the large dining room for a Continental buffet breakfast, which includes an uncommon assortment of fresh fruit and homemade breads and muffins. Afterward, you can relax on one of the two spacious porches or participate in a myriad of family-oriented activities offered in the Lakeside community.

White Tor ✪
1620 OREGONIA ROAD, LEBANON, OHIO 45036

Tel: **(513) 932-5892**
Best Time to Call: **Before 9 AM; after 6 PM**
Hosts: **Eric and Margaret Johnson**
Location: **25 mi. N of Cincinnati**
No. of Rooms: **1 suite**
No. of Private Baths: **1**
Suite: **$75**

Open: **All year**
Breakfast: **Full**
Pets: **No**
Children: **No**
Smoking: **No**
Social Drinking: **Permitted**
Foreign Languages: **French**

Just a half hour's drive from both Cincinnati and Dayton, this handsome farmhouse, built in 1862, crowns a hilltop on seven wooded acres. Margaret's full English breakfast will give you stamina for a day of antique shopping or viewing artful stitchery at local quilt shows. Area attractions range from Kings Island and the Beach Waterpark to the Honey and Sauerkraut festivals. Or simply relax on the porch in view of the pretty Miami Valley, with a good book and cold drink.

The Mainstay ✪
1320 EAST MAIN STREET, LOUISVILLE, OHIO 44641

Tel: **(330) 875-1021**
Hosts: **Mary and Joe Shurilla**
Location: **7 mi. E of Canton**
No. of Rooms: **3**
No. of Private Baths: **3**
Double/pb: **$50–$60**
Single/pb: **$40–$50**
Suite: **$50; sleeps 3**

Open: **All year**
Reduced Rates: **15% weekly**
Breakfast: **Full**
Pets: **No**
Children: **Welcome, over 3**
Smoking: **No**
Social Drinking: **Permitted**

Enjoy a step backward in time at this century-old Queen Anne Victorian with its richly carved oak woodwork, spacious rooms, original tin ceilings, and numerous antiques. Louisville was the home of Charles Juilliard, founder of the famous New York City music school that bears his name; his house, listed on the National Register of Historic Places, may be toured by arrangement. If you prefer halftime shows to string quartets, you'll probably want to visit the Pro Football Hall of Fame in nearby Canton. Mary and Joe, both educators, greet newly arrived guests with fruit, cheese, and a sparkling beverage. In the morning, have your choice of full or Continental breakfast, with specialties like quiche and home-baked biscuits.

Mulberry Inn ✪
53 NORTH FOURTH STREET, MARTINS FERRY, OHIO 43935

Tel: **(614) 633-6058; (800) 705-6171 ext. 3136**

Hosts: **Charles and Shirley Probst**
Location: **5 mi. W of Wheeling, W. Va.**

No. of Rooms: **3**	Reduced Rates: **5% seniors**
Max. No. Sharing Bath: **4**	Breakfast: **Continental, plus**
Double/pb: **$65**	Credit Cards: **AMEX, DISC, MC, VISA**
Single/pb: **$50**	Pets: **No**
Double/sb: **$55**	Children: **Welcome, over 5**
Single/sb: **$45**	Smoking: **No**
Open: **All year**	Social Drinking: **Permitted**

Built in 1880, this frame Victorian is on a tree-lined street within walking distance of a Civil War cemetery and the Sedgwick Museum. (Martins Ferry is the oldest settlement in Ohio.) Beautiful woodwork, antiques, and mantels grace the large rooms, and air-conditioning cools the house in summer. A retired medical secretary, Shirley devotes her time to making her guests feel comfortable and welcome, tempting them with her unusual French toast recipe. Dog races, recreational activities, the Fostoria Glass Outlet, the Jamboree-in-the-Hills, Ohio University, and Bethany College are less than 10 miles away.

The Outback Inn Bed & Breakfast ✪
171 EAST UNION AVENUE, McCONNELSVILLE, OHIO 43756

Tel: **(740) 962-2158; (800) 542-7171**	Open: **All year**
Best Time to Call: **9 AM–9 PM**	Breakfast: **Full**
Hosts: **Carol and Bob Belfance**	Pets: **No**
No. of Rooms: **3**	Children: **Sometimes**
No. of Private Baths: **3**	Smoking: **No**
Double/pb: **$62.50–$69.50**	Social Drinking: **Permitted**

This restored 1880s banker's home is located in the heart of a small historic village, midway between Zanesville and Marietta. You'll find original oak woodwork, antiques, memorabilia, and stained glass throughout the Inn and all three rooms air-conditioned. Works by local artists are also on display. Breakfast delicacies are served in the dining room or in the private fenced-in yard. Excellent restaurants, a restored 1890 opera house (showing movies on weekends), covered bridges, and a wildlife preserve where rare and vanishing species are bred are just a few of the attractions in this historic area.

English Manor ✪
505 EAST LINDEN AVENUE, MIAMISBURG, OHIO 45342

Tel: **(937) 866-2288; (800) 676-9456**	Reduced Rates: **10% after 3 nights**
Best Time to Call: **9 AM–10 PM**	Breakfast: **Full**
Hosts: **Jeannette and Ken Huelsman**	Other Meals: **Available**
Location: **9 mi. SW of Dayton**	Credit Cards: **AMEX, DC, DISC, MC,**
No. of Rooms: **5**	**VISA**
No. of Private Baths: **3**	Pets: **No**
Max. No. Sharing Bath: **4**	Children: **Welcome**
Double/pb: **$75–$95**	Smoking: **No**
Double/sb: **$65**	Social Drinking: **Permitted**
Open: **All year**	Airport Pickup: **Yes**

Jeannette and Ken Huelsman welcome you to their antique-filled 1920s home in historic Miamisburg. Read by the fireplace, lounge in the hammock, sip lemonade on the wicker porch. Then wander past charming neighborhood homes, or head toward the Great Miami River walking and bike trail. Antique shops, ancient Indian mounds, golf courses, tennis courts, and fine restaurants are all nearby. To start your day, a sumptuous breakfast is served on antique china, with silver, and linens.

Gastier Farm Bed & Breakfast

1902 STRECKER ROAD, MILAN, OHIO 44846

Tel: **(419) 499-2985**
Best Time to Call: **After 5 PM**
Hosts: **Ted and Donna Gastier**
Location: **60 mi. W of Cleveland**
No. of Rooms: **3**
Max. No. Sharing Bath: **3**
Double/sb: **$50**
Single/sb: **$35**

Open: **All year**
Breakfast: **Continental**
Credit Cards: **MC, VISA**
Pets: **No**
Children: **Welcome**
Smoking: **No**
Social Drinking: **No**
Aiport/Station Pickup: **Yes**

Ted and Donna's working farm has been a family tradition for more than one hundred years, providing the local community with grain, fresh produce, cattle, and a variety of house plants. Now the farmhouse has become a bed and breakfast. The rooms have all been decorated in a homey country atmosphere. Nearby attractions include Edison Birthplace, Milan Museum, Lake Erie, Cedar Point Amusement Park, and antique shops.

Morgan Manor ✪
154 WEST MAIN STREET, NEW LONDON, OHIO 44851

Tel: **(419) 929-4046**
Hosts: **Henry and Sue Morgan**
Location: **60 mi. W of Akron**
No. of Rooms: **3**
No. of Private Baths: **2**
Max. No. Sharing Bath: **4**
Double/pb: **$90**
Single/pb: **$85**
Double/sb: **$80**

Single s/b: **$75**
Open: **All year**
Reduced Rates: **10% seniors**
Breakfast: **Full**
Credit Cards: **MC, VISA**
Pets: **Sometimes**
Children: **By arrangement**
Smoking: **No**
Social Drinking: **Permitted**

This grand, one-hundred-forty-year-old manor and past boarding house has a signatured cupola—guests are invited to add their names. Morgan Manor is located in a quaint village with many homes of historical background. Inside you will see twelve-foot ceilings, marble fireplaces, and in-room tubs with folding screens. Nearby you can enjoy biking, golf, cross-country skiing, fishing, sail boarding, and boating. The Buckeye Trail is three miles away. Sue was a social services specialist and art major. Henry, chemist generalist and plant manager, used to be involved in a local community theater. The upper-level sitting room is always open to guests.

St. George House ✪
33941 LORAIN ROAD, NORTH RIDGEVILLE, OHIO 44039

Tel: **(440) 327-9354**
Best Time to Call: **Early mornings;**
  evenings until 9 PM
Hosts: **Helen Bernardine and**
  Muriel Dodd
Location: **22 mi W of Cleveland**
No. of Rooms: **4**
No. of Private Baths: **1**
Max. No. Sharing Bath: **4**
Double/pb: **$55**
Single/pb: **$50**
Double/sb: **$45**

Single/sb: **$40**
Open: **All year**
Reduced Rates: **Weekly**
Breakfast: **Continental**
Other Meals: **Available**
Pets: **Sometimes**
Children: **Welcome, over 12**
Smoking: **Permitted**
Social Drinking: **Permitted**
Minimum Stay: **2 nights**
Airport/Station Pickup: **Yes**

This spacious Colonial home sits on an acre of scenic country. You may want to enjoy the renaissance of nearby downtown Cleveland. For those of you who enjoy night life, a trip to the Flats, which boasts comedy halls, saloons, galleries, and microbreweries, is in order. Flats restaurants offer dockside service for boaters. Playhouse Square has top-shelf theater, and Gateway is the home of the Cleveland Indians and the Cavaliers. Also nearby are the Rock and Roll Hall of Fame, Case Western Reserve, Oberlin College, and University Circle (home of the Cleveland Orchestra, Museum of Art, Cleveland Playhouse, and Cleveland Clinic). Freeway access is within two minutes.

Inn at the Green ✪
500 SOUTH MAIN STREET, POLAND, OHIO 44514

Tel: **(330) 757-4688**	Open: **All year**
Best Time to Call: **After 12 PM**	Breakfast: **Continental**
Hosts: **Ginny and Steve Meloy**	Other Meals: **No**
Location: **7 mi. SE of Youngstown**	Credit Cards: **DISC, MC, VISA**
No. of Rooms: **4**	Pets: **No**
No. of Private Baths: **4**	Children: **Welcome, over 10**
Double/pb: **$60**	Smoking: **Permitted**
Single/pb: **$55**	Social Drinking: **Permitted**

The Inn at the Green is an 1876 Victorian town house located on the south end of the village green. The rooms have the grandeur of bygone days, with original moldings, 12-foot-high ceilings, and original poplar floors. There are five Italian marble fireplaces and extensive public rooms furnished with gracious antiques. Guests are welcome to relax in the parlor, greeting room, and enclosed porch. Sleeping quarters are air-conditioned, and are furnished with poster beds, Posturepedic mattresses, antiques, and working fireplaces. Coffee, croissants, muffins, and French jam are served in the greeting room in winter and on the wicker-furnished porch during moderate weather. Enjoy a glass of sherry on the porch overlooking the garden before dinner. Your hosts will gladly direct you to gourmet dining as well as cross-country ski trails, golf, tennis, and the Butler Institute, home of one of the nation's finest American art collections.

The Signal House ✪
234 NORTH FRONT STREET, RIPLEY, OHIO 45167

Tel/Fax: **(937) 392-1640**	Open: **All year**
Best Time to Call: **Morning**	Reduced Rates: **Available**
Hosts: **Vic and Betsy Billingsley**	Breakfast: **Full**
Location: **1 hr. E of Cincinnati**	Credit Cards: **DISC, MC, VISA**
No. of Rooms: **2**	Pets: **No**
Max. No. Sharing Bath: **4**	Smoking: **Permitted**
Double/sb: **$75**	Social Drinking: **Permitted**

This stately 1830 historic home overlooks the scenic Ohio River. The Signal House offers relaxing porches and beautiful sunsets for romantic getaways or a rural business trip. Two Civil War officers lived in this house; legend tells of the house's role in the Underground Railroad. Ripley has 55 acres on the National Register of Historic Places. Two of our museums, The Runkin House and John Parker's House, are now listed with the National Park Service. Guests can enjoy central air, fireside parlor games, gardens, and the yard. Places to visit include antique and specialty shops, restaurants, and a winery. Nearby is the Ohio River, for fishing and boating.

The Red Gables Bed & Breakfast ✪

421 WAYNE STREET, SANDUSKY, OHIO 44870
www.bbonline.com/oh/redgables

Tel: **(419) 625-1189**
Best Time to Call: **9 AM–9 PM**
Host: **Jo Ellen Cuthbertson**
Location: **60 mi. W of Cleveland**
No. of Rooms: **4**
No. of Private Baths: **2**
Max. No. Sharing Bath: **4**
Double/pb: **$80–$100**
Double/sb: **$70–$85**
Open: **Feb.–Dec.**

Reduced Rates: **Oct. 1–May 1 all rooms are $50–$65**
Breakfast: **Continental, plus**
Credit Cards: **MC, VISA**
Pets: **No**
Children: **By arrangement**
Smoking: **No**
Social Drinking: **Permitted**
Station Pickup: **Yes**

A lovely old Tudor Revival home finished in 1907, The Red Gables is located in the historic Old Plat District. Guests are welcomed into the great room, which features a massive fireplace and large bay window where breakfast is served. The home's many interesting architectural details include lots of oak woodwork. The Red Gables is decorated in a very eclectic style, from Oriental artifacts in the great room to flowered chintz in the bedrooms. The innkeeper, a semi-retired costume maker, has filled the rooms with handmade slipcovers, curtains, and comforters. Guest rooms are light and airy, with easy access to a wicker-filled sitting room, a refrigerator, and coffeemaker or teakettle. Guests have said, "It's like going to grandma's house!" Guest rooms have air-conditioning.

Wagner's 1844 Inn ✪

230 EAST WASHINGTON STREET, SANDUSKY, OHIO 44870

Tel: **(419) 626-1726**
Hosts: **Walt and Barb Wagner**
Location: **8 mi. from Ohio Tpke., Exit 7**
No. of Rooms: **3**
No. of Private Baths: **3**
Double/pb: **$70–$100**
Single/pb: **$60–$90**
Open: **All year**

Reduced Rates: **Oct.–Apr.**
Breakfast: **Continental**
Credit Cards: **DISC, MC, VISA**
Pets: **Sometimes**
Children: **No**
Smoking: **No**
Social Drinking: **Permitted**
Airport/Station Pickup: **Yes**

This elegantly restored Italianate home, built in 1844, is listed on the National Register of Historic Places. The warm interior features old-fashioned amenities like a billiard room, an antique piano, and a wood-burning fireplace. The screened porch and enclosed courtyard provide tranquil settings for conversation with your hosts Walt, an attorney, and Barb, a registered nurse. Within easy walking distance are parks, tennis courts, antique shops, art galleries, and ferries to Cedar Point Amusement Park and the Lake Erie Islands.

Somer Tea B&B ✪
200 SOUTH COLUMBUS STREET, BOX 308, SOMERSET, OHIO 43783

Tel: **(740) 743-2909**	Open: **All year**
Hosts: **Richard and Mary Lou Murray**	Breakfast: **Full**
Location: **40 mi. SE of Columbus**	Pets: **Welcome**
No. of Rooms: **2**	Children: **Welcome**
Max. No. Sharing Bath: **4**	Smoking: **No**
Double/sb: **$55**	Social Drinking: **Permitted**
Single/sb: **$45**	

Somerset was the boyhood home of the Civil War general Phil Sheridan. Two of his nieces lived in the Somer Tea, a stately brick residence listed on the National Register of Historic Places. And yes, tea is always available here; guests are encouraged to sit with a cup on the porch swing. Ask Mary Lou to show you her collection of more than 300 teapots. If you'd like to do some collecting yourself, she'll direct you to the region's numerous antique shops and crafts stores. Full country breakfasts, with an egg casserole, a fruit dish, home fries, and raisin bran muffins, are served in the elegant dining room.

Lakewood Farm Bed & Breakfast, Inc. ✪
8495 ROUTE 48, WAYNESVILLE, OHIO 45068

Tel: **(937) 885-9850**	Open: **Mar.1–Dec. 31**
Best Time to Call: **8 AM–11 AM**	Reduced Rates: **Available**
Hosts: **Liz and Jay Jorling**	Breakfast: **Full**
Location: **15 mi. S of Dayton**	Credit Cards: **MC, VISA**
No. of Rooms: **4**	Pets: **Sometimes**
No. of Private Baths: **4**	Children: **Welcome, over 2**
Double/pb: **$80**	Smoking: **No**
Suites: **$125**	Social Drinking: **Permitted**

Lakewood Farm, built in the early 1830s, is a year-round 25-acre estate with a 5-acre lake, 17 acres of forest, a horse stable, several pastures, and plenty of wildlife. Guests are invited to experience breath-taking views, miles of hiking trails, fishing, sunbathing, tennis, croquet, horseshoes, sledding, and ice skating. The guest rooms are all furnished with turn-of-the-century decor, queen-size beds, telephone service within the rooms, and air-conditioning. Breakfast is served in the courtyard dining room, or in the garden.

Amish Country Log Cabin ✪
2658 COON HILL ROAD, WINCHESTER, OHIO 45697

Tel: **(937) 386-3144; (800) 738-3332**
Best Time to Call: **9 AM–9 PM**
Hosts: **Donna and Glenn Sorrell**
Location: **58 mi. E of Cincinnati**
No. of Rooms: **4**
No. of Private Baths: **4**
Double/pb: **$69–$75**
Single/pb: **$60**
Open: **All year**

Reduced Rates: **10% Sun.–Thurs. 55 and older**
Breakfast: **Full**
Credit Cards: **MC, VISA**
Pets: **No**
Children: **Welcome**
Smoking: **No**
Social Drinking: **No**

Amish Country Log Cabin Bed & Breakfast was built in 1788, and was moved to its present location in 1988. Rooms are decorated with a mix of antiques and traditional furniture, queen-size beds, TVs, and VCRs. Guests are invited to walk on the well-trodden paths, which cover 27 acres of woods. Fish in the pond or have a barbecue in the picnic shelter. Places to visit include Serpent Mound, the Amish bakery and auction, Herb Festivals, Ohio River towns, Ohio Brush Creek, and many nature preserves for bird watching and hiking.

Millennium Classic Bed & Breakfast ✪
1626 BEALL AVENUE, WOOSTER, OHIO 44691

Tel: **(330) 264-6005**
Best Time to Call: **8 AM–9 PM**
Host: **John Byler**
Location: **50 mi. S of Cleveland**
No. of Rooms: **4**
No. of Private Baths: **3**
Max. No. Sharing Bath: **4**
Double/pb: **$65–$75**
Double/sb: **$60–$70**
Single/sb: **$45–$55**
Suites: **$75–$85**

Open: **All year**
Reduced Rates: **10% seniors, 10% less Mon–Thurs**
Breakfast: **Continental**
Credit Cards: **AMEX, DISC, MC, VISA**
Pets: **No**
Children: **Welcome**
Smoking: **No**
Social Drinking: **No**
Airport/Station Pickup: **By arrangement**
Foreign Languages: **German**

Built in 1911, the Millennium Classic Bed & Breakfast is located in the heart of Wooster, one block from the college, hospital, and shopping center and three doors north of Friendly's Ice Cream. The world's largest Amish community and tourist center is twenty minutes away. Millennium's exterior is post-Victorian and the interior is traditional classic. Outside there are quiet sitting areas with a lot of shade trees and a second-story deck that overlooks the backyard.

OKLAHOMA

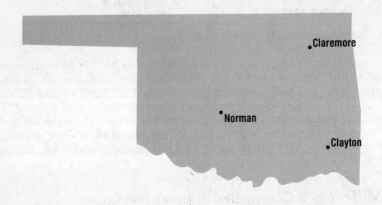

Country Inn ✪
20530 EAST 430 ROAD, CLAREMORE, OKLAHOMA 74017

Tel: **(918) 342-1894**
Best Time to Call: **8 AM–8 PM**
Hosts: **Dennis and Linda Coons**
Location: **25 mi. NE of Tulsa**
No. of Rooms: **3**
No. of Private Baths: **3**
Double/pb: **$54**
Single/pb: **$35**

Suite: **$65**
Open: **All year**
Reduced Rates: **Available**
Breakfast: **Full**
Children: **No**
Smoking: **No**
Social Drinking: **Permitted**

Located fifteen minutes from Claremore, this small inn has a tranquil, friendly atmosphere. Guests are invited to swim in the in-ground pool or just swing in the hammock. A full breakfast including gourmet coffee is served daily. Nearby are numerous antique shops, Davis Gun Museum, and Will Rogers Memorial. Guest quarters are separate from the main house, and each smoke-free room has a private bath.

Clayton Country Inn ☺
ROUTE 1, BOX 8, HIGHWAY 271, CLAYTON, OKLAHOMA 74536

Tel: **(918) 569-4165, 747-1990**
Best Time to Call: **8 AM–9 PM**
Hosts: **Betty Lundgren, Rita and Bill Lyons**
Location: **140 mi. SE of Tulsa**
No. of Rooms: **11**
No. of Private Baths: **11**
Double/pb: **$47**
Single/pb: **$39**

Guest Cottage: **$55; for 2**
Open: **All year**
Breakfast: **Continental**
Other Meals: **Available, dinner only**
Credit Cards: **AMEX, DISC, MC, VISA**
Pets: **No**
Children: **Welcome**
Smoking: **Permitted**
Social Drinking: **Permitted**

Perched on a hill amid 140 acres and surrounded by the Kiamichi Mountains is this 50-year-old, two-story, stone and wood inn. It's furnished in a simple, traditional style with a beamed ceiling and fireplace. The on-premises restaurant is noted for its fine cooking. Bass fishing at Lake Sardis is two miles away, and an 18,000-acre game preserve is just across the highway. Feel free to bring your horse and enjoy trail rides under the vast Western skies. Enjoy the casual elegance of the Inn.

Holmberg House Bed & Breakfast ☺
766 DEBARR, NORMAN, OKLAHOMA 73069

Tel: **(405) 321-6221; (800) 646-6221**
Host: **Jo Meacham and Michael Cobb**
Location: **17 mi. S of Oklahoma City**
No. of Rooms: **4**
No. of Private Baths: **4**
Double/pb: **$75–$85**
Single/pb: **$65–$75**
Open: **All year**

Reduced Rates: **$10 less Sun.–Thurs.**
Breakfast: **Full**
Credit Cards: **AMEX, DISC, MC, VISA**
Pets: **No**
Children: **Welcome, over 12**
Smoking: **No**
Social Drinking: **Permitted**

Located in Norman's National Register Historic District and across the street from the University of Oklahoma's campus, this handsome 1914 Craftsman house was built by Professor Frederick Holmberg and his wife Signy. Jo bought the house in 1993 and it now accommodates many of the university's visiting scholars and parents. Guest rooms are individually decorated with antiques, private baths with claw-footed tubs, and color cable TVs. A parlor with a fireplace, porches with rockers, and gardens are for your pleasure. A hearty breakfast is served in the dining room.

OREGON

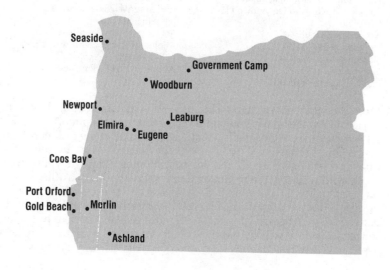

Seaside

Government Camp

Woodburn

Newport

Leaburg

Elmira

Eugene

Coos Bay

Port Orford

Gold Beach • Merlin

Ashland

Northwest Bed and Breakfast Reservation Service
1067 HANOVER COURT SOUTH, SALEM, OREGON 97302-6002

Tel: **(503) 243-7616, 370-9033; fax:**
  (503) 316-9118
Best Time to Call: **8 AM–5 PM**
Coordinator: **David and Betty**
  Hickerson
States/Regions Covered: **Pacific**
  Northwest, British Columbia

Rates (Single/Double):
  Modest: **$60–$80**
  Average: **$80–$100**
  Luxury: **$100–up**
Credit Cards: **AMEX, DISC, MC, VISA**

Northwest Bed and Breakfast Reservation Service is a network established in 1979. The Hickersons list hundreds of homes and inns throughout the Pacific Northwest, including British Columbia.

Cowslip's Belle Bed & Breakfast ✪

159 NORTH MAIN STREET, ASHLAND, OREGON 97520
stay@cowslip.com; www.cowslip.com/cowslip

Tel: **(800) 888-6819; (541) 488-2901;**
   fax: **(541) 482-6138**
Hosts: **Jon and Carmen Reinhardt**
Location: **3 blocks to Downtown Plaza**
No. of Rooms: **4**
No. of Private Baths: **4**
Double/pb: **$95–$135**
Single/pb: **$85–$130**
Open: **All year**
Reduced Rates: **Available**

Breakfast: **Full**
Credit Cards: **MC, VISA**
Pets: **No**
Children: **Welcome, over 10**
Smoking: **No**
Social Drinking: **Permitted**
Minimum Stay: **2 nights weekends**
   June–Sept.
Airport/Station Pickup: **Yes**

From the moment you step inside this 1913 Craftsman bungalow or its adjacent carriage house, you will receive modern-day comfort sprinkled with old-fashioned hospitality. Snuggle up to one of the resident teddy bears. Guest rooms have luxurious queen beds, caressed by soft white linens, down comforters, and air-conditioning. Indulge your sweet tooth with a melt-in-your-mouth homemade chocolate truffle, placed on your pillow when your bed is turned down each evening. Daily fare includes a scrumptious breakfast with a hearty serving of lively conversation. Whether you wish to explore Ashland by foot or by car, Jon and Carmen will be happy to help you plan your itinerary and assist you with reservations for dinner, bike rentals, and raft trips.

The Woods House Bed & Breakfast Inn ✪

333 NORTH MAIN STREET, ASHLAND, OREGON 97520
woodshse@mind.net; www.mind.net/woodshouse/

Tel: **(541) 488-1598; (800) 435-8260;**
   fax: **(541) 482-8027**
Best Time to Call: **10 AM–10 PM**
Hosts: **Françoise and Lester Roddy**
Location: **4 blks. N of Downtown Plaza**
No. of Rooms: **6**
No. of Private Baths: **6**
Double/pb: **$75–$120**
Single/pb: **$75–$110**
Open: **All year**

Reduced Rates: **Available**
Breakfast: **Full**
Credit Cards: **DISC, MC, VISA**
Pets: **No**
Children: **Welcome, over 12**
Smoking: **No**
Social Drinking: **Permitted**
Minimum Stay: **2 days June–Oct.;**
   weekends Nov.–May
Station Pickup: **Yes**

The Woods House is located in Ashland's historic district four blocks from the Shakespearean theater, shops, restaurants, and 100-acre Lithia Park. The Inn, a 1908 Craftsman home renovated in 1984, has six sunny and spacious guest rooms. Simple furnishings, comprising warm woods, antique furniture and linens, watercolors, oriental carpets, and leather books, combine with high-quality amenities to create a sophisticated comfortable atmosphere. The terraced English gardens provide many areas for guests to relax and socialize. Françoise previously worked in human resources and event planning and is skilled in calligraphy, cooking, and needlecrafts. Lester has spent the past 25 years in business management and consulting. Their aim is to make each guest feel like a special friend, not just a paying customer. They strive to anticipate guests' needs and cheerfully accommodate the unexpected, always maintaining the highest standards of cleanliness, cordiality, and fine food.

Old Tower House B&B ✪
476 NEWMARK AVENUE, COOS BAY, OREGON 97420

Tel: **(541) 888-6058; fax: (541) 888-6058**
Hosts: **Don and Julia Spangler**
Location: **5 mi. W of Coos Bay**
No. of Rooms: **3**
Max. No. Sharing Bath: **4**
Double/sb: **$65–$85**
Guest Cottage: **$65**
Suites: **$85**

Open: **All year**
Breakfast: **Full**
Credit Cards: **DISC, MC, VISA**
Pets: **No**
Children: **Welcome, over 10, by arrangement**
Social Drinking: **No**
Airport Pickup: **Yes**

Built in 1872, this Victorian home is on the National Historic Register and is furnished with antiques throughout. All three guest rooms have pedestal sinks and share two full baths with clawfoot tubs. For relaxing, a spacious parlor is offered. For seclusion you might want to enjoy the Carriage House loft suite with a queen-size bed, clawfoot tub, kitchen, and sitting room with TV, or the Ivy Cottage with a double bed and a private bath.

McGillivray's Log Home Bed and Breakfast ✪
88680 EVERS ROAD, ELMIRA, OREGON 97437

Tel: **(541) 935-3564**
Best Time to Call: **8 AM–8 PM**
Host: **Evelyn McGillivray**
Location: **14 mi. W of Eugene**
No. of Rooms: **2**
No. of Private Baths: **2**
Double/pb: **$70–$80**
Single/pb: **$60–$70**

Open: **All year**
Breakfast: **Full**
Credit Cards: **MC, VISA**
Pets: **No**
Children: **By arrangement**
Smoking: **No**
Social Drinking: **Permitted**

This massive home is situated on five acres covered with pines and firs. The air-conditioned structure is designed with six types of wood, and features a split-log staircase. Guests may choose from a spacious, wheelchair-accessible bedroom, or an upstairs room that can accommodate a family. All are beautifully decorated in a classic Americana motif. Evelyn usually prepares buttermilk pancakes using an antique griddle of her mother's. She also offers fresh-squeezed juice from farm-grown apples and grapes, fresh bread, eggs, and all the trimmings. It's just three miles to a local vineyard; country roads for bicycling and a reservoir for fishing and boating are close by.

Maryellen's Guest House

1583 FIRCREST, EUGENE, OREGON 97403
maryellen@continet.com; www.continet.com/blarson

Tel: **(541) 342-7375**
Best Time to Call: **9 AM–9 PM**
Hosts: **Maryellen and Bob Larson**
Location: **1 mi. off I-5, Exit 191-192**
No. of Rooms: **2**
No. of Private Baths: **2**
Double/pb: **$89**
Single/pb: **$79**
Open: **All year**

Reduced Rates: **10% weekly**
Breakfast: **Full**
Other Meals: **Available**
Credit Cards: **MC, VISA**
Pets: **No**
Children: **Welcome, over 12**
Smoking: **No**
Social Drinking: **Permitted**
Airport/Station Pickup: **Yes**

Maryellen's Guest House is a contemporary hillside home with casual elegance. This B&B is close to the University of Oregon, Hendrick's Park, and shopping. Each guest room is private and spacious, with a sitting area, TV, VCR, and phone. Amenities include a guest refrigerator, games, books, videos, and a pool and hot tub located on spacious cedar decks. A bountiful breakfast is served in the dining room, or you may request room service.

The Oval Door Bed & Breakfast ✪

988 LAWRENCE STREET, EUGENE, OREGON 97401

Tel: **(541) 683-3160**; fax: **(541) 485-5339**; **(800) 882-3160**
Hosts: **Judith McLane and Dianne Feist**
No. of Rooms: **4**
No. of Private Baths: **4**
Double/pb: **$75–$100**
Single/pb: **$65–$90**
Open: **All year**

Breakfast: **Full**
Credit Cards: **AMEX, DC, MC, VISA**
Pets: **No**
Children: **By arrangement**
Smoking: **No**
Social Drinking: **Permitted**
Minimum Stay: **2 nights during conventions, University functions**

This inviting 1920s-style farmhouse was rebuilt as a B&B in 1990. From its location in the heart of downtown Eugene, it's an easy walk to fine restaurants and the Hult Performing Arts Center. The University of Oregon campus is also nearby. Scrumptious breakfasts include a seasonal fruit dish, homemade breads, and a special entree, such as zucchini filbert waffles. You'll also find extra touches like terry robes, Perrier water, Frango Mints, and the Tub Room with its whirlpool bath for two, music, candles, and bubbles.

Pookie's Bed 'n' Breakfast on College Hill

2013 CHARNELTON STREET, EUGENE, OREGON 97405

Tel: **(541) 343-0383**; **(800) 558-0383**
Hosts: **Pookie and Doug Walling**
Location: **110 mi. S of Portland**

No. of Rooms: **3**
No. of Private Baths: **2**
Max. No. Sharing Bath: **4**

Double/pb: **$85–$95**
Single/pb: **$70–$80**
Double/sb: **$65**
Single/sb: **$55**
Open: **All year**

Breakfast: **Full**
Pets: **No**
Children: **Welcome, over 6**
Smoking: **No**
Social Drinking: **Permitted**

Although it has been remodeled on the outside, this Craftsman-style house, built in 1918, retains much of its original interior charm. One room has antique mahogany furniture and a queen-size bed; the other has oak furnishings and either a king or twin beds. Pookie's is in a quiet older neighborhood just south of downtown, where you'll find great shopping, excellent dining, and access to the Hult Performing Arts Center. The University of Oregon campus is all of a mile away. Early morning coffee is served in the small sitting room upstairs. A full breakfast, with specialties like quiche and orange custard–baked French toast, follows.

Endicott Gardens ✪

95768 JERRY'S FLAT ROAD, GOLD BEACH, OREGON 97444

Tel: **(541) 247-6513**
Best Time to Call: **10 AM–noon**
Hosts: **Beverly and Mary Endicott**
No. of Rooms: **4**
No. of Private Baths: **4**
Double/pb: **$55**
Single/pb: **$45**

Open: **All year**
Breakfast: **Continental, plus**
Pets: **No**
Children: **Welcome**
Smoking: **Restricted**
Social Drinking: **Permitted**

This classic contemporary B&B is across the road from Rogue River, famous for fishing and riverboat trips to white water. The guest rooms are located in a private wing of the house with decks overlooking the forest, mountains, and beautiful grounds. Homegrown strawberries, blueberries, apples, and plums are often featured in delicious breakfast treats served on the deck or in the dining room. In cool weather, the living room with its cozy fireplace is a favorite gathering spot. Beverly and Mary will be happy to share their collection of restaurant menus from nearby eating establishments with you.

Falcon's Crest Inn ✪

87287 GOVERNMENT CAMP LOOP HIGHWAY (MAILING ADDRESS: P.O. BOX 185, GOVERNMENT CAMP, OREGON 97028)

Tel: **(503) 272-3403; (800) 624-7384**
Hosts: **BJ and Melody Johnson**
Location: **54 mi. E of Portland**
No. of Rooms: **5**
No. of Private Baths: **5**
Double/pb: **$95–$99.50**

Suites: **$169–$179; sleeps 2**
Open: **All year**
Reduced Rates: **Nov.–Mar.; with ski package, multiple nights**
Breakfast: **Full**
Other Meals: **Available**

Credit Cards: **AMEX, DISC, MC, VISA**	Smoking: **No**
Pets: **No**	Social Drinking: **Permitted**
Children: **Welcome, over 6**	Airport/Station Pickup: **Yes**

Falcon's Crest Inn is nestled among the firs on the 4000-foot level of Mount Hood. The two-story glass front of this elegant, intimate B&B provides a spectacular view of Ski Bowl, a year-round recreational area. Duffers can head to the 27-hole championship course just 12 miles from the front door, and those who love water sports can occupy themselves with fishing, swimming, and white-water rafting. The bedrooms, which are decorated with family heirlooms and keepsakes, have forest or mountain views. In the morning, fresh muffins and a beverage are delivered to your door. Then you'll breakfast on hearty fare like buttermilk pancakes, waffles, or French toast.

Marjon Bed and Breakfast Inn ✪
44975 LEABURG DAM ROAD, LEABURG, OREGON 97489

Tel: **(541) 896-3145**	Open: **All year**
Host: **Marguerite Haas**	Breakfast: **Full**
Location: **24 mi. E of Eugene**	Pets: **No**
No. of Rooms: **2**	Children: **No**
No. of Private Baths: **2**	Smoking: **Permitted**
Double/pb: **$95**	Social Drinking: **Permitted**
Suite: **$125**	Airport/Station Pickup: **Yes**

This cedar chalet is located on the banks of the McKenzie River. The suite overlooks the river and a secluded Japanese garden, and features a sunken bath. The other room has a fish bowl shower and a view of a 100-year-old apple tree. Relax in the living room with its wraparound seating and massive stone fireplace. One of the walls is made entirely of glass with sliding doors that lead to a terrace that faces the river. A multicourse breakfast is served there on balmy days. Waterfalls, trout fishing, white-water rafting, and skiing are all nearby.

Pine Meadow Inn B&B ✪
1000 CROW ROAD, MERLIN, OREGON 97532
pmi@pinemeadowinn.com; www.pinemeadowinn.com

Tel: **(541) 471-6277; (800) 554-0806**	Breakfast: **Full**
Hosts: **Maloy and Nancy Murdock**	Credit Cards: **DISC, MC, VISA**
Location: **10 mi. NW of Grants Pass**	Pets: **No**
No. of Rooms: **4**	Children: **Welcome, over 8**
No. of Private Baths: **4**	Smoking: **No**
Double/pb: **$80–$110**	Social Drinking: **Permitted**
Open: **All year**	Minimum Stay: **No**
Reduced Rates: **10% weekly**	

Secluded on nine acres of meadow and woods, Pine Meadow Inn B&B is styled after Midwestern farmhouses, and features a wraparound porch with comfortable wicker furniture. There are many exciting choices of things to do: white-water rafting, walking, biking, jogging, visiting the California redwoods, Crater Lake, the Shakespeare Festival, or historic Jacksonville. When your day is complete you might want to read a book from the library in the quiet sitting room, which has a fireplace. Or take a dip in the hot tub. All guest rooms have queen-size beds with private baths, window seat, or sitting area. Awake in the morning to a healthful gourmet breakfast.

Oar House Bed & Breakfast ✪

520 SOUTHWEST 2ND STREET, NEWPORT, OREGON 97365
www.newportnet.com/oarhouse

Tel: **(800) 252-2358; (541) 265-9571**	Breakfast: **Full**
Best Time to Call: **10 AM–9 PM**	Credit Cards: **DISC, MC, VISA**
Host: **Jan LeBrun**	Pets: **No**
No. of Rooms: **5**	Children: **No**
No. of Private Baths: **5**	Smoking: **No**
Double/pb: **$95–$115**	Social Drinking: **Permitted**
Suites: **$125**	Minimum Stay: **2 nights holidays and**
Open: **All year**	**special events; summer**
Reduced Rates: **$10 less Nov.–May; $5 less multiple nights Mon.–Thurs. off-season**	

The Oar House Bed & Breakfast was built over 100 years ago, and was renovated in 1993 to provide modern amenities. Its location allows guests to walk to the beach, the historic bay front, performing and visual arts centers, and excellent restaurants. A spacious living room with a bar area for beverages and snacks and a sitting room with a fireplace and a music system provide guests with both comfort and ambience. Following early coffee, Jan serves a gourmet-inspired breakfast. A unique feature of the inn is its lighthouse tower, from which guests have spectacular views.

Tyee Lodge Oceanfront Bed & Breakfast ✪

4925 NORTHWEST WOODY WAY, NEWPORT, OREGON 97365
www.newportnet.com/tyee/home.htm

Tel: **(888) 553-8933; (541) 265-8953**	Breakfast: **Full**
Best Time to Call: **10 AM–10 PM**	Credit Cards: **AMEX, DISC, MC, VISA**
Hosts: **Mark and Cindy McConnell**	Pets: **No**
Location: **130 mi. SW of Portland**	Children: **Welcome, over 15**
No. of Rooms: **5**	Smoking: **No**
No. of Private Baths: **5**	Social Drinking: **Permitted**
Double/pb: **$85–$115**	Minimum Stay: **2 nights, special events,**
Single/pb: **$75–$105**	**holidays**
Open: **All year**	Station Pickup: **Yes**
Reduced Rates: **Oct.–May, midweek**	Foreign Languages: **Spanish, German**

Tyee Lodge Oceanfront Bed & Breakfast boasts a breathtaking setting, true to your image of the Oregon Coast, with windswept trees, waves crashing on headlands, and flat sandy beaches. Northwest decor and colors enhance the oceanfront view from every room. From the secluded half-acre gardens, an easy trail leads to tide pools and miles of beach. You can walk to Yaquina Head Lighthouse. Newport attractions are a five-minute drive away.

Home by the Sea Bed & Breakfast

444 JACKSON STREET, PORT ORFORD, OREGON 97465-0606
www.homebythesea.com

Tel: **(541) 332-2855**	Open: **All year**
Best Time to Call: **8 AM–8 PM**	Breakfast: **Full**
Hosts: **Alan and Brenda Mitchell**	Credit Cards: **MC, VISA**
Location: **54 mi. N of California border**	Pets: **No**
No. of Rooms: **2**	Children: **No**
No. of Private Baths: **2**	Smoking: **No**
Double/pb: **$95–$105**	Social Drinking: **Permitted**
Suite: **$105; sleeps 2**	

Alan and Brenda built this contemporary home overlooking a stretch of the Oregon coast that could take your breath away. Both guest rooms have private baths, queen Oregon myrtlewood beds, cable TV, and laundry privileges. It's a short walk to restaurants and direct beach access. The Mitchells provide current Oregon coast travel tips at homebythesea.com/CST-Tips.html.

Anderson's Boarding House Bed & Breakfast ✪
208 NORTH HOLLADAY DRIVE, SEASIDE, OREGON 97138

Tel: **(503) 738-9055; (800) 995-4013**	Open: **All year**
Host: **Barb Edwards**	Reduced Rates: **Available**
Location: **1/2 mi. from Rte. 101**	Breakfast: **Full**
No. of Rooms: **6**	Credit Cards: **MC, VISA**
No. of Private Baths: **6**	Pets: **No**
Double/pb: **$80–$90**	Children: **Welcome**
Single/pb: **$75–$85**	Smoking: **No**
Guest Cottage: **$120; sleeps 6, $650**	Social Drinking: **Permitted**
weekly	Airport/Station Pickup: **Yes**

Located on the banks of the Necanicum River, this rustic Victorian was built as a private residence in 1898. During World War I, the house became a boarding home. After an extensive renovation, the wood walls and beamed ceilings have been restored to their original charm. Guest rooms feature brass or white iron beds, down quilts, family heirlooms, wicker, and wood. Claw-footed tubs, window seats, antiques, and a picture of grandma make you feel as if this house is your own. A fire is often burning in the fir-paneled parlor, and an old melody sounds just right on the old-fashioned Victrola. A 100-year-old guest cottage with wood paneling, country furnishings, bedroom, loft, and river view is also available. Breakfast specialties such as cheese-and-egg strata, orange French toast, and blueberry scones are served in the dining room or outside on the wraparound porch. The house is just four blocks from the ocean and two blocks from downtown.

The Carriage House ✪
515 SOUTH PACIFIC HIGHWAY, WOODBURN, OREGON 97071

Tel: **(503) 982-6321**	Open: **All year**
Best Time to Call: **Before 9 AM; after 6**	Breakfast: **Full**
PM	Credit Cards: **MC, VISA**
Hosts: **Lawrence and Marilyn Paradis**	Pets: **Sometimes**
Location: **30 mi. S of Portland**	Children: **Welcome**
No. of Rooms: **2**	Smoking: **No**
Max. No. Sharing Bath: **4**	Social Drinking: **Permitted**
Double/sb: **$55**	Airport/Station Pickup: **Yes**
Single/sb: **$50**	Foreign Languages: **French**

The Carriage House is a 1906 Victorian known for its peaceful country elegance. Completely restored, it is furnished with family treasures and heirloom quilts. Lawrence and Marilyn keep horses and an antique buggy in a carriage house next to the inn. This is an excellent location for visiting the Enchanted Forest, the Oregon State Fair, the Octoberfest in Mt. Angel, the Bach Festival, historic Champoeg, and numerous antique shops and wineries. There is a private bath for $65; inquire about availability.

For key to listings, see inside front or back cover.

✪ This star means that rates are guaranteed through December 31, 1999, to any guest making a reservation as a result of reading about the B&B in *Bed & Breakfast U.S.A.*—1999 edition.

Important! To avoid misunderstandings, always ask about cancellation policies when booking.

Please enclose a self-addressed, stamped, business-size envelope when contacting reservation services.

For more details on what you can expect in a B&B, see Chapter 1.

Always mention *Bed & Breakfast U.S.A.* when making reservations!

We want to hear from you! Use the form on page 593.

PENNSYLVANIA

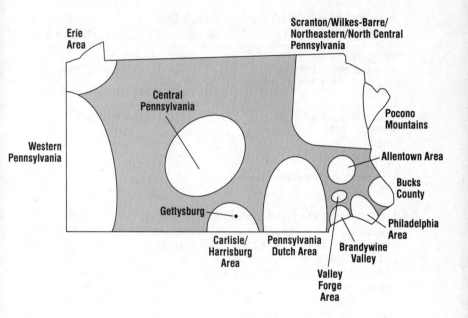

ALLENTOWN AREA

Brennans B&B ✪
3827 LINDEN STREET, ALLENTOWN, PENNSYLVANIA 18104

Tel: **(610) 395-0869**
Best Time to Call: **7 AM–11 PM**
Hosts: **Lois and Edward Brennan**
Location: **1 mi. from 78 and 22**
No. of Rooms: **2**
No. of Private Baths: **1**
Max. No. Sharing Bath: **2**
Double/pb: **$40**
Single/pb: **$35**

Double/sb: **$30**
Single/sb: **$25**
Open: **Apr.–Dec.**
Breakfast: **Full**
Pets: **Sometimes**
Children: **Welcome**
Smoking: **Permitted**
Social Drinking: **Permitted**
Airport/Station Pickup: **Yes**

Furnished in Early American fashion, accented with lush plants and family treasures, this comfortable brick ranch-style house can be your home away from home. The Brennans are history buffs who, now that they're retired, enjoy traveling and entertaining travelers. Breakfast features bacon and eggs with home fries, or sausages and pancakes, or delicious muffins to go with the homemade jam. You can walk off the calories on your way to the Haines Mill, Dorney Park, or one of the area's many museums.

Around the World Bed & Breakfast ✪
30 SOUTH WHITEOAK STREET, KUTZTOWN, PENNSYLVANIA 19530

Tel: **(610) 683-8885**
Hosts: **Jean and Joel Masiko**
Location: **15 mi. E/W of Allentown/ Reading**
No. of Rooms: **2**
No. of Private Baths: **2**
Double/pb: **$79**
Single/pb: **$69**
Suites: **$75–$125**
Open: **All year**
Reduced Rates: **$10 less Dec.–March; 10% seniors**

Breakfast: **Full**
Credit Cards: **DISC, MC, VISA**
Pets: **No**
Children: **Welcome, over 12**
Smoking: **No**
Social Drinking: **Permitted**
Minimum Stay: **2 nights Renninger's Antique Show, last week Apr., June, Sept.**
Airport/Station Pickup: **Yes**

Around the World Bed & Breakfast is located one half-block from Main Street, an antique lover's paradise in the heart of Pennsylvania Dutch countryside. Built in 1830, this brick Victorian still maintains the charm and character of a well-kept home. Rooms are authentically decorated with artifacts from around the world to suggest Australia, the Pacific Coast, western parts of North America, and the local Amish culture. All guest rooms have queen-size beds, phone, and air-conditioning. The suites have TV. Jean and Joel invite you to enjoy the landscaped gardens, complete with a lily pond and gazebo.

Longswamp Bed and Breakfast ✪
1605 STATE STREET, MERTZTOWN, PENNSYLVANIA 19539

Tel: **(610) 682-6197**
Hosts: **Elsa and Dean Dimick**
Location: **12 mi. SW of Allentown**
No. of Rooms: **10**
No. of Private Baths: **6**
Max. No. Sharing Bath: **4**
Double/pb: **$83–$88**
Single/pb: **$73–$78**
Double/sb: **$83–$88**

Single/sb: **$73–$78**
Open: **All year**
Breakfast: **Full**
Credit Cards: **AMEX, MC, VISA**
Pets: **No**
Children: **Welcome**
Smoking: **No**
Social Drinking: **Permitted**
Foreign Languages: **French**

This guesthouse was originally built around 1750 and served as the first post office in town. The main house, completed in 1863, was a stop on the Underground Railroad. Today, Longswamp is a comfortable place with high ceilings, antiques, large fireplaces, plants, and bookcases full of reading pleasure. Breakfast specialties include home-dried fruits, *pain perdu*, quiche, and homemade breads. Elsa offers wine, cheese, and coffee anytime. She will gladly direct you to antique shops, auction houses, Reading, and the Amish country.

Classic Victorian ✪
35 NORTH NEW STREET, NAZARETH, PENNSYLVANIA 18064

Tel: **(610) 759-8276**	Breakfast: **Full**
Best time to call: **Morning–evenings**	Credit Cards: **AMEX, MC, VISA**
Hosts: **Irene and Dan Sokolowski**	Pets: **No**
No. of Rooms: **3**	Children: **Welcome**
No. of Private Baths: **3**	Smoking: **No**
Double/pb: **$80–$85**	Social Drinking: **Permitted**
Suite: **$105**	Minimum Stay: **2 nights holiday**
Open: **All year**	**weekends, special events**
Reduced Rates: **10% weekly**	

Step into this circa 1908 brick Colonial Revival located in the historic district of Nazareth, the oldest Moravian settlement of North America. Classic Victorian offers a comfortable mix of antique and traditional furnishings coupled with a warm and relaxed atmosphere. Amenities include down-filled comforters, classical music, evening turn-down service, air-conditioning, TVs, and a three-course breakfast served on Wedgwood in the dining room, front veranda, or second-floor balcony. The Bach Festival in May and the Music Fest in August are 15 minutes away. Manhattan, N.Y., and Philadelphia are $1^1/_2$ hrs. away. Jacobsburg Environmental Education Center, within a ten-minute drive, offers hiking, bird-watching, nature photography, horseback riding, and 1166 acres of the great outdoors. Irene and Dan enjoy entertaining and restoring their Colonial Revival.

BRANDYWINE VALLEY

Bed & Breakfast at Walnut Hill ✪
541 CHANDLER'S MILL ROAD, AVONDALE, PENNSYLVANIA 19311

Tel: **(610) 444-3703; fax: (610) 444-6889**	Single/sb: **$70**
	Open: **All year**
Best Time to Call: **Anytime**	Breakfast: **Full**
Hosts: **Sandy and Tom Mills**	Pets: **No**
Location: **2 mi. S of Kennett Square**	Children: **Welcome, over 2**
No. of Rooms: **2**	Smoking: **Permitted**
Max. No. Sharing Bath: **4**	Social Drinking: **Permitted**
Double/sb: **$85**	

Sandy and Tom's 1844 mill house is in Kennett Square (despite the mailing address above) in the heart of the Brandywine Valley, midway between Philadelphia and Amish country. Longwood Gardens, Chadds Ford Winery, Winterthur, Brandywine River (Wyeth) Museum, and other museums are all within an eight-mile radius. But nature lovers may want to stay on the B&B grounds, where horses graze in the meadow and a great blue heron fishes in the stream. Deer, Canada geese, and the occasional red fox also put in appearances. Guests enjoy walking along the country road, sitting on the wicker-filled porch, or relaxing in the hot tub. However you plan to spend your day, you'll begin it with breakfast specialties like cottage cheese pancakes with blueberry sauce, fresh mushroom omelettes, and French toast. Sandy welcomes guests with lemonade, iced tea, hot cider, and homemade sweets.

Old Country Bed & Breakfast
1260 MIDDLETOWN ROAD, GLEN MILLS, PENNSYLVANIA 19342

Tel: **(610) 358-0504**
Hosts: **Roger and Claire Poulet**
Location: **15 mi SW of Philadelphia**
No. of Rooms: **3**
No. of Private Baths: **3**
Double/pb: **$75**
Single/pb: **$65**
Open: **All year**

Reduced Rates: **10% weekly**
Breakfast: **Continental**
Credit Cards: **AMEX, MC, VISA**
Pets: **No**
Children: **Welcome**
Smoking: **No**
Social Drinking: **Permitted**
Foreign Languages: **French**

Old Country Bed & Breakfast is a renovated 1800s barn built of stone and wood siding, located on five acres. The renovated rooms have exposed beams and cathedral ceilings. You will enjoy the American and European antiques throughout the house. Guests are offered soft drinks, wine, and cheese upon arrival. In the morning, a continental breakfast consisting of coffee cake, muffins, or pastries, fresh fruit, and juices is served. Ridley Creek Park is a short walk away; Brandywine attractions are 20 minutes away by car. Your innkeepers are a teacher and interior architect. Both speak French and enjoy traveling.

Bankhouse Bed & Breakfast ✪
875 HILLSDALE ROAD, WEST CHESTER, PENNSYLVANIA 19382

Tel: **(610) 344-7388**
Best time to call: **2–10 PM**
Hosts: **Diana and Michael Bove**
No. of Rooms: **2**
No. of Private Baths: **1**
Max. No. Sharing Bath: **4**
Double/pb: **$90**
Double/sb: **$70**
Suite: **$90**

Open: **All year**
Reduced Rates: **Available**
Breakfast: **Full**
Pets: **No**
Children: **Welcome, over 12**
Smoking: **No**
Social Drinking: **Permitted**
Minimum Stay: **2 nights weekends May–Oct.**

This 18th-century stuccoed stone bankhouse overlooks a 10-acre horse farm and pond. Bankhouse is conveniently located to Brandywine Valley attractions such as Longwood Gardens, Winterthur, and Brandywine River Museum. Philadelphia and Lancaster are only a 45-minute drive away. Guests have a private entrance, porch, and sitting room.

The house is charmingly decorated with country antiques, folk art, stenciling, and a wall full of books and games. Michael is a production engineer in the media services department of a local college. Diana markets her cross-stitch and quilting projects, and prides herself on having more than 100 muffin recipes—you're sure to sample some of her homemade snacks.

BUCKS COUNTY

Maplewood Farm Bed & Breakfast ✪
5090 DURHAM ROAD, P.O. BOX 239, GARDENVILLE, PENNSYLVANIA 18926

Tel: **(215) 766-0477**	Reduced Rates: **Mon.–Thurs.**
Best Time to Call: **10 AM–9:30 PM**	Breakfast: **Full**
Hosts: **Cindy and Dennis Marquis**	Credit Cards: **AMEX, DISC, MC, VISA**
Location: **45 mi. NW of Philadelphia**	Pets: **No**
No. of Rooms: **5**	Children: **Welcome, Sun.–Thurs.**
No. of Private Baths: **5**	Smoking: **No**
Double/pb: **$85**	Social Drinking: **Permitted**
Suite: **$135**	Minimum Stay: **2 nights weekends, 3**
Open: **All year**	**nights holidays**

Near New Hope and Peddler's Village, Maplewood Farm offers you gentle country living. One-hundred-year-old trees shelter this farmhouse that dates back to 1792. The five-acre property has a beautiful shaded creek for picnicking, pastures for grazing sheep, chickens who provide fresh eggs for morning breakfast, and a two-story bank-barn that houses playful barnyard cats. Guest rooms are decorated country casual with hand-painted murals, stenciling, colorful quilts, and country antiques. Breakfast specialties include fresh fruit salad topped with yogurt, homemade granola, baked apples, omelets filled with fresh vegetables, pancakes, and Pennsylvania sausage. Upon returning from your day's adventures, enjoy seasonal refreshments by fireside or poolside. A soothing evening cordial is offered before or after dinner.

Aaron Burr House ✪
80 WEST BRIDGE STREET, NEW HOPE, PENNSYLVANIA 18938

Tel: **(215) 862-2343, 862-2570**	Reduced Rates: **Mon.–Thurs., corporate**
Best Time to Call: **10 AM–10 PM**	**guests**
Hosts: **Jesse and Carl Glassman**	Breakfast: **Continental, plus**
Location: **20 mi. N of Philadelphia**	Pets: **Sometimes**
No. of Rooms: **6**	Children: **Welcome**
No. of Private Baths: **6**	Smoking: **No**
Double/pb: **$75**	Social Drinking: **Permitted**
Single/pb: **$70**	Minimum Stay: **2 nights on weekends, 3**
Suites: **$95–$195; sleeps 3**	**nights holidays**
Open: **All year**	Station Pickup: **Yes**

This 1874 Victorian is tucked onto a tree-lined street in the town's historic district, just steps from the village center. New Hope was founded in 1681, so visitors can absorb three centuries of architecture and American history, plus fine antique shops, excellent restaurants, and art galleries and crafts shops. At the end of the day, join your host in the parlor for reading, games, refreshments, and friendly conversation. After a peaceful night's rest in a canopy bed, you'll wake up to the aroma of fresh coffee and home-baked muffins.

Wedgwood Inn of New Hope ✪
111 WEST BRIDGE STREET, NEW HOPE, PENNSYLVANIA 18938-1401

Tel: **(215) 862-2520**
Best Time to Call: **10 AM–10 PM**
Hosts: **Carl Glassman and Nadine Silnutzer**
Location: **62 mi. SW of New York City**
No. of Rooms: **12**
No. of Private Baths: **12**
Double/pb: **$70–$125**
Single/pb: **$65–$115**
Double/sb: **$65–$85**
Single/sb: **$60–$80**
Suites: **$90–$185**
Open: **All year**

Reduced Rates: **Available**
Breakfast: **Continental, plus**
Credit Cards: **AMEX, MC, VISA**
Pets: **Sometimes**
Children: **Welcome**
Smoking: **No**
Social Drinking: **Permitted**
Minimum Stay: **3 holiday weekends, 2 nights if stay includes Saturday**
Station Pickup: **Yes**
Foreign Languages: **French, Hebrew, Spanish**

Wedgwood pottery is displayed throughout this aptly named two-and-a-half-story home with lots of 19th-century details: a gabled roof, veranda, porte cochere, and gazebo. Rooms are decorated with antiques, original art, handmade quilts, and fresh flowers. You can breakfast on house specialties like lemon yogurt poppyseed bread and ricotta pineapple muffins on the sunporch, in the gazebo, or in the privacy of your room. Carl and Nadine are such accomplished hosts that they conduct workshops and seminars on innkeeping, and Carl has taught courses on buying and operating country inns.

CARLISLE/HARRISBURG AREA

Line Limousin Farmhouse B&B ✪

2070 RITNER HIGHWAY, CARLISLE, PENNSYLVANIA 17013
bline@pa.net

Tel: **(717) 243-1281; fax: (717) 249-2865**	Single/sb: **$55**
Hosts: **Bob and Joan Line**	Open: **All year**
Location: **22 mi. W of Harrisburg**	Breakfast: **Full**
No. of Rooms: **4**	Pets: **No**
No. of Private Baths: **2**	Children: **Welcome, over 8**
Max. No. Sharing Bath: **4**	Smoking: **No**
Double/pb: **$85**	Social Drinking: **Permitted**
Single/pb: **$65**	Minimum Stay: **3 nights car shows**
Double/sb: **$65**	Airport/Station Pickup: **Yes**

Bob's great-grandfather built this eleven-room stone and brick house in 1864, using walnut wood from the farm for all the woodwork. Rooms are furnished with family heirlooms—some older than the house—and have fresh flowers, air-conditioning, and cable TV. A hearty breakfast is served in an antique-filled dining room on Limoges china. A refrigerator for guest use is stocked with juice and soft drinks. Bob and Joan raise Limousin beef cattle from Limoges, France. If you're tired of artificial, mass-produced country decor, come and experience the real thing.

CENTRAL PENNSYLVANIA

Rest & Repast Bed & Breakfast Service ✪
P.O. BOX 126, PINE GROVE MILLS, PENNSYLVANIA 16868
iul.com/bnbipa

Tel: **(814) 238-1484**; fax: **(814) 234-9890**
Best Time to Call: **8:30–11:30 AM Mon.–Fri.**
Coordinators: **Linda and Brent Peters**
States/Regions Covered: **Aaronsburg,**
Bellefonte, Boalsburg, Clearfield, Phillipsburg, Potters Mills, Spruce Creek, State College, Tyrone
Rates (Single/Double):
Average: **$50–$55 / $55–$65**
Luxury: **$60–$75 / $75–$100**

Since 1982, Rest & Repast has represented inspected bed and breakfasts throughout central Pennsylvania. The fifty-plus properties include scenic farms near famous fly fishing streams, estates listed on the National Register of Historic Places, contemporary homes within walking distance to Penn State, apartments, guest houses, and cottages. Visit the many historical sites, hike the mountainsides at the many parks, or tour the area's charming 19th-century villages and shops.

Christopher Kratzer House ✪
101 EAST CHERRY STREET, CLEARFIELD, PENNSYLVANIA 16830

Tel: **(814) 765-5024; (888) 252-2632**
Hosts: **Bruce and Ginny Baggett**
No. of Rooms: **3**
No. of Private Baths: **1**
Max. No. Sharing Bath: **4**
Double/pb: **$70**
Single/pb: **$55**
Double/sb: **$55**
Single/sb: **$45**
Open: **All year**
Reduced Rates: **10% after 3rd night**
Breakfast: **Full**
Credit Cards: **MC, VISA**
Pets: **No**
Children: **Welcome**
Smoking: **Permitted**
Social Drinking: **Permitted**
Airport/Station Pickup: **Yes**

This Classic Revival House, located in the Old Town Historic District, was built prior to 1840 by Christopher Kratzer, a noted lumberman, carpenter, architect, politician, and owner of the county's first newspaper. Bruce and Ginny have filled the rooms with an interesting mix of historical and contemporary pieces that reflect their interest in music and art. The house has views of the river and park, white picket fences, a spacious yard and large old trees. You'll be within walking distance of shops, an antique emporium, library, restaurants, movie theater, and the Clearfield County Historical Society Museum. Activities nearby include boating, fishing, and hiking; Penn State University football stadium is less than an hour away.

Victorian Loft Bed & Breakfast ✪
216 SOUTH FRONT STREET, CLEARFIELD, PENNSYLVANIA 16830
pdurant@csrlink.net; www.virtualcities.com/ons/pa/z/paza601.htm

Tel: **(814) 765-4805; (800) 798-0456**	Suites: **$85–$110**
Best Time to Call: **Evenings**	Open: **All year**
Hosts: **Tim and Peggy Durant**	Reduced Rates: **10% after 3rd night**
Location: **40 mi. NW of State College**	Breakfast: **Full**
No. of Rooms: **3**	Credit Cards: **AMEX, DISC, MC, VISA**
Max. No. Sharing Bath: **4**	Pets: **Sometimes**
Double/pb: **$65–$80**	Children: **Welcome**
Single/pb: **$60–$75**	Smoking: **No**
Double/sb: **$50–$65**	Social Drinking: **No**
Single/sb: **$45–$60**	Airport/Station Pickup: **Yes**
Cabin: **$65–$105**	

Victorian charm fills this elegant 1894 riverfront home in the historic district, from the double-decker gingerbread porches to the grand staircase and original stained glass windows. This B&B is located just off Exit 19 PA of I-80 and minutes from myriad outdoor recreational activities. Guest rooms have air conditioning with skylights or balcony. The suite has a private kitchen, dining room, entertainment center, and whirlpool bath. There is a weaving studio, and spinning demonstrations are given upon request. Also off-premises is a three-bedroom mountain cabin near the state parks.

North Bend Bed & Breakfast ✪
P.O. BOX 214, ROUTE 120, JOHN AVENUE, NORTH BEND,
PENNSYLVANIA 17760

Tel: **(717) 923-2927**	Open: **All year**
Best Time to Call: **6 PM–10 PM**	Reduced Rates: **Jan.–Feb. 2 nights $99**
Hosts: **Barbara and John Mastriania**	Breakfast: **Full**
Location: **24 mi. W of Lock Haven**	Credit Cards: **AMEX, DISC, MC, VISA**
No. of Rooms: **4**	Pets: **No**
Max. No. Sharing Bath: **4**	Children: **Welcome**
Double/sb: **$56**	Smoking: **Permitted**
Single/sb: **$54**	Social Drinking: **Permitted**

Nestled in the heart of Pennsylvania's Keystone Mountain country, North Bend Bed & Breakfast offers a peaceful getaway. Barbara and John operate an antique shop located on the premises. Breakfast features homemade breads and is served in a large dining room. Guests are invited to have early morning coffee in the cozy kitchen featuring a radiator with a built-in warmer, or on the front porch in warm weather. This area is ideal for outdoor enthusiasts and those who love to visit the roads less traveled.

ERIE AREA

Raspberry House Bed & Breakfast ✪
118 ERIE STREET, ROUTE 99, EDINBORO, PENNSYLVANIA 16412

Tel: **(814) 734-8997**	Reduced Rates: **Available**
Best Time to Call: **After 6 PM weekdays, anytime on weekends**	Breakfast: **Full**
	Pets: **No**
Hosts: **Betty and Hal Holmstrom**	Children: **Welcome**
Location: **20 mi. S of Erie**	Smoking: **No**
No. of Rooms: **4**	Social Drinking: **Permitted**
No. of Private Baths: **4**	Minimum Stay: **2 nights on Edinboro**
Double/pb: **$80**	**homecoming weekend**
Single/pb: **$55**	Airport/Station Pickup: **Yes**
Open: **All year**	

Raspberry House Bed & Breakfast is an 1860 Victorian home that has been restored to its original charm. Located in the heart of Edinboro, this B&B allows guests the opportunity to enjoy biking, skiing, boating, golf, historical attractions, shopping, and university activities. Breakfast is served daily, with accommodation for special dietary needs; wake-up coffee can be served in your room. A common room for guests is furnished with a TV, VCR, and telephone. All guest rooms are individually decorated and have a private bath.

GETTYSBURG AREA

Shultz Victorian Mansion Bed & Breakfast ✪
756 PHILADELPHIA AVENUE, CHAMBERSBURG, PENNSYLVANIA 17225

Tel: **(717) 263-3371**	Open: **All year**
Best Time to Call: **8 AM–9 PM**	Reduced Rates: **10% Jan.–Mar.; after 4th night**
Hosts: **Doris and Joe Shultz**	
Location: **23 mi. W of Gettysburg**	Breakfast: **Full**
No. of Rooms: **9**	Credit Cards: **MC, VISA**
No. of Private Baths: **9**	Pets: **No**
Double/pb: **$63–$85**	Children: **Welcome, over 10**
Single/pb: **$58–$80**	Smoking: **No**
Suites: **$115**	Social Drinking: **Permitted**

Shultz Victorian Mansion Bed & Breakfast is located twenty-four miles north of Hagerstown, Maryland, along a tree-lined street in a charming neighborhood. This 1880 Victorian brick home has an onion-topped turret and elaborate wood carving throughout. Guests are invited to enjoy three common rooms, large porches and gardens, balcony, air-conditioning, and the family collection of antiques. Wilson College, Shippensburg University, two state parks, Mercersburg Academy, and Dickenson College and Law School are all within minutes of this bed and breakfast. Breakfast is served by candlelight.

The Brafferton Inn

44 YORK STREET, GETTYSBURG, PENNSYLVANIA 17325

Tel: **(717) 337-3423**	Suites: **$125**
Best Time to Call: **9 AM–9 PM**	Open: **All year**
Hosts: **Jane and Sam Back**	Breakfast: **Full**
Location: **90 mi. N of Washington, D.C.;**	Credit Cards: **AMEX, DISC, MC, VISA**
2 mi. from Rte 15 York Street exit	Pets: **No**
No. of Rooms: **10**	Children: **Welcome, over 7**
No. of Private Baths: **10**	Smoking: **No**
Double/pb: **$90–$105**	Social Drinking: **Permitted**

Listed on the National Register of Historic Places, the Brafferton Inn is a landmark in the historic town of Gettysburg. This 1786 fieldstone home has been fully restored and decorated with exquisite antiques and original artistry throughout. The Inn combines elegance and ease. Warm-colored oriental rugs, comfortable wingbacks, and a tall 1800 grandfather clock grace the living room. The dining room boasts a stunning folk art mural. A deck and an in-town garden provide guests with quiet getaway spots.

Country Escape ✪

275 OLD ROUTE 30, P.O. BOX 195, MCKNIGHTSTOWN, PENNSYLVANIA 17343

Tel: **(717) 338-0611**	Open: **All year**
Hosts: **Merry V. Bush and Ross Hetrick**	Breakfast: **Full**
Location: **6 mi. W of Gettysburg**	Credit Cards: **AMEX, DISC, MC, VISA**
No. of Rooms: **3**	Pets: **Sometimes**
No. of Private Baths: **1**	Children: **Welcome**
Max. No. Sharing Bath: **4**	Smoking: **No**
Double/pb: **$80**	Social Drinking: **Permitted**
Double/sb: **$65**	

Country Escape Bed and Breakfast is located on the road the Confederates took to Gettysburg. The house was built in 1868, and is located 5 miles from the famous battlefield. Rooms are furnished in country decor with some antiques. Local crafts are displayed throughout and are for sale. The extensive gardens include a pond, and the mountains can be seen in the distance. Merry and Ross invite you to come and immerse yourself in history or relax in a quiet atmosphere. Merry runs a desktop publishing company, and Ross owns a used bookshop/coffee bar in Gettysburg.

Fox Run Inn ✪
14873 BAIN ROAD, MERCERSBURG, PENNSYLVANIA 17236

Tel: **(717) 328-3570**
Best Time to Call: **After 7 PM**
Hosts: **Dick and Elsie Secrest**
Location: **54 mi. NW of Washington, D.C.**
No. of Rooms: **4**
No. of Private Baths: **4**
Double/pb: **$65**

Open: **All year**
Reduced Rates: **6th night free**
Breakfast: **Full**
Credit Cards: **MC, VISA**
Pets: **No**
Children: **Welcome, over 12**
Smoking: **No**
Social Drinking: **Permitted**

Built in 1786, this authentically restored farmhouse is surrounded by 170 acres of fields with walking trails. The inn's views of the country-side and Tuscarora Mountain are spectacular. The kitchen and dining area have open beamed ceilings and an exposed log wall in the dining area. Each of the four bedrooms has private baths and three have queen-size beds. Guests have full use of the house including the always full cookie jar. Barbecue facilities are also provided. Whitetail Ski Resort, Mercersburg Academy, State Parks, Antietam Battlefield, country auctions and antique shops, golfing, and Fort Frederick are among the nearby attractions.

PENNSYLVANIA DUTCH AREA

Adamstown Inns ✪
62 WEST MAIN STREET, ADAMSTOWN, PENNSYLVANIA 19501

Tel: **(717) 484-0800; (800) 594-4808**
Hosts: **Tom and Wanda Berman**

Location: **10 mi. SW of Reading**
No. of Rooms: **7**

No. of Private Baths: **7**
Double/pb: **$70–$80**
Suite: **$105–$135**
Open: **All year**
Reduced Rates: **10% after 4th night**
Breakfast: **Continental, plus**

Credit Cards: **MC, VISA**
Pets: **No**
Children: **Welcome, over 12**
Smoking: **Restricted**
Social Drinking: **Permitted**

In the heart of Adamstown's antique district, and just a short drive from Pennsylvania Dutch country and Reading's factory outlets, you'll find Victorian B&B—the Adamstown Inn and the Amethyst Inn. Inside, lace and balloon curtains and oriental rugs complement the chestnut woodwork and leaded-glass doors. Five rooms feature two-person Jacuzzis. Three rooms also include gas log fireplaces. Your hosts are avid antiquers and will gladly direct you to their favorite haunts. Coffee or tea will be brought to your door in the morning; refills, as well as juice, fresh fruit, cheese, and home-baked goodies, are served during a Continental breakfast.

Mill Creek Homestead Bed & Breakfast ✪
2578 OLD PHILADELPHIA PIKE, BIRD-IN-HAND, PENNSYLVANIA 17505

Tel: **(717) 291-6419; (800) 771-2578**
Hosts: **Vicki and Frank Alfone**
Location: **5 mi. E of Lancaster**
No. of Rooms: **3**
No. of Private Baths: **3**
Double/pb: **$75–$80**
Single/pb: **$65–$70**
Suites: **$95–$130**
Open: **All year**

Reduced Rates: **Available**
Breakfast: **Full**
Credit Cards: **DISC, MC, VISA**
Pets: **No**
Children: **Welcome, over 10**
Smoking: **No**
Social Drinking: **Permitted**
Minimum Stay: **2 nights holidays**

Mill Creek Homestead is the second oldest home in Bird-In-Hand. This fieldstone farmhouse was built in the eighteenth century, but it has central air-conditioning, and is gracefully decorated with treasured family pieces and locally made Amish quilts. Before beginning your day of activities, enjoy a hearty breakfast served in the formal dining room. Upon returning, enjoy complimentary light refreshments and a dip in the pool on those hot summer days. Or pull up a rocking chair on the porch and watch the horse and buggies while sipping your first cup of coffee or that cool glass of iced tea. There are so many things to do and see that there will be no time for phones or TV.

The Enchanted Cottage ✪
RD 4, 22 DEER RUN ROAD, BOYERTOWN, PENNSYLVANIA 19512

Tel: **(610) 845-8845**
Hosts: **Peg and Richard Groff**
Location: **16 mi. S of Allentown**
No. of Private Baths: **1**

Double/pb: **$90**
Single/pb: **$80**
Open: **All year**

Reduced Rates: **$5 less Mon.–Thurs.**
except holidays and special events
Breakfast: **Full**
Pets: **No**

Children: **Welcome, over 12**
Smoking: **Permitted**
Social Drinking: **Permitted**

Complete privacy awaits you in this cozy cottage nestled in a clearing in the woods. Downstairs, the exposed beams, wood-burning fireplace, quilts, and antique furniture lend themselves to quiet, romantic evenings. On the second floor you'll find an air-conditioned double bedroom and a Laura Ashley bathroom. Gourmet breakfasts are served in the main house in front of either the garden or a cheerful fire, depending on the season. While the cottage is a destination in itself, you'll have easy access to the Pennsylvania Dutch area, the Reading factory outlets, antique shops, historic sites, and country auctions. An excellent restaurant is within walking distance.

The Columbian ✪
360 CHESTNUT STREET, COLUMBIA, PENNSYLVANIA 17512
bedandb@aol.com; user.aol.com/bedandb

Tel: **(717) 684-5869; (800) 422-5869**
Hosts: **Chris and Becky Will**
Location: **8 mi. W of Lancaster**
No. of Rooms: **6**
No. of Private Baths: **6**
Double/pb: **$65–$105**
Suites: **$105**
Open: **All year**
Reduced Rates: **10% seniors; after 4th night**

Breakfast: **Full**
Credit Cards: **MC, VISA**
Pets: **No**
Children: **Welcome**
Smoking: **No**
Social Drinking: **Permitted**
Minimum Stay: **2 nights June–Oct., holiday weekends**
Airport/Station Pickup: **Yes**

Built in 1896, this brick Colonial Revival mansion features an ornate stained glass window, tiered staircase, and unique wraparound porches. The Columbian is centrally located minutes from the local attractions in the historic river town of Columbia, a onetime stop on the Underground Railroad that came within two votes of becoming the capital of the United States. This is a porch-sitting town where you can still get a malted at the local drugstore. Come relax with Becky and Chris in their lovely bed and breakfast and browse through nearby antique shops, art galleries, and museums.

Sheep Hill Bed & Breakfast ✪
1322 SHEEP HILL ROAD, EAST EARL, PENNSYLVANIA 17519

Tel: **(717) 355-2041; (717) 354-3146**
Best Time to Call: **11 AM–9 PM**
Hosts: **Laura and Greg Sabasino**
Location: **17 mi. E of Lancaster**
No. of Rooms: **3**

No. of Private Baths: **2**
Max. No. Sharing Bath: **4**
Double/pb: **$65–$75**
Double/sb: **$55**
Open: **All year**

Reduced Rates: **10% seniors**
Breakfast: **Full**
Pets: **No**

Children: **Welcome, over 12**
Smoking: **No**
Social Drinking: **Permitted**

Escape to a bygone era in this circa 1870 farmhouse, warmly furnished with antiques and personal collections. The smells of a family-style breakfast will awaken you. Sheep Hill is located close to antique shops (Antique Capital of the U.S.), outlet shopping museums, farmers' markets, craft shops, and many excellent restaurants. As you travel to your destination you will see Amish farmers working the fields just as it was done years ago. After a long day of enjoyment in Lancaster County, set a spell on the large wraparound porch, sip lemonade, and watch the sunset melt into the farmland. Laura and Greg will be happy to make special arrangements for you, including dinner with a local Amish family.

George Zahm House Bed & Breakfast ✪
6070 MAIN STREET, EAST PETERSBURG, PENNSYLVANIA 17520

Tel: **(717) 569-6026**
Hosts: **Robyn Kemple-Keeports and Jeff Keeports**
Location: **4 mi. N of Lancaster**
No. of Rooms: **4**
No. of Private Baths: **4**
Double/pb: **$65–$75**
Suites: **$70–$85**
Open: **All year**

Reduced Rates: **10% seniors, weekly, corporate**
Breakfast: **Continental, plus**
Credit Cards: **MC, VISA**
Pets: **No**
Children: **Welcome, over 12**
Smoking: **No**
Social Drinking: **Permitted**
Minimum Stay: **2 nights holidays**

A Federal home built in 1854 and restored, George Zahm House boasts ten-foot ceilings throughout and is richly furnished with an eclectic collection of family heirlooms and antiques. Three restaurants are within walking distance and Lancaster City is only a ten-minute drive away. Robyn, her mother Daneen, and Jeff all planned and worked on the renovations and decor of the inn and enjoy refinishing furniture, antiquing, and going to auctions. Breakfast is served on Blue Willow china in the formal dining room and includes homemade breads, jams, Belgian waffles, granolas, and seasonal fresh fruit.

Elm Country Inn Bed & Breakfast ✪
P.O. BOX 37, ELM AND NEWPORT ROADS, ELM, PENNSYLVANIA 17521

Tel: **(717) 664-3623; (800) 245-0532;**
  fax: **(717) 664-2734**
Best Time to Call: **After 4:30 PM**
Hosts: **Betty and Melvin Meck**
Location: **12 mi. N of Lancaster**
No. of Rooms: **2**
Max. No. Sharing Bath: **4**
Double/pb: **$65**
Double/sb: **$50–$55**
Single/sb: **$40**

Open: **Mar.–Dec.**
Reduced Rates: **Families**
Breakfast: **Full**
Credit Cards: **MC, VISA**
Pets: **No**
Children: **Welcome**
Smoking: **No**
Social Drinking: **Permitted**
Airport/Station Pickup: **Yes**

Located in a small country village, this 1860 brick farmhouse overlooks beautiful farmland. The large, sunny rooms feature original wood trim and are furnished with a pleasing blend of antiques and collectibles. Antique shops, crafts shops, and opportunities to fish or canoe are available. Betty and Melvin thoroughly enjoy having visitors and do their best to make them feel instantly at home.

Gibson's Bed & Breakfast ✪
141 WEST CARACAS AVENUE, HERSHEY, PENNSYLVANIA 17033

Tel: **(717) 534-1305**
Hosts: **Frances and Bob Gibson**
Location: **One block off Rte. 422**
No. of Rooms: **3**
Max. No. Sharing Bath: **3**
Double/sb: **$55**
Single/sb: **$45**

Open: **All year**
Breakfast: **Full**
Pets: **No**
Children: **Welcome, over 5**
Smoking: **No**
Social Drinking: **Permitted**
Airport/Station Pickup: **Yes**

Bob and Frances Gibson have a 65-year-old Cape Cod, located in the center of Hershey, within walking distance to many local attractions. The house has been recently renovated to enhance the charm of the hardwood floors, wood trim, and original windows. The atmosphere is friendly and informal. The Gibsons will gladly help you find local sights such as Hershey Park, Chocolate World, Founders Hall, and the Amish country.

Walkabout Inn ✪
837 VILLAGE ROAD, LAMPETER (LANCASTER COUNTY), PENNSYLVANIA 17537

Tel: **(717) 464-0707**	Open: **All year**
Best Time to Call: **9 AM–9 PM**	Reduced Rates: **Available**
Hosts: **Richard and Maggie Mason**	Breakfast: **Full**
Location: **3 mi. S of Lancaster**	Credit Cards: **AMEX, MC, VISA**
No. of Rooms: **5**	Pets: **No**
No. of Private Baths: **5**	Children: **Welcome, over 10**
Double/pb: **$99**	Smoking: **No**
Single/pb: **$79**	Social Drinking: **Permitted**
Suites: **$149**	

The Walkabout Inn takes its name from the Australian word that means to go out and discover new places. Australian-born host Richard Mason and his wife, Margaret, will help you explore the Amish country that surrounds their brick Mennonite farmhouse. The twenty-two-room house was built in 1925 and features a large wraparound porch with wicker furniture, wildflower gardens, and an exotic fish pond. The house was built by a master cabinetmaker and features chestnut wood-work, decorative flooring, and floor-to-ceiling cabinets. Guest rooms are decorated with antiques, Oriental rugs, and fireplaces; most have can-opy beds. Honeymoon and anniversary suites have Jacuzzis or hot tubs, and all have cable TV. When it's time to say "Good day," a candlelight gourmet breakfast is served on silver and crystal in the dining room. Homemade Australian bread, pastries, and imported tea from Down Under are always on the menu. Special packages are available between December and April, including a dinner for two.

Lincoln Haus Inn Bed & Breakfast ✪
1687 LINCOLN HIGHWAY EAST, LANCASTER, PENNSYLVANIA 17602

Tel: **(717) 392-9412**	Suites: **$80–$85**
Best Time to Call: **Before 11 PM**	Open: **All year**
Host: **Mary K. Zook**	Reduced Rates: **Available**
Location: **2 mi. E of Lancaster**	Breakfast: **Full**
No. of Rooms: **5**	Pets: **No**
No. of Private Baths: **5**	Children: **Welcome**
Double/pb: **$55–$70**	Smoking: **No**
Single/pb: **$53–$68**	Social Drinking: **No**

Ten minutes east of historic Lancaster and five minutes from Route 30 and the Pennsylvania Dutch Visitors Bureau in Lancaster County, you'll find this 1915 stucco home with distinctive hip roofs and burgundy trim. Above the living room door, your host has hung a "Welcome" sign. Mary prides herself on giving guests a glimpse of the Amish life-style; the farmers' market, horse auctions, buggy rides, quilt sales, and traditional Amish farmlands are all within ten to twenty minutes by car. But before you set out, you'll have a hearty family-style breakfast including juice, fruit, quiche, sausage, and different kinds of muffins.

The Loom Room ✪

1458 OLD BERNVILLE ROAD, LEESPORT, PENNSYLVANIA 19533
gsmith1458@aol.com

Tel: **(610) 926-3217; fax: (610) 926-3217**	Double/sb: **$45**
Best Time to Call: **9 AM–9 PM**	Open: **All year**
Hosts: **Mary and Gene Smith**	Reduced Rates: **Weekly**
Location: **4 mi. N of Reading**	Breakfast: **Full**
No. of Rooms: **3**	Pets: **No**
No. of Private Baths: **1**	Children: **Welcome (crib)**
Max. No. Sharing Bath: **4**	Smoking: **No**
Double/pb: **$50**	Social Drinking: **Permitted**
	Airport/Station Pickup: **Yes**

The Loom Room is a stucco-covered stone farmhouse dating back to 1812. It is located in the Berks County countryside, surrounded by shade trees, flowers, and herb gardens. The spacious rooms feature country antiques, open beams, and handwoven accessories. Mary, once a weaver and now a sculptor, works in a 1760 log studio attached to the main house. Gene, an avid golfer, is the breakfast chef. Breakfast offers hearty fare, like eggnog French toast, homemade muffins, country fries, chipped beef, apple cinnamon pancakes, country sausage, bacon, and a variety of fruits. This lovely homestead is minutes from Reading's outlets, antiquing, numerous hiking trails, golf courses, and many historical sites.

Market Sleigh Bed & Breakfast ✪

BOX 99, 57 SOUTH MAIN STREET, LOGANVILLE, PENNSYLVANIA 17342-0099

Tel: **(717) 428-1440**	Reduced Rates: **After 3rd day**
Best Time to Call: **3–6 PM**	Breakfast: **Full**
Hosts: **Judy and Jerry Dietz**	Credit Cards: **MC, VISA**
Location: **7 mi. S of York**	Pets: **No**
No. of Rooms: **2**	Children: **Welcome (no crib)**
No. of Private Baths: **1**	Smoking: **No**
Suite: **$65–$85; $20 each additional person**	Social Drinking: **Permitted**
	Minimum Stay: **2 nights convention weekends**
Open: **All year**	

This bed and breakfast takes its name from the 19th-century sleigh sitting by the entrance as if stranded after the snow melted. A peaceful night's sleep and a hearty farmer's breakfast await you. Walk the paths of the 22-acre farm through the meadows, enjoy the stream and the quiet of the woodland, or just relax near the water garden and enjoy the view of the sheep and horses grazing in the valley. Judy and Jerry will direct you to fine dining, rail excursions, a dozen golf courses, parks, museums (including the Harley-Davidson Motorcycle Museum, only minutes away), farm markets, wineries, antiques, and historic areas. The Dietz home is on the bicycle crossroad, and near the York County Rail Trail, which extends into Maryland.

Cedar Hill Farm ✪

305 LONGENECKER ROAD, MOUNT JOY, PENNSYLVANIA 17552

Tel: **(717) 653-4655**	Reduced Rates: **Weekly**
Hosts: **Russel and Gladys Swarr**	Breakfast: **Continental, plus**
Location: **10 mi. W of Lancaster**	Credit Cards: **AMEX, DISC, MC, VISA**
No. of Rooms: **5**	Pets: **No**
No. of Private Baths: **5**	Children: **Welcome (crib)**
Double/pb: **$75–$80**	Smoking: **No**
Single/pb: **$65–$70**	Social Drinking: **Permitted**
Open: **All year**	Airport/Station Pickup: **Yes**

This historic 1817 stone farmhouse overlooks a peaceful stream and was the birthplace of the host. An open winding stairway leads to the comfortably furnished rooms, each with a private bath and central air conditioning. One room has a whirlpool tub and shower. Breakfast is served beside a walk-in fireplace. Stroll the acreage, bike or hike on country roads, or relax on rockers or a hammock on the large front porch. Cedar Hill lies midway between Lancaster and Hershey, where farmers' markets, antiques, and quilt shops abound.

Country Gardens Farm Bed & Breakfast

686 ROCK POINT ROAD, MOUNT JOY, PENNSYLVANIA 17552

Tel: **(717) 426-3316**	Open: **All year**
Best Time to Call: **Anytime**	Reduced Rates: **Available**
Hosts: **Andy and Dottie Hess**	Breakfast: **Full**
Location: **16 mi. W of Lancaster**	Credit Cards: **AMEX, MC, VISA**
No. of Rooms: **3**	Pets: **No**
No. of Private Baths: **3**	Children: **Welcome**
Double/pb: **$60–$70**	Smoking: **No**
Single/pb: **$50–$60**	

Country Gardens offers the friendly down-home hospitality that made Lancaster County famous. Colorful flower gardens accent the 1860s brick farmhouse with large porches and spacious lawns. The farmhouse is graced with handmade crafts, houseplants, original oil paintings, and family heirlooms. The host and hostess spent most of their lives working on the farm and delight in sharing it with you. Relax in clean comfortable bedrooms, air-conditioning, electric heat, and private baths.

There's easy access to farmers' markets, quilt shops, antique shops, and historic sites, and other attractions are available year-round. Country Gardens is also close to Amish country and Hershey Park.

Hillside Farm B&B ☉
607 EBY CHIQUES ROAD, MOUNT JOY, PENNSYLVANIA 17552-8819

Tel: **(717) 653-6697**	Open: **All year**
Hosts: **Gary and Deb Lintner**	Reduced Rates: **Available**
Location: **10 mi. W of Lancaster**	Breakfast: **Full**
No. of Rooms: **5**	Credit Cards: **DISC, MC, VISA**
No. of Private Baths: **3**	Pets: **No**
Max. No. Sharing Bath: **4**	Children: **Welcome, over 10**
Double/pb: **$70**	Smoking: **No**
Double/sb: **$60**	Social Drinking: **Permitted**

Quiet and secluded, this 1863 two-acre brick Pennsylvania Dutch farm homestead overlooks Chiques Creek with its waterfall and dam. Hillside is located 10 miles from downtown Lancaster, and entirely surrounded by farmland. The house is filled with country furnishings, dairy antiques, milk bottles, and a cow motif. Things to do include exploring the large barn for friendly cats, watching a modern milking at a neighboring farm, and enjoying the colorful gardens. Relax on the second-floor balcony or sit on the porch swing and watch the fireflies. Dinner with the Amish can be arranged with advance reservations. Gary and Deb will be happy to help you plan your itinerary. Biking tour trails and maps are available, as well as seasonal packages.

Churchtown Inn B&B ☉
2100 MAIN STREET, ROUTE 23 W, NARVON, PENNSYLVANIA 17555

Tel: **(717) 445-7794; fax: (717) 445-0962**	Open: **All year**
Best Time to Call: **9 AM–9 PM**	Reduced Rates: **Weekly**
Hosts: **Jim Kent Hermine and Stuart Smith**	Breakfast: **Full**
	Other Meals: **Available**
Location: **4 mi. off Pennsylvania Turnpike, Exit 22**	Credit Cards: **MC, VISA**
	Pets: **No**
No. of Rooms: **8**	Children: **Welcome, over 12**
No. of Private Baths: **8**	Smoking: **No**
Double/pb: **$80–$95**	Social Drinking: **Permitted**
Single/pb: **$75–$85**	Foreign Languages: **German**

Churchtown Inn is a lovely fieldstone Federal Colonial mansion built in 1735. Located in the heart of Pennsylvania Dutch country, this B&B is close to Amish attractions, antique markets, and manufacturers' outlets. Rooms are decorated with the hosts' personal treasures: antique furniture, original art, and music boxes. Stuart (a former music director) and Jim (a former accountant who moonlighted as a ballroom dance instruc-

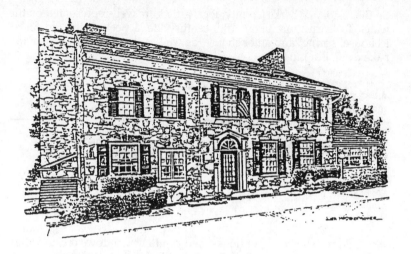

tor) stage events throughout the year. The schedule includes concerts, costume balls, carriage rides, walks, and holiday celebrations. Every Saturday, guests have the opportunity of joining Amish or Mennonite families for dinner at an additional fee. Of course, after a Churchtown Inn breakfast, you may not have room for any more meals; the table groans with English oatmeal custard, apple pancakes, Grand Marnier French toast, homemade coffee cake, and other delectables. Churchtown Inn is on the National Register of Historic Places.

Reiff Farm Bed & Breakfast ✪
495 OLD STATE ROAD, OLEY, PENNSYLVANIA 19547

Tel: **(610) 987-6216**	Cabin: **$120**
Host: **John Moxon**	Open: **Apr.–Dec.**
Location: **8 mi. E of Reading**	Reduced Rates: **10% seniors**
No. of Rooms: **5**	Breakfast: **Full**
No. of Private Baths: **2**	Pets: **No**
Max. No. Sharing Bath: **4**	Children: **Welcome**
Double/pb: **$60**	Smoking: **Permitted**
Double/sb: **$60**	Social Drinking: **Permitted**

Established in the early 1700s, this Pennsylvania Dutch homestead is listed on the National Register of Historic Places. Reiff Farm is nestled in the hills overlooking the Oley Valley, one mile from the center of town. The grounds feature over 200 acres of accessible foot and horse trails. The two-bedroom log cabin can be a family retreat or a honeymoon cottage. The main house has four bedrooms decorated with period antiques and lots of fireplaces. Guests are invited to spend a chilly evening in the library in front of the fire reading one of the many books on the history of Berks County; local artists are well-represented on the walls. To learn more about 18th-century life, a peek at the old forge, icehouse, spring, and smokehouse, as well as the summer kitchen and bake oven, is a must.

The "Hen-Apple" Bed and Breakfast ✪

409 SOUTH LINGLE AVENUE, PALMYRA, PENNSYLVANIA 17078

Tel: **(717) 838-8282**	Open: **All year**
Best Time to Call: **9 AM–9 PM**	Reduced Rates: **Available**
Hosts: **Flo and Harold Eckert**	Breakfast: **Full**
Location: **E of Hershey**	Credit Cards: **AMEX, MC, VISA**
No. of Rooms: **6**	Pets: **No**
No. of Private Baths: **6**	Children: **No**
Double/pb: **$75**	Smoking: **No**
Single/pb: **$65**	

Wood floors, stenciling, antiques, and candlelit windows create a cozy country atmosphere at this 1825 farmhouse five minutes from Hershey. Home-baked breads and muffins, served on old china, make breakfast a treat, whether you enjoy it on the screened porch or in the dining room. In warm weather, guests may relax in the orchard on lawn furniture, a swing, and a hammock. The local attractions are many and varied: antique and crafts shops, horse racing and ice hockey, theaters and museums, even a winery and a bologna factory that welcome visitors.

Nine-Patch Bed & Breakfast ✪

726 PENN AVENUE, WEST READING, PENNSYLVANIA 19611

Tel: **(610) 372-2711**	Reduced Rates: **25% weekly**
Best Time to Call: **6 PM**	Breakfast: **Full**
Hosts: **Suzanne R. Romig**	Credit Cards: **MC, VISA**
Location: **1½ mi. W of Reading**	Pets: **No**
No. of Rooms: **3**	Children: **Welcome, over 12**
No. of Private Baths: **3**	Smoking: **No**
Double/pb: **$55–$65**	Social Drinking: **Permitted**
Open: **All year**	

This turn-of-the-century home has been renovated to provide air conditioning, and a breakfast room with hospitality center. Two rooms have balconies for warm weather enjoyment. The charm of this bed and breakfast is enhanced with antique furnishings and a variety of quilts. Guests can walk across the street and bargain hunt at Reading's famous Vanity Fair Outlet Village. History buffs will find it a short drive to the Ephrata Cloister, Daniel Boone Homestead, or Hopewell Furnace. Antique lovers will enjoy Lancaster County's "antique row," only twenty minutes away. Nine-Patch is within walking distance to restaurants, churches, and specialty shops in West Reading.

PHILADELPHIA AREA

A Bed and Breakfast Connection/Bed & Breakfast of Philadelphia ✪
P.O. BOX 21, DEVON, PENNSYLVANIA 19333
bnbphiladelphia.com; www.bnbphiladelphia.com

Tel: **(610) 687-3565; (800) 448-3619;**
  fax: **(610) 995-9524**
Best Time to Call: **9 AM–6 PM**
  Mon.–Fri.; 9 AM–1 PM Sat.
Coordinators: **Peggy Gregg and Mary**
  Alice Hamilton
States/Regions Covered: **Amish country,**

Philadelphia and Main Line suburbs;
Reading, Valley Forge, York County
Rates (Single/Double):
  Modest: **$30 / $40**
  Average: **$45 / $85**
  Luxury: **$75 / $175**
Credit Cards: **AMEX, MC, VISA**

A Bed and Breakfast Connection/Bed & Breakfast of Philadelphia invites you to select a personally inspected host home in the greater Philadelphia area, from historic Center City to Revolutionary Valley Forge. It also serves the scenic Brandywine Valley and Pennsylvania Dutch country. While the locations range from country farmhouses to downtown high-rises, they all offer an inviting atmosphere and dedicated, attentive hosts.

POCONO MOUNTAINS

La Anna Guest House ✪
RD 2, BOX 1051, CRESCO, PENNSYLVANIA 18326

Tel/fax: **(717) 676-4225**
Host: **Kay Swingle**

Location: **9 mi. from I-80 and I-84**
No. of Rooms: **4**

Max. No. Sharing Bath: **4**
Double/sb: **$40**
Single/sb: **$30**
Open: **All year**
Breakfast: **Continental**

Pets: **No**
Children: **Welcome (crib)**
Smoking: **Permitted**
Social Drinking: **Permitted**

This Victorian home has large rooms furnished with antiques; it is nestled on 25 acres of lush, wooded land, and has its own pond. Kay will happily direct you to fine dining spots that are kind to your wallet. Enjoy scenic walks, waterfalls, mountain vistas, Tobyhanna and Promised Land state parks; there's cross-country skiing right on the property. Lake Wallenpaupack is only 15 minutes away.

The Shepard House ✪
P.O. BOX 486, 108 SHEPARD AVENUE, DELAWARE WATER GAP, PENNSYLVANIA 18327

Tel: **(717) 424-9779**
Best Time to Call: **9 AM–9 PM**
Host: **Jeanni Buonura**
Location: **3 mi. E of Stroudsburg**
No. of Rooms: **7**
Max. No. Sharing Bath: **4**
Double/sb: **$79–$110**
Single/sb: **$69–$79**

Open: **All year**
Reduced Rates: **Available**
Breakfast: **Full**
Pets: **No**
Children: **Welcome, over 8**
Smoking: **No**
Social Drinking: **Permitted**
Minimum Stay: **2 nights holidays**

Originally called "The Far View House," this large Victorian operated as a summer vacation boardinghouse in the early 1900s. Today, from its site just off the Appalachian Trail, The Shepard House greets visitors year-round. Guest rooms are filled with antiques and special touches. Take a seat in the comfortable parlor or on the veranda that wraps around the entire house. Your host serves a gourmet breakfast and offers afternoon tea and refreshments.

Morning Glories ✪
204 BELLEMONTE AVENUE, HAWLEY, PENNSYLVANIA 18428

Tel: **(717) 226-0644**
Best Time to Call: **5–10 PM**
Hosts: **Roberta Holcomb and Jessica Brooks**
Location: **35 mi. E of Scranton**
No. of Rooms: **3**
No. of Private Baths: **1**
Max. No. Sharing Bath: **4**
Double/pb: **$65**
Double/sb: **$50**

Guest cottage: **$90, sleeps 4**
Suites: **$90, sleeps 4**
Open: **All year**
Reduced Rates: **Weekly**
Breakfast: **Full**
Credit Cards: **DISC, MC, VISA**
Pets: **No**
Children: **No**
Smoking: **No**
Social Drinking: **Permitted**

From this B&B's location in the small town of Hawley, you can walk to the downtown shopping area, summer theater, and several fine restaurants. Your own transportation will allow you to enjoy the area's attractions, such as Lake Wallenpaupack, the Delaware River, train rides, canoeing, rafting, skiing, horseback riding, antiquing, hunting, and fishing. The house has a front porch and a deck in the rear for relaxation, and the living room makes a nice gathering place. The oak staircase leads to the guest rooms on the second floor.

Bonny Bank ✪
P.O. BOX 481, MILL RIFT, PENNSYLVANIA 18340

Tel: **(717) 491-2250**	Open: **May 15–Sept. 15**
Best Time to Call: **9 AM–9 PM**	Reduced Rates: **10% weekly**
Hosts: **Doug and Linda Hay**	Breakfast: **Full**
Location: **5 mi. from I-84**	Pets: **No**
No. of Rooms: **1**	Children: **No**
No. of Private Baths: **1**	Smoking: **No**
Double/pb: **$50**	Social Drinking: **Permitted**
Single/pb: **$45**	

The rush of the rapids will lull you to sleep in this quaint cottage, located on the banks of the Upper Delaware National Scenic & Recreational River. The remodeled guest room has windows on three sides for spectacular panoramic views. Privacy is what you get as the only guests, with your own entrance and river area use. Canoe and raft rentals are nearby, or borrow one of Doug and Linda's inner tubes to float through the rapids. Hike or mountain bike in the surrounding forest, abundant in wildlife—deer, bear, and a variety of birds. Nearby attractions include Zane Gray's house, Gray Towers National Historic Site, the Victorian village of Milford, riding stables, and the variety of recreation and restaurants the Poconos are known for. Your hosts will be happy to guide you to points of interest.

The Lampost Bed & Breakfast ✪
HCR BOX 154, ROUTE 507, PAUPACK, PENNSYLVANIA 18451

Tel: **(717) 857-1738**	Single/sb: **$50**
Best Time to Call: **6–9 PM**	Open: **May–Oct.**
Hosts: **Cheryl and Mike Seagaard**	Breakfast: **Continental**
Location: **Rte. 507 Lake Wallenpaupack**	Credit Cards: **MC, VISA**
No. of Rooms: **4**	Pets: **No**
No. of Private Baths: **3**	Children: **Welcome, over 10**
Max. No. Sharing Bath: **4**	Smoking: **No**
Double/pb: **$95**	Social Drinking: **Permitted**
Double/sb: **$60**	

An assortment of lampposts line the driveway leading to this white Colonial home on two acres overlooking Lake Wallenpaupack. This is an ideal stopover for those who love waterfront activities—swimming, boating, fishing, and water skiing. If you'd rather stay high and dry, there are facilities for golfing, tennis, and horseback riding nearby. Other recreational options include scenic train excursions and balloon rides.

SCRANTON/WILKES-BARRE/NORTHEASTERN/ NORTH CENTRAL PENNSYLVANIA

Harts' Content ✪
P.O. BOX 97, HUNTINGTON MILLS, PENNSYLVANIA 18622

Tel: **(717) 864-2499**	Open: **All year**
Best Time to Call: **After 5 PM**	Breakfast: **Full**
Hosts: **Kenneth and Gerry Hart**	Pets: **No**
Location: **25 mi. SW of Wilkes-Barre**	Children: **Welcome**
No. of Rooms: **3**	Smoking: **No**
No. of Private Baths: **3**	Social Drinking: **Permitted**
Double/pb: **$50–$55**	Airport/Station Pickup: **Yes**

Harts' Content is nestled on twenty-seven wooded acres in the old 19th-century mill town of Huntington Mills. The area abounds in wildlife. Fish in the B&B's private pond or quietly wander through the woods to Huntington Mills Creek. Delight in a leisurely country breakfast with friendly conversation around an oak table. Nearby, enjoy golf, Rickett's Glen State Park, covered bridges, and antiquing. Gerry and Ken will gladly help you plan your stay.

The Bodine House ✪
307 SOUTH MAIN STREET, MUNCY, PENNSYLVANIA 17756

Tel: **(717) 546-8949**	Carriage House: **$125**
Hosts: **David and Marie Louise Smith**	Open: **All year**
Location: **15 mi. S of Williamsport;**	Breakfast: **Full**
10 mi. from I-80, Exit 31B	Credit Cards: **AMEX, DISC, MC, VISA**
No. of Rooms: **4**	Pets: **No**
No. of Private Baths: **4**	Children: **Welcome, over 6**
Double/pb: **$65–$70**	Smoking: **No**
Single/pb: **$60**	Social Drinking: **Permitted**

Built in 1805, this restored Federal townhouse in the Muncy National Historic District offer guests the opportunity to enjoy an era of days gone by. Candlelight is used in the living room, where the fireplace and baby grand piano add to the ambience. A full breakfast is served in the dining room, by the fire on chilly mornings. Guest rooms are furnished with antiques and are air conditioned. The Carriage House, a two-story cottage on the premises, is also available. The garden patio is a favorite of guests in the warm weather. Bodine House is located three blocks from the village center, where you can enjoy a movie, shopping, restaurants, or the library.

The Weeping Willow Inn ✪
RR 7, BOX 254, TUNKHANNOCK, PENNSYLVANIA 18657

Tel: **(717) 836-7257**
Best Time to Call: **6–9 PM**
Hosts: **Patty and Randy Ehrenzeller**
Location: **25 mi. NW of Scranton**
No. of Rooms: **3**
No. of Private Baths: **3**
Double/pb: **$65–$80**

Single/pb: **$60–$70**
Open: **All year**
Breakfast: **Full**
Pets: **No**
Children: **Welcome**
Smoking: **No**

Patty and Randy have lovingly restored this charming Colonial home and cordially invite you to experience its warmth and rich history. Antiques can be seen throughout the house, and breakfast is served by candlelight each morning. The Susquehanna River offers opportunities for hiking, canoeing, and fishing. Or travel the Endless Mountains region of northeastern Pennsylvania and partake of the antique and craft shops along the way. A relaxing bed and breakfast experience awaits you at the Weeping Willow Inn.

Ponda-Rowland Bed & Breakfast Inn ✪
RR 1, BOX 349, WILKES-BARRE, PENNSYLVANIA 18612

Tel: **(717) 639-3245; (800) 854-3286**
Best Time to Call: **11 AM–9 PM**
Hosts: **Jeanette and Cliff Rowland**
Location: **20 mi. W of Scranton**

No. of Rooms: **5**
No. of Private Baths: **5**
Double/pb: **$75–$95**
Open: **All year**

Breakfast: **Full**	Smoking: **No**
Credit Cards: **AMEX, DISC, MC, VISA**	Social Drinking: **Permitted**
Pets: **Welcome (outside)**	Airport Pickup: **Yes**
Children: **Welcome**	

You'll have a memorable stay at this large scenic farm in the Endless Mountains region of northeast Pennsylvania. The farmhouse (circa 1850) features a big stone fireplace, beamed ceilings, and museum-quality antiques. Outside you'll see farm animals as well as the less domesticated kind—the property includes a private 34-acre wildlife refuge with six ponds and walking and skiing trails. Athletic types can go canoeing, ice skating and ice fishing, or play horseshoes, volleyball, and badminton. Over a full breakfast, your hosts can tell you about local horse rentals, air tours, state parks, hunting and trout fishing sites, restaurants, country fairs, and ski slopes. They now have horses and give free wagon rides.

VALLEY FORGE AREA

Association of Bed & Breakfasts in Philadelphia, Valley Forge, Brandywine ✪

P.O. BOX 562, VALLEY FORGE, PENNSYLVANIA 19481
pa@BNBAssociation.com

Tel: **(610) 783-7838; (800) 344-0123;** fax: **(610) 783-7783**	Descriptive Directory: **Free**
Best Time to Call: **9 AM–9 PM**	Rates (Single/Double):
Coordinator: **Carolyn J. Williams**	Modest: **$45–$55**
States/Regions Covered: **Philadelphia,**	Average: **$55–$85**
Valley Forge, Main Line, Brandywine	Luxury: **$85–$150**
Valley, Bucks County, Lancaster	Credit Cards: **AMEX, DC, DISC, MC,**
County	**VISA**

Even George Washington would applaud the manner in which Carolyn has brought the British tradition of bed and breakfast to his former headquarters. Choose from more than 130 sites in southeast Pennsylvania. Whether you are on vacation, business, personal getaway or using a gift certificate, Carolyn says, "There is a B&B for you!" Her roster includes modest homestays, city/country inns and town houses, historic and farm homes, ski lodges, guest cottages, carriage houses, and elegant, grand estates close to where you need to be.

WESTERN PENNSYLVANIA

Weatherbury Farm ✪

1061 SURGAR RUN ROAD, AVELLA, PENNSYLVANIA 15312

Tel: **(724) 587-3763**	Location: **20 mi. SW of Pittsburgh**
Hosts: **Dale, Marcy, and Nigel Tudor**	No. of Rooms: **8**

No. of Private Baths: **8**
Double/pb: **$65–$75**
Single/pb: **$60–$70**
Suites: **$85–$95**
Open: **All year**
Breakfast: **Full**
Credit Cards: **AMEX, DISC, MC, VISA**

Pets: **No**
Children: **Welcome, crib**
Smoking: **No**
Social Drinking: **Permitted**
Airport Pickup: **Yes**
Foreign Languages: **German**

One hundred acres of meadows, gardens, fields, and valleys create a tranquil setting at the Tudors' B&B, the perfect getaway from everyday pressures. Guest rooms at this 1860s farm have been lovingly furnished with an old-fashioned country charm. Awake to a bountiful farm breakfast, which might include apple cinnamon pancakes, garden vegetable eggs, or creamy peach-filled French toast. Later, get acquainted with the chickens, sheep, and cattle. Opportunities for golf, fishing, boating, and antiquing abound. Or visit the historic nineteenth-century Meadowcroft Village, Starlake Amphitheater, or West Virginia attractions nearby.

Mountain View Bed and Breakfast Inn ✪
MOUNTAIN VIEW ROAD, DONEGAL, PENNSYLVANIA 15628

Tel: **(724) 593-6349; (800) 392-7773**
Hosts: **Lesley and Jerry O'Leary**
Location: **1 mi. E of Pa. Tpke. Exit 9**
No. of Rooms: **8**
No. of Private Baths: **8**
Double/pb: **$130–$155**
Open: **All year**

Breakfast: **Full**
Credit Cards: **AMEX, DC, DISC, MC, VISA**
Pets: **No**
Children: **Welcome, over 10**
Smoking: **No**
Social Drinking: **Permitted**

In a quiet pastoral setting in the heart of the Laurel Highlands, you can enjoy lodging and breakfast in a restored 1850s farmhouse and barn furnished with period American furniture. Mountain View is a Westmoreland County historic landmark which affords a magnificent view of the Laurel Ridge. This location is convenient to several mountain resorts, state parks, white-water rafting, and Frank Lloyd Wright's Fallingwater. Lesley's restaurant is open daily for dinner, and there is a bar on premises.

The Lamberton House ✪
1331 OTTER STREET, FRANKLIN, PENNSYLVANIA 16323-1530

Tel: **(814) 432-7908; (800) 481-0776**
Hosts: **Jack and Sally Clawson**
Location: **80 mi. N of Pittsburgh**
No. of Rooms: **6**
No. of Private Baths: **4**
Max. No. Sharing Bath: **4**
Double/pb: **$60–$75**
Double/sb: **$50–$65**

Open: **All year**
Reduced Rates: **Available**
Breakfast: **Full**
Pets: **Sometimes**
Children: **Welcome**
Smoking: **Restricted**
Social Drinking: **Permitted**

Named for its original occupant, this Queen Anne Victorian was built in 1874 and is listed in the National Register of Historic Places. The rooms feature beautiful glass, original brass chandeliers, and woodwork of old-world craftsmanship. When they aren't exploring nearby recreational and historic sites, guests can relax in the drawing room, watch TV, play the piano, read in the library, swing on the front porch, or walk in the flower garden. A full country breakfast is served in the elegant dining room each morning.

Lynnrose Bed & Breakfast ✪
114 WEST MAIN STREET, GROVE CITY, PENNSYLVANIA 16127

Tel: **(724) 458-6425**
Hosts: **Dave and Susie Lynn**
Location: **60 mi. N of Pittsburgh**
No. of Rooms: **5**
No. of Private Baths: **5**
Double/pb: **$65–$75**
Single/pb: **$50**
Open: **All year**

Reduced Rates: **10% seniors**
Breakfast: **Full**
Credit Cards: **DISC, MC, VISA**
Pets: **Sometimes**
Children: **Welcome, over 12**
Smoking: **No**
Social Drinking: **Permitted**
Airport/Station Pickup: **Yes**

Lynnrose Bed & Breakfast is decorated in Victorian style, with beautiful antiques and lace curtains. The large foyer and living room, with beamed ceilings and hardwood floors, are tastefully furnished, so guests may relax in front of the fireplace or enjoy TV and the VCR. All guest rooms have air-conditioning. Dave and Susie offer afternoon tea and provide a bountiful, nutritious breakfast. Lynnrose is located within walking distance of Grove City College and the downtown area and only a short way from Slippery Rock University, outlet shops, and wonderful restaurants.

Snow Goose Inn ✪

112 EAST MAIN STREET, GROVE CITY, PENNSYLVANIA 16127
www.bbonline.com/pa/snowgoose

Tel: **(724) 458-4644; (800) 317-4644**	Open: **All year**
Best Time to Call: **10 AM–10 PM**	Breakfast: **Full**
Hosts: **Orvil and Dorothy McMillen**	Credit Cards: **MC, VISA**
Location: **60 mi. N of Pittsburgh**	Pets: **No**
No. of Rooms: **4**	Children: **Welcome**
No. of Private Baths: **4**	Smoking: **No**
Double/pb: **$65**	Social Drinking: **Permitted**
Single/pb: **$60**	Airport/Station Pickup: **Yes**

Formerly a country doctor's home and office, the Snow Goose Inn, built around 1895, has a large porch with an old-fashioned swing. Inside, you'll find tastefully furnished bedrooms with a cozy, warm atmosphere. Each morning, freshly brewed coffee and a complete breakfast, including homemade muffins and nut breads, await guests in the dining room. The Inn is conveniently located across from Grove City College, next door to a restaurant, and two blocks from the business district. Orvil and Dorothy will be glad to direct you to all the local points of interest.

As Thyme Goes By ✪

214 NORTH MAIN STREET, BOX 493, HARRISVILLE,
PENNSYLVANIA 16038

Tel: **(724) 735-4003**	Hosts: **Susan Haas**
Best Time to Call: **Afternoon**	Location: **60 mi. N of Pittsburgh**

No. of Rooms: **3**
No. of Private Baths: **3**
Double/pb: **$50–$70**
Open: **All year**
Reduced Rates: **10% after 3rd night;
    10th night free**

Breakfast: **Full**
Pets: **No**
Children: **No**
Smoking: **No**
Social Drinking: **Permitted**

Gracious hospitality, elegance, and lovingly decorated guest rooms await you in this restored home built in the late 1800s. As Thyme Goes By is the perfect setting for special celebrations or simply an escape from everyday life. Pick a bestseller from the library shelves or slip a classic video into the VCR, pour yourself a cup of hot tea, fill a plate with homemade goodies, and curl up in front of the fireplace for the evening. Breakfast, complete with homemade baked goods and jams, is served by candlelight with classical music. This B&B is located just minutes from the Grove City Factory Shops, Grove City College, and Slippery Rock University.

Foursquare B&B ✪
250 SOUTH FIFTH STREET, INDIANA, PENNSYLVANIA 15701

Tel: **(724) 465-6412**
Best Time to Call: **Before 10 PM**
Hosts: **Mary Ann and Walt Ballard**
Location: **60 mi. NE of Pittsburgh**
No. of Rooms: **3**
Max. No. Sharing Bath: **4**
Double/sb: **$50**
Single/sb: **$37**

Open: **All year**
Breakfast: **Full**
Credit Cards: **MC, VISA**
Pets: **No**
Children: **Welcome**
Smoking: **Restricted**
Social Drinking: **Permitted**

Come stay at this buff brick American Foursquare house, built in the 1920s. Guests will admire Mary Ann's handmade quilts, and everyone will enjoy Walt's breakfast specialties. Indiana, the "Christmas Tree Capital of the World," is also Jimmy Stewart's birthplace and the home of Indiana University of Pennsylvania. Local attractions include an Amish community and a fine winery. Indiana is now the home of a Jimmy Stewart museum.

Woolley Fox ✪
61 LINCOLN HIGHWAY EAST, LIGONIER, PENNSYLVANIA 15658

Tel: **(412) 238-3004**
Hosts: **Barbara and Wayne Carroll**
Location: **50 mi. E of Pittsburgh**
No. of Rooms: **3**
No. of Private Baths: **3**
Double/pb: **$85**
Suites: **$125–$175**
Open: **All year (main house weekends
    only)**

Breakfast: **Full**
Pets: **No**
Children: **Welcome, over 13**
Smoking: **Restricted**
Social Drinking: **Permitted**
Minimum Stay: **2 nights holidays,
    Highland Games, Fort Ligonier Days**

The Woolley Fox is located on a wooded hillside in Pennsylvania's Laurel Highlands, one and a half miles from historic Ligonier. The main house resembles an English stone cottage and features a cheerfully decorated bedroom with a queen-size bed and an adjacent sitting area with a TV. The Guest House is Swiss chalet–style, with a queen bed, sitting room, fireplace, and balcony that overlooks the koi pond and the natural woodlands. The Woolley Cottage has a large living room with a stone fireplace and cathedral ceiling plus an awning-covered deck surrounded by forest. All houses are furnished with country antiques and crafts, including Barbara's primitive hooked rugs. The front porch of the main house offers guests a place to relax with beverages, look at the stars, or watch the deer.

John Orr Guest House ✪

320 EAST BUTLER STREET, MERCER, PENNSYLVANIA 16137
www.pathway.net/jorrbandb; jorrbandb@pathway.net

Tel: **(724) 662-0839**
Hosts: **Ann and Jack Hausser**
Location: **60 mi. N of Pittsburgh**
No. of Rooms: **3**
No. of Private Baths: **3**
Double/pb: **$70–$80**
Single/pb: **$65–$75**
Open: **All year**

Reduced Rates: **Available**
Breakfast: **Full**
Credit Cards: **AMEX, DISC, MC, VISA**
Pets: **No**
Children: **Welcome**
Smoking: **No**
Social Drinking: **Permitted**
Airport/Station Pickup: **Yes**

The John Orr Guest House is located just a short walk from the Courthouse Square. The surrounding area of this quaint Victorian town offers the richness of Western Pennsylvania's history, culture, education, recreation, shopping, and fine dining. Comfort and charm are a part of this turn-of-the-century home featuring beautifully restored quarter-sawn oak woodwork and a historic Reznor gas fireplace. Accommodations include a large front porch, living room, den with cable TV, and dining room. Breakfast fare is prepared with an emphasis on health and nutrition, always fresh and always home-baked. Guests are greeted with fresh fruit and a full cookie jar.

Mehard Manor ✪
146 NORTH PITT STREET, MERCER, PENNSYLVANIA 16137

Tel: **(724) 662-2489**
Best Time to Call: **8 AM–8 PM**
Hosts: **Jerry and Lucille Carlson**
Location: **60 mi. N of Pittsburgh**
No. of Rooms: **4**
No. of Private Baths: **4**
Double/pb: **$75–$90**
Open: **All year**

Reduced Rates: **Available**
Breakfast: **Full**
Credit Cards: **DISC, MC, VISA**
Pets: **No**
Children: **By arrangement**
Smoking: **No**
Social Drinking: **Permitted**

Mehard Manor is a 1913 vintage, sixteen-room Georgian Colonial located near the historic courthouse square. The house features turn-of-the-century architectural details, including rich moldings, wainscot paneling, molded plaster ceilings, balustrade, Doric columns, fireplaces, and a leaded-glass skylight. Guest rooms are uniquely decorated with antique beds, richly carved headboards, and other period pieces that blend warmth with the elegance of the structure itself. Breakfast is served in the formal dining room or in the sunlit solarium.

Zephyr Glen Bed and Breakfast ✪
205 DEXTER ROAD, SCOTTDALE, PENNSYLVANIA 15683

Tel: **(724) 887-6577**
Best Time to Call: **8 AM–10 PM**
Hosts: **Noreen and Gil McGurl**
Location: **45 mi. SE of Pittsburgh**
No. of Rooms: **3**
No. of Private Baths: **3**
Double/pb: **$75**
Single/pb: **$65**
Open: **All year**
Breakfast: **Full**

Credit Cards: **DISC, MC, VISA**
Pets: **No**
Children: **Welcome, over 12**
Smoking: **No**
Social Drinking: **Permitted**
Minimum Stay: **2 nights Christmas, Easter, Labor Day and October weekends**
Airport/Station Pickup: **Yes**

Would a trip back to the mid-19th century appeal to you? If so, Zephyr Glen Bed and Breakfast is the place to stay. This Federal farmhouse was built in 1822 and has been restored to its original condition: oak floors and handsome woodwork, period antiques, Noreen's stenciling, and fireplaces. The house sits on a hillside in the midst of mature maple, oak, linden, and fruit trees, herb gardens, and a fish pond. Breakfast may include fruit, juice, homemade granola, jams, baked goodies, yogurt, a cooked entree, coffee, and tea. Noreen and Gil enjoy meeting new people, making them feel at home and sharing experiences with them. Hiking, biking, skiing, Fallingwater, and historic attractions are all within a thirty-minute drive.

Charbert Farm Bed and Breakfast ✪
RR 3, BOX 68, LAUREL ROAD, SHELOCTA, PENNSYLVANIA 15774

Tel: **(724) 726-8264; (800) 475-8264**
Best Time to Call: **8–9 AM**
Hosts: **Barbara and Bob Rago; Laura Herrington**
Location: **7 mi. S of Indiana**
No. of Rooms: **4**
Max. No. Sharing Bath: **4**
Double/pb: **$85**
Single/pb: **$65**
Double/sb: **$75**

Single/sb: **$55**
Suites: **$95**
Open: **All year**
Reduced Rates: **Available**
Breakfast: **Full**
Pets: **Sometimes**
Children: **Welcome**
Smoking: **No**
Social Drinking: **Permitted**

A stay here is like coming to grandma's house. The rural mystique and nostalgic images begin as you approach this bed and breakfast. Built in the mid-1800s and restored, Charbert Farm has not eliminated the antiques or country atmosphere. Guests have full use of the house during their stay. Rooms are spacious, each with its own decor. Visit the music room and sing along with the player piano or relax in the cozy Country Western room with a fireplace, TV, and VCR. If you prefer the outdoors, there are 108 scenic acres with a gazebo, hiking, biking, golf, and three stocked ponds.

Dodson's Valentine House ✪

99 OLD NATIONAL PIKE, WEST ALEXANDER, PENNSYLVANIA 15376

Tel: **(724) 484-7843**
Best Time to Call: **8 AM–9 PM**
Hosts: **Bryce and Pam Dodson**
Location: **45 mi. W of Pittsburgh**
No. of Rooms: **2**
No. of Private Baths: **2**
Double/pb: **$60**

Single/pb: **$50**
Open: **All year**
Breakfast:**Full**
Pets: **No**
Children: **Welcome, over 10**
Smoking: **No**
Social Drinking: **Permitted**

Step into one of the most popular stopping places along the Old National Park. Built in 1810, the house served as an inn, and has been restored and furnished with antiques from various periods of American history. Each guest has a chance to experience the aura of the days of stagecoaches and Conestoga wagons. Located one mile off Interstate 70, Dodson's is just minutes from Wheeling's Festival of Lights, Oglebay Park, Jamboree U.S.A., and Washington's Trolley Museum. You are welcome to spend time relaxing in the Colonial living room, family TV room, or perhaps spot a deer or a wild turkey while on a nature walk around the ten-acre estate. Every morning, you'll awaken to the aroma of homemade muffins and breads.

The Inn on Grandview ✪

310 EAST GRANDVIEW AVENUE, ZELIENOPLE, PENNSYLVANIA 16063

Tel: **(724) 452-0469**
Best Time to Call: **Mornings, evenings**
Hosts: **Richard and Juanita Eppinger**
Location: **30 mi. N of Pittsburgh**
No. of Rooms: **4**
No. of Private Baths: **4**
Double/pb: **$85–105**
Open: **All year**

Breakfast: **Full**
Credit Cards: **DISC, MC, VISA**
Pets: **No**
Children: **Welcome**
Smoking: **No**
Social Drinking: **No**
Airport Pickup: **Yes**

Built in the early 19th century, when it was known as the Zimmerman Hotel, The Inn on Grandview is now beautifully restored. Furnished with antiques and reproductions, each room has a different feel. But the feeling is that of elegance and warmth. Guest rooms have cable TV, computer hook-up, and telephones. Wake up to a large breakfast of sweet rolls, pancakes, fresh fruit, and sausage from the local smokehouse. What makes the Inn so successful is the warmth of your hosts. Rich is a barber and enjoys golfing. Juanita has an interior design shop, and enjoys showing hospitality to her guests. You will leave feeling refreshed, satisfied, and wanting to return.

RHODE ISLAND

- **Providence**
- **Bristol**
- **Newport**
- **Westerly**

Rockwell House Inn ✪
610 HOPE STREET, BRISTOL, RHODE ISLAND 02809-1945
rockwellinn@ids.net

Tel: **(401) 253-0040; (800) 815-0040;**
  fax: **(401) 253-1811**
Hosts: **Debra and Steve Krohn**
Location: **15 mi. SE of Providence; 12
  mi. NE of Newport, 60 mi. S of
  Boston**
No. of Rooms: **4**
No. of Private Baths: **4**
Double/pb: **$80–$125**
Open: **All year**
Reduced Rates: **Weekly; off-season,
  corporate**

Breakfast: **Full**
Credit Cards: **AMEX, DISC, MC, VISA**
Pets: **No**
Children: **Welcome, over 12**
Smoking: **No**
Social Drinking: **Permitted**
Minimum Stay: **Major holidays,
  weekends**
Foreign Languages: **Spanish**

This beautifully restored Federal-style home, built in 1809, is located in
the heart of Bristol's historic waterfront district, 20 minutes from New-

port and within walking distance of museums and antique shops. Rooms feature fireplaces, king-size beds, terrycloth robes, hair dryers, English bath amenities, and a casual elegance that will immediately put you at ease. Enjoy afternoon tea in the garden, read in one of the parlors, and meet new friends over evening sherry. Your hosts Steve and Debra will share their passion for wines, cooking, and entertaining.

William's Grant Inn ✪

154 HIGH STREET, BRISTOL, RHODE ISLAND 02809

Tel: **(401) 253-4222; (800) 596-4222**	Reduced Rates: **Off-season**
Best Time to Call: **8 AM–9 PM**	Breakfast: **Full**
Hosts: **Mary and Michael Rose**	Credit Cards: **AMEX, DISC, DC, MC, VISA**
Location: **15 mi. SE of Providence**	
No. of Rooms: **5**	Pets: **No**
No. of Private Baths: **3**	Children: **Welcome, over 12**
Max. No. Sharing Bath: **4**	Smoking: **No**
Double/pb: **$65–$115**	Social Drinking: **Permitted**
Double/sb: **$55–$105**	Minimum Stay: **2 nights, holidays and graduation**
Suites: **$95**	
Open: **All year**	

Just two blocks from Bristol's unspoiled harbor you'll find the sea captain's house that Deputy Governor William Bradford granted to his grandson in 1808. Mary and Mike restored and remodeled the five-bay Federal house, turning it into a gracious, beautifully appointed Inn decorated with traditional and folk art. Breakfasts are always a treat, with home-baked goodies, granola, and perhaps Mike's huevos rancheros or Mary's pesto omelettes. Each guest room has a firm queen-size bed, a

comfortable chair to read in, and a fireplace. Within a 3-mile radius you'll find seven museums and a 30-mile bike/walking path. Your hosts are Mary, a development coordinator with the Nature Conservancy and part-time innkeeper, and Mike, a full-time innkeeper. They enjoy kayaking, exercise, gardening, and many other activities too numerous to mention.

The Melville House ✪

39 CLARKE STREET, NEWPORT, RHODE ISLAND 02840

Tel: **(401) 847-0640**
Hosts: **Vince DeRico and David Horan**
Location: **35 mi. from I-95, Exit 3**
No. of Rooms: **7**
No. of Private Baths: **5**
Max. No. Sharing Bath: **4**
Double/pb: **$85–$145**
Double/sb: **$60–$125**
Suite: **$165 (winter only)**

Open: **All year**
Breakfast: **Full**
Credit Cards: **AMEX, DISC, MC, VISA**
Pets: **No**
Children: **Welcome, over 12**
Smoking: **No**
Social Drinking: **Permitted**
Minimum Stay: **2 nights weekends; 3 nights holidays**

The Melville House is a 1750s shingled home set in Newport's historic Hill section. This quiet street is just one block from the Brick Market and wharfs, and around the corner from Touro Synagogue and Trinity Church. Vince and Dave welcome you to guest rooms decorated with oak furnishings, braided rugs, and lace curtains, with special touches such as fresh flowers and a bowl of fruit. Your hosts will start your day off with homemade muffins, granola, and other home-baked items served at polished wood tables in the sunny breakfast room. When you want to relax, the country parlor with its collection of old grinders and gadgets and comfortable wing chairs awaits. Vince and Dave will be glad to provide sightseeing advice, and when the day is at a close, you can enjoy a 4 o'clock sherry at the house.

Cady House ✪
127 POWER STREET, PROVIDENCE, RHODE ISLAND 02906

Tel: **(401) 273-5398**
Hosts: **Anna and Bill Colaiace**
Location: **1 mi. from Rte. 195 E, Exit 2**
No. of Rooms: **3**
No. of Private Baths: **3**
Double/pb: **$80**
Single/pb: **$70**

Open: **All year**
Breakfast: **Continental**
Pets: **Sometimes**
Children: **Welcome**
Smoking: **No**
Social Drinking: **Permitted**

Cady House is a beautiful Classical Revival house (circa 1839) on College Hill, in the heart of the Brown University campus and within walking distance of the Rhode Island School of Design and Johnson and Wales University. The interior is decorated with antique furnishings, oriental carpets, and the owners' extensive collection of American and international folk art. A screened veranda overlooks a large landscaped garden and patio for warm weather relaxation. The hosts are health professionals, cooks, and musicians. They enjoy helping guests discover the attractions of Providence and Rhode Island.

Historic Jacob Hill Farm Bed & Breakfast Inn ✪
P.O. BOX 41326, PROVIDENCE, RHODE ISLAND 02940

Tel: **(888) 336-9165; (508) 336-9165**
Hosts: **Bill and Eleonora Rezek**

Reduced Rates: **Weekly**
Breakfast: **Full**

Location: **3 mi. E of Providence, R.I.**
No. of Rooms: **5**
No. of Private Baths: **5**
Open: **All year**
Suites: **$95–$225**

Credit Cards: **AMEX, DISC, MC, VISA**
Pets: **Horses only**
Children: **Welcome, over 12**
Smoking: **No**
Social Drinking: **Permitted**

Minimum Stay: **2 nights holiday weekends, 3 nights Memorial Day & Labor Day**

Airport/Station Pickup: **Yes**
Foreign Languages: **Polish**

Built in 1722, Jacob Hill Farm was once known as the Jacob Hill Hunt Club, where the legendary Vanderbilts once displayed their horses and coach. Today guests are entertained with the same old-fashioned hospitality. Rooms are spacious, with queen- and king-size beds. Some have fireplaces and Jacuzzi tubs. The Inn is furnished with antiques and charming fireplaces. An inground pool and tennis courts are available. After a busy day of shopping and sightseeing, relax at the Inn and enjoy the magnificent sunsets.

Woody Hill B&B ✪

149 SOUTH WOODY HILL ROAD, WESTERLY, RHODE ISLAND 02891

Tel: **(401) 322-0452**
Best Time to Call: **After 5 PM during school year**
Host: **Ellen L. Madison**
Location: **¾ mi. from Rte. 1**
No. of Rooms: **4**
No. of Private Baths: **4**
Double/pb: **$85–$130**

Open: **All year**
Reduced Rates: **Off-season**
Breakfast: **Full**
Pets: **No**
Children: **Welcome**
Smoking: **No**
Social Drinking: **Permitted**

You'll feel as though you've stepped into a bygone era in this reproduction Colonial with wide floorboards, tiny windowpanes, antiques, quilts, fresh flowers from the perennial gardens, and twenty acres of woods and fields. Guests are invited to enjoy the 40-foot in-ground pool, snuggle up with a good book in the library, and savor breakfast by the walk-in colonial fireplace. The rooms are spacious, easily accommodating families, but far enough apart to provide peace and quiet as you crawl under the canopy or pull the bedhangings closed. Nearby, visit Newport, Block Island, ocean beaches, Mystic, and Foxwoods Casino.

SOUTH CAROLINA

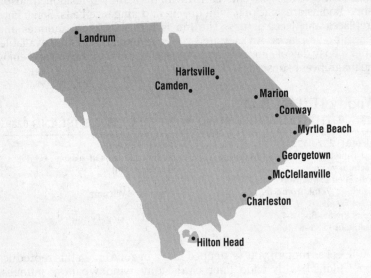

Candlelight Inn ✪
1904 BROAD STREET, CAMDEN, SOUTH CAROLINA 29020

Tel: **(803) 424-1057**
Hosts: **George and JoAnn Celani**
Location: **30 mi. N of Columbia**
No. of Rooms: **3**
No. of Private Baths: **3**
Double/pb: **$75–$125**
Open: **All year**
Breakfast: **Full**

Credit Cards: **AMEX, DISC, MC, VISA**
Pets: **No**
Children: **Welcome, over 12**
Smoking: **No**
Social Drinking: **Permitted**
Minimum Stay: **2 nights Carolina and Colonial Cup Steeplechase**

The Candlelight Inn is located in Camden's Historic District, on two acres surrounded by azaleas and camellias and shaded by a canopy of grand old oaks. A brick drive will guide you to the inn, where the glow of candles illuminates the windows. In addition to family antiques, vintage quilts, and queen-size beds, the decor is highlighted by hand stitchery, needlepoint, and reproduction samplers. Breakfast is served on the sunporch and may include fresh fruit, featherbed eggs, or banana walnut pancakes with strawberry syrup, accompanied by frizzled ham, coffee cake, or muffins. Guests can enjoy antique shops, a steeplechase track, golf, and fine restaurants.

Historic Charleston Bed & Breakfast
57 BROAD STREET, CHARLESTON, SOUTH CAROLINA 29401

Tel: **(843) 722-6606; (800) 743-3583**	Rates (Single/Double):
Best Time to Call: **9 AM–5 PM**	Modest: **$65 / $75**
Mon.–Fri.	Average: **$80 / $95**
Coordinator: **Jo Bacon, manager**	Luxury: **$120 / $225**
States/Regions Covered: **South Carolina**	Credit Cards: **MC, VISA**
Descriptive Directory: **Free**	Minimum Stay: **2 nights Mar. 15–June 15, Oct.**

This port city is one of the most historic in the United States. Through the auspices of this service, you will enjoy your stay in a private home, carriage house, or mansion in a neighborhood of enchanting walled gardens, cobblestoned streets, and moss-draped oak trees. Each home is unique, yet each has a warm and friendly atmosphere provided by a host who sincerely enjoys making guests welcome. All are historic properties dating from 1720 to 1890, yet all are up to date with air-conditioning, phones, and television. Reduced rates may be available for weekly stays. There is a one-time $15 reservation fee charged with each reservation.

Ann Harper's Bed & Breakfast
56 SMITH STREET, CHARLESTON, SOUTH CAROLINA 29401

Tel: **(843) 723-3947**	Breakfast: **Full**
Best Time to Call: **Before 11 AM; after 6 PM**	Pets: **No**
	Children: **Welcome, over 10**
Host: **Ann D. Harper**	Smoking: **Restricted**
Location: **Downtown Charleston**	Social Drinking: **Permitted**
Suite: **$70–$85**	Minimum Stay: **2 nights weekends**
Open: **All year**	

This attractive home is a traditional single house, circa 1870, located in Charleston's historic residential district. The suite consists of two rooms (one double and one single), a sitting area with cable TV, and a private bath. The morning starts with a southern breakfast. Ann is a retired medical technologist. As a former guide in the museum houses and a native of the area, she can direct you to the many interesting sites in the area, all within easy walking distance. There is a $10 surcharge for one-night stays.

Country Victorian Bed and Breakfast ✪
105 TRADD STREET, CHARLESTON, SOUTH CAROLINA 29401

Tel: **(843) 577-0682**
Host: **Diane Deardurff Weed**
Location: **96 mi. S of Myrtle Beach**
No. of Rooms: **2**
No. of Private Baths: **2**
Double/pb: **$85–$125**
Suites: **$145–$185**

Open: **All year**
Breakfast: **Continental**
Pets: **No**
Children: **Welcome, over 8**
Smoking: **No**
Social Drinking: **Permitted**

As tourists pass in horse-drawn carriages, their eyes are drawn to the beautiful screen doors of this Victorianized house, built in 1820. Rooms have private entrances and are comfortably decorated with antique iron and brass beds, old quilts, and antique oak and wicker furniture. You'll find homemade cookies waiting for you when you arrive. Coffee and tea can be prepared in your room at any time, and snacks are served in the afternoon. Restaurants, churches, antique shops, museums, and art galleries are all within walking distance.

Johnson's Six Orange Street B&B
6 ORANGE STREET, CHARLESTON, SOUTH CAROLINA 29401

Tel: **(843) 722-6122**
Hosts: **Becky and Bill Johnson**
Location: **Located in historic district of Charleston**
No. of Rooms: **1**
No. of Private Baths: **1**
Apartment: **$100–$125**
Open: **All year**

Breakfast: **Continental**
Credit Cards: **No**
Pets: **No**
Children: **Welcome (crib)**
Smoking: **No**
Social Drinking: **Permitted**
Foreign Languages: **French, German**

Within Charleston's historic district, Becky and Bill maintain an attached guesthouse complete with sitting room, efficiency kitchen, upstairs bedroom, and private bath and entrance. The bedroom sleeps three and features an antique sleigh bed plus an iron and brass single bed. A crib is also available for families with an infant. Enjoy scrumptious home-baked coffee cakes, pastries, and breads before you explore the numerous sights, shopping, and attractions this city has to offer.

The Cypress Inn ✪
16 ELM STREET, CONWAY, SOUTH CAROLINA 29526
www.bbonline.com/sc/cypress/

Tel: **(843) 248-8199**
Best Time to Call: **After 10 AM**
Hosts: **Jim and Carol Ruddick**
Location: **15 mi. W of Myrtle Beach**
No. of Rooms: **12**

No. of Private Baths: **12**
Double/pb: **$95–$140**
Open: **All year**
Reduced Rates: **10% corporate; 15% weekly**

Breakfast: **Full**
Credit Cards: **AMEX, MC, VISA**
Pets: **No**

Children: **Welcome, over 10**
Smoking: **No**
Social Drinking: **No**

At the Cypress Inn you can slip into a divine realm where you'll find excellence in the little details. Your hosts never forget that this is where your precious memories are being made. Guest rooms are a gentle mix of old and new, all with TVs, and phones with dataports for the business traveler. Each morning enjoy the sunny breakfast room, alive with delicious aromas and enthusiastic voices. Enjoy bird watching, boating, nature or history trails, sculpture gardens, golf, tennis, walks on pristine beaches, or strolls along a five-million-year-old black water river.

1790 House ✪

**630 HIGHMARKET STREET, GEORGETOWN,
SOUTH CAROLINA 29440**

Tel: **(803) 546-4821; (800) 890-7432**
Best Time to Call: **9 AM–9 PM**
Hosts: **Patricia and John Wiley**
Location: **60 mi. N of Charleston; 35 mi.
  S of Myrtle Beach**
No. of Rooms: **6**
No. of Private Baths: **6**
Double/pb: **$85–$110**
Guest Cottage: **$135**
Suites: **$95**

Open: **All year**
Reduced Rates: **Nov.–Feb. 10% less
  Sun.–Thurs., 10% seniors**
Breakfast: **Full**
Credit Cards: **AMEX, DISC, MC, VISA**
Pets: **No**
Children: **Welcome**
Smoking: **No**
Social Drinking: **Permitted**
Minimum Stay: **Holiday weekends**

This meticulously restored, 200-year-old Colonial plantation-style inn in Georgetown's historic district has spacious, luxurious rooms, 11-foot ceilings, and seven fireplaces. Slaves once slept in the Slave Quarters, while the elegant Rice Planters and Indigo Rooms have four-poster beds, sitting areas, and fireplaces. Your other options include the Prince George Suite, a hideaway under the eaves; Gabrielle's Library, with built-in bookcases and a fireplace; and the Dependency Cottage, with its private entrance, patio, and spacious bath with a Jacuzzi. Whichever you pick, you can walk to shops, restaurants, and historic sites. Or take a short drive to Myrtle Beach, golfing on the Grand Strand, the Brookgreen Gardens, Pawleys Island, and downtown Charleston.

Missouri Inn B&B ✪

314 EAST HOME AVENUE, HARTSVILLE, SOUTH CAROLINA 29550

Tel: **(803) 383-9553**
Best Time to Call: **Noon–9 PM**
Hosts: **Kyle and Kenny Segars, and Lucy
  Brown**
Location: **28 mi. NW of Florence**
No. of Rooms: **5**

No. of Private Baths: **5**
Double/pb: **$85**
Single/pb: **$75**
Open: **All year**
Reduced Rates: **Corporate**
Breakfast: **Full**

Credit Cards: **AMEX, MC, VISA**
Pets: **No**
Children: **Welcome, over 10**

Smoking: **Restricted**
Social Drinking: **Permitted**

An elegant Southern mansion built around the turn of the century and completely renovated in 1990, the Missouri Inn offers discriminating guests exceptional peace, quiet, and privacy in a small, luxurious setting. Located in Hartsville's official historic district, the Inn stands opposite the lovely Coker College campus, on about five acres landscaped with stately trees and flowering shrubs. The distinctively furnished rooms not only have telephones and TVs, but terry robes, bath sheets, towel warmers, hair dryers, and fresh floral arrangements. Amenities include afternoon tea and complimentary beverages at all times.

Ambiance Bed & Breakfast

8 WREN DRIVE, HILTON HEAD, SOUTH CAROLINA 29928

Tel: **(843) 671-4981**
Host: **Marny Kridel Daubenspeck**
Location: **40 mi. from I-95, Exit 28**
No. of Rooms: **2**
No. of Private Baths: **2**
Double/pb: **$80**
Single/pb: **$75**

Open: **All year**
Breakfast: **Continental**
Pets: **No**
Children: **Welcome, over 12**
Smoking: **No**
Social Drinking: **Permitted**

Marny welcomes guests to sunny Hilton Head Island. This cypress home, nestled in subtropical surroundings, is in Sea Pines Plantation. Ambiance reflects the hostess's interior decorating business by the same name. All the amenities of Hilton Head are offered in a contemporary, congenial atmosphere. The climate is favorable year-round for all sports. Ambiance is across the street from a beautiful beach and the Atlantic Ocean.

The Red Horse Inn ✿

**310 NORTH CAMPBELL ROAD, LANDRUM,
SOUTH CAROLINA 29356**

Tel: **(864) 895-4968**
Best Time to Call: **After 6:30 PM**
Hosts: **Roger and Mary Wolters**
Location: **8 mi. S of Landrum**
Guest Cottages: **$85–$105**
Open: **All year**
Reduced Rates: **Jan.–Feb.; 10% seniors,
 AAA, guests using *Bed & Breakfast
 U.S.A.* guide book**

Breakfast: **Continental**
Pets: **Sometimes**
Children: **Welcome**
Smoking: **No**
Social Drinking: **Permitted**
Airport Pickup: **Yes**

Located on 190 mountain-view acres, the Red Horse Inn offers five romantic Victorian-style cottages. Each has a kitchen, living room with fireplace, decks or patios, color TV, and air-conditioning. Three have sleeping lofts and Jacuzzis. The equestrian sport of fox hunting takes place in the fall to early spring, and golfing, tennis, hiking, antiquing, sporting clays, hunting, and parks beckon year-round. The Flatrock Playhouse and the Peace Center offer professional performing arts productions. Or guests can simply relax and consume the mountain views from the rocking porch. Breakfast is served in baskets containing muffins or croissants, fruit or juice, and coffee.

Montgomery's Grove ✪

408 HARLEE STREET, MARION, SOUTH CAROLINA 29571
www.bbonline.com/sc/montgomery

Tel: **(843) 423-5220**	Single/sb: **$70**
Hosts: **Coreen and Rick Roberts**	Open: **All year**
Location: **20 mi. E of Florence**	Reduced Rates: **10% weekly, seniors**
No. of Rooms: **4**	Breakfast: **Full**
No. of Private Baths: **3**	Other Meals: **Available**
Max. No. Sharing Bath: **4**	Pets: **No**
Double/pb: **$80**	Children: **Welcome**
Single/pb: **$70**	Smoking: **No**
Double/sb: **$80**	Social Drinking: **Permitted**

Nestled among five acres of century-old trees and gardens, Montgomery's Grove is a beautiful Victorian mansion known for its exceptional architectural features. Dramatic fourteen-foot archways and elaborate woodwork greet all guests. Yet it is easy to relax in the five beautifully decorated rooms, on the wraparound porches, or with a stroll through the woods. Walk beneath the Spanish moss to historic downtown Marion, or travel just thirty minutes to Myrtle Beach. Only 15 minutes from I-95, Montgomery's Grove is the perfect midway stopping point to and from Florida. Visit Marion, the pretty little town on the way to the beach. It'll be a visit you won't forget.

Laurel Hill Plantation ✪

8913 NORTH HIGHWAY 17, P.O. BOX 190, McCLELLANVILLE, SOUTH CAROLINA 29458

Tel: **(888) 887-3708**	Single/pb: **$85**
Best Time to Call: **Before 9 PM**	Open: **All year**
Hosts: **Jackie and Lee Morrison**	Breakfast: **Full**
Location: **30 mi. N of Charleston**	Pets: **No**
No. of Rooms: **4**	Children: **No**
No. of Private Baths: **4**	Smoking: **No**
Double/pb: **$95**	Social Drinking: **Permitted**

The original Laurel Hill, an 1850s plantation house listed on the National Register of Historic Places, was destroyed by Hurricane Hugo in 1989. Nestled in a nook by a picturesque tidal creek, the spacious reconstruction retains the romance of the past while affording the convenience of the contemporary. Wraparound porches provide a sweeping panorama of the Atlantic Ocean and Cape Romain's salt marshes, islands, and waterways. Four charming guest rooms feature fascinating views of the landscape and are furnished with carefully chosen primitives and antiques reflecting the renowned hospitality of South Carolina's low country.

Brustman House

400 25TH AVENUE SOUTH, MYRTLE BEACH,
SOUTH CAROLINA 29577
wcbrustman@worldnet.att.net; www.home.att.net/~wcbrustman

Tel: **(803) 448-7699; (800) 448-7699;** fax: **(803) 626-2478**
Best Time to Call: **Early evening**
Host: **Dr. Wendell C. Brustman**
Location: **90 mi. N of Charleston**
No. of Rooms: **5**
No. of Private Baths: **5**
Double/pb: **$59–$85**
Single/pb: **$54–$80**
Suites: **$89–$135**

Open: **All year**
Reduced Rates: **Extended stay; Oct. 26–Apr. 4**
Breakfast: **Full**
Pets: **No**
Children: **Welcome, over 10**
Smoking: **No**
Social Drinking: **Permitted**
Airport/Station Pickup: **Yes**

Maybe you can't have it all, but Brustman House comes close. This Georgian-style home is two short blocks from the beach, and without leaving the almost 2-acre, tree-studded property you can admire the fresh herb garden or have a tête-à-tête on the glider in the rose garden gazebo. Located nearby are golf courses, seafront restaurants, discount shops, and country music theaters. Afternoon tea includes wines, waters, and sweets served on exquisite Scandinavian dinnerware. Sleep late in your quiet room, its snug bed warmed by a down comforter. The Rosewood Room has a Jacuzzi tub for two. The breakfast menu includes healthful specialties, such as ten-grain buttermilk pancakes.

Serendipity, An Inn ✪

407 71ST AVENUE NORTH, MYRTLE BEACH,
SOUTH CAROLINA 29572

Tel: **(803) 449-5268; (800) 762-3229**
Best Time to Call: **8 AM–10 PM**
Hosts: **Terry and Sheila Johnson**
Location: **60 mi. from Rte. 95**
No. of Rooms: **14**
No. of Private Baths: **14**
Double/pb: **$79–$109**
Suites: **89–$139**

Open: **Feb.–Nov.**
Breakfast: **Continental**
Credit Cards: **MC, VISA**
Pets: **No**
Children: **Welcome**
Smoking: **Permitted**
Social Drinking: **Permitted**

Serendipity is a Spanish Mission–style inn surrounded by lush tropical plants and flowers. The setting is peaceful, the street is quiet, and the ocean is less than 300 yards away. Bedrooms are highlighted with antiques drawing from Victorian, Oriental, wicker, and pine motifs. The Garden Room is the place for a generous breakfast of homemade breads, fresh fruit, eggs, and cereal. Your hosts invite you to use the heated pool and spa, play shuffleboard, Ping-Pong, or just share a quiet moment beside the patio fountain. Myrtle Beach is known for its fine restaurants, but the Johnsons have a gas grill if you want to do your own cooking. Terry and Sheila will gladly direct you to nearby shops, fishing villages, golf courses, miles of beaches, and music theaters.

For key to listings, see inside front or back cover.

✪ This star means that rates are guaranteed through December 31, 1999, to any guest making a reservation as a result of reading about the B&B in *Bed & Breakfast U.S.A.*—1999 edition.

Important! To avoid misunderstandings, always ask about cancellation policies when booking.

Please enclose a self-addressed, stamped, business-size envelope when contacting reservation services.

For more details on what you can expect in a B&B, see Chapter 1.

Always mention *Bed & Breakfast U.S.A.* when making reservations!

We want to hear from you! Use the form on page 593.

SOUTH DAKOTA

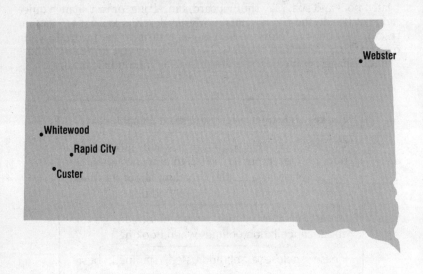

Webster

Whitewood

Rapid City

Custer

Custer Mansion Bed & Breakfast ✪
35 CENTENNIAL DRIVE, CUSTER, SOUTH DAKOTA 57730

Tel: **(605) 673-3333**
Hosts: **Millard and Carole Seaman**
Location: **42 mi. W of Rapid City**
No. of Rooms: **5**
No. of Private Baths: **5**
Double/pb: **$68–$98**
Suite: **$115, sleeps 4**
Open: **All year**
Reduced Rates: **Off-season, extended stays**

Breakfast: **Full**
Pets: **No**
Children: **Welcome**
Smoking: **No**
Social Drinking: **No**
Minimum Stay: **2 nights, holidays, peak season**
Foreign Languages: **Spanish**

Built in 1891, this Victorian Gothic home is listed on the National Register of Historic Places and features a blend of Victorian elegance, country charm, and Western hospitality. Guests enjoy clean quiet accommodations and a delicious home-cooked breakfast. Custer Mansion is centrally located to all Black Hills attractions, including Mt. Rushmore, Cus-

ter State Park, Crazy Horse Memorial, and much more. Afternoon tea is served between 4 and 5 PM.

Abend Haus Cottages & Audrie's Bed & Breakfast ✪

23029 THUNDERHEAD FALLS ROAD, RAPID CITY, SOUTH DAKOTA 57702-8524
www.pahasapa.com/wp/audries

Tel: **(605) 342-7788**
Best Time to Call: **9 AM–9 PM MST**
Hosts: **Hank and Audrie Kuhnhauser**
Location: **¼ mi. from Hwy. 44**
No. of Rooms: **9**
No. of Private Baths: **9**
Double/pb: **$95**
Guest Cottages: **$145**

Suites: **$95**
Open: **All year**
Breakfast: **Full**
Pets: **No**
Children: **No**
Smoking: **No**
Social Drinking: **Permitted**

At this country home and 5-acre estate in a secluded Black Hills setting just 30 miles from Mt. Rushmore and 7 miles from Rapid City, you can experience charm and old-world hospitality. There are free trout fishing, biking, and hiking on the property, which is surrounded by thousands of acres of national forest land. Each suite and cottage has a private entrance, bath, hot tub, patio, cable TV, VCR, coffee pot, microwave, and refrigerator. Full breakfast is provided for you to heat and serve at your convenience.

Bed and Breakfast Domivara ✪
2760 DOMIVARA ROAD, RAPID CITY, SOUTH DAKOTA 57702-6008

Tel: **(605) 574-4207**
Best Time to Call: **Mornings; 6–8 PM**
Host: **Betty Blount**
Location: **26 mi. SW of Rapid City**
No. of Rooms: **4**
No. of Private Baths: **4**
Double/pb: **$70–$75**
Single/pb: **$60–$65**

Open: **All year**
Breakfast: **Full**
Pets: **Sometimes**
Children: **Welcome**
Smoking: **No**
Social Drinking: **Permitted**
Minimum Stay: **2 nights**

Enjoy Western hospitality in a unique log home located in the picturesque Black Hills of South Dakota. The homey wood interior is decorated with comfortable antiques and accents of stained glass. A large picture window overlooks the countryside where you may see an occasional wild turkey or deer. Betty Blount offers complimentary snacks served with coffee. She prepares a variety of special breakfast dishes including sourdough pancakes, egg soufflés, fresh trout, and homemade blueberry muffins. There are good restaurants nearby. Domivara is conveniently located just 20 minutes from Mt. Rushmore and the Crazy Horse Memorial.

Lakeside Farm ✪
RR 2, BOX 52, WEBSTER, SOUTH DAKOTA 57274

Tel: **(605) 486-4430**
Hosts: **Joy and Glenn Hagen**
Location: **60 mi. E of Aberdeen on Hwy. 12**
No. of Rooms: **2**
Maximum No. Sharing Bath: **4**
Double/sb: **$45**

Single/sb: **$35**
Open: **All year**
Breakfast: **Full**
Pets: **No**
Children: **Welcome**
Smoking: **No**
Social Drinking: **No**

This 750-acre farm where Joy and Glenn raise oats and corn is located in the Lake Region where recreational activities abound. You are certain to be comfortable in their farmhouse, built in 1970 and furnished in a simple, informal style. You will awaken to the delicious aroma of Joy's heavenly cinnamon rolls or bread and enjoy breakfast served on the enclosed porch. Nearby attractions include Fort Sisseton and the June festival that recounts Sam Brown's historic ride. You will also enjoy the Blue Dog fish hatchery and the Game Reserve. Dakotah, Inc., manufacturers of linens and wall hangings, is located in Webster. It has an outlet shop where great buys may be found.

Rockinghorse Bed & Breakfast ✪
RR 1, BOX 133, WHITEWOOD, SOUTH DAKOTA 57793

Tel: **(605) 269-2551**
Hosts: **Bob and Sherry St. Andre;**
 Margaret Saxton
Location: **30 mi. NW of Rapid City**
No. of Rooms: **3**
No. of Private Baths: **1**
Double/pb: **$60–$85**
Guest Cottage: **$100–$150**

Open: **All year**
Reduced Rates: **Available**
Breakfast: **Full**
Pets: **Sometimes**
Children: **Welcome**
Smoking: **No**
Social Drinking: **No**

A cedar clapboard–sided house, built in 1914 to accommodate local timber teams, Rockinghorse was moved in 1991 and restored. Handsome wood floors, columns, and trims grace the living and dining areas, and the original stairway is still usable. Antiques, lace, and country delights complement the homey atmosphere. Rockinghorse is situated at the base of the rustic Black Hills, where deer graze in nearby fields and wild turkeys strut across the valley below the house. Nature walks and panoramic views will appeal to the artist/photographer. Domestic animals abound—after a rooster's crow awakens you, you may pet a bunny in the petting zoo or visit the horses.

TENNESSEE

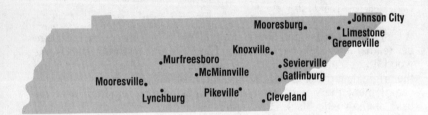

Bed & Breakfast—About Tennessee ✪
P.O. BOX 110227, NASHVILLE, TENNESSEE 37222-0227

Tel: **(615) 331-5244 for information;**
  fax: **(615) 833-7701**
Coordinator: **Fredda Odom**
States/Regions Covered: **Statewide**

Rates (Single/Double):
  Average: **$40–$50 / $65**
  Luxury: **$80–$100 / $80–$150**
Credit Cards: **AMEX, DISC, MC, VISA**

From the Great Smoky Mountains to the Mississippi, here are diverse attractions that include fabulous scenery, Tennessee's Grand Ole Opry and Opryland, universities, Civil War sites, horse farms, and much more. Fredda will arrange sightseeing tours, car rentals, tickets to events, and everything she can to assure you a pleasant stay.

Chadwick House ✪

2766 MICHIGAN AVENUE, RD NORTH EAST, CLEVELAND, TENNESSEE 37323

Tel: **(423) 339-2407**
Host: **Winnie A. Chadwick**
Location: **35 mi. N of Chattanooga**
No. of Rooms: **3**
No. of Private Baths: **1**
Max. No. Sharing Bath: **4**
Double/pb: **$52**
Double/sb: **$47**
Single/sb: **$35**

Open: **All year**
Reduced Rates: **10% seniors**
Breakfast: **Full**
Other Meals: **Available**
Pets: **No**
Children: **Welcome**
Smoking: **Permitted**
Social Drinking: **Permitted**
Airport/Station Pickup: **Yes**

White shutters and trim accent the multicolored bricks of this hand-some ranch home just a half hour from Chattanooga. White-water rafting, Red Clay's historic Indian meeting grounds, and Cherokee National Forest are close by, and golfing and tennis are available right in Cleveland. In their spare moments B&B guests can watch the squirrels and birds in the back garden or relax by the fireplace with a glass of locally made wine. Winnie's full country breakfasts include homemade rolls and muffins.

Butcher House in the Mountains ✪

1520 GARRETT LANE, GATLINBURG, TENNESSEE 37738

Tel: **(423) 436-9457**
Best Time to Call: **10 AM–9 PM**
Hosts: **Hugh and Gloria Butcher**
Location: **50 mi. SE of Knoxville**
No. of Rooms: **5**
No. of Private Baths: **5**
Double/pb: **$79–$129**
Open: **Mar.–Dec.**
Reduced Rates: **Mon.–Thurs.**

Breakfast: **Full**
Credit Cards: **AMEX, MC, VISA**
Pets: **No**
Children: **Welcome, over 12**
Smoking: **No**
Social Drinking: **Permitted**
Minimum Stay: **2 nights**
Foreign Languages: **Italian**

Butcher House is literally a part of the Smokey Mountain chain and provides one of the most spectacular panoramic views of the mountains in the state of Tennessee. Four of the guest rooms have queen beds, the suite has a king, and all have color TVs. Two elegant living rooms furnished with Victorian antiques, a guest kitchen complete with microwave, and complimentary desserts add to your enjoyment. Awaken to the smell of fresh-baked muffins to be served with fresh fruit covered with almond granola, then topped with black cherry yogurt. The second course may consist of eggs Sebastian, crêpes Italian, eggs Josephine, and much more. Butcher House is a favorite destination for photographers and artists who say, "It's the most beautiful view in Gatlinburg."

Hilltop House Bed and Breakfast Inn ✪
6 SANFORD CIRCLE, GREENEVILLE, TENNESSEE 37743

Tel: **(423) 639-8202**
Best Time to Call: **5 PM–7 PM**
Host: **Denise M. Ashworth**
Location: **7 mi. S. of Greeneville**
No. of Rooms: **3**
No. of Private Baths: **3**
Double/pb: **$80**
Single/pb: **$75**
Open: **All year**

Reduced Rates: **Available**
Breakfast: **Full**
Other Meals: **Available**
Credit Cards: **AMEX, MC, VISA**
Pets: **No**
Children: **Welcome, over 3 years**
Smoking: **No**
Social Drinking: **Permitted**
Airport/Station Pickup: **Yes**

Hilltop House is a 1920s manor house on a hillside above the Noli-chucky River Valley, with the Appalachian Mountains in the background. All the guest rooms, which are furnished in 18th-century English antiques and period reproductions, have mountain views; two have verandas. In keeping with her British birth, the innkeeper sets out a proper English tea every afternoon. The family-style breakfast consists of fruit, cereal, egg dishes, and homemade biscuits or muffins. Then it's time to explore the great outdoors: white-water rafting, hiking, biking, trout fishing, golfing, hunting, horseback riding, and bird-watching are among your options. Cherokee National Forest is within striking distance, as are the Great Smoky Mountains and the Blue Ridge Parkway.

Nolichuckey Bluffs B&B ✪
400 KINSER PARK LANE, GREENEVILLE, TENNESSEE 37743

Tel: **(800) 842-4690; (423) 787-7947**
Best Time to Call: **8 AM–8 PM**
Hosts: **Patricia and Brooke Sadler**
Location: **80 mi. NE of Knoxville**
No. of Rooms: **3**
No. of Private Baths: **3**
Double/pb: **$65–$85**
Guest Cabins: **$75–$85**
Open: **All year**

Reduced Rates: **Available**
Breakfast: **Full**
Credit Cards: **DISC, MC, VISA**
Pets: **Sometimes**
Children: **Welcome**
Smoking: **No**
Social Drinking: **Permitted**
Minimum Stay: **2 nights**
Airport/Station Pickup: **Yes**

Nolichuckey Bluffs bed and breakfast is your invitation to enjoy old-fashioned hospitality. Choose from three bedrooms with private baths in the main house and two cabins located in the foothills of the Smokies. Guests enjoy a full breakfast each morning, and in the evening see the sun set behind the mountains. You may want to enjoy the five-person hot tub in the gazebo high on the bluff. Activities include golf, swimming, hiking, tennis, waterslides, go-carts, and much more. Nearby you can visit the birthplace of Davy Crockett, or tour the home of Andrew Johnson, the seventeenth president. You can ski the best in the North Carolina mountains. Or visit Gatlinburg, Great Smokey Mountain National Park, Asheville, Baltimore Estate, and historic Jonesborough, all within 1 to $1^1/2$ hours' drive.

Natchez Trace B&B Reservation Service
P.O. BOX 193, HAMPSHIRE, TENNESSEE 38461
www.bbonline.com/natcheztrace

Tel: **(800) 377-2770; (931) 285-2777**
Best Time to Call: **Evening; weekends**
Coordinator: **Kay Jones**
States/Regions Covered:
  Alabama—Florence, Cherokee;
  Mississippi—Church Hill, Corinth,
  French Camp, Jackson, Kosciusko,
  Lorman, Natchez, New Albany, Port
  Gibson, Vicksburg; Tennessee—

  Columbia, Mt. Pleasant, Culleoka,
  Fairview, Franklin, Hohenwald,
  Leiper's Fork, Nashville
Descriptive Directory of B&Bs: **Free**
Rates (Single/Double):
  Modest: **$55 / $65**
  Average: **$70 / $80**
  Luxury: **$90 / $175**
Credit Cards: **MC, VISA**

Kay's reservation service is unique in that the homes are all convenient to the Natchez Trace National Parkway, the historic Nashville-to-Natchez route that was first designated by President Thomas Jefferson. The parkway is known for both its natural beauty and the charming Southern towns along the way. Kay can help you plan your trip and give you access to homes ranging from rustic, woodsy sites to fine antebellum mansions. Call her for a free list of homes, as well as literature about the Natchez Trace.

Hart House Bed and Breakfast ✪
207 EAST HOLSTON AVENUE, JOHNSON CITY, TENNESSEE 37601

Tel: **(423) 926-3147**
Hosts: **Francis and Vanessa Gingras**
Location: **90 mi. NE of Knoxville**
No. of Rooms: **3**
No. of Private Baths: **3**
Double/pb: **$65**
Single/pb: **$55**
Open: **All year**

Reduced Rates: **10% seniors**
Breakfast: **Full**
Credit Cards: **AMEX, DISC, MC, VISA**
Pets: **Sometimes**
Children: **Welcome**
Smoking: **No**
Social Drinking: **Permitted**

Hart House is named after the original owner of this 1910 Dutch Colonial, which Francis and Vanessa have filled with antiques and collectibles. Johnson City is located in the heart of upper northeast Tennessee, an area brimming with both notable sites and scenic beauty. For history buffs, Jonesborough, the oldest town in the state, is five miles away, and those who love the great outdoors—camping, hiking, fishing, whitewater rafting—will find plenty to do here. Each morning, guests wake up to an elegant breakfast of fresh fruit, homemade muffins, eggs, and fresh brewed coffee.

The Jam N Jelly Inn Bed and Breakfast
1310 INDIAN RIDGE ROAD, JOHNSON CITY, TENNESSEE 37604

Tel: **(423) 929-0039; fax: (423) 929-9026**
Best Time to Call: **9 AM–11 PM**
Hosts: **Bud and Carol Kidner**

Location: **5 mi. SW of I-81, Exit 35**
No. of Rooms: **6**
No. of Private Baths: **6**
Double/pb: **$65**

Single/pb: **$55**
Suites: **$75**
Open: **All year**
Reduced Rates: **Available**
Breakfast: **Full**
Credit Cards: **AMEX, DISC, MC, VISA**

Pets: **No**
Smoking: **No**
Social Drinking: **Permitted**
Minimum Stay: **2 nights on special event
   weekends**
Airport Pickup: **Yes**

The Jam N Jelly Inn is centrally located and provides a unique lodging experience. The inn is a custom-built log home that offers comfort and privacy to guests. The decor is a tasteful blend of country casual elegance in a home-like atmosphere. Guest rooms are furnished with antique reproductions, TVs, and queen-size beds. Amenities include a well-stocked video library, fifty-two-inch TV, VCR, 8–10-person hot tub, spacious front porch, large covered rear deck for quiet reflection, fax and copy machine, and central heat and air. Rooms are available with telephones for the business traveler. One room is accessible to the disabled visitor. The Inn's main entrance has a ramp accessible by the well-lit, off-street parking lot. Snacks and complimentary beverages are provided in the evenings.

"Mitchell's" ✪
1031 WEST PARK DRIVE, KNOXVILLE, TENNESSEE 37909

Tel: **(423) 690-1488**
Host: **Mary M. Mitchell**
Location: **1.6 mi. from I-75-40,
   Exit 380**
No. of Rooms: **1**
No. of Private Baths: **1**
Double/pb: **$40**
Single/pb: **$35**

Open: **All year**
Breakfast: **Continental**
Pets: **Sometimes**
Children: **Welcome**
Smoking: **Permitted**
Social Drinking: **Permitted**
Airport/Station Pickup: **Yes**

Located in a pleasant, quiet neighborhood with numerous shade trees, Mary's B&B is air-conditioned and has a private entrance with no steps to climb. There's a double bed, and a rollaway is available. Breakfast features homemade muffins or cinnamon rolls with coffee. "Mitchell's" is convenient to the University of Tennessee; Oak Ridge is only a 15-minute drive while Great Smoky Mountains National Park is an hour away.

Snapp Inn B&B ✪
1990 DAVY CROCKETT PARK ROAD, LIMESTONE, TENNESSEE 37681

Tel: **(423) 257-2482**	Single/pb: **$55**
Best Time to Call: **Before 10 AM;**	Open: **All year**
after 7 PM	Breakfast: **Full**
Hosts: **Dan and Ruth Dorgan**	Pets: **Welcome**
Location: **4 mi. from Rte. 11 E**	Children: **Welcome (one at a time)**
No. of Rooms: **2**	Smoking: **No**
No. of Private Baths: **2**	Social Drinking: **Permitted**
Double/pb: **$65**	Airport/Station Pickup: **Yes**

Built in 1815 and situated in farm country, this Federal brick home has lovely mountain views. The house is decorated with antiques, including a Victorian reed organ. Now retired, Ruth and Dan have the time to pursue their interests in antiques restoration, history, needlework, and bluegrass music. It is an easy walk to Davy Crockett Birthplace State Park, and 15 minutes to historic Jonesborough or the Andrew Johnson Home in Greeneville. A swimming pool, golf, and fishing are close by. You are welcome to use the laundry facilities, television, and pool table.

Cedar Lane Bed and Breakfast ✪
ROUTE 3, BOX 155E, LYNCHBURG, TENNESSEE 37352

Tel: **(931) 759-6891**	Reduced Rates: **10% weekly**
Best Time to Call: **After 4 PM**	Breakfast: **Continental, plus**
Hosts: **Elaine and Chuck Quinn**	Other Meals: **Available**
Location: **45 mi. N of Huntsville,**	Credit Cards: **AMEX, MC, VISA**
Alabama	Pets: **No**
No. of Rooms: **4**	Children: **Welcome, over 10**
No. of Private Baths: **4**	Smoking: **No**
Double/pb: **$70–$75**	Social Drinking: **Permitted**
Single/pb: **$65**	Foreign Languages: **Hungarian**
Open: **All year**	

On the outskirts of historic Lynchburg, home of the Jack Daniel's Distillery, this newly built farmhouse offers guests comfort and relaxation. Whether it be a weekend or a week's stay, guests can spend time antiquing in nearby shops or reading a book in the sunroom. Rooms are beautifully decorated in rose, blue, peach, and green, with queen- and twin-size beds. Dinner is available by reservation.

Historic Falcon Manor✪

2645 FAULKNER SPRINGS ROAD, McMINNVILLE, TENNESSEE 37110
falconmanor@falconmanor.com; www.falconmanor.com

Tel: **(931) 668-4444**
Best Time to Call: **Anytime**
Hosts: **George and Charlien McGlothin**
Location: **72 mi. SE of Nashville**
No. of Rooms: **5**
No. of Private Baths: **5**
Double/pb: **$105**
Open: **All year**

Reduced Rates: **10% 3 days or more**
Breakfast: **Full**
Credit Cards: **MC, VISA**
Pets: **No**
Children: **Welcome, over 12**
Smoking: **No**
Social Drinking: **Permitted**

This historic Victorian mansion re-creates the romance of the 1890s. Relax in the friendly warmth of this fine old house and savor the luxury of its museum-quality antiques. The huge gingerbread veranda is well stocked with rocking chairs and shaded by giant trees. Falcon Manor is a favorite for couples celebrating anniversaries. It's also the ideal base for a middle Tennessee vacation—halfway between Nashville and Chattanooga and just thirty minutes from four state parks. McMinnville is "the nursery capital of the world" and the home of America's second largest cave. George left a career in retail management to spend four years restoring the house, while Charlien pitched in during time off from her job as a NASA public affairs writer. They love sharing stories about Falcon Manor's history and their adventures, bringing it back to life.

The Home Place ✪
132 CHURCH LANE, MOORESBURG, TENNESSEE 37811

Tel: (800) 521-8424; (423) 921-8424;
  fax: (423) 921-8003
Best Time to Call: 9 AM–5 PM
Host: Priscilla Rogers
Location: 50 mi. NE of Knoxville
No. of Rooms: 4
Max. No. Sharing Bath: 4
Double/pb: $65
Single/pb: $45

Double s/b: $55
Suites: $100
Open: All year
Reduced Rates: 10% seniors, 3 nights or
  more
Breakfast: Continental
Pets: No
Children: Welcome (crib)
Smoking: No

Built as a log cabin, The Home Place has been in the family since the early 1800s. Located on Cherokee Lake, Home Place offers four guest rooms; one suite has a Jacuzzi. The first floor is accessible to guests with disabilities. Amenities include a guest refrigerator and microwave, a TV in the family room, and a phone jack in every room. A special room is available for receptions, parties, and meetings. Wedding parties are welcome. The breakfast menu varies from fresh fruit to ham biscuits, depending upon guest's request.

Clardy's Guest House ✪
435 EAST MAIN STREET, MURFREESBORO, TENNESSEE 37130

Tel: (615) 893-6030
Best Time to Call: After 10 AM
Hosts: Robert and Barbara Deaton
Location: 2 mi. from I-24
No. of Rooms: 3
No. of Private Baths: 2
Max. No. Sharing Bath: 4
Double/pb: $53
Single/pb: $45

Double/sb: $45
Single/sb: $36
Open: All year
Breakfast: Continental
Pets: Sometimes
Children: Welcome (crib)
Smoking: Restricted
Social Drinking: Permitted

Located in the heart of Murfreesboro's East Main Historic District, this 20-room Victorian Romanesque-style home offers guests an opportunity to enjoy unusual architectural features, antique furnishings throughout, and beautiful flowers in the courtyard. Guests can survey the historic homes and restored town square, all within walking distance and featured on the local walking tour. This area is rich in history and has much to offer antiques shoppers. Centrally located, it's close to Nashville and lots of mid-state attractions. For over 50 years, the guest house has hosted visitors who wish to visit this area or simply stop over.

Fall Creek Falls Bed & Breakfast ✪
ROUTE 3, BOX 298B, PIKEVILLE, TENNESSEE 37367

Tel: (423) 881-5494
Hosts: Doug and Rita Pruett

Location: 50 mi. N of Chattanooga
No. of Rooms: 7

No. of Private Baths: **7**
Double/pb: **$75–$105**
Single/pb: **$65**
Suite: **$125**
Open: **All year (except Jan.)**
Breakfast: **Full**

Pets: **No**
Children: **Welcome, over 10**
Smoking: **No**
Social Drinking: **No**
Minimum Stay: **2 nights, weekends in October and holidays**

Enjoy the relaxing atmosphere of a new country manor home on forty acres of rolling hillside one mile from the nationally acclaimed Fall Creek Falls State Resort Park. Beautiful guest rooms have pickled oak floors and antique furniture with two common sitting areas. Lodging includes a full breakfast served in a cozy country kitchen or an elegant dining room. Touring, dining, and shopping information is always available. A special occasion suite is available with a gas log fireplace and a heart whirlpool for two.

Blue Mountain Mist Country Inn & Cottages ✪
1811 PULLEN ROAD, SEVIERVILLE, TENNESSEE 37862

Tel: **(800) 497-2335; (423) 428-2335**
Best Time to Call: **10 AM–9 PM**
Hosts: **Norman and Sarah Ball**
Location: **4 mi. E of Pigeon Forge**
No. of Rooms: **12**
No. of Private Baths: **12**
Double/pb: **$98**
Guest Cottage: **$140**

Suites: **$110–$130**
Open: **All year**
Breakfast: **Full**
Pets: **No**
Children: **Welcome (2 rooms)**
Smoking: **No**
Social Drinking: **Permitted**

This Victorian-style farmhouse inn with country cottages is located on 60 acres in the foothills of the Great Smoky Mountains. Away from the congestion you can enjoy beautiful views of rolling meadows and mountains while rocking on the huge front porch. The Inn is filled with country antiques, handmade quilts, and local art. In the morning awake to a hearty Tennessee breakfast, in the evening indulge in a delicious homemade dessert. Each cottage has a large Jacuzzi and a fireplace designed for a peaceful romantic getaway. Nearby attractions include Gatlinburg, the Crafts Community, Pigeon Forge, and Dollywood.

Calico Inn ✪

757 RANCH WAY, SEVIERVILLE, TENNESSEE 37862

Tel: **(423) 428-3833; (800) 235-1054**	Reduced Rates: **Jan.–Feb.**
Best Time to Call: **11 AM–9 PM**	Breakfast: **Full**
Hosts: **Lill and Jim Katzbeck**	Pets: **No**
Location: **35 mi. N of Knoxville**	Children: **Welcome, over 6**
No. of Rooms: **3**	Smoking: **No**
No. of Private Baths: **3**	Social Drinking: **Permitted**
Double/pb: **$85–$95**	Minimum Stay: **2 nights holidays and**
Open: **All year**	**special events**

Nestled among trees atop a peaceful ridge, Calico Inn offers guests a serene panoramic view of the Smoky Mountains. Lill and Jim invite you to start your day with a delicious breakfast, guaranteed to be more than you can eat. The Calico Inn has been voted "Inn of the Year" by their many guests from the United States and around the world. Nearby attractions include Dollywood, shopping, fishing, golfing, live entertainment, and hiking in the mountains. After a full day of fun, you will enjoy returning to the quiet Calico Inn.

Little Greenbrier Lodge ✪

3685 LYON SPRINGS ROAD, SEVIERVILLE, TENNESSEE 37862

Tel: **(423) 429-2500; (800) 277-8100**	Double/pb: **$95–$110**
Best Time to Call: **Anytime**	Double/sb: **$75**
Hosts: **Charles and Susan LeBon**	Single/sb: **$65**
No. of Rooms: **10**	Open: **All year**
No. of Private Baths: **8**	Breakfast: **Full**
Max. No. Sharing Bath: **4**	Credit Cards: **DISC, MC, VISA**

Pets: **No**

Children: **Welcome, over 12; under 12 by arrangement**

Smoking: **No**

Social Drinking: **Permitted**

Airport Pickup: **Yes**

Nestled in the hills of the Great Smoky Mountains, Little Greenbrier Lodge was built in 1939 and renovated in 1993. All rooms offer guests modern comforts with the Victorian decor. The view of the valley provides a perfect backdrop for a delicious country breakfast. Cades Cove, Dollywood, outlet malls, and numerous antique and craft shops are all within 30 minutes. If you enjoy hiking, the lodge is located right next to a park and just 150 yards from Little Greenbrier Trailhead, which will connect you to other interesting paths in the park.

For key to listings, see inside front or back cover.

✪ This star means that rates are guaranteed through December 31, 1999, to any guest making a reservation as a result of reading about the B&B in *Bed & Breakfast U.S.A.*—1999 edition.

Important! To avoid misunderstandings, always ask about cancellation policies when booking.

Please enclose a self-addressed, stamped, business-size envelope when contacting reservation services.

For more details on what you can expect in a B&B, see Chapter 1.

Always mention *Bed & Breakfast U.S.A.* when making reservations!

We want to hear from you! Use the form on page 593.

TEXAS

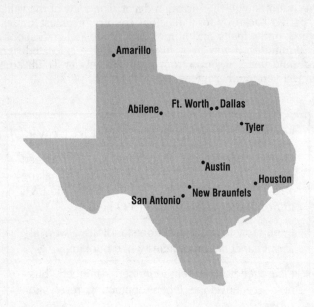

Bed & Breakfast Texas Style ✪
4224 WEST RED BIRD LANE, DALLAS, TEXAS 75237

Tel: **(972) 298-8586; (800) 899-4538**
Best Time to Call: **9 AM–4:30 PM CST**
Coordinator: **Ruth Wilson**
States/Regions Covered: **Austin, Dallas, Fort Worth, Lake Travis, San Antonio, Tyler**

Descriptive Directory: **$8**
Rates (Single/Double):
   Modest: **$60 / $70**
   Average: **$70 / $90**
   Luxury: **$100 / $150**
Credit Cards: **AMEX, DISC, MC, VISA**

The above cities are only a small sample of the locations of hosts waiting to give you plenty of warm hospitality. Ruth's register includes comfortable accommodations in condos, restored Victorians, lakeside cottages, and ranches. The University of Texas, Southern Methodist University, Baylor University, Rice University, and Texas Christian University are convenient to many B&Bs.

Bolin's Prairie House Bed & Breakfast ✪
508 MULBERRY, ABILENE, TEXAS 79601

Tel: **(915) 675-5855; (800) 673-5855**	Double/pb: **$65**
Best Time to Call: **8AM–8 PM**	Double/sb: **$55**
Mon.–Sat.	Open: **All year**
Hosts: **Sam and Ginny Bolin**	Breakfast: **Full**
Location: **180 mi. W of Dallas**	Credit Cards: **AMEX, MC, VISA**
No. of Rooms: **4**	Children: **Welcome, over 12**
No. of Private Baths: **2**	Smoking: **No**
Max. No. Sharing Bath: **4**	

Tucked into the heart of this famous frontier town is Bolin's Prairie House, a 1902 house furnished with antiques and modern luxuries. The warm, homey atmosphere puts guests at their ease. Relax in the living room with its wood-burning stove, or settle in the den for a little TV. Each of the four bedrooms—named Love, Joy, Peace, and Patience—has its own special charm. Breakfast features Ginny's delicious baked egg dishes, fresh fruit, and homemade bread, all lovingly served in the dining room, where fine china and cobalt Depression glass are displayed.

Parkview House Bed and Breakfast ✪
1311 SOUTH JEFFERSON STREET, AMARILLO, TEXAS 79101
members.aol.com/parkviewb; parkviewbb@aol.com

Tel: **(806) 373-9464; fax: (806) 373-3166**	Suite: **$85**
	Open: **All year**
Best Time to Call: **Before 10 PM**	Breakfast: **Continental**
Hosts: **Carol and Nabil Dia**	Credit Cards: **AMEX, MC, VISA**
Location: **1/2 mi. from I-40**	Pets: **No**
No. of Rooms: **5**	Children: **By arrangement**
No. of Private Baths: **3**	Smoking: **No**
Max. No. Sharing Bath: **4**	Social Drinking: **Permitted**
Double/pb: **$75**	Airport/Station Pickup: **Yes**
Double/sb: **$65**	Foreign Languages: **Arabic**

Enjoy friendly Texas hospitality in a Victorian setting. Historical Parkview House is near all local attractions. Decorated with period antiques, collectibles, and memorabilia, the inn is cozy and inviting. Guests may relax on the porch with a favorite beverage, stroll through the English garden, or at day's end take a soothing soak in the hot tub under the stars. After a restful night, wake up with your hosts' special coffee blend. The gourmet breakfast is served in the dining room or in the eclectic country kitchen, with a view of the gardens. The menu consists of homemade goodies served with cinnamon butter, herbal omelets, fresh fruits, and a variety of juices.

Austin's Wildflower Inn ✪

1200 WEST 22½ STREET, AUSTIN, TEXAS 78705
Kjackson@io.com; www.io.com/~Kjackson

Tel: **(512) 477-9639; fax: (512) 474-4188**	Single/pb: **$79**
Best Time to Call: **Anytime**	Double/sb: **$74**
Host: **Kay Jackson**	Single/sb: **$70**
Location: **2 mi. from Rte. IH35, Exit MLK**	Open: **All year**
No. of Rooms: **4**	Reduced Rates: **10% seniors**
No. of Private Baths: **2**	Breakfast: **Full**
Max. No. Sharing Bath: **4**	Credit Cards: **AMEX, MC, VISA**
Double/pb: **$89**	Pets: **No**
	Smoking: **No**
	Social Drinking: **Permitted**

Built in the early 1930s and nestled on a quiet, tree-lined street, this central Austin home is within a few blocks of the University of Texas and within minutes of the State Capitol complex. Outdoor enthusiasts will love the hike and bike trails at Shoal Creek or tennis at Caswell Courts. Kay prides herself on her warm Texas hospitality and delights in serving you her hearty gourmet specialties each morning.

B & G's ✪

15869 NEDRA WAY, DALLAS, TEXAS 75248
bgbed@netgazer.net; www.bg-bed-and-breakfast.com

Tel: **(972) 386-4323; fax: (972) 386-9010**	Reduced Rates: **Available**
Best Time to Call: **Before 8 AM**	Breakfast: **Full**
Hosts: **George and Betty Hyde**	Other Meals: **Available**
No. of Rooms: **2**	Pets: **No**
No. of Private Baths: **2**	Children: **Welcome**
Double/pb: **$60**	Smoking: **No**
Single/pb: **$50**	Social Drinking: **Permitted**
Open: **All year**	Airport/Station Pickup: **Yes**

Betty and George are retirees who have had visitors from around the world since 1980. They want you to think of their home—furnished with "an eclectic collection of family heirlooms and junk"—as your own. Upon your arrival, they'll pour you something to drink, ascertain your interests, and direct you to appropriate activities in the Dallas–Fort Worth area. This B&B is close to prestigious shopping malls, the University of Texas at Dallas, Southern Methodist University, and the sights of downtown Dallas, such as the Kennedy Assassination Museum and the new Arts District. You'll start the day with conversation and a three-course breakfast at a lovely table set with grandma's antique silver and good crystal.

The Texas White House ✪
1417 8TH AVENUE, FORT WORTH, TEXAS 76104

Tel: **(817) 923-3597; (800) 279-6491**	Reduced Rates: **Available**
Best Time to Call: **7 AM–10:30 PM**	Breakfast: **Full**
Host: **Jamie Sexton**	Other Meals: **Available**
Location: **2 mi. SW of downtown Fort Worth**	Credit Cards: **AMEX, DISC, MC, VISA**
	Pets: **No**
No. of Rooms: **3**	Children: **Welcome**
No. of Private Baths: **3**	Smoking: **Restricted**
Double/pb: **$105**	Social Drinking: **Permitted**
Open: **All year**	Airport/Station Pickup: **Yes**

This historically-designated, award-winning country-style home has been restored to its original 1910 grandeur of simple, elegant decor. The inn is centrally located within five minutes of downtown, the medical center, Fort Worth Zoo, Cultural District, Botanic Gardens, Water Gardens, and Texas University. Guest rooms have queen-size beds with your choice of pillows, sitting areas, and private baths with claw-footed tubs for showers or bubble baths by candlelight. Guests are afforded complete privacy; however, they may enjoy the parlor, living room with fireplace, dining room, and large wraparound porch. Breakfast, a gourmet treat, may be served in the dining room or delivered to your room. Amenities include telephone, TV, early-morning coffee service upon request, afternoon snacks and beverages, laundry service for extended stays, and off-street parking.

The Lovett Inn ✪
501 LOVETT BOULEVARD, HOUSTON, TEXAS 77006
www.lovettinn.com

Tel: **(713) 522-5224; (800) 779-5224;** fax: **(713) 528-6708**	Suites: **$75–$150**
	Open: **All year**
Best Time to Call: **10 AM–6 PM**	Reduced Rates: **Weekly**
Host: **Tom Fricke**	Breakfast: **Continental**
Location: **Downtown Houston**	Credit Cards: **AMEX, DISC, MC, VISA**
No. of Rooms: **8**	Pets: **Sometimes**
No. of Private Baths: **8**	Children: **By arrangement**
Double/pb: **$75–$105**	Smoking: **Restricted**
Town House: **$75–$150**	Social Drinking: **Permitted**

It's easy to be fooled by the Lovett Inn: although it looks far older, this stately Federalist-style mansion, attractively furnished with 19th-century reproductions, was actually built in 1924. Its convenient museum-district location puts visitors within easy striking distance of downtown Houston, the Galleria, and the Houston Medical Center. After spending the day in the city, guests are sure to appreciate a dip in the pool. Each room has a color TV.

Aunt Nora's Bed and Breakfast ✪

120 NAKED INDIAN TRAIL, NEW BRAUNFELS, TEXAS 78132-1865
www.texasbedandbreakfast.com/AuntNoras.htm

Tel: **(830) 905-3989; (800) 687-2887**	Reduced Rates: **Available**
Best Time to Call: **9 AM–5 PM**	Breakfast: **Full, Continental**
Hosts: **Iralee and Alton Haley**	Pets: **No**
Location: **15 mi. NW of New Braunfels**	Children: **Welcome**
Guest Cottages: **$95–$125**	Smoking: **No**
Open: **All year**	Social Drinking: **Permitted**

In the Texas hill country at Canyon Lake, just minutes from New Braunfels and Guadalupe River, is a country house with old-time Victorian charm, nestled on four tree-covered acres with a meadow. Walk to the top of the hill to view Canyon Lake, or breathe the fresh country air from the front porch swing. Relax amid handmade furnishings, antiques, a woodstove, and natural wood floors. Tastefully decorated queen rooms have handmade quilts. The cottages have private decks, kitchens, beautiful decor, private baths, and a view.

River Haus Bed & Breakfast ✪

817 EAST ZIPP ROAD, NEW BRAUNFELS, TEXAS 78130

Tel: **(830) 625-6411**	Open: **All year**
Hosts: **Dick and Arlene Buhl**	Breakfast: **Full**
Location: **25 mi. NE of San Antonio**	Pets: **No**
No. of Rooms: **1**	Children: **No**
No. of Private Baths: **1**	Smoking: **No**
Double/pb: **$75**	Social Drinking: **No**
Single/pb: **$70**	Foreign Languages: **German**

Historic New Braunfels, a major tourist destination, offers museums, antique shopping, and unparalleled canoeing and river sports, all in the charming setting of the German Hill Country. River Haus is a delightful hill country–style home located on the Guadalupe River at Lake Dunlap. Watch the sun set over the lake from your spacious bedroom or sitting room. On the enclosed porch, with its deck overlooking the lake, you can sip a cool drink or enjoy the warmth of a wood-stove fire. The complete gourmet breakfasts include local specialties and homemade bread and preserves.

The White House

217 MITTMAN CIRCLE, NEW BRAUNFELS, TEXAS 78132

Tel: **(830) 629-9354**	No. of Private Baths: **4**
Best Time to Call: **9 AM–8 PM**	Double/pb: **$60–$95**
Hosts: **Beverly and Jerry White**	Single/pb: **$55–$90**
Location: **20 mi. N of San Antonio**	Double/sb: **$45–$50**
No. of Rooms: **4**	Single/sb: **$40–$45**

Open: **All year**
Breakfast: **Full**
Pets: **No**

Children: **Welcome (crib)**
Smoking: **No**
Social Drinking: **Permitted**

This Spanish-style white brick home is on acreage in the Texas Hill Country. Guests are welcomed with tea and pastries, then shown to their room either in the main house or the spacious cottage by the pond. Nearby attractions include river rafting, the largest water park in Texas, and the Alamo and Riverwalk in San Antonio.

Beckmann Inn and Carriage House ✪
222 EAST GUENTHER STREET, SAN ANTONIO, TEXAS 78204
www.beckmanninn.com

Tel: **(210) 229-1449; (800) 945-1449**
Best Time to Call: **8 AM–10 PM**
Hosts: **Betty Jo and Don Schwartz**
Location: **³/₄ mi. S of downtown San Antonio**
No. of Rooms: **5**
No. of Private Baths: **5**
Double/pb: **$99–$140**
Single/pb: **$90–$130**
Open: **All year**

Reduced Rates: **Available**
Breakfast: **Full**
Credit Cards: **AMEX, DC, DISC, MC, VISA**
Pets: **No**
Children: **Welcome, over 12**
Smoking: **No**
Social Drinking: **Permitted**
Minimum Stay: **2 nights, weekends**

Enjoy gracious hospitality in an elegant Victorian inn located in San Antonio's King William historic district. The beautiful wraparound porch welcomes guests. Inside, rooms are colorfully decorated, with high-back, queen-size, antique Victorian beds. Gourmet breakfast, complete with dessert, is served in the formal dining room on a table set with china, crystal, and silver. Then guests may stroll over to the Riverwalk or ride the trolley to the sights of San Antonio.

A Yellow Rose Bed & Breakfast ✪
229 MADISON, SAN ANTONIO, TEXAS 78204

Tel: **(800) 950-9903; (210) 229-9903**
Best Time to Call: **10 AM–8 PM**
Hosts: **Kit and Deb Field-Walker**
Location: **Downtown San Antonio**
No. of Rooms: **5**
No. of Private Baths: **5**
Double/pb: **$100–$150**
Open: **All year**

Reduced Rates: **Available**
Breakfast: **Full**
Credit Cards: **AMEX, DISC, MC, VISA**
Pets: **No**
Children: **Welcome, over 12**
Smoking: **No**
Social Drinking: **Permitted**
Minimum Stay: **2 nights weekends**

A Yellow Rose Bed & Breakfast is an 1878 Victorian home in the King William Historic District of San Antonio. The guest rooms are appointed with turn-of-the-century antiques, cable TV, and queen-size beds. Off-street covered parking is also provided. Breakfast is served in the 18th-century dining room, and afterward you are invited to enjoy relaxing on one of the B&B's comfortable porches. Your hosts have an art gallery that includes many of their favorite artists. The Riverwalk and the trolley are only two blocks away.

Rosevine Inn Bed and Breakfast ✪
415 SOUTH VINE AVENUE, TYLER, TEXAS 75702

Tel: **(903) 592-2221**
Best Time to Call: **After 9:30 AM**
Hosts: **Bert and Rebecca Powell**
Location: **100 mi. E of Dallas**
No. of Rooms: **7**
No. of Private Baths: **7**
Double/pb: **$85**
Suites: **$150**
Open: **All year**
Reduced Rates: **Available**

Breakfast: **Full**
Other Meals: **Available**
Credit Cards: **AMEX, DC, DISC, MC, VISA**
Pets: **No**
Children: **Welcome, over 3**
Smoking: **No**
Social Drinking: **Permitted**
Airport/Station Pickup: **Yes**

Rosevine Inn combines the best qualities of a bed & breakfast, offering hospitality, comfort, convenience, and a sense of history. The house sits on a hill and overlooks the Historic Brick Street District that has become a favorite of tourists because of the specialty shops and restored homes. You may also want to visit the Azalea District, where homes are notable for architectural styles representing many periods in Tyler's past. Guest rooms are cheerfully decorated with antiques. Guests are encouraged to use all areas, including the lodge game room with a fireplace, hot tub, and courtyard. Breakfast is a grand affair of homemade delights served in the dining room.

UTAH

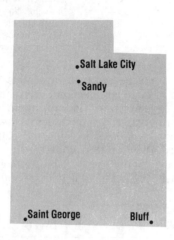

.Salt Lake City
•Sandy

.Saint George   Bluff.

Mi Casa–Su Casa/Old Pueblo Bed and Breakfast ✪
Reservation Service—Utah
P.O. BOX 950, TEMPE, ARIZONA 85280-0950
www.mi-casa.org

Tel: **(602) 990-0682; (800) 456-0682;**
  fax: **(602) 990-3390**
Best Time to Call: **8 AM–8 PM**
Coordinator: **Ruth T. Young**
States/Regions Covered: **Utah: Alton,**
  Cedar City, Moab, Monroe,
Monticello, Salt Lake City,
Springdale, Torrey, Tropic; Arizona;
New Mexico; Nevada
Descriptive Directory of B&Bs: **$9.50**
Rates (Single/Double): **$65–$135**
Credit Cards: **AMEX, MC, VISA**

Ruth offers travelers unique accommodations from historic inns in Salt
Lake City to a contemporary home in Alton. Many of the B&Bs are near
national parks and scenic areas with sites for hiking, mountain biking,
fishing, and white-water boating.

Bluff Bed & Breakfast ✪
BOX 158, BLUFF, UTAH 84512

Tel: (801) 672-2220
Hosts: **Rosalie Goldman**
Location: **At intersection of 163 and 191**
No. of Rooms: **2**
No. of Private Baths: **2**
Double/pb: **$75**
Singe/pb: **$70**
Open: **All year**

Breakfast: **Full**
Other Meals: **Available**
Pets: **No**
Children: **Welcome**
Smoking: **No**
Social Drinking: **Permitted**
Airport/Station Pickup: **Yes**
Foreign Languages: **French**

Just outside of town on the San Juan River, this Frank Lloyd Wright-style home nestles in huge boulders on desert land at the foot of red-rock cliffs. Twenty-seven picture windows frame four different canyon views. The Navajo reservation is directly across the river. This Four Corners region abounds in prehistoric ruins and petroglyphs; archaeologists have identified a few on this property. There are dozens of wild canyon hikes and explorations nearby. Bluff is central to nine national parks and monuments, all within one to three hours' driving distance.

Seven Wives Inn ✪
217 NORTH 100 WEST, ST. GEORGE, UTAH 84770

Tel: **(435) 628-3737; (800) 600-3737**
Best Time to Call: **After 9 AM**
Hosts: **Jay and Donna Curtis**
Location: **125 mi. NE of Las Vegas**
No. of Rooms: **13**
No. of Private Baths: **13**
Double/pb: **$55–$100**
Single/pb: **$55–$100**
Suites: **$125**

Open: **All year**
Reduced Rates: **Special business rate (single occupancy) $50 Mon.–Thurs.**
Breakfast: **Full**
Credit Cards: **AMEX, DC, MC, VISA**
Children: **By arrangement**
Smoking: **No**
Social Drinking: **Permitted**

This delightful Inn is featured on the walking tour of St. George; it is just across from the Brigham Young home and two blocks from the historic Washington County Court House. Your hosts offer traditional Western hospitality. Their home is decorated with antiques collected in America and Europe. Bedrooms are named after some of the seven wives of Donna's polygamous great-grandfather. A gourmet breakfast is served in the elegant dining room that will give you a hint of the past. St. George is located near Zion and Bryce national parks, boasts eight golf courses, and is noted for its mild winters. Dixie College is nearby. There's a swimming pool for your pleasure.

The Log Cabin on the Hill B&B ✪
2275 EAST 6200 SOUTH, SALT LAKE CITY, UTAH 84121

Tel: **(800) 639-2969; (801) 272-2969**
Best Time to Call: **9 AM–9 PM**

Host: **Geri M. Symes**
No. of Rooms: **4**

No. of Private Baths: **4**	Pets: **No**
Double/pb: **$75–$95**	Children: **Welcome**
Open: **All year**	Smoking: **No**
Reduced Rates: **Available**	Social Drinking: **Permitted**
Breakfast: **Full**	Minimum Stay: **4 nights Dec. 20–**
Credit Cards: **AMEX, DISC, MC, VISA**	**Apr. 15**

Nestled in a natural hollow of the canyon foothills, this B&B is located just minutes from every major ski resort and area attraction. Guest rooms have down-filled comforters, fresh flowers, and terrycloth robes. Mornings begin with a hearty breakfast. After a day of skiing, sightseeing, or shopping, you're invited to sit by the fire and visit with other guests, curl up with a good book, or soak in the hot tub under the stars.

Alta Hills Farm Bed & Breakfast ○

10852 SOUTH 2000 EAST, SANDY, UTAH 84092

Tel: **(801) 571-1712; (800) 571-1713**	Reduced Rates: **10% weekly, seniors**
Hosts: **Blaine and Diane Knight**	Breakfast: **Continental**
Location: **15 mi. S of Salt Lake**	Credit Cards: **DISC, MC, VISA**
No. of Rooms: **4**	Pets: **Yes**
No. of Private Baths: **2**	Children: **Welcome**
Max. No. Sharing Bath: **4**	Smoking: **No**
Double/pb: **$89**	Social Drinking: **Permitted**
Double/sb: **$69**	Airport/Station Pickup: **Yes**
Open: **Sept. 1–May 31**	

This B&B is nestled at the base of the Rocky Mountains fifteen minutes from the Alta and Snow Bird ski resorts. Alta Hills Farm has been an English Huntseat Equestrian Center for the past twenty years. In the summer the Knights run a riding camp for children of all ages. Their home has a warm, spacious English country style. Every evening, guests can relax with hot apple cider in a private living room with a fireplace. You are also invited to join the Knights downstairs. Blaine and Diane love kids and welcome families who come to ski or to enjoy beautiful Salt Lake.

VERMONT

North Troy

North Hero

Morgan

Jericho

Stowe

Waterbury

Cabot

Montpelier

Warren

Fairlee

Bethel

Fair Haven

Rutland

Brownsville

Wallingford

Dorset

Townshend

Greenhurst Inn
RIVER STREET, BETHEL, VERMONT 05032

Tel: **(802) 234-9474**
Hosts: **Lyle and Claire Wolf**
Location: **30 mi. E of Rutland**
No. of Rooms: **13**
No. of Private Baths: **7**
Max. No. Sharing Bath: **4**
Double/pb: **$80–$100**
Single/pb: **$65–$85**
Double/sb: **$50–$70**

Single/sb: **$35–$55**
Open: **All year**
Breakfast: **Continental**
Credit Cards: **MC, VISA**
Pets: **Welcome (no cats)**
Children: **Welcome (crib)**
Smoking: **Permitted**
Social Drinking: **Permitted**

Located 100 yards from the White River, this elegant Queen Anne mansion, built in 1890, is listed on the National Register of Historic Places. The heavy brass hinges, embossed floral brass doorknobs, and etched windows at the entry have withstood the test of time. The cut-crystal collection is magnificent, and the stereoscope and old Victrola add to the old-fashioned atmosphere. The mansion is close to many points of historic interest, and seasonal recreational activities are abundant. Vermont Law School is close by.

The Pond House at Shattuck Hill Farm ✪
SHATTUCK HILL ROAD, BROWNSVILLE, VERMONT 05037
www.windsor.K12.vt.us/pondhse.html

Tel: **(802) 484-0011**	Other Meals: **Dinner included with rate**
Best Time to Call: **5–9 PM**	Credit Cards: **MC, VISA**
Hosts: **David Raymond and Gretel Schuck**	Pets: **Sometimes**
	Children: **Welcome, over 6**
Location: **10 mi. S of Woodstock**	Smoking: **No**
No. of Rooms: **3**	Social Drinking: **Permitted**
No. of Private Baths: **2**	Minimum Stay: **2 nights holiday weekends**
Max. No. Sharing Bath: **4**	
Double/pb: **$125–$150**	Airport/Station Pickup: **Yes**
Open: **All year**	Foreign Languages: **French**
Breakfast: **Full**	

The Pond House is nestled in the mountains on 10 secluded acres just south of Woodstock. The farm dates from 1779, with miles of stone walls and a traditional white cape. The inn is cozy with antiques, Oriental rugs, and touches of Laura Ashley. Your hosts offer custom bicycle tours designed for all skills. Guests are invited to take a dip in the spring-fed pond, explore the flower and herb gardens, or relax with a glass of wine during a round of croquet. Winter brings day or night torch-lit skating or sledding and back country cross-country tours. Pond House is only minutes from three major ski resorts. Dinners with Northern Italian flair set with family silver and linen are included in the rates.

Creamery Inn Bed & Breakfast ✪
P.O. BOX 187, CABOT, VERMONT 05647

Tel: **(802) 563-2819**	Open: **All year**
Hosts: **Dan and Judy Lloyd**	Reduced Rates: **Families, Nov.–June**
Location: **18 mi. NE of Montpelier**	Breakfast: **Full**
No. of Rooms: **3**	Other Meals: **Available**
No. of Private Baths: **3**	Pets: **Sometimes**
Double/pb: **$65**	Children: **Welcome**
Single/pb: **$45**	Smoking: **No**
Suites: **$75**	Social Drinking: **Permitted**

Enjoy lovely year-round accommodations in this Federal-style home, circa 1835. Guest rooms are tastefully decorated, with stenciling, old-fashioned wallpaper, a canopy bed, and old trunks. Located one mile from Cabot Creamery, the Inn is on two acres in a country setting beautiful in any season. New lambs each spring attract many visitors. It's a great area for joggers, hikers, bicyclists, and nature lovers—walk up the road and delight in ponds and waterfalls along the way. Full breakfasts

include Finnish pancakes and other homemade fare. Candlelight dinner is available by advance reservation.

The Little Lodge at Dorset ✪
ROUTE 30, BOX 673, DORSET, VERMONT 05251

Tel: **(802) 867-4040; (800) 378-7505**	Open: **All year**
Best Time to Call: **Anytime**	Breakfast: **Continental, plus**
Hosts: **Allan and Nancy Norris**	Credit Cards: **AMEX, DISC**
Location: **6 mi. N of Manchester**	Pets: **No**
No. of Rooms: **5**	Children: **Welcome**
No. of Private Baths: **5**	Smoking: **No**
Double/pb: **$85–$105**	Social Drinking: **Permitted**
Single/pb: **$75–$95**	

Situated in one of the prettiest little towns in Vermont, this delightful 1820 Colonial house, on the Historic Register, is perched on a hillside way back from the road, overlooking the mountains and its own trout pond that's used for skating in winter or swimming in summer. The original paneling and wide floorboards set off the splendid antiques. After skiing at nearby Stratton or Bromley, toast your feet by the fireplace while sipping hot chocolate. If you prefer, bring your own liquor, and Nancy and Allan will provide Vermont cheese and crackers.

Maplewood Inn

ROUTE 22A SOUTH, FAIR HAVEN, VERMONT 05743
www.sover.net/~maplewd

Tel: **(802) 265-8039; (800) 253-7729**	Reduced Rates: **After 5th night**
Best Time to Call: **9 AM–9 PM**	Breakfast: **Continental, plus**
Hosts: **Cindy and Doug Baird**	Credit Cards: **AMEX, DISC, MC, VISA**
Location: **18 mi. W of Rutland**	Pets: **No**
No. of Rooms: **5**	Children: **Welcome, over 8**
No. of Private Baths: **5**	Smoking: **No**
Double/pb: **$75–$95**	Social Drinking: **Permitted**
Suites: **$115–$130**	Minimum Stay: **Parents college**
Open: **All year**	**weekends, holidays, foliage**

The Inn is a beautifully restored National Register Greek Revival–style home, built in 1843, with lovely country views from every window. Chippendale furnishings, original pine floors polished to a warm glow, four-poster or brass beds, wingback chairs, and carefully chosen accessories provide a soothing backdrop for a relaxing visit. Rooms and suites feature air-conditioning, TVs, and phones, and four out of the five rooms have fireplaces. After a multicourse breakfast, enjoy a walk in the historic village or participate in the recreational activities at nearby Lakes Bomoseen and St. Catherine, or take a short drive to ski the slopes of Killington or Pico. Linger on the porch, play croquet on the lawn, enjoy a board game, book or complimentary liqueur in the parlor. The gourmet restaurants and shops of Rutland are close by. Reserve early for the fall foliage season.

Silver Maple Lodge and Cottages ✪

SOUTH MAIN STREET, RR1, BOX 8, FAIRLEE, VERMONT 05045

Tel: **(802) 333-4326; (800) 666-1946**	Double/pb: **$64–$84**
Hosts: **Scott and Sharon Wright**	Single/pb: **$59–$79**
Location: **20 mi. N of White River**	Double/sb: **$56**
Junction	Single/sb: **$52**
No. of Rooms: **14**	Open: **All year**
No. of Private Baths: **12**	Reduced Rates: **10% seniors, AAA**
Max. No. Sharing Bath: **4**	Breakfast: **Continental**

Credit Cards: **AMEX, MC, VISA**
Pets: **Sometimes**
Children: **Welcome**

Smoking: **Permitted**
Social Drinking: **Permitted**
Airport/Station Pickup: **Yes**

Built as a farmhouse in 1855, Silver Maple Lodge became an inn some seventy years later. To accommodate extra guests, several cottages were added, constructed from lumber cut on the property. It's easy to see why this B&B remains popular. There's swimming, boating, and fishing at two local lakes. Other outdoor activities in the area include golf, tennis, horseback riding, canoeing, hiking, and skiing. If you're tired of feeling earthbound, Post Mills Airport, seven miles away, offers flights in a hot-air balloon and gliding rides. (Special packages, combining a flight in a hot-air balloon and other activities of your choice, can be arranged.) And for concerts, theater, and art exhibits, it's an easy drive to Dartmouth College, in Hanover, New Hampshire.

Millikens ✪

65 VT ROUTE 15, JERICHO CORNERS, VERMONT 05465
maha11@aol.com

Tel: **(802) 899-3993**
Hosts: **Rick and Jean Milliken**
Location: **12 mi. E of Burlington**
No. of Rooms: **2**
Double/pb: **$50**
Single/pb: **$35**
Suites: **$65**

Open: **May 20–Nov. 15**
Breakfast: **Full**
Pets: **No**
Children: **Welcome**
Smoking: **No**
Social Drinking: **Permitted**
Airport/Station Pickup: **Yes**

Rick and Jean host this Second Empire early Victorian B&B. The house has the high ceilings and large windows typical of the period, and original woodwork. Rick is a hotel manager and Jean-Marie is a dance teacher. There are various musical instruments available, including a grand piano, which is eager to be played by guests. A leisurely breakfast is served on the glassed-in porch, weather permitting, and a goodnight snack is usually offered. In residence are Patrick, age 14, two dogs, Sandy and Bailey, and two guinea pigs, Hootie and Patootie. Millikens is located 10 minutes from the foot of Mt. Mansfield and one half-hour from the big city of Burlington.

Betsy's B&B ✪

74 EAST STATE STREET, MONTPELIER, VERMONT 05602

Tel: **(802) 229-0466**	Reduced Rates: **Available**
Hosts: **Jon and Betsy Anderson**	Breakfast: **Full**
Location: **Downtown Montpelier**	Credit Cards: **AMEX, DISC, MC, VISA**
No. of Rooms: **12**	Pets: **No**
No. of Private Baths: **12**	Children: **Welcome**
Double/pb: **$55–$90**	Smoking: **No**
Single/pb: **$50–$85**	Social Drinking: **Permitted**
Suites: **$95–$180**	Airport/Station Pickup: **Yes**
Open: **All year**	

This fancy Queen Anne B&B in the historic district near downtown, Statehouse, Vermont College, and history and art museums is a real find. It is lavishly furnished with period antiques. Great restaurants and interesting book, crafts, and sporting goods shops are nearby. Walk or run in nearby parks or neighborhoods with Victorian homes, then relax on the porch or decks. Betsy's boasts award-winning building restoration and landscaping. Amenities include in-room cable TV and telephone, exercise room, and fax. Your hosts are interested in historic preservation, gardening, antiques, law, and politics.

Hunt's Hideaway ✪

RR 1, BOX 570, WEST CHARLESTON, MORGAN, VERMONT 05872

Tel: **(802) 895-4432, 334-8322**	Open: **All year**
Best Time to Call: **7 AM–11 PM**	Reduced Rates: **Available**
Host: **Pat Hunt**	Breakfast: **Full**
Location: **6 mi. from I-91**	Pets: **Sometimes**
No. of Rooms: **3**	Children: **Welcome**
Max. No. Sharing Bath: **4**	Smoking: **Restricted**
Double/sb: **$40**	Social Drinking: **Permitted**
Single/sb: **$30**	

This modern, split-level home is located on 100 acres of woods and fields, with a brook, pond, and large swimming pool. Pancakes with Vermont maple syrup are featured at breakfast. Ski Jay Peak and Burke, or fish and boat on Lake Seymour, two miles away. Visiting antique shops or taking a trip to nearby Canada are other local possibilities.

Charlie's Northland Lodge ✪

BOX 88, NORTH HERO, VERMONT 05474

Tel: **(802) 372-8822**
Best Time to Call: **Before 8 PM**
Hosts: **Charles and Dorice Clark**
Location: **60 mi. S of Montreal, Canada**
No. of Rooms: **2**
Max. No. Sharing Bath: **4**
Double/sb: **$55–$65**
Guest Cottage: **$400–$600 weekly;**
  sleeps 6

Open: **All year**
Breakfast: **Continental**
Pets: **No**
Children: **Welcome, over 5**
Smoking: **Permitted**
Social Drinking: **Permitted**

Located in a quiet village on the shores of Lake Champlain, this 1800s guest house has a view of the Green Mountains. Guest rooms are furnished in country antiques, with a private entrance and guest parlor. Activities include fishing, biking, sailing, canoeing, and kayaking. There is a sport and gift shop, and boat rentals are available.

Rose Apple Acres Farm ✪

RR 2, BOX 300, EAST HILL ROAD, NORTH TROY, VERMONT 05859

Tel: **(802) 988-4300**
Best Time to Call: **Evenings**
Hosts: **Jay, Camilla, and Courtney Mead**
Location: **30 minutes from I-91, Exit 26**
No. of Rooms: **3**
No. of Private Baths: **1**
Max. No. Sharing Bath: **4**
Double/pb: **$60**

Double/sb: **$50**
Single/sb: **$45**
Open: **All year**
Breakfast: **Continental, plus**
Pets: **No**
Children: **Welcome, over 6**
Smoking: **No**

Situated on fifty-two acres of fields, woods, gardens, and ponds, Rose Apple Acres Farm is located on the Vermont–Canada line, only four hours north of Boston and two hours from Montreal. The atmosphere is peaceful and quiet, with panoramic views that are especially spectacular during the fall foliage. In addition to the B&B, the farm is home to Alpine goats, Lincoln sheep, Belgian horses, and of course, the collies. Hiking, cross-country skiing, and snowshoeing can be enjoyed on the premises; horse-drawn sleigh or wagon rides are also offered. Downhill skiing is only twenty minutes away. Also on the premises is Henderson Forge, with wrought-iron creations by Courtney, and Camilla's Porcelain Doll Studio.

Hillcrest Guest House ✪

RR 1, BOX 4459, RUTLAND, VERMONT 05701
Pegdombro@aol.com

Tel: **(802) 775-1670**	Open: **All year**
Hosts: **Bob and Peg Dombro**	Breakfast: **Continental**
Location: **³/₁₀ mi. from Rte. 7**	Pets: **No**
No. of Rooms: **3**	Children: **Welcome, over 5**
Max. No. Sharing Bath: **5**	Smoking: **No**
Double/sb: **$50**	Social Drinking: **Permitted**
Single/sb: **$45**	Airport/Station Pickup: **Yes**

This 150-year-old farmhouse, with a comfortable screened porch for warm-weather relaxing, is furnished with country antiques. Pico and Killington ski areas are 7 and 16 miles away, respectively. Summer brings the opportunity to explore charming villages, covered bridges, and antiques and crafts centers. Country auctions, marble quarries, trout streams, and Sunday-evening band concerts are pleasant pastimes. Bob and Peg always offer something in the way of between-meal refreshments.

Bittersweet Inn

692 SOUTH MAIN STREET, STOWE, VERMONT 05672

Tel: **(802) 253-7787; (800) 387-8789**	Suites: **$145–$180**
Best Time to Call: **7 AM–10 PM**	Open: **All year**
Hosts: **Barbara and Paul Hansel**	Reduced Rates: **5-night stays**
Location: **36 mi. E of Burlington**	Breakfast: **Continental, plus**
No. of Rooms: **8**	Credit Cards: **AMEX, DISC, MC, VISA**
No. of Private Baths: **5**	Children: **Welcome (play area)**
Max. No. Sharing Bath: **4**	Smoking: **No**
Double/pb: **$68–$86**	Social Drinking: **Permitted**
Double/sb: **$45–$56**	

Bittersweet Inn is a brick Cape with converted clapboard carriage house, dating back to 1835. The house is set on eleven and a half acres, overlooking Camel's Hump Mountain. Inside you'll find comfortable rooms decorated with a combination of antiques and family pieces. It's just a half mile to the center of town and minutes to ski lifts and a cross-country touring center. A good-size swimming pool is located out back with plenty of room for laps or just taking it easy. In the winter season, the indoor hydro-spa will be waiting after your last ski run. Your hosts, Barbara and Paul, invite you to relax in the game room with BYOB bar and will help you plan your evening.

Ski Inn ✪
ROUTE 108, STOWE, VERMONT 05672
www.ski-inn.com/bb

Tel: **(802) 253-4050**
Best Time to Call: **Before 11 AM; after 7:30 PM**
Hosts: **The Heyer Family**
Location: **47 mi. NE of Burlington**
No. of Rooms: **10**
No. of Private Baths: **5**
Max. No. Sharing Bath: **5**
Double/pb: **$50–$65**
Double/sb: **$45–$50**

Single/sb: **$30–$45**
Open: **All year**
Reduced Rates: **Off-season**
Breakfast: **Continental**
Other Meals: **In winter, full breakfast and dinner (additional fee)**
Pets: **Sometimes**
Children: **Welcome**
Smoking: **No**
Social Drinking: **Permitted**

This traditional New England inn is set back from the highway on a gentle sloping hillside, offering guests total relaxation and a peaceful night's sleep. In the winter this is a skier's delight. This B&B is located close to Stowe's challenging downhill ski area, or you can cross-country ski for miles on the trails right at the back door. The Heyer family assures you of warm hospitality in all seasons.

Boardman House Bed & Breakfast ✪
P.O. BOX 112, TOWNSHEND, VERMONT 05353

Tel: **(802) 365-4086**
Hosts: **Sarah Messenger and Paul Weber**
Location: **125 mi. N of Boston**
No. of Rooms: **6**
No. of Private Baths: **5**
Max. No. Sharing Bath: **4**
Double/pb: **$70–$80**
Single/pb: **$65–$75**
Suites: **$90–$100**

Open: **All year**
Reduced Rates: **10–15% seniors; off-season; weekly**
Breakfast: **Full**
Pets: **Sometimes**
Children: **Welcome**
Smoking: **No**
Social Drinking: **Permitted**

If you tried to imagine an idealized New England home, it would resemble this white 19th-century farmhouse set on Townshend's Village Green. This is a prime foliage and antiquing area. Direct access to State Routes 30 and 35 allows you to pursue other interests, from skiing at Stratton to canoeing on the West River. Gourmet breakfasts feature pear pancakes, individual soufflés, hot fruit compotes, and more.

White Rocks Inn ✪
RR 1, BOX 297, ROUTE 7, WALLINGFORD, VERMONT 05773

Tel: **(802) 446-2077**
Best Time to Call: **Mornings; evenings**
Hosts: **June and Alfred Matthews**
Location: **20 mi. N of Manchester**
No. of Rooms: **5**

No. of Private Baths: **5**
Double/pb: **$75–$110**
Single/pb: **$70–$100**
Guest Cottage: **$130–$140**
Open: **Dec. 1–Oct. 31**

Breakfast: **Full**
Credit Cards: **AMEX, MC, VISA**
Pets: **No**
Children: **Welcome, over 8**
Smoking: **No**

Social Drinking: **Permitted**
Minimum Stay: **2 nights holidays, fall
    foliage season**
Foreign Languages: **French, Spanish**

Escape to this century-old Greek Revival farmhouse and Gothic barn, both listed on the Register of Historic Places. The inn is located in a pastoral setting with mountain views. Guest rooms are decorated with antiques, canopy beds, and Oriental and braided rugs. A country breakfast is served outdoors on warm summer mornings, other days in the dining room. Fresh juice, homemade muffins, eggs, banana pancakes with real maple syrup, and freshly brewed coffee are just a few morning delights you may enjoy. Things to do include swimming, canoeing, antiquing, cross-country and downhill skiing, and hiking on the Appalachian and Long trails. Otter Creek is perfect for fishing. White Rocks is close to four major downhill ski areas. At the end of the day, chat with June and Al over tea or play cards on the veranda.

West Hill House

RR1, BOX 292, WEST HILL ROAD, WARREN, VERMONT 05674
dotty@westhillhouse.com; www.westhillhouse.com

Tel: **(802) 496-7162; (800) 898-1427**
Best Time to Call: **7 AM–10 PM**
Hosts: **Dotty Kyle and Eric Brattstrom**
Location: **25 mi. SW of Montpelier**
No. of Rooms: **7**
No. of Private Baths: **7**
Double/pb: **$95–$145**
Single/pb: **$85–$135**
Open: **All year**

Reduced Rates: **Available**
Breakfast: **Full**
Credit Cards: **AMEX, MC, VISA**
Pets: **No**
Children: **Welcome, over 10**
Smoking: **No**
Social Drinking: **Permitted**
Minimum Stay: **2 nights weekends**

Up a quiet country lane, on nine wooded and open acres with stunning mountain views, gardens, pond and apple orchard, this 1860s farmhouse is one mile from Sugarbush Ski Resort, adjacent to its golf course and cross-country ski trails. Take advantage of an outdoor sports paradise near fine restaurants, quaint villages, covered bridges, and unique shops. After a busy day, enjoy the comfortable front porch or a roaring fire, eclectic library, oriental rugs, art, antiques, and the interesting company of other guests. Bedrooms feature premium linens, down comforters, and good reading lights. The inn is state-licensed for the sale of beer and wine. Dotty and Eric pride themselves on their memorable breakfasts and afternoon and bedtime snacks.

Grünberg Haus B&B and Cabins ✪
RR2, BOX 1595, BU ROUTE 100 SOUTH, WATERBURY,
VERMONT 05676

Tel: (802) 244-7726; (800) 800-7760
Hosts: **Christopher Sellers and Mark
  Frohman**
Location: **25 mi. E of Burlington**
No. of Rooms: **14**
Max. No. Sharing Bath: **4**
Double/pb: **$80–$150**
Single/pb: **$65–$135**
Double/sb: **$59–$75**
Single/sb: **$45–$60**

Open: **All year**
Reduced Rates: **10% after 3rd night**
Breakfast: **Full**
Credit Cards: **DISC, MC, VISA**
Pets: **No**
Children: **Welcome**
Smoking: **No**
Social Drinking: **Permitted**
Airport/Station Pickup: **Yes**

You'll think you're in the Alps when you see this hand-built Tyrolean chalet perched on a secluded hillside. The living room features an eight-foot grand piano, a massive fieldstone fireplace, and a long breakfast table overlooking the valley and distant forest. All eleven guest rooms open onto the quaint balcony that surrounds the chalet. There are two secluded bedroom cabins with wood stoves hidden along the walking trails. The BYOB rathskeller features hand-stenciled booths; the formal dining room is furnished with antiques. Outside, cleared logging trails provide cross-country skiing and hiking access to hundreds of acres of meadows and woodlands. And Waterbury's central location makes it easy to get to ski resorts like Stowe and Sugarbush. Whatever you plan to do, bring an appetite; Grünberg Haus serves memorable gourmet breakfasts, and other meals can be arranged.

Inn at Blush Hill ✪
BOX 1266, BLUSH HILL ROAD, WATERBURY, VERMONT 05676

Tel: (802) 244-7529; (800) 736-7522
Hosts: **Gary and Pam Gosselin**
Location: **22 mi. E. of Burlington**
No. of Rooms: **5**
No. of Private Baths: **5**
Double/pb: **$59–$130**
Open: **All year**
Reduced Rates: **Available**

Breakfast: **Full**
Credit Cards: **AMEX, DISC, MC, VISA**
Pets: **No**
Children: **Welcome, over 6**
Smoking: **No**
Social Drinking: **Permitted**
Airport/Station Pickup: **Yes**

This 1790 brick farmhouse, the oldest Inn in Waterbury, is located halfway between the Stowe and Sugarbush ski areas. The atmosphere is warm and homey, with antiques, old-time rockers, books, and lots of fireplaces. Your host Pam is a gourmet cook and enjoys making her own bread and muffins each morning. A huge lake with boating, swimming, and fishing is located just one and a half miles from the house, and a nine-hole golf course is located directly across the street. The Inn is back to back to Ben & Jerry's Ice Cream Factory. At the end of the day, sit back and enjoy the surroundings, relaxing on the large, old-fashioned porch. Afternoon and evening refreshments are served. One room has a fireplace, another has a canopy queen-size bed with a 13-foot-wide window view of the sunrise over the mountains. The newest room has a queen-size bed with a sitting room and Jacuzzi tub.

For key to listings, see inside front or back cover.

✪ This star means that rates are guaranteed through December 31, 1999, to any guest making a reservation as a result of reading about the B&B in *Bed & Breakfast U.S.A.*—1999 edition.

Important! To avoid misunderstandings, always ask about cancellation policies when booking.

Please enclose a self-addressed, stamped, business-size envelope when contacting reservation services.

For more details on what you can expect in a B&B, see Chapter 1.

Always mention *Bed & Breakfast U.S.A.* when making reservations!

We want to hear from you! Use the form on page 593.

VIRGINIA

Woodstock
Winchester
New Market
Flint Hill
Manassas
Luray
Fredericksburg
Chincoteague Island
Staunton
Waynesboro
Goshen
Arrington
Onancock
Montross
Rockville
Urbanna
Lexington
Lynchburg
Williamsburg
Cape Charles
Blacksburg
Smith Mountain Lake
Capron
Abingdon
Damascus
Cluster Springs
Virginia Beach

River Garden ✪
19080 NORTH FORK, RIVER ROAD, ABINGDON, VIRGINIA 24210

Tel: **(540) 676-0335; (800) 952-4296**
Best Time to Call: **11 AM–4 PM**
Hosts: **Bill Crump and Carol Schoenherr-Crump**
Location: **9 mi. NE of Abingdon**
No. of Rooms: **4**
No. of Private Baths: **4**

Double/pb: **$65–$70**
Open: **All year**
Breakfast: **Full**
Pets: **Caged only**
Children: **Welcome, infants, over 4**
Smoking: **No**
Social Drinking: **Permitted**

River Garden is tucked into the foothills of the Clinch Mountains, on the bank of the Holston River's North Fork. Each room has its own riverside deck, private entrance, and a king- or queen-size bed. Guests are encouraged to try their hand at weaving on the antique loom. More contemporary challenges can be had in the recreation room, which is equipped with a Ping-Pong table, board games, and exercise equipment. Fishing equipment, a picnic table, and inner tubes are also at your disposal. The center of Abingdon, fifteen minutes away, is home to the historic Barter Theater, as well as many eateries. Lovers of the outdoors will want to head for the Virginia Creeper Trail—34 miles of scenic mountain trails for hikers, bikers, and horseback riders.

Alexandria and Arlington Bed and Breakfast Network ✪

P.O. BOX 25319, ARLINGTON, VIRGINIA 22202-9319
AABBN@erols.com; www.AABBN.com

Tel: **(703) 549-3415; (888) 549-3415**	**Church, Fairfax; D.C.; Maryland,**
Best Time to Call: **10 AM–5 PM**	**Pennsylvania, West Virginia**
Mon.–Fri.	Rates (Single/Double):
Coordinator: **Leslie C. and Ann L.**	Modest: **$65 / $75**
Garrison	Average: **$75 / $85**
States/Regions Covered:	Luxury: **$295**
Virginia—Alexandria, Arlington, Falls	Credit Cards: **AMEX, MC, VISA**

The range of listings in the Alexandria and Arlington Bed & Breakfast Network is breathtaking. Homes range from Colonial town houses of Old Towne Alexandria to modern, high-rise urban dwellings. Locations outside the D.C. metro area allow travelers to experience the quiet civility of the countryside and expand sightseeing possibilities to nearby areas of historic interest. Hosts are eclectic, including civil servants, political activists, veterans, diplomats, and yuppies.

Harmony Hill Bed & Breakfast ✪

929 WILSON HILL ROAD, ARLINGTON, VIRGINIA 22922

Tel: **(804) 263-7750**	Breakfast: **Full**
Best Time to Call: **4–7 PM**	Pets: **No**
Hosts: **Joanne and Robert Cuoghi**	Children: **Welcome, over 6**
Location: **30 mi. N of Lynchburg**	Smoking: **No**
No. of Rooms: **5**	Social Drinking: **Permitted**
No. of Private Baths: **5**	Minimum Stay: **2 nights holiday**
Double/pb: **$80–$100**	**weekends**
Open: **All year**	Airport/Station Pickup: **Yes**

Harmony Hill Bed and Breakfast is a new log home, set on 17 acres of rolling farmland in the foothills of the Blue Ridge. Guest rooms are spacious and offer air conditioning, queen-size beds, handmade quilts, and ceiling fans. Some feature a fireplace, whirlpool tub, or sitting room. In keeping with a country log home, the style is unpretentious and unfussy. Within easy driving distance are Natural Bridge, Monticello, and Appomattox. Fishing, golf, skiing, antiques, and wineries are nearby. Your hosts are Revolutionary War reenactors and are interested in all crafts of the 18th and 19th centuries, especially quilting and woodworking.

Clay Corner Inn ✪

401 CLAY STREET SOUTHWEST, BLACKSBURG, VIRGINIA 24060
claycorner@aol.com

Tel: **(540) 953-2604; fax: (540) 951-0541**
Best Time to Call: **9 AM–9 PM**
Hosts: **John and Joanne Anderson**
Location: **35 mi. SW of Roanoke**
No. of Rooms: **12**
No. of Private Baths: **12**
Double/pb: **$75–$105**

Single/pb: **$68–$85**
Open: **All year**
Breakfast: **Full**
Credit Cards: **AMEX, MC, VISA**
Pets: **No**
Children: **Welcome, over 12**
Smoking: **No**
Social Drinking: **Permitted**

Clay Corner Inn is a cluster of houses on a corner a few blocks from downtown and the Virginia Tech campus. The main house is decorated with a mix of traditional and Southwestern decors. The Huckleberry House next door, circa 1913, has four guest rooms. Each of the two Cape-style guesthouses has a kitchen, dining area, living room, and three guest rooms. The main house, circa 1929, has two guest rooms. A heated swimming pool is located in the center of the complex and is open May through September. Wood decks with benches and rockers provide wonderful places to relax, read, visit, and enjoy coffee, tea, or breakfast.

Bay Avenue's Sunset Bed & Breakfast ✪

108 BAY AVENUE, CAPE CHARLES, VIRGINIA 23310
www.baysunsetbb.com

Tel: **(757) 331-2424; 888-4BAYAVE**
Best Time to Call: **After 10 AM**
Hosts: **Al Longo and Joyce Tribble**
Location: **35 mi. N of Norfolk**
No of Rooms: **4**

No. of Private Baths: **4**
Double/pb: **$75–$95**
Single/pb: **$70–$90**
Open: **All year**
Reduced Rates: **Available**

Breakfast: **Full**
Credit Cards: **AMEX, DISC, MC, VISA**
Pets: **No**
Children: **Welcome, over 10**
Smoking: **Restricted**

Social Drinking: **Permitted**
Minimum Stay: **2 nights, holiday weekends**
Airport Pickup: **Yes**

Look out at the Chesapeake Bay from this charming 1915 Victorian B&B. The convenient in-town location allows you to walk across the street to the beach or to town for dinner, explore the historic district, or just relax, unwind, and watch spectacular sunsets from rockers on the front porch. Experience a bygone era in charming Cape Charles, which has no traffic lights or parking meters. Biking, bird watching, tennis, golf, and fishing are nearby. Guest rooms are spacious and cheery, featuring central air, Hunter fans, TVs, VCRs, and fireplaces. A hearty breakfast features delicious award-winning hot entrees, fresh fruit, and homemade baked goods.

Sandy Hill Farm B&B ✪
11307 RIVERS MILL ROAD, CAPRON, VIRGINIA 23829

Tel: **(804) 658-4381**
Best Time to Call: **6:30–8 AM; 7:30–11:30 PM**
Host: **Anne Kitchen**
Location: **11 mi. from I-95**
No. of Rooms: **2**
Double/pb: **$50**
Single/pb: **$40**

Open: **Mar. 20–Dec. 5**
Reduced Rates: **Families; 5 nights**
Breakfast: **Full**
Other Meals: **Available**
Pets: **Welcome**
Children: **Welcome**
Smoking: **Permitted**
Social Drinking: **Permitted**

Experience the pleasures of an unspoiled rural setting at this ranch-style farmhouse. There are animals to visit, quiet places to stroll, and a lighted tennis court on the grounds. This is an ideal hub from which to tour southeastern and central Virginia. Day trips to Williamsburg, Norfolk, and Richmond are possibilities. Fresh fruits and homemade breads are served at breakfast. Rooms are booked by reservation only.

Guesthouses Reservation Service ✪

P.O. BOX 5737, CHARLOTTESVILLE, VIRGINIA 22905

www.va-guesthouses.com

Tel: **(804) 979-7264**	Rates (Single/Double):
Best Time to Call: **12–5 PM Mon.–Fri.**	Modest: **$60 / $68**
Coordinator: **Mary Hill Caperton**	Average: **$72 / $80**
States/Regions Covered: **Albemarle**	Luxury: **$100 / $150**
County, Charlottesville	Estate Cottages: **$100 up**
Descriptive Directory: **$1**	Credit Cards: **AMEX, MC, VISA**

Charlottesville is a gracious town. The hosts in Mary's hospitality file offer you a genuine taste of Southern hospitality. All places are close to Thomas Jefferson's Monticello and James Madison's Ash Lawn, as well as the University of Virginia. Unusual local activities include ballooning, steeplechasing, and wine festivals. Reduced rates are available for extended stays, and most hosts offer a full breakfast.

Miss Molly's Inn ✪

4141 MAIN STREET, CHINCOTEAGUE ISLAND, VIRGINIA 23336

Tel: **(757) 336-6686; (800) 221-5620**	Reduced Rates: **10% seniors;**
Best Time to Call: **10 AM–10 PM**	**Oct. 1–Memorial Weekend**
Hosts: **Barbara and David Wiedenheft**	Breakfast: **Full**
Location: **50 mi. S of Salisbury,**	Other Meals: **Available**
Maryland	Pets: **No**
No. of Rooms: **7**	Children: **Welcome, over 8**
No. of Private Baths: **5**	Smoking: **No**
Max. No. Sharing Bath: **4**	Social Drinking: **Permitted**
Double/pb: **$69–$155**	Minimum Stay: **2 days, weekends**
Single/pb: **$59–$115**	Airport/Station Pickup: **Yes**
Double/sb: **$75–$109**	Foreign Languages: **French, Dutch,**
Single/sb: **$65–$99**	**German**
Open: **Mar. 15–New Year**	

This bayside Victorian Inn has been lovingly restored to its 19th-century charm; lace curtains, stained glass windows, and period pieces add to the ambience. While writing her book *Misty of Chincoteague*, Marguerite Henry stayed here. The ponies celebrated by that story roam wild at the nearby National Wildlife Refuge close to the unspoiled beaches of Assateague Island. You, too, may find Miss Molly's cool breezes, five porches, and traditional English tea—complete with superlative scones—worth writing about.

The Watson House ✪
4240 MAIN STREET, CHINCOTEAGUE, VIRGINIA 23336

Tel: **(757) 336-1564; (800) 336-6787**
Hosts: **Tom and Jacque Derrickson,**
   David and Joanne Snead
Location: **180 mi. SE of Washington,**
   D.C.
No. of Rooms: **6**
No. of Private Baths: **6**
Double/pb: **$59–$85**
Suites: **$79–$99**
Open: **Apr.–Nov.**

Reduced Rates: **Available**
Breakfast: **Full**
Credit Cards: **MC, VISA**
Pets: **No**
Children: **Welcome, over 10**
Smoking: **No**
Social Drinking: **Permitted**
Minimum Stay: **2 nights, weekends;**
   3 nights, holidays

Friendly hosts and Southern hospitality await you at this newly restored country Victorian home. Guest rooms are tastefully decorated with antiques, wicker, and nostalgic pieces; each room has a ceiling fan and air-conditioning. Watson House is within biking distance of Assateague National Wildlife Refuge, where you can enjoy numerous nature trails, guided tours, crabbing, fishing, clamming, or swimming. Your hosts will equip you with bicycles, beach chairs, and towels. In the mornings, you can mingle with other guests over a hearty breakfast, which includes fruit, eggs, breads, pastries, and aromatic coffee and tea. Some guest baths have whirlpool tubs.

Oak Grove Plantation Bed & Breakfast ✪
P.O. BOX 45, 1245 CLUSTER ROAD, CLUSTER SPRINGS, VIRGINIA 24535

Tel: **(804) 575-7137**
Host: **Pickett Craddock**
Location: **60 mi. N of Durham, N.C.**
No. of Rooms: **4**
Max. No. Sharing Bath: **4**

Double/sb: **$60–$80**
Single/sb: **$55–$75**
Open: **May and Sept. weekends, full-**
   time June–Aug.
Breakfast: **Full**

Other Meals: **Available**
Pets: **No**
Children: **Welcome**
Smoking: **No**

Social Drinking: **Permitted**
Airport/Station Pickup: **Yes**
Foreign Languages: **Spanish**

Thomas Easley, a prominent Virginia legislator, built this estate in 1820 and it has remained in the family ever since. Pickett, the director of a preschool in Washington, D.C., is a fifth-generation descendant. She encourages guests to hike, bike, and look at the wildlife on the 400-acre grounds. All bedrooms have fireplaces and are decorated with comfortable period pieces and family heirlooms. Guests will enjoy reading or chatting in the elegant parlor or on the cheerful sunporch. Breakfast is served in the Victorian dining room. Historic Danville, last capital of the Confederacy, and Buggs Island Lake are within a half-hour drive. Appomattox is one hour away.

Apple Tree Bed & Breakfast ✪
P.O. BOX 878, 115 EAST LAUREL AVENUE,
DAMASCUS, VIRGINIA 24236
www.clarkenet.org/appletree/; Appletree@naxs.com

Tel: **(800) 231-7626; (540) 475-5261**
Best Time to Call: **After 11 AM**
Hosts: **John and Beth Reese**
Location: **13 mi. SE of Abingdon**
No. of Rooms: **3**
No. of Private Baths: **3**
Double/pb: **$60**
Suites: **$90**

Open: **All year**
Reduced Rates: **Available**
Breakfast: **Continental**
Credit Cards: **MC, VISA**
Pets: **No**
Smoking: **No**
Social Drinking: **Permitted**
Minimum Stay: **2 nights, Jun.–Aug., Oct.**

Located in the heart of the Virginia Highlands, this 96-year-old home could be a great spot for a romantic weekend. But it never seems to work out that way! Once guests arrive at Apple Tree, their time is filled with mountain biking, hiking, horseback riding, trout fishing, golfing, antique shopping, cross-country skiing, and porch swing sitting. Even though guest rooms are decorated in antiques and luxury touches, you will not spend much time in them. Nearby are the Appalachian Trail, Virginia Creeper Trail, 76 Bike Trail, and historic Abingdon.

Caledonia Farm—1812 ✪
47 DEARING ROAD, FLINT HILL, VIRGINIA 22627
www.bnb-N-va.com/cale1812.htm

Tel: **(540) 675-3693; (800) BNB-1812**
Best Time to Call: **10 AM–6 PM**
Host: **Phil Irwin**
Location: **68 mi. SW of Washington, D.C.; 4 mi. N of Washington, Va.**
No. of Rooms: **3**

Max. No. Sharing Bath: **4**
Double/sb: **$80**
Suite: **$140**
Open: **All year**
Breakfast: **Full**
Credit Cards: **DISC, MC, VISA**

Pets: **No**
Children: **Welcome, over 12**

Smoking: **No**
Social Drinking: **Permitted**

This charming 1812 stone manor house and its companion "summer kitchen" are located on a working beef cattle farm adjacent to Shenandoah National Park. Each accommodation has a fireplace, period furnishings, individual temperature controls for heat or air-conditioning, and spectacular views of the Blue Ridge Mountains. A candlelight breakfast is served from a menu that offers a choice of omelette, smoked salmon, or eggs Benedict. The Skyline Drive, fine dining, caves, wineries, hayrides, hot tub, antiquing, historic sites, and sporting activities are a few of the possible diversions. Caledonia Farm is a Virginia Historic Landmark and on the National Register of Historic Places.

La Vista Plantation ✪

4420 GUINEA STATION ROAD, FREDERICKSBURG, VIRGINIA 22408
LaVistaBB@aol.com; www.bbonline.com/va/lavista/

Tel: **(540) 898-8444; (800) 529-2823;**
   fax: **(540) 898-9414**
Best Time to Call: **Before 9:30 PM**
Hosts: **Michele and Edward Schiesser**
Location: **60 mi. S of Washington, D.C.;**
   4.5 mi. from I-95
No. of Rooms: **2**
No. of Private Baths: **2**
Double/pb: **$95**
Single/pb: **$75**

Guest Apartment: **$95; sleeps 6**
Open: **All year**
Reduced Rates: **7th night free; families**
Breakfast: **Full**
Credit Cards: **MC, VISA**
Pets: **No**
Children: **Welcome**
Smoking: **No**
Social Drinking: **Permitted**

Built in 1838, this Classical Revival country home is nestled amidst ancient tulip poplars, cedars, and hollies, and surrounded by pastures, woods, and fields. The site is close to historic Fredericksburg, but in a quiet rural area. The house retains its original charm, with intricate acorn and oak leaf moldings, high ceilings, wide pine floors and a two-story front portico. Guest rooms have private baths, air-conditioning, working fireplaces, TV, radio, and refrigerator. Enjoy brown egg breakfasts from resident hens. The Schiessers also have a stocked pond.

The Hummingbird Inn

30 WOOD LANE, P.O. BOX 147, GOSHEN, VIRGINIA 24439
hmgbird@cfw.com; www.hummingbirdinn.com

Tel: **(540) 997-9065; (800) 397-3214**
Best Time to Call: **8 AM–5 PM**
Hosts: **Jeremy and Diana Robinson**
Location: **23 mi. NW of Lexington**
No. of Rooms: **5**
No. of Private Baths: **5**
Double/pb: **$75–$125**
Open: **All year**

Reduced Rates: **10% seniors, AAA, military**
Breakfast: **Full**
Credit Cards: **AMEX, DISC, MC, VISA**
Pets: **Sometimes**
Children: **Welcome, over 12**
Smoking: **No**
Social Drinking: **Permitted**

Located on an acre of landscaped grounds in the Shenandoah Valley, this Victorian Carpenter Gothic villa has accommodated Eleanor Roosevelt and Efrem Zimbalist, Sr. Wraparound verandas, original pine floors, a rustic den and a solarium give Hummingbird Inn an old-fashioned ambiance. In keeping with its architecture, the B&B is decorated in an early Victorian style and furnished with antiques. Nearby recreational facilities offer golf, swimming, hiking, skiing, canoeing, tubing, fishing, and hunting. Head out in your car for scenic routes like the Blue Ridge Parkway and Skyline Drive. Or visit the Garth Newell Music Center, historic Staunton, the Museum of American Frontier Culture, Virginia Military Institute, and Washington and Lee University. On Saturdays dinner is included for $135 per person.

A B&B at Llewellyn Lodge ✪

603 SOUTH MAIN STREET, LEXINGTON, VIRGINIA 24450
www.llodge.com; lll@rockbridge.net

Tel: **(800) 882-1145; (540) 463-3235;** **fax: (540) 464-3122**	Open: **All year**
Best Time to Call: **8 AM–10 PM**	Breakfast: **Full**
Hosts: **Ellen and John Roberts**	Credit Cards: **AMEX, DISC, MC, VISA**
Location: **50 mi. N of Roanoke**	Pets: **No**
No. of Rooms: **6**	Children: **Welcome, over 10**
No. of Private Baths: **6**	Smoking: **Restricted**
Double/pb: **$65–$98**	Social Drinking: **Permitted**
Single/pb: **$55–$88**	Airport/Station Pickup: **Yes**

The location of this brick Colonial makes it the perfect home base for exploring historic Lexington and the beautiful surrounding areas. Your comfort and satisfaction are Ellen and John's main concern. Ellen's breakfast—including incredible omelets, Belgian waffles with Virginia maple syrup, sausage, bacon, ham, and her famous blueberry muffins—brings many repeat guests. John, a Lexington native, takes special delight in sharing his knowledge of the area; an avid outdoorsman, he invites you to one of his top twenty hikes. The lodge is an easy walk to the Robert E. Lee Chapel, Stonewall Jackson House, George Marshall

Museum, Washington and Lee University, and Virginia Military Institute. A B&B at Llewellyn Lodge's terrific value and location make it the place to stay.

Brierley Hill
RT 2, BOX 21A BORDEN ROAD, LEXINGTON, VIRGINIA 24450

Tel: **(540) 464-8421; (800) 422-4925**	Reduced Rates: **Available**
Best Time to Call: **8 AM–8 PM**	Breakfast: **Full**
Hosts: **Barry and Carole Speton**	Other Meals: **Available**
Location: **50 mi. N of Roanoke**	Credit Cards: **MC, VISA**
No. of Rooms: **5**	Pets: **No**
No. of Private Baths: **5**	Children: **Welcome, over 14**
Double/pb: **$85–$145**	Smoking: **No**
Open: **All year**	Social Drinking: **Permitted**

This charming B&B sits on eight acres of farmland. Guests are sure to appreciate the spectacular views of the Blue Ridge Mountains and the Shenandoah Valley. Located nearby are Blue Ridge Parkway, the Natural Bridge area, and historic Lexington. All rooms are furnished with antique brass or canopy beds, plus Laura Ashley wall coverings and linens. A TV room and a sitting room with a fireplace are at your disposal, and the dining room also has a fireplace. Barry, a retired Canadian lawyer, is interested in antique prints and refinishing furniture. Carole likes cooking, gardening, and quilting. Together, they offer relaxed comfort, wonderful food, and friendly hospitality.

Lavender Hill Farm B&B ✪
ROUTE 1, BOX 515, LEXINGTON, VIRGINIA 24450

Tel: **(540) 464-5877; (800) 446-4240**	Reduced Rates: **Available**
Best Time to Call: **9 AM–9 PM**	Breakfast: **Full**
Hosts: **Sarah and John Burleson**	Other Meals: **Available**
Location: **50 mi. N of Roanoke**	Credit Cards: **MC, VISA**
No. of Rooms: **3**	Pets: **No**
No. of Private Baths: **3**	Children: **Welcome**
Double/pb: **$69–$74**	Smoking: **No**
Single/pb: **$59–$64**	Social Drinking: **Permitted**
Suites: **$105–$115**	Minimum Stay: **2 nights on holidays or**
Open: **All year**	**special events**

Situated on a 20-acre working farm in the beautiful Shenandoah Valley, this restored farmhouse (circa 1790) is located five miles from historic Lexington. It has been carefully renovated to blend old and new for your comfort and relaxation. Enjoy the large front porch, fishing, hiking, bird-watching, panoramic mountain views, and lambs frolicking on the hillside. Breakfast specialties include homemade bread, stuffed French toast, fresh farm eggs, and much more. Dinner, served to guests by advance reservation, is highly recommended. John is the chef whose specialties involve fresh herbs and vegetables from the garden. Sarah will be glad to direct you to nearby attractions, introduce you to farm animals, or arrange a horseback riding package for you.

The Woodruff House Bed & Breakfast ✪
330 MECHANIC STREET, LURAY, VIRGINIA 22835

Tel: **(540) 743-1494**
Hosts: **Lucas and Deborah Woodruff**
Location: **89 mi. W of Washington, D.C.**
No. of Rooms: **6**
No. of Private Baths: **6**
Double/pb: **$98–$175**
Suites: **$165–$195**
Open: **All year**
Reduced Rates: **20% Mon.–Thurs.,**
  5% after 3 nights

Breakfast: **Full**
Other meals: **Dinner, included with**
  room rate
Credit Cards: **DISC, MC, VISA**
Pets: **No**
Children: **Welcome, Mon.–Thurs. only**
Smoking: **No**
Social Drinking: **Permitted**
Minimum Stay: **2 nights weekends**

jim joggins

This fairy-tale Victorian, beautifully appointed with period antiques, hallmarked silver and fine china, is chef-owned and -operated. Escape from reality and come into this fairy tale, where the ambiance never ends. Awaken to your choice of freshly brewed coffees delivered to your door. The price includes a gourmet breakfast and dinner, and afternoon tea. You may want to relax in the fireside candlelit garden spa, or enjoy the canoes and bicycles provided by your hosts. Each guest room has a working fireplace and a private bath. The Woodruff House is located in the beautiful Shenandoah Valley of Virginia. Some rooms offer Jacuzzis for two.

Federal Crest Inn B&B ✪
1101 FEDERAL STREET, LYNCHBURG, VIRGINIA 24504

Tel: **(804) 845-6155; (800) 818-6155**
Best Time to Call: **10 AM–10 PM**
Hosts: **Phil and Ann Ripley**
Location: **50 mi. E of Roanoke**
No. of Rooms: **5**
No. of Private Baths: **4**
Max. No. Sharing Bath: **4**
Double/pb: **$85**
Single/pb: **$80**
Double/sb: **$55**
Suites: **$100–$125**
Open: **All year**

Reduced Rates: **10% Sun.–Thurs.,
  business rates, seniors**
Breakfast: **Full**
Other Meals: **Available**
Credit Cards: **AMEX, DISC, MC, VISA**
Pets: **No**
Children: **Welcome, over 10**
Smoking: **No**
Social Drinking: **Permitted**
Minimum Stay: **May–Oct. 2 nights
  weekends**
Airport/Station Pickup: **Yes**

This elegant 1909 Georgian Revival home has over 8000 square feet and is located in the Federal Hill Historic District. The original charm is seen in the woodwork and the interior columns that lead to the grand central staircase in the front foyer. Guests are invited to enjoy the antiques, the unique mantels of the seven fireplaces and the '50s cafe which offers delightful surprises. Perhaps there will be a special visitation to the third floor, where the original owner constructed a stage for his children to give plays. All rooms have queen beds, down comforters, plush robes and towels, snack baskets, and clock radios. In one room, atmosphere is meant to be shared in the romantic Jacuzzi tub, as the lights dim on a painted mural of Virginia's Blue Ridge Mountains. Federal Crest lies within walking distance to many attractions.

Lynchburg Mansion Inn B&B ✪
405 MADISON STREET, LYNCHBURG, VIRGINIA 24504

Tel: **(804) 528-5400; (800) 352-1199**
Hosts: **Bob and Mauranna Sherman**
Location: **65 mi. S of Charlottesville**
No. of Rooms: **5**
No. of Private Baths: **5**
Double/pb: **$109–$124**
Suites: **$139–$144**
Open: **All year**

Reduced Rates: **Available**
Breakfast: **Full**
Credit Cards: **AMEX, DC, MC, VISA**
Pets: **No**
Children: **Welcome**
Smoking: **No**
Social Drinking: **Permitted**

Restored with your every comfort in mind, this Spanish Georgian mansion has pretty gardens, a spacious veranda, oak floors, tall ceilings, pocket doors, and cherry woodwork. Bedrooms are lavish, with either king- or queen-size beds, luxurious linens, fireplaces, TVs, and turn-down service. Bob and Mauranna have also added an outdoor hot tub for guests to use. Fine china, silver, and crystal complement the sumptuous full breakfasts. The mansion surveys a half-acre in downtown Lynchburg's Garland Hill Historic District, which is listed on the National Register of Historic Places; impressive Federal and Victorian

homes line Madison Street, still paved in its turn-of-the-century brick. Plus there are Civil War sites, antique shops, art galleries, and countless programs offered by the city's colleges and universities.

Sunrise Hill Farm ✪
5590 OLD FARM LANE, MANASSAS, VIRGINIA 20109

Tel: **(703) 754-8309**
Best Time to Call: **Anytime**
Hosts: **Frank and Sue Boberek**
Location: **35 minutes W of Washington, D.C.**
No. of Rooms: **2**
No. of Private Baths: **1**
Max. No. Sharing Bath: **4**
Double/pb: **$90**

Double/sb: **$78**
Open: **All year**
Breakfast: **Full**
Credit Cards: **MC, VISA**
Pets: **Horses boarded**
Children: **Welcome, over 10**
Smoking: **No**
Social Drinking: **Permitted**

Standing in the heart of the 6000-acre Manassas National Battlefields, this Civil War treasure overlooks Bull Run Creek. Sunrise Hill Farm is an uncommonly charming, Federal-era country home furnished in period style. This B&B is a haven for Civil War buffs and guests visiting northern Virginia and the nation's capital. Situated within the renowned Virginia hunt country, it is just 35 minutes from Washington, D.C., and close to Harpers Ferry, Antietam, Skyline Drive, Luray Caverns, and numerous historic sites and antique-filled towns.

Porterville Bed & Breakfast ✪
14201 KING'S HIGHWAY, MONTROSS, VIRGINIA 22520

Tel: **(804) 493-9394**
Best Time to Call: **7–8 AM; evenings**
Host: **Mary P. Hall**
No. of Rooms: **2**
Max. No. Sharing Bath: **4**
Double/sb: **$55–$95**

Single/sb: **$45–$85**
Open: **All year**
Reduced Rates: **10% seniors, Tues. only**
Breakfast: **Full**
Pets: **No**
Children: **Welcome, over 8**

Smoking: **No**
Social Drinking: **No**

Airport Pickup: **Yes, Richmond only**

Porterville Bed & Breakfast is a brick home nestled behind lovely shade trees near Chandler's Mill Pond. The property was originally owned by two Baptist churches, and the home was built for a parsonage. Mary offers your choice of two guest rooms. The Cornelia room has an antique double bed, and the Juanita room has twin beds. Nearby attractions include Stratford Hall Plantation, Popes Creek Plantation, and Colonial Beach. Historic Fredericksburg and the battlegrounds are only 45 minutes away. A home-cooked breakfast is served with Southern hospitality.

The Jacob Swartz House ✪
574 JIGGADY ROAD, NEW MARKET, VIRGINIA 22844
www.shenwebworks.com/j.s.house; jshouse@shentel.net

Tel: **(540) 740-9208**
Best Time to Call: **Before 9 PM**
Host: **Virginia Dicken Harris**
Location: **110 mi. SW of Washington, D.C.**
Guesthouse: **$100–$215**
Open: **Mar.–Dec.**

Reduced Rates: **Available**
Breakfast: **Full**
Pets: **No**
Smoking: **No**
Social Drinking: **Permitted**
Minimum Stay: **2 nights holidays, weekends, special events**

Perched on a bluff overlooking the Shenandoah River, the Jacob Swartz House is the perfect place for the angler, nature lover, or history buff. This 1852 clapboard farmhouse and adjacent cobbler shop survived the Battle of New Market and raid by General Custer in 1864. The traditionally furnished two-bedroom, two-bath converted shop features an intimate living room with a wood-burning stove, sun room, full kitchen, screened porch, and terrace. The central location makes this bed and breakfast an ideal place for those who want to explore the entire Shenandoah Valley. A lavish breakfast is served daily in the main house.

A Touch of Country Bed & Breakfast ✪
9329 CONGRESS STREET, NEW MARKET, VIRGINIA 22844

Tel: **(540) 740-8030**
Hosts: **Jean Schoellig and Dawn Kasow**
Location: **18 mi. N of Harrisonburg**
No. of Rooms: **6**
No. of Private Baths: **6**
Double/pb: **$60–$75**
Single/pb: **$50–$65**

Open: **All year**
Breakfast: **Full**
Credit Cards: **AMEX, DISC, MC, VISA**
Pets: **No**
Children: **Welcome, over 12**
Smoking: **No**
Social Drinking: **Permitted**

This restored 1870s home is located in a historic town in the beautiful Shenandoah Valley. It displays the original hardwood floors and is decorated with antiques and collectibles in a country motif. You'll start your day with a hearty breakfast of pancakes, meats, gravy, and biscuits. Daydream on the porch swings or stroll through town with its charming shops, dine at a variety of restaurants or visit the legendary New Market Battlefield and Park. Close by are Skyline Drive, George Washington National Forest, caverns, and vineyards.

The Spinning Wheel Bed & Breakfast ✪

31 NORTH STREET, ONANCOCK, VIRGINIA 23417

Tel: **(757) 787-7311**	Breakfast: **Full**
Hosts: **David and Karen Tweedie**	Credit Cards: **MC, VISA**
Location: **60 mi. N of Virginia Beach**	Pets: **No**
No. of Rooms: **5**	Children: **Welcome, over 12**
No. of Private Baths: **5**	Smoking: **No**
Double/pb: **$75–$95**	Social Drinking: **Permitted**
Open: **Apr.–Oct.**	Minimum Stay: **2 nights, weekends**
Reduced Rates: **Over 4 nights**	

This 1890s folk Victorian home is in the historic waterfront town of Onancock, on the Eastern Shore peninsula separating the Chesapeake Bay from the Atlantic Ocean. The B&B is decorated with antiques and, true to its name, spinning wheels. Guest rooms have queen-size beds and air-conditioning. Kerr Place (a 1799 museum), restaurants, shops, the town wharf, and the ferry to Tangier Island are all within walking distance. David is a college professor and Karen is a teacher of the deaf. Their guests are greeted by Nelly, the resident old English sheepdog.

Woodlawn ✪

2211 WILTSHIRE ROAD, ROCKVILLE, VIRGINIA 23146

Tel: **(804) 749-3759**	Open: **All year**
Best Time to Call: **3–10 PM**	Breakfast: **Full**
Host: **Ann Nuckols**	Pets: **No**
Location: **20 mi. W of Richmond**	Children: **No**
No. of Rooms: **2**	Smoking: **No**
No. of Private Baths: **2**	Social Drinking: **Permitted**
Double/pb: **$75**	

An ideal hub from which to tour many historic points of interest in the area, this circa 1813 farmhouse is set on 40 acres of peaceful, grassy slopes, just 3 miles from the interstate. The interior has been completely restored, tastefully decorated, and furnished with antiques. The house has central air-conditioning for summer comfort. Each of the two guest rooms has its own fireplace. Both guest rooms are furnished with majestic hand-carved double beds and down pillows and comforters. Breakfasts with sourdough rolls, bran muffins, homemade jellies, and juice are served on the screened porch or in the dining area in the English basement.

The Manor at Taylor's Store B&B Country Inn ✪

P.O. BOX 510, SMITH MOUNTAIN LAKE, VIRGINIA 24184
taylors@symweb.com; www.symweb.com/taylors

Tel: **(540) 721-3951; (800) 248-6267**
Hosts: **Lee and Mary Lynn Tucker**
Location: **20 mi. E of Roanoke**
No. of Rooms: **10**
No. of Private Baths: **8**
Double/pb: **$90–$185**
Guest Cottage: **$95–$190; sleeps 2–6**
Open: **All year**
Reduced Rates: **$300–up weekly for cottage**

Breakfast: **Full**
Credit Cards: **MC, VISA**
Pets: **No**
Children: **Welcome in cottage**
Smoking: **Cottage only**
Social Drinking: **Permitted**
Airport/Station Pickup: **Yes**

Situated on 120 acres in the foothills of the Blue Ridge Mountains, this elegant manor house, circa 1799, was the focus of a prosperous tobacco plantation. It has been restored and refurbished, and you'll experience the elegance of the past combined with the comfort of tasteful modernization. The estate invites hiking, swimming, and fishing. The sunroom, parlor, and hot tub are special spots for relaxing. Smith Mountain Lake, with its seasonal sporting activity, is five miles away. Breakfast, designed for the health-conscious, features a variety of fresh gourmet selections.

Frederick House ✪

28 NORTH NEW STREET, STAUNTON, VIRGINIA 24401
ejharman@frederickhouse.com; www.frederickhouse.com

Tel: **(540) 885-4220; (800) 334-5575;**
fax: **(540) 885-5180**
Best Time to Call: **7 AM–10 PM**
Hosts: **Joe and Evy Harman**
Location: **2.7 mi. from I-81 exit 222; on 250 W**
No. of Rooms: **14**
No. of Private Baths: **14**
Double/pb: **$75–$170**
Single/pb: **$65–$150**
Suites: **$115–$170**

Open: **All year**
Reduced Rates: **Available**
Breakfast: **Full**
Credit Cards: **AMEX, DC, DISC, MC, VISA**
Pets: **No**
Children: **Welcome**
Smoking: **No**
Social Drinking: **Permitted**
Station Pickup: **Yes**

Frederick House is located across from Mary Baldwin College in downtown Staunton, the oldest city in the Shenandoah Valley and two blocks from Woodrow Wilson's birthplace on Frederick Street. The five separate buildings that are listed in the National Register of Historic Places have been tastefully restored and furnished with antiques. The large rooms and suites feature oversize beds, modern baths, remote cable TV, air-conditioning, ceiling fans, robes, telephones, and private entrances. Some have fireplaces or balconies. A full breakfast, prepared by the owners, is served in Chumley's Tearoom between 7:30 and 10:30 AM.

Breakfast choices include ham and cheese pie, apple raisin quiche, waffles, stratta, fresh fruit, juice, coffee, tea, warm bread, and hot or cold cereal. Joe and Evy Harman previously worked in banking and insurance. Since 1984 they have enjoyed informing guests about the area and suggesting trips to many nearby interesting sights.

The Sampson Eagon Inn ✪
238 EAST BEVERLEY STREET, STAUNTON, VIRGINIA 24401

Tel: **(540) 886-8200; (800) 597-9722**
Best Time to Call: **10 AM–9 PM**
Hosts: **Laura and Frank Mattingly**
Location: **35 mi. W of Charlottesville**
No. of Rooms: **5**
No. of Private Baths: **5**
Double/pb: **$95**
Suites: **$120**

Open: **All year**
Breakfast: **Full**
Pets: **No**
Children: **Welcome, over 12**
Smoking: **No**
Social Drinking: **Permitted**
Minimum Stay: **Weekends May–Nov.**

This circa 1840 in-town Greek Revival mansion provides affordable luxury accommodations in a preservation award–winning setting. Comfort and hospitality are key. Guest rooms are spacious, air-conditioned, and have modern ensuite baths. Canopied beds and antique furnishings reflect various periods of this elegant building's past. Scrumptious gourmet breakfasts are served daily. Within two blocks of shops and restaurants, the Inn is adjacent to the Woodrow Wilson Birthplace and Mary Baldwin College. Nearby, guests can enjoy the natural and historic attractions and recreational activities of the central Shenandoah Valley. Charlottesville and Lexington are within a 40-minute drive.

Thornrose House at Gypsy Hill ✪
531 THORNROSE AVENUE, STAUNTON, VIRGINIA 24401
www.bbhsv.org/thornrose

Tel: **(540) 885-7026; (800) 861-4338**
Best Time to Call: **9 AM–9 PM**
Hosts: **Suzanne and Otis Huston**

Location: **3¹/₂ mi. from Rte. I-81, Exit 222**
No. of Rooms: **5**

No. of Private Baths: **5**
Double/pb: **$65–$85**
Single/pb: **$55–$75**
Open: **All year**
Reduced Rates: **Available**
Breakfast: **Full**
Credit Cards: **AMEX, MC, VISA**

Pets: **No**
Children: **Welcome, over 5**
Smoking: **No**
Social Drinking: **Permitted**
Minimum Stay: **Apr.–Oct. weekends**
Airport/Station Pickup: **Yes**

This 1912 Georgian Revival home is six blocks from the center of Victorian Staunton and adjacent to 300-acre Gypsy Hill Park, which has facilities for golf, tennis, swimming, and summer concerts. A wraparound veranda, Greek colonnades, and an acre of lovely gardens grace the exterior of the house. Inside, there's a cozy parlor with a fireplace and a grand piano. A relaxed, leisurely breakfast is set out in the dining room, which offers the comfort of a fireplace on chilly mornings. Local attractions include Blue Ridge National Park, Natural Chimneys, Skyline Drive, Woodrow Wilson's birthplace, and the Museum of American Frontier Culture.

The Duck Farm Inn ✪
P.O. BOX 787, RTES. 227 AND 639, URBANNA, VIRGINIA 23175

Tel: **(804) 758-5685**
Host: **Fleming Godden**
Location: **55 mi. E of Richmond**
No. of Rooms: **6**
No. of Private Baths: **2**
Max. No. Sharing Bath: **4**
Double/pb: **$85**
Single/pb: **$70**
Double/sb: **$75**

Single/sb: **$60**
Open: **All year**
Reduced Rates: **After first visit**
Breakfast: **Full**
Pets: **No**
Children: **Welcome**
Smoking: **No**
Social Drinking: **Permitted**
Airport/Station Pickup: **Yes**

This elegant, contemporary Inn is situated on Virginia's middle peninsula, surrounded by 800 secluded acres and bordered by the Rappahannock River. Guests are welcome to hike along the shore or through the woods, fish in the river, sunbathe on the private beach, lounge on the deck, or retire to the cozy library with a good book. Fleming has traveled all over the world and thoroughly enjoys her role as full-time innkeeper. One of her breakfast menus consists of seasonal fresh fruit, jumbo blueberry muffins, cheese-and-egg scramble served with spiced sausage, and a variety of hot beverages.

Angie's Guest Cottage ✪
302 24TH STREET, VIRGINIA BEACH, VIRGINIA 23451

Tel: **(757) 428-4690**
Best Time to Call: **10 AM–9 PM**
Host: **Barbara G. Yates**
Location: **20 mi. E of Norfolk**

No. of Rooms: **6**
No. of Private Baths: **1**
Max. No. Sharing Bath: **4**
Double/pb: **$84**

Single/pb: **$72**
Double/sb: **$54–$78**
Single/sb: **$44–$68**
Guest Cottage: **$450–$600 weekly;
    sleeps 2–6**
Open: **Apr. 1–Oct. 1**
Reduced Rates: **Off-season**

Breakfast: **Continental, plus**
Pets: **Sometimes**
Children: **Welcome**
Smoking: **No**
Social Drinking: **Permitted**
Minimum Stay: **2 nights**

Just a block from the beach, shops, and restaurants is this bright and comfortable beach house. Former guests describe it as "cozy, cute, and clean." Deep-sea fishing, nature trails, and harbor tours are but a few things to keep you busy. Freshly baked croissants in various flavors are a breakfast delight. You are welcome to use the sundeck, barbecue, and picnic tables.

Barclay Cottage ✪
400 16TH STREET, VIRGINIA BEACH, VIRGINIA 23451

Tel: **(757) 422-1956**
Hosts: **Peter and Claire**
Location: **20 mi. E of Norfolk**
No. of Rooms: **5**
No. of Private Baths: **3**
Max. No. Sharing Bath: **2**
Double/pb: **$105–$125**
Double/sb: **$75–$85**

Open: **Apr.–Oct.; special holidays**
Breakfast: **Full**
Credit Cards: **AMEX, MC, VISA**
Pets: **No**
Smoking: **No**
Social Drinking: **Permitted**
Minimum Stay: **2 nights**

The Barclay is a historic building designed in turn-of-the-century, Southern Colonial style. Your hosts bring you casual sophistication in a warm, innlike atmosphere two blocks from the beach and fishing pier. The inn has been completely restored to add the feeling of yesterday to the comfort of today. Peter and Claire look forward to welcoming you to their B&B, where the theme is, "We go where our dreams lead us."

The Iris Inn ✪

191 CHINQUAPIN DRIVE, WAYNESBORO, VIRGINIA 22980
www.irisinn.com

Tel: **(540) 943-1991**
Best Time to Call: **10 AM–8 PM**
Hosts: **Wayne and Iris Karl**
Location: **25 mi. W of Charlottesville**
No. of Rooms: **9**
No. of Private Baths: **9**
Double/pb: **$80–$140**
Single/pb: **$75**
Suites: **$130–$140**
Open: **All year**

Reduced Rates: **Corporate, Sun.–Thurs.**
Breakfast: **Full**
Credit Cards: **MC, VISA**
Pets: **No**
Children: **Welcome, over 10**
Smoking: **No**
Social Drinking: **Permitted**
Minimum Stay: **2 nights weekends**
Airport Pickup: **Yes**

Situated on a 21-acre wooded tract on a western slope of the Blue Ridge overlooking the Shenandoah Valley, this inn is spacious, casual, and comfortable. Built and designed by an architect in 1991, the inn was expanded in 1996 with the addition of two luxury suites. Rooms are decorated with nature and wildlife motifs; some have whirlpools, fireplaces, and kitchenettes. The great room features a 20-foot original mural, rockers, hot tub, and splendid views.

Candlewick Inn B&B ✪

800 JAMESTOWN ROAD, WILLIAMSBURG, VIRGINIA 23185

Tel: **(800) 418-4949; (757) 253-8695;**
　fax: (755) 253-6547
Host: **Mary L. Peters**
Location: **2 miles from Rte. 64, Exit 242A**
No. of Rooms: **3**
No. of Private Baths: **3**
Double/pb: **$95–$125**
Open: **All year**
Reduced Rates: **Available**

Breakfast: **Full**
Credit Cards: **AMEX, MC, VISA**
Pets: **No**
Children: **Welcome, over 12**
Smoking: **No**
Social Drinking: **Permitted**
Minimum Stay: **2 nights**
Station Pickup: **Yes**
Foreign Languages: **German**

A candle in the window is an old Virginia tradition, a gesture of welcome. At Candlewick Inn you will see a candle in every window: inside the Colonial white clapboard exterior, 18th-century and reproduction candles glow. All guest rooms have king or queen canopy beds and private baths. Breakfast is served in the keeping room and may include homemade sticky buns, butter cake muffins, and hot entrees. Candlewick is located near the historic area and across from the College of William and Mary.

Colonial Capital Bed & Breakfast ✪

501 RICHMOND ROAD, WILLIAMSBURG, VIRGINIA 23185
ccbb@widomaker.com; www.ccbb.com

Tel: **(800) 776-0570; (757) 229-0233;** fax: **(757) 253-7667**	Open: **All year**
	Breakfast: **Full**
Hosts: **Barbara and Phil Craig**	Credit Cards: **AMEX, DISC, MC, VISA**
Location: **2.5 mi. from I-64, Exit 238**	Pets: **No**
No. of Rooms: **5**	Children: **Welcome, over 8**
No. of Private Baths: **5**	Smoking: **Restricted**
Double/pb: **$84–$135**	Social Drinking: **Permitted**
Suites: **$120–$150**	Airport/Station Pickup: **Yes**

Barbara and Phil offer a warm welcome to guests in their three-story Colonial revival (c. 1926) home only three blocks from the historic area. The B&B is decorated with period antiques, oriental rugs, and many of the original lighting and plumbing fixtures; all guest rooms feature king or queen four-poster beds crowned with charming canopies and remote control ceiling fans. In the morning you can look forward to such treats as a soufflé, French toast, fluffy omelette, or yeast waffles complemented with a choice of juices, fresh seasonal fruits, and specially blended coffees and tea. The sunny solarium or formal dining room invite guests to linger over breakfast and get to know one another as does the plantation parlor, where tea and wine are served during afternoons and evenings. Games, books, and puzzles are provided for your pleasure. Jamestown, Yorktown, some of the state's finest plantations, Busch Gardens, and Water Country USA are only a few minutes away. Personalized gift certificates and lighted off-street parking are available.

For Cant Hill Guest Home

4 CANTERBURY LANE, WILLIAMSBURG, VIRGINIA 23185-3410

Tel: **(757) 229-6623;** fax: **(757) 229-1863**	Open: **All year**
	Reduced Rates: **Available**
Best Time to Call: **9 AM–9 PM**	Breakfast: **Full**
Hosts: **Martha and Hugh Easler**	Pets: **No**
No. of Rooms: **2**	Children: **Welcome, over 10**
No. of Private Baths: **2**	Smoking: **No**
Double/pb: **$85**	Social Drinking: **Permitted**

Situated in a lovely wooded area in the heart of town, only 5–6 blocks from the Colonial historic area, overlooking a lake, For Cant is part of the College of William and Mary. The rooms are beautifully decorated in antiques and collectibles for your complete comfort. The house has central heat and air, and a TV in each room. A hearty breakfast is served every morning. Your hosts will be happy to make dinner reservations for you, and provide helpful information on the many attractions offered in the area. Telephone and fax are available.

Fox & Grape Bed & Breakfast ✪

701 MONUMENTAL AVENUE, WILLIAMSBURG, VIRGINIA 23185

Tel: (757) 229-6914; (800) 292-3699
Best Time to Call: 9 AM–9 PM
Hosts: Bob and Pat Orendorff
Location: 2 mi. from I-64, Exit 238
No. of Rooms: 4
No. of Private Baths: 4
Double/pb: $85–$95

Open: All year
Breakfast: Full
Pets: No
Children: No
Smoking: No
Social Drinking: Permitted
Station Pickup: Yes

Warm hospitality awaits you upon entering this renovated two-story Colonial, with a spacious wraparound porch. Attention to detail can be seen throughout the house. The parlor is filled with folk art-style Noah's Arks and Shaker-style furniture made by your host. The dining room displays a collection of carved roosters and duck decoys. Guest rooms are furnished with antiques, counted cross-stitch samplers, handmade quilts, and queen beds. After breakfast stroll five blocks to see Virginia's restored Colonial capital.

Governor's Trace ✪

303 CAPITOL LANDING ROAD, WILLIAMSBURG, VIRGINIA 23185

Tel: (757) 229-7552; (800) 303-7552;
  fax: (757) 220-2767
Best Time to Call: 9 AM–10 PM
Hosts: Sue and Dick Lake
Location: 2 mi. from I-64, exit 238
No. of Rooms: 3
No. of Private Baths: 3
Double/pb: $75–$125

Suites: $105–$125
Open: All year
Breakfast: Full
Credit Cards: MC, VISA
Pets: No
Children: No
Smoking: No
Social Drinking: Permitted

This Georgian brick home featured on the back cover of the 1992 edition of *Bed & Breakfast U.S.A.* is Colonial Williamsburg's closest B&B neighbor, just one door away. Hardy patriot, loyal royalist, or plantation gentry travelers would have found the rooms here comfortably familiar but with modern exceptions, king- and queen-size beds, and private baths. Special amenities include a fireplace in one bedroom and a screened-in porch off another. Private romantic candlelit breakfast is served in each room. Sue and Dick provide refuge from the modern world's hectic pace to let you discover unexpected treasures in an 18th-century atmosphere. Make "take away" memories at the Governor's Trace.

The Homestay Bed & Breakfast ✪

517 RICHMOND ROAD, WILLIAMSBURG, VIRGINIA 23185

Tel: (757) 229-7468; (800) 836-7468
Best Time to Call: 9 AM–9:30 PM
Hosts: Barbara and Jim Thomassen

Location: 3 mi. from Rte. I-64, Exit 238
No. of Rooms: 3
No. of Private Baths: 3

Double/pb: **$80–$110**
Single/pb: **$70–$100**
Open: **All year**
Reduced Rates: **20% less Jan. 2–
    Mar. 15**
Breakfast: **Full**
Credit Cards: **MC, VISA**

Pets: **No**
Children: **Welcome, over 10**
Smoking: **No**
Social Drinking: **Permitted**
Minimum Stay: **2 nights, weekends,
    holidays, and special events**
Airport/Station Pickup: **Yes**

The Homestay is cozy and convenient. Enjoy the comfort of a lovely Colonial Revival home furnished with turn-of-the-century family antiques and country charm. Guest rooms are decorated with attention to detail and have either king- or queen-size beds. Guests can relax in the second-floor sitting room, or by the fire in the living room. Breakfast is served in the formal dining room and may feature homemade breads and delicious hot dishes. Only a 10–15-minute walk to Colonial Williamsburg, the Homestay is adjacent to the College of William & Mary, and just minutes away from Jamestown, Yorktown, and Busch Gardens.

War Hill ✪

4560 LONG HILL ROAD, WILLIAMSBURG, VIRGINIA 23188
wmbg.com/its/visit/bnb/wh.html; inngetaways.com/va/warhill.html

Tel: **(757) 565-0248; (800) 743-0248;
    fax: (757) 565-4550**
Best Time to Call: **9 AM–9 PM**
Hosts: **Shirley, Bill, and Will Lee**
Location: **2 mi. from Williamsburg**
No. of Rooms: **5**
No. of Private Baths: **5**
Double/pb: **$75–$90**
Guest Cottage: **$125–$180; sleeps 2–5**

Suite: **$105–$160; sleeps 2–5**
Open: **All year**
Breakfast: **Full**
Credit Cards: **MC, VISA**
Pets: **No**
Children: **Welcome**
Smoking: **No**
Social Drinking: **Permitted**

War Hill is situated in the center of a 32-acre working farm, just three miles from the tourist attractions. Built in 1968, this Colonial replica couples the charm of yesteryear with contemporary conveniences. The wide heart pine floors came from an old school, the stairs from a church, overhead beams from a barn; the oak mantel is over 200 years old. Whether you are looking for a romantic retreat or a family adventure, War Hill has the room for you. Fruits from a variety of trees in the orchard are yours to pick in season. In autumn, the Lees serve delicious homemade applesauce and cider. Angus show cattle graze in the pasture, and in the evening you'll drift off to the soothing sounds of owls, frogs, and crickets.

Williamsburg Sampler Bed and Breakfast ✪

922 JAMESTOWN ROAD, WILLIAMSBURG, VIRGINIA 23185
WbgSampler@aol.com

Tel: **(800) 722-1169; (757) 253-0398;
    fax: (757) 253-2669**
Best Time to Call: **9 AM–10:30 PM**

Hosts: **Helen and Ike Sisane**
No. of Rooms: **2**
No. of Private Baths: **4**

Double/pb: **$100**
Suites: **$150**
Open: **All year**
Breakfast: **Full**
Pets: **No**

Children: **Welcome, over 12**
Smoking: **No**
Social Drinking: **Permitted**
Airport/Station Pickup: **Yes**

Welcome to one of Williamsburg's finest 18th-century plantation-style homes. This three-story brick Colonial is located in the Architectural Corridor Protection District, and is furnished with antiques, pewter, and samplers. This elegant home complements those located in the Restored area. Accommodations include four-poster beds in king or queen sizes, TVs, fireplaces, rooftop garden, and your hosts' famous "skip lunch" breakfast. Personalized gift certificates are available.

Brownstone Cottage ✪
161 MCCARTY LANE, WINCHESTER, VIRGINIA 22602
www.nvim.com/brownstonebnb; brnstone@winchesterva.com

Tel: **(540) 662-1962**
Best Time to Call: **9 AM**
Hosts: **Chuck and Sheila Brown**
Location: **3 mi. E of Winchester**
No. of Rooms: **2**
No. of Private Baths: **2**
Double/pb: **$95**
Single/pb: **$75**
Suites: **$95**

Open: **All year**
Reduced Rates: **15% seniors; 10% families**
Breakfast: **Full**
Credit Cards: **MC, VISA**
Pets: **No**
Children: **Welcome, over 12**
Smoking: **No**
Social Drinking: **Permitted**

Enjoy the peaceful setting of Brownstone Cottage, nestled in the Shenandoah Valley outside historic Winchester. The minute you enter,

Chuck and Sheila will make you feel at home. Relax in your room, the sitting room, or on the outside deck. In the morning, awake to the smell of freshly brewed coffee and enjoy a country breakfast featuring Chuck's homemade pancakes. The Browns offer wedding, anniversary, and honeymoon packages. Sheila is licensed to perform a wedding ceremony or officiate as you renew your vows.

Azalea House
551 SOUTH MAIN STREET, WOODSTOCK, VIRGINIA 22664

Tel: **(540) 459-3500**
Hosts: **Margaret and Price McDonald**
Location: **35 mi. N of Harrisonburg**
No. of Rooms: **4**
No. of Private Baths: **4**
Double/pb: **$55–$75**
Open: **All year**

Breakfast: **Full**
Credit Cards: **AMEX, MC, VISA**
Pets: **No**
Children: **Welcome, over 6**
Smoking: **No**
Social Drinking: **Permitted**

This spacious home, built in the early 1890s, served as a parsonage for 70 years. It has been restored following its Victorian tradition and has porches, bay windows, and a white picket fence—in spring, one hundred blooming azaleas enhance its beauty. The interior is made particularly lovely with family heirlooms and pretty color schemes. Azalea House is within walking distance of a fine restaurant. It is convenient to antique shops, wineries, orchards, trails, horseback riding, and fishing. Air-conditioning assures your summer comfort.

WASHINGTON

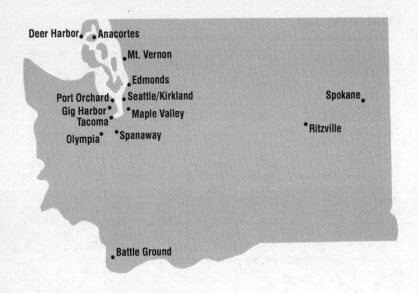

Deer Harbor, Anacortes, Mt. Vernon, Edmonds, Port Orchard, Seattle/Kirkland, Gig Harbor, Maple Valley, Tacoma, Olympia, Spanaway, Battle Ground, Spokane, Ritzville

Pacific Bed & Breakfast Agency ✪
P.O. BOX 46894, SEATTLE, WASHINGTON 98146
PacificB@nwlink.com; www.seattlebedandbreakfast.com

Tel: **(206) 439-7677; fax: (206) 431-0932**
Best Time to Call: **9 AM–5 PM**
Coordinator: **Greg Kaminski**
States/Regions Covered: **Statewide; Canada—Vancouver, Victoria**
Descriptive Directory: **$5**

Rates (Single/Double):
Modest: **$45 / $55**
Average: **$55 / $85**
Luxury: **$85 / $200**
Credit Cards: **AMEX, MC, VISA**
Minimum Stay: **2 nights in Seattle**

Victorians, contemporaries, and private suites, apartments, and condos are available. Most are close to downtown areas, near bus lines, in fine residential neighborhoods. Many are near water, some with views and near beaches.

A Burrow's Bay B&B
4911 MACBETH DRIVE, ANACORTES, WASHINGTON 98221

Tel: **(360) 293-4792**
Best Time to Call: **8 AM–8 PM**
Hosts: **Beverly and Winfred Stocker**
Location: **92 mi. N of Seattle**
Suites: **$95; sleep 2–4**
Open: **All year**

Breakfast: **Continental, Plus**
Credit Cards: **MC, VISA**
Children: **Welcome**
Smoking: **No**
Social Drinking: **Permitted**
Airport/Station Pickup: **Yes**

Enjoy a sweeping view of the San Juan Islands from your deck in this lovely contemporary Northwest home. The 1200-square-foot suite has its own entrance, a sitting room with a fireplace, TV, built-in bar with refrigerator, microwave, and the same spectacular view from the sitting room to the bedroom, which has a king-size bed. Beverly and Winfred offer a sumptuous continental breakfast, served in your room at your convenience. Burrow's Bay lies within walking distance to nearby ferries that go to the San Juan Islands and Victoria, British Columbia, Canada. Beautiful Washington Park and restaurants are close by. Your hosts provide a seven-day agenda of things to do upon your arrival.

Sunset Beach B&B ✪
100 SUNSET BEACH, ANACORTES, WASHINGTON 98221

Tel: **(360) 293-5428; (800) 359-3448**
Best Time to Call: **8 AM–10 PM**

Hosts: **Joann and Hal Harker**
Location: **80 mi. NW of Seattle**

No. of Rooms: **3**
No. of Private Baths: **3**
Double/pb: **$82–$115**
Open: **All year**
Reduced Rates: **Available**
Breakfast: **Full**

Credit Cards: **MC, VISA**
Pets: **No**
Children: **Welcome, over 12**
Smoking: **No**
Social Drinking: **Permitted**

This B&B is located on exciting Rosario Straits. Relax and enjoy the view of seven major islands from every room and deck. Stroll on the beach or walk in beautiful Washington Park, adjacent to the private gardens. Guest rooms all have private baths with a Jacuzzi shower. A hot tub is available upon request. This guest house is five minutes from San Juan Ferry, fine restaurants, marina, and convenience store. The sunsets are outstanding.

Teddy Bear House ✪

18404 NORTHEAST 109 AVENUE, BATTLE GROUND, WASHINGTON 98604
bdasher@worldaccess.com

Tel: **(360) 687-4328**
Hosts: **Bertha and Bill Dasher**
Location: **20 mi. NE of Portland, Oregon**
No. of Rooms: **2**
Max. No. Sharing Bath: **4**
Double/sb: **$60**

Open: **All year**
Breakfast: **Full**
Pets: **Sometimes**
Children: **Welcome, over 12**
Smoking: **No**
Social Drinking: **No**

Located in southwest Washington, the heart of the beautiful Pacific Northwest, this home can be your hub for exploring the Columbia Gorge National Scenic Area, Mt. St. Helens National Monument, and the historic Fort Vancouver Restoration. A working grist mill is a few miles away and the Lewis and Clark Railroad excursion train station is nearby. Teddy Bear House is named for Bertha's large collection of teddy bears and teddy bear memorabilia, which are used in the decor throughout the house. You will enjoy this quiet secluded country home surrounded by flowers, lawn, and large fir, dogwood, and maple trees.

Palmer's Chart House ✪

P.O. BOX 51, ORCAS ISLAND, DEER HARBOR, WASHINGTON 98243

Tel: **(360) 376-4231**
Hosts: **Majean and Don Palmer**
Location: **50 mi. N of Seattle**
No. of Rooms: **2**
No. of Private Baths: **2**
Double/pb: **$60–$70**
Single/pb: **$45–$50**

Open: **All year**
Breakfast: **Full**
Pets: **No**
Children: **Welcome, over 10**
Smoking: **No**
Social Drinking: **Permitted**
Foreign Languages: **Spanish**

Palmer's Chart House was the first bed and breakfast on Orcas Island—open since 1975—with a magnificent water view. The thirty-three-foot yacht, *Amante,* is available for a minimal fee with skipper Don. Palmer's Chart House's private, low-key, personal attention makes this bed and breakfast unique and attractive.

The Harrison House ❂
210 SUNSET AVENUE, EDMONDS, WASHINGTON 98020

Tel: **(425) 776-4748**
Hosts: **Jody and Harve Harrison**
Location: **15 mi. N of Seattle**
No. of Rooms: **2**
No. of Private Baths: **2**
Double/pb: **$55–$65**
Single/pb: **$45–$55**

Open: **All year**
Breakfast: **Continental**
Pets: **No**
Children: **No**
Smoking: **No**
Social Drinking: **Permitted**

This new, informal, waterfront home has a sweeping view of Puget Sound and the Olympic Mountains. It is a block north of the ferry dock and two blocks from the center of this historic town. Many fine restaurants are within walking distance. Your spacious room has a private deck, TV, wet bar, telephone, and king-size bed. The University of Washington is nearby.

Hudgens Haven ❂
9313 190 SOUTH WEST, EDMONDS, WASHINGTON 98020

Tel: **(206) 776-2202**
Best Time to Call: **4–8 PM**
Hosts: **Lorna and Edward Hudgens**
Location: **20 min. from downtown Seattle**
No. of Rooms: **1**
No. of Private Baths: **1**
Double/pb: **$60**

Single/pb: **$55**
Open: **All year**
Breakfast: **Full**
Pets: **No**
Children: **Welcome, over 10**
Smoking: **No**
Social Drinking: **Permitted**

Hudgens Haven is located in a picture postcard town on Puget Sound. Windows on the west side boast a lovely view of the waterfront. The guest room is furnished with antiques as well as a queen-size bed, rocker, and plenty of drawer space. Edmonds, located 20 minutes from downtown Seattle, is a former lumber town with interesting old houses and an abundance of small shops and excellent restaurants.

The Maple Tree ❂
18313 OLYMPIC VIEW DRIVE, EDMONDS, WASHINGTON 98020

Tel: **(425) 774-8420**
Hosts: **Marion and Hellon Wilkerson**

Location: **15 mi. N of Seattle**
No. of Rooms: **1**

No. of Private Baths: **1**
Double/pb: **$60**
Single/pb: **$55**
Open: **All year**
Breakfast: **Continental**

Pets: **No**
Children: **Welcome, over 5**
Smoking: **No**
Social Drinking: **Permitted**

The Maple Tree is a beautifully restored older home with landscaped grounds. Located across the street from Puget Sound, it commands a stunning view of the Olympic Mountains. You're welcome to watch the activity on Puget Sound through the telescope in the solarium. Lounge on the brick patio or watch the sun set over the snowcapped mountains as you sip a glass of Washington State wine. Hellon and Marion enjoy having guests and exchanging travel experiences with them. Hellon loves to cook; both like to work in their rose garden.

Olde Glencove Hotel ❂
9418 GLENCOVE ROAD, GIG HARBOR, WASHINGTON 98329

Tel: **(206) 884-2835**
Hosts: **Lawrence and Luciann Nadeau**
No. of Rooms: **4**
No. of Private Baths: **2**
Max. No. Sharing Bath: **4**
Double/sb: **$65**
Suites: **$85**

Open: **All year**
Breakfast: **Full**
Pets: **No**
Children: **Welcome**
Smoking: **No**
Social Drinking: **Permitted**

Built in 1897, this historic landmark is a perfect location for honeymoons, anniversaries, or any romantic weekend. Located on the water, the Olde Glencove Hotel offers guests a lovely view and a unique peaceful atmosphere. Lawrence and Luciann have painstakingly restored their lovely home to its authentic 1890s ambiance, complete with antiques of the period, wood-burning stoves, velvet chairs, and stained glass windows and lamps. They want to share their home with experienced world travelers, interesting local folks, and gentle people who appreciate antiques and fine accommodations.

Peacock Hill Guest House ❂
9520 PEACOCK HILL AVENUE, GIG HARBOR, WASHINGTON 98332

Tel: **(206) 858-3322; (800) 863-2318**
Best Time to Call: **10 AM–8 PM**
Hosts: **Steven and Suzanne Savlov**
Location: **50 mi. S of Seattle**
No. of Rooms: **2**
No. of Private Baths: **2**
Double/pb: **$85**
Suites: **$115**

Open: **All year**
Breakfast: **Full**
Pets: **No**
Children: **Welcome, over 10**
Smoking: **No**
Social Drinking: **Permitted**
Minimum Stay: **2 nights weekends**
Station Pickup: **Yes**

As you descend toward the quaint fishing village of Gig Harbor you take in a panoramic view of majestic Mount Rainier towering over ship masts, galleries, restaurants, and a potpourri of shops. This contemporary home sits on a wooded hilltop and has large picture windows that offer a postcard view of the harbor. In the morning you'll awaken to the aroma of a gourmet breakfast; it will give you the energy you need for a picturesque walk around the marina, or a drive to the nearby museums, gardens, zoo, and aquarium. The Scandinavian village of Poulsbo is 40 minutes away. It's a little bit farther to the Bainbridge Island Ferry, which takes you to Seattle's Pike Place Market where you can sample the sights and smells of a large open market. Summit Winter Sports Area is one hour away and has excellent skiing.

Shumway Mansion
11410-99 PLACE NORTH EAST, KIRKLAND, WASHINGTON 98033

Tel: **(425) 823-2303; fax: (425) 822-0421**	Suites: **$105 for 2**
Best Time to Call: **9 AM–7 PM**	Open: **All year**
Hosts: **Richard and Sallie Harris, and Julie and Marshall Blakemore**	Breakfast: **Full**
	Credit Cards: **AMEX, MC, VISA**
Location: **5 mi. NE of Seattle**	Pets: **No**
No. of Rooms: **8**	Children: **Welcome, over 12**
No. of Private Baths: **8**	Smoking: **No**
Double/pb: **$70–$95**	Social Drinking: **Permitted**

This stately 24-room mansion, built in 1909, has a regal presence overlooking Lake Washington. The eight antique-filled guest rooms, including a charming corner suite, pair today's comforts with intricately carved pieces from yesteryear. Richard and Sallie will indulge your palate with variety-filled breakfasts that always feature homemade scones and jams. Within a short distance are water and snow recreation, an athletic club, downtown Seattle, and lots of shopping. After a busy day, return ''home'' and relax in front of the fire with a seasonal treat.

Maple Valley Bed & Breakfast ✪
20020 SOUTHEAST 228, MAPLE VALLEY, WASHINGTON 98038

Tel: **(425) 432-1409; fax: (425) 413-1459**	Open: **All year**
	Reduced Rates: **Families**
Best Time to Call: **9 AM–9 PM**	Breakfast: **Full**
Hosts: **Jayne and Clarke Hurlbut**	Pets: **Sometimes**
Location: **26 mi. SE of Seattle**	Children: **Welcome**
No. of Rooms: **2**	Smoking: **No**
Max No. Sharing Bath: **4**	Social Drinking: **Permitted**
Double/sb: **$75**	Airport Pickup: **Yes**

After a good night's sleep in either of the B&B's guest rooms—one with a four-poster log bed and the other complete with a pink rosebud tea set—you'll come down to breakfast at a table that overlooks the lawn, the Hurlbuts' resident peacocks, and a wildlife pond teeming with a variety of Northwestern birds. If the morning is cool, you'll be warmed by a stone fireplace and you won't go away hungry after orange juice, lemon-blueberry muffins, a plate-size hootenanny pancake (served with whipped cream, strawberries, slivered almonds, and syrup), ham, sausage or bacon, fresh-ground coffee, tea, or hot chocolate.

The White Swan Guest House ✪
1388 MOORE ROAD, MT. VERNON, WASHINGTON 98273

Tel: **(360) 445-6805**
Best Time to Call: **Mornings; evenings**
Host: **Peter Goldfarb**
Location: **60 mi. N of Seattle, 6 mi. SE of La Conner**
No. of Rooms: **3**
Max. No. Sharing Bath: **3**
Double/sb: **$80**
Single/sb: **$70**

Guest Cottage: **$125–$165; sleeps 4**
Open: **All year**
Reduced Rates: **Weekly in cottage**
Breakfast: **Continental**
Credit Cards: **MC, VISA**
Pets: **No**
Children: **Welcome (in cottage)**
Smoking: **No**
Social Drinking: **Permitted**

Surrounded by farmland and country roads, this storybook Victorian farmhouse, built in 1898, is painted crayon yellow and framed by English-style gardens. There's a wood stove in the parlor, wicker chairs on the porch, books for browsing, and a unique collection of old samplers. A platter of homemade chocolate chip cookies is waiting for you on the sideboard. It's only 6 miles to LaConner, a delightful fishing village brimful of interesting art galleries, shops, waterfront restaurants, and antique stores. The San Juan ferries are a half hour away.

Puget View Guesthouse ✪

7924 61ST NORTHEAST, OLYMPIA, WASHINGTON 98516
Pugetview@aol.com; www.innsite.com/inns/A002245.html

Tel: **(360) 413-9474**	Reduced Rates: **Families; weekly;**
Best Time to Call: **Evenings**	**off-season**
Hosts: **Dick and Barbara Yunker**	Breakfast: **Continental, plus**
Location: **4½ mi. from I-5, Exit 111**	Credit Cards: **MC, VISA**
No. of Rooms: **1 cottage**	Pets: **Sometimes**
No. of Private Baths: **1**	Children: **Welcome**
Guest Cottage: **$89–$102; sleeps 4**	Smoking: **No**
Open: **All year**	Social Drinking: **Permitted**

This charming waterfront guest cottage is located next to Tolmie State Park and adjacent to Dick and Barbara's log home. The panoramic Puget Sound setting makes it a popular, romantic getaway. You are apt to discover simple pleasures such as beachcombing or bird-watching and activities such as kayaking or scuba diving. Your breakfast, an elegant repast, is brought to the cottage. You are welcome to use the beachside campfire for an evening cookout or to barbecue on your deck.

Swantown Bed and Breakfast Inn

1431 11TH AVENUE SOUTHEAST, OLYMPIA, WASHINGTON 98501

Tel: **(360) 753-9123**	Open: **All year**
Best Time to Call: **Evenings**	Reduced Rates: **Weekly**
Hosts: **Lillian and Ed Peeples**	Breakfast: **Full**
Location: **½ mi. from I-5 Exit 105**	Credit Cards: **MC, VISA**
(Port of Olympia)	Pets: **No**
No. of Rooms: **4**	Children: **Welcome, over 12**
No. of Private Baths: **4**	Smoking: **No**
Double/pb: **$75–$115**	Social Drinking: **Permitted**
Single/pb: **$65–$105**	

Built in 1893, this stately Queen Anne/Eastlake mansion is an Olympia landmark, listed on both the state and city historical registers. Guests are invited to relax with a hot beverage in the drawing room or stroll among the Inn's half-acre gardens and orchard. It is conveniently located near the State Capitol campus, Farmers Market, downtown shops, restaurants, and waterfront boardwalk. The Inn has a great location for day trips to the Olympic peninsula, Mount St. Helens, Mount Rainier, and the city of Seattle. Accommodations include queen-size beds, and most rooms have a view of the Capitol dome. Breakfast entrees may include German apple pancakes, crepes benedict, and cream cheese French toast with homemade syrups.

Laurel Inn ✪
7914 BEACH DRIVE EAST, PORT ORCHARD, WASHINGTON 98366

Tel: **(360) 769-9544; (888) 888-9661**
Host: **Judy McQueen**
Location: **35 mi. N of Tacoma**
No. of Rooms: **3**
No. of Private Baths: **1**
Max. No. Sharing Bath: **4**
Double/pb: **$75**
Single/pb: **$70**
Double/sb: **$55–$65**
Single/sb: **$50–$60**

Open: **All year**
Reduced Rates: **10% after 3 nights**
Breakfast: **Full**
Credit Cards: **DISC, MC, VISA**
Pets: **No**
Children: **Welcome, over 12**
Smoking: **No**
Social Drinking: **Permitted**
Minimum Stay: **2 nights holidays**
Airport/Station Pickup: **Yes**

Located across the Puget Sound from West Seattle, this contemporary home is furnished with family heirlooms and needlework from three generations. Large windows frame the view of Mt. Rainier and Blake Island. Ocean-bound vessels, local sailboats, and ferries dot the seascape of Manchester. This charming community northeast of Port Orchard is on a popular bicycle route from the Southworth Ferry north to Bremerton, and Laurel Inn is just two miles from Manchester State Park. Wake to the aroma of a gourmet breakfast, which may include poached eggs with salmon cakes and lemon sauce, or cinnamon French toast with bananas and coconut syrup.

The Portico, Victorian Bed & Breakfast ✪
502 SOUTH ADAMS STREET, RITZVILLE, WASHINGTON 99169

Tel: **(509) 659-0800**
Best Time to Call: **Day or evening**
Hosts: **Mary Anne and Bill Phipps**
Location: **60 mi. SW of Spokane**
No. of Rooms: **2**
No. of Private Baths: **2**
Double/pb: **$59–$79**
Single/pb: **$53–$73**

Open: **All year**
Breakfast: **Full**
Other Meals: **Available**
Credit Cards: **AMEX, DISC, MC, VISA**
Pets: **No**
Children: **Welcome**
Smoking: **No**
Social Drinking: **Permitted**

The Portico is regarded as one of the finest bed and breakfast experiences in the region, where cordial hospitality, delectable food, and tastefully appointed accommodations offer superior ease and comfort in Victorian style. The historic 1902 mansion combines Classical Revival and Queen Anne architecture. The interior displays gleaming oak woodwork, inglenooks, columns, spindled screens, and a grand entry. Victorian wallpapers, furnishings, and lighting will delight antique lovers. Rooms have exceptionally comfortable beds and discreetly hidden TVs. This B&B is set in a rural community with easy access to I-90 and Highway 395.

Chelsea Station on the Park
4915 LINDEN AVENUE NORTH, SEATTLE, WASHINGTON 98103

Tel: **(206) 547-6077; (800) 400-6077**
Best Time to Call: **10 AM–6 PM**
Hosts: **John Griffin and**
   Karen Carbonneau
Location: **Seattle's North End**
No. of Rooms: **9**
No. of Private Baths: **9**
Double/pb: **$95–$135**
Open: **All year**

Reduced Rates: **Off-season, weekly**
Breakfast: **Full**
Credit Cards: **AMEX, DC, DISC, MC,**
   VISA
Pets: **No**
Children: **Welcome, over 12**
Smoking: **No**
Social Drinking: **Permitted**

Refresh your spirit! Feel the warmth and comfort in one of Seattle's finest neighborhood inns. Built in 1929, Chelsea Station on the Park offers unique rooms, including large suites with peek-a-boo mountain views. Relax in the Mission-style furniture and enjoy the antiques throughout. Stroll to Woodland Park, the zoo, the Rose Garden, and wonderful restaurants. This B&B is within ten minutes to the heart of downtown and city activities. A sumptuous breakfast is served each morning, and guests are invited to eat from the bottomless cookie jar.

Mildred's Bed & Breakfast ✪
1202 15TH AVENUE EAST, SEATTLE, WASHINGTON 98112

Tel: **(206) 325-6072**
Best Time to Call: **Mornings**
Hosts: **Mildred and Melodee Sarver**

Location: **Capitol Hill area**
No. of Rooms: **3**
No. of Private Baths: **3**

Double/pb: **$95–$120**
Single/pb: **$85–$105**
Open: **All year**
Breakfast: **Full**
Credit Cards: **AMEX, DC, MC, VISA**

Pets: **No**
Children: **Welcome**
Smoking: **No**
Social Drinking: **Permitted**

Mildred's is the ultimate trip-to-grandmother's fantasy come true. A large white 1890 Victorian, it's the perfect setting for traditional, caring B&B hospitality. Guest rooms on the second floor have sitting alcoves, lace curtains, and antiques. Mildred's special touches, like coffee and juice delivered to your room one-half hour before breakfast, and tea and cookies on arrival, make her guests feel truly pampered. Across the street is historic 44-acre Volunteer Park with its art museum, flower conservatory, and tennis courts. An electric trolley stops at the front door and there is ample street parking. It is just minutes to the city center, freeways, and all points of interest.

Prince of Wales ✪
133 THIRTEENTH AVENUE EAST, SEATTLE, WASHINGTON 98102

Tel: **(206) 325-9692; (800) 327-9692;**
  fax: **(206) 322-6402**
Best Time to Call: **10 AM–7 PM**
Host: **Faith Addicott**
Location: **In heart of Seattle**
No. of Rooms: **4**
No. of Private Baths: **4**
Double/sb: **$90–$99**
Suites: **$100–$125**

Open: **All year**
Reduced Rates: **10% 4 days or more**
Breakfast: **Full**
Pets: **No**
Children: **Welcome**
Smoking: **No**
Social Drinking: **Permitted**
Foreign Languages: **Spanish**

Prince of Wales is just a brief walk to the convention center and a short bus ride to the Space Needle, Pikes Place Market, and downtown Seattle's many other attractions. In the evening you're sure to be tempted by the menus of neighborhood restaurants. Theaters, coffee shops, and plenty of unique shopping opportunities are all within walking distance. All rooms have queen beds and great views.

Roberta's Bed and Breakfast
1147 SIXTEENTH AVENUE EAST, SEATTLE, WASHINGTON 98112
robertasbb@aol.com; www.roberta'sbb.com

Tel: **(206) 329-3326;**
  fax: **(206) 324-2149**
Host: **Roberta Barry**
No. of Rooms: **5**
No. of Private Baths: **5**
Double/pb: **$90–$125**
Single/pb: **$85–$110**

Open: **All year**
Breakfast: **Full**
Credit Cards: **MC, VISA**
Pets: **No**
Children: **Welcome, over 12**
Smoking: **No**
Social Drinking: **Permitted**

Roberta's is a 1903 frame Victorian with a large, old-fashioned front porch. The house is located in a quiet, historic neighborhood near the heart of the city. The cheerful rooms all boast queen-size beds. The Peach Room has bay windows, oak furniture, and Grandma's fancy desk; the Rosewood Room has a window seat and built-in oak bookcase; all five rooms have phones and are filled with books; the Hideaway has a long clawfoot tub for relaxing and skylights over the bed for stargazing. In the morning you'll smell a pot of coffee right beside your door. That's just a warm-up for the breakfast to come. The specialty of the house is Dutch Babies, a local dish, served with powdered sugar or fresh berries. For your convenience the *New York Times* and local newspapers are available every morning.

Seattle Guest Suite ✪
701 NORTHWEST 60TH STREET, SEATTLE, WASHINGTON 98107

Tel: **(206) 783-2169**	Breakfast: **Continental**
Host: **Inge Pokrandt**	Pets: **No**
Location: **1 mi. from I-5**	Smoking: **No**
No. of Rooms: **1**	Social Drinking: **Permitted**
No. of Private Baths: **1**	Minimum Stay: **2 nights**
Double/pb: **$65**	Foreign Languages: **German**
Open: **All year**	

This private garden-level guest suite offers everything a traveler may need: a quiet neighborhood, privacy, nearby parks, beaches, and the University of Washington. Guests enjoy many special touches such as fresh flowers, a fully stocked refrigerator, chocolates on their pillow, daily maid service, and much more. One guest from Florida wrote, "This must be the best value we ever experienced in all our travels."

English Gardens B&B ✪

8305-201ST STREET EAST, SPANAWAY, WASHINGTON 98387

Tel: **(253) 846-5220**
Best Time to Call: **10 AM–10 PM**
Hosts: **Earl and Emy Atchley**
No. of Rooms: **1**
Double/pb: **$60**
Open: **May–Sept.**

Breakfast: **Full**
Pets: **Sometimes**
Children: **No**
Smoking: **No**
Airport/Station Pickup: **Yes**

Stress and tension melt away in the peaceful surroundings of English Gardens B&B. During the day guests can enjoy the many sights, including Mount Rainier, located just minutes away. At the end of the day unwind on the spacious patio. Depending on your appetite, Emy will serve you a full country breakfast or a lighter Continental fare.

Marianna Stoltz House ✪

427 EAST INDIANA, SPOKANE, WASHINGTON 99207

Tel: **(509) 483-4316; (800) 978-6587;**
   fax: **(509) 483-6773**
Best time to Call: **8 AM–8 PM**
Hosts: **James and Phyllis Maguire**
No. of Rooms: **4**
No. of Private Baths: **2**
Max. No. Sharing Bath: **4**
Double/pb: **$85–$95**
Single/pb: **$75–$95**

Open: **All year**
Breakfast: **Full**
Credit Cards: **AMEX, DC, DISC, MC, VISA**
Pets: **No**
Children: **Welcome, over 4**
Smoking: **No**
Social Drinking: **Permitted**
Airport/Station Pickup: **Yes**

Established in 1987, the Marianna Stoltz House, a Spokane landmark, was designed in the classic American foursquare tradition. Built in 1908, and surrounded by 100-year-old maples, the house offers modern-day comforts with vintage ambiance. Period furnishings complement the house's maple floors, tile fireplace, fir woodwork, leaded glass bookshelves, and china cupboard. Awaken to a full breakfast, which may include Stoltz House strada or peach Melba parfait. This B&B is located minutes from I-90, Gonzaga University, the opera house/convention center, arena, downtown, Northtown, and Central Trail.

A Greater Tacoma B&B Reservations Service ✪

3312 NORTH UNION AVENUE, TACOMA, WASHINGTON 98407
reservations@tacoma-inns.org; www.tacoma-inns.org

Tel: **(253) 759-4088; fax: (253) 759-4025; (800) 406-4088**	Descriptive Directory: **Free**
	Rates (Single/Double):
Best Time to Call: **9 AM–9 PM**	Modest: **$55–$70**
Coordinator: **Sharon Kaufmann**	Average: **$75 / $90**
States/Regions Covered: **Auburn, Federal Way, Fox Island, Gig Harbor, Mt. Rainier, Olalla, Puyallup, Tacoma, University Place**	Luxury: **$95 / $165**
	Credit Cards: **AMEX, DISC, MC, VISA**

Greater Tacoma B&B Reservations Service offers more than twenty-five inspected and licensed accommodations. Prefer full or Continental breakfast? Shared or private bath? Have your choice of homes that range from a cozy cottage to a historic waterfront mansion. Some sites have extra amenities like hot tubs, romantic Jacuzzis, and fireplaces.

Commencement Bay B&B ✪

3312 NORTH UNION AVENUE, TACOMA, WASHINGTON 98407
greatviews@aol.com; www.bestinns.net/USA/WA/cb.html.

Tel: **(253) 752-8175; fax: (253) 759-4025**	Reduced Rates: **Available**
	Breakfast: **Full**
Best Time to Call: **9 AM–9 PM**	Credit Cards: **AMEX, DISC, MC, VISA**
Hosts: **Bill and Sheri Kaufmann**	Pets: **No**
Location: **1 mi. N of Tacoma**	Children: **Welcome, over 12**
No. of Rooms: **3**	Smoking: **Restricted**
No. of Private Baths: **3**	Social Drinking: **Permitted**
Double/pb: **$85–$125**	Airport/Station Pickup: **Yes**
Open: **All year**	

An elegantly decorated Colonial home overlooking scenic north end Tacoma, this B&B has dramatic bay and mountain views from both the rooms and the common areas. Guests can enjoy a quiet, relaxing fireside reading area, an outdoor hot tub in a lovely garden, weight room, bicycles, covered outdoor smoking deck, a casual game room with TV, VCR, microwave, and refrigerator—even an office for business travelers (with a fax/modem available). The B&B offers guests cable TV, VCR, and telephone in rooms, an early businessman's breakfast on weekdays, and transportation to nearby universities or downtown business areas. It is close to several waterfront parks, jogging/hiking trails, great restaurants, quaint shops (including antiques), and easy freeway access. A delicious breakfast and different gourmet coffees and teas are served daily.

Inge's Place
6809 LAKE GROVE SW, TACOMA, WASHINGTON 98499

Tel: **(253) 584-4514**	Suites: **$60**
Host: **Ingeborg Deatherage**	Open: **All year**
Location: **3 mi. from !-5**	Reduced Rates: **Available**
No. of Rooms: **3**	Breakfast: **Full**
No. of Private Baths: **1**	Pets: **No**
Max. No. Sharing Bath: **4**	Children: **Welcome**
Double/pb: **$50**	Smoking: **No**
Single/pb: **$40**	Social Drinking: **Permitted**
Double/sb: **$45**	Airport/Station Pickup: **Yes**
Single/sb: **$40**	Foreign Languages: **German**

This spic-and-span home is in a lovely Tacoma suburb called Lakewood. Feel welcome to use the hot tub, large backyard, and patio. There are many restaurants and shopping centers within walking distance, and several nearby lakes where fishing is excellent. Tacoma is the gateway to Mount Rainier. Inge is a world traveler, teacher, and enthusiast about B&Bs.

WEST VIRGINIA

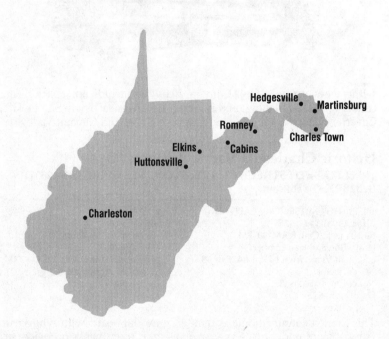

North Fork Mountain Inn ✪
P.O. BOX 114, CABINS, WEST VIRGINIA 26855

Tel: **(304) 257-1108**
Best Time to Call: **Evenings**
Hosts: **Joan and Art Ricker**
Location: **7 mi. from Rte. 55**
No. of Rooms: **6**
No. of Private Baths: **6**
Double/pb: **$70–$95**
Guest Cottage: **$125, sleeps 6**
Open: **All year**

Breakfast: **Full**
Other Meals: **Available**
Credit Cards: **MC, VISA**
Pets: **Welcome, in guest house**
Children: **Welcome, in guest house**
Smoking: **Permitted, in guest house**
Social Drinking: **Permitted**
Minimum Stay: **2 nights**

North Fork Mountain Inn is a haven from today's fast-paced world. The atmosphere is relaxed and friendly, yet the rooms and service are impeccable. The inn's guest rooms are uniquely decorated, with twin or queen beds; some have Jacuzzis and fireplaces. For guests who would like privacy or have a large family, the guest house offers three bedrooms, two baths, kitchen, living room, satellite TV, and a large porch

with a view of Smoke Hole Canyon. Activities include horseback riding, canoeing, hiking, fishing, and hunting. Located nearby are Smoke Hole Caverns, Seneca Rock, Dolly Sod, Spruce Knob, and Canaan Valley.

Historic Charleston Bed & Breakfast ✪
110 ELIZABETH STREET, CHARLESTON, WEST VIRGINIA 25311
Bed2BRKST@aol.com

Tel: **(304) 345-8156; (800) CALL-WVA;** **fax: (304) 342-1572**	Single/pb: **$65** Open: **All year**
Best Time to Call: **8 AM–11 PM**	Reduced Rates: **Available**
Hosts: **Bob and Jean Lambert**	Breakfast: **Full**
Location: **½ mi. from I-77, I-64, Exit 99**	Credit Cards: **AMEX, MC, VISA**
No. of Rooms: **3**	Children: **By arrangement**
No. of Private Baths: **3**	Smoking: **No**
Double/pb: **$75**	

This French country home is painted gray clapboard with white trim. Guest accommodations are spacious—each room has a fireplace, private sitting area, and central heating and air-conditioning. The entrance hall is furnished with a Victorian loveseat, candle table, and a claw-footed desk, setting the tone for the rest of the house, which is decorated with antiques, collectibles, and handicrafts. Breakfast is served in the dining room, on an early 1930s dining suite. Then you can explore the area, starting with the state capitol and cultural center one block away.

Washington House Inn ✪
216 SOUTH GEORGE STREET, CHARLES TOWN,
WEST VIRGINIA 25414
mnvogel@intrepid.net; www.intrepid.net/whib&b

Tel: **(304) 725-7923; (800) 297-6957**	No. of Rooms: **6**
Best Time to Call: **8 AM–10 PM**	No. of Private Baths: **6**
Hosts: **Nina and Mel Vogel**	Double/pb: **$75–$150**
Location: **60 mi. NW of Washington,** **D.C., and Baltimore**	Open: **All year** Reduced Rates: **Available**

Breakfast: **Full**
Credit Cards: **AMEX, DISC, MC, VISA**
Pets: **No**
Children: **Welcome, over 10**

Smoking: **No**
Social Drinking: **Permitted**
Airport/Station Pickup: **Yes**

George Washington didn't sleep here—but his relatives did. Built in 1899 by descendants of the president's brothers, John Augustine and Samuel, Washington House Inn is a wonderful example of Late Victorian architecture. From the three-story turret and wraparound porch to the carved oak mantels, this home echoes a bygone era. As you enter the main foyer, period antiques help you step back in time. In the morning, a hearty full breakfast is served in the dining room. Located in West Virginia's eastern gateway, the Inn is convenient to a host of activities. Within a ten-minute drive you will find Harpers Ferry National Park, white-water rafting, biking, and hiking on the restored C&O Canal towpath, thoroughbred horse racing, history museum, theater, and Grand Prix–style sports car racing.

The Post House Bed and Breakfast ✪
306 ROBERT E. LEE AVENUE, ELKINS, WEST VIRGINIA 26241

Tel: **(304) 636-1792**
Hosts: **Toni Eddy, innkeeper; JoAnn Post Barlow, owner**
Location: **120 mi. S of Pittsburgh, Pa.**
No. of Rooms: **5**
No. of Private Baths: **2**
Max. No. Sharing Bath: **4**
Double/pb: **$65**
Single/pb: **$55**

Double/sb: **$60**
Single/sb: 55
Open: **July–Oct.**
Breakfast: **Continental**
Pets: **No**
Children: **Welcome**
Smoking: **No**
Social Drinking: **Permitted**
Airport Pickup: **Yes**

Located in the heart of the mountains, the Post House Bed and Breakfast offers individual or group accommodations. Guests are invited to relax on the front porch, the lounge, or in the spacious backyard complete with a children's playhouse. To really unwind, enjoy a massage by a certified masseuse. Handmade quilts are available for purchase. Nearby attractions include Monongahela Forest, Seneca Rocks, and Blackwater Falls. Cultural events are offered by Davis and Elkins College, including the world-famous six-week instruction at the Augusta Heritage Arts Center.

The Warfield House
318 BUFFALO STREET, ELKINS, WEST VIRGINIA 26241

Tel: **(304) 636-4555; (888) 636-4555**
Best Time to Call: **10 AM–8 PM**
Hosts: **Connie and Paul Garnett**
No. of Rooms: **5**
No. of Private Baths: **3**

Max No. Sharing Bath: **4**
Double/pb: **$75**
Single/pb: **$65**
Double/sb: **$75**
Single/sb: **$65**

Open: **All year**
Reduced Rates: **Available**
Breakfast: **Full**
Pets: **No**

Children: **Welcome, over 12**
Smoking: **No**
Social Drinking: **Permitted**

Nestled on a corner in a small scenic town, The Warfield House faces the forested City Park. Restaurants, shops, and theaters are within walking distance. Built in 1901 of shingle and brick, the house has been restored with turn-of-the-century reproduction carpets and wallpaper, and boasts spectacular woodwork and stained glass. Guest rooms provide comfort and privacy. You will awaken to a hearty breakfast before you begin your day of hiking, biking, rafting, bird-watching, photography, mountain climbing, downhill and cross-country skiing, antiquing, and much more. Your hosts, both musicians, are waiting to share the beauty of the mountains and their home with you.

The Farmhouse on Tomahawk Run

1 TOMAHAWK RUN PLACE, HEDGESVILLE, WEST VIRGINIA 25427

Tel: **(304) 754-7350**
Best Time to Call: **10 AM–noon, 6–9 PM**
Hosts: **Hugh and Judy Erskine**
Location: **12 mi. W of Martinsburg**
No. of Rooms: **5**
No. of Private Baths: **5**
Double/pb: **$65–$75**
Guest Cottage: **$140**
Open: **Mar.–Dec.**

Reduced Rates: **10% March**
Breakfast: **Full**
Credit Cards: **DISC, MC, VISA**
Pets: **No**
Children: **Welcome, by arrangement**
Smoking: **No**
Social Drinking: **Permitted**
Minimum Stay: **2 nights weekends**

Nestled in a quiet valley next to the historic Tomahawk-shaped spring for which the area was named, the farmhouse was built by Judy's great-grandfather during the Civil War. The land itself has been occupied by her ancestors since 1740. Two of the guest rooms inside the farmhouse have balconies. The self-contained carriage house sleeps five to seven and is available for weekend or week-long stays. A peaceful, bubbling brook winds its way through the 280 acres of woods and meadows, where walking paths are maintained for your pleasure. A Jacuzzi on the back porch of the farmhouse will ensure a restful visit.

The Hutton House ✪

ROUTES 219 AND 250, HUTTONSVILLE, WEST VIRGINIA 26273

Tel: **(304) 335-6701; (800) 234-6701**
Best Time to Call: **Anytime**
Hosts: **Dean and Loretta Murray**
Location: **17 mi. S of Elkins**
No. of Rooms: **6**
No. of Private Baths: **6**
Double/pb: **$70–$80**

Single/pb: **$60–$70**
Open: **All year**
Reduced Rates: **Available**
Breakfast: **Full**
Other Meals: **Available**
Credit Cards: **MC, VISA**
Pets: **No**

Children: **Welcome**
Smoking: **No**

Social Drinking: **Permitted**
Airport/Station Pickup: **Yes**

Built in 1899 by a scion of Huttonsville's founder, Hutton House commands a broad view of the Tygart Valley and Laurel Mountain ridges. This ornate Queen Anne mansion, with its extraordinary woodwork and windows, is listed on the National Register of Historic Places. Travelers come here to ski at Snowshoe, visit Cass Railroad, and hike in the Monongahela National Forest. Civil War buffs will find plenty of battle sites to study, and the Augusta Heritage Arts Festival, in nearby Elkins, also merits a detour. For breakfast, your hosts dish out cantaloupe sorbet and whole wheat pancakes drizzled with maple syrup made from their own trees.

Pulpit & Palette Inn ✪
516 WEST JOHN STREET, MARTINSBURG, WEST VIRGINIA 25401

Tel: **(304) 263-7012**
Hosts: **Bill and Janet Starr**
Location: **20 mi. S of Hagerstown**
No. of Rooms: **2**
Max. No. Sharing Bath: **4**
Double/sb: **$80**
Single/sb: **$65**
Open: **Mar.–Dec.**

Breakfast: **Full**
Credit Cards: **DISC, MC, VISA**
Pets: **No**
Children: **Welcome, over 12**
Smoking: **No**
Social Drinking: **Permitted**
Station Pickup: **Yes**

Built in 1870, this Italianate Victorian is furnished with American antiques, Oriental objets d'art, Tibetan rugs, paintings, and stained glass work done by the hostess. Bill and Janet's objective is to give personalized attention to guests with afternoon tea, complimentary evening drinks and hors d'oeuvres, a morning bed tray, and a full gourmet breakfast. Bill and Janet are retired educators; their interests include drama production, stained glass work, art appreciation, travel, and community service. The Pulpit & Palette Inn is located 30 minutes from Harpers Ferry National Park and the Antietam National Battlefield, and 80 minutes from historic Gettysburg.

Hampshire House 1884 ✪
165 NORTH GRAFTON STREET, ROMNEY, WEST VIRGINIA 26757

Tel: **(304) 822-7171**
Hosts: **Jane and Scott Simmons**
Location: **35 mi. W of Winchester, Va.**
No. of Rooms: **5**
No. of Private Baths: **5**
Double/pb: **$70–$95**
Single/pb: **$55–$75**
Open: **All year**
Reduced Rates: **Available**

Breakfast: **Full**
Credit Cards: **AMEX, DC, DISC, MC, VISA**
Pets: **No**
Children: **Welcome**
Smoking: **No**
Social Drinking: **Permitted**
Airport/Station Pickup: **Yes**

Only two and a half hours west of Washington, D.C., via Route 50, lies Romney, the oldest town in West Virginia. Surrounded by beautiful rolling hills, Hampshire House is conveniently located to the downtown area. You will enjoy touring the town, with its quaint shops and historic buildings, and winery tours are nearby. The bedrooms are attractively furnished with old-fashioned furniture and wallpapers and kept comfortable with central heating and air-conditioning. Jane and Scott graciously offer complimentary snacks and invite you to enjoy the old pump organ, television, VCR, or a variety of games. There's a small spa on the premises, with appointments for massage available.

For key to listings, see inside front or back cover.

❂ This star means that rates are guaranteed through December 31, 1999, to any guest making a reservation as a result of reading about the B&B in *Bed & Breakfast U.S.A.*—1999 edition.

Important! To avoid misunderstandings, always ask about cancellation policies when booking.

Please enclose a self-addressed, stamped, business-size envelope when contacting reservation services.

For more details on what you can expect in a B&B, see Chapter 1.

Always mention *Bed & Breakfast U.S.A.* when making reservations!

We want to hear from you! Use the form on page 593.

WISCONSIN

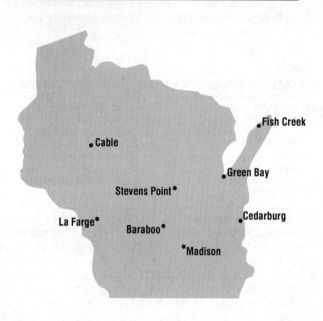

The Gollmar Guest House B&B ✪
422 3RD STREET, BARABOO, WISCONSIN 53913

Tel: **(608) 356-9432**	Breakfast: **Full**
Best Time to Call: **6–10 PM**	Credit Cards: **MC, VISA**
Host: **Thomas Luck**	Pets: **No**
Location: **200 mi. NW of Chicago**	Children: **Welcome, over 7**
No. of Rooms: **3**	Smoking: **No**
No. of Private Baths: **3**	Social Drinking: **Permitted**
Double/pb: **$75**	Station Pickup: **Yes**
Open: **All year**	

Welcome to the Gollmar Guest House B&B, an exquisite Victorian circus home laden with charming treasures, unique features, and a wealth of history. Original hand-painted ceiling frescoes, beveled glass, chandeliers, furniture, and antiques will delight antiques connoisseurs. Guest rooms all have queen beds and are named after the exceptional Gollmar women. Isabell's room is pristine and elegant in white and periwinkle. Leora's Country Meadow Room is soft and romantic, with hearts and flowers. Viola's Attic Room is peachy and private with French Impressionist prints. Guests may relax in the parlor or sit on the porch and enjoy the view. Breakfast may include apple pancakes, French toast, pastries, and fruit. The Inn is located within four blocks of downtown Baraboo. Your hosts will be happy to supply you with maps and acquaint you with the area.

Pinehaven ○
E13083 STATE HIGHWAY 33, BARABOO, WISCONSIN 53913

Tel: **(608) 356-3489**	Open: **All year**
Best Time to Call: **Before 10 PM**	Breakfast: **Full**
Hosts: **Lyle and Marge Getschman**	Credit Cards: **MC, VISA**
Location: **10 mi. from I-90**	Pets: **No**
No. of Rooms: **4**	Children: **Welcome, over 5**
No. of Private Baths: **4**	Smoking: **No**
Double/pb: **$79–$135**	Social Drinking: **Permitted**
Single/pb: **$69–$125**	

Lyle and Marge's home is nestled in a pine grove with a beautiful view of the Baraboo Bluffs and a small private lake. Guest rooms have air-conditioning. The full breakfast may include fresh-baked muffins, coffee cakes, egg dishes, meat, fruit, and juice. Eat in the dining room, on the deck, or on the screened-in porch. Play the baby grand piano. Feel free to take a leisurely stroll in these inviting surroundings. A tour to see your hosts' Belgian draft horses and antique wagons and sleighs on the farm side of the highway, and wagon or sleigh rides pulled by the Belgians, may be arranged. Fine restaurants and numerous activities abound in the area. A guest cottage with a double whirlpool is available.

The Victorian Rose ○
423 THIRD AVENUE, BARABOO, WISCONSIN 53913

Tel: **(608) 356-7828**	Open: **All year**
Hosts: **Bob and Carolyn Stearns**	Breakfast: **Full**
Location: **40 mi. N of Madison**	Pets: **No**
No. of Rooms: **3**	Children: **No**
No. of Private Baths: **3**	Smoking: **No**
Double/pb: **$70–$90**	Social Drinking: **Permitted**

The Victorian Rose is located on a large corner lot, surrounded by sugar maples and pine trees, within walking distance of Baraboo's historical sites, specialty shops, and galleries. The Stearns family welcomes you to their beautifully restored 19th-century "Painted Lady," furnished with roses, lace, antiques, and heirloom collectibles. Guests can enjoy a game or book in the library parlor or watch old classic movies by the fireplace with a cup of tea and sweet treats. Appropriately enough, guest rooms are decorated in Victorian style. A full gourmet candlelight breakfast awaits guests in the morning.

Connors Bed & Breakfast
ROUTE 1, BOX 255, CABLE, WISCONSIN 54821

Tel: **(715) 798-3661; (800) 848-3932**	Open: **All year**
Hosts: **Alex and Mona Connors**	Breakfast: **Full**
Location: **1.7 mi. N of Cable**	Credit Cards: **MC, VISA**
No. of Rooms: **4**	Pets: **No**
No. of Private Baths: **2**	Children: **Welcome**
Max. No. Sharing Bath: **4**	Smoking: **No**
Double/sb: **$50**	Social Drinking: **Permitted**
Cabin: **$70 for 2**	Minimum Stay: **2 nights cabin**
Suites: **$85**	Airport/Station Pickup: **Yes**

Once a 77-acre farm, Connors Bed & Breakfast lies approximately 40 miles south of Lake Superior, surrounded by the Chequamegon National Forest. This central location gives guests easy access to nearby lakes, golf, casinos, numerous day trips, and downhill and cross-country skiing—there is a private trail on the property. A 107-year-old cabin, located in the apple orchard, is perfect for an unusual honeymoon getaway, or can accommodate up to six people. It has a kitchenette, wood-burning stove, gas heater, and a claw-footed tub in the master bedroom. The second floor has one room with a full bed and one with two singles.

Stagecoach Inn Bed & Breakfast ✪
W61 N520 WASHINGTON AVENUE, CEDARBURG, WISCONSIN 53012
www.stagecoach-inn-wi.com

Tel: **(414) 375-0208; (888) 375-0208;**	Open: **All year**
fax: **(414) 375-6170**	Breakfast: **Continental**
Hosts: **Brook and Liz Brown**	Credit Cards: **AMEX, DISC, MC, VISA**
Location: **20 mi. N of Milwaukee**	Pets: **No**
No. of Rooms: **12**	Children: **Welcome, over 12**
No. of Private Baths: **12**	Smoking: **No**
Double/pb: **$75**	Social Drinking: **Permitted**
Suites: **$115–$130**	

The Inn, listed on the National Register of Historic Places, is housed in a completely restored 1853 stone building in downtown historic Cedarburg. The rooms are decorated with period antiques. Suites include two-person whirlpools and fireplaces. A secret garden area is available to guests. A candy shop and a pub that is a popular gathering place for guests occupy the first floor. Specialty stores, antique shops, a winery, a woolen mill, and a variety of fine restaurants are within walking distance.

Thorp House Inn & Cottages ✪
4135 BLUFF LANE, P.O. BOX 490, FISH CREEK, WISCONSIN 54212

Tel: **(920) 868-2444**
Best Time to Call: **8 AM–10 PM**
Hosts: **Christine and**
   Sverre Falck-Pedersen
No. of Rooms: **3**
No. of Private Baths: **3**
Double/pb: **$85–$105**
Cottages: **$85–$145**
Open: **All year**

Reduced Rates: **Weekly**
Breakfast: **Continental**
Pets: **No**
Children: **Welcome, in cottages**
Smoking: **Yes, in cottages**
Social Drinking: **Permitted**
Minimum Stay: **3 nights summer, fall**
   and holiday weekends
Foreign Languages: **Norwegian**

Thorp House is a turn-of-the-century country Victorian inn perched on a wooded hill overlooking Green Bay. The beach, shops, restaurants, and Peninsula State Park are just a stroll away. Four elegant guest rooms re-create romantic periods of the past with fine antiques and accessories, documentary wall coverings, and European lace. Each room has a private bath (one with a whirlpool), central air-conditioning, and ceiling fans. Guests have their own parlor with its original granite fireplace. A delicious home-baked breakfast is included. Also available: country cottages with wood-burning fireplaces, full kitchens and baths (some with whirlpools), decks, and views of the bay. The inn and cottages are listed on the National Register of Historic Places.

The Astor House ✪

637 SOUTH MONROE AVENUE, GREEN BAY, WISCONSIN 54301

Tel: **(920) 432-3585**
Best Time to Call: **8 AM–8 PM**
Host: **Doug Landwehr**
Location: **In Green Bay**
No. of Rooms: **5**
No. of Private Baths: **5**
Double/pb: **$79–$129**
Suites: **$89–$149**
Open: **All year**
Reduced Rates: **Business travelers, multi-night**

Breakfast: **Continental**
Credit Cards: **AMEX, DISC, MC, VISA**
Pets: **No**
Children: **No**
Smoking: **No**
Social Drinking: **Permitted**
Minimum Stay: **2 nights holiday weekends**

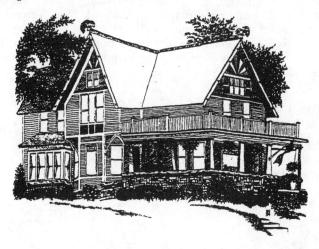

Welcome to the 1888 Astor House, where gracious seclusion, peace, and personal attention are yours from the time you enter the Astor Historic Neighborhood, near Green Bay's City Center. The five distinctive guest suites are incredibly decorated and equipped with queen or king beds, private shower or whirlpool bath, telephones, cable TV, VCR, CD and tape decks, refrigerators, and air-conditioning. Breakfast includes homemade baked goods, fruit, and gourmet coffee. Enjoy the public and private gardens, luxuriate in a gentle whirlpool for two, bask before a roaring fire, or sample the many shops, restaurants, theaters, events, and activities in the Green Bay area. The Astor House is designed for either the vacationer or the business visitor.

Trillium ✪

E-10596, EAST SALEM RIDGE ROAD, LA FARGE, WISCONSIN 54639-8015

Tel: **(608) 625-4492**
Best Time to Call: **Mornings; evenings**
Hosts: **Joe Swanson and Rosanne Boyett**
Location: **40 mi. SE of La Crosse**
Guest Cottage: **$80 for 2**
Open: **All year**

Breakfast: **Full**
Reduced Rates: **Single guest; weekly; winter, after first night**
Pets: **No**
Children: **Welcome (crib)**
Smoking: **No**
Social Drinking: **Permitted**

This private cottage is on a working farm located in the heart of a thriving Amish community. It has a large porch and is surrounded by an orchard, garden, and a lovely tree-shaded yard. There's a path beside the stream that winds through woods and fields. The cottage is light and airy, with comfortable country furnishings. Nearby attractions include the Elroy-Sparta Bike Trail, Mississippi River, trout streams, and cheese factories.

Annie's Bed & Breakfast

2117 SHERIDAN DRIVE, MADISON, WISCONSIN 53704
www.bbinternet.com/annies

Tel: **(608) 244-2224**
Hosts: **Anne and Larry Stuart**

No. of Rooms: **2 suites**
No. of Private Baths: **2**

Suites: **$96–$134 for 2; $160–$214
for 4**
Open: **All year**
Reduced Rates: **4th night free weekdays
only**
Breakfast: **Full**
Credit Cards: **AMEX, MC, VISA**

Pets: **No**
Children: **Welcome, over 12**
Smoking: **No**
Social Drinking: **Permitted**
Minimum Stay: **2 nights**
Airport/Station Pickup: **Yes**

When you want the world to go away, come to Annie's, a quiet inn with a beautiful view of meadows, water, and woods. This charming, fully air-conditioned cedar shake home has been a getaway for travelers since 1985. The house is a block from a large lake and directly adjoining Warner Park, allowing guests a broad selection of activities, including swimming, boating, tennis, hiking, and biking during summer, and cross-country skiing and skating in winter. The four antique-filled guest rooms are full of surprises and unusual amenities. There is a great-hall dining room, a pine-paneled library with a lannen stone fireplace and a soothing double whirlpool surrounded by plants. The unusually lovely gardens, with romantic gazebo and pond, have been selected for the annual Madison Garden Tours.

Dreams of Yesteryear Bed & Breakfast ✪
1100 BRAWLEY STREET, STEVENS POINT, WISCONSIN 54481

Tel: **(715) 341-4525**
Best Time to Call: **After 4 PM**
Hosts: **Bonnie and Bill Maher**
Location: **30 mi. S of Wausau**
No. of Rooms: **6**
No. of Private Baths: **4**
Double/pb: **$55–$135**
Single/pb: **$50–$130**

Open: **All year**
Breakfast: **Full**
Credit Cards: **AMEX, DISC, MC, VISA**
Pets: **No**
Children: **Welcome, over 12**
Smoking: **No**
Social Drinking: **Permitted**
Airport/Station Pickup: **Yes**

Dreams, listed on the National Register of Historic Places and featured in *Victorian Homes* magazine, was designed by architect J. H. Jeffers, who also designed the Wisconsin Building at the St. Louis World's Fair of 1904. Lavish in Victorian detail, the home is handsomely decorated, with floral wallpapers, and period furniture. One bathroom has a clawfooted tub and a pedestal sink. Bonnie, a University of Wisconsin secretary, and Bill, owner of a water-conditioning business, love to talk about the house and its furnishings. Skiing, canoeing, shopping, and university theater, among other activities, are in close proximity.

WYOMING

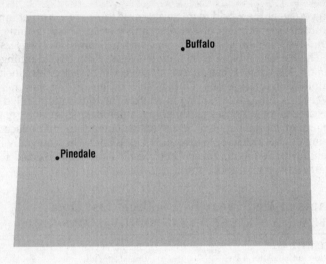

Cloud Peak Inn ✪
590 NORTH BURRITT AVENUE, BUFFALO, WYOMING 82834

Tel: **(307) 684-5794; (800) 715-5794**
Best Time to Call: **Anytime**
Hosts: **Rick and Kathy Brus**
Location: **115 mi. N of Casper**
No. of Rooms: **5**
No. of Private Baths: **3**
Max. No. Sharing Bath: **4**
Double/pb: **$55–$80**
Single/pb: **$50–$65**
Double/sb: **$45–$60**
Single/sb: **$40–$50**

Open: **All year**
Reduced Rates: **Available**
Breakfast: **Full**
Other Meals: **Available**
Credit Cards: **AMEX, MC, VISA**
Pets: **No**
Children: **Welcome**
Smoking: **No**
Social Drinking: **Permitted**
Airport/Station Pickup: **Yes**

Built in 1912, this home is an expanded bungalow with a generous front porch. The grand curved staircase leads to spacious guest rooms decorated with period antiques. In the parlor and dining room, ten-foot wood-beamed ceilings enhance the feeling of luxury. Guests are encouraged to relax by the fossilized fireplace or in the Jacuzzi sunroom. You'll wake up to a three-course breakfast ranging from full country entrees to gourmet delights. The Big Horn Mountains offer something for everyone, including fishing, hiking, sightseeing, horseback riding, and boating. During spring, the wildflower display is unrivaled. Come and see what the West is all about.

Window on the Winds ✪
10151 HIGHWAY 191, P.O. BOX 996, PINEDALE, WYOMING 82941

Tel: **(307) 367-2600**	Reduced Rates: **Available**
Host: **Leanne McClain**	Breakfast: **Full**
Location: **75 mi. S of Jackson**	Other Meals: **Available**
No. of Rooms: **4**	Credit Cards: **MC, VISA**
Max. No. Sharing Bath: **4**	Pets: **Welcome**
Double/sb: **$60–$95**	Children: **Welcome**
Single/sb: **$50**	Smoking: **No**
Open: **All year**	Social Drinking: **Permitted**

Pinedale, at the base of the Wind River Mountains in western Wyoming, is on one of the major routes to Grand Teton and Yellowstone National Parks. The Winds offers world-class hiking and fishing in the summer and snowmobiling and Nordic skiing in the winter. The comfortable log home, decorated in striking Western and Plains Indians themes, is a rustic retreat—the perfect base for your Wyoming vacation. There is room for pets and kids and a large garage to store extra gear. Host Leanne is an archaeologist who enjoys sharing her unique perspective on the cultural heritage of the area.

6

Canada

ALBERTA

Note: All prices listed in this section are quoted in Canadian dollars.

B&B at Harrison's ✪
6016 THORNBURN DRIVE NW, CALGARY, ALBERTA, CANADA T2K 3P7

Tel: **(403) 274-7281, 531-0065;**
  fax: (403) 531-0069
Best Time to Call: **7–8 AM; 4–7 PM**
Host: **Susan Harrison**
Location: **In Calgary**
No. of Rooms: **3**
Max. No. Sharing Bath: **2**
Double/pb: **$75**

Single/pb: **$50**
Open: **All year**
Breakfast: **Full**
Pets: **No**
Children: **Welcome, over 10**
Smoking: **No**
Social Drinking: **Permitted**

Situated in a quiet residential area, B&B at Harrison's is a cozy bungalow located ten minutes from the city center and fifteen minutes from Calgary International Airport. Spend a peaceful afternoon walking to the nearby 1090-hectare, natural prairie Nose Hill Park, where you can view the distant Canadian Rockies, or eat at one of the many restaurants. One room features twin beds with a 1940s-style decor. Modern decor and a queen-size bed set the tone for the second room. And for the single traveler, a third room has a single bed with ensuite bath. Guests share a lounge with a TV and library, and a sheltered patio with their host. The Calgary Exhibition and Stampede, the Calgary Zoo and Prehistoric Park, and the University of Calgary are within six miles. Banff and Kananaskis Country are a one-hour drive west.

Brink Bed and Breakfast ✪
79 SINCLAIR CRESCENT S.W., CALGARY, ALBERTA, CANADA T2W 0M1

Tel: **(403) 255-4523**	Suite: **$70–$75**
Best Time to Call: **Mornings**	Open: **All year**
Host: **Helen G. Scrimgeour-Brink**	Breakfast: **Full**
Location: **In Calgary**	Other Meals: **Available**
No. of Rooms: **2**	Pets: **Sometimes**
No. of Private Baths: **1**	Children: **Welcome**
Max. No. Sharing Bath: **4**	Smoking: **Permitted**
Double/pb: **$60–$65**	Social Drinking: **Permitted**
Double/sb: **$55**	Airport/Station Pickup: **Yes**
Single/sb: **$45**	

Helen is a native Calgarian and a retired registered nurse who decided to open a bed and breakfast. Each bedroom is tastefully decorated. The suite "Sarah's Garden" is a private retreat with a queen-size bed, TV, armoire, and complete bath. The "Bed of Roses" room, on another level, has a comfortable double bed and is adjacent to a half-bath and a family room with a TV and a wide collection of books. Breakfast, served in a sunny dining room, features specialties like homemade scones, muffins, French toast, pancakes, fruit compote, and freshly squeezed juice. There is a large deck and well-landscaped private backyard. A traditional British afternoon tea, picnic baskets, or an evening meal are offered at an additional cost. There is a $5 surcharge for one-night stays.

BRITISH COLUMBIA

Note: All prices listed in this section are quoted in Canadian dollars.

Canada-West Accommodations ✪
P.O. BOX 86607, NORTH VANCOUVER, BRITISH COLUMBIA, CANADA V7L 4L2
ellison@b-b.com; www.b-b.com

Tel: **(604) 990-6730; (800) 561-3223;** fax: **(604) 990-5876**	Regions Covered: **Greater Vancouver, Victoria, Kelowna, Whistler**
Best Time to Call: **Daily to 10 PM**	Rates (Single/Double):
Coordinator: **Ellison Massey**	Average: **$65–$95 / $85–$135**
	Credit Cards: **AMEX, MC, VISA**

This registry has over 100 hosts with comfortable bed-and-breakfast accommodations. All serve a full breakfast, and most have a private bath for guest use. When traveling through British Columbia, visitors should note that B&Bs are available within a day's drive of one another. Canada-West features friendly host families eager to share their knowledge of cultural and scenic attractions.

Moonshadows Guest House

771 GEORGESON BAY ROAD, S16, C16, RR1, GALIANO ISLAND, BRITISH COLUMBIA, CANADA V0N 1P0
moonshadowsbb@bc.sympatico.ca

Tel/Fax: **(250) 539-5544; (888) 666-6742**
Hosts: **Pat Goodwin and Dave Muir**
No. of Rooms: **3**
No. of Private Baths: **3**
Double/pb: **$100–$110**
Single/pb: **$90–$95**
Suites: **$135**
Open: **All year**

Reduced Rates: **Winter, extended stays**
Breakfast: **Full**
Credit Cards: **MC, VISA**
Pets: **No**
Children: **Welcome, over 12**
Smoking: **No**
Social Drinking: **Permitted**
Minimum Stay: **2 nights holidays, Suite—2 nights**

This modern architect-designed home is welcoming, with plenty of natural light on its oak floors, paneled ceilings, and massive stone fireplace. The two-acre property is nestled in the center of tranquil Galiano Island, allowing easy access to hiking, cycling, kayaking, beaches, shops, and restaurants. Each guest room is individually decorated, featuring queen beds, complete privacy, and plenty of space to relax. The suite has a private entrance, indoor Jacuzzi tub, and walk-in shower. Breakfasts are an event to be anticipated, with fresh fruit and baked goods, followed by a frittata, soufflé, French toast, or perhaps feather-light pancakes. Guests can pamper themselves outdoors by soaking in the hot tub, or inside, snuggled in a chair next to the wood-burning fireplace with a good book.

Deep Cove Bed & Breakfast ✪

2590 SHELLEY ROAD, NORTH VANCOUVER, BRITISH COLUMBIA, CANADA V7H 1J9
deepcove@istar.ca

Tel: **(604) 929-3932; fax: (604) 929-9330**
Hosts: **Diane and Wayne Moore**
Location: **8 mi. NE of Vancouver**
No. of Rooms: **2**
No. of Private Baths: **2**
Double/pb: **$90**
Single/pb: **$80**

Open: **All year**
Reduced Rates: **Available**
Breakfast: **Full**
Credit Cards: **MC, VISA**
Pets: **No**
Smoking: **No**
Social Drinking: **Permitted**

Only fifteen minutes from downtown Vancouver, Deep Cove Bed & Breakfast combines the privacy of a large secluded property with easy access to all major points of interest. The separate guest cottage is ideally suited for honeymoons and getaways. Guest rooms in the cottage have private baths, entrances, parking, and TV. Guests are invited to relax in the garden and in the outdoor cedar hot tub. Breakfast is served in the morning room or on the patio. Diane will be happy to direct you to all the special places that make Vancouver so exciting.

Poole's Bed & Breakfast ✪
421 WEST ST. JAMES ROAD, NORTH VANCOUVER, BRITISH COLUMBIA, CANADA V7N 2P6
rapoole@lightspeed.bc.ca

Tel: **(604) 987-4594; fax: (604) 987-4283**	Single/sb: **$45**
Best Time to Call: **9 AM–9 PM**	Open: **All year**
Hosts: **Doreen and Arthur Poole**	Reduced Rates: **Available**
Location: **5 mi. N of Vancouver**	Breakfast: **Full**
No. of Rooms: **3**	Pets: **No**
Max. No. Sharing Bath: **4**	Children: **Welcome**
Double/sb: **$60**	Smoking: **No**
	Social Drinking: **Permitted**

On a lovely tree-lined street near the North Shore Mountains sits this quiet Colonial home. The Pooles' residential neighborhood is close to the bus, restaurants, downtown Vancouver, Stanley Park, Capilano Suspension Bridge, Grouse Mountain Skyride, and Vancouver Island Ferry. Doreen and Arthur are retirees who are happy to assist you with information and directions. They'll serve you an abundant candlelight breakfast in the dining room.

"Mandeville" Tudor Cottage by the Sea ✪
1064 LANDSEND ROAD, SIDNEY, BRITISH COLUMBIA, CANADA V8L 5L3

Tel: **(250) 655-1587**	Open: **All year**
Best Time to Call: **8 AM–10 PM**	Reduced Rates: **Oct.–Apr. $80 double**
Hosts: **Averil and Maurice Clegg**	Breakfast: **Full**
Location: **20 mi. N of Victoria**	Pets: **No**
No. of Rooms: **2**	Children: **Welcome**
No. of Private Baths: **2**	Smoking: **No**
Double/pb: **$80–$100**	Social Drinking: **Permitted**
Single/pb: **$80**	Airport/Station Pickup: **Yes**
Suites: **$100**	

"Mandeville" Tudor Cottage, located at the north end of the Saanich Peninsula on Vancouver Island, is nestled in one acre of forest. Beautiful lawns and gardens lead to the beach. "Mandeville" is just minutes from British Columbia and Washington State ferry terminals, and Victoria

International Airport. The capital city of Victoria is twenty miles away. The suites have private entrances, queen-size beds, private baths with tub and shower, and large sitting rooms with cable TV.

Beautiful Bed & Breakfast
428 WEST 40 AVENUE, VANCOUVER, BRITISH COLUMBIA, CANADA V5Y 2R4

Tel: **(604) 327-1102; fax: (604) 327-2299**
Best Time to Call: **Evenings**
Hosts: **Corinne and Ian Sanderson**
Location: **In Vancouver**
No. of Rooms: **4**
No. of Private Baths: **1**
Max. No. Sharing Bath: **4**
Double/sb: **$115–$210**

Single/sb: **$115–$210**
Open: **All year**
Reduced Rates: **10% less weekly**
Breakfast: **Full, Continental**
Pets: **No**
Children: **Welcome, over 14**
Smoking: **No**
Social Drinking: **Permitted**
Foreign Languages: **French**

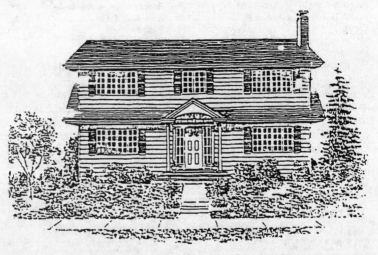

Relax in elegance in a gorgeous new Colonial home furnished with antiques, views, and fresh flowers. This is a great central location on a quiet residential street, just five minutes from downtown and within walking distance of Queen Elizabeth Park, Van Dusen Gardens, tennis, golf, three cinemas, wonderful restaurants, swimming, and a major shopping center. It's one block from bus to downtown, ferries, airport, and University of British Columbia. Enjoy a view of the north shore mountain peaks or Vancouver Island and Mount Baker, comfortable beds, a large attractive backyard—and friendly helpful hosts who will assist you with your travel plans.

Johnson Heritage House Bed & Breakfast ✪

**2278 WEST 34TH AVENUE, VANCOUVER, BRITISH COLUMBIA,
CANADA V6M 1G6**

johnsonBB@bc.sympatico.ca; www.vancouver-bc.com/JohnsonHouseBB

Tel/Fax: **(604) 266-4175**
Best Time to Call: **9 AM–9 PM**
Hosts: **Sandy and Ron Johnson**
Location: **1½ mi. W of Hwy. #99 on
33rd Ave.**
No. of Rooms: **3**
Max. No. Sharing Bath: **4**
Double/pb: **$85–$110**
Single/pb: **$75–$100**

Double/sb: **$75–$85**
Single/sb: **$65–$75**
Suite: **$115–$145**
Open: **All year**
Breakfast: **Full**
Pets: **No**
Children: **Welcome, over 12**
Smoking: **No**
Social Drinking: **Permitted**

Centrally located on a quiet, tree-lined avenue, the Johnson Heritage
House is a restored 1920s Craftsman-style home. Features include rhododendron and rock gardens, ancient stone sculptures, large front
porch, extensive interior woodwork, and a unique antique decor including brass and iron beds, wooden carousel horses, and painted horn gra-
mophones. Relax in the guest living room with a large brick fireplace
and TV/VCR. Two guest rooms have mountain views, private baths,
and very comfy beds. Sandy and Ron provide guidebooks with maps
that will direct you to all the attractions and calendar events. The B&B
is within walking distance to buses, banks, shops, and restaurants. Airport, beaches, downtown, and attractions are five to fifteen minutes
away. A hearty breakfast is served between 8:15–9:30.

Kenya Court Ocean Front Guest House ✪

2230 CORNWALL AVENUE, VANCOUVER, BRITISH COLUMBIA, CANADA V6K 1B5

Tel: **(604) 738-7085**	Pets: **No**
Hosts: **Dr. and Mrs. H. Williams**	Children: **Welcome, over 8**
Location: **20 mi. from the U.S. border**	Smoking: **No**
Suites: **$85 up**	Social Drinking: **Permitted**
Open: **All year**	Foreign Languages: **French, German,**
Breakfast: **Full**	**Italian**

There is an unobstructed view of the park, ocean, mountains, and downtown Vancouver from this heritage building on the waterfront. Across the street are tennis courts, a large heated outdoor saltwater pool, and walking and jogging paths along the water's edge. Just minutes from downtown, it's an easy walk to Granville Market, the Planetarium, and interesting shops and restaurants. All the suites are large and tastefully furnished. Breakfast is served in a glass solarium with a spectacular view of English Bay.

Town & Country Bed & Breakfast Reservation Service

BOX 74542, 2803 WEST 4TH AVENUE, VANCOUVER, BRITISH COLUMBIA V6K 1K2

Tel: **(604) 731-5942**	Rates (Single/Double):
Coordinator: **Helen Burich**	Modest: **$55–$75 / $75–$105**
States/Regions Covered: **Vancouver,**	Luxury: **$75–$125 / $125–$225**
Vancouver Island, Victoria	Minimum Stay: **2 nights**

Helen has the oldest reservation service in British Columbia. She has dozens of host homes, many of which have been accommodating guests for ten years. Ranging from modest homes to lovely heritage homes, they are a 15- to 20-minute drive to Stanley Park, beaches, Capilano and Lynn Canyons, Grouse Mountain Skyride, museums, and galleries; neighborhood restaurants and shopping areas are usually within walking distance. There are also a couple of cottages and self-contained suites. There is a $5 surcharge for Victoria and Vancouver Island reservations. In addition to normal business hours, Helen is often available evenings and weekends.

Beachside Bed and Breakfast

**4208 EVERGREEN AVENUE, WEST VANCOUVER,
BRITISH COLUMBIA, CANADA V7V 1H1**
beach@uniserve.com; www.vancouver-bc.com/BeachsideBB/

Tel: **(604) 922-7773; (800) 563-3311;**
  fax: **(604) 926-8073**
Hosts: **Gordon and Joan Gibbs**
Location: **4 mi. NW of Vancouver Ctr.**
No. of Rooms: **3**
No. of Private Baths: **3**
Double/pb: **$120–$225**

Open: **All year**
Breakfast: **Full**
Credit Cards: **MC, VISA**
Pets: **No**
Children: **By arrangement**
Smoking: **No**
Social Drinking: **Permitted**

Guests are welcomed to this beautiful waterfront home with a fruit basket and fresh flowers. The house is a Spanish-style structure, with stained glass windows, located at the end of a quiet cul-de-sac. Its southern exposure affords a panoramic view of Vancouver. A sandy beach is just steps from the door. You can watch the waves from the patio or spend the afternoon fishing or sailing. The hearty breakfast features homemade muffins, French toast, and Canadian maple syrup. Gordon and Joan are knowledgeable about local history and can gladly direct you to Stanley Park, hiking, skiing, and much more.

Dorrington B&B ✪

**13851 19A AVENUE, WHITE ROCK, BRITISH COLUMBIA,
CANADA V4A 9M2**
www.bbcanada.com/508.html

Tel: **(604) 535-4408; fax: (604) 535-
4409**
Best Time to Call: **7 PM**
Hosts: **Pat Gray**
Location: **20 mi. S of Vancouver**
No. of Rooms: **3**
No. of Private Baths: **3**
Double/pb: **$75–$90**
Single/pb: **$65–$75**
Open: **All year**

Reduced Rates: **Oct.–Apr., 5th night
free**
Breakfast: **Full**
Credit Cards: **VISA**
Pets: **No**
Children: **No**
Smoking: **No**
Social Drinking: **Permitted**
Minimum Stay: **2 nights**

Dorrington B&B is a magnificent brick and stone estate set on one half-acre of ponds and gardens featuring an outdoor hot tub, tennis court, and game room for guests to enjoy. A four-poster double bed graces the Victorian room with an en suite bathroom. The St. Andrews has a unique queen bed hewn from maple branches, and a private bath. The Mountie Post is decorated like a Northwest Mounted Police cabin, offering RCMP memorabilia and a custom-built queen fourposter log bed and en suite bath. Breakfast is served in the hunt salon or on the patio overlooking the gardens. Dorrington B&B is located close to the U.S. border, and 20 minutes from the ferry terminal to Victoria.

NEWFOUNDLAND

Note: All prices listed in this section are quoted in Canadian dollars.

Terra Nova Hospitality Home & Cottages ✪
PORT BLANDFORD, NEWFOUNDLAND, CANADA A0C 2G0

Tel: **(709) 543-2260;**
 fax: **(709) 543-2241**
Host: **Rhoda Parsons**
Location: **130 mi. W of St. Johns**
No. of Rooms: **3**
Max. No. Sharing Bath: **5**
Double/pb: **$55**
Single/pb: **$45**
Double/sb: **$55**
Single/sb: **$45**
Guest Cottage: **$75–$100**

Cabins: **$75**
Suites: **$65**
Open: **All year**
Reduced Rates: **Available**
Breakfast: **Full**
Other Meals: **Available**
Credit Cards: **MC, VISA**
Pets: **No**
Children: **Welcome, under 12 free**
Smoking: **Permitted**
Social Drinking: **Permitted**

Terra Nova is located three miles east of Terra Nova National Park and seventy miles east of Gander. Nearby there are three salmon rivers, a golf course, and hiking trails. Guide service is available for skidooing, hiking, and fishing. Kitchen and barbecue facilities are available, as well as a satellite TV, laundromat, sauna, and exercise equipment. For relaxing, there is a large room with cathedral ceiling, hardwood floor, and a fireplace, or a large deck that overlooks the ocean. Children will enjoy the play area and swings. Rhoda provides home-cooked meals with fresh-baked muffins, bread, and homemade jam. A new conference room and boat charter are available.

NOVA SCOTIA

Note: All prices listed in this section are quoted in Canadian dollars.

Fairfield Farm Inn ✪
10 MAIN STREET, BOX 1287, MIDDLETON, NOVA SCOTIA, CANADA B0S 1P0

Tel: **(902) 825-6989; (800) 237-9896**
Best Time to Call: **9 AM–9 PM**
Hosts: **Richard and Shae Griffith**
Location: **90 mi. W of Halifax**
No. of Rooms: **5**
No. of Private Baths: **5**
Double/pb: **$60–$90**
Single/pb: **$50–$80**
Open: **All year**

Breakfast: **Full**
Credit Cards: **AMEX, DC, DISC, ER, MC, VISA**
Pets: **No**
Children: **Welcome**
Smoking: **No**
Social Drinking: **Permitted**
Airport/Station Pickup: **Yes**

Rated four stars, this elegant 1886 Victorian country inn features antique furnishings, air conditioning, king- or queen-size beds, and cable TV. One hundred and ten acres of garden, meadow, and woodland surround the inn, yet it is within walking distance to museums and boutiques. A country breakfast is served with fresh-picked fruit and homemade jams. Lunch and dinner are available by advance reservation. Richard and Shae offer help planning day trips around the Annapolis Valley and the Bay of Fundy shore.

ONTARIO

Note: All prices listed in this section are quoted in Canadian dollars.

Cozy Corner ✪
2 MORTON CRESCENT, BARRIE, ONTARIO, CANADA L4N 7T3

Tel: **(705) 739-0157**
Best Time to Call: **10 AM–9 PM**

Hosts: **Charita and Harry Kirby**
Location: **36 mi. N of Toronto**

No. of Rooms: **3**
No. of Private Baths: **2**
Max. No. Sharing Bath: **4**
Double/sb: **$65**
Single/sb: **$55**
Suites: **$100**
Open: **All year**
Breakfast: **Full**
Other Meals: **Available**

Credit Cards: **VISA**
Pets: **No**
Children: **No**
Smoking: **No**
Social Drinking: **Permitted**
Minimum Stay: **2 nights**
Airport/Station Pickup: **Yes**
Foreign Languages: **Spanish, German**

Charita and Harry welcome you to their lovely home, where you will enjoy modern features such as central air, electronic air cleaning, VCR lounge with Old World charm, secluded patio, and front porch. Choose from two rooms with double beds, shared bath and TV, or the Simcoe Suite with a queen bed, sitting area, and a private bath with Jacuzzi and shower. The outgoing style of your hosts will make you extremely comfortable. Their *joie de vivre* is infectious. Harry, a retired European chef, will make you a superb breakfast.

Glen Mhor Guesthouse ✪
5381 RIVER ROAD, NIAGARA FALLS, ONTARIO, CANADA L2E 3H1

Tel: **(905) 354-2600; fax: (905) 354-2600**
Host: **Vi Moncur**
Location: **Between Rainbow and Whirlpool Bridges to USA**
No. of Rooms: **4**
No. of Private Baths: **2**
Max. No. Sharing Bath: **5**
Double/pb: **$85**
Single/pb: **$65**
Double/sb: **$75**

Single/sb: **$45–$55**
Open: **All year**
Reduced Rates: **Jan. 4–Apr. 30**
Breakfast: **Full**
Credit Cards: **MC, VISA**
Pets: **No**
Children: **Welcome, infants and over 7**
Smoking: **Restricted**
Social Drinking: **Permitted**
Station Pickup: **Yes**

You can expect a friendly welcome at this turn-of-the-century home. Glen Mhor Guesthouse is situated on the lovely Niagara River, only a short drive from Niagara-on-the-Lake, home of the Shaw Theatre. A leisurely walk takes you to the falls; cyclists may bring bicycles or rent them for a ride on the riverfront path. At all times you can relax in comfortable wicker chairs on the restored veranda overlooking the Niagara's awesome gorge. A hearty breakfast is served on the sunporch or in the antique-furnished dining room. For light snacks, a refrigerator is available.

Gretna Green ✪
5077 RIVER ROAD, NIAGARA FALLS, ONTARIO, CANADA L2E 3G7

Tel: **(905) 357-2081**
Hosts: **Stan and Marg Gardiner**
Location: **25 mi. NE of Buffalo, N.Y.**

No. of Rooms: **4**
No. of Private Baths: **4**
Double/pb: **$60–$75**

Single/pb: **$45–$50**
Open: **All year**
Reduced Rates: **10% Oct. 1–Apr. 30**
Breakfast: **Full**

Pets: **No**
Children: **Welcome**
Smoking: **Restricted**
Social Drinking: **No**

Gretna Green is an easy stroll from the falls—the front porch of this 90-year-old brick home overlooks Niagara Gorge. With Marineland, the Imax Theatre, the local museums, and year-round festivals, this area is rich in diversions. But you won't miss out on your favorite shows because each bedroom has a TV and queen beds. Marg loves to bake, and prides herself on the homemade muffins and scones she serves at breakfast.

Almar House Bed & Breakfast ✪

339 MARY STREET, BOX 1103, NIAGARA-ON-THE-LAKE, ONTARIO, CANADA L0S 1J0
almar.niagara@sympatica.ca

Tel: **(905) 468-1368**; fax: **(905) 468-2409**
Hosts: **Marie-Jane and Alan Johnson**
Location: **15 mi. N of Niagara Falls**
No. of Rooms: **3**
No. of Private Baths: **3**
Double/pb: **$65–$80**
Single/pb: **$60–$75**
Open: **All year**

Reduced Rates: **Winter**
Breakfast: **Full**
Pets: **No**
Children: **Welcome, prior arrangement**
Smoking: **No**
Social Drinking: **Permitted**
Station Pickup: **Yes**
Foreign Languages: **French, German**

Situated in a peaceful part of a historic town, this Georgian-style home is within walking distance of shopping, restaurants, and the renowned Shaw Festival Theatres. Nearby you can visit Niagara Falls, battlefields, forts of the 1812 war, wineries, and the Welland Ship Canal. Breakfast is gourmet, served in the dining room. A guest lounge is available on the bedroom level, and the house is air-conditioned. Relax and meet new friends in the elegant living room or mingle in the beautifully landscaped garden. Enjoy Marie-Jane and Alan's hospitality in your home away from home when visiting the Niagara region.

Hiebert's Guest House ✪

BOX 1371, 275 JOHN STREET, NIAGARA-ON-THE-LAKE, ONTARIO, CANADA L0S 1J0
hieberts@sprint.ca; www.vip.com/hieberts

Tel: **(905) 468-3687**	Open: **All year**
Hosts: **Otto and Marlene Hiebert**	Reduced Rates: **10% Nov.–Apr.**
Location: **15 mi. N of Niagara Falls**	Breakfast: **Full**
No. of Rooms: **3**	Pets: **No**
No. of Private Baths: **3**	Children: **Welcome**
Double/pb: **$75–$85**	Smoking: **No**
Double/sb: **$60–$65**	Social Drinking: **Permitted**
Single/sb: **$55–$60**	

Hiebert's Guest House is located in a peaceful setting in the old historic town of Niagara-on-the-Lake. Area attractions include the Shaw Festival Theatre (open April–October), numerous local wineries, historic Fort George, many boutiques, restaurants, and the natural beauty of the area. Stay in queen or twin rooms with ensuite baths and central air. Home-cooked breakfasts include locally grown fresh fruit in season. Relax under the arbor in the large treed yard. Otto and Marlene look forward to your arrival.

The Turner House ✪

P.O. BOX 1509, 293 REGENT STREET, NIAGARA-ON-THE-LAKE, ONTARIO, CANADA L0S 1J0

Tel: **(905) 468-4440**	Double/sb: **$85**
Best Time to Call: **9 AM–9 PM**	Open: **All year**
Hosts: **Donna and Larry Turner**	Reduced Rates: **Jan.–Apr.**
Location: **20 mi. N of Niagara Falls**	Breakfast: **Full**
No. of Rooms: **3**	Pets: **No**
No. of Private Baths: **1**	Children: **Welcome, over 12**
Max. No. Sharing Bath: **4**	Smoking: **No**
Double/pb: **$95**	Social Drinking: **No**

Located in a historic town near Niagara Falls, this 1880s Victorian home provides a quiet base for your tour of the battlefields and forts of the War of 1812, Niagara Falls, the Welland Ship canal, and local vineyards and wineries. Then attend one of the many plays at the Shaw Festival Theatre. Turner House is within walking distance of shops, dining, and three theaters. Enjoy your hosts' fine home, full breakfast, and knowledge of the area. Sit in the parlor, the upstairs sitting room, by the pool, or on the porch and relax before your next activity in this scenic and historic area.

Ottawa Bed & Breakfast ✪
488 COOPER STREET, OTTAWA, ONTARIO, CANADA K1R 5H9

Tel: **(613) 563-0161; (800) 461-7889**
Best Time to Call: **9 AM–9 PM**
Coordinators: **Robert Rivoire and R. G. Simmens**

Regions Covered: **Ontario—Ottawa**
Rates (Single/Double):
   Average: **$54 / $64**
Credit Cards: **No**

If you are seeking an interesting but inexpensive holiday, then Canada's capital, Ottawa, is the place for you. The city is packed with activities including museums, the House of Parliament, art galleries, and historic sites. You can skate on the Rideau Canal or bike on miles of parkways and trails. Our fully inspected homes await you.

Australis Guest House ✪
35 MARLBOROUGH AVENUE, OTTAWA, ONTARIO, CANADA K1N 8E6

Tel/Fax: **(613) 235-8461**
Best Time to Call: **After 4 PM**
Hosts: **Brian, Carol, and Olivia Waters**
Location: **1 mi. from Parliament**
No. of Rooms: **3**
No. of Private Baths: **1**
Max. No. Sharing Bath: **4**
Double/pb: **$78**
Single/pb: **$65**
Double/sb: **$65**
Single/sb: **$55**

Open: **All year**
Reduced Rates: **10% seniors; 10% less Nov.–Mar.**
Breakfast: **Full**
Pets: **No**
Children: **Welcome, over 6**
Smoking: **Restricted**
Social Drinking: **No**
Station Pickup: **Yes**
Foreign Languages: **French**

Located on a quiet tree-lined street in Sandy Hill, one of Ottawa's first residential areas, Australis House is next to the Rideau River and Strathcona Park. It is but a twenty-minute walk to the Parliament buildings, museums, and the art gallery. This handsome brick house boasts leaded windows, fireplaces, oak floors, and eight-foot stained glass windows overlooking the hall. Your hosts have lived in Africa, Asia, and Latin America, and mementos from their travels are displayed throughout. Hearty, delicious breakfasts, with fruit salads and home-baked breads and pastries, ensure that guests start the day in the right way.

Sleeping Giant Bed & Breakfast—Cambrian Place ✪
532 CAMBRIAN CRESCENT, THUNDER BAY, PROVIDENCE, ONTARIO, CANADA P7C 5B9

Tel: **(807) 475-3105**
Best Time to Call: **9 AM–8 PM**
Hosts: **Sonja Isaksen and Finn Anderson**

No. of Rooms: **2**
Max. No. Sharing Bath: **4**
Double/sb: **$60**

Single/sb: **$50**
Open: **All year**
Reduced Rates: **Weekly, winter ski packages**
Breakfast: **Full**
Other Meals: **Available**

Credit Cards: **VISA**
Pets: **No**
Children: **Welcome (no crib)**
Smoking: **No**
Social Drinking: **Permitted**
Foreign Languages: **Danish**

Cambrian Place is a spacious elegant home newly decorated with hardwood floors, broadloom carpeting, large picture windows, French patio doors, and two gas fireplaces. The house is situated in a quiet, tree-lined residential area of Thunder Bay of the North of Superior Region. Enjoy a full breakfast with specialties such as Danish pancakes or abelskivers, homemade sausages, bread, jams, and jellies. Special attention is paid to detail such as fresh flowers, fruit baskets, and homemade chocolates. Guests will be close to golf courses, skiing, walking, biking trails, shopping, and many other attractions.

Bed and Breakfast Homes of Toronto ✪

P.O. BOX 46093, COLLEGE PARK POST OFFICE, TORONTO, ONTARIO, CANADA M5B 2L8

Tel: **(416) 363-6362**
Best Time to Call: **8 AM–11 PM**
Coordinator: **May Jarvie**
States/Regions Covered: **Toronto**
Descriptive Directory of B&Bs: **Free**

Rates (Single/Double):
Modest: **$45–$55**
Average: **$60–$75**
Luxury: **$80–$125**

Bed and Breakfast Homes of Toronto is a friendly cooperative of fourteen homes located in various downtown and surrounding neighborhoods, all serviced by safe public transportation. Hosts offer individual rooms or private suites at about half the cost of hotels. Each bed and breakfast has its own unique ambience and decor, a high standard of cleanliness, comfort, and, in most cases, free parking.

The Downtown Toronto Association of B&B Guest Houses ✪

P.O. BOX 190, STATION B, TORONTO, ONTARIO, CANADA M5T 2W1

Tel: **(416) 368-1420; fax: (416) 368-1653**
Best Time to Call: **9 AM–6 PM Mon.–Fri.; 9 AM–noon Sat.–Sun.**
Coordinator: **Linda Lippa**
Region Covered: **Toronto**

Rates (Single/Double):
Modest: **$45–$55**
Average: **$65–$85**
Luxury: **$95–$110**
Credit Cards: **MC, VISA**
Minimum Stay: **2 nights**

Quality, charm, and safety are the three main elements of the roster, which includes accommodations in more than thirty restored older homes throughout Toronto. A free brochure contains a map listing each neighborhood where the homes are located. All provide ample parking and are within 10 minutes of Eaton Centre, theaters, fine restaurants, and 24-hour public transit lines.

Beaconsfield B&B ✪

38 BEACONSFIELD AVENUE, TORONTO, ONTARIO,
CANADA M6J 3H9
beacon@idirect.com

Tel: **(416) 535-3338**; fax: **(416) 535-3338**	Single/sb: **$59**
	Suites: **$99**
Best Time to Call: **Anytime**	Open: **All year**
Hosts: **Bernie and Katya McLoughlin**	Breakfast: **Full**
No. of Rooms: **4**	Pets: **No**
No. of Private Baths: **1**	Children: **Welcome**
Max. No. Sharing Bath: **4**	Smoking: **No**
Double/pb: **$99**	Social Drinking: **Permitted**
Single/pb: **$89**	Foreign Languages: **Spanish, Russian**
Double/sb: **$69**	

Bernie and Katya, an artist-actress couple, invite you to their colorful 1882 Victorian home full of fun and sun, art and heart. Beaconsfield is in a quiet, multicultural downtown neighborhood just beyond the commercial center. A short trolley ride takes you to major theaters, CN Tower, SkyDome, Chinatown, and Eaton Centre. Choose between imaginatively decorated rooms or the very private Mexican honeymoon suite with its treetop terrace. All come with top-of-the-line beds and full, creative breakfasts presented musically in an eclectic dining room. Parking, TV, air-conditioning, sundecks, refrigerator, and microwave are among the amenities at guests' disposal.

Orchard View ✪

92 ORCHARD VIEW BOULEVARD, TORONTO, ONTARIO, CANADA
M4R 1C2

Tel: **(416) 488-6826**	Double/sb: **$70**
Hosts: **Donna and Ken Ketchen**	Single/sb: **$60**
Location: **In Toronto**	Open: **All year**
No. of Rooms: **2**	Breakfast: **Full**
No. of Private Baths: **1**	Pets: **Cats only**
Max. No. Sharing Bath: **3**	Children: **No**
Double/pb: **$75**	Smoking: **No**
Single/pb: **$60**	Social Drinking: **Permitted**

Built in 1911, this spacious home is uniquely decorated for the 1990s. Choose between the queen-size bedroom with private bath or the twin room with sitting area and separate entrance to the main bath. Free parking close to the subway, shops, and restaurants.

Vanderkooy Bed & Breakfast ✪

53 WALKER AVENUE, TORONTO, ONTARIO, CANADA M4V 1G3

Tel: **(416) 925-8765**	Location: **In Toronto**
Best Time to Call: **7 AM–11 PM**	No. of Rooms: **3**
Host: **Joan Vanderkooy**	No. of Private Baths: **1**

Max. No. Sharing Bath: **4**
Double/pb: **$75**
Single/pb: **$60**
Double/sb: **$65**
Single/sb: **$50**
Open: **All year**

Reduced Rates: **Available**
Breakfast: **Full**
Pets: **No**
Children: **Welcome, over 12**
Smoking: **No**
Social Drinking: **Permitted**

Joan and the resident cat, Jazz, welcome you to this charming home where you will enjoy comfortable guest rooms and breakfast served in an open dining room overlooking the garden. A short walk to Summerhill station on the Younge subway line allows easy access to downtown attractions, including Harbourfront, SkyDome, the Eaton Centre, and theaters. Restaurants and shopping districts are all within walking distance. Feel free to watch TV by the fire, enjoy the waterfall and pond in the garden, or relax on the flower-filled deck in the summer.

PRINCE EDWARD ISLAND

Note: All prices listed in this section are quoted in Canadian dollars.

The Home Place Inn & Restaurant ✪
P.O. BOX 88, 21 VICTORIA STREET EAST, KENSINGTON, PRINCE EDWARD ISLAND C0B 1M0

Tel: **(902) 836-5686**
Host: **Glenda Burt**
Location: **44 mi. W of Charlottetown**
No. of Rooms: **3**
No. of Private Baths: **3**
Double/pb: **$85**
Single/pb: **$75**
Suite: **$125**
Open: **All year**

Reduced Rates: **10% seniors, families**
Breakfast: **Full**
Other Meals: **Available**
Credit Cards: **AMEX, MC, VISA**
Pets: **No**
Children: **Welcome, over 12**
Smoking: **No**
Social Drinking: **Permitted**

Located in the heart of Kensington is the Home Place Inn & Restaurant. Built in 1915 by the prominent Orr family, this inn is rich in history. Each room is uniquely furnished with antiques; the spacious honeymoon suite features a four-poster king-size bed and Jacuzzi. Start your day with a hearty breakfast. Then use the Home Place as a base from which to explore the many scenic splendors that led island author Lucy Maud Montgomery to create Anne of Green Gables, one of the world's favorite fictional heroines. Discover the island's famous Malpeque oysters, a specialty served here. After dinner, relax in the sitting room or sample the theater offerings.

Thompson Tourist Home ✪
KENSINGTON RR6, MARGATE, PRINCE EDWARD ISLAND, CANADA C0B 1M0

Tel: **(800) 567-7907; (902) 836-4160**
Best Time to Call: **Morning**
Hosts: **Don and Valerie Thompson**
No. of Rooms: **4**
No. of Private Baths: **1**
Max. No. Sharing Bath: **5**
Double/pb: **$70**
Single/pb: **$65**
Double/sb: **$40**
Single/sb: **$35**

Suites: **$70**
Open: **June 1–Sept. 30**
Reduced Rates: **Available**
Breakfast: **Continental**
Credit Cards: **VISA**
Pets: **Sometimes**
Children: **Welcome**
Smoking: **No**
Social Drinking: **Permitted**
Station Pickup: **Yes**

Situated on three acres, this family farmhouse has a water view from every window, balcony, and veranda. The Thompsons live 30 minutes from Charlottetown and fifteen to twenty minutes from most major attractions; their location approximately in the center of the island makes either end easily accessible. Don and Valerie live up to the motto "home away from home." There are usually baby goats and kittens for guests to enjoy. The B&B's proximity to beaches and restaurants makes it a convenient, pleasant place to holiday.

QUEBEC

Note: All prices listed in this section are quoted in Canadian dollars.

Bed & Breakfast Montréal: A City-Wide Network
P.O. BOX 575, SNOWDON STATION, MONTREAL, QUEBEC, CANADA H3X 3T8
bbmtlnet@total.net

Tel: **(514) 738-9410; (800) 738-4338;**
  fax (514) 735-7493
Coordinator: **Marian Kahn**
Regions Covered: **Montreal, Quebec
  City**

Rates (Single/Double):
  Modest: **$40 / $60**
  Average: **$45 / $70**
  Luxury: **$55 / $85**
Credit Cards: **AMEX, MC, VISA**
Foreign Languages: **German, Polish,
  Spanish**

Marian established the province's first reservation service in 1980. Most of the fifty hosts in her group have been welcoming guests ever since and have seen many travelers return for repeat visits. Homes are located downtown, in the Latin Quarter, in fashionable Westmount, and in other attractive neighborhoods. Accommodations are in Victorian row-houses, condo apartments, and even a contemporary ranch-style house overlooking a golf course. The standard of gracious hospitality is assured in all. Gift certificates are available.

Bed & Breakfast—A Downtown Network ✪

3458 LAVAL AVENUE, MONTREAL, QUEBEC, CANADA H2X 3C8
bbdtown@cam.org; www.cam.org/~drivard/bedbreak/index.htm

Tel: **(514) 289-9749; (800) 267-5180;** fax: **(514) 287-7386**	Rates (Single/Double):
Best Time to Call: **8:30 AM–6 PM**	Modest: **$35–$45**
Coordinator: **Bob and Mariko Finkelstein**	Average: **$45–$65**
	Luxury: **$75–$95**
Regions Covered: **Montreal, Outremont, Westmount**	Credit Cards: **AMEX, MC, VISA**
	Foreign Languages: **Japanese, French**

Bob and Mariko specialize in the city center, Old Montreal, and the Plateau. Hosts with inside knowledge of the city can recommend great shopping, places of special interest, and fine restaurants. They will make every effort to ensure that your stay is as comfortable as possible.

A Montreal Oasis ✪

3000 DE BRESLAY ROAD, MONTREAL, QUEBEC, CANADA H3Y 2G7

Tel: **(514) 935-2312**	Open: **All year**
Host: **Lena Blondel**	Breakfast: **Full**
No. of Rooms: **3**	Pets: **No**
Max. No. Sharing Bath: **3**	Children: **Welcome, over 10**
Double/sb: **$60–$90**	Smoking: **No**
Single/sb: **$50–$70**	Social Drinking: **Permitted**
Guest Cottage: **$80–$85; sleeps 3**	Minimum Stay: **June–Sept.**

This spacious home is located in the Priest Farm district. According to the Canadian Center for Architecture, this is the only 1920s residential development of interest in downtown Montreal. In downtown's select West End you can enjoy the Fine Art Museum and Crescent and St. Catherine's streets. The bed and breakfast is decorated with Quebec and Swedish furniture, and the art is African, Asian, and Swedish. Lena is Swedish and lives in Montreal by choice, although she has lived in many other parts of the world. She also operates a small network of homes in downtown Montreal, including the Latin Quarter and the Old City.

Bay View Farm/La Ferme Bay View ✪

P.O. BOX 21, 337 MAIN HIGHWAY ROUTE 132, NEW CARLISLE WEST,
QUEBEC, CANADA G0C 1Z0

Tel: **(418) 752-2725, 752-6718**
Best Time to Call: **7–8 AM**
Host: **Helen Sawyer**
No. of Rooms: **5**
No. of Private Baths: **1**
Max. No. Sharing Bath: **4**
Double/pb: **$35**
Double/sb: **$35**
Single/sb: **$25**
Guest Cottage: **$350 weekly; sleeps 10**

Open: **All year**
Breakfast: **Full**
Other Meals: **Available**
Pets: **No**
Children: **Welcome**
Smoking: **No**
Social Drinking: **No**
Airport/Station Pickup: **Yes**
Foreign Languages: **French**

A spacious wooden home on the ruggedly beautiful Gaspé Peninsula coast. Your host offers quiet, comfortable accommodations and a generous breakfast of fresh farm eggs, homemade muffins and jams, fresh seasonal fruit, bacon, and coffee. Guests can enjoy golf, tennis, canoeing, horseback riding, bird watching, beachcombing, sunsets over the water, and a nearby lighthouse. Visit Acadian and United Empire Museums, archaeological and fossil sites, Perce Rock, Bonaventure Island, bird sanctuaries, and natural parks. This is a photographer's paradise.

Aux Berges Fleuries ✪

1028 PRINCIPALE, PRÉVOST, QUÉBEC, CANADA J0R 1T0

Tel: **(450) 224-7631; fax: (450) 436-5997**
Best Time to Call: **Days and evenings**

Hosts: **Fransois Laroche**
Location: **35 mi. N of Montreal**
No. of Rooms: **4**

Max. No. Sharing Bath: **4**
Double/sb: **$64**
Single/sb: **$44**
Open: **All year**
Reduced Rates: **10% 3 nights and longer**

Breakfast: **Full**
Pets: **Sometimes**
Children: **Welcome**
Smoking: **Permitted**
Social Drinking: **Permitted**
Foreign Languages: **French**

Experience the warmth of France without crossing the ocean. The Aux Berges Fleuries, a hundred-year-old manor, offers it. Hiking, bicycling, cross-country skiing, horseback riding, golfing, canoeing, and nature await your arrival. This B&B is situated in the historic section of a small village. Fransois, a young retired analyst, is available to help you understand the French way of living in North America. He welcomes you, cooks for you, and will often accompany you to outside activities.

For key to listings, see inside front or back cover.

✪ This star means that rates are guaranteed through December 31, 1999, to any guest making a reservation as a result of reading about the B&B in *Bed & Breakfast U.S.A.*—1999 edition.

Important! To avoid misunderstandings, always ask about cancellation policies when booking.

Please enclose a self-addressed, stamped, business-size envelope when contacting reservation services.

For more details on what you can expect in a B&B, see Chapter 1.

Always mention *Bed & Breakfast U.S.A.* when making reservations!

We want to hear from you! Use the form on page 593.

Appendix:
UNITED STATES AND CANADIAN TOURIST OFFICES

Listed here are the addresses and telephone numbers for the tourist offices of every U.S. state and Canadian province. When you write or call one of these offices, be sure to request a map of the state and a calendar of events. If you will be visiting a particular city or region, or if you have any special interests, be sure to specify them as well.

State Tourist Offices

Alabama Bureau of Tourism
Box 4927, 401 Adams Avenue
Montgomery, Alabama 36103-4927
alaweb.asc.edu/ala_tours/tours.html
(205) 242-4169; (800) ALABAMA [252-2262]; fax (334) 242-4554

Alaska Division of Tourism
P.O. Box 110801
Juneau, Alaska 99811
www.state.akus
(907) 465-2010

Arizona Office of Tourism
2702 N 3rd Street
Suite 4015
Phoenix, Arizona 85004
www.arizonaguide.com
(800) 842-8257 (602) 230-7733; fax: (602) 277-9289

Arkansas Department of Park and Tourism
1 Capitol Mall
Little Rock, Arkansas 72201
(501) 682-7777 or (800) NATURAL [628-8725]

California Office of Tourism
P.O. Box 1499
Sacramento, California 95812
(800) 462-2543 or (800) TO-CALIFORNIA [862-2254]
www.gocalif.ca.gov

Colorado Travel & Tourism Authority
3554 N. Academy Blvd.
Colorado Springs, Colorado 80917
(800) 265-6723; fax: (718) 591-7068

Connecticut Vacation Center
865 Brook Street
Rocky Hill, Connecticut 06067
www.2.uconn.edu/CTSTATE/vacguide.html
(860) 258-4355 or (800) CT-BOUND [282-6863]; fax (860) 258-4275

Delaware Tourism Office
99 Kings Highway, P.O. Box 1401
Dover, Delaware 19903
www.state.de.us/govern/agencies/dedo/index
(302) 739-4271 or (800) 441-8846

Washington, D.C. Convention and Visitors' Association
1212 New York Avenue N.W.
Suite 600
Washington, D.C. 20005
www.washington.org
(202) 789-7000; (800) 422-8644 in USA; fax: (202) 789-7037

Florida Division of Tourism
126 W. Van Buren Street
Tallahassee, Florida 32399
(904) 487-1462; fax: (904) 921-9158
www.state.fl.us/commerce

Georgia Tourist Division
Box 1776 Dept TIA
Atlanta, Georgia 30301
www.georgia-on-my-mind.org/
(404) 656-3590 or (800) 847-4842 in USA

Hawaii Visitors Bureau
2270 Kalakaua Avenue
Suite 801
Honolulu, Hawaii 96815
www.visit.hawaii.org/
(808) 923-1811; (800) 353-5846 in USA;
    fax: (808) 922-8991

Idaho Travel Council
700 W. State Street
Boise, Idaho 83720-2700
(800) 635-7820 in USA or (208) 334-2470

Illinois Office of Tourism
100 W. Randolph Street
Suite 3-400
Chicago, Illinois 60601
www.enjoyillinois.com
(800) 223-0121

Indiana Tourism Development
    Division
1 North Capitol, Suite 100
Indianapolis, Indiana 46204-2288
(317) 232-8860 or (800) 232-8860 in USA

Iowa Tourism Office
200 East Grand Avenue
Des Moines, Iowa 50309
www.state.ia.us/tourism/
(515) 242-4705 or (800) 345-IOWA
    [4692] in USA

Kansas Travel and Tourism Division
700 SW Harrison Street, Suite 1300
Topeka, Kansas 66603
(913) 296-2009 or (800) 252-6727 in USA

Kentucky Department of Travel
    Development
500 Mero St.
Frankfort, Kentucky 40601
(800) 225-8747 in USA; (502) 564-4930
TDD-equipped

Louisiana Office of Tourism
P.O. Box 94291
Baton Rouge, Louisiana 70804-9291
(504) 342-8119 (within Louisiana) or
    (800) 334-8626 in USA

Maine Publicity Bureau
P.O. Box 2300
325-B Water Street
Hallowell, Maine 04347
(207) 623-0363 or (800) 533-9595 in USA

Maryland Office of Tourist
    Development
217 E. Redwood Street
Baltimore, Maryland 21202
www.mdisfun.org/
(800) 543-1036; (410) 333-6611

Massachusetts Office of Tourism
100 Cambridge Street—13th Floor
Boston, Massachusetts 02202
(617) 727-3201 or (800) 447-MASS
    [6277] in USA

Michigan Travel Bureau
P.O. Box 3393
Livonia, Michigan 44851
www.travel-michigan.state.mi.us/
(517) 373-0670 or (800) 543-2YES [2937]
    in USA

Minnesota Tourist Information Center
121 7th Place East
#100 Metro Square
St. Paul, Minnesota 55101-2112
www.tccn.com/mn.tourism/
    mnhome.html
(612) 296-5029 or (800) 657-3700
    (out of state)

Mississippi Division of Tourism
Box 1705
Ocean Springs, Mississippi 39566
www.mississippi.org
(601) 364-2163 or (800) 927-6378 in USA

Missouri Division of Tourism
P.O. Box 1055
Jefferson City, Missouri 65102
(314) 751-4133 or (800) 877-1234 in USA

Travel Montana
P.O. Box 200533
Helena, Montana 59620
(800) 847-4868; fax: (406) 844-1800

Nebraska Division of Travel and
    Tourism
P.O. Box 98913
Lincoln, Nebraska 68509
www.ded.state.ne.us/tourism.html
(800) 228-4307 in US

Nevada Commission on Tourism
Capitol Complex
Carson City, Nevada 89710
www.travelnevada.com/
(702) 687-4322 or (800) NEVADA 8
[638-2328] in USA

New Hampshire Office of Travel and
  Tourism Development
P.O. Box 1856
Concord, New Hampshire 03302-1856
www.visitnh.gov
(800) FUN-IN-NH [386-4664] or (603)
  271-2343, Ext. 162

New Jersey Division of Travel and
  Tourism
20 West State St. C.N. 826
Trenton, New Jersey 08625-0826
www.state.nj.us/travel/index.htm/
(609) 292-2470 or (800) JERSEY-7 [537-
  7397]

New Mexico Department of Tourism
491 Old Santa Fe Trail
Santa Fe, New Mexico 87503
(800) 545-2040, or (800) 545-2040 (out of
  state), (505) 827-7402 (FAX)

New York State Division of Tourism
1 Commerce Plaza
Albany, New York 12245
www.iloveny.state.ny.us
(518) 474-4116 or (800) CALL-NYS
  [225-5697]

North Carolina Travel and Tourism
  Division
430 North Salisbury Street
Raleigh, North Carolina 27603
(919) 733-4171 or (800) VISIT NC
  [847-4862] in USA

North Dakota Tourism Promotion
Liberty Memorial Building
604 E. Boulevard
Bismarck, North Dakota 58505
(701) 224-2525 or (800) HELLO ND
  [435-5663]

Ohio Division of Travel and Tourism
P.O. Box 1001
Columbus, Ohio 43216-0101
www.travel.state.oh.us
(800) BUCKEYE [282-5393]; fax: (513)
  794-0878

Oklahoma Division of Tourism
500 Will Rogers Bldg.
Oklahoma City, Oklahoma 73105
www.otrd.state.ok.us
(405) 521-3981 or (800) 652-OKLA
  [6552]

Oregon Tourism Division
775 Summer Street N.E.
Salem, Oregon 97310
(503) 986-0000 or (800) 547-7842

Pennsylvania Bureau of Travel
  Marketing
Department of Commerce
453 Forum Building
Harrisburg, Pennsylvania 17120
www.state.pa.us/visit/info-trav.htm/
(717) 787-5453 or (800) VISIT-PA [847-
  4872]

Puerto Rico Tourism Company
23rd Floor
575 Fifth Avenue
New York, New York 10017
(212) 599-6262 or (800) 223-6530
  or (800) 866-STAR [7827]

Rhode Island Tourism Division
7 Jackson Walkway
Providence, Rhode Island 02903
www.visitrhodeisland.com/(401) 277-
  2601 or (800) 556-2484; fax: (401) 273-
  8720

South Carolina Division of Tourism
P.O. Box 71
Columbia, South Carolina 29202
(803) 734-0122; (800) 346-3634;
  fax: (803) 273-8270

South Dakota Division of Tourism
711 East Wells Avenue
Pierre, South Dakota 57501-3369
www.state.sd.us/state.sd.us
(605) 773-3301 or (800) 732-5682;
  fax: (605) 773-3256

Tennessee Tourist Development
P.O. Box 23170
Racheal Jackson Bldg., 5th Floor
Nashville, Tennessee 37202-3170
www.tennessee.net
(615) 741-2158; (800) 836-6200;
  fax: (615) 741-7225

Texas Dept. of Commerce
Division of Tourism
P.O. Box 12728
Austin, Texas 78711-2728
www.traveltex.com/RightMain.html
(512) 462-9191 or (800) 8888-TEX [888-8839]

Utah Travel Council
Council Hall
Capitol Hill Dept. TIA
Salt Lake City, Utah 84114
www.utah.com/
(801) 538-1030 or (800) 200-1160

Vermont Department of Travel and
Tourism
134 State Street
Montpelier, Vermont 05602
vtinfo@dca.state.vt.us
(802) 828-3237 or (800) VERMONT
[837-6668]; fax: (802) 828-3367

Virginia Division of Tourism
1021 E. Cary Street 14th Floor #500
Richmond, Virginia 23219
www.virginia.org/cgi-shl/VISITVA/
Tourism/Welcome
(804) 786-4484 or (800) VISIT-VA [847-4882]

Washington State Tourism
Development Division
P.O. Box 42500
Olympia, Washington 98504
(360) 586-2012 or (800) 544-1800 (out of
state)

Travel West Virginia
Capital Complex, Bldg. 17
Charleston, West Virginia 25305-0312
(800) CALL WVA [225-5982] or
(304) 345-2286

Wisconsin Division of Tourism
P.O. Box 7976
Madison, Wisconsin 53707-7606
(608) 266-2161; (800) 432-8747

Wyoming Travel Commission
I-25 and College Drive
Cheyenne, Wyoming 82002
www.state.wy.us/state/welcome.html
(307) 777-7777 or (800) CALL-WYO
[225-5996]

Canadian Province Tourist Offices

Alberta Tourism, Parks, and Recreation
City Center Building
P.O. Box 2500
Edmonton, Alberta, Canada T5J 2Z4
(403) 427-4321 (from Edmonton area)
or (800) 661-8888 (from the U.S. and
Canada)

Tourism British Columbia
Parliament Bldgs.
Victoria, British Columbia, Canada
V8V 1X4
(604) 663-6000 or (800) 663-6000

Travel Manitoba
Department 6020
7th Floor
155 Carlton Street
Winnipeg, Manitoba, Canada
R3C 3H8
www.gov.mb.ca/itt/travel/explore/
(204) 945-3777 or (800) 665-0040 (from
mainland U.S. and Canada)

New Brunswick Tourism
P.O. Box 6000
Fredericton, New Brunswick, Canada
E3B 5C3
(506) 453-8745 or (800) 561-0123 (from
mainland U.S. and Canada)

Newfoundland/Labrador Tourism
Branch
Department of Tourism & Culture
P.O. Box 8730
St. John's, Newfoundland, Canada
A1B 4K2
info@tourism.gov.nf.ca
(709) 729-2830 (from St. John's area)
or (800) 563-6353 (from mainland
U.S. and Canada)

Nova Scotia Tourism
P.O. Box 456
Halifax, Nova Scotia B3S 2M7
(800) 565-0000 or (902) 425-5781

Prince Edward Island
P.O. Box 940
Charlotte Town, Prince Edward Island,
CIA 7M5
(800) 463-4734 or (902) 368-4444

Tourisme Quebec
C.P. 979
Montreal, Quebec H3C 2W3
(800) 363-7777 or (514) 873-2015

Tourism Saskatchewan
500-1900 Albert St.
Regina, Saskatchewan, Canada
  S4P 4L9
www.sasktourism.sk.ca/
(306) 787-2300 or (800) 667-7191

Northwest Territories Tourism
Box 610, Yellowknife
www.edt.gov.nt.ca/guide/index.html
(403) 873-7200 or (800) 661-0788

Tourism Yukon
P.O. Box 2703
Whitehorse, Yukon, Canada Y1A 2C6
www.touryukon.com/
(403) 667-5340

BED AND BREAKFAST RESERVATION REQUEST FORM

Dear _____
       Host's Name

I read about your home in *Bed & Breakfast U.S.A. 1999,* and would
be interested in making reservations to stay with you.

My name: _____

Address: _____
          street

_____
    city   state   zip
Telephone: _____
           area code
Business address/telephone: _____

_____

Number of adult guests: _____

Number and ages of children: _____

Desired date and time of arrival: _____

Desired length of stay: _____

Mode of transportation: _____
(car, bus, train, plane)

Additional information/special requests/allergies: _____

_____

_____

_____

_____

_____

_____

I look forward to hearing from you soon.

Sincerely,

APPLICATION FOR MEMBERSHIP
(Please type or print)
(Please refer to Preface, pages xxxvii–xxxviii, for our membership criteria.)

Name of Bed & Breakfast: _____

Address: _____

City: _____ State: _____ Zip: _____ Phone: ( ) _____

E-mail address: _____

URL: _____

Best Time to Call: _____

Host(s): _____

Located: No. of miles _____ compass direction _____ of Major

City _____ Geographic region _____

No. of miles _____ from major route _____ Exit: _____

No. of guest bedrooms with private bath: _____
No. of guest bedrooms that share a bath: _____
How many people (including *your* family) must use the shared
bath? _____
How many bedrooms, if any, have a sink in them? _____

Room Rates:
$ _____ Double—private bath $ _____ Double—shared bath
$ _____ Single—private bath $ _____ Single—shared bath
$ _____ Suites
Separate Guest Cottage $ _____ Sleeps _____

Are you open year-round? ☐ Yes   ☐ No
If "No," specify when you are open: _____

How many rooms are wheelchair accessible? _____

Are you qualified to have your listing appear in the Wheelchair
   Accessible section? (see page 35) _____

Do you require a minimum stay? _____

Do you discount rates at any time? ☐ No ☐ Yes

If "yes," specify when you discount rates: _____

Do you offer a discount to senior citizens? ☐ No ☐ Yes: _____ %

Do you offer a discount for families? ☐ No ☐ Yes: _____ %

Breakfast: Type of breakfast included in rate:
    ☐ Full ☐ Continental

Describe breakfast specialties: _____
_____

Are any other meals provided? ☐ No ☐ Yes
    Lunch ☐ cost: $ _____ Dinner ☐ cost: $ _____

Do you accept credit cards? ☐ No ☐ Yes:
☐ AMEX ☐ DINERS ☐ DISCOVER ☐ MASTERCARD ☐ VISA

Will you GUARANTEE your rates from January through December
2000? ☐ Yes ☐ No

Note: This Guarantee applies only to those guests making reservations having read about you in *Bed & Breakfast U.S.A. 2000*.

If you have household pets, specify how many:
    ☐ Dog(s) ☐ Cat(s) ☐ Other

Can you accommodate a guest's pet?
    ☐ No ☐ Yes ☐ Sometimes

Are children welcome? ☐ No ☐ Yes If "Yes," specify age
restriction _____

Do you permit smoking somewhere inside your house?
☐ No ☐ Yes

Do you permit social drinking? ☐ No   ☐ Yes

Guests can be met at ☐ Airport _____   ☐ Train _____   ☐ Bus _____

Can you speak a foreign language fluently? ☐ No   ☐ Yes
Describe: _____

GENERAL AREA OF YOUR B&B (e.g., Boston historic district; 20 minutes from Chicago Loop):

GENERAL DESCRIPTION OF YOUR B&B (e.g., brick Colonial with white shutters; Victorian mansion with stained glass windows):

AMBIENCE OF YOUR B&B (e.g., furnished with rare antiques; lots of wood and glass):

THE QUALITIES THAT MAKE YOUR B&B SPECIAL ARE:

THINGS OF HISTORIC, SCENIC, CULTURAL, OR GENERAL INTEREST NEARBY (e.g., one mile from the San Diego Zoo; walking distance to the Lincoln Memorial):

YOUR OCCUPATION and SPECIAL INTERESTS (e.g., a retired teacher of Latin interested in woodworking; full-time host interested in quilting):

If you do welcome children, are there any special provisions for them (e.g., crib, playpen, high chair, play area, baby-sitter)?

Do you offer snacks (e.g., complimentary wine and cheese; pretzels and chips but BYOB)?

Can guests use your kitchen for light snacks? ☐ No   ☐ Yes

Do you offer the following amenities? ☐ Guest refrigerator
  ☐ Air-conditioning ☐ TV ☐ Piano ☐ Washing machine
  ☐ Dryer ☐ Hot tub ☐ Pool ☐ Tennis court
  Other _____

What major college or university is within 10 miles?
_____

Please supply the name, address, and phone number of three personal references from people not related to you (please use a separate sheet).

Please enclose a copy of your brochure along with color photos including exterior, guest bedrooms, baths, and breakfast area. Bedroom photos should include view of the headboard(s), bedside lamps, and night tables. Please show us a typical breakfast setting. Use a label to identify the name of your B&B *on each.* If you have a black-and-white line drawing, send it along. If you have an original breakfast recipe that you'd like to share, send it along, too. (Of course, credit will be given to your B&B.) **Nobody can describe your B&B better than you. Limit your description to 100 words and submit it typed, double-spaced, on a separate sheet of paper. We will of course reserve the right to edit.** As a member of the Tourist House Association of America Inc., your B&B will be described in the next edition of our book, *Bed & Breakfast U.S.A.*, published by Plume, an imprint of Dutton Signet, a member of Penguin Putnam Inc., and distributed to bookstores and libraries throughout the U.S. The book is also used as a reference for B&Bs in our country by major offices of tourism throughout the world.

Note: The following will NOT be considered for inclusion in *Bed & Breakfast U.S.A.:* Rental properties or properties where a host doesn't reside on the premises. B&Bs having more than fifteen guest rooms. Rates exceeding $35 where six people share a bath. Rates exceeding $45 where five people share a bath. Applications received after March 15, 1999. Incomplete applications, no photos, etc. Applications received in states that are overcrowded; this is due to space limitations. Higher-priced B&Bs and inns will only be included according to space availability.

Note: If the publisher or author receives negative reports from your guests regarding a deficiency in standards of CLEANLINESS, COMFORT, and CORDIALITY, and/or failure to honor the rate guarantee, we reserve the right to cancel your membership.

This membership application has been prepared by:

_____

(Signature)

Please enclose your $40 membership dues.   Date: _____

I am insured by _____ .

Return to:
Tourist House Association of America, Inc.
RD 1, Box 12A
Greentown, Pennsylvania 18426

To ensure that your listing will be considered for the 2000 edition of *Bed & Breakfast U.S.A.*, we MUST receive your completed application by March 15, 1999. Thereafter, listings will be considered only for the 2001 edition.

APPLICATION FOR MEMBERSHIP FOR A
BED & BREAKFAST RESERVATION SERVICE

NAME OF BED & BREAKFAST SERVICE: _____

ADDRESS: _____

CITY: _____ STATE: _____ ZIP: _____ PHONE:(   ) _____

E-MAIL: _____

URL: _____

COORDINATOR: _____

BEST TIME TO CALL: _____

Do you have a telephone answering ☐ machine?   ☐ service?

Names of state(s), cities, and towns where you have hosts (in alpha-
betical order, please, and limit to 10):

Number of hosts on your roster: _____

THINGS OF HISTORIC, SCENIC, CULTURAL, OR GENERAL
INTEREST IN THE AREA(S) YOU SERVE:

Range of Rates:
   Modest: Single $ _____   Double $ _____
   Average: Single $ _____   Double $ _____
   Luxury: Single $ _____   Double $ _____

Will you GUARANTEE your rates through December 2000?
☐ Yes   ☐ No

How often do you reinspect listings? _____
Do you require a minimum stay? _____
Surcharges for one-night stay? _____
Do you accept credit cards? ☐ No   ☐ Yes:
☐ AMEX ☐ DINERS ☐ DISCOVER ☐ MASTERCARD
☐ VISA

Is the guest required to pay a fee to use your service?
☐ No ☐ Yes—The fee is $ _____

Do you publish a directory of your B&B listings?
☐ No ☐ Yes—The fee is $ _____

Are any of your B&Bs within 10 miles of a university? Which? ____
_____

Briefly describe a sample host home in each of the previous categories: e.g., a cozy farmhouse where the host weaves rugs; a restored 1800 Victorian where the host is a retired general; a contemporary mansion with a sauna and swimming pool.

Please supply the name, address, and phone number of three personal references from people not related to you (please use a separate sheet of paper). Please enclose a copy of your brochure.

This membership application has been prepared by:

_____
(Signature)

Please enclose your $40 membership dues.   Date: _____

If you have a special breakfast recipe that you'd like to share, send it along. (Of course, credit will be given to your B&B agency.) As a member of the Tourist House Association of America, Inc., your B&B agency will be described in the next edition of our book, *Bed & Breakfast U.S.A.*, published by Plume, an imprint of Dutton Signet, a member of Penguin Putnam Inc. Return to: Tourist House Association of America, Inc., Greentown, PA 18426.

To ensure that your listing will be considered for the 2000 edition, we must receive your completed application by March 15, 1999. Thereafter, listings will be considered only for the 2001 edition.

INFORMATION ORDER FORM

We are constantly expanding our roster to include new members in the Tourist House Association of America, Inc. Their facilities will be fully described in the next edition of *Bed & Breakfast U.S.A.* In the meantime, we will be happy to send you a list including the name, address, telephone number, etc.

For those of you who would like to order additional copies of the book, and perhaps send one to a friend as a gift, we will be happy to fill mail orders. If it is a gift, let us know and we'll enclose a special gift card from you.

ORDER FORM

To:
Tourist House
Association of
America, Inc.
Book Dept.
Greentown, PA
18426

From: _____
               (Print your name)
Address: _____

_____
City   State   Zip

Date: _____

Please send:

☐ _____ copies of *Bed & Breakfast U.S.A.* @ $18.95 each (includes 4th class mail)

Send to: _____

Address: _____

_____
City   State   Zip

☐ Enclose a gift card from:

Please make check or money order payable to Tourist House Association of America, Inc.

WE WANT TO HEAR FROM YOU!

Name: _____

Address: _____
      street

_____
      city   state   zip

Please contact the following B&Bs; I think that they would be great additions to the next edition of *Bed & Breakfast U.S.A.*

Name of B&B: _____

Address: _____
      street

_____
      city   state   zip

Comments:

Name of B&B: _____

Address: _____
      street

_____
      city   state   zip

Comments:

_____

The following is our report on our visit to the home of:

Name of B&B: _____ Date of visit: _____

Address: _____ I was pleased. ☐

_____ I was disappointed. ☐

Comments:

Just tear out this page and mail it to us. It won't ruin your book!

Return to:
Tourist House Association of America, Inc.
Greentown, Pennsylvania 18426